$11.70

Human Sexuality 88/89

Editor

Ollie Pocs

Illinois State University

Ollie Pocs is in the Department of Sociology,
Anthropology, and Social Work at Illinois State University.
He received his B.A. in Sociology in 1958 and his M.A. in
1960 from University of Illinois. In 1978 he completed his
Ph.D. in Family Studies from Purdue University. His
primary areas of interest are marriage and family, human
sexuality and sexuality education, sex roles, and
counseling/therapy. He has published several articles in
those areas.

A Library of Information from the Public Press

Cover illustration by Mike Eagle

The Dushkin Publishing Group, Inc.
Sluice Dock, Guilford, Connecticut 06437

The Annual Editions Series

Annual Editions is a series of over forty volumes designed to provide the reader with convenient, low-cost access to a wide range of current, carefully selected articles from some of the most important magazines, newspapers, and journals published today. Annual Editions are updated on an annual basis through a continuous monitoring of over 200 periodical sources. All Annual Editions have a number of features designed to make them particularly useful, including topic guides, annotated tables of contents, unit overviews, and indexes. For the teacher using Annual Editions in the classroom, an Instructor's Resource Guide with test questions is available for each volume.

VOLUMES AVAILABLE

Africa
Aging
American Government
American History, Pre-Civil War
American History, Post-Civil War
Anthropology
Biology
Business and Management
China
Comparative Politics
Computers in Education
Computers in Business
Computers in Society
Criminal Justice
Drugs, Society, and Behavior
Early Childhood Education
Economics
Educating Exceptional Children
Education
Educational Psychology
Environment
Geography
Global Issues
Health

Human Development
Human Sexuality
Latin America
Macroeconomics
Marketing
Marriage and Family
Middle East and the Islamic World
Nutrition
Personal Growth and Behavior
Psychology
Social Problems
Sociology
Soviet Union and Eastern Europe
State and Local Government
Third World
Urban Society
Western Civilization,
    Pre-Reformation
Western Civilization,
    Post-Reformation
Western Europe
World History, Pre-Modern
World History, Modern
World Politics

Library of Congress Cataloging in Publication Data
Main entry under title: Annual editions: Human sexuality.
    1. Sexual behavior—Addresses, essays, lectures—Periodicals. 2. Sexual hygiene—Addresses, essays, lectures—Periodicals. 3. Sex education—Addresses, essays, lectures—Periodicals. 4. Human relations—Addresses, essays, lectures—Periodicals. I. Title: Human sexuality.
155.3'05   75-20756
ISBN 0-87967-716-3

Thirteenth Edition

Manufactured by The Banta Company, Harrisonburg, Virginia 22801

Editors/ Advisory Board

Members of the Advisory Board are instrumental in the final selection of articles for each edition of Annual Editions. Their review of articles for content, level, currency, and appropriateness provides critical direction to the editor and staff. We think you'll find their careful consideration well reflected in this volume.

EDITOR

Ollie Pocs
Illinois State University

ADVISORY BOARD

John Baldwin
University of California
Santa Barbara

Janice Baldwin
University of California
Santa Barbara

Beverly Battle
Thomas Nelson Community
College

Harry F. Felton
The Pennsylvania State University

Robert T. Francoeur
Fairleigh Dickinson University
Madison

Marylou Hacker
Modesto Junior College

Narendra Kalia
SUNY College, Buffalo

Gary F. Kelly
Clarkson University

Owen Morgan
Arizona State University

Phillip Patros
Southern Connecticut State University

Fred L. Peterson
The University of Texas
Austin

Robert Pollack
University of Georgia

Marlise Riffel-Gregor
Rochester Community College

Mina Robbins
California State University
Sacramento

Laurna Rubinson
University of Illinois
Urbana-Champaign

Robin Sawyer
University of Maryland
College Park

Helene Sloan
CUNY, Brooklyn College

Jeffrey S. Victor
Jamestown Community College

STAFF

To The Reader

In publishing ANNUAL EDITIONS we recognize the enormous role played by the magazines, newspapers, and journals of the *public press* in providing current, first-rate educational information in a broad spectrum of interest areas. Within the articles, the best scientists, practitioners, researchers, and commentators draw issues into new perspective as accepted theories and viewpoints are called into account by new events, recent discoveries change old facts, and fresh debate breaks out over important controversies.

Many of the articles resulting from this enormous editorial effort are appropriate for students, researchers, and professionals seeking accurate, current material to help bridge the gap between principles and theories and the real world. These articles, however, become more useful for study when those of lasting value are carefully *collected, organized, indexed,* and *reproduced* in a *low-cost format,* which provides easy and permanent access when the material is needed. That is the role played by *Annual Editions.* Under the direction of each volume's *Editor,* who is an expert in the subject area, and with the guidance of an *Advisory Board,* we seek each year to provide in each *ANNUAL EDITION* a current, well-balanced, carefully selected collection of the best of the public press for your study and enjoyment. We think you'll find this volume useful, and we hope you'll take a moment to let us know what you think.

Sex lies at the root of life, and we can never learn to reverence life until we know how to understand sex.

Havelock Ellis

The above quote by one of the first sexologists highlights the objective of this book. Learning about sex is a lifelong process that can occur informally and formally. With knowledge comes the understanding that we are all born sexual, and that sex, per se, is neither good nor bad, beautiful nor ugly, moral nor immoral.

While we are all born with basic sexual interests, drives, and desires, human sexuality is a dynamic and complex force that involves psychological and sociocultural dimensions in addition to the physiological. That is, sexuality includes an individual's whole body and personality. We are not born with a fully developed body or mind, but instead grow and learn; so it is with respect to our sexuality. Sexuality is learned. We learn what "appropriate" sexual behavior is, how to express it, when to do so, and under what circumstances. We also learn sexual feelings: positive feelings for accepting our sexuality or negative and repressive feelings such as guilt.

Sexuality, which affects human life so basically and powerfully, has, until recently, received little attention in scientific research and even less attention within communities of higher education. Yet, our contemporary social environment is expanding its sexual and social horizons toward greater freedom for the individual, especially women. Without proper understanding, this expansion in sexual freedom can lead to new forms of sexual bondage as easily as to increased joy and pleasure. The celebration of sexuality today is most likely found somewhere between the traditional, rigid, repressive morality that is our sociosexual heritage, and a new performance-oriented, irresponsible, self-seeking mentality.

Our goal in trying to understand sexuality is to seek a joyful acceptance of being sexual and to express this awareness in the most considerate way for ourselves and our sexual partners, while at the same time taking society and consequences into account. This anthology is aimed at helping all of us achieve the sexuality goals we seek.

The articles selected for this edition cover a wide range of important topics and are written primarily by professionals for a nonprofessional audience. Health educators, psychologists, sociologists, sexologists, and sex therapists writing for professional journals and popular magazines present their views on how and why sexual attitudes and behaviors are developed, maintained, and changed. This edition of *Annual Editions: Human Sexuality 88/89* is organized into six sections. *Sexuality and Society* notes historical and cross-cultural views, and our continually changing society and sexuality. *Sexual Biology and Health* explains the responses of the human body and new concerns with sexual hygiene. *Reproduction* discusses some recent technologies related to pregnancy and childbirth and deals with the reproductive cycle from conception to contraception. *Interpersonal Relationships* provides suggestions for establishing and maintaining intimate relationships of quality and responsibility. *Sexuality Through the Life Cycle* looks at what happens sexually throughout one's lifetime from childhood to later years. Finally, *Old/New Sexual Concerns* deals with such topics as sexual orientation, sexual abuse and violence, and AIDS.

The articles in this anthology have been carefully reviewed and selected for their quality, currency, and interest. They present a variety of viewpoints. Some you will agree with, some you will not, but you will learn from all of them.

Appreciation and a thank you goes to Sally Tone for her untiring organizational work and editorial expertise. We feel that *Human Sexuality 88/89* is one of the most useful and up-to-date books available. Please let us know what you think. Return the article rating form on the last page of this book with your suggestions and comments. Any book can be improved. This one will continue to be—annually.

Ollie Pocs

Ollie Pocs
Editor

Contents

Unit 1

Sexuality and Society

Eight selections trace sexuality from a historical and cross-cultural perspective to today's changing attitudes toward human sexual interaction.

The concepts in bold italics are developed in the article. For further expansion please refer to the Topic Guide, the Index, and the Glossary.

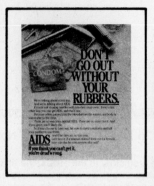

Unit 2

Sexual Biology and Health

Nine selections examine the biological aspects of human sexuality and emphasizes the importance of a better understanding of sexual hygiene.

The concepts in bold italics are developed in the article. For further expansion please refer to the Topic Guide, the Index, and the Glossary.

Unit 3

Reproduction

Nine articles discuss the roles of both males and females in pregnancy and childbirth. The latest birth control methods and practices are considered as they impact on society and the individual.

The concepts in bold italics are developed in the article. For further expansion please refer to the Topic Guide, the Index, and the Glossary.

Unit
4

Interpersonal
Relationships

Seven selections examine the dynamics of establishing
sexual relationships and the need to make these
relationships responsible and effective.

The concepts in bold italics are developed in the article. For further expansion please refer to the Topic Guide, the Index, and the Glossary.

Unit 5

Sexuality Through the Life Cycle

Ten articles consider human sexuality as an important element throughout the life cycle. The topics covered include sexuality and its relationship to children's feelings about themselves, responsible adolescent sexuality, sex in and out of marriage, and sex in old age.

Unit
6

Old/New Sexual Concerns

Twelve selections discuss continuing sexual concerns: sexual orientation, sexual harassment and violence, pornography, and the growing concern over AIDS.

The concepts in bold italics are developed in the article. For further expansion please refer to the Topic Guide, the Index, and the Glossary.

The concepts in bold italics are developed in the article. For further expansion please refer to the Topic Guide, the Index, and the Glossary.

Topic Guide

This topic guide suggests how the selections in this book relate to topics of traditional concern to human sexuality students and professionals. It is very useful in locating articles which relate to each other for reading and research. The guide is arranged alphabetically according to topic. Articles may, of course, treat topics that do not appear in the topic guide. In turn, entries in the topic guide do not necessarily constitute a comprehensive listing of all the contents of each selection.

TOPIC AREA	TREATED AS AN ISSUE IN:	TOPIC AREA	TREATED AS AN ISSUE IN:
Abuse, Sexual	34. Sex in Childhood 48. The Incest Controversy 49. Shattered Innocence 50. Kids for Sale	Childbirth	19. New Study of Teenage Pregnancy 20. Young, Innocent, and Pregnant 21. Saying No to Motherhood
Acquired Immune Deficiency Syndrome (AIDS)	8. Sex and Schools 23. Kids and Contraceptives 37. Teen Lust 52. The Facts About AIDS 53. AIDS and the College Student 54. Speaking Out on AIDS 55. Fighting the Plague	Conception Couples	18. Miracle Babies: The Next Generation 4. Erotic Wisdom of the Orient 11. The Power of Touch 18. Miracle Babies: The Next Generation 33. Making Love
Adolescence/ Teenagers	8. Sex and Schools 19. New Study of Teenage Pregnancy 20. Young, Innocent, and Pregnant 25. How We Can Prevent Teen Pregnancy 36. Children Having Children 37. Teen Lust 38. Formal vs. Informal Sources of Sex Education	Fallopian Tubes Friends/Friendship Health	14. Fragile Fallopian Tubes 30. Bruised Friendships 17. A Consumer's Guide to Over-the-Counter Tests 40. Sexual Passages 55. Fighting the Plague
Aging	40. Sexual Passages 41. Some Hard (and Soft) Facts About Sex and Aging 42. Never Too Late 43. Love, Sex, and Aging	History of Sex	1. 20 Greatest Moments in Sex History 2. New Directions for the Kinsey Institute 4. Erotic Wisdom of the Orient 16. A Gift From Mother Nature
Attitudes/Values	7. Re-Making Love 8. Sex and Schools	Homosexuality Incest	44. Women Who Have Lesbian Affairs 45. Hostile Eyes 48. The Incest Controversy 49. Shattered Innocence
Birth Control/ Contraception	19. New Study of Teenage Pregnancy 22. The Crisis in Contraception 23. Kids and Contraceptives 24. A Second Look at the Pill 25. How We Can Prevent Teen Pregnancy	Intimacy, Sexual	4. Erotic Wisdom of the Orient 6. How Important Is Sex? 11. The Power of Touch 33. Making Love
Child/Children	8. Sex and Schools 23. Kids and Contraceptives 27. Considering the Way Most of Us Learned About Sex. . . 34. Sex in Childhood 35. What Kids Need to Know 48. The Incest Controversy 49. Shattered Innocence 50. Kids for Sale	Love Men/Males	6. How Important Is Sex? 29. The Three Faces of Love 43. Love, Sex, and Aging 12. Prostate 13. The Secret "Gynecological" Disorders of Men 41. Some Hard (and Soft) Facts About Sex and Aging 42. Never Too Late 43. Love, Sex, and Aging

Sexuality and Society

- Historical and Cross-Cultural Perspective (Articles 1-4)
- Changing Society/Changing Sexuality (Articles 5-8)

People of different civilizations in different historical periods have engaged in a variety of different modes of sexual expression and behavior. Despite this cultural and historical diversity, one important principle should be kept in mind: Sexual awareness, attitudes, and behaviors are learned within sociocultural contexts that define appropriate sexuality for society's members. That is, our sexual attitudes and behaviors are in large measure social and cultural phenomena.

For several centuries, Western civilization has been characterized by an "antisex ethic" which has normatively limited sexual behavior to the confines of monogamous pair bonds (marriage) for the sole purpose of procreation. Today changes in our social environment—the widespread availability of effective contraception, the liberation of women from the home, the reconsideration of democratic values of "individual freedom" and the "pursuit of happiness"—are strengthening our concept of ourselves as sexual beings and posing a challenge to the "antisex ethic" that has traditionally served to orient sexuality.

As a rule, social change is not easily accomplished. Sociologists generally acknowledge that changes in the social environment are accompanied by the presence of interest groups that offer competing versions of what "is" or "should be" appropriate social behavior. The contemporary sociocultural changes surrounding sexuality are highly illustrative of such social dynamics. Many of the articles in this section document such tensions and conflicts between groups and their definitions of what is or should be social policy regarding sexuality. Sexologists, along with many individuals and groups in society, have a vital interest in the translation of social consciousness and sexuality into meaningful and rewarding sexual awareness and expression among society's members.

The fact that human sexuality is primarily a learned behavior can be both a blessing and a curse. The learning process enables humans to achieve a range of sexual expression and meaning that far exceeds their biological programming. Unfortunately, however, our society's lingering "antisex ethic" tends to foreclose constructive learning experiences and contexts. Often, prevailing sociocultural myths and misconceptions are learned in-

stead. Anachronistic ideas and educational opposition drive the learning process underground.

The past should be studied to improve the present. The cross-cultural perspective should provide us with a view beyond our immediate borders, thus increasing our eclectic choices. A better future for our fast-changing society and sexuality calls for quality sex education programs to counteract the locker room, commercial sex, and trial by error contexts in which most individuals in our society gain misinformation as opposed to knowledge.

The first subsection *Historical and Cross-Cultural Perspective* looks at some of the greatest discoveries in the sexual area and describes some of the struggles that the pioneers of sex research had to overcome. It also looks at the revitalization of the Kinsey Institute in recent years, provides an overview of the changes in childbirth during the past 200 years, and explores the ancient erotica of the Orient.

The subsection on *Changing Society/Changing Sexuality* begins with an article which reports on the Meese Commission on Pornography and the ramification of its proposals and actions for our society. The next article looks at the different perceptions males and females have of sex, and the differences between sex and intimacy. The resurging controversy over female autonomy in sexuality is the topic of "Re-Making Love." The final article deals with the importance of sex education, especially in light of the threat of AIDS.

Looking Ahead: Challenge Questions

What would you like to see added to the greatest moments in sex history? Why do you think that your suggestion would qualify?

What were the challenges for early sex researchers and how have things changed?

How might the teachings of the Orient enhance sexual relationships of today?

Is censorship in line with the basic ideas on which the United States was founded? What are the social ramifications of censorship?

What is meant by "value-free" sex education? Why is this an important issue? How can sex education help to protect children from contracting AIDS?

Unit 1

—20—
GREATEST MOMENTS IN SEX HISTORY

The annals of human sexuality are crowded with invention

PHILIP NOBILE

Sex has a long history and even longer prehistory. In fact, earth would not be a very interesting planet without it. Generally speaking, grass would not grow, birds would not fly and men would not be men unless the male and female of every species of flora and fauna got down to merging their DNA through an act of sex.

But how many moments in this erotic vastness can truly be called great? What turn of events have altered and illuminated the history of sex for good and for ill? Should the accounting begin on Mount Sinai when Yahweh dictated the Ten Commandments, including two divine admonitions against committing adultery and coveting a neighbor's wife? Probably more sex lives have been affected by these proscriptions than by technical miracles of the modern age. But the route to Mt. Sinai is too easy. The 20 moments that follow in chronological order may seem quirky, capricious and sometimes obvious. But so, too, is sex.

1. INTERCOURSE FACE-TO-FACE (PREHISTORY)

Perhaps the supreme moment in human sexual history was the popularization of frontal intercourse. Our animal forbears, including primate relatives, mated from the rear (*a tergo*) which hampered intimacy and discouraged female orgasm. (The latter is almost unknown among female mammals.) But when our evolutionary line started walking erect, and the female pelvis shifted around, face-to-face intercourse was en-couraged and spread like herpes.

Coitus *a tergo* is now a minor variation occurring, said Kinsey, in less than 15 percent of the population on a regular basis.

2. LOSS OF ESTRUS (PREHISTORY)

Human females are unlike their mammalian sisters in one crucial sexual respect: they have no estrus cycle, that is, periods of heat in which they are receptive to males and without which they are cold as ice. With the disappearance of estrus, primitive women became available to the amorous attentions of their mates all year-round. Anthropologists attribute the development of the pair-bonded family structure to this evolutionary curve.

3. PORNOGRAPHY (PREHISTORY)

Men have always had an eye for an ankle, a thigh, a breast or some other female part. This predilection is obviously prehistoric, although cave art from the Old Stone Age reveals no depictions of animal or human copulation. One exception from a cave in Laussel, France shows a couple in an odd embrace, but its pornographic intent is debatable.

The oldest known representation of human intercourse, depicting a Mesopotamian couple, goes as far back as 3000 B.C. Incidentally, the most common position in the ancient porn of Peru, India, China and Japan is the woman on top.

4. PROSTITUTION (PREHISTORY)

Although it is the world's oldest profession, nobody knows how old. But it is not unreasonable to guess that prostitution was born in prehistory when women realized that exchanging sex for enhancement of one kind or another was better than giving it away. The earliest records of prostitution are religious: sacred whores assisted worshippers in the temple of Hammurabi (c. 1750 B.C.) in Babylonia and worked the holy spots of ancient Egypt, Greece and Rome. Ever since then, prostitutes have satisfied the physical needs and fantasy requirements of polyerotic men.

5. AQUINAS CONDEMNS HOMOSEXUALITY (13th CENTURY)

Homosexuals got a relatively free ride during the Middle Ages. Despite ups and downs in early Christianity—Emperor Justinian outlawed all homosexual relations in 533—those of the sodomite persuasion were not considered moral outcasts in the Church's eyes until Thomas Aquinas testified against them in the late thirteenth century. He called homosexual acts an "unnatural vice" in his *Summa Theologica* and compared this behavior to cannibalism, beastiality and eating dirt. Given the authority of Aquinas' work and his extreme position on this matter, homosexuals never again got an even break in the Christian west.

6. THE CONDOM (1564)

Gabriello Fallopio, a sixteenth-century Italian anatomist, claimed the discovery of the linen sheath, which is the first documented prophylactic for the male member.

The English term supposedly derived from a Dr. Condom, a physician at Charles II's court, but this origin is dubious.

Casanova (1725–1798) called them "English overcoats" in his memoirs: "a little coat of very fine and transparent skin, eight inches long and closed at one end, with a narrow pink ribbon slotted through the open end."

After rubber was vulcanized in 1843–44, the modern variety gained popularity in Europe. Packages of condoms were sold with portraits of Queen Victoria on the cover.

Although it is said that condoms are "armor against pleasure and cobwebs against danger," they have spared men from disease and women from pregnancy on millions of happy occasions.

7. SPERMATOZOA (1677)

Antonie van Leeuwenhoek, a Dutch haberdasher, was the first human to see actual spermatozoa. Looking through his primitive microscope in 1677, he saw and described the spermatozoa of dogs and men. Prior to Leeuwenhoek, physicians believed that spermatic fluid contained homunculi or little men who grew into bigger human beings after being deposited in the uterus.

8. VASECTOMY (17th CENTURY)

The first vasectomy was performed more than 300 years ago. By 1925 it had become a routine method of male sterilization. But not until the 1970s did the feminist movement pressure men into taking more responsibility for birth control. In the absence of a male pill, vasectomy operations prospered—with good reason. This minor surgical procedure takes only a half-hour, can be done under a local anesthetic, costs about $150, and is 99 to 100 percent effective. Side-effects are minimal. Hormone production, erection capability and orgasm remain unaffected. Better yet, vasectomies are now sometimes reversible with microsurgery.

9. THE DIAPHRAGM (1870)

Dr. Wilhelm Mensinga, a German anatomy professor, invented the "occlusive pessary" in the 1870s. Also known as the Dutch Cap, it consisted of a hollow rubber hemisphere with a watch-spring rim. Mensinga's device, which closely resembles the modern diaphragm, permitted women to control contraception reliably for the first time in

history When used properly, the diaphragm provides 97 to 98 percent protection.

10. THREE ESSAYS ON THE THEORY OF SEXUALITY (1905)

When Freud's biographer Ernest Jones asked him to name his favorite writings from his oeuvre, Freud pulled down from his shelves *Interpretation of Dreams* and *Three Essays* and said that the latter "should last longer." Diverging from the crudities of Richard Krafft-Ebing's *Psychopathologia Sexualis (1902)*, Freud invented a new language and psychology of the sex instinct that cleared the erogenous zones of prigs and priests and made way for the science of sex. His boldest ideas—the Oedipus complex, the seduction theory, castration anxiety, bisexuality, sublimation, repression, etc.—were expressed in *Three Essays*, a book that was considered wicked and obscene in its day.

11. IDEAL MARRIAGE (1926)

An efflorescence of sex manuals occurred during the first two decades of this century. *Ideal Marriage* by Dutch gynecologist Th. H. Van de Velde was the *Joy of Sex* of its time and has remained in print ever since. Although quaint by today's standards, Van de Velde risked condemnation by praising foreplay, orgasm, variety in intercourse positions and the "genital kiss" (otherwise called oral sex) in grandly lyric terms.

12. ULYSSES DECISION (1933)

Until 1933 any book with sexually descriptive passages was pornographic in the eyes of the law. But then a mild-mannered U.S. District Court Judge, John M. Woolsey, ruled that James Joyce's masterpiece *Ulysses* was not obscene when read "in its entirety" by "a person with average sex instincts." The U.S. Attorney's office in New York had asked the government to authorize the forfeiture, confiscation, and destruction of the book because of its allegedly prurient content. In an opinion that sexually liberated literature and revolutionized obscenity laws, Judge Woolsey declined the motion, stating, "The words which are criticized are old Saxon words known to almost all men and, I venture, to many women, and are such words as would be naturally and habitually used, I believe, by the types of folk whose life, physical and mental, Joyce is seeking to describe. In respect of the recurrent emergence of the theme of sex in the minds of his characters, it must always be remembered that his locale was Celtic and his season spring."

13. PENICILLIN (1940)
Syphilis was a frequent killer until penicillin mold, discovered by Sir Alexander Fleming in 1928, was manufactured in usable quantities in England in the early 1940s. This antibiotic drug is effective in treating syphilis in both early and late stages. Unfortunately, gonorrhea has proved resistant to penicillin.

14. THE KINSEY REPORTS
(1948–1953)
More was known about the mating habits of animals than the mating game of human beings until Alfred Kinsey gave up the study of wasps in 1938 and began interviewing 18,000 real people about their sexual behavior. Kinsey and his small team produced a Himalaya of original data (much of which remains untapped at the Kinsey Institute in Bloomington, Indiana) that rescued sex from the whims of misinformed psychologists and physicians.

Unlike previous sexologists who researched miscellaneous and patient populations, Kinsey cast his net broadly to find out "what average people do sexually." He established baselines for certain practices (e.g., 37 percent of white American males had a homosexual encounter to the point of orgasm after adolescence), demonstrated that individual variations were so divergent that concepts of normality and abnormality were nonsense, devised a 0–6 scale to measure the spectrum of heterosexual and homosexual response, and confirmed the myth that erotic preferences developed according to social level (sex indeed was the poor man's grand opera).

15. THE FIRST SEX CHANGE
(1952)
George Jorgensen, a 26-year-old ex-

GI, became the world's first transsexual in 1952. A team of Danish surgeons and endocrinologists, led by Dr. Christian Hamburger, undid nature's plan with a combination of therapy, hormones and scalpels.

In 1966, the first American clinic for gender reversal problems opened at Johns Hopkins Hospital despite the objections of some resident psychiatrists.

During the first decade of transsexual surgery, an estimated two thousand people had their bodies altered. The vast majority went from male to female (only 28 of 368 early transsexuals studied by the pioneering researcher Dr. Harry Benjamin asked to go from Ms. to Mr).

16. THE PILL
The Food and Drug Administration approved G.D. Searle's pill in 1960. Simple, certain and relatively safe for younger women, the first oral contraceptive revolutionized birth control and, in its heyday, American sexual behavior. Not exactly a panacea, the pill is used by only half of American women who are contraceptors. Worldwide use lags far behind other means—including prolonged lactation and abortion.

17. HUMAN SEXUAL RESPONSE
(1966)
Despite latter day demolitions of their overrated therapy books *Human Sexual Inadequacy* and *Homosexuality in Perspective*, Masters and Johnson brought forth a masterwork of physiology in *Human Sexual Response*. By direct observation and physical measurement of couples in the lock of passion, Masters and Johnson mapped for the first time the unknown region of orgasm. Spelunking in previously unexplored vaginal zones, they threw considerable light on female sexuality—although they seemed to have missed the recently hallowed Gräfenberg Spot.

A special oak leaf cluster is owed to the St. Louis team for witnessing over 7,500 climaxes by women and over 2,500 male ejaculatory episodes in 11 years.

18. DEEP THROAT (1972)
Porn films languished in the backrooms of the entertainment industry before fellatrice Linda Lovelace turned her esophagus into an erogenous zone and thereby made *Deep Throat* a mass cult classic in 1972. With a gross of $50 million plus, it was the most profitable movie in history. But the real significance of *Deep Throat* was cultural: its campy oragenitalism conquered social resistance to X-rated films and paved the way for hardcore acceptability.

19. HOMOSEXUALS DECLARED
HEALTHY (1973)
Until 1973, health professionals treated homosexuality as a mental illness. It was included in the American Psychiatric Association's official classification of diseases, and agencies like the Immigration and Naturalization Service used this category to keep "sick" homosexuals out of the United States.

When the APA's *Diagnostic and Statistical Manual of Disorders* was revised 12 years ago, homosexuality was removed from its pages. Distress about one's homosexuality is still listed as an illness, but homosexuality alone can no longer be considered a mental defect.

20. SEXAHOLIC PLAGUE (1984)
According to a recent report in *The New York Times*, as many as one in 12 people may be addicted to sex, that is, they use "sex as a psychological narcotic." If this estimate is accurate, the world population of sexaholics is approximately 375 million, a figure greater than the combined populations of the United States, Italy, South Africa, Romania, Morocco and Argentina.

PROFILE
JUNE REINISCH

New Directions for the Kinsey Institute

ITS THIRD DIRECTOR STRESSES BIOMEDICAL AND PSYCHOBIOLOGICAL RESEARCH, A MOVE SHE BELIEVES KINSEY WOULD APPROVE.

ELIZABETH HALL

Elizabeth Hall, coauthor of Sexuality *and* Child Psychology Today, *both published by Random House, has conducted numerous conversations for* Psychology Today.

In 1948, a book popularly known as the *Kinsey Report* launched the modern era of sex research. *Sexual Behavior in the Human Male*, followed five years later by *Sexual Behavior in the Human Female*, helped demystify sex and make public discussion acceptable. To house and protect the nearly 18,000 interviews collected for the books and for other use, researcher Alfred Kinsey founded the Institute for Sex Research at Indiana University.

Today, after decades of virtual silence, the voice of the Kinsey Institute is again being heard throughout the land. Since pressure from conservative groups convinced the Rockefeller Foundation to withdraw funding in the 1950s, the institute has kept such a low profile that many people thought it had gone out of business. Then in 1982, June Machover Reinisch became the institute's third director. A developmental psychobiologist known for her work on the behavioral influences of exposure to prenatal hormones, she immediately broadened the organization's scope, changed its name to the Kinsey Institute for Research in Sex, Gender, and

Reproduction and set out to make it a household name once again.

Reinisch, a 43-year-old whose energy is always in overdrive, told me of her plans and her research during an interview at the institute. She firmly believes that she is moving in a direction Kinsey would have favored. In a voice that for an unsettling moment makes it seem Joan Rivers is seated beside you, Reinisch points out that Kinsey was a biologist. Once he was satisfied with the survey research that launched the institute, she suggests, he would have headed in the same biomedical and psychobiological directions. He had, after all, advised William Masters and Virginia Johnson when they began their physiologically oriented research on human sexuality.

At the time Reinisch was nominated to apply for the institute director's job, she was an associate professor of psychology at Rutgers University. A New Yorker by birth and conviction, she had no intention of moving to the heartland and believed she was merely a token woman in the group of 20 candidates. But her research record, combined with a presentation full of new directions for the institute, apparently convinced the selection committee that she was the right leader for the Kinsey Institute in the 1980s and beyond.

The path from the sidewalks of New York to the Bloomington campus had

Gwen Verdon of her generation. She tried, becoming a singer with a rock group called the Seagulls before she discovered she couldn't stand the constant auditions.

"I have a lot of physical bravery," she says. "I can fly planes and skydive and scuba dive and go into the jungles, but I can't handle rejection. Even if you become a star, you have to start from square one every time you go after a new part. I loved to entertain, but that didn't make up for the constant tryouts and rejections."

So Reinisch tried other things. She sold airplanes, she became a sales representative for a cosmetics firm and,

had left her speaking "bop talk," a music and show-business jargon that made the university vocabulary seem like a foreign language.

During that first semester, Reinisch was intrigued by Eleanor Maccoby's book, *The Development of Sex Differences*. She was especially fascinated by the discussion of sex hormones and the suggestion—based on research by psychologist John Money of Johns Hopkins University—that prenatal exposure to androgens (male hormones) might make girls tomboyish. Through childhood and adolescence, she had hung out with the boys because she shared their interest in motorcycles, cars and adventure. Yet she always longed to be exactly like her doll-like mother and couldn't understand why she was so different.

As she puts it, "I was delighted to discover that there might be biological reasons for my being a tomboy. I've noticed that most good research (and I hope mine is good) reflects the researcher's private questions. It took me a long time to see that my work grew out of my own concerns."

The influence of biology on behavior was an unpopular topic in 1969, but Brian Sutton-Smith, then program coordinator for developmental psychology at Teachers College in New York, supported Reinisch. He saw to it that she had a predoctoral fellowship and introduced her to Money, his fellow New Zealander, whose work had intrigued her. Money had originated the concept of gender identity (the inner feeling of being male or female) as distinct from gender roles (outward masculine or feminine behavior).

Reinisch forgot show business and started a doctoral program at Columbia, under an arrangement that allowed Money to act as her major adviser. For her dissertation, she looked at 42 children whose mothers had been given steroid hormones during pregnancy. Each of the children had a sibling who had not been exposed to the hormones, and she used them as a comparison group. She found significant personality differences. The youngsters who had been exposed to progestins (which act like male hormones) scored consistently higher on traits considered masculine than their siblings of the same sex did. That is, they were more independent, individualistic, self-assured and self-sufficient. Youngsters who had been ex-

*P*RENATAL EXPOSURE TO SYNTHETIC MALE HORMONES HAS A POWERFUL EFFECT ON WHETHER CHILDREN EXPECT TO HANDLE CONFLICT THROUGH PHYSICAL AGGRESSION OR OTHER MEANS.

many turnings. Reinisch's interest in prenatal development may have begun in Greenwich Village, where 6-year-old June became fascinated with the jars of human fetuses that lined a shelf in the science room of the progressive City and Country School. She became so adept at sneaking into the room, which was off-limits for first- and second-graders, that she was soon leading regular tours of first-graders to see the awesome sight.

Her teachers could hardly have suspected that Reinisch would become a researcher in human behavioral endocrinology. She's dyslexic; she didn't learn to read until she entered public school and found herself the only fourth-grader who couldn't. In college, she prepared to be an elementary school teacher, but her heart wasn't in it. She went to Florida and helped train dolphins. She learned to skydive and got a pilot's license. But always, in the back of her mind, Reinisch saw herself as a musical comedy star, the

finally, found her way back to show business, managing nightclubs and promoting and managing rock groups. Soon she was traveling 100,000 miles a year for Sly and The Family Stone, but she had no time for herself and wanted a change. Dealing with record companies had convinced her that she would be good at what the trade calls "A & R" (artists and repertoire), a sort of executive producer's job. But in 1969 no women held that position. Executives at a record company suggested that she might break the sex barrier if she had a master's degree in anything.

Few people were getting MBA's in 1969; if they had, Reinisch might never have reached the Kinsey Institute. Instead, she decided that a master's in psychology would appeal to the artists she'd be dealing with and trotted off to Columbia University in her miniskirt and white boots. It was tough at first. Dyslexia made reading difficult, and her years with the music industry

posed to estrogens, particularly synthetic diethylstilbestrol (DES), which acts like a female hormone, scored higher on feminine characteristics; they were more group-oriented and dependent on the group.

Serendipity then took Reinisch to Rutgers, which needed another developmental psychologist. The search committee, largely composed of researchers in animal behavior, had interviewed candidate after candidate who smugly told them that such research had no relevance for human development. When Reinisch described her work and mentioned that it would have been impossible without the foundation provided by animal research, she got the job.

At Rutgers, she studied the effects of hormones on behavior and discovered that prenatal exposure to male hormones had a powerful effect on whether children expected to handle conflict with physical aggression or through other means. Because most psychologists were still attributing nearly all behavior to learning, she was careful to eliminate possible sources of bias. No one who interviewed or tested the children was allowed to know which ones had been exposed. She studied children who showed no physical evidence of their exposure, whose mothers had forgotten, or had never known, they had been given hormones; most thought they had been given vitamins.

Some of her findings were so strong (see the box, "The Fighting Hormones") that Reinisch herself had a hard time believing them. She waited for almost a year, checking and rechecking her data with several respected colleagues, before submitting them for publication. She still shakes her head with disbelief when she talks about those findings. "You don't expect effects like that," she says. "You expect delicate little effects that you need fancy-schmantzy statistics to bring out. Not this time. The simplest tests were all we needed."

Her research has convinced Reinisch that sex differences in perception, cognition and personality exist but are built on a foundation of "biological differences that are really quite small." These original differences are highly magnified by experience and by complicated interactions between the person and the environment.

Looking for an example of the way temperament is expressed, she cites aggression. "One person might go out and rob banks or beat up old ladies in the park, while someone with the same propensity in a different environment might run a multinational corporation." She suddenly becomes serious and perches on the edge of the couch, her voice urgent. "We don't know enough about what aggression is. Does it have to do with the impulse? Or with physiological responses? Perhaps if you respond slowly, you have time to think, 'My God, if I hit him, he'll hit me. Maybe I better not do that.'"

THE SEXUAL REVOLUTION IS MAINLY IN THE MEDIA. IN OUR HOMES, WE'RE STILL STRUGGLING.

We are interrupted by the insistent ring of the telephone, and Reinisch puts on a headset that allows her to talk, pace the carpet and gesture at the same time. A researcher in human sexuality wants the institute to take a position on pornography. Reinisch refuses. "I can't do it," she tells me later. "The institute is a place to develop information, to collect it and to disseminate it. It must be a place that all people, whatever their ideas or political beliefs, can rely on as a source of unbiased information."

That position is reflected in "The Kinsey Report," a thrice-weekly syndicated newspaper column on sexuality that Reinisch began in 1984. Some people were nervous when Reinisch proposed writing a column to share research-generated information with the public. "They were afraid it would be filled with 'Dear Abby' type of advice," Reinisch says, "and there was great concern about that." But Reinisch, who writes the column with

the help of other staff members, gives information, not advice.

She soon discovered that, despite all the cultural small talk, the skin magazines and the triple-X movies, many Americans needed the basics. "All the talk about a sexual revolution makes me laugh," she says. "The sexual revolution is mostly in the media. In our homes, we're still struggling. Sex is so scary that students in sex education classes devote most of their energy to sitting quietly, trying not to giggle or blush. They often don't even hear the information they need."

Reinisch started the column, in part, to answer the desperate calls she got from people who needed simple information about sexuality. "They can't put their problems into words. They keep saying 'it, it' until finally I have to say, 'Now tell me what you're really talking about. Is your problem that your penis will not stay erect?' Then you hear them take a deep breath, pause and say, 'Yes.' They can't tell their physicians, and when they try, the physicians are sometimes as embarrassed as the patients."

It's clear that the column is not read just by teenagers. Reinisch has had questions from readers as young as 14 and as old as 96 but says that more than half the letters come from people over 40 and 30 percent come from people over 50. The questions tend to fo-

ONE NEWSPAPER AXED THE COLUMN WHEN THE PUBLISHER'S WIFE FOUND IT EMBARRASSING.

cus on two issues: "Am I normal?" and "Should I go to a doctor?"

Most attempts to ban the column have failed. When the editor of the Evansville (Indiana) Press asked his readers if the column should be sent back to Bloomington in a brown paper

---

Lifestyle

Sensitivity, accuracy needed in fertility testing

The Kinsey report
By June Reinisch

QUESTION — I've been trying to conceive for one year and had a test (PVC) that showed that my husband's sperm lacks motility.

I told him it's from smoking too much marijuana. He doesn't agree. His reply is, "If that's true, why don't they prescribe pot for birth control?"

I don't know how to answer him. The doctor wants to do a sperm count on him but my husband is extremely reluctant. What should I do?

ANSWER — I'm not sure what test you had. Was it called a "post-coital test"?

In this test, the couple abstains from intercourse for two days before the day ovulation is expected. Following coitus, the woman's upper vagina and cervical area are carefully cleaned, and a sample of cervical mucus taken within two to four hours. This sample is then examined through a microscope as quickly as possible.

Post-coital test results include number and movement (motility) of any sperm seen and the quality of the woman's cervical mucus (whether it is too thick, etc.).

But a number of things can affect the validity of the test results, including the timing of coitus, the use of a lubricant, a delay in reaching the mucus [...] the ovulation [...] cycle. There a[...] the stress of ha[...] timed sex cause[...] ence ejaculator[...] curs, but littl[...] emitted).

If there were[...] post-coital testi[...] ing, the woman[...] factory, and the[...] five forwardly[...] mucus sample,[...] sis is impor[...] whether the r[...] tains sperm s[...] tion. In fact,[...] analysis is u[...] doing the mo[...] coital test.

Many men find it difficult to provide a semen sample, but a sensitive physician can discuss various options with your husband and arrange the procedure so that your husband's comfort is maintained without jeopardizing the test validity.

There are many causes of low sperm motility. The effect of marijuana has not been clearly established as a cause of low fertility.

the testicle), having a fever or a virus, some medications (such as steroids) or wearing underwear that holds the testicles too close to the body.

Nearly all of these problems can be successfully treated and the sperm motility increased; in fact, there is even a 25 percent pregnancy rate in couples where the man has been tested and categorized as having a poor sperm count or motility and has had no treatment.

You should seriously discuss with your husband whether he's really interested in parenthood right now.

If he is, then he should participate in selecting the specialist or clinic. Making this decision may reduce his reluctance about tests and examinations.

To return to the issue of marijuana: I recommend that both men and women stop ingesting all substances not absolutely required for their health beginning several [...]ore conception is [...] nother should contin[...] nce throughout preg[...] breast-feeding. This [...] egal drugs, alcohol, [...] n drugs (even aspi[...] ription drugs unless

absolutely necessa[...] Science simply d[...] effects of exposu[...] stances on the fe[...] abstinence is the [...] healthiest possible

Send questions t[...] The Kinsey Report, Telephone, P.O. Bo[...] ton, IN 47402. Volu[...] its personal replies [...] general interest m[...] future columns.

June Reinisch i[...] Kinsey Institute for [...] Gender and Repro[...] University.

Lifestyle

Circumcision: cultural choice

The Kinsey report
By June Reinisch

QUESTION — We're expecting our first child. If it's a boy, should he be circumcised?

We've understand there is no medical reason for circumcision, but is there an effect on sexuality?

We've heard two views: That circumcision removes sensitive penile nerve endings that would make sex more enjoyable for both the man and his partner, and the opposite — that circumcised men have hardened glans that minimize premature ejaculation. Which is true?

You might be interested to know that the American Academy of Pediatrics (in 1971 and again in 1975) and the American College of Obstetricians and Gynecologists have reevaluated the health value of routine circumcision.

Good hygiene for boys doesn't involve forcible retraction of the foreskin. Daily washing of the external penile surface with soap and water is all that is necessary. The foreskin will eventually retract naturally and older boys can be taught the importance of retracting the foreskin and cleaning beneath it as a part of the daily bath or shower.

This is a decision that parents should make based on their personal feelings. But circumcision is no longer thought to be medically or hygienically necessary. For a brochure on this topic, write to The

Sex three times a week: The column provides research-based information, not advice to the lovelorn.

---

wrapper, they overwhelmingly urged him to keep printing it. But the column was axed by a major Midwestern newspaper when the publisher's wife found it embarrassing.

Despite signs of growing social conservatism, Reinisch believes that the VCR will keep Victorian primness from dominating the culture. She often gets letters saying things like, "My wife and I belong to the church, have three children and do everything right. But once a week we like to spice up our private life with an erotic video. Why are people trying to take them away from us?"

When I asked her whether she believed the triple-X tapes were educational, she hesitated. "Everybody learns from them," she said, "but we don't know whether it's good or bad. If they learn new ways to make each other happy, that's fine. But most of the actors suffer from delayed ejaculation, and if men get the idea that there's something wrong with them because they can't hold an erection for 25 minutes, that's bad.

"But we don't have data on anything." She comes down hard on each word. "We ought to be interviewing people who use videotapes to find out whether their marriages have changed. And how. We could find out if we had the money."

Reinisch is keenly aware that ultimately taxpayers pay for all scientific research and thinks that one way to

pay them back is to pass along what the researchers learn. She believes that scientists who speak only to other scientists are making a mistake, one that could dry up research funds.

"If people don't know what researchers have done," she says, "how can they be expected to keep giving us money? Why do you think they always cut research funds first? Nobody understands, least of all Congress and the President, that you don't cure cancer by throwing $800 million into the construction of elaborate cancer cen-

THE LASTING INFLUENCE OF SUCH HORMONES MAKES HER LOOK CLOSELY AT OTHER SUBSTANCES THAT AFFECT THE UNBORN CHILD.

ters. You cure cancer by throwing money into the pool of scientific research and letting researchers do their own thing. Maybe somebody will find

a cure for cancer while studying mushrooms. How many senators know that some guy studying the engineering of feathers discovered the information that enabled us to keep submarines from being crushed on the ocean floor? Our column might help people to understand that it's basic research that needs the support."

A belief in the public's right to know also guides Reinisch's research. When she studies a family to see how prenatal hormones or barbiturates affect children, she provides voluminous feedback. "My team always interviews and tests every child who wants to be included," she says. "I don't believe in picking two children out of eight for special attention. The kind of testing we do—IQ, specific mental abilities, personality—would cost the family $500 to $1,000 per child." She always sandwiches any necessary negative information into positive reports. "In many cases," she says, "we've changed families' views of children and children's views of themselves, always for the better."

In one family, for example, "the first and third children were sent to college, but the middle one was working in a gas station. Everybody, including the kid, agreed that he was the dumb one. When I looked at the test, it was clear that the boy's IQ was at least 15 points ahead of anybody in the family. The tester took the kid aside

THE FIGHTING HORMONES

In the early 1970s, when psychologists Eleanor Maccoby and Carol Jacklin analyzed studies to look for sex differences in behavior, the only clear-cut difference they found was in aggression. In every culture, boys were more physically aggressive than girls. Studies of girls whose mothers had taken synthetic hormones to prevent a miscarriage suggested some biological basis to other sex differences in behavior, but no one had found tomboyish girls particularly aggressive.

Reinisch looked at the question from another perspective, to see whether prenatal hormones changed the way children see aggressiveness in themselves. She questioned 54 youngsters about how they thought they would respond to six typical conflicts children have with one another, such as arguments over a game. After hearing each situation described, they were asked to choose one of four possible reactions: hit someone, use aggressive words, beat a hasty retreat or find a nonaggressive way to handle the conflict, such as appealing to a teacher.

Half of these children (17 girls and 8 boys) had been exposed to synthetic progestins (substances that can have masculinizing effects) before they were born. The others were their brothers and sisters of the same sex who had not been exposed. When Reinisch looked at the replies, she found that both sex and prenatal exposure to hormones influenced whether a child expected to use physical force. Girls who had been exposed to the hormones were much more likely to pick a physically aggressive response than were their unexposed sisters. Boys who had been exposed were considerably more apt to choose physical aggression than were their brothers. But gender differences still held: As a group, the unexposed boys chose more physically aggressive responses than the unexposed girls (see chart).

No other factors seemed to influence the results. Age made no dif-

HORMONES AND AGGRESSION

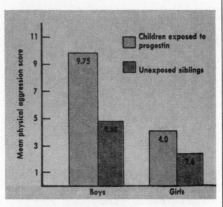

Mean physical aggression scores for 17 girls and 8 boys. The maximum score would be 18 if someone picked the physical option in all situations.

ference, nor did a child's birth order. And the effects held only for physical aggression. Hormone exposure had no effect on the children's choice of verbal aggression.

Reinisch can't be certain, of course, that the children would behave the same way in real conflicts as they did on the test. But the data show that boys are more likely than girls to imagine themselves reacting to conflict with physical aggression, and that prenatal exposure to synthetic hormones increases both sexes' belief that they would act that way.

Reinisch's findings are consistent with other research indicating that prenatal exposure to masculinizing hormones often makes girls act more like boys in various ways. But the effect in boys was even greater, which was a surprise. "Based on animal research," Reinisch says, "we had assumed that any hormones with masculinizing properties in addition to those normally produced by the male fetus would not influence behavior. What we found suggested that if higher levels of these hormones reached boys' brains before birth, the differences between male and female behavior would be even greater."

and told him that he had the highest IQ in the family. If he wanted to be a gas station attendant, that was OK, but he had the intelligence to do just about anything he wanted with his life. Two weeks later he was enrolled in college."

What she's learned about the lasting effects of prenatal hormones makes Reinisch look closely at other substances that affect the unborn child. She's especially worried by our ignorance about various drugs. "The fact that babies look OK when they're born doesn't tell you very much. You've got to wait until they're 2 or 3 to find out if they can talk, until they're 6 to find out if they can read. You've got to wait until 12 to find out if they can do higher mathematics, until 18 or 20 to find out if they are capable of falling in love and until their 20s to find out if they can have babies.

"It takes even longer to know if they can be decent parents. A drug that affects the development of the brain before birth may not show itself until very late along that path. And you can't get that kind of information from studying rats. You have to spend money to follow children throughout the life span."

Alarmed by her review of the animal literature, Reinisch has been looking at young men whose mothers were given barbiturates while they were pregnant. It's been estimated that up to 25 percent of women in Europe and the United States between 1950 and 1980 took barbiturates at some time during pregnancy. Reinisch prefers not to reveal any findings of this research—or of another, five-year study of Danish children born between 1959 and 1961 whose mothers took hormones while they were pregnant—until she finishes her analyses.

In another, earlier study of 4,653 infants, she found that the length of gestation has a powerful effect on how quickly infants reach such developmental milestones as sitting, crawling and standing. All these babies were considered full-term, but they were born anywhere from 38 to 41 weeks after the mother's last menstrual period. Reinisch has found that those born closer to 41 weeks consistently reached the milestones sooner than the others. The same pattern applies to premature babies; the less time in the womb, the slower their development.

I TELL PARENTS OF PREMATURE BABIES, 'LOOK. YOU WANT TO HAVE A HAPPY FIRST TWO YEARS? LIE ABOUT YOUR CHILD'S BIRTHDAY.'

When she talks to parents of premature babies, Reinisch says, she tells them, "Look. You want to have a happy first two years? Lie about your child's birthday. Start the birthday on the day the baby should have been born, nine months after conception. You'll feel better about your baby and your baby will feel better about herself or himself. And you won't have to hear people say, 'Gee, that doesn't look like a 6-month-old baby. You mean he doesn't sit up?'"

In the same study, Reinisch found that baby boys and girls generally reach milestones on different timetables. "The areas of development that each sex concentrates on seem roughly analogous to the psychological characteristics of adult maleness and femaleness," Reinisch says. "For example, little girls may start sitting without support earlier but spend more time at it than little boys do before they stand with support. Boys may start crawling earlier than girls but crawl for a longer period before they walk with support. Perhaps sitting permits more face-to-face interaction with the caretaker, and crawling results in separation from the caretaker—reflecting earlier independence. In a sense, the boy is being independent and the girl is being social."

The demands of the Kinsey Institute keep Reinisch from spending as much time on her research as she would like. The institute needs a $5 million endowment to end worries about another dark age like the 1950s. The need has pushed Reinisch into spending more time fundraising, a skill enhanced by her stage presence. The way she warms up an audience also comes in handy when she talks to journalists and appears on television programs.

The institute buzzes with activity these days. Seminars meet regularly in the conference room. In 1984, the first Kinsey symposium brought experts from all disciplines to discuss masculinity and femininity, and summer institutes provide education and training for professionals. Scholars come from all over the world to use the collection, and Reinisch hopes to increase the number of postdoctoral fellows at the institute.

One of Reinisch's ambitions is to get enough funds to reinterview the people Kinsey talked to 40 years ago. Knowing how well they remembered their sex lives in the 1940s would tell a lot about the reliability of retrospective data. By comparing the replies of the people who are now 60 with those given by the 60-year-olds Kinsey interviewed, researchers might discover whether sexual practices have really changed or whether people just talk about them more.

Men and women in their 50s, 60s, 70s and 80s keep turning up at the institute to say that the Kinsey interview was the greatest experience of their lives. Reinisch would like to know if their reaction is typical and how a person's sex life over the years affects longevity. So far this is a million-dollar dream; $300,000 a year for three and a half years would enable her to reinterview 2,000 of the original group. You leave the institute feeling that she has the drive to make the dream come true.

200 Years of Childbirth

Advances in the management of labor and delivery
have led to reactions that
emphasize the pregnant woman's own role.

Andrea Boroff Eagan

Andrea Boroff Eagan is the author of
"The Newborn Mother: Stages of Her Growth"
(Little, Brown, and Company).

A woman begins to feel the first pangs of labor. Her husband or perhaps one of her older children is dispatched to alert the midwife and probably several other women in the community, who rapidly gather. The women remain with their laboring friend, talking and praying, helping with household and farm chores, as long as necessary. The labor, like most, is painful but uneventful. Eventually, the baby is born, the mother rests. The midwife and one or more of the other women stay to attend the new mother and to help for a few days or even a few weeks.

This was childbirth in America until the nineteenth century. Women attended women at childbirth, and the death of a woman in childbirth, as far as we can determine, was a very uncommon event. The babies, of course, were more fragile, and it is not unusual to read of a family in which only one or two of eight or more children survived to adulthood.

Things changed by the mid-nineteenth century. Childbirth, for many women, became something to be feared as an unbearably painful and quite often fatal event. Victorian morals and the growth of cities made women, at least middle-class women, less active than their rural grandmothers had been. A woman whose diet was probably seriously deficient (the Victorians were not much for eating vegetables), who had no exercise at all, whose knowledge of the processes of labor and delivery was very limited if not nonexistent, and who had kept herself tightly corseted throughout her pregnancy, then faced birth without even the comfort that her eighteenth-century grandmother would have had of a knowledgeable midwife and probably several other older, more experienced women. A respectable, middle-class woman was likely to be delivered in her home by a doctor, one of the new breed of "scientific practitioners" who promised to employ the latest advances—forceps and other instruments and bloodletting—to speed labor.

Advances in the management of childbirth always come as a reaction to the standard practices and problems of the times. And, for that reason among others, what is an improvement for one age often turns out to be a major problem of the next. Thus, many people who were considered heroes at the time they practiced later became symbols of interference, mismanagement, and disaster.

Forceps.

In England, where by the seventeenth century the population was more urbanized (and less healthy) than in colonial America, the midwives' custom was to call in the barber-surgeon when a normal delivery appeared impossible. These men had a number of instruments that they used to extract the infant, living or dead, from the mother when all else had failed.

Early in the seventeenth century, a surgeon named Peter Chamberlen developed an instrument, called the forceps, which was shaped like two large spoons, to be inserted one at a time into the birth canal around the infant's head. The handles were then joined, and the infant could be extracted. To protect this very lucrative practice, the design of the forceps was kept secret. The instruments were carried about in a huge, carved, locked wooden box. When a member of the Chamberlen family arrived to attend a birth, the patient was blindfolded and the door was locked. One of the family would make noises, ringing bells and such, to cover the clanking sound of the instruments. The Chamberlen family kept the design of their device secret for over a century, becoming famous for successful deliveries in difficult cases, and rich in the process.

Eventually, the secret was stolen, and forceps gradually came into wide use, in England, Europe, and America. As their use increased, however, untrained practitioners or doctors in a hurry damaged or killed a great many babies, as they were saving others. As a result, forceps developed a bad reputation with midwives, but retained their popularity with doctors. As the training of doctors improved in the twentieth century, their use of forceps became less dangerous. Nonetheless, the development, in the 1970's, of suction devices for delivering a baby who is stuck in the birth canal, was seen by some as a significant advance in safety, since forceps, even in skilled hands, can still cause injury to both the infant and the mother.

Puerperal fever.

In America in the nineteenth century, members of the middle class were born and died at home; hospitals were considered to be places for the fallen and the destitute. The death rate in many hospitals from puerperal (or childbed) fever was high—20 percent of the patients in one Boston hospital died of the disease in 1883, according to historians Richard and Dorothy Wertz. The fact that puerperal fever was contagious had been deduced by Alexander Gordon, M.D., of Aberdeen, as early as 1793, but the medical texts of the nineteenth century made no mention of contagion. Oliver Wendell Holmes, a doctor practicing in Boston (and the father of the Oliver Wendell Holmes who later became a Justice of the Supreme Court), knowing of Gordon's theory, published an eloquent paper in the *New England Quarterly Journal of Medicine and Surgery* in 1843, laying out the horrors of the disease and the evidence for its extreme contagiousness. Holmes believed that the disease-causing agent was carried from one woman to another on the unwashed hands of the attending physician. Holmes was ridiculed and at-

tacked: one prominent Philadelphia physician, Dr. Charles D. Meigs, wrote furiously that doctors, being gentlemen, could not possibly have dirty hands. In 1855, Holmes published another monograph on the subject, which eventually, and fortunately, had widespread influence, especially after Pasteur's discovery of germs in the 1880's.

But the preventive measures taken against the contagion were truly horrendous, even to read, and must have been unbearable for the poor women subjected to them. Holmes' very simple suggestion that the hands be thoroughly washed between patients might have been rejected, but repeated injections of carbolic acid into a woman's genitalia were acceptable. The increased use of instruments and surgical intervention, which caused easily infected wounds, made puerperal fever a continuing problem into the 1930's and 40's, when it finally came under control as a result of better sterile procedures, improved general health, and antibiotics. But were it not for Holmes and some of his European colleagues, the death rate from this terrible scourge would undoubtedly have been even higher than it was.

Chloroform.

The discovery of an apparently safe way to spare women the agonies of childbirth seemed to some a tremendous advance in its time. To others, including Dr. Meigs, who believed that gentlemen doctors could not have dirty hands, pain in labor (or even during surgery) was considered a beneficial, cleansing experience. Did not the Bible, after all, say that "in sorrow thou shalt bring forth children"?

Dr. James Simpson, a Scot, who first used chloroform for anesthesia in childbirth in 1847, argued that God himself had put Adam to sleep before removing his rib. In 1853, because of one woman who used chloroform, it became acceptable, even fashionable, to be put to sleep during labor. Queen Victoria accepted chloroform from one of her doctors, John Snow, M.D., during her eighth confinement, at the birth of Prince Leopold. Though the Palace tried to keep it quiet, the news rapidly spread. Women were assured that suffering was not inevitable, though, of course, it was subsequently learned that chloroform was dangerous for both mother and infant.

Cesarean.

Cesarean section (named for the myth that the Roman Emperor Julius Caesar was delivered by surgery) was performed for centuries when it became necessary to try to deliver a live baby from a mother who had already died. It was not performed on living women, because it was always fatal. Some historians believe that the first cesarean in which both mother and baby survived was performed by an eighteenth-century Irish midwife named Mary Dunally. The first successful cesarean section that is documented, however, was performed in 1882 by a German physician, Max Sänger, who had the good sense to attempt to use sterile techniques and to sew up the uterine wall as well as the abdomen. The death rate from cesarean section remained high until after the first quarter of the twentieth century, when the timing and the techniques for the procedure were properly developed.

Confinement.

A middle-class woman in 1900, pregnant for the first time, had no way of confirming the pregnancy. When she was reasonably certain that she was indeed pregnant—missed periods (assuming she understood the significance of that), nausea, a spreading middle, and perhaps the baby's first stirrings—she would, with some embarrassment, confess the news to her husband and female relatives and thereupon be "confined" until well after the baby was born. "Confinement" was not a figure of speech: pregnant women did not leave their homes or even receive any but the most intimate visitors. Some health experts denounced the inactivity and the wearing of corsets during pregnancy, but most women felt there was little alternative to hiding their state. With the turn of the twentieth century, women began taking a more public role, and confinement during pregnancy became more and more onerous. In 1904, a young dressmaker was asked by a client to make a gown which she could wear for entertaining at home during her pregnancy. The seamstress, Lena Bryant, produced a tea gown, which had an accordion-pleated skirt attached to an elastic band at the waist. It was an instant hit. More clothing—loose and concealing, but still fashionable—including some that could be worn *out of doors*, followed. A change in Bryant's first name from "Lena" to "Lane" resulted from a mistake made in filling out a check by the nervous and newly-successful young designer. The chain of Lane Bryant retail stores was built on this line of maternity clothes.

Intervention.

Joseph DeLee is scarcely a hero. His patients qualify better than he does for heroism. But as a shaper of modern obstetrics, he is unparalleled. DeLee, a prominent Chicago obstetrician, did as much as anyone to promote the idea that childbirth is "decidedly pathologic" and to popularize routine intervention.

In 1920, DeLee spoke at a meeting of the American Gynecological Society, and his paper was subsequently published in the *American Journal of Obstetrics and Gynecology*. DeLee believed that modern women were too "nervous" and inefficient to withstand childbirth. Therefore, he recommended a regimen that included "twilight sleep" (which was already becoming very popular) for early labor, general anesthesia for the second stage, along with an extensive episiotomy and the use of forceps to extract the infant from its unconscious mother. Although twilight sleep, accomplished by giving the woman a combination of morphine to suppress pain and scopolamine to make her forget everything that happens, has fallen out of favor, anesthesia and forceps for the actual delivery remain standard procedure in many hospitals today. And, as any woman who has delivered in a hospital knows, episiotomy remains an almost inevitable part of every American birth.

DeLee argued that normal labor was harmful not only to the mother, who would suffer unbearable pain and exhaustion and risk tearing of the tissues, but that it was perhaps even more dangerous for the baby whose head was subjected to "prolonged pounding" during delivery. The large and repeated doses of drugs necessary to maintain twilight sleep were eventually, of course, found to be dangerous to the baby. The routine use of forceps, especially in unskilled hands, could and often did cause brain damage resulting in retardation, cerebral palsy, and other conditions. The episiotomy was necessary because the woman, then as now, usually delivered lying on her back with her legs in high stirrups, a position which made the forceps delivery easier for the doctor. This position stretches the

perineum, making it virtually impossible to deliver the baby's head without tearing or cutting. DeLee, however, like many doctors since, argued that the cut had an advantage, because its repair would restore the mother to "virginal conditions."

The rebirth of midwifery.

In the United States, until the late nineteenth century, most babies were delivered by midwives. It took many years and a concerted campaign against midwives by doctors to convince American women that doctors were better qualified to attend women in childbirth. (In fact, doctors received little or no training in labor and delivery and for centuries had to deliver by touch alone, since no halfway respectable woman would allow any doctor to see the relevant parts of her anatomy.)

By the 1930's, however, midwives had fallen out of favor in most communities. There was little formal opportunity for training in this country, and in some states the practice of midwifery was actually outlawed.

Two institutions kept midwifery alive until obstetrics would find a way to integrate it into standard practice. One was started by Mary Breckinridge, an American, who saw midwives practicing when she went to France to do relief work after World War I. She later went to England (where midwifery had never died out) to receive training on her own. Returning to the United States and inheriting a considerable sum, she looked around for a way to make herself useful. In the Kentucky mountains, she learned, women were giving birth, unattended, under filthy and primitive conditions, and the death rate for both mothers and babies was predictably high. Breckinridge founded the Frontier Nursing Service, hiring British-trained nurse-midwives who rode on horseback through the Kentucky hills giving prenatal care, educating women about health and sanitation, and delivering babies. Today, the Frontier Nursing Service runs a network of rural health centers, which delivers services to a still poor and relatively isolated population. But their standards of care and their record of successful home delivery and low maternal and child mortality with a high-risk population stood for decades as the only evidence of the potential value of midwives.

The other institution is the Maternity Center Association of New York, founded in 1918 to provide prenatal care and education for the poor. In 1932, in a program begun by a midwife from the Frontier Nursing Service, the MCA began offering the first professional midwifery training in the United States. In 1958, the MCA began the first hospital-based midwifery-training program in the United States, at King's County Hospital in Brooklyn, where midwives continue to deliver a majority of clinic patients. Today, the MCA functions as a freestanding birthing center, where midwives have achieved an impressive record of safe, family-centered, out-of-hospital delivery. And now there are over over 3,000 certified nurse-midwives in the country, giving American women a significant choice, not only in birth attendants but in philosophy as well, since midwifery historically (and in contrast to obstetrics) has always been founded on a belief in letting nature take its course.

Pregnancy testing.

You don't hear about the "rabbit test" very often anymore, except occasionally in a stand-up comic's routine. Most women today have only the experience of a test that involves mixing a few drops of urine with something else in a test tube. Before 1928, there was no reliable test for pregnancy; women simply had to wait to know whether they were pregnant. In that year, two Germans, Selmar Aschheim and Bernhard Zondek, developed a test in which a woman's urine could be injected into a mouse to detect the presence of urinary gonadotropins, hormones excreted in large quantities in the urine of pregnant women. A few days later, the mouse was killed and its ovaries examined for signs that it had ovulated. If the woman was pregnant, the hormones caused the mouse to ovulate. Later tests used rabbits (hence "rabbit test"), South African toads (which laid eggs when injected with pregnant urine), or male frogs, which would produce sperm. The tests, generically known as the A-Z test, made early diagnosis of pregnancy, certainly a convenience for women, possible for the first time.

Natural childbirth.

By the late 1930's, some women had begun to object to the routine intervention they faced in childbirth.

When *Childbirth Without Fear*, by the British obstetrician Grantly Dick-Read, was published, it rapidly became enormously popular. Read, as a young doctor, had been taught that childbirth was always unbearably painful and that every woman needed relief. But not long into his practice, he was startled while attending a birth to have the woman refuse chloroform. Asked why, she replied, to Read's amazement, "It didn't hurt. It wasn't meant to, was it, Doctor?"

Read came to believe that pain in childbirth resulted primarily from fear and that, if women were taught to look upon birth as a natural process, to understand the process of labor, to exercise to strengthen the muscles and to breathe through contractions, they would suffer little (or at least less) pain than their unprepared sisters. Although Read had great success with his own patients, the method never really caught on in the United States. One requirement of Read's method was that every woman have emotional support, preferably from someone close to her, throughout labor. Read recommended that this be the husband, but it would be years before American hospitals were willing to have anyone but regular hospital personnel present during labor and delivery. Hospitals also rarely had sufficient staff to permit someone to stay with an unmedicated woman in labor, and American doctors had long since given up staying with a patient through labor. A woman all alone through many hours of labor was less troublesome (and may have been better off) if she was medicated. Read's work, however, planted the idea in the minds of American women that childbirth could be something natural, normal, satisfying, and even joyful. It would take a woman, however, to really start the revolution.

The Lamaze method.

Russian doctors were the first to apply Pavlov's principles of conditioned reflex, combined with some old midwives' tricks, to the problem of labor pain, in a technique they called psychoprophylaxis. In 1951, two French doctors, Fernand Lamaze, M.D., and Pierre Vellay, M.D., visited the Soviet Union, and on their return began applying the method with their patients at a metalworkers' clinic near Paris. The method stressed the woman's control over the birth process. As most Americans now know, the Lamaze method teaches a series of breathing techniques designed to block the sensation of pain. The method had been in use in France for about five years when it was discovered by an American, Marjorie Karmel (who was living in France and looking for someone to deliver her baby by the Read method), whose first child was delivered by Dr. Lamaze. On her return, she wrote *Thank You, Dr. Lamaze*, which described the birth of her first child and Lamaze's method. The book was immensely popular, and Karmel, with several others, founded the American Society for Psychoprophylaxis in Obstetrics, which led the battle to get American doctors and hospitals to accept the method.

Most significant perhaps, for American women, Karmel's book described her struggle to deliver her *second* baby in an American hospital as she had delivered the first in France. American doctors resisted the Lamaze method for the same reasons that they didn't like Read: they preferred to be in charge. However, as the Lamaze method became adapted to the American hospital, the doctor *was* able to remain in charge. While in France the woman had a trained *monitrice* with her for aid and encouragement, the American woman had her husband. While he might also give support and encouragement, he had, as American couples rapidly discovered, no standing in the hospital; he was there only as long as he and his wife behaved themselves.

American women fought hard for the Lamaze method. Eventually, it became widely accepted by doctors because it reduced the need for drugs, which everyone was coming to understand were harmful to babies. Nonetheless, most Lamaze patients continue to receive some medication, and delivery is rarely accomplished without local anesthesia and episiotomy. The Lamaze method also makes women more cooperative and less noisy in childbirth, with the doctor still in control. The most popular American text on the Lamaze method counsels: "If your doctor himself suggests medication, you should accept it willingly—even if you don't feel the need for it."

Full circle: Leboyer.

In 1975, Frederick Leboyer, M.D., another French obstetrician, published *Birth Without Violence*, which has had a tremendous impact on the way that we in America think about newborns, although its effect on hospital practice has been less than profound. Recognizing the newborn's ability to see, hear, and feel, Leboyer argues that ordinary delivery-room conditions and practices—air conditioning, bright lights, shouted orders, clanking equipment, and seizing the just-emerged infant, holding her upside down by the feet and slapping her on the buttocks—provides a rather shocking entry into the world.

Leboyer's techniques, which include very low light, quiet, warmth, and a body-temperature bath, undoubtedly provide not only a smoother transition for the newborn but probably also a more relaxed atmosphere for the mother. The Leboyer "method" is now frequently offered to parents whose babies are delivered in hospital birthing rooms and in many out-of-hospital birth centers. With the exception of the bath, the Leboyer techniques, of course, resemble the ordinary conditions of that eighteenth-century birth, where bustling staff, operating-room lights, and scissors clinking in a metal basin were not a problem.

Leboyer's sensitivity to the feelings of the newborn is counterbalanced a bit, in the minds of some critics, with his apparent obliviousness to the mother. He is the infant's deliverer. Instead of the mother being given the baby to hold, the infant is taken by the doctor or the father to be bathed. But Leboyer has educated us, more than anyone else, to look at the effects of our practices on the child as it is born.

Back to nature.

In the face of rising rates of intervention, routine use of electronic fetal monitors, and the rocketing increase in cesarean section, Michel Odent, another Frenchman, may become a hero of obstetrics in the future. The proponent of what he himself calls anti-obstetrics, Michel Odent brings us full circle, back to nature. His goal, in his own words, is to "give birth back to women."

At the maternity clinic he runs in Pithiviers, outside Paris, women of all ages and classes deliver in a dark, warm room, with a cushioned platform to sit or lie on. A pool of warm water is also available for relaxing in during labor, and some women deliver in the water. Many, however, seem to prefer to deliver in a semi-squatting position, supported from behind by the midwife, the doctor, or their husband.

What is revolutionary about Odent

is that he insists that the woman be in charge. It is she who decides to walk or to lie down, to eat or to drink, to scream or to moan. No one directs her; the doctor and the midwife accede to her wishes. Odent believes that women need no preparation for birth, that we instinctively know how to do it. The midwife and the doctor are there for encouragement, to help the woman relax, to be a comforting presence, and in case of the rare emergency. Pain is expected; so is joy.

The cesarean-section rate at Pithiviers is under 7 percent, in a population of women that is *not* selected (compared to 19 percent in the United States, 15 percent in France, by Odent's estimate); many women come to Pithiviers because they have been told that the birth will be complicated or that they are at high risk. Episiotomies, which are common practice in most United States hospitals, are performed on only 7 percent, usually when the baby is in the breech position, to allow it to be born more quickly. The safety record at Pithiviers is impressive, and the satisfaction of the women who deliver there is reported to be considerable.

The parents.

The history of obstetrics is, by and large, one of establishment resistance to change and of ongoing tension and struggle for control, between women and doctors and between doctors and midwives. Pregnant women still find themselves caught between the philosophy articulated by most midwives and a few doctors, like Odent, that birth is a completely natural process that under the vast majority of circumstances requires no intervention at all, and the present direction of American obstetrics, which prescribes the utmost in technological interference, from routine ultrasound examination to determine pregnancy to surgical delivery at term.

Whether the ideas of Odent and the midwives will ever be accepted, even in modified form, by American doctors and hospitals will depend on those who can, if they wish to, really shape American obstetrics: the parents whose choices, made with their feet and their pocketbooks, can be the key influence on the future of childbirth in America.

EROTIC
WISDOM OF THE ORIENT

Jeannie Sakol

Jeannie Sakol has been writing about sex and history for 20 years. She is currently working on a novel about the private life of Alexander Hamilton.

Loving is an art form, and the erotic lore of the East (over 1,000 years old) has perfected it in poetry, perfume, and pictures—the total indulgence of the senses. Add a dash of Oriental spice to your love life. It might just shake up some old routines.

A JAPANESE WOMAN IN A FLOWING KI-mono supports her lover's neck in one arm and tenderly raises a cup of wine to his lips. The woman's face conveys utter confidence. The man appears relaxed; with her, he is in good hands. A mirror is positioned so that they can gaze at the sensual scene they create.

While this may sound like an X-rated commercial for next year's hot perfume, it is actually a description of a classic Japanese *Shunga* print from the eighteenth century. A popular art form for over 200 years, *Shunga* love scenes were painted on silk and rice paper, depicting with *explicit* detail an astonishing variety of sexual pleasures in luxurious settings.

Although the *Shunga* art form has been around for only 200 years, the paint-ings are based on a sexual and spiritual wisdom that dates back to the first century A.D., when the Oriental philosophy of lovemaking was published in Taoist and Tantric love manuals such as the famed *Kama Sutra* and the *pillow books* of India, Nepal, China, and Japan (called "pillow books" because couples would keep them under their pillows—at close reach for aid in lovemaking).

Today, classic Oriental erotica tends to arouse feelings of wistfulness. After all, it presents us with a distant civilization comprised of exquisitely beautiful, limber men and women who make love with skill and generosity of spirit amid lush colors and exotic settings. We wonder, how can their example be of help to us, in a time and culture when women are more likely to be called dynamic than sultry? And, while possessing considerable sexual knowledge, many American women aren't supple or coordinated enough to achieve the gymnastic positions that often are depicted in Oriental paintings.

Also, while Oriental wisdom already has infiltrated Western society in many ways (massage, meditation, deep breathing, hot tubs, and diets of fish and rice all originated in the East), specific sexual practices and attitudes are more difficult to change. While none can doubt that American women have come a long way from the sexual repression of earlier generations, many of us are still seeking a broader education. After all, we were the generation of women to experiment openly with our sexuality, and many of us had few role models—in fact, many of us probably were unable to utter the word

Oriental lovemaking is seen as a private, *theatrical* event. Often, the woman functions as the director, set designer, and props manager—in addition to playing the female lead.

sex in front of our mothers. Unless we had a courtesan in the family (like the grandmother in *Gigi*, who taught her granddaughter love secrets), we've had to put our own act together to find the road to happiness.

From sources such as the *Kama Sutra* (the title translates as "aphorisms on love") and the teachings of the Tantra (a form of sexual yoga practiced in India and Tibet), we can learn things that mother couldn't—or wouldn't—teach us.

Variety is the spice of sex. In the *Kama Sutra*, the section "Of Sexual Union" describes the many different ways of making love. It suggests, for example, that lovers vary the way in which they touch: don't only kiss and hug but also "scratch and bite," it advises.

There are detailed descriptions of possible sexual positions as well: for instance, if your lover tires easily or you're simply feeling more assertive than he is, the *Kama Sutra* encourages you to "act the part of the man" and tells you, more specifically: "Lay him down on his back." Whatever is done by a man for giving pleasure to a woman is called the "work of man." So, in other words, do to your beloved what he does—or what you wish he would do—to you. As advised by the *Kama Sutra*, press your body against his and overwhelm him with kisses.

The legendary pillow books, illustrated love manuals originally designed as wedding gifts to help newly married couples consummate their union—and help them stave off any later sexual boredom—are another source of erotic inspiration from the East. One pillow book from the Ming Dynasty (1368-1644) portrays 24 love postures. As with the *Kama Sutra,* variety in technique and touch is seen as the key to a couple's sexual bliss.

Know where your lover's heart is. In Eastern philosophy, there is a focus on commitment between lovers—two people must have a basis of absolute trust and mutual caring. In cases where bonds of trust have been broken and your lover has strayed or lied, the *Kama Sutra*'s wisdom is as sound today as when it was written: "A wise woman should *only* renew her connection with a former lover if she is satisfied that good fortune, gain, love, and friendship are likely to result."

Your body makes the difference. Tantric yoga stresses the development of the body and of the five senses in order to make sex its best. What you eat and drink, how much you exercise, and your attention to bathing, sleep, meditation, and massage all contribute to a feeling of being at your sexual peak.

Bathing and scrupulous cleanliness are basic to daily Eastern ritual. Yet yoga texts condemn the Western tendency to wash immediately after lovemaking. They instruct that the perspiration produced during sex contains minerals and secretions that are highly beneficial to you—if you give them a chance to be absorbed. Lovers are advised to wait at least one hour before hopping into the shower.

Sex as a state of elevated consciousness. The Tantra, known as the "yoga of sexual ecstasy," has been practiced in India and Tibet for centuries. Whereas some forms of yoga repress sex or renounce it entirely, Tantric yoga seeks to achieve an elevated state of consciousness through the power of sex and the art of love.

In his preface to Omar Garrison's *Tantra: The Yoga of Sex*, William S. Kroger, M.D., defines the yoga of sex as the philosophy that the sexual relationship of the male and female is an integral part of achieving a more advanced stage of hu-

mankind: "The female is not less than the male; one does not antagonize the other. Both seek and achieve a unity which reflects the deeper, fuller, and higher joys of living."

Similarly, an early Chinese pillow book praises the "bedroom arts" as the means of averting calamity, changing bad luck to good, and achieving immortality.

The theatrics of sex. Much can be learned from the love postures illustrated in the pillow books. No matter how varied they are, there is one constant: lovemaking is perceived as a private, *theatrical* event. In many instances, the woman functions as the director, set designer, and props manager—in addition to playing the female lead.

Exquisite fabrics, flowers, pillows, mirrors, and art objects enhance the various scenes. In one, a couple makes love on a canopied red-lacquer bed surrounded by gauze curtains and floral tapestry, while a crimson candle burns on a nearby table. Elsewhere, a willow tree suggests constancy, and a pink lotus, bursting open, conveys sexual awakening. Nowhere is there any suggestion of sexual shame. Lovers display their nakedness with casual aplomb and explore each other with joy.

All of this may seem a bit much in your daily scheme of things. But even if you sleep in a Mickey Mouse T-shirt and your bedside lamp holds a 150-watt bulb so you can read without squinting, you might want to consider a more sensual "love chamber" atmosphere just for the fun of it.

▨ Sprinkle your sheets or comforter with scent.

▨ Scatter props around your bedroom: musical instruments, books illustrating love postures, books of love poems.

▨ Arrange lights so that they create dramatic shadows on the walls, or set up mirrors for reflecting.

▨ Ornament your bed with many pillows and cover with a canopy—or make it into a tent, even if it's makeshift.

▨ Place bottles of refreshments and glasses within easy reach.

Sex talk. In contrast to the often crude and demeaning names given to the genitals in Western society, Oriental erotica uses such euphemisms as *love grotto, citadel, precious peony, pleasure portal, secret cavern, valley of joy,* and *cinnabar crevice.* There is elegance in a pillow-book description of a man's *jade stalk* seeking entry into his beloved's *jade gateway.* A woman caresses her lover's *ambassador* while he, in turn, gently approaches her *honey pot.*

As an extension of this idea, you and your lover might want to invent your own humorous, affectionate, and imaginative euphemisms.

The scents of sensuality. Aro-

ma in general plays a vivid role in Eastern sensibility. From the days of Marco Polo and the spice trade, the fragrant gifts of the Orient have invigorated, restored, and refreshed the body and spirit. People's increased interest in aroma therapy today highlights a growing awareness of the benefits of scent.

Jasmine, saffron, and patchouli are especially uplifting. Combine them with baby oil for massaging yourself and your lover. Add some to bath water. Your bathroom may not be the baths of Caracalla, but bathing together in fragrance can make it seem just as divine.

Having an awareness of ordinary, everyday aromas can add pleasure and intimacy to your life. Take fruit, for example: try keeping a bowl of fresh fruit in your bedroom. At room temperature it emits a fragrance that permeates the room and intoxicates the senses.

Remember the obvious, too, such as candles. They're not just for dinner parties. In Eastern tradition, they're used as frequently as flowers to enhance a setting.

The art of foot massage. And then there is the Oriental art of massage—especially the massaging of the feet. Did you know that it's erotically stimulating to massage both big toes simultaneously? Next time you and your lover are watching sports or listening to music, take his bare feet in your lap and firmly knead his big toes before moving to his heels, which connect through nerve endings to his genitals.

Literature and lovemaking. Sharing erotica with your lover can be emotionally intimate and physically rewarding. One ancient Chinese pillow book illustrates a noble couple in a fond embrace, tenderly caressing each other while looking at a painting of another couple likewise caressing each other: a clear case of love imitating art.

Reading aloud to a lover (or being read to) is another joyful part of love. *Sonnets from the Portuguese, The Prophet, The Waste Land,* Shelley, Keats, Ferlinghetti—if you love it, share it. Just as your singing voice is enhanced in the shower, the speaking voice acquires a special nuance and passion within the confines of intimacy.

Love poetry of the East conveys a rare fusion of erotic delicacy and ardor. From among the hundreds of exquisite examples in translation, this one stands out:

We slip beneath the silken covers,
All warm and scented; our moment comes,
The dew falls; the Precious Flower opens
In the tenderness of love; the Clouds And Rain complete us, complete us.
—Huang Ching □

Sex Busters

*A Meese commission and the Supreme Court
echo a moral militancy*

Americans have always wanted it both ways. From the first tentative settlements in the New World, a tension has existed between the pursuit of individual liberty and the quest for Puritan righteousness, between the pursuit of individual liberty and the quest for Puritan righteousness, between Benjamin Franklin's open road of individualism and Jonathan Edwards' Great Awakening of moral fervor. The temper of the times shifts from one pole to the other, and along with it the role of the state. Government intrudes; government retreats; the state meddles with morality, then washes its hands and withdraws. The Gilded Age gave way to the muscular governmental incursions of the Age of Reform. The Roaring Twenties gave rise to the straitlaced Hays Office of the '30s. The buttoned-up '50s ushered in the unbuttoned '60s. And, most recently, a reaction to the sexual revolution spurred a spirited crusade to reassert family values that helped sweep Ronald Reagan into the presidency.

Each swing brings to the fore a series of questions. What is the role of the state in enforcing the morality of its citizenry? How far should government go in regulating private conduct? Is morality a question of individual rights? Or should the state play an active role in nurturing values deemed worthy by the community?

These questions were at the heart of the debate last week surrounding the release of the final report of Attorney General Edwin Meese's Commission on Pornography and a series of restrictive Supreme Court decisions that, among other things, allowed states to outlaw homosexual sodomy. Though significant, neither the report's findings nor the court's rulings were, on their own, momentous. Taken together, however, they seemed emblematic of a new moral militancy evident in communities around the country and of a willingness of government officials, from federal to local levels, to help enforce traditional values. In addition to the pornography report and the sodomy ruling, consider:

• More than 10,000 stores across the country, including such mammoth chains as 7-Eleven and Rite Aid, have removed *Playboy* and *Penthouse* from their shelves, many of them acting after receiving a letter from the Meese commission suggesting that they might be cited for distributing pornography.

• The Supreme Court last week upheld a New York State public-health nuisance law that would permit officials in Buffalo to close an adult bookstore for one year because of solicitation for prostitution on the premises.

• In another decision last week, the court gave a narrow interpretation to the First Amendment in a case involving the suspension of a student who gave a speech colored by sexual innuendo.

• The court ruled two weeks ago, in a case involving advertising by gambling casinos in Puerto Rico, that even truthful ads for lawful goods and services could be restricted by the state to protect the "health, safety and welfare" of its citizens.

• The Justice Department issued a ruling that would allow businesses to discriminate against workers with AIDS if there was a fear that the health of other employees was jeopardized.

• A proposal that could quarantine AIDS victims, sponsored by followers of Lyndon LaRouche, has gathered nearly 700,000 signatures to win a spot on the ballot in a California referendum this fall.

• Despite a voter referendum in Maine last month in which citizens soundly rejected an antipornography measure, large-scale efforts to restrict the sale of sexually explicit material are under way in more than a dozen states from Massachusetts to Arizona.

To civil libertarians, these actions raise the specter of an invasive moral vigilantism that could erode the constitutional right of free speech and penetrate the protected realm of privacy. Democrats who have long advocated federal activism note with irony that the traditional Republican principle of getting government off the back of its people has been subverted by the evangelical right, seemingly intent on transforming Big Brother into a bedroom busybody. Conservatives and many mainstream Americans, on the other hand, view the trend as a welcome response to the breakdown of sexual and family values. The reassertion of traditional moral values, they say, is part of a broad conservative realignment in the political process.

The current atmosphere does seem to be part of a national retrenchment from the giddy permissiveness of the '60s and '70s. As the baby-boom generation settles into respectable middle age, many of the trends associated with it are in decline: singles bars seem to be on the wane, promiscuity is becoming a fickle memory. The sexual revolution, which celebrated polymorphous diversity, ended with cruel jolts: first herpes, then AIDS. Says Michael Novak, a social philosopher at the American Enterprise Institute: "The coming theme for the liberal society is virtue and character. In its youth liberal society could claim that the sex shops on 42nd Street represented emancipation. Adulthood means learning to choose, and above all, to say no."

Yes . . . and no. There it is, the old duality, the split personality of the American character. While polls show that many Americans have a renewed appreciation for traditional values, their tolerance of their neighbor's right to reject those values has not declined at all. Notes California Pollster Gary Lawrence: "More people than ever are embracing moral traditional values. But they're saying, I don't want anything to be repressed or oppressed, either."

The debate has been crystallized by the completion of a government-sponsored study that was initially dismissed as a small sop to Reagan's New Right constituency. After hearing testimony in half a dozen cities on topics ranging from sex with fish to baroque forms of bondage, making three field trips to porn shops like Mr. Peepers in Houston, and spending $500,000, the Attorney General's Commission on Pornography issued a two-volume, 1960-page report. In ceremoniously accepting it from Chairman Henry Hudson at a Justice Department news conference, Meese seemed both proud and sheepish as he stood before a seminaked statue of a female figure called *Spirit of Justice.*

The commission's conclusions were couched amid careful clauses that only partly tempered the strong attack on pornography: the panel stated that there is a causal link between violent pornography and aggressive behavior toward women. Furthermore, it said that exposure to sexually explicit material that is not violent but nevertheless degrades women—a category that "constitutes somewhere between the predominant and the overwhelming portion of what is currently standard fare heterosexual pornography"—bears "some causal relationship to the level of sexual violence." The Meese panel's findings are diametrically opposed to those

of the 1970 report of the President's Commission on Obscenity and Pornography, which asserted that pornography was not a significant cause of sexual crime and recommended better sex education in schools. The 1970 analysis, the new report claims, is now "starkly obsolete." Since 1970, according to the Meese panel, pornography that is far more violent and explicit has flooded the market, and this has been accompanied by a commensurate increase in the number of sex crimes.

In addition to being a catalyst for violence, the report said, sexually violent pornography "leads to a greater acceptance of the 'rape myth' in its broader sense—that women enjoy being coerced into sexual activity, that they enjoy being physically hurt in a sexual context." The commission was less certain about material it labeled nonviolent but "degrading"; such items, it said, foster a similarly lax and accepting attitude toward rape, but do not necessarily arouse violence. A third category, erotica that is neither violent nor degrading, proved to be the most problematic; the commission acknowledged that there was no evidence to suggest it promotes violence, but did say that "none of us think the material in this category, individually or as a class, is in every instance harmless."

Although the panel rejected any efforts to expand the legal definition of obscenity (which the Supreme Court has declared depends partly on the "community standards" of each locality), it did call for the enactment of federal laws to make it easier to seize the assets of those involved in the trade. It also proposed that Congress enact unfair-labor-practice laws to be used against producers who pay performers in pornographic films. The Federal Communications Commission, it said, should restrict pornographic cable television shows and "Dial-a-Porn" telephone services. It also recommended that peep-show booths not be equipped with doors, so that the occupants can be clearly seen, thereby discouraging sexual activity.

The commission placed a special emphasis on the problem of child pornography, which it says has undergone the greatest growth since the 1970 commission. To combat what it calls the rise of the "kiddie-porn industry," the commission proposed that the knowing possession

of child pornography be considered a felony.

In addition, the report contains 37 pages of suggestions that are, in effect, a how-to guide for citizen action against pornography. The text includes suggestions on how to conduct a "court watch" program ("Citizens . . . will write to the prosecutor, judge or police officer and relay their opinions of the investigation, prosecution and disposition of the case") and how to monitor the lyrics of rock music ("Many popular idols of the young commonly sing about rape, masturbation, incest, drug usage, bondage, violence, homosexuality and intercourse").

The social significance of the report goes beyond its specific findings. It serves to document the evolving attitudes toward sexual morality that have gained acceptance during the Reagan era. In many ways it reflects society's ambivalence, mixing some moderate views about the rights of individuals with some visceral moralizing about pornography and promiscuity. Says the commission: "There are undoubtedly many causes for what used to be called the 'sexual revolution,' but it is absurd to suppose that depictions or descriptions of uncommitted sexuality were not among them." At times the report hesitantly departs from an examination of pornography and discusses the need for a moral compass in society. "We all agree that some degree of individual choice is necessary in any free society, and we all agree that a society with no shared values, including moral values, is no society at all." While they refrain from seeking to impose their view by legislation, the commissioners make clear what they feel about sex outside the framework of love and marriage: "Although there are many members of this society who can and have made affirmative cases for uncommitted sexuality, none of us believes it to be a good thing."

The $35 report could prove to be a best seller partly because of a straight-faced 300-page section that provides graphic descriptions of sex scenes and no-expletives-deleted excerpts of steamy dialogue from such movies as *Deep Throat* and *Debbie Does Dallas.* In addition, it gives a clinical accounting of pictures in magazines like *Tri-Sexual Lust,* along with a list of 2,370 film titles and 725 book titles ranging from *Horny Holy Roller Family* to *Thoroughly Amorous Amy.*

1. SEXUALITY AND SOCIETY: Changing Society/Changing Sexuality

During its intermittent, yearlong investigation, there were times when the commission seemed to be on a kind of surrealist mystery tour of sexual perversity, peeping at the most recondite forms of sexual behavior known—though mostly unknown—to society. The report details testimony about practices involving human excretions, asphyxiation and anilingus, along with even more arcane fetishes, such as collecting toenail clippings and sniffing sweat. The panel heard from a Houston police officer whose vice squad had confiscated and was storing some 27,000 "rubber goods." Many of the so-called victims described the harm that had befallen them after being lured into the world of pornography. In Miami, for example, Larry Madigan, 38, told the commission he had been "a typically normal, healthy boy," whose subsequent life of solitary masturbation, bestiality and drug addiction could all be traced to the finding of a deck of pornographic playing cards when he was twelve.

An early draft of the report seemed to several commissioners to be an overzealous reaction to such testimony. It had been written by a number of commission staff members and overseen by the group's executive director, Alan Sears, a former assistant U.S. Attorney and an ardent antipornography crusader. One panel member, Frederick Schauer, a respected University of Michigan law professor, criticized its oversimplification and reliance on the bizarre. To avoid having it become a laughingstock, he wrote a 200-page draft that became the basis for the main part of the final report. As a result, more consideration is given to the need to protect the rights of free speech and privacy as defined by the federal courts.

Nevertheless, two members of the commission, Judith Becker, director of the Sexual Behavior Clinic at the New York State Psychiatric Institute, and Ellen Levine, editor of *Woman's Day,* objected to the premise that there is evidence linking pornography and violence and wrote an 18-page rebuttal. In it they noted that the panel's "efforts to tease the current data into proof of a causal link . . . simply cannot be accepted."

The fundamental issue involved—whether certain forms of pornography are harmful to the public and thus might be legitimately restricted by the government—is unlikely to

be settled by the publication of the Meese commission's report. Because the group had limited funds, it was not able to commission academic research of its own on the topic. Instead it relied on past academic studies, testimony from victims and law-enforcement officials, and "common sense."

A small amount of work done in the past decade does in fact suggest that hardcore pornography involving violence has a certain harmful effect. Other evidence, mostly of the anecdotal variety, is far more murky. Edward Donnerstein, a University of Wisconsin psychologist who has studied the effects of sexually violent material, was billed as one of the committee's star witnesses. But in his testimony he refused to make a direct causal link between pornography and violence. Although he does not repudiate the report, he suggests that the crucial variable is not explicit sex but graphic violence. Violent films without sex, like *Rambo,* he suggests, cause the same changes in attitude as sexually violent ones. "If you take out the sex and leave the violence, you get the increased violent behavior in the laboratory setting, and these 'changes in attitude.' If you take out the violence and leave the sex, nothing happens."

Donnerstein is particularly perturbed by what he sees as the pervasive depiction of violence toward women on broadcast television and in movies. "Why all the sudden talk about sex?" he says. "Why do people find it offensive and violence acceptable?" The emphasis, he suggests, should be on controlling violence. The columnist TRB in the *New Republic* pointed out recently that while the Reagan Administraton decries the spread of sexual pornography, the President has invited Sylvester Stallone, whose movies glamourize violence (and whose wife appears undraped in the current issue of *Playboy*), to the White House on more than one occasion.

Many social scientists believe that an individual's sexual attitudes are determined long before he or she is exposed to pornography and that pornography is a symptom of deviant sexuality rather than a cause of it. Says A. Nicholas Groth, who runs the sex-offender program at the Connecticut Correctional Institution: "We've had men who were very much turned on by looking at the underwear ads of kids that appear in the Sears, Roebuck catalog,

which doesn't make the Sears, Roebuck catalog a kiddie-porn magazine."

Even before the commission issued its report, the American Civil Liberties Union published a critique by Barry Lynn, a lawyer who attended meetings in each of the six cities where they occurred and obtained its internal papers under the Federal Advisory Committee Act. Lynn dismissed the report as "little more than prudishness and moralizing masquerading behind social-science jargon." He charged that the conclusions were precooked, and labeled the commissioners "quintessential censors," noting that six of the eleven were already committed to stamping out pornography before the hearings began. (Chairman Hudson, for example, is a U.S. Attorney in Virginia who made his name by clamping down on adult bookstores.) "They truly want to regulate everyone's sex life," Lynn says. "If they had their way, they'd like to crawl into your bedroom and tell you what is and is not appropriate."

Members of the commission emphasized that they had refrained from advocating any form of censorship. "Those people that anticipated a document supporting censorship are going to be disappointed," said Hudson. Park Dietz, a sociologist who is a member of the panel, felt vindicated after the report was released: "The big news here is that . . . the report says exactly the opposite of what the A.C.L.U. claims. It says that 'slasher' films are bad, *Playboy* is O.K., and no books should be prosecuted."

But Lynn, paraphrasing Justice Potter Stewart's standard for obscenity, said he knew censorship when he saw it. "He can say that this is not about censorship. In fact, whenever you use the powers of the state or Federal Government to punish, to criminalize, to imprison people who sell certain kinds of sexually explicit material, that is censorship." Leanne Katz, executive director of the National Coalition Against Censorship, charges the approach is similar to ones used in the past: "I have been working in the anti-censorship cause for about 30 years, and I have never encountered a censorship controversy in which the other side wasn't saying 'This isn't censorship.' They also always argue that they are talking about harm. It's always harm to women, harm to children, harm to somebody. In truth, however, it is

Reagan's Moral Point Man

He did not establish the Commission on Pornography, he did not sit in on its hearings, and even late last week he maintained that he had not read the report. Yet Attorney General Edwin Meese is widely regarded as the driving force behind the commission that he inherited from his predecessor, William French Smith. Indeed, in his 16 months in office, the former Presidential Counsellor has emerged as the Administration's chief crusader for Ronald Reagan's social agenda. It is Ed Meese who speaks out against judicial activism, openly challenges Supreme Court decisions through Justice Department briefs, and selects conservative ideologues for nomination to the federal judiciary in an effort to realize the Reagan Revolution in America's courts.

While the President makes plain his conservative views on abortion, school prayer and affirmative action, he has shunned active involvement in the right-wing campaigns on social causes. Meese is more than happy to jump into the fray and get his hands dirty. "He represents us on the conservative social issues. It's his franchise," says White House Communications Director Patrick Buchanan. "He speaks with the voice of the President if not at his specific direction."

Despite his adversarial zeal, Meese contends that his actions reflect the will of the people. "I hope we've been successful," he said in a TIME interview last week. "The President stands high in the opinion polls and the electoral polls because he stands for mainstream values. We wouldn't have been successful if his views hadn't struck a response chord with society."

Meese is quick to point out that the Justice Department has not called for sweeping bans on pornography or abortion. He thinks that state and local governments should be left to rule on such issues without federal intervention. Says Meese: "What's happening here is that over the years, people favoring a more permissive atmosphere **tried to impose their views on** society through the courts and through legislation. People are now resisting that, trying to reverse it. Our view is that these are legal issues that ought to be left to legislatures, as close to the people as possible."

So far the Attorney General's initiatives have encountered some stinging rebuffs. Rejecting arguments by the Justice Department, the Supreme Court has, in recent weeks, reiterated its commitment to abortion rights and affirmative action. Political pragmatists in the Administration have thus far thwarted Meese in his efforts to wipe out minority quotas for Government contracts through an Executive Order. Earlier this year when Meese endorsed a plan for random drug-testing of federal employees, a number of top Reagan aides criticized it as an invasion of privacy. And, of course, the methods and findings of the pornography commission have provoked a downpour of derision from liberals.

Because of his strongly conservative beliefs and his pugnacious demeanor, Meese is perhaps the most controversial figure in the Administration. Matters did not begin well with a year-long struggle for confirmation, during which he admitted to helping get Government jobs for friends who had granted him loans, some of them interest free. Today, polls show that he is the only Reagan aide whose negative ratings exceed his positive marks. Liberal fund raisers, who find it difficult to run campaigns criticizing the popular President, have discovered that political literature condemning Meese can inspire generous donations. Ira Glasser, executive director of the American Civil Liberties Union, dubs the Attorney General the "James Watt of the Constitution."

Meese's name is often whispered as a potential Supreme Court nomination. The Attorney General seems equally unfazed by the criticism and the rumors of his one day sitting on the hallowed bench. For the time being, he appears focused on carrying out the President's social philosophy. "We're neither arbitrating morals nor trying to impose policy choices on others," declares Meese. "We're trying to enforce the law."

—By Jacob V. Lamar Jr.
**Reported by David Beckwith/
Washington**

harm to our precious idea that all of us are supposed to be able to decide for ourselves what we can see and read and think."

Critics asserted that the commission's guidelines for citizens' actions, which the panel specifically noted could be undertaken against publications that were not legally obscene, indirectly amounts to censorship by seeming to give a government imprimatur to efforts to prevent the sale of various publications. Noted Legal Scholar Geoffrey Stone of the University of Chicago: "To the extent the report directs private citizens to protest against constitutionally protected acts, there are serious First Amendment problems. The government has no business encouraging people to do things that it can't do."

Christie Hefner, president of Playboy Enterprises, objected that the commission, despite its claims to have focused on pornography dealing with children or violence, implicitly coupled *Playboy* with raunchier material, especially in its advocacy of citizens' action against magazine sellers. This was accomplished in part through the panel's extremely broad definition of the type of erotic material that could be considered "degrading." There was also the feeling expressed by some panel members that magazines such as *Playboy* and *Penthouse* can be in effect an appetizer that inculcates a taste for hard porn. "What the report does," said Hefner, "is condemn everything that has a sexual content." First, she says, the commission talks about violence, "and then there's a little bit of a soft shoe and a shuffle, and all of a sudden we're talking about *Playboy* magazine."

One example of how the commission, in its zeal, apparently infringed on the rights of *Playboy* and other mainstream publications involved a letter sent out by Director Sears. He cited testimony from an unnamed witness (who turned out to be the Rev. Donald Wildmon, head of a group called the National Federation for Decency, in Tupelo, Miss.) accusing convenience stores like 7-Eleven of being purveyors of pornography. Sears asked those mentioned to respond to the accusations, warning that failure to do so would be interpreted as acquiescence. This was followed rather rapidly by the decision by some chains and stores to remove *Playboy* and other magazines from their shelves. *Playboy,* joined by the Magazine Publishers Association, went to court to have the letter rescinded and prevent publication of what it called a blacklist.

Judge John Garrett Penn of the federal district court in Washington, in an emphatic ruling, ordered the commission to send out new letters retracting the implied threat, and he prohibited publication of Wildmon's list. Said Penn: "It is clear that something has occurred in the marketplace. A deprivation of a First Amendment right, that is, a prior restraint on speech, a right so precious in this nation, constitutes irreparable injury." *Playboy* has even managed to retain its trademark smoking-jacket smirk: it put out a call to female employees of 7-Eleven stores for a December pictorial titled—What else?—"Women of 7-Eleven."

The findings of presidential commissions are often a kind of mirror of the public sensibility at the time—one reason, perhaps, that the latest porn report is so different from the 1970 one. The Supreme Court, too, reads the papers and looks at election returns. The tenor of the decision allowing a state to outlaw sodomy among homosexuals is an echo of cultural conservatism, a statement that is in tune with the times. Notes Harvard Law Professor Randall Kennedy: "The law is now catching up with the rightward swing politically and culturally."

What is disquieting about the decision for many constitutional scholars is that it could unravel the evolving constitutional right of privacy, the court's creation of a realm of personal life that the state cannot enter. This concept of privacy has been enshrined during the past two decades in decisions such as those allowing the use of contraceptives and asserting a woman's right to have an abortion. "What's

frightening," says Kennedy, "is that if what [Justice Byron] White's decision says is true, the history of these other decisions is in trouble." The principle of liberty, wrote Justice Harry Blackmun in his dissent, includes intimate associations and private conduct central to one's fulfillment as a person, and those include sexual activity. Some scholars, however, like Stanford Law Professor Thomas Grey, have maintained that the court has never given support to the notion that the right of privacy protects sexual freedom.

Justice White's invocation of the "ancient roots" proscribing homosexuality is not unlike the Meese commission's homage to family values. But there is a kind of fallacy in resorting to the presumed wisdom of the ancients. Slavery has ancient roots. So too did laws forbidding marriage between people of different races. Says Kennedy: "The court makes ancient roots into something which we, ipso facto, should pay deference. We should critically see if these practices are complementary with a just society."

Many conservatives saw the sodomy decision as a laudable attempt to adhere to a strict interpretation of the Constitution rather than read into it new rights that are more suitably left to the discretion of elected legislatures. Whether or not they favor laws restricting homosexual activities, they argue that there is nothing in the Consitution that specifically prohibits such laws. Religious-rights activists went even further, saying that the decision was a clear statement about the "unnaturalness" of homosexuality.

If Jerry Falwell had a divine plan for America, then the Supreme Court's sodomy decision and the Meese report would both be on his drawing board. Falwell views these two events as the trophies of the New Right's gradual rise to power. "The new moralism in this country," he says, "has been growing for the past two decades. The awakening is manifesting itself in the change in the national lifestyle." Falwell sees the court's decision as a kind of last-straw vote, a moral denunciation of Sodom. "It was a clarion call that enough is enough." Enough is much too much in the case of pornography: "We recognize the existence of pornography and the impossibility of stamping it all out. But we do want to push it back to

Sleaze Town to live amongst the roaches where it belongs."

Pat Robertson, head of the Christian Broadcasting Network and the favorite son among evangelical Christians for the Republican nomination in 1988, envisions a moral resurgence in America. "I see a definite spiritual revival that is touching the standards of conduct of the entire society, which has gone too far toward sexual freedom . . . Americans perceive a serious crisis to the long-range stability of the American family. The American people are looking for a return to moral values that strengthen the family." The theme is not just limited to the preachers of the right. Jesse Jackson, for one, has spoken out against "sex without love," arguing that teenage pregnancy is blighting the next generation of blacks.

Falwell sees Reagan as both a cause and an effect of the conservative moral movement. "The country is moving politically to the right, and Ronald Reagan is a product of that phenomenon. He has been produced by it and has contributed to it." Reagan marches to his own drummer, but he also manages to be in step with the parade. "The trick," says Deputy White House Chief of Staff Dennis Thomas, "is to be far enough ahead to be a leader, but not so far that you're out of touch."

Though he has never departed from his ideological passions, Reagan has proved to be consistently pragmatic about avoiding crusades that could forfeit his popular support. He has long preached family values but has not pushed any significant legislation advancing the conservative social agenda into law. He sends staunch messages of support to anti-abortion rallies but never appears himself; he makes the right noises about school prayer but does not press for a constitutional amendment to legalize it.

Reagan's greatest contribution to the conservative moral agenda has been through his appointments to the federal judiciary. So far, however, he has had only mixed success with the Supreme Court. Although the high court has recently shown a willingness to be more restrictive in its interpretation of free speech and privacy rights, it is still at least one vote away from reversing its 1973 abortion decision.

White House Communications Director Patrick Buchanan predicts a new, more vigorous incarnation for social conservatives. "The right-to-life movement is as strong or stronger than ever. The number of gay-rights marchers at various demonstrations has been a fraction of their old strength. The Christians are taking over the Republican Party in Missouri, Washington and Michigan."

One of the most active groups of antipornography crusaders is Wildmon's National Federation for Decency, which grew from its Tupelo headquarters to encompass 350 chapters nationwide. Leslie and Ronald Pasquini run the chapter in Springfield, Mass., which coordinates efforts in New England. It claims 1,000 members and has staged pickets at 30 adult-magazine outlets in the region. The group's relentless pressure on the Rhode Island-based CVS drugstore chain, along with the commission letter, apparently bore fruit last month: the company announced it was removing *Playboy* and *Penthouse* from its 600 shops.

A similar organization, the Dallas-based American Renewal Foundation, distributes window decals for store owners to proclaim their refusal to sell porn. The group is currently threatening to boycott Circle K convenience stores, whose chairman has thus far withstood pressure to remove offending magazines. Another chain that has resisted is Dairy Mart convenience stores, with 950 outlets in the East and Midwest. Following a boycott organized by an affiliate of the N.F.D. in April, Dairy Mart conducted a survey of its patrons in four states, asking whether it should stock magazines like *Playboy*. The result: 55% said yes, 35% no, and the rest had no opinion.

Frank Herrera, president of ICD/Hearst, which distributes 120 magazines ranging from *Cosmopolitan* to *Popular Mechanics*, says distributors are under growing pressure from Fundamentalist groups. "We're extremely sensitive," he says, "be-

Pornography: The Feminist Dilemma

According to various feminists, the Meese commission report was good for the women's movement (Law Professor Catharine MacKinnon), bad for the movement (A.C.L.U. Attorney Nan Hunter) or basically irrelevant to feminist interests (Movement Pioneer Betty Friedan). "Today could be a turning point in women's rights," MacKinnon told a news conference in a cramped storefront near the Times Square porno district that serves as the offices of Women Against Pornography. "Women actually succeeded in convincing a national governmental body of a truth that women have long known: pornography harms women and children." Hunter tapped a different strand of feminist thinking: women should seek liberation, not special protection from the state. "Protectionist attitudes," she said, "ultimately hurt women." Friedan once again declared that the war against porn is a woeful waste of energies needed on the economic and legal fronts. Said she: "As repulsive as pornography can be, the obsession with it **is a dangerous diversion for the women's movement.**"

Almost all feminists are troubled by pornography. By its very nature it tends to degrade women and treat them as sexual playthings for men. The problem: how to take an effective stance without seeming prudish or giving comfort to the antifeminist right. Gloria Steinem has tried to promote a distinction between pornography, which should be opposed, and erotica, healthy sexual materials marked by mutuality and respect, presumably the kind of material men should be interested in, but usually aren't. Some feminists see porn as repellent but harmless masturbatory material for shuttins, or as an expression of anxiety by males who are threatened by the women's movement. But some of the more militant feminists take a darker view: porn is a conscious assault against women, comparable to antiblack and anti-Semitic literature. "Pornography is virulent propaganda against women," says Author Susan Brownmiller. "It promotes a climate in which the ideology of rape is not only tolerated but encouraged." In her book *Pornography,* Andrea Dworkin calls violence "the prime component of male identity" and says porn is an expression of men's abusive control of women.

Dworkin and MacKinnon have been pushing antiporn legislation framed as ways to protect the civil rights of women. One such bill passed the Minneapolis city council twice, but was vetoed each time by the Mayor. A similar ordinance, passed in Indianapolis, was declared unconstitutional by a federal appeals court, a decision upheld in February by the Supreme Court. An uneasy alliance of Women Against Pornography and right-wing groups supported the legislation. Prominent feminists such as Friedan, Kate Millett and Rita Mae Brown opposed it, and the National Organization for Women avoided taking a position. The Meese Commission recommended hearings on a national version of the Dworkin-MacKinnon proposal.

To underscore their civil rights strategy and distinguish themselves from the religious Right, some militants rejected the commission's first 36 recommendations, which call for stronger anti-obscenity measures. Other feminists consider porn a symptom of sexism, not a cause. Says Nan Hunter: "Sexual abuse is not caused by violent sexual movies any more than war is caused by *Rambo*." But many agree with the commission that porn is linked to sexual assault. NOW President Eleanor Smeal says that feminist work with rape victims and battered wives points up "the influence of violent pornography firsthand." But, she adds, "we don't want to suppress sexually explicit material that is not harmful or violent." The problem, similar to the one faced by the Meese Commission, is sorting out what is and is not damaging. Says Deborah Chalfie, a Washington attorney active in Feminists Against Pornography: "I still have problems with defining what we are trying to get at."

—By John Leo. Reported by Cathy Booth/New York and Alessandra Stanley/ Washington

cause of the apparent success of the Wildmons and Falwells in putting their own definition on pornography." One recent confrontation took place in Tyler, Texas, where a city ordinance bans nudity below the navel. Local marshals warned stores in the city that the July issue of *Cosmopolitan* had to be taken off the shelf because of an article showing tummy-tucking operations for chubby women; the local district attorney stepped in, however, and told the marshals that the law did not apply in this case.

The antipornography movement has some close cousins. One prominent grassroots movement is the Parents Music Resource Center, led by Tipper Gore, the wife of Democratic Senator Albert Gore Jr. of Tennessee. The P.M.R.C., through well-publicized hearings and letter-writing campaigns, has succeeded in persuading record companies voluntarily to identify recordings with explicit lyrics. Says Gore: "This is where the action is these days. I think it's very exciting what's happening all over the country. People in the communities are reawakening and reaffirming their commitment to values."

In Iowa, militant moralism is making its way into the mainstream after a group of evangelical and Fundamentalist Christians seized control of the Polk County Republican convention. Iowa Governor Terry Branstad penciled in child-porn laws as one of his top legislative priorities for 1986. The legislature responded by passing a bill that makes it a crime to purchase child porn. The trickle-down theory of antiporn was in evidence when a planned fund-raising softball game south of Des Moines, featuring a group of Playboy Bunnies and Rabbits, was canceled after phone calls to the local athletic booster club protested that the game would be promoting pornography.

In Kansas, the legislature passed a law that makes retailers of pornography responsible for the content of what they sell. The legislature also expanded a law prohibiting "sexual exploitation of a child" (previously defined as under 16, now under 18) and outlawed possession of "kiddie porn" materials. Another measure this year banned vibrators, artificial vaginas and any device

primarily used for the "stimulation of human genital organs."

The clean-living capital of the antipornography crusade might be Cincinnati, where Charles Keating Jr. began a moral crusade in the 1950s that residents have carried on ever since. Arthur Ney, the county prosecutor, says, "There is not one X-rated movie house or bookstore in the county today. They know if they bring them in here, we're going to enforce the law." The Meese commission report, says Steve Hallman, director of Citizens Concerned for Community Values of Greater Cincinnati, "will give momentum nationwide to obscenity-law enforcement."

In the tiny town of Belgrade, Mont., a legislative committee was formed to ban pornographic materials inside the city limits. It so happens that there are no adult bookstores in Belgrade (pop. 3,200); the city elders just want to make sure that it's kept that way.

Campaigns against pornography are not being orchestrated solely by conservative Republicans from the heartland. Boston Mayor Raymond Flynn, a populist Democrat in the cradle of liberty, has been trying to clean up the city's "combat zone," which was officially designated an adult-entertainment area in 1974.

Opposition to government intervention in individual lives has always been a pillar of conservative thought. In the 1960s and '70s, while liberals agitated for federal intervention on civil rights and the Viet Nam War, conservatives felt smothered by a leftist tyranny of activism. The roles have now reversed. As the New Right presses its case against pornography and homosexual activities, liberals argue that this amounts to unwarranted government intrusiveness into the homes of private citizens. There are, of course, distinctions among the issues, yet the sea change reveals the inherent contradictions in the way Americans feel about Government. As Gunnar Myrdal, the Swedish Nobel laureate, once pointed out, Americans will say, practically in the same breath, "No one can tell me what to do" and "There ought to be a law against that."

For Republicans, the moral revival has been a distinct political

blessing. But it could turn into a risky one. "Morality is a very dangerous issue for the Republican Party," says William Schneider, a political analyst at the conservative American Enterprise Institute. "Religion is to Republicans what race is to Democrats. Religion could tear the G.O.P. apart in the next election." Tony Podesta, executive director of People for the American Way, which was formed as a foil to Falwell's Moral Majority, says that Republicans are in danger of becoming dominated by a narrow segment of the ideological spectrum. "In many places," he says, "the Republican Party machine thought it would be good to broaden their base and ended up getting swallowed up by the religious-right movement."

Both Democrats and Republicans are jealously eyeing the votes of baby boomers, who do not, as a rule, share all the values or the goals of the religious right. "The key word for 1988 is tolerance," insists Republican Strategist Roger Stone. A fellow analyst of baby-boom voters, George Bush's strategist Lee Atwater says that whoever succeeds Reagan will have to emulate him: "Reagan won the baby-boom vote in 1984 because he projected tolerance. They did not think that Reagan would impose his personal views on them. A Republican can afford to be more conservative on social issues as long as he conveys the notion of tolerance."

Tolerance: a word seldom heard from those engaged in a crusade. But on issues like sexual freedom, those who ignore it do so at their peril. In every era when moral fervor held sway, a counterreaction began to build when the community became intolerant of individual liberties. That is why the Meese commission, even while helping to foment a more repressive stance toward pornography, made a point of mentioning that tolerance for private choices must still be respected. Political and social leaders who carry their moral zeal too far are in danger of being left stranded when the pendulum swings the other way. And it always does.

—By Richard Stengel. Reported by Howard G. Chua-Eoan/New York, Anne Constable/ Washington and Elizabeth Taylor/ Chicago

HOW IMPORTANT IS SEX?

THE BIGGEST MISUNDERSTANDING BETWEEN MEN AND WOMEN – HOW TO CLEAR IT UP

SUE WOODMAN

Sue Woodman is a freelance writer and broadcaster living in New York.

Today, when love partners have busy jobs and overpacked lives, they seem to make sex less and less a priority, accepting the diminishment of desire and excitement as natural over time. People complain that the "chemistry" goes, says Theresa L. Crenshaw, M.D., director of the Crenshaw Clinic in San Diego and author of *Bedside Manners,* "but they're not really right. Chemistry doesn't just disappear. We tend to drive it away by accepting that it inevitably fades."

Making chemistry last takes some thought and planning. But lately there's been some question about whether it's worth it. Although sex therapists and psychologists believe sex is a vital ingredient in lasting love, recent studies of contented couples reveal that many don't rank sex as a major component of their happiness. Why the discrepancy?

How important *is* sex?

Experts in the field believe that sex is about far more than simply physical need. "It represents identity, desirability, an affirmation of one's self," says Edward M. Shelley, M.D., assistant clinical professor of psychiatry at Columbia University College of Physicians and Surgeons. "We attach many important psychological needs to our sexuality. That's why it's such a revealing area."

"Anyone can say 'I care about you,' and you may believe it or not," says Gene Abel, M.D., professor of psychiatry at Emory University School of Medicine in Atlanta. "But during sex we naturally evaluate how our partner seems to feel about us. If loving feelings are there, they come through. If they are lacking, that comes through, too."

At its best, lovemaking attunes couples so finely that they feel merged with their partners—a marvelous and healthy experience, says psychologist Marilyn Ruman, Ph.D., director of Clinical and Counseling Associates in Encino, California. "While you are getting your needs met, you are ideally also giving pleasure to your partner—and vice versa. The best lovemaking is where what is *taken* by one is seen as *giving* by the other. Your partner feels given to by his ability to give you pleasure. This kind of true give-and-take fulfills an adult erotic need and also a primal, childlike need to be joined with someone."

These needs may be what makes sex such a driving force early in a relationship. "During courtship, people are uncertain of their role in their partner's life and need reassurance that they are loved," says Dr. Shelley. Sex can create a sense of closeness between partners more quickly than other forms of togetherness.

In some ways sexual intimacy becomes even more necessary later in a relationship, when the mundane problems of daily life—bills to pay, cars to repair—encroach on romance. "Being desired and made love to by someone who pays bills with you and sees you at your worst is terribly important," says Dr. Ruman. "Over the long run, sex acts as a sort of 'relationship lubricant,'" agrees Joseph LoPiccolo, Ph.D., professor of psychology at Texas A&M University. "It allows you to live together day by day without grinding against each other. When a couple can have good sex, the minor irritations of life don't seem to bother them as much."

Love without lovemaking

Yet for many people, all these reasons do not seem to make sex a vital ingredient for happiness. "I feel quite satisfied with my sex life," said one woman, "but I often think it's the part of my relationship I would miss the least if I had to give it up. For me, what's special is the talking and laughing and companionship."

Several surveys seem to bear out this sentiment. In a study of 100 happily married couples published in *The New England Journal of Medicine*, one-third reported having intercourse no more than three times a month. Nevertheless, all these couples said they "still feel very positive about their sexual relations and their marriages." When *Self* asked readers (in October 1984) to list the most rewarding ingredients in their lives, sex ranked fifth, after love, health/ fitness, friendship and children. Sex therapists and psychologists confirm that some couples have happy, stable relationships even though they have little or no sex.

If desire is disrupted

Contrary to the importance experts today put on it, sex was never considered the binding glue of marriage and family in the past; financial, religious and social codes were. Even without such bonds and sex more in the forefront, there are things in life that disrupt desire. Events like pregnancy, illness or the death of a loved one may all negate the urge for sex. Usually, desire returns spontaneously after a while, and the couple simply resume their sex life. But that shouldn't be taken for granted. "It's up to the pregnant or grieving person to talk to her mate about it," says Dorothy Cantor, Psy.D., president of the New Jersey Psychological Association. "Simply saying 'It's a phase, it will pass' may be interpreted by the partner as withdrawal from him rather than a response to an external event."

In some cases, a temporary lack of desire can become chronic if not treated properly. One woman had an exciting new boyfriend when her father died and she lost interest in sex completely. "By the time my grief had subsided, my lover and I had become so used to not having sex that we didn't know how to get it back in our lives," she said. This couple sought professional help.

But often it's possible to restore desire with our imaginations, says Dr. Ruman. "Sex is about more than just the physical act—it's about the layers we impose on it that make it satisfying: expectation, eroticism, fantasy. Fantasy is healthy; it allows us to heighten sex, to make it more than it may be in reality."

When lovemaking becomes too familiar, our minds can help us restore the mystery and novelty of early romance. "Don't wait to be turned on by your partner," advises Dr. Ruman. "Find ways to arouse yourself so you can feel good and be responsive."

Alternating roles with your partner, so that sometimes you respond to his lead and sometimes you take the lead, is important in preventing staleness. "Most couples have fixed roles—one is the initiator, the other the responder—and develop a set of signals that indicate desire," says Dr. Shelley. "It can be stimulating to vary

those well-known signals, so lovemaking doesn't get stuck in a rut." Similarly, try making love in different ways, different places or at different times of day.

When sex goes bad

"We have to work to keep up with changes in our partners—in sex as well as in other areas of life," says Dr. Abel. When partners change in major ways and seem to be growing more apart than together, sex is often the first area to show the strain. "Lovemaking becomes something to be avoided," says Dr. LoPiccolo. "The sexual arousal and release can't make up for the alienation the partners feel elsewhere in the relationship."

"There is a saying that when sex goes well, it is 15 percent of a relationship, but if it goes badly, it's 85 percent," says David Knox, Ph.D., director of the marriage therapy program at East Carolina University and author of *Human Sexuality: The Search for Understanding*. "I think that's so. When a couple's sex life is fine, it seems less important. But if it sours, it can seem all-consuming."

One woman who has not had a satisfactory sex life with her husband for several years finds this saying painfully true. "Not having sex in a relationship is very different from just not having sex," she said. "In a relationship, you're with someone you want to be with, including sexually, yet that person may not be willing or able to make love to you. That really hurts."

"Rejecting someone sexually is like rejecting their very essence," says Dr. Ruman. It's hard for most people to believe someone loves them, no matter how many times they are told, if they are not desired physically.

Finding out what underlies sexual rejection is a complex process and may require professional help. But partners can accomplish a lot if they talk over their feelings, especially what makes them feel inhibited. Howard Markman, Ph.D., associate professor of psychology at the University of Denver, suggests that partners "approach each other lovingly, not defensively or in an accusatory manner. A good strategy is to discuss something less highly charged first, then move on to sex."

Intimacy vs. intercourse

Sex is a very individual human drive; there is huge variety in the frequency with which couples make love, and in the satisfaction they need from it. "As long as they are both satisfied, it doesn't matter in the least how infrequently they make love," says Dr. Ruman. "Often the party line, the 'optimum amount of sex' couples should have, makes people believe they're not having enough— even if it's enough for them. People need to develop a sense of their own needs and of what's important to them."

Even the experts are wary of surveys that try to establish a "norm" of sexual activity—for example, that most couples make love twice a week. Such surveys are far from conclusive. For one, it is difficult to define what couples mean by "sex": intercourse and orgasms every time? Opinions vary. "Sex is equally about touching and kissing and holding," says Dr. Knox. "Couples can certainly experience sexual fulfillment in these ways without necessarily having intercourse every time." Notes Dr. Ruman, "It isn't so much intercourse that's important as erotic, sensual interplay. Sex changes in the course of a relationship from three-days-in-bed-withtakeout-food to something quieter, more tender and affectionate. What matters is that desire and intimacy remain."

But Dr. Shelley points out that "if there is never intercourse, people tend to feel a kind of coolness, a sense of sterility about their relationship. Although sexual expression doesn't always have to lead to intercourse, if it doesn't happen occasionally it's likely that at least one partner will feel unfulfilled."

It is probably the male who will feel the loss first since, as Dr. Shelley observes, he is traditionally more performance-oriented. "Many men need to express their tenderness and sensuality in an active way—through intercourse. For them, intercourse is how they get affirmation," he says. "But if a woman wants to be cuddled more, she can tell her mate and help him become a better lover."

Compromise in sex is a need to be recognized, not resented. "Lovemaking needn't always be slow and leisurely and result in orgasms for both partners," says Dr. Abel. "If only one partner feels like having sex, it's perfectly okay for it to be short and sweet, with only one partner climaxing." The pace should vary—next time long and tender—but no score-keeping. The "one for you, one for me" sort of pressure should be avoided. In the area of sex—where there is such infinite variety and possibility—agreement is the key to a happy relationship. Depending on the couple, sex can be one of the most or least important elements in their life. Whether you make love every night or every other month, what really matters is that both of you feel satisfied with the sex you share. In that, most people *and* experts concur.

RE-MAKING LOVE
The Real Sexual Revolution

*Sex has changed more than
any other part of our lives.
But the backlash is now
trying to tell us that female
autonomy is female promiscuity.
Beware.*

Barbara Ehrenreich, Elizabeth Hess, and Gloria Jacobs

Barbara Ehrenreich is a "Ms." contributing editor. Elizabeth Hess is a free-lance journalist who has written for the Washington "Post," "The Village Voice," and "Ms." Gloria Jacobs is an editor at "Ms."

Ellen* at 34 has made what she considers a "nice little life" for herself. She works for the local telephone company and has managed to buy a small house on the outskirts of Santa Fe. She has what used to be called "all-American" good looks—straight, gleaming hair and clear blue eyes. She is single, has had numerous boyfriends, and is currently seeing one man, whom she has been dating for the last two years. By her own description she is a "cowgirl" with a rough-and-ready attitude toward sex. Her present

*The names and background details have been altered to protect anonymity.

relationship is just one more phase in her continuing sexual exploration. The late sixties, when she made her first discoveries of her sexuality, were, she says, "one of the most intense periods of my life. I had learned nothing about sex at home and was constantly randy as a teenager. It was a relief to let my needs explode. I had a chance to discover what I liked sexually, who I liked. I made a lot of demands on men too; I chose them for their sexiness or sensuality. Amazing discovery that I could do that."

Ellen's enthusiasm is typical of the generation of women who came of age sexually at a time when repression was coming undone. Their newfound sexual freedom brought the added benefit of a healthy confidence in their bodies—and in their ability to live, at least part of the time, without being seriously involved with a man. If they were heterosexuals, other women might still offer the

warmth and emotional intimacy that was previously expected of a sexual relationship. They could also, if they chose, experiment with bisexuality or eliminate men from their lives altogether. Such women were realistic: casual sex was neither heaven nor hell, but it was an important part of their sexual experience.

Nevertheless by the early 1980s a backlash was brewing against what was pejoratively called female "promiscuity." The media began to metamorphose the modern woman, who had been practicing her sexual negotiating skills throughout the seventies, into an old-fashioned girl looking for moonlight, flowers, and commitment. Despite the enthusiasm women brought to the sexual revolution, this new revisionism inevitably began to feed on their doubts, undermining the positive feelings of many who had enjoyed the freedoms of casual sex.

Given the extent of the changes women's sexual revolution had brought to heterosexuality in one brief generation, it is not surprising that some people *were* confused. In any revolution, political or cultural, the old verities disappear; choices have to be made where none were demanded before. Freedom may be exhilarating, or it may just bring on a bad case of anxiety—or both.

Under the circumstances, a backlash may have been inevitable. But this backlash was ignoring, and in some cases, actively denying, the very real statistics and testimony that pointed to women's increasing enjoyment of sexual independence. According to surveys in several major magazines, by the late 1970s a majority of women—of all ages—had accepted with pleasure progressive attitudes toward sex. *Redbook*'s editors were awash in responses when they published their questionnaire on sex in 1975. The comments left the surprised editors declaring, "Women are becoming increasingly active sexually and are less likely to accept an unsatisfactory sex life as part of the price to be paid for marriage." The study also found that a "considerable number" of readers were having affairs while happily married to men they loved, and nine out of ten of the newly married women who responded were engaging in intercourse before they married.

As statistics, these women were remarkably on target with a survey five years later of *Cosmo* readers. Many of *Cosmo*'s readers were as sexually satisfied as *Redbook*'s (the median reported was nine lovers per woman) and a little more brazen to boot: "I have lovers because sex feels good," said one, and, claimed another, "I have lovers because what else is there in life that's so much fun as turning on a new man, interesting him, conquering him?" Among *Playboy*'s readers in 1983, young married wives were "fooling around" more than their husbands.

Women's sexual revolution had a great many committed converts, but men were lagging behind. In a 1985 Roper poll 43 percent of the men surveyed wanted a traditional marriage "in which he [the husband] was the provider and she [the wife] ran the house." The traditional man seemed to have equally conservative sexual views. Many surveys still showed a large majority of men who did not think women should engage in premarital sex or have extramarital affairs. As one female veteran of the New York singles scene said, "It's the same old 1950s rules of the game . . . I've found

The true heart of the sexual revolution was a change in women's behavior, not men's.

a lot of fear of my own sexuality. Beneath the rhetoric lie the same old attitudes."

The Death of Sex?

At the end of 1982 *Esquire* magazine ran a cover story entitled "The End of Sex." The article, by George Leonard, was illustrated with a photograph of a funeral wreath of dying roses laid over a tombstone which read "The Sexual Revolution, R.I.P." Sex, as we have just seen, was far from dead. But a certain notion of sex—loving, nurturing, long-term sex—was gone, said Leonard. "The trivialization of the erotic," he wrote, "climaxes in the practice of 'recreational sex' in which sexual intercourse becomes a mere sport, divorced not only from love and creation, but also from empathy, compassion, morality, responsibility, and sometimes even common politeness."

Was Leonard bemoaning the death of sex, after all, or the birth—already over a decade old—of female sexual autonomy? He implied that women were making it too easy: "Recreational sex

palls not so much from its immorality as from its dullness. The plot can be summed up, Hollywood style, in three sentences: Boy meets girl. Boy gets girl. They part." Many of the women reading that article had experienced enough of heterosexuality, whether pre- or post-sexual revolution, to know that recreational sex had always been part of the traditional male repertoire. Whether in 1950 or 1980, casual sex had always been *the* macho symbol, and very few men were complaining as long as they controlled the action. Men like Leonard were responding to the little-discussed fact that the true heart of the sexual revolution was a change in women's behavior, not men's.

Where women had once participated wholeheartedly, some were now having second thoughts when confronted with male ambivalence—and sexism. Despite all the talk of the sensitive, feminist "new man," too many women claimed to be meeting men who simply could not let them participate with equal control in a sexual relationship. "You have no idea what it's like out there," a woman bus driver in Philadelphia says. Married and divorced, she's been happy to "date around and sleep around." But, she says, "sometimes they treat me like just another woman who 'puts out' for them. Or they think *I* want commitment and to some men that justifies treating a woman like dirt." It seemed that the kind of man who insists on lighting a lady's cigarette or opening the door for her wasn't ready for a woman who would open the door to new sexual experiences.

The relationship between sex and intimacy was confusing for both sexes. Women's sexual liberation had touched social bedrock, threatening ideas about gender, dependence, family, and marriage. Some people didn't like to be touched there, and the media was quick to pick up on a new mood of hesitation and nostalgia. By the mid-eighties, the nearly unanimous message presented by the mainstream media was that women were fed up with casual sex. There were few criticisms of men: this was a campaign against women and their sex lives.

TV Fights Casual Sex

When NBC television ran a documentary report, "Second Thoughts on Being Single," early in 1984, it implied that women's primary goals are love and security: they need to get married, while men try to avoid marriage. The program began with the statement that women of the "baby boom generation" are "fed up with modern American men, and modern morality.'' They want ''to get married,'' they want ''a family,'' but, said one of the program's experts, sociologist Pepper Schwartz, ''men [don't] like them to be very sexually experienced.''

The program showed attractive, educated women with good jobs who seemed hopelessly lost at singles' gatherings; others were working out every day—not for pleasure, but to simulate the body of a teenager. Then there were women mooning over other people's babies, proof positive to the viewer that they needed a man and a family. A long parade of academics was called upon to show that women were naturally monogamous, or if they weren't, had better be. Tired clichés emanated from experts like sociologist Nancy Moore Clatworthy, of Ohio State University, who said, ''The farmer used to say that a man certainly wouldn't buy the cow if he could milk the cow through the fence.''

These experts all assumed that women hated casual sex, but they offered no explanation for why so many were engaged in it. In fact, several women on the program explained that the problem wasn't with the sex, it was the attitudes of the men they were sleeping with. The only solution, according to one woman, was to become a ''born-again prude.'' If there were women who were still willing to fight with men over their right to sexual freedom, NBC never found them.

Sex Radicals
Searching for Love

Another serious blow to mainstream acceptance of casual sex came when two women, famous as sexual mavericks themselves—if only in their writing—executed their own about-faces. Erica Jong, who had delighted many female readers with her breezy, picaresque approach to sex in *Fear of Flying*, was, by the mid-eighties, not so sure that women had benefited from the sexual revolution. Her 1984 book, *Parachutes & Kisses*, brought Isadora Wing, her alter ego and heroine of *Fear of Flying*, up to date sexually, and while it documented the frequency and variety of Isadora's sexual encounters, one soon discovered that the pleasure of the hunt had given way to the search for true love. Passion was no longer an end in itself. Jong began her book with Isadora's musings on the sexual balance sheet 10 years after the revolution: "The world has certainly changed. For one thing

Given the choice between promiscuity and repressiveness, some women will choose promiscuity.

there is more oral sex. For another, more impotence. For a third, sex is ubiquitous and yet also somehow devoid of its full charge of mystery."

Wing is, after all, a fictional character. Yet Erica Jong had clearly given some thought to the drawbacks of the sexual revolution. "Many women discovered," she commented in a 1985 article in *Us* magazine surveying the influence of the birth-control pill, "that the freedom to say yes to everyone and anyone was really another form of slavery. Repeated, meaningless, one-night stands without commitment did not satisfy their hunger for love and connection, and so the so-called sexual revolution was really more a media myth than a reality." The author who had once celebrated the joys to be found when women chose and experimented with lovers, now called the sexual revolution a "pseudoevent."

Another, equally influential woman was on the same trail. Germaine Greer, one of the more glamorous exponents of early feminism, had been the perfect

media spokeswoman for some very radical sexual ideas. But, after years of espousing sexual freedom, Greer reverted to a philosophy suspiciously like that of the fundamentalist right. In 1984, during an interview following the publication of her new book, *Sex and Destiny*, she told a reporter that by exchanging "fidelity" for "promiscuity," women had traded one form of restriction for another: "The sexual revolution never happened. Permissiveness happened and that's no better than repressiveness." But in *The Female Eunuch* she had asked women to refuse "to commit themselves with pledges of utter monogamy and doglike devotion" as a "revolutionary measure." Once she had called for the destruction of "the polarity of masculine-feminine." To achieve this, "individual women [must] agree to be outcasts, eccentrics, perverts, and whatever the powers-that-be choose to call them."

Soon after the publication of *Sex and Destiny*, Greer was asked by a reporter if she regretted waiting to have a child: "Like many women, I chose not to have a child when I could have. Then when I thought I could fit one into my life I found out I couldn't conceive." Critic Linda Gordon believes this is at the heart of Greer's revisionism. A book "about fertility ... written by a woman suffering from infertility ... elicited my sympathy," wrote Gordon. But, she continued, Greer is "generalizing on the basis of what seems to be her personal response"—and forgetting, one might add, that millions of women, including herself, have fought for the idea that their sexuality is not linked absolutely and eternally to their reproductive capacity.

While women were trying to sort out the mixed messages they received from the media about their sexuality, important medical events influenced the public dialogue on sex. The 1980s brought very real fears about Acquired Immune Deficiency Syndrome (AIDS). Once it became clear that AIDS could be spread during heterosexual intercourse, and was not restricted to gay men, the hysteria surrounding the disease was an epidemic in itself. Sexually transmitted diseases such as syphilis, gonorrhea, and herpes, as well as AIDS, lend themselves to public moralizing. But in this case, the backlash against sexual promiscuity was well established before AIDS became a topic of general concern. When it did, it was all too easy to use the tragic new disease to reinforce the developing sexual conservatism.

A Revolution Just Begun

In the midst of reaction, the women's sexual revolution was being reappraised as part of an attempt to make sense of the events of the past two decades. Since the analysis the conservatives were offering was inherently anti-woman, the question of who controlled the direction of the revolution became one of the most critical issues to be debated. But feminism, which had helped initiate the sexual revolution in the first place, was now deeply divided over it. Some women, described as "cultural feminists," advocated an ideology which, in emphasizing women's "natural" traits, ended up glorifying attributes painfully similar to the reactionary clichés the conservatives were pushing. To cultural feminists, women's sexuality could be described in terms of gentleness, nurturance, and "circularity," as opposed to aggressive penetration. Others—the new "radical" feminists?—argued that the women's sexual revolution had to be open to all possibilities or a new tyranny would be created. Any attempt at this stage to define women's sexuality was premature and too limiting.

Australian-born British feminist Lynne Segal suggested that we still had a long way to go in the sexual revolution before most women would experience a real change in their lives. "Whatever the questioning which is going on, and whatever the tolerance for 'deviance,'" said Segal, "sexuality is still seen in terms of its reproductive functioning, symbolized by a genital heterosexuality which men initiate and control." Segal offered a reminder that love, romance, and marriage could be just as painful in a sexist society as anything a sexual adventurer might experience.

If women could acknowledge that the problem was greater than the particular man they slept with, they could also insist on their right to continue pushing forward the frontiers of female sexuality. Lesbian activist Amber Hollibaugh seemed to be speaking for more than just the gay women she was describing when she called for a new kind of "speak-out" in which women admitted their "secret" yearnings: "Who are all the women who don't come gently and don't want to; don't know yet what they like but intend to find out; are the lovers of butch or femme women; who like fucking with men; practice consensual s/m; feel more like faggots than dykes; love dildos, penetration, costumes; like to sweat, talk dirty, see expressions of need sweep across their lovers' faces; are confused and need to experiment with their own tentative ideas of passion; think gay male porn is hot; are into power?"

The media was not telling the story of the women who spoke up and questioned sexual orthodoxy, nor was it looking for the women who had become, essentially, the avant-garde of sexuality. They were women like Diane, who, with her short, bright-red hair, flashy clothes, and uproarious laugh is a mixture of punkette and flash: "I have what I call the 'gang boyfriend motif.' I have one boyfriend I've had for eleven years [she's 38]. He's been married twice in that time, and I know and his wife knows we're both better off not having him full-time. He's my main man. Then I have other boyfriends, usually out of town, who I see fairly regularly. I also have one other boyfriend in town, who I really like a lot.

They all add up to one big boyfriend, and all my needs get taken care of. It keeps me out of the bars—that's what I call the 'desperado motif.'"

Diane represents a small but important cadre of independent women who *are* promoting sexual solutions. These are the women who, given the choice between promiscuity and repressiveness, as Greer saw it, will choose promiscuity, although they would prefer not to be faced with such absolute choices. These are women like the one who said, "I love the mystery of something new...the physical and emotional possibilities of testing myself and him. The variety *is* the turn-on."

It is not necessary that these women speak for all of us. But their solutions are more than symbols; their choices are not so extreme that they have no relevance. Those on the frontier of sexual choice keep alive options which might otherwise be buried under a reactionary avalanche. What seems experimental and marginal at one time may become an important option—for all women—at another time. Shulamith Firestone, for example, was once regarded as a radical feminist whose ideas were provocative (she recommended separating reproduction from sexuality by having all babies born outside the womb) but could have little application in the "real" world. But she also wrote in 1970 in *The Dialectic of Sex*, her ground-breaking study of the need for feminist revolution, that the "most important characteristic to be maintained in any revolution is *flexibility*" and that "a program of multiple options [should] exist simultaneously...some transitional, others far in the future."

As Firestone thought, casual sex should be a choice, not a duty imposed by ideology, and not a privilege to be whisked away as soon as the political climate turns conservative. Women have come too far to surrender the range of possibilities opened up by a sexual revolution.

Sex and Schools

AIDS and the Surgeon General add a new urgency to an old debate

It took only a single paragraph (four sentences, 91 words) to change the course of an ancient debate. "There is now no doubt," said Surgeon General C. Everett Koop in his grim report on AIDS last month, "that we need sex education in schools and that it must include information on heterosexual and homosexual relationships." With characteristic bluntness, Koop made it clear that he was talking about graphic instruction starting "at the lowest grade possible," which he later identified as Grade 3. Because of the "deadly health hazard," he said later, "we have to be as explicit as necessary to get the message across. You can't talk of the dangers of snake poisoning and not mention snakes."

Some people would clearly prefer not to talk about poison at all. Sex educators face a powerful array of detractors and doubters: Fundamentalist and Roman Catholic leaders, antiabortionists, opponents of the gay lobby, psychologists worrying about the impact of AIDS messages on the young, blacks who consider sex education racist, and even a few capitalists who think that school clinics offering birth-control information should be turned over to private enterprise.

But Koop's speech has thrown the naysayers on the defensive and increased the odds that comprehensive sex education will at last overcome its critics. For years, surveys have shown that about 80% of Americans favor sex education in the public schools. In the wake of Koop's dramatic report, a poll for TIME by Yankelovich, Clancy, Shulman found that instruction is now favored by 86%, perhaps the highest number ever; 89% want such courses for children age 12 to deal with birth-control information, and about three-quarters say homosexuality and abortion should be included in the curriculum (*see box*). "AIDS will definitely change the nature of sex education as we know it," said Harvey Fineberg, dean of the Harvard School of Public Health. "It will lead to more open, explicit discussions about condoms and other strategies for safe sex." Though some people will be shocked, he said, "we are at a point where sex education is no longer a matter of morals—it's a matter of life and death."

For opponents of sex ed, that is precisely the problem: the recommendation to students that they use condoms as an anti-AIDS measure helps erode moral opposition to premarital sex and contraception, just as the impartial listing of "options" such as homosexuality and abortion undermines other traditional teachings. Critics of abortion fear that its mention in classes will make it seem like an easy solution to an offhand mistake. "The way sex education is taught in the schools encourages experimentation," says Right-Wing Crusader Phyllis Schlafly. "It's the cause of promiscuity and destroys the natural modesty of girls."

Since President Reagan and Koop have strongly opposed sex education in the past, the Surgeon General's report was particularly galling to conservatives. So was the spectacle of Koop's virtually writing off the family as a reliable source of sexual guidance. Though he insisted that parents stay involved, he said, "Most parents are so embarrassed and reluctant, you can't count on getting the message across at home." Most Americans seem to agree: the TIME poll showed that 69% believe parents are not doing as much as they should to educate their youngsters about sex.

Politically, Koop's statements last month came one step ahead of an AIDS study that might have proved embarrassing to the Administration: a National Academy of Sciences report warned that the AIDS epidemic "could become a catastrophe" without strong White House leadership and a campaign of education and research that would probably cost $2 billion by 1990. Whether Koop's motive was political or not, his report plunged the nation into a thicket of legal and moral questions. Is it unwise to tell third-graders about anal sex and the connection between sex, AIDS and death? Is it the proper function of a public school to push either abstinence or birth control? Is value-free sex education possible, and if not, whose values will be taught?

Sex education has been a program searching for a consensus since it arrived in the schools at the turn of the century, the brainchild of stern progressive-era reformers, mostly doctors and other upper-crust male professionals. The idea, the only idea, was to enforce sexual restraint. Reformers believed that enlightened mass education could help banish venereal disease, prostitution, masturbation and sex outside marriage. The notion of "scientific" sex education arose as a way of deflecting the curious from actual sexual behavior. Instruction, said a 1912 committee, "should aim to keep sex consciousness and sex emotions at the minimum." Then, as now, there were heavy implications that parents, particularly impoverished ones, could not be counted on to teach restraint to the young.

About 80% of public-school children in major U.S. cities now take some kind of sex-education course. As for national figures, no one knows for sure: sex education is strictly a local matter, varying widely from one community to the next, and few accurate statistics are kept. Only Maryland, New Jersey and Washington, D.C., require the subject in all schools.

In a number of schools, sex education turns out to be nothing more than a brief bout with a safely biological "swimming sperm and Fallopian tube" course that has put students to sleep for generations. Or, hardly more energizing, it may be a three-hour course taught by a gym teacher, followed by a display of condoms or foam brought along by a speaker from Planned Parenthood. In Kansas, the curriculums for phys ed, drivers' ed and sex ed are all overseen by the same state board of education official. "No matter what is written in the curriculum, there is not much going on out there," says Mary Lee Tatum, a sex-education consultant. "Under 15% of U.S. children get really good sex education. We are only beginning to institute adequate programs."

Many communities, of course, have outstanding programs, including Arlington, Va., Baltimore, and Irvington, N.J. Teaching can be impressively broad, running from kindergarten through twelfth grade and based on developmental psychology, emphasizing assertiveness training, the mechanics of decision making and assigned essays on topics like sex in the media.

At P.S. 42 on New York City's Lower East Side, Principal Anthony Barry takes the formal sex-ed curriculum "with a grain of salt": teaching the children of fairly conservative parents, most of them Chinese American and Hispanic, means playing things by ear. Says he: "We want parents to know that we're not undermining what they are trying to do."

One technique at the school is to raise animals in the classroom. When they mate, the children understand that they produce babies of the same species—a smooth introduction to sex education known to every farm child. Nurse Mary Tang teaches anatomy to fifth- and sixth-graders and answers explicit questions, but she does not bring up subjects like abortion and birth control. That is the only formal part of the instruction; most of the rest of the sex-ed time is spent in rap sessions, fielding questions about sex and trying to build personal responsibility.

Good or bad, adequate or not, is some better than none? Does sex education work? So far, studies on the subject have been fragmentary, unconvincing or massively inconclusive. A six-volume 1984 analysis by Mathtech Inc. of nine programs around the country came to the deflating conclusion after a seven-year investigation that sex-ed courses had almost no effect on contraceptive use, views about premarital sex, or such social skills as assertiveness and self-understanding. The only significant changes in behavior and attitude came in the two programs with strong backing from parents and the local community. And the only increased use of birth control came when the sex-ed program was combined with ready access to a health clinic. The study offered a nugget of hope to conservative parents: graduates of sex-ed programs were less permissive about premarital sex than control groups.

After studying 3,600 students at six high schools in Indiana, Texas and Mississippi, the Center for Population Options found little discernible impact. "Formal sex education appears to have no consistent effect on the subsequent probability that a teenager will begin to have intercourse, neither postponing it nor hastening it," said Douglas Kirby, the head researcher. "Typically, students who take sex-education courses report more tolerant attitudes toward the sexual behavior of others but little change in the values that govern their own personal behavior."

The Surgeon General's intervention brought new doubts about sex education. Some critics who spoke out reacted angrily at the prospect of explicit teaching about homosexuality and anal sex. "Where do we draw the line?" roared Joseph Casper, an outspoken member of the elected Boston school committee. "The gay community would love to come in and say theirs is an alternative life-style that's really O.K. But then what's next? Do we bring in people who want to talk about safe bondage too? Chimps making it with chickens? It's insane." A few people talked as if AIDS were ushering in a new puritan era in which sex-ed courses would be used as a bully pulpit for abstinence. "As awful as it sounds, AIDS is almost a blessing in disguise," said Mary Ann Briggs, a health teacher at Fairview High School in Boulder. "Many kids are very scared by AIDS, and it makes it easier to say, 'Do you really want to get involved with sex?'"

Some proponents of sex education had reservations about Koop's report. Stanford Education Professor Michael Kirst said schools are overburdened enough without becoming the official problem-solving arena for the nation's sex problems. Said Kirst: "Every time schools take on value-laden topics, they end up losing overall public support. It's a no-win ball game." The national president of Planned Parenthood, Faye Wattleton of New York City, offered Koop only cold praise. Reason: she wants upbeat instruction, not just education "within the context of preventing a deadly disease."

By far Koop's most explosive proposal is the idea of teaching eight-year-olds about AIDS. Only 23% of those surveyed in the TIME poll agreed with the suggestion. Most professional educators seem opposed. "If you brought up anal sex to third-graders, they would be in a state of shock," said Marilyn Huriwitz, a health teacher at South Boston High School. "How are you going to talk to kids that age about anal sex?" asks Al Wardell, a Chicago high school teacher and a gay activist. "I guess that's my teacher's prudishness." Young children's brains cannot assimilate such information, warns William Chambers, director of pediatric psychiatry at Manhattan's Columbia-Presbyterian Medical Center. "For them, anal sex is going to the bathroom."

A few experts believe the Surgeon General's suggestion makes sense. Observes Harold Harris, a child psychiatrist at Duke Medical Center: "At four or five, they're playing doctor games. Sexuality is what that's all about. We should bring it out of the closet and talk about it in school and home." It would not be necessary to give third-graders the full hair-raising message, only a few basics. Child Psychologist Lee Salk would not favor including the subject as part of sex education, but he thinks that AIDS could be explained as a disease if care is taken to avoid raising undue fear. He would describe anal sex as well as drug use. "One of the ways grown-ups protect themselves is to avoid doing these things," he would continue. But, he points out, "notice I am avoiding alarming language and not saying, 'If you do this, you'll be dead in no time.'"

Pragmatically, Koop might be well advised to abandon campaigning for vivid AIDS instruction in the third grade. The delay of a couple of years would not greatly undermine his overall goal. But the largest problem entwined in sex-ed courses cannot be so easily evaded or resolved. The subject is impossible to teach without plunging into the question of values. Many educators assert that curriculums can be made value free, a dubious idea at best.

The difficulties of remaining value free show up clearly in an 18-minute anti-AIDS videotape prepared for the New York City school system and purchased by groups in 35 states. The narrator is the young movie actress Rae Dawn Chong. She discusses the two riskiest behaviors involved in AIDS, unambiguously advising viewers to avoid intravenous drug use but shying away from a similar warning on anal sex. Instead, she suggests use of condoms for vaginal and anal intercourse and adds offhandedly, "If you decide not to have sex, that's O.K. too."

The videotape is earnestly intent on deflecting criticism of homosexuals for spreading AIDS. In the tape's one emotional scene, the brother of an AIDS victim says, "If I ever hear anyone talking about how gays are to blame for AIDS . . . I swear to God, I'm gonna punch 'em in the head!" New York City is still debating whether to accept the tape. Board of Education President Robert Wagner Jr. has criticized it for not clearly opposing adolescent sex and drug use, but he has not directly objected to its gingerliness about homosexuality and anal sex.

Wagner and Schools Chancellor Nathan Quinones must deal with a minefield of conflicting views. The city's sex-education curriculum is described as "value neutral" but, like many other school systems' courses, is actually based on a generalized secular ethic of caring and respect for others. Parents dissatisfied with the version of the city curriculum served up in their district can pull their children out of particular classes by informing the principal. The program is sometimes popular, as it is at P.S. 42, but the effort to accommodate everyone is unacceptable to many. Last month the board of education mandated sex education for the remaining eleven school districts without it. Last week 250 protesters showed up at city hall to object.

Mary Cummins, head of School Board 24 in Queens, threatens to fight the imposed course plans in court. She complains that chastity is not taught as a value and homosexuality is depicted as an "acceptable alternative life-style." Her board, she said, supports the concept of sex education but not a curriculum that "violates social values and moral principles without consideration of our views and values." Deriding the idea of value-free instruction, Cummins says, "I defy anyone to teach it, including myself, without getting his own moral values across. I know, if I were teaching it, I'd stress morality."

Education Secretary William Bennett supports that kind of concern. His fear, he told a New York City audience last month, is that instead of a clear ethic of right and wrong, sex-ed students are frequently exposed to a hodgepodge of "feel-good philosophy." Bennett accepts sex education "provided that people do not try to make it value free." He would require instruction to include a message on abstinence. "Such courses should take place only if the community wants them and the parents are involved and know what is going to be taught."

One group has confronted value-free teaching by devising and marketing a model curriculum that states traditional conservative values throughout. Teen-Aid Inc., with headquarters in Spokane and 25 affiliates in the U.S. and Canada, urges youngsters to "resist the tide" of a sex-saturated culture. The program tries to sharpen the "refusal skills" of students and sends summaries of lessons home to parents. Students are told to be careful about what clothes they wear on dates, and not to drink or take drugs while on a date.

The feistiest combatants are fighting against not school curriculums but school clinics. These health facilities are attached to or near public schools around the country, and they are spreading rapidly. Most are funded with a mix of public and private money. All offer across-the-board medical care. Some 28% dispense contraceptives, 52% prescribe them, and the rest make referrals to family-planning agencies. So far there are 72, mostly in poor neighborhoods of big cities. A hundred more are in the works.

The Roman Catholic Church, which on the whole has reacted mildly to the growing clamor for more sex education, has been anything but docile about the clinics' birth-control services. Two weeks ago Archbishop Roger Mahony of Los Angeles issued a heated pastoral letter calling for "all those who value the family and have hope for the future of our children" to join him in vigorous protest against a proposal to establish three school-based clinics. In Boston, Bernard Cardinal Law denounced four proposed health clinics that would provide contraceptives in junior and senior high schools. In an 86-page attack, the archdiocese challenged the constitutionality of school clinics and argued that contraceptives increase the amount of teen sex by eroding "cautions and reluctance." Replied Nancy Drooker of Massachusetts' Planned Parenthood: "Most teenagers are sexually active for over a year before they get contraception, so you can hardly say birth control was the cause."

A few black leaders in Boston and New York City have denounced the clinics as racist. In Chicago, 13 black clergymen are suing to block distribution of contraceptives at the DuSable High School clinic. Says the Rev. Hiram Crawford: "If these clinics are so good for black kids, why don't they put them in white areas? It's a form of genocide. Why do they so readily recommend abortion?"

The conservative belief is that such clinics lead students to be more promiscuous, but clearly established facts are difficult to come by. In St. Paul, records show that birth rates fell 40% in schools with clinics, though Health Supervisor Wanda Miller was hesitant to claim full credit for the clinics. Of the adolescent mothers who used the services, 80% stayed in school, and repeat pregnancies were almost nonexistent. Follow-ups are important, says Miller, because teens are "rotten contraceptors."

Other clinics report lower birth rates among those counseled or treated. And a survey of two inner-city schools, released this year by a team headed by Laurie Schwab Zabin of Johns Hopkins' School of Public Health, reported that sexually inactive high school students who used the clinic postponed their first sexual encounter about seven months, to age 16.2

How the Public Feels

Adults do not think they are doing a very good job of teaching their children about the facts of life: 69% of 1,015 Americans polled for TIME *last week by Yankelovich, Clancy, Shulman* said parents are not doing as much as they should to* educate their children about sex; 39% of the parents who were polled admit they have had "frank and open" discussions about sex with their teenagers only a few times or not at all. Those questioned overwhelmingly support sex-education courses in school, and 47% of them said they wished they had been better informed about sex when they were teenagers. Some of the poll's other findings:

What to teach—and when

Eighty-six percent of the respondents agree that sex-education courses should be taught in school, and 83% agree with the Surgeon General's recommendation that schools should teach children about AIDS. Only 23% agree with the Surgeon General's recommendation to teach children about AIDS as early as age 8; even fewer people (17%) think sex-education courses should be offered to 8-year-olds. However, large majorities support the idea of giving older children specifics about sex.

Should sex-education courses teach 12-year-olds about:

	Yes
The dangers of AIDS	95%
Sexually transmitted diseases	93%
Birth control	89%
Premarital sex	78%

How men and women have sexual intercourse	76%
Homosexuality	76%
Abortion	72%
Practices such as oral and anal sex	40%

(Other respondents answered "No" or "Not sure")

Teaching morality

If most people want schools to teach children about sex, they also want teachers to be preachers. Seventy percent say sex-education programs should try to teach moral values—what students should or should not do sexually; moreover, 58% do not think it is possible to teach sex-related issues without discussing moral values.

*The survey was conducted by telephone Nov. 10 to 12 among Americans 18 years or older. The potential sampling error is plus or minus 3% for the entire population. Among the smaller group of 150 parents, the potential error is larger.

instead of the 15.7 that otherwise was typical. Zabin's study is one of the most frequently cited by activists who support sex education and school clinics. In the first two-plus years of the study, the pregnancy rate fell 30% among teenagers who had access to birth-control supplies at a clinic near their school, while the pregnancy rate rose 57% among a control group.

But conservatives have their own favorite research, described by one of the authors in the *Wall Street Journal* but not yet generally available: two studies by Utah researchers named Stan Weed and Joseph Olsen. Their major finding is that during a period when the number of teens using family-planning clinics rose from 300,000 to 1.5 million, the teen pregnancy rate actually increased 19%. Births were down, they said, but only because of abortion. "Apparently the programs are more effective at convincing teens to avoid birth than to avoid pregnancy," Weed wrote in the *Journal*. The point: teens tend to get pregnant not because of lack of information or birth-control devices but because of social and psychological factors, including low self-esteem, impulsiveness and a bleak economic future. In response, the Alan Guttmacher Institute charged that the *Journal* piece contained "numerous inaccuracies." The number of adolescent pregnancies has decreased for the past three years on record, 1980-83, said the institute, and the pregnancy rate has declined as well.

Another study tends to back the Weed-Olsen view. Deborah Anne Dawson, as a doctoral student at Johns Hopkins, found that two-thirds of girls between 15 and 19 have had some instruction about birth control and pregnancy, with only 16% lacking any such education at all. Her conclusion: teaching about birth control and pregnancy has no significant effect on the pregnancy rate among teens, presumably because teenagers are more emotional than rational about sex and its risks. Says Boston's Huriwitz: "Adolescent sex is spontaneous, based on passion and the moment, not thought and reason. They don't worry about AIDS because they think it will never happen to them, no matter what we tell them. And I don't know how we change that."

A few programs incorporating discussions of AIDS were already under way before Koop's report. Last spring, after a student and staff member in two public schools were diagnosed as having AIDS, Boston prepared a 28-minute AIDS videotape filled with medical facts but also polite circumlocutions, including the message that AIDS spreads through blood and semen and "intimate sexual contact." For Boston, that was a shift. "Look, ten years ago, you couldn't even mention intimate sexual contact in this town," says Michael Grady, medical director for the Boston public schools. Grady's defense of the vagueness: "We'd rather do a little education than none at all." This fall Greater Miami began offering comprehensive AIDS information as part of its sex-education program. AIDS is mentioned briefly to seventh-graders as one of many sexually transmitted diseases. Tenth-graders get a more thoroughgoing five hours focused on it. Parents are mostly pleased.

In Omaha, where a beleaguered committee is now cautiously preparing the city's first sex-ed program, there is still controversy about whether to teach the subject at all. In such an atmosphere, school officials tend to talk a lot about the family and the bracing wonders of abstinence. School Superintendent Norbert Schuerman has called for "educational experiences that do not violate the social and moral standards of the total community." He said schools need the help of parents and suggested that any sex-ed program underline the message "It's O.K. to Say No." In a spasm of candor, School Board Member Bill Pfeffer admitted that a lot of sidestepping and shuffling is going on. "Everyone is afraid that the Catholic Church and the other groups are going to get very angry." One board member, John

Should sex-education courses:	Yes	No
Teach students that sex at too early an age is harmful	**79%**	15%
Urge students not to have sexual intercourse	**67%**	25%
Urge students to practice birth control when having casual sex	**84%**	11%
Tell students that abortion is an option when pregnancy occurs	**56%**	35%
Tell students that abortion is immoral	**44%**	44%
Tell students that homosexuality is just an alternative sexual activity	**24%**	64%
Tell students that homosexuality is immoral	**56%**	36%

Only 24% think sex education would make students more likely to engage in sex at an earlier age. (Opponents of sex education disagree: 49% think the courses would make students more likely to experiment with sex.) Most people (78%) think sexually active youngsters would be more likely to practice birth control if they had some sex education. People also say schools should provide students with birth-control information—but not with contraceptives.

	Yes	No
Should school health clinics make birth-control information available?	**84%**	12%
Should school health clinics provide students with contraceptives?	**36%**	53%

Catholics and Protestants tend to agree on these issues: 83% of Catholics and 84% of Protestants think sex-education courses should urge students to practice birth control when having casual sex; 51% of Catholics and 57% of Protestants say abortion should be presented as an alternative when pregnancy occurs.

Parents and children

Many adults feel their own sexual education was inadequate: 73% say they were "only somewhat informed" or "poorly informed" about sex when they were teenagers. Women feel this way more often than men: 52% of the women (and 40% of the men) wish they had been better informed about sex as teenagers; 32% of the women said they knew nothing at all about birth control when they became sexually active. Only 9% of men and women say they learned about sex from sex-education courses. Forty percent say they got much of their information from friends; 23% learned from their parents. While more than half of the parents polled say they have discussed sexual matters with their teenage children, few have talked about the birds and bees with preteens. When parents do tell youngsters about sex, the job often falls to Mother.

Have you ever told your 8- to 12-year-old children:	Mothers Yes	Fathers Yes
About the dangers of AIDS	**48%**	**42%**
About homosexuality	**37%**	**35%**
About abortion	**36%**	**25%**
How men and women have intercourse	**34%**	**21%**
About birth control	**26%**	**17%**

How Much Do They Know?

"There's nothing they're not aware of but a lot they don't know," muses New York City Assistant Principal Herbert Silkowitz. What was true a generation ago is true today: children know both too much and not enough about sex. Now it's just more of the same, at a younger age, with misinformation running wild.

This is hardly a surprise, considering where children get their concepts about sex. Three-fifths of teenagers pick them up from friends or "on their own," according to a 1985 Planned Parenthood poll, while only a third get their information from parents or school. Pornography is part of the on-their-own category, with the soft-core pages of *Penthouse* sometimes supplemented by an X-rated videocassette Dad left lying around. The increasingly unfettered use of sex as a come-on in the mass media is a new and unsettling factor, overwhelming the young in stimulation—soap operas, cable television, blatantly erotic ads for Obsession perfume. But apart from saying "watch" or "buy," these sensations offer no guiding context. Says Nancy Olin, teen-education coordinator for Boston Planned Parenthood: "The daytime soaps show constant and irresponsible sexual behavior: no waiting, very few morals."

Professional sex educators agree that when it comes to guidance, parents are the best source. "This is probably the first generation of parents that believes sex is normal and natural, and that leaves plenty of room for the moral questions—when it is right and with whom. People are entitled to their own views and to pass them on to their children," says Ron Moglia, director of the human-sexuality research and teaching program at New York University. "Any parent who relinquishes the right to talk to his child about sex is giving up one of the most wonderful experiences he can have."

But it is not an easy one. What should children be told, and when? Clearly there are no absolute rules. Variations depend on how each child is maturing, even where a family lives. Children from rural backgrounds, particularly farms, are more in tune with sex and reproductive cycles than their supposedly sophisticated urban counterparts. The experts offer general guidelines based on experience. Leah Lefstein, acting director of the Center for Early Adolescence in Chapel Hill, N.C., notes, "Kids are aware of human sexuality at an earlier age than we give them credit for. They are three years old when they want to know where babies come from." And they can understand simple, descriptive answers. Says Sharon Shilling, a Denver sex-education expert: "When they come into kindergarten, they generally have a knowledge of body parts, and they know about basic bodily functions."

Olin stresses that it is appropriate to explain things differently at different ages. Until perhaps age eight, the questions are mainly biological and the answers should be too. But at ten, parents and educators need to explain masturbation, wet dreams and menstruation, for example. At that age, she says, children do not need to know about birth control. Sex educators agree that girls should understand in advance the most important and indeed shocking physical changes that will affect their bodies during their lifetimes. And boys, who mature more slowly and undergo less dramatic physical changes, should nonetheless be told what is about to happen to them. It may also be appropriate to describe the changes in the opposite sex.

By the early teenage years, the full range of sexuality can be discussed in concrete terms; explanations should not be overly complex but may require a little reading up and planning beforehand. Parents should not be put off by shrugs of "I know all that." Exposure to explicit pictures or peer-group whispers is no substitute, and ignorance can mean disaster. Says Olin: "We have pregnant teenagers now at age 13 or 14." Dr. Marion Howard, of Atlanta's Grady Memorial Hospital, lists some myths that are, appallingly, still prevalent at this age: "If you think the time of the month you can get pregnant is near the time of your menstrual cycle, or douching with Coke keeps you from getting pregnant, or using Saran Wrap as a condom is effective, or sexual intercourse standing up prevents pregnancy—that's all harmful." Such misinformation flourishes best when parents shy away from the responsibility and reward of guiding their children.

year public debate before starting sex-education programs in the schools in 1983. Grateful to be asked for their input, the bishops endorsed the state's sex-education plans, but "with reservations," mostly about instruction on abortion and contraception.

One of the state's model programs, designed for the Irvington school system, which is 92% black and Hispanic, runs from kindergarten through twelfth grade, starting with simple instruction on bodily functions and child abuse, then moving on during high school years to instruction in family planning. Fourth-Grade Teacher Linda Lichtenberger conducts her sex-ed classes like rap sessions, and designs homework assignments that encourage students to discuss what they are learning with their parents.

The course does not slip by controversial areas. Lichtenberger shows her nine- and ten-year-olds a chart on contraceptive methods and their efficiency rates. "We really have to arm children with something," she says. "They don't have to be abused or taken advantage of. We want them to protect themselves so they don't become one of the wounded adults that take it out on the next generation." Latasha Gadsden remembers taking the course last year and learning about "VD, how babies are born and how babies form in the uterus." Sometimes "the boys all laughed," she adds. But Latasha thinks "sex education makes people more mature because it's not really funny, it's your own body."

In Rockford, Ill., Teacher Thomas Lundgren's seventh-grade "Family Life and Health" course separates the sexes for two or three days each year because girls do not want to discuss sanitary protection in front of boys, and boys are just as embarrassed to talk about wet dreams in a mixed class. When students talk about the emergence of heterosexuality and homosexuality, Lundgren says, "we tell them we're just giving them an educated guess, and use an analogy with right- and left-handedness, that sexual orientation is something that is established very early in life."

Lundgren talks about condoms ("No glove, no love" is a popular class mnemonic), and abortion is presented as a fact of life. "We explain how suction curettage happens and what happens with a saline injection," says the teacher. "We tell them to keep reading, keep thinking and keep talking about it." Lundgren starts discussions of oral and anal sex by saying, "We're not telling you this to gross you out." Only six or seven youngsters out of 850 are excused from the class each year because of parents' objections. Says the popular Lundgren, one of eight finalists for state teacher of the year in 1985: "Everybody we talk to in the community is positive about what we're doing."

By national standards, St. Paul's sex-

Haller, 77, said he will keep opposing any program because "the kids are getting too inquisitive; we're arousing their curiosity." The difficulty with sex, contended the Rev. Bob Thone of the Omaha Gospel Tabernacle, is that "the more you talk about it, the more it excites the desire to experiment."

New Jersey appears to have managed the task of eroding the conservative beachhead. There are still some angry dissenters who have lawsuits and other protests pending. But the state board of education defused much opposition and won the support of the state's five Roman Catholic dioceses by conducting a three-

ed program is one of the frankest and most thriving. It touches on homosexuality without either endorsing or criticizing it. "We say the gay community defines homosexuality as a trait that is born into them, and we are not putting our own construction on that because we don't have research to substantiate it," says Wanda Miller. Teachers also explain exactly how one gets or avoids AIDS. "We are clear and explicit about semen and blood being the roots of transmission and that condoms offer protection." Despite such directness, St. Paul's program operates without much criticism from parents.

The popular acceptance of these programs seems to rest on their adjustment to their individual communities, something not easily outlined in a lesson plan. Says Harvard Psychology Professor Jerome Kagan: "Human sexuality is a moral issue in every society. But while some societies have a consensus on sex, ours doesn't." The conflicting moral values touch the most seemingly innocuous issues. Everyone, for example, agrees that self-esteem and psychological factors are crucial, particularly to demoralized ghetto youngsters. But even building self-esteem divides proponents and critics of sex education. One side tends to talk of right and wrong, the other of self-enhancement and the importance of feelings. UCLA Health Educator Adrienne Davis says she teaches "that nothing is good that decreases your self-esteem, that you don't feel good about and that hurts another person," the essence of what Secretary Bennett cites when he harrumphs about "feel-good philosophy."

The struggle over sex education echoes the right-left battles over public school textbooks around the nation, notably in Tennessee, where Fundamentalist parents successfully sued to shield their children from basic school readers they considered offensive. The Roman Catholic Archdiocese of Boston has begun to use language similar to Southern Fundamentalists', charging that school clinics would establish an "official state philosophy of situation ethics and moral relativism" that contradicts the teachings of most major religions. Psychiatrist Thomas Szasz, author of Sex by Prescription, thinks pressures on the public schools are bound to mount. "A covert struggle is going on to see who will control the free schools and mold the minds of other people's children," he says. "You can see a pattern with the Tennessee case—when one group imposes its values on the schools, everyone else feels mugged." Szasz believes the current debate may foreshadow the breakup of the public school system, something that, as a libertarian, he would not mind in the least.

A sex-ed solution, however, need not await or depend on the crumbling of the public school system. Some towns are evolving their own compromises. In Lindenhurst, N.Y., after a fierce conservative protest against an eleventh-grade sex-ed program, the school decided to offer three different courses. About 60% of the students attend the liberal "Family Life" course; 25% take the conservative option, "Sexuality, Commitment and Family"; and 15%, including those who make no choice at all, end up in a health course without sex ed.

Another promising answer to fundamental differences may lie in an emerging agreement on one basic. A number of cities are turning up evidence that most youngsters are looking for an excuse to abstain. In 1980 the teen services program at Atlanta's Grady Memorial Hospital found that of the thousand or so girls under age 16 it saw each year, the overwhelming majority (87%) wanted to learn how to say no without hurting anyone's feelings. Grady responded with a program for eighth-graders called "Postponing Sexual Involvement." It is now taught in 23 Atlanta-area schools, focusing on decision making, assertiveness and how to articulate values and feelings.

Older teenagers, paid $8 an hour, are the teachers. "The girls who took the program see themselves differently," says Marion Howard, clinical director of the Grady teen services. "They didn't think having sex meant they were grown up. They didn't think it would earn them respect." And only 5% of them started having sex in the eighth grade, in contrast to 16.5% of girls outside the program.

Many educators think the prochastity movement is a pipe dream. "We can't fool ourselves into thinking that abstinence is the solution," says Mary Luke of San Francisco/Alameda Planned Parenthood. "These kids have made their decisions, and we're going to have to deal with the reality of it." But there is no doubt that the threat of AIDS and the need to defuse conservative critics have made the abstinence message politically popular to left and right alike. "Our preferred way to deal with sexual activity is to say no," says Patricia Davis-Scott, clinic director at two Chicago high schools. In the California school system, notes Bill Honig, state superintendent of public instruction, when a boy says, "If you love me, you will," a girl is taught to answer, "If you love me, you won't ask me." Illinois Governor James Thompson told a Republican meeting last month, " 'Just Say No' is a good slogan for drugs, and it is a good slogan for teen sex."

This popular fervor for abstinence, undreamed of just a few years ago, surely is no harbinger of a new puritanism. But it may open up some room for sex education to overtake its critics. In exchange for the abstinence message being treated with respect, many conservative opponents seem likely to follow Surgeon General Koop and accept sex instruction in the schools. As Koop himself seems to argue, there is really no other choice. —By John Leo.
Reported by Patricia Delaney/Washington and Leslie Whitaker/New York, with other bureaus

Sexual Biology and Health

- **The Body and Its Responses (Articles 9-11)**
- **Sexual Hygiene (Articles 12-17)**

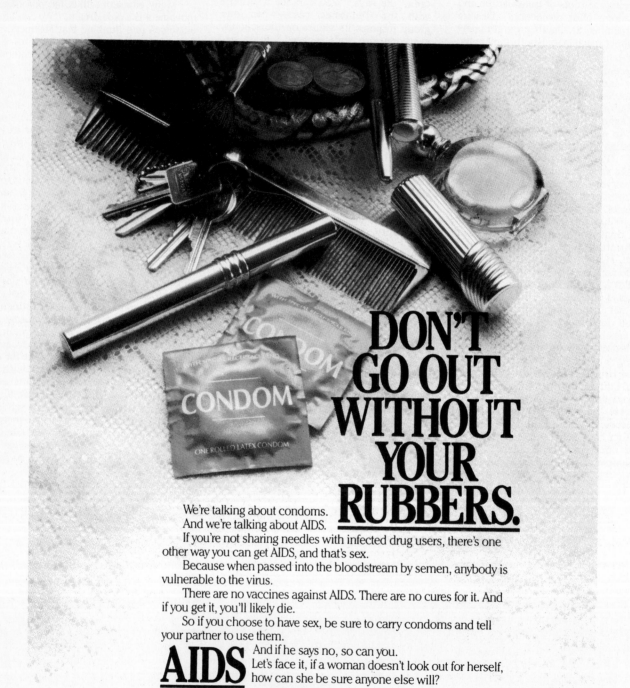

DON'T GO OUT WITHOUT YOUR <u>RUBBERS.</u>

We're talking about condoms. And we're talking about AIDS.

If you're not sharing needles with infected drug users, there's one other way you can get AIDS, and that's sex.

Because when passed into the bloodstream by semen, anybody is vulnerable to the virus.

There are no vaccines against AIDS. There are no cures for it. And if you get it, you'll likely die.

So if you choose to have sex, be sure to carry condoms and tell your partner to use them.

AIDS And if he says no, so can you.

Let's face it, if a woman doesn't look out for herself, how can she be sure anyone else will?

If you think you can't get it, you're dead wrong.

Changing attitudes toward sexuality is instrumental in opening avenues for more humanistic sexual relations. Indeed, freeing the mind for awareness and acceptance of bodily sensations is an important measure for maximizing sexual expression. But this is only half of the story. Of parallel importance is developing a clear understanding and appreciation of the working of the human body. This section directs attention toward these goals.

Males and females have a great number of misconceptions and a general lack of knowledge concerning bodily responses of the opposite sex. This less than optimal situation is further denigrated by the fact that many individuals have less than a working knowledge of their own bodily responses and functioning during sexual activity. In an effort to develop an understanding of and an appreciation for a healthy sexual awareness, quality physiological information is desperately needed and sought after by females and males alike. Several articles in this section focus on the physical sexual response of females and males, laying to rest many of the fallacies that individuals have come to believe. Other articles explain some of the recent discoveries concerning the sexual functioning of males and females.

The physiological dimension of sexuality also includes sexual hygiene. Sexually transmitted diseases (STDs) are often inappropriately labeled "social diseases." This stigmatization may be a reflection of the general negative aura that surrounds sexuality in American culture. Such diseases might be a lesser social problem if people could deal with them as medical problems and seek immediate treatment for themselves and their sexual contacts.

As you read through the articles in this section, you may come to realize that sexual biology and health are not merely matters of physiology, but—as with sexuality in general—are frequently psychological, social, and cultural in origin. The awareness, appreciation, and health of our bodies extends far beyond organic determinants.

The first two articles in the subsection *The Body and Its Responses* review many often asked questions about the body and its sexual responses and provide short answers to some common myths and misinformation. The next article deals with the importance of touch, adding that sex is more than the act of intercourse.

The *Sexual Hygiene* subsection begins with a discussion of the latest news about problems and treatments of the prostate gland. The next article is about disorders that can have an effect on men's sexuality. The problems women deal with are considered in two articles. One discusses the fallopian tubes and ways to keep them healthy. The other suggests that the historically negative view of menstruation should be improved, and that both females and society in general should look upon menstruation in a more positive way. In "Sex, With Care" the changes in sexual activity across the nation are reviewed in light of increasing rates of Sexually Transmitted Diseases (STDs). Different types, symptoms, and treatments of STDs are described. Finally, a consumer's guide to self health tests is included which specifically lists several brand name products available on the market.

Looking Ahead: Challenge Questions

Why does American society seem to have such an overabundance of myths and misinformation in the area of sexuality? What are some questions that you would like to add to the lovemaking IQ test?

Are there such things as aphrodisiacs? If so, what are they?

Why is touch an important issue? How can the use of touch be implemented in sex therapy?

What are some of the potential problems a male may encounter with his prostate gland? How can some of the diseases explained in the article affect a man's sexual performance if he is uninformed?

In the past, how well prepared were most women for menarche, their first menstruation? Do you feel women are more prepared today than in the past? Why or why not? What are the general societal feelings about menstruation?

What might be some solutions for improving the ever increasing problems of STDs? Besides finding better medical treatments, what needs to be done at the psychosocial and cultural levels?

In your opinion, are self-tests beneficial? Why or why not? Under what circumstances or conditions would you rely on their use? Are there some dangers in self-testing?

WHAT'S YOUR LOVE-MAKING IQ?

Of course you've experimented with different techniques, laughed at the old taboos—...but sometimes even the most aware girl gets her facts a bit scrambled. Dare to find out how sexually savvy you really are?

Arthur Foster

☐ The following quiz is designed to help you evaluate the state of your erotic knowledge. The questions are those most frequently asked of me in my practice as a marriage counselor and sex therapist; each deals with an issue that has created confusion and/or concern in the love relationships of many young couples. Answer truthfully, according to what you really know, not what you *think* you should know.

1 Who gets the most pleasure from love-making?
a. Men.
b. Women.
c. Both sexes enjoy lovemaking equally.

2 Your lover says you're undersexed, while you think he's oversexed. Could you both be right?
a. Yes.
b. No.

3 Overall, how satisfied are most married couples with their sexual relationship?
a. Dissatisfied.
b. Highly satisfied.
c. Moderately satisfied.

4 What percentage of men fail to maintain an erection sufficient to achieve penetration during sex?
a. Seven.
b. Twenty.
c. Forty.
d. Sixty.
e. Seventy-five.
f. One hundred.

5 How much time does the average couple devote to foreplay before going on to intercourse?
a. Five minutes or less.
b. Six to ten minutes.
c. Eleven to fifteen minutes.
d. Sixteen minutes to half an hour.
e. More than a half hour.

6. An erection is a sure sign that a man is highly aroused.
a. True.
b. False.

7. Your lover likes you to touch his breasts. Does this mean he has homosexual tendencies?
a. Yes.
b. No.

8. For the most part, male and female orgasms are identical.
a. True.
b. False.

9. On the average, how many minutes do most men maintain an erection after the penis enters the vagina?
a. Less than one.
b. One to five.
c. Five to ten.
d. Over ten.

10. One night you're thrilled when your lover caresses you in a certain way. But the next time you have sex, the same touch is a total turnoff. What's wrong?
a. You have any one of a number of sexual problems.
b. Your lover is not sensitive to your needs.
c. Nothing.

11. How often do most couples make love?
a. Once a day or more.
b. Five or six times a week.
c. Two to four times a week.
d. Once a week.
e. Less than once a week.

12. Your lover wants to have anal sex. Are there any problems you should be aware of before you consent?
a. Yes.
b. No.

13. How many orgasms is it possible for a woman to have during a single lovemaking session?
a. One.
b. Three to five.
c. As many as ten.
d. More than ten.

14. Though you've read that women have little sensation beyond the opening and outer third of the vagina, you're extremely turned on when your man thrusts deeply. Is your case unusual?
a. Yes.
b. No.

15. Who initiates lovemaking most often?
a. Men.
b. Women.

ANSWERS

1. a. Men. In a national sampling of married couples, husbands and wives were asked separately to rate how much pleasure they derived from a wide range of lovemaking activities. Men gave themselves higher scores on every single activity.

2. b. No. Like unicorns, undersexed and oversexed people are figments of the imagination. Differences in libido have more to do with such factors as conditioning, personality, than innate drive.

3. c. According to a recent poll, a little less than half the American married population rated their sexual relationship as "moderately satisfying." A surprising one third said their love life was unsatisfactory, and the remainder were highly satisfied.

4. a. Seven percent—but the answer depends on how you interpret the question. Nearly every man struggles with a sputtering penis at some point in his life. Looked at in this way, the incidence of impotence hovers close to 100 percent. Happily, most men pass through these temporary setbacks quickly. About 7 percent of American men are not so lucky and may be impotent for months, years, even a lifetime.

5. c. Eleven to fifteen minutes. This is unfortunate, because although an occasional "quickie" can be fun, as a general rule spending less than a half hour making love is inadequate.

6. b. False. As any man who has been embarrassed by an unexpected swelling in public will tell you, erections can and do occur at times when arousal is absent or mild. Conversely, a man may feel very passionate and obtain little in the way of an erection.

7. b. No. Male breasts have exactly the same nerve endings for pleasure that female breasts do. Some men find it highly stimulating to have their breasts touched.

8. a. True. Except that males ejaculate during orgasm and females do not, the physiological processes involved are identical for both sexes.

9. b. According to a study conducted at the Phoenix Psychological Institute, approximately 40 percent of American husbands maintain an erection for between one and five minutes following entry of the penis into the vagina. Eighteen percent for less than one minute; 27 percent between five and ten minutes, and the remaining fifteen are the marathoners of marital sex, maintaining erection for more than ten minutes.

10. c. Nothing is wrong. Body sensitivity changes from day to day and often from moment to moment. Tension, state of arousal, resentment, and many other factors determine how a touch feels.

11. c. According to a recent poll, 49 percent of American married couples reported they made love two to four times a week. Ten percent said they had sex more often than that; 41 percent, less.

12. a. Yes. A few precautions should be observed. The rectum was not designed for sexual purposes, so a lubricant will make this sort of activity more comfortable. Also, to avoid infection, do not immediately proceed from anal to vaginal intercourse, and gentleness on your man's part is vital to avoiding possible injury.

13. d. More than ten. Scientists have recorded as many as fifty female orgasms in a single lovemaking session. How many times you climax depends upon both your body and personality. Whatever that number is, it's most likely normal for you.

14. a. Yes. Some women experience intense pleasure from deep pelvic pressure, especially those who've had children. If this is true for you, your man does not need to be generously endowed. By shifting your position or raising your hips on a pillow, you can get the desired results.

15. a. Men. When polled, however, both men and women said they'd prefer initiating to be equally shared.

SCORING

Give yourself one point for each question you answered correctly. The sum is your lovemaking IQ.

10 to 15 points: Excellent. Your partner is sure to revel in such a knowledgeable lover.

5 to 10 points: Average. A bit of homework could change your love life from so-so to super!

Less than 5 points: Shaky. By clinging to sexual myths, you're probably not enjoying lovemaking as fully as possible.

HITS & MYTHS IN THE BEDROOM:

Test Your Sexual Assumptions

Is small-breasted sexier? Do big, big hands mean
he'll be sizable someplace *else?* Separate fact from funky fiction
with this compendium of libidinous lore.

Bonnie Davidson

☐ Misconceptions about sex have been around since Eve first whispered to Adam, "That's okay, honey, women don't need to have orgasms every time." Some old wives' tales have thankfully gone to shibboleth heaven (for example, that the touch of a menstruating woman causes flowers to wilt, milk to sour, and iron to rust), but many still linger, confounding our understanding of lovemaking, the act that novelist Henry Miller described as "one of the nine reasons for reincarnation. The other eight are unimportant." Is your pet sexual aphorism a hit or a myth? The truth begins here:

Sex saps your energy.

It's not the sex that hurts your performance, baseball legend Casey Stengel once said, but rather, the energy you expend convincing people to go to bed with you. Stengel's wisdom notwithstanding, physicians are only now discovering what lovers and other athletes have known for years: Sex does *not* drain energy. On the contrary, a round of spirited lovemaking can actually be quite invigorating.

No one is exactly sure what causes this phenomenon—some sexperts credit the release of postorgasm hormones; others point to a "rebound effect" in the nervous system following acute physical activity. Whatever it may be, we all know that vigorous, tender lovemaking makes us feel exuberant, sexy, and positively power-charged (no wonder they call it "afterglow").

Many athletes insist that squelching their libidinous yens before a big event can actually *hurt* rather than help their performance. "If I disrupt any part of my regular routine, whether it's eating, sleeping, warming up, or having sex," says a thirty-

three-year-old marathon runner, "then my concentration falls apart. On those unfortunate occasions when I have no sexual outlet, my time drops off."

According to William Masters, M.D., chairman of the board of directors of the Masters and Johnson Institute in St. Louis, sex uses about as much energy as climbing two flights of stairs. "There are very few athletes who would refuse to walk up a flight of stairs before a football game," he observes.

People who are always tense and uptight just need to "get laid."

Okay, there *are* more effective ways to relieve stress than sex. Indeed, it's not a panacea for anyone experiencing chronic emotional turmoil (those people may benefit more by lying down on a shrink's couch than a lover's king-size Posturepedic). However, as an aid in dealing with the normal psychic fatigue that comes from keeping up a hectic schedule and working superhard, it's not bad.

According to Helen Singer Kaplan, M.D., director of the Human Sexuality Program at New York Hospital–Cornell Medical Center and author of *The New Sex Therapy: Active Treatment of Sexual Dysfunctions*, erotic activity—especially orgasm—may stimulate the body's release of certain neuroproteins called endorphins (meaning "the morphine within"), the same soothing, painkilling, mood-elevating hormones that are probably responsible for "runner's high." Having sex, says Kaplan, has an analgesic effect similar to what you experience after taking a mild drug, such as aspirin. As a matter of fact, some doctors even prescribe sex for arthritis sufferers as a means of physically distracting them and relieving their pain. So the next time your inamorato complains that his tyrannical new boss is winding him up as tight as a clock spring, tell him you've got the perfect remedy.

The more sex you have, the more sex you want.

Happily, this one is true. It describes one of life's most wondrous cycles: The more testosterone there is in a man's system, the stronger his sexual impulses become and the more sex he's likely to want. The more sex he has, the more testosterone there is in his system, since the male hormone that governs the libido is released *in response* to sex. According to Marilyn Fithian, a marriage counselor and codirector of the Center for Marital and Sexual Studies in Long Beach, California, women experience a similar pattern, although research in this area has yet to be completed. What we do know, she says, is that "the hormones released with sexual activity increase desire." In other words, having sex makes you feel zestful, rested, even slightly intoxicated—pleasurable feelings that tempt you to start all over again.

Sex clears up your acne.

Some people insist their skin looks most radiant when they're newly in love, but Lia Schorr, a Manhattan skin-care specialist, knows better: *Sex* is actually what perks up the complexion. "I wish I could hang a sign in my salon that says, 'Have plenty of sex; it clears up acne,' " she says. People with very active sex lives "look well, happy, and satisfied. Sex brings a glow to their skin."

Schorr gets little argument from John F. Romano, an attending dermatologist at New York Hospital–Cornell Medical Center. Some adult acne, he advises, is stress induced—and given that sex is a stress reliever, regular and gratifying lovemaking can help those prone to breakouts. "It's not that the activity of the sebaceous glands decreases when you have an orgasm. Still, these glands do seem to be very keyed in to hormonal changes that may be triggered by tension. If the sex is really good," he explains, "then it will help complexion problems." Not that all in love is fair to the face: *Bad* sex can actually cause pimples because, "if someone feels pressured to perform, it causes tension."

Because semen is vitamin-rich, rubbing it on your face improves your complexion.

A beautiful forty-two-year-old public-relations account executive I know insists that the secret to her wrinkle- and blemish-free complexion is a thrice-weekly semen mask. In dermatological circles, however, her theory is considered seriously pockmarked.

According to Dr. John Romano, vitamins are not absorbed through the skin. "They need a cofactor even to be absorbed through the intestine," he says. "Vitamin preparations have a limited effect on only the very top layer of skin." Therefore, semen does nothing to nourish the skin or prevent wrinkles. If anything, its use as a topical skin treatment is unhealthy—semen is very high in fructose, a form of sugar.

Sex is better than dieting if you want to lose weight.

That's true—if you skip meals and make love around the clock. If not, forget it.

No one has been able to calculate the exact number of calories burned up during the act of love, but here are the most popular estimates: foreplay, 100 calories an hour; intercourse, 100 calories an hour; orgasm, 400 calories an hour. The Big O may sound like a dieter's dream come true, but given that an orgasm lasts, on the average, only two to fifteen seconds, that's a whopping 1.6 calories *at most* per seismic event. The grand total is 201.6 calories for two hours and fifteen seconds of lovemaking.

Being physically fit makes you a better lover.

"A man can have poor ejaculatory control if he's in the best or the worst of shape," says William Masters. Clearly, even a triathlon champion can lack sexual prowess and sensitivity, but Masters does allow that "if you're physically fit, any natural function works better."

Others find a stronger link between keeping in shape and being a great lover. Physical fitness is a definite boon in the bedroom, says marriage counselor Marilyn Fithian, because it enhances endurance. "We've found that nonorgasmic women who are out of shape tend to tire often and give up before they get anyplace." Similarly, orgasmic women who *are* in shape experience more forceful pelvic contractions during orgasm, because their muscles are stronger. Regular exercisers, she continues, also put less strain on their heart during orgasm than do sedentary types.

In addition, the health-conscious eighties has redefined our perception of "sexy"—for women, at least. Marilyn Monroe-type curves are much less titillating than a tight bottom, trim hips, and taut thighs. If you work out and your body is fit, you look and feel sexier—which may not make you a better lover, but it does make you a more desirable one. Staying fit might even make you more emotionally balanced as well. Joggers claim that a long-distance run helps to relieve depression and anxiety—the two major causes of sexual dysfunction. Running may not *cure* sexual problems, but as a reliable mood-elevator, it could make you feel happier when you're snuggling up to Mr. Right Now.

Small penises are just as good.

Once upon a time, everyone believed that big penises gave women more pleasure. Cures for the underendowed included this pearl from *The Perfumed Garden*, a sixteenth-century manual of Arabian erotic technique: "Wash the member in warm water until it becomes red and enters into erection. Then take a piece of soft leather, upon which spread hot pitch, and envelop the member in it. It will not be long before the member raises its head, trembling with passion."

New methods of penile enlargement include everything from injecting oneself with ground up ram's testicles to applying a mail-order suction pump. These days, however, sex researchers have proclaimed penis size irrelevant to female pleasure, thus bringing this myth full circle.

But what *is* the truth? According to Masters and Johnson, most penises are from 4½ to 8 inches long when erect, with the majority 5¾ to 6 inches long. However, most women I know worry less about length than about circumference. "A thin penis just doesn't cause enough friction against the vaginal walls," complains a twenty-eight-year-old secretary. Masters' research, however, proves otherwise. He describes the vagina as a wonderfully elastic organ that automatically dilates in order to welcome a penis, then expands or constricts so that it can hug whatever is encountered. "If the coital connection lasts for a minute and a half to two minutes," he says, "then the vagina has enough time to obviate the difference in penile size. The only exceptions are the macro, or horse-size, penis, and the micro, or infantile-size."

Still, many women tell New York psychosexual therapist Betti Krukofsky that they just don't experience the same feeling of vaginal containment from a thin penis. "I advise a woman with this complaint to experiment," says Krukofsky. "Maybe if she's on top, she'll feel more pressure. Or he can enter her from behind." Personally, Krukofsky believes that small penises *are* just as good and that women who are dissatisfied with them are victims of cultural conditioning. "If one looks at sculpture and painting throughout history, one is aware that the penis is always big, thick, and very prominent. So we expect big penises to be able to bring more pleasure. But they don't."

Flat-chested women have strong libidos.

This myth was probably hatched to cheer those on the skimpy size—A-cup women everywhere. Once the organs that put the "sex" in "sex symbol," breasts are now widely considered—in these days of fitness fanaticism—most attractive when they're firm rather than full. Perhaps those who've perpetuated the myth mistake a megalibido for what is *really* some small-breasted women's eagerness to please. After all, they know that no man will look at their chest and keel over, so they've devised plenty of wily ways to be seductive with *all* the body they *do* have. Meanwhile, some less enlightened men, as they salivate over centerfolds, still cling to the primitive notion that the bigger the breasts, the hotter the female. The truth, however, comes from William Masters, who says, "Breast size has absolutely nothing to do with a woman's sexual interest or her ability to be orgasmic. Some women are stimulated by breast play; to them the breast is an extremely erotic organ. To others, it's not."

You can tell the size of a man's penis by the size of his feet.

Our historic fascination with the phallus long ago gave rise to the notion that penis size and foot size are somehow related (although debate rages over whether the *real* giveaway may actually be the hands, thumbs, or forearms). Not surprisingly, research in this area is skimpy; no urologist questioned for this article would take the issue seriously enough to answer on the record. However, a random sampling of women surveyed agreed that foot dimension is not a reliable indicator of penile proportion. "I used to go out with a guy whose sneakers were size thirteen and a half," confesses a thirty-year-old advertising copywriter, "and believe me, what you hear people say about feet is false."

Other physical characteristics fared no better as penis meters. A twenty-seven-year-old boutique manager admits that although she finds thick forearms sexy, she's never met a man with the genitals to match. A twenty-four-year-old graduate student recalls her one-night stand with a college basketball star who had "tremendous hands, long sinewy fingers, and a very average penis." And a thirty-two-year-old freelance illustrator laughs, "I fell in love with my boyfriend's thumbs on our first date. I wasn't disappointed by the rest of his body, but let's just say that he has singular thumbs."

Being on the Pill gives a woman a stronger sex drive.

My friend Kristin swears that birth-control pills are an aphrodisiac; since she's been taking them, her sexuality has soared. Some women who take oral contraceptives are liable to feel sexier and to make love more often, but the reason, says Marilyn Fithian, may be less chemical than cerebral: Because these women are no longer afraid of getting pregnant, they feel freer to let go and really enjoy themselves.

Statistics show, however, that the majority of Pill users experience no major psychosexual changes, with a small percentage actually reporting loss of libido. Says Fithian, "Subconsciously, they may *want* to get pregnant, so the Pill detracts from their sexual interest." Other experts claim that earlier brands of progesterone-dominant pills were responsible for thwarting sex drive. These medications are rarely prescribed anymore, but if you find oral contraceptives adversely affecting your appetite, check with your doctor. He may want to switch you to a pill with more estrogen.

Masturbation causes blindness, insanity, and hairy palms.

Of course we all know that masturbation is natural, healthy, and, in the case of preorgasmic women, even therapeutic. If the masturbation myths were true, Masters estimates that 90 percent of all men and 85 percent of all women in the civilized world would foam at the mouth and sport a permanent pair of fur gloves.

How, then, did such a normal, pleasurable activity fall into such contempt? The answer, it's been said, is rooted in early biblical writing. Poor Onan was commanded to marry (and mate with) his childless, widowed sister-in-law in order to produce a son and perpetuate his dead brother's name. At the moment of truth, he did not impregnate her and instead spilled his precious juices on the ground—the usual consequences of self-abuse. For his sin, he was put to death, and forevermore masturbation has been called "onanism." (The term *masturbation* itself also boasts a less-than-flattering derivation. From Latin: *manus stuprare* means "to defile with the hand.")

The stigma lives on even today, as young mothers, largely unaware of this biblical dictum but nevertheless influenced by it, cringe at the sight of their child exploring his or her own body. "Whenever my mother found me touching my vagina," recalls a twenty-nine-year-old health-education teacher, "she used to scowl and say, 'Take your hand out of your pants.' But it felt so good that I would actually make a date with myself to continue that night when I got into bed, where my mother would never see me. Of course, I felt guilty the next day."

Before the advent of the Judeo-Christian tradition, ancient Egyptians considered masturbation a sacred ritual. Men manipulated their penises wildly, offering semen as a solemn sacrifice to the gods. Far from generating guilt, male masturbation was credited with creating the universe; the Nile, Euphrates, and Ganges Rivers were depicted as glorious liquid gushing from an enormously erect, divine phallus.

Modern sexologists assure us that although self-manipulation is not responsible for creating heaven and earth, it never hurt anyone either.

The ultimate sign of sexual compatibility is simultaneous orgasm.

Compulsive striving for both partners to climax at one time causes some couples more pain than pleasure. Often lovers are so preoccupied with getting their orgasmic convulsions in sync that they inhibit their pleasure. Lovemaking becomes, for them, a nerve-racking game of hurry-up-and-wait, which leaves them feeling sexually and psychologically distraught.

It is important to remember that there *are* advantages to climaxing sequentially rather than together. For one thing, it enables partners to concentrate on really exciting each other, to dawdle in their love-mate's secret erogenous zones, and to vicariously enjoy their rolling waves of pleasure. The majority of women do not climax during penetration anyway (researchers estimate that 70 percent of the sexually active female population requires some form of clitoral stimulation in order to enjoy release), so for many couples mutual orgasm during intercourse requires heroic—if not contortionistic—effort. While it does feel terrific to reach Pluto in unison, it's no less lovely taking turns getting there. Indeed, for some this may even be the preferred itinerary.

With every orgasm, you feel like your bed is straddling the San Andreas Fault and the "big quake" has finally hit.

Orgasms may make seismographs go haywire in the movies, but in real life they come in a variety of intensities—from mildly pleasurable to industrial strength. While the basic physiological process of arousal, contraction, and release is uniform, the size of the tremor depends on such variables as time of day and month, mood, feelings about one's bedmate, and which technique used.

Believing the myth of the regular ten-points-on-the-Richter-scale orgasm can cause considerable—and unnecessary—worry for both men and women. "Many women experience very quiet orgasms that can be quite pleasurable," says sex therapist Betti Krukofsky. "A man likes to see a woman climax very noisily, thrashing about in bed, so he can enjoy a macho pride in having given her such ecstasy. If she's quiet, the man feels that on some level he's failed." And the woman ends up feeling inadequate.

If you're worried that your orgasms aren't "big" enough, Krukofsky's got some advice: "Listen to your body during masturbation. *Experience* your feelings." Then just relax and enjoy your distinct brand of pleasure.

There are two different kinds of female orgasms.

As every sexually alert woman knows by now, Masters and Johnson proved that Freud's theory of the "immature" clitoral orgasm and the "mature" vaginal orgasm has about as much validity as the concept of penis envy. Female orgasm is a physiological reaction that can be triggered by stimulation of the clitoris, vagina, nipples and breasts, or even by fantasizing. Betti Krukofsky says, however, that many women still report feeling a difference between vaginally sparked orgasms during intercourse and clitorally stimulated orgasms brought about by masturbation. "This is probably because when they're having intercourse, they're sharing the experience with a loved partner, and that makes the orgasm feel fantastic. Masturbation is pleasurable, but it's basically a lonely activity." The difference, she concludes, is mainly a psychological one, not a physiological one.

Women don't need to climax every time they have sex.

As we become sexually aroused, blood rushes to our pelvic region and our labia swell, engorged with blood, much like an erect penis. If orgasm does not follow, the blood takes a while to dissipate, and we may be left with an uncomfortable, throbbing, bloated feeling called chronic pelvic congestion (what men experience as "blue balls"). We don't *need* to have an orgasm, but we do feel much, much better when we have one (or two, or three . . .). In her book *Good Sex*, psychosexual therapist and media personality Ruth Westheimer writes, "Fully ninety-five percent of all women are capable of experiencing orgasm in some way—if not during intercourse, then by manual or oral stimulation. It may not always be necessary for a woman to have an orgasm, but by the same logic, it should be equally acceptable for a man to bring his partner to orgasm without ejaculating himself."

Most married couples make love an average of two or three times a week.

Did you hear the one about the guy who smokes only after sex? He's down to a pack a year. But as long as he and his wife are happy, says Marilyn Fithian, then they have absolutely no sexual problem.

Statistics show that, generally speaking, couples in their twenties are likely to make love every day, thirty- to forty-year-olds have intercourse between two and three times a week, forty- to fifty-year-olds once a week, and sixty-plus less than once a week. But these should *not* be considered rigid requirements for a healthy sexual relationship, and Fithian warns against feeling that if you don't meet these standards you are sick, not really in love, libidinal midgets, or abnormal in any way at all.

Objective norms don't really exist, she insists. A couple can be perfectly fulfilled by having sex twenty times a week, once a week, or only on birthdays and their anniversary. "There's a problem only if one partner wants more than the other."

A famed soft drink's "secret formula" is also a spermicide; used as a vaginal douche, this beverage becomes a carbonated contraceptive.

Three Harvard Medical School doctors caused an international sensation recently when, as a joke, they scientifically tested this age-old fable (reportedly still practiced in developing nations) and discovered that Coca-Cola does indeed kill sperm—in the test tube, that is.

The researchers obtained semen from a healthy, fertile donor, placed it in test tubes containing three incarnations of Coca-Cola (Diet, Classic, and New Coke), incubated the samples at room temperature for one minute, and observed sperm motility under a microscope. Their surprising findings: Absolutely no sperm were moving in Diet Coke, only 8.5 percent were moving in Classic Coke, and 41.6 percent in New Coke.

However, Joseph Hill, a fellow in reproductive endocrinology and infertility at Boston's Brigham and Women's Hospital—and one of the doctors who participated in the experiment—is quick to point out that despite these results, Diet Coke is not destined to replace the Pill as the safest means of contraception. "Coke did have a strong spermicidal effect in vitro, but the chances of it working in vivo are very small." After ejaculation, explains Dr. Hill, "the sperm are in the fallopian tubes within minutes, so a woman would not have time to douche before an egg there was fertilized. Even if you douched before coitus, a significant number of sperm would still make their way to the fallopian tubes." A pre- or postlovemaking douche with soda pop, or anything else for that matter, he cautions, "would not be efficacious at all, and we do not recommend it for contraception."

Marijuana is an aphrodisiac.

Smoking pot will *not* make your beloved more attracted to you, cure his sexual hang-ups (or yours), or make him more imaginative in bed. But will it put him in the mood? And will it heighten your pleasure? Maybe, if sex was good before you got high. If it was bad, pot will make it worse. You may also be endangering your health in the process. According to Marilyn Fithian, while a pot smoker may *perceive* her orgasms as more intense, what's really happening is that her drug-and-sex-stimulated heart is racing perilously fast, up to 240 beats each minute. "It's terribly frightening," she says. Other research shows that although marijuana does increase skin sensitivity slightly, it may reduce a man's ability to maintain an erection. This drug also induces an obsessive state of mind—as he gently nibbles your neck, you just can't take your mind off your friend's brother's girlfriend, who said that she lost twenty-six pounds while she was on the cold seaweed diet. Perhaps the only factor in pot's favor is that getting high can very easily distort your perception of time, making you *think* sex is lasting much longer than it really is.

Sex prolongs your life.

Countless studies have shown that aging does not mean the end of lovemaking (two out of three men over seventy are sexually active), and information abounds on sex and the older man (his erection may not be as rigid, and more direct stimulation is required to attain it; his orgasms may be fewer, but just as enjoyable). But do we have research data linking frequency of lovemaking to longevity? According to William Masters, the answer is no. "Sex makes you want to live longer, if that's what you're talking about," he says.

THE POWER OF TOUCH

A lover's touch can heal a bruised ego and calm a raging fever. It can also be the most tender, sensual experience of your life, if you take a moment to learn the language of touch.

Sherry Suib Cohen

ALL GOOD SEXUAL TOUCH IS sensual. A sensual touch is one that gratifies the senses—all the senses. It is voluptuous. It is slow, searching, and attentive to reactions. It gives and receives. It is enjoyed as much by the giver as by the receiver. Although sensual touch is related to sexual touch, it doesn't necessarily lead to sex. Sensual touch is glorious in itself. Wise lovers know that sex does not necessarily mean intercourse but rather sharing the exquisite delight of exploring one another's bodies. A sensitive toucher can evoke wonders. With sensual fingers, a partner's touch can instantly cool head and eyes that are burning with fever. With sensual touch, he or she can instantly gentle your damaged psyche and send it to a calming sleep. And then, when the time is ripe, he or she knows how to transform the sensual touch into the sexual.

Fingers and hands that have practiced the craftsmanship of sensuality can touch your libido, make it surge with desire and burn brighter than you ever imagined possible. The same language of sensual touch that nourishes the infant comes into adult fruition during erotic play.

William H. Masters, M.D., and Virginia E. Johnson, Ph.D., and the many sex therapists who use their methods, allow no intercourse at all in the first few weeks of sex therapy. Couples practice touch— gentle, appreciative, sensual touch—of one another's feet, arms, legs, face, hands . . . and bodies. They carefully learn the art of touch as a process in it- self. Intercourse is *not* a goal, they teach. If it happens because both lovers are in the mood, fine. If not, sensual touching is golden anyway.

Intercourse as a goal seems to be a big hang-up in our culture. Most sex thera- pists warn against it as a sure way to de- crease sensual enjoyment. In *Touching for Pleasure: A Guide to Sensual En- hancement,* Susan Dean, Ph.D., a special- ist in human sexuality, and Adele P. Ken- nedy, a sex therapist, advise: "When you are goal-oriented you are no longer in the present. You interrupt your re- sponses when you try to anticipate the next step. Stay focused on the moment, so that you receive all that is being of- fered. Touch is, in and of itself, the plea- sure. Any by-product is coincidental to the experience, although it is to be en- joyed and appreciated. The motivation is to sensitize your body to its intrinsic ca- pacity for pleasure."

Alexandra Penney, author of several popular books on sex, agrees. Great sex, she says, is between two people and not two bodies. It goes far beyond mechan- ics; there are all kinds of great sex be- sides intercourse.

We are sexual creatures from the mo- ment of birth. We are sexual because we are sensual, and, once having experi- enced the pleasure of body electricity, we can anticipate it and even simulate it in our brain. Ever feel a rush of flutters in your groin while reading a sexy passage? You *remember.* Touch is so powerful that it lingers in our bodies even when it's not actually there. That's why audiences flock to superbly written sexual scenes in movies or in print.

The skin, the medium for touch, is such a wondrous conductor of sensual sig- nals that it changes either visibly or in ways that can be felt when it is touched, when it anticipates being touched, or even when it remembers being touched. How many of us have felt an actual warming of the skin, a literal heating-up at the very thought of a single touch from a special person?

But there are many receptors of sexual touch, besides the skin. There's the brain, for example. It interprets touch and tells you whether you should let a caress be enjoyable or despicable. If your brain tells you that the man in front of you is your dream of an ideal sex object, you will enjoy the feel of him. On the other hand, if your brain tells you that he turns you off, the *feel* of him may still be enjoyable, though you *think* it shouldn't be.

Of course, you don't always have to love someone to respond to sexual touch. As Mae West put it, "Honey, sex with love is the greatest thing in life, but sex without love—that's not so bad either." So sensitive are the erogenous zones that if you look forward to being aroused, if you concentrate on responding to sexual touch, if you *think* you'll be turned on, the odds are you will be. After all, people are the sexiest primates on earth; while females in other species are limited in sexual receptivity to times of ovulation, the human female loves making love any time—*if* she's in the mood.

Still, as the sex therapists point out, it does help a lot when caring is present. Tenderness, respect, and practice have a way of intensifying physical pleasure. Knowledgeable sexual touch gives us heightened sexual pleasure that a one-night stand never can, as Kennedy realized in a recent encounter with her lover: "[He] had arrived at my house one night to take me out to dinner and a film. We sat down in the living room to discuss which restaurant to go to. As we were talking, he was running his fingers gently over my knuckles, and I was looking through a magazine for dining suggestions. Before I knew it, I was aroused.

"We were both surprised, as there was nothing outwardly conducive to it. Although our conversation or nuances had in no way been sexual, we were connected; and since I had allowed that connection to flow freely, my body responded long before sexual thoughts ever reached my consciousness. It was at that point that I knew that the possibilities of stimulation and response were infinite."

HOW DO MEN AND WOMEN differ in their relationship to touch? Generally, young girls are more likely to be touched than boys are—although that is slowly changing as people become aware of how such actions perpetuate the notion of woman as nurturer. In the meantime, while extra touching may make women warm and affectionate, it also makes them tend to take what they get and not to be assertive in the getting. Many women learn to let themselves accept sexual touching rather than initiate it. They are believed to be more passive sexually, and thus they train themselves to be so. They worry that men will find them pushy, unfeminine, or grabby if they are sexually aggressive in touching. Boys, on the other hand, learn to be the touching aggressors. When they are men, they often have little patience for lying back and receiving touches in foreplay. Lie back and just enjoy? Is that really manly?

Although this attitude seems old-fashioned, it still persists in spite of many studies and books to the contrary. Our

If one doesn't love to experiment with touch as a conveyance of affection and friendliness, one may never reach the zenith of sexual achievement.

generation is supposed to be one of sexual sophistication, yet insidious double standards continue.

Touch is then relegated to a sexual provocation instead of being a mutual and enduring pleasure in its own right. If one doesn't love to experiment with touch as a conveyance of affection and friendliness, one may never reach the zenith of sexual achievement. Sensual touches must precede sexual intents for both men and women.

A man may place his hand on his partner's breast two seconds after they tumble into bed. Or perhaps he heads straight for her genital area before she has time to catch her breath. He expects that once he touches these sensitive zones her sexual motor will automatically shift into high gear.

But, of course, it doesn't. She feels annoyed, outraged, or, at best, unaroused. Her motor remains in idle position, or perhaps it stalls, chokes, and turns off.

He feels confused or nervous. Is there something wrong with him if his touch doesn't spark a conflagration? He may feel irritated; what a cold potato his partner is! It's not his fault, surely.

And therein, note Masters and Johnson, lies a basic dead-end approach for many relationships. He thinks she's frigid, either because she didn't let him touch her in the crucial place or because, when he did, she wasn't thrilled. She decides he's a boor and a lousy lover. They learn to settle for mediocre. They consider touch merely as a means to an end. They buy sex manuals that teach them how to manipulate body parts—the science of stimulation of disembodied parts. How much better to have a philosophy that celebrates caring, that celebrates sensual touch as an extension of everyday life. Sensual touching should not be chained to the bedroom.

The bottom line is this: we—both men and women—miss sensual touch. We confuse it with sexual intercourse, and so we deny its casual use. And then, ironically, we separate it from sexual touch, which depends on sensuality for its goodness.

Masters and Johnson point out that too many people interpret every sensually loving touch as an invitation to copulate. Bodies hunger for holding as a sensation quite apart from genital penetration. Marc H. Hollender, M.D., a psychiatrist with the Department of Psychiatry at Vanderbilt University School of Medicine in Tennessee, has said that the need to be held is so compelling for some women that they have intercourse when they may not really want it in exchange for being held.

"The need for touch is a kind of ache," says one woman.

"I'd rather have my husband hold me than have a Cadillac convertible," says another.

"The reason I like to wear big, fuzzy sweaters and be bundled up and held in warm blankets is that it makes me feel like I'm being held," says yet another.

When you know yourself, you'll know when your body and soul need to be touched. What feels like sadness can simply be your disguised need to be held; what feels like hunger or fatigue can be your disguised wish for lovemaking. Your response to touch can help you build a personal and a sensual sense of well-being. Touch is glorious. And perfecting it can be a life's work.

PROSTATE: THE MISUNDERSTOOD GLAND
The Latest News About Problems and Treatments

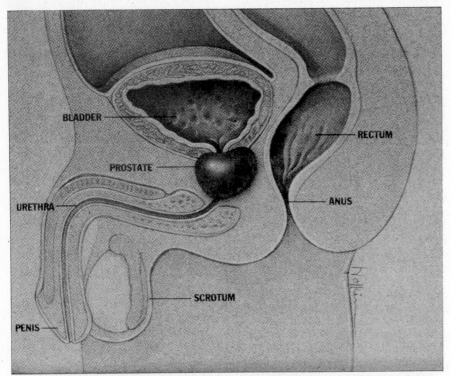

The prostate, which at puberty begins to produce seminal fluid, is tiny in boys but continues to grow with age and can become a source of numerous urologic discomforts, infections, and diseases that can affect potency and fertility.

MICHAEL CASTLEMAN

Michael Castleman, author of "Sexual Solutions" (Touchstone/Simon & Schuster), a self-help guide to men's common sexual concerns, is the managing editor of "Medical Self-Care" magazine, Point Reyes, California 94956.

WAYNE NOTICED THAT HE HAD to urinate more frequently than usual but thought nothing of it. The World Series was on, and his beer consumption had increased. Then his low-back pain returned. He'd had it on and off for years, and his exercises usually helped, but this time the aching persisted. Wayne thought he was simply getting older. Then he noticed a strange tingling in the head of his penis. That night, he and wife Martha made love. When he ejaculated, Wayne felt a sharp, stabbing pain in his penis. He said nothing; it was probably just some irritation from Martha's diaphragm. But that night he slept badly. He felt hot. By morning his pajamas were

soaked. He had a fever and his penis hurt. Now he was worried. He told Martha his symptoms. He did not tell her his fears: impotence, cancer, AIDS.

Martha had no idea what might be wrong. She urged him to see their doctor. The only penile illness she'd heard of was gonorrhea. Wayne had been away on business the previous month. Their relationship was good, but what if he had cheated on her?

Martha spent an anxious morning. Then Wayne called. "The doctor says it's prostatitis." "Prosta-what?" Martha asked. The word sounded suspiciously like "prostitute."

"Prostatitis," Wayne repeated. "In my prostate. I'm taking antibiotics."

Wayne sounded relieved, but Martha still felt upset. How did he get this whatever-it-was? An hour later, she called their physician, suddenly thankful they had a woman doctor. Dr. Mary Stevens reassured her that her husband's case of prostatitis was not gonorrhea and not a sexually transmitted disease.

The prostate is a doughnut-shaped gland that sits below the male bladder and about two inches above the rectum. The urethra (the urine and semen tube) passes through the "doughnut" hole. Muscles at the base of the bladder neck act as a valve allowing urine—but not semen—to flow when the penis is flaccid; and blocking urine—and freeing semen—when the penis is erect. The prostate is tiny in young boys, but at puberty, testosterone stimulates its growth and the production of seminal fluid. Unlike most organs, this gland continues to grow with age.

Until recently, three conditions were believed to account for most prostate problems: inflammation (bacterial prostatitis), noncancerous overgrowth (benign hypertrophy), and prostate cancer. Recently, however, urologists have determined that much of what was once called bacterial prostatitis may involve nonbacterial microorganisms or no microorganisms at all. Nonbacterial prostatitis is a relatively new concept, and urologists have not settled on a name for the condition, which is variously known as "prostatosis," "prostadynia," and "urinary sphincter hypertonicity" (USH).

PROSTATITIS

Prostatitis was considered the most common urologic problem in men under 50. Symptoms could include fever; pain in the penis, lower abdomen, lower back, or perineum (the area between the scrotum and the anus); pain or burning on ejaculation; and various troubles with urinating (voiding dysfunction). Prostatitis was assumed to be caused by either gonorrhea or the bacteria usually responsible for urinary tract infections in women. But prostatitis symptoms varied tremendously, and bacteria could be cultured only rarely. The reason was that the germs often responsible for prostatitis were not ordinary bacteria, but other microorganisms that did not grow in standard cultures.

"Chlamydia and mycoplasma may cause the majority of prostatitis in men under fifty," says Dr. John Owen Marks, a urologist affiliated with Beth Israel Hospital in New York City. Recently a simple test has been developed to detect chlamydia, but more extensive laboratory work is required to detect mycoplasma.

Bacterial prostatitis is either acute or chronic. Both types require treatment with antibiotics, but the latter, though less painful, may last longer.

If a man has voiding dysfunction and pain, but no identifiable microorganisms and no fever or elevated white blood cell count, the current thinking is that he does not have prostatitis but the related condition.

"Prostatosis and prostadynia," says Dr. Marks, "are catchall diagnoses that mean we don't know what's causing the problem. In such cases, I try a variety of antibiotics and recommend sitz baths, changes in sexual activity, and eliminating caffeine, alcohol, and spicy foods."

Other urologists believe that prostatosis/prostadynia is actually stress-related tension in the muscle that controls urination and prefer to call the condition urinary sphincter hypertonicity (USH). "The man is uptight and so is his urinary sphincter," says Dr. Ira Sharlip, an assistant clinical professor of urology at the University of California San Francisco Medical Center. Dr. Sharlip usually treats USH with sitz baths, stress management techniques, and possibly a prescription muscle relaxant.

Prostatitis was once thought to be associated with irregular or bingeing sexual activity. It was called "the sailor's disease" because after months of presumed sexual abstinence at sea, sailors have been known to binge on shore and develop prostatitis. But there is no evidence that sailors abstain from sex at sea, and many sexually active men never develop prostatitis. Sexual abstinence, however, may contribute to nonbacterial prostatitis. For many men, sex is a key means—for some their *only* means—of stress management. Without reasonably regular sexual release, some may focus their stress burdens below the belt.

What about sex during episodes of prostatitis? Says Dr. Sharlip, "Some urologists recommend regular ejaculation. Others recommend temporary abstinence to rest the prostate. I advise men to do what feels most comfortable for them."

ENLARGED PROSTATE

A 20-year-old's prostate is about the size of a chestnut, but by age 50 it may have grown many times larger. *This growth is not cancer, nor does it predispose a man to cancer.* But it may

pinch the urethra and cause voiding dysfunction, particularly a need to get up at night. Eventually, the man may decide to have it surgically corrected with a transurethral resection of the prostate (TURP). With the man under spinal or general anesthesia, a urologist inserts an instrument into the urethra, and uses electrocautery to snip away prostate overgrowth and widen the urethral path.

TURPs have become routine, but they are major surgery. Recovery usually involves three to five days of hospitalization and a week of rest at home. Although surgical complications are uncommon, several are possible: infection (1 percent risk), bleeding that requires transfusion (1 percent), urinary sphincter damage that causes incontinence (1 percent), and erection impairment (1 to 5 percent).

"TURP-related erection problems," Dr. Sharlip says, "are both physiological and psychological in origin. There is often no physiological reason why this operation, when performed properly, should damage the nerves that control erection."

In most cases, however, TURPs result in "dry orgasm" and infertility. Scarring from the electrocautery usually closes the ejaculatory ducts, thus blocking the flow of seminal fluid. After a TURP, orgasm feels as pleasurable as ever, but the man does not ejaculate. If seminal fluid still flows, the man experiences retrograde ejaculation, release backward into the bladder. (In a few cases, some seminal fluid does leave the penis, making conception possible.) Although TURP usually signals the end of male fertility, this is rarely a problem because the operation is typically performed on men over 60. But sometimes, a man must choose between enlarged prostate symptoms and fertility.

PROSTATE CANCER

Prostate cancer is the number-two cancer in men (after lung). It accounts for 19 percent of men's cancers and 10 percent of male cancer deaths. The American Cancer Society estimates 25,500 prostate cancer deaths for 1985.

Prostate cancer is quite common—some say almost inevitable—in older men, but it is by no means always fatal. Fortunately, most prostate tumors are slow-growing, and they usually do not spread beyond the gland. Cancerous prostate cells are found in 10 percent of men in their fifties, 30 percent in their sixties, and 80 percent of men over 80.

Early prostate cancer symptoms include blood in the urine, voiding dysfunction, and possibly pain. The first diagnostic step is a prostate exam. The physician inserts a gloved finger into the rectum and feels for hard lumps. Periodic prostate exams are recommended for men over 40, and annual exams for men over 50. If the physician finds any lumps, a biopsy and other tests provide definitive diagnosis and show whether the cancer is slow-growing. If it is slow-growing, most urologists advise no treatment, just checkups once or twice a year, unless the man is young or has an advanced stage of cancer.

In about 20 percent of cases, fast-growing prostate cancer is diagnosed before it has spread beyond the gland. Treatment includes radiation and/or complete prostate removal (radical prostatectomy). This operation involves an abdominal or perineal incision, and until recently resulted in impotence because the nerves that control erection run along the gland and were severed to remove it.

But that has changed. Dr. Patrick Walsh, professor and director of the Brady Neurological Institute at Johns Hopkins University has developed a new potency-sparing technique in cases where the cancer remains localized in the gland. "Previously, 10 percent of men remained potent after a total prostatectomy. Now we're preserving potency in up to 70 percent of cases," says Walsh. This technique, developed in 1982, is still new and therefore only available at some health-care facilities and from some practitioners.

Even if it spreads beyond the gland, prostate cancer is still quite treatable, if caught before advanced stages. Prostate cancer is testosterone dependent. Deprived of the male hormone, which is produced chiefly by the testicles, most go into dramatic remission.

"When prostate cancer metasticizes," Dr. Sharlip says, "it usually goes to the bones, where it causes terrible pain. But once testosterone has been eliminated, I've seen men experience sudden improvement and live many more years. It's almost miraculous."

But such miracles have a price. The testicles must be either removed surgically (castration) or hormonally disabled with estrogen, usually diethylstilbestrol (DES). Either way, the results are impotence, decreased body hair, and possibly breast development and breast pain. Currently, researchers are investigating two new chemical treatments for fast-growing prostate cancer—drugs that suppress the pituitary hormones that stimulate the testicles to make testosterone, and ketoconazole, an antifungal drug known to suppress testosterone production.

Both appear to have sexual side effects similar to surgery and DES, with perhaps less breast development.

ZINC

Recently, alternative health practitioners have touted zinc as a possible preventive for the entire range of prostate ills. Zinc is an essential trace mineral found in milk, whole grains, peas, carrots, and particularly in oysters, long considered a "virility food" in the folk wisdom of several cultures. The prostate has the male body's highest concentration of zinc, and men with prostate problems often show abnormally low zinc levels. Several studies point to therapeutic possibilities, but the role of zinc in prostate health remains controversial.

"I know of no good data indicating that zinc prevents or cures prostate problems," Dr. Sharlip says. "But a zinc-rich diet doesn't do any harm."

The same cannot be said, however, for commercial zinc supplements. Nonfatal but nonetheless toxic overdoses are possible, though rare. Any man who takes a zinc supplement should not exceed the recommended dose.

PROSTATE EROTICISM

Some men find prostate massage a turn-on during lovemaking, either by itself, or as part of fellatio. External massage involves caressing the perineum. Internal massage requires short fingernails, adequate lubrication, and tender loving care. Insert the finger slowly; rotate it slowly. Some men don't care for prostate massage. As in all matters sexual, a little discussion beforehand is the way to go.

THE SECRET "GYNECOLOGICAL" DISORDERS OF
MEN

Hedda Garza

Ever heard of twisted testicle or constant erection? Well, neither have most of us. Yet these and other ailments affecting male sex organs can do just as much damage as any female complaint . . . maybe more . . .

Carrie hadn't heard from Jack in over a week, and she was frantic. She'd been dumped, neglected, and generally mistreated by a few men in the past, but the relationship with Jack had been different. For six months now, they had been best friends, lovers . . . open, honest, real on every level. But this was Monday, and she had last seen him a week ago Saturday. He'd behaved weirdly at the time—not touching her, moping around the apartment. He'd gone home early, and then—a week of silence. She'd left several messages on his answering machine and at his office, but he hadn't returned her calls.

By midweek Carrie's imagination had soared: Jack had eloped with his next-door neighbor. He'd been hit by a truck. She'd even scurried around searching for her savings-account passbook to make sure she hadn't been swindled by Jack-the-madman-forger.

On Thursday, she dialed Jack's number again, and this time, he answered. They spoke for exactly three minutes. He was busy, he said; he'd get back to her in a few days. Of course he loved her. But he sounded depressed, cold, all wrong. And there sat Carrie—not known for flaming neuroses—tearfully wondering whether the man she'd been so close to would ever call again.

A few blocks away, Jack was scrambling himself some eggs, trying to push away the dread he felt. Four weeks before, he had found a dime-size hardened area under the skin of his penis. Then, a couple of weeks later, in the midst of a passionate weekend with Carrie, he'd noticed the lump had enlarged and that

another one was forming not far from the first. Even worse, when he was sexually aroused, his penis clearly twisted in the two directions of the mysterious plaques, giving it the appearance of a damaged ram's horn. He managed to conceal this from Carrie—candlelight had its advantages—but it was obvious the situation was steadily worsening. His imagination took off even faster than Carrie's: He would die from some strange sexual disease . . . infect his beloved Carrie if he touched her. He thought about going to the doctor, but he was so consumed with terror, he was afraid to hear what the diagnosis might be. When Carrie had called, he'd wanted to confide in her, but he couldn't get the words out . . .

Jack's reaction is not unusual. This type of response sometimes springs from male pride or lingering Victorianism, but mostly, such avoidance is the direct result of ignorance. Amazingly, in an era in which people talk glibly about erotic technique, revel in x-rated movies, the subject of male sex organs is still taboo.

Every educated person knows the basics of venereal disease—gonorrhea, syphilis, herpes. Most men have at least a vague idea about women's gynecological complaints—missed menstrual periods, too much bleeding, infections. And no woman would be afraid or ashamed to tell her husband, father, or lover that she is plagued by one of those problems. But neither men nor women tend to be aware of the not uncommon afflictions that can affect *males—causing as much or more permanent damage as any female disorder.* Sex experts and others in the almost-no-holds-barred media rarely even *mention* these ailments, despite the fact that many men are left sterile, impotent, or both simply because they did not seek treatment until it was too late. Ask a supposed authority to tell you about Peyronie's disease or thrombotic penile vein or twisted testicle, and you're likely to draw a laugh—or a total blank.

Peyronie's disease—twisted penis. In plain language—was the disorder that engendered so much terror in Jack. No one knows the cause, but the facts are not half as frightening as the ailment's dramatic appearance. The plaques can cause so many twists and turns in an erect penis that it begins to look like a primitive country road. Dozens of quaint "cures" abound—a mystery drug called Potoba, which does nothing and costs a lot; massive doses of vitamin E, which may help circulation but leave the plaques unscathed; potassium pills in huge quantities (the twists stay and an ulcer arrives to keep them company); steroids, with the possibility of unpleasant side effects and no change in the twists; and, most dangerous of all, radiation therapy. The latter can not only cause painful surface burns on the penis but can also bring on total sterility months later. The reality is that Peyronie's disease often goes away as quickly as it arrives. The ailment is painless, and except in the most extreme cases, having intercourse is not only perfectly possible but can be just as enjoyable as before. In long-lasting and severe cases, surgery can be used to remove the plaques.

There are two other conditions that can suddenly threaten the penis, one requiring no medical attention and the other necessitating immediate surgery. Sometimes, after a particularly Olympic-style bout of lovemaking, a strange, cord-like structure appears all along the top of the penis. It's only an alarming-looking bruise, first cousin to a good old black-and-blue mark on your knee. One of the veins in the penis is injured, and the blood inside of it clots and hardens. It will heal—just the way a bruise disappears—but the term **thrombotic penile vein** sounds ominous. The cure: talk, read—but no fooling around!

Priapism, the second condition, is by far more threatening. Its slang name would have to be "constant erection"—supposedly a condition some men would favor. But the reality is quite the contrary. The sufferer suddenly finds himself with a painful erection that refuses to return to normal, even though he has no sexual desire. No one knows what sets priapism off. In a normal erection, the two major corporal bodies of the penis and the area called the corpus spongiosum that surrounds the urinary tube are filled with blood. During priapism, however, the corpus spongiosum fails to fill, so as the penis keeps filling with blood, the two corporal bodies become superfilled. If the pool of noncirculating blood remains in the penis, scar tissue will destroy the normal internal structures in a few weeks, making it impossible to ever have an erection again.

In cases of priapism, emergency surgery, during which a small connection is made between the corporal bodies and the spongiosum, is an absolute must. Blood is released through this opening and pain immediately disappears. Many a man has nursed his constant erection, believing that he is simply oversexed, and become permanently impotent.

Less dramatic, but often causing misery and flight reactions, are a number of skin conditions that can appear on the penis in the same way that they appear on other parts of the body. Most of them go away by themselves, but a variety of antibiotics and other creams and lotions are available that speed up their demise. Any competent doctor can quickly distin-

guish between venereal diseases and these rashes, but again, despite sexual liberation, many men are so terrified that they wait in itching, burning agony until the condition simply goes away by itself or is so severe that it's a real struggle to clear up. Among the most common rashes are lichen planus, pityriasis rosea, ringworm, warts, and yeast infections (the same ones women get). They are often confused with each other and misdiagnosed.

Lichen planus is extremely common. Starting with a small flaky and horribly itchy spot almost anywhere on the penis or scrotum, it turns an odd silvery color and is totally unreceptive to antibiotics. Strangely, a month or two later, the condition tends to jump mainly to the wrists and inside of the mouth. Completely untreated, it disappears in another two or three months, but the misery and anxiety can make those months seem like forever. A steroid cream applied to the affected areas can ease itching and speed up healing. It's also comforting to know that lichen planus is not contagious.

Pityriasis rosea launches a sneak attack. It begins with one almost unnoticeable ring-shaped rash on virtually any part of the body and then disappears after a few days. Two or three weeks later, however, large areas of itching scales pop out on the penis and other areas of the body. This condition, too, will go away by itself. Annoying as it is, pityriasis rosea is *not* a veneral disease. While the cause may be unknown, the ailment will definitely leave as mysteriously as it appeared.

Yeast and **ringworm** are both fungal infections that appear often in the area of the penis. As is the case with pityriasis rosea, they are not veneral diseases . . . but they *can* be spread through sexual contact. Women are frequent victims of yeast infections in the vagina and can pass such ailments on to their lovers—especially if the man is not circumcised. Ringworm attacks in such a similar way that it is difficult to distinguish between it and a yeast infection. There are several creams available that clear up both.

Warts on the genitals, which can also be passed to and fro in bed, were once treated with painful cutting and scraping surgery, followed by a long healing process. Now, drying solutions are dabbed on them, and they slowly and painlessly disappear.

The penis, then, is a tough instrument, hard to damage and easy to cure—but even so, needless suffering is often endured. When a reluctance to seek help, coupled with ignorance, is applied to disorders of the *testicles*, however, the consequences are far more serious.

Pain and swelling in the testicles are terrifying, and so they should be. Such

symptoms are often left unattended or are all too frequently misdiagnosed . . . which can quickly lead to permanent impotence. The two most confusing ailments, both causing enormous swelling, often to the size of a grapefruit, are **torsion of the testicle** and **epididymitis.**

Torsion is a mechanical problem, whereas epididymitis is a bacterial infection. Their symptoms are identical—severely swollen testicles—but confusing the two can be an irreversible error.

The testicles hang by the cremasteric muscles, which permits them to pull up to a safer, warmer environment when it is cold and descend again when the surrounding temperature rises. This mechanism operates to keep sperm alive. There are times, however, when a testicle can literally twist around its own cord, cutting off one direction of the blood flow. Blood gets in because it is driven in by high pressure, but it can't return through the blocked veins. The testicle swells tremendously, and if surgery is not performed to untwist the testicle within four to eight hours, it will slowly die. Gradually, over a period of the next three months, the swelling does subside, and the man thinks he's cured . . . but by the end of the following few months, he discovers that his testicle has shrunk to the size of a pebble. If this happens to the other testicle as well (if the weakness is structural it sometimes happens on both sides), he will be left in the same condition as a castrated man—a eunuch. A simple emergency operation could have prevented the whole nightmare, but even doctors find diagnosis tricky.

Often, doctors believe that the swelling is caused by epididymitis, a common bacterial infection that inflames the duct bringing sperm into the vas deferens—the tube that carries manufactured sperm into the ejaculatory fluid. In that mistaken belief, antibiotics are prescribed. The swelling indeed subsides, but if torsion was the problem, the antibiotic has no effect and the testicle dies. It's vital to know that there are two diagnostic tests which definitely and quickly determine if torsion of the testicle exists. One is nuclear scanning with a Geiger counter tracing irradicated fluid through each testicle; even safer is ultrasound, where sound waves trace a path through the affected area. Obviously then, a man with swollen testicles should not be afraid to ask for diagnostic tests before he takes antibiotics.

Finally, you can play a key role in seeing that your man gets the care he needs. You wouldn't think twice aout dragging a lover or husband to the doctor if his head were bleeding, his ear aching, his back twinging. Knowing about possible threats to the penis and testicles and being sure your partner *does* something about them could help to save the manhood of many a good man!

FRAGILE FALLOPIAN TUBES

Keeping these tiny, vital conception and birth-control organs healthy

MARY GARNER

The fallopian tubes may be just about the smallest link in the reproductive tract, but that's no measure of their importance. These four-inch tubes between ovaries and uterus play a vital role in fertility. They are, however, as delicate as they are small, and it's worth knowing what you can do to ensure their smooth operation. In addition, the fallopian tubes are the focal points of the most common and most effective method of birth control—sterilization.

A multifaceted transit system

As bodily organs go, the tubes are highly movable parts: Each month at ovulation, one of the pair reaches down to an ovary (about an inch to an inch-and-a-half away) and swallows up an egg. A few days later it has resumed its hovering-over-the-ovary position.

Egg is actually snared from ovary by feathery tendrils called fimbria, which line the flared end of each tube. From here, microscopic "oars," called cilia, propel it onward by stoking 1,200 times a minute. Two minutes and inches later, the egg becomes lodged in the mid-portion of the tube where it narrows to about the width of a telephone cord. And here it sits for up to 24 hours, available for fertilization.

To increase the chances this will successfully take place, the tubes detain sperm as they try to enter, filtering out some abnormal ones, allowing the rest to trickle in slowly. This ensures that fresh sperm from one ejaculation will be supplied for up to 48 hours should a ripe egg happen along.

Once inside the tube, sperm are faced with the challenge of swimming against the cilia-created current in search of an egg. When fertilization does occur, fluids in the tube provide nourishment for the developing embryo for the next two to three days. Contractions then usher it into the uterus, ending the tubes' almost balletically choreographed role in reproduction.

The two most common tube troubles

Because of their delicate design, however, the tubes don't always perform with such fluidity. In fact, damaged fallopian tubes are the number-one cause of infertility, with infection being the most common problem to plague them.

Tubal infection, known as *salpingitis,* is triggered when a sexually transmitted disease (STD), most often gonorrhea or chlamydia, makes its way through the vagina and uterus and into one or both fallopian tubes. Once there, the bacteria behind these infections can impair a woman's fertility by killing off the cilia necessary to sweep eggs along, as well as destroying cells on the walls of the tubes' inner lining. The body replaces these damaged tubal cells with thick layers of scar tissue, which further thwart an egg's journey by narrowing the tubes or, in some cases, blocking them altogether, explains Jessica L. Thomason, M.D., associate professor, department of obstetrics and gynecology, University of Wisconsin Medical School, Milwaukee Campus.

Those at high risk for contracting salpingitis are women who: 1) have more than one sexual partner, since their lifestyle may increase the odds they'll be exposed to STDs; 2) have had abdominal surgery or an abortion, after which it is possible to get an unnoticeable infection that may spread bacteria into the tubal area; 3) are past or present IUD users (some experts suspect that the tail acts like a wick to draw bacteria from the vagina into the uterus) and 4) have a history of STDs or tubal infections. In addition, salpingitis can recur, particularly if a woman stops taking her antibiotics before it has completely cleared up.

The chance of infection can be decreased, on the other hand, by using a condom or diaphragm during lovemaking. Both help defend against sexually transmitted bacteria, according to Homer Chin, M.D., assistant professor of reproductive medicine, University of California, San Diego, Medical Center.

Diagnosing salpingitis is particularly tricky because its symptoms—cramplike abdominal pain and, sometimes, vaginal discharge and fever—may not all be present at the same time and can mimic many other conditions, from menstrual cramps to urinary tract infections. What's more, in many cases, no symptoms surface at all.

Because salpingitis can have devastating effects—permanent tube damage if not intercepted rapidly—it's important to report even the vaguest suspicion to a physician (especially if you believe you've been exposed to an STD) in order to have salpingitis either confirmed or ruled out. The first steps are a pelvic exam (in which cells are gathered from the vagina and cervix and checked out for bacteria) and, possibly, a blood test. Depending upon the results, a doctor may decide it's necessary to take a closer look at the tubes with one or more of the following tests. Which ones are done depends upon symptom severity, as well as your and your gynecologist's preference.

● *Ultrasound*, a continuous picture of the tubes which is painlessly "snapped" by bouncing high-frequency sound waves off the woman's abdomen.

● *Culdocentesis*, an in-office procedure done under local anesthesia in which a doctor inserts a needle through the vaginal wall and into the cul-de-sac (space behind the uterus) to remove fluid and check it for salpingitis-related bacteria, which may also be inhibiting the nearby tubes.

● *Laparoscopy*, a direct look at the tubes by way of a thin telescope slipped through a small incision in the abdomen. Laparoscopy is usually done on an outpatient basis and requires general anesthesia.

Treatment for salpingitis consists of a ten- to 14-day course of antibiotics to wipe out the offending bacteria. In severe cases, several days of hospitalization may be recommended to deliver a higher dose of medication intravenously. (The stomach can digest only a moderate amount of these drugs at once.)

In order to know which antibiotics to prescribe, the doctor has to pin down the bacteria to blame. If a laparoscopy (during which infected tubal cells are harvested and sent to a lab for analysis) wasn't done, experts have to rely on some educated guesswork. In this case they base their decision on cells gathered from the easier-to-reach vagina and cervix. Bacteria from these two spots don't always match what's affecting the tubes, though, which is why a few different antibiotics are sometimes tried before the right one is found.

The second most common tube trouble is endometriosis. In this condition, tissue that normally lines the uterus seems to stray (most likely during menstruation), attaching to abdominal organs, such as the tubes and the ovaries. Although misplaced, this tissue still responds to fluctuating hormones just as it would in the uterus. Each month it enlarges and is partially sloughed off, bleeding into the abdomen.

Bleeding from errant tissue clinging to the fallopian tubes can result in infertility by causing the tubes to scar over. This leaves them too inflexible to snag an egg. Researchers are still not sure, however, why lesions in other areas are also associated with infertility. Nor can they explain with certainty the intense cramping some women experience, although one common theory attributes at least some of it to blood irritating the sensitive lining of the pelvic cavity.

Once endometriosis is diagnosed—usually via laparoscopy—if pain is minimal and a woman isn't having trouble conceiving, some doctors merely suggest mild painkillers and twice-annual pelvic exams to keep an eye on things. Others take a more aggressive stance regardless of symptom severity and prescribe hormones

that mimic either pregnancy or menopause—two times when endometrial growth shuts down. This gives the lesions time to shrivel up. Hormones are taken for at least six months, or until a woman wants to start a family.

If endometrial growths are hampering tube mobility and a woman is unable to conceive, surgery may be recommended. Endometrial lesions and residual scar tissue can be cauterized, surgically removed or, more recently, vaporized with a laser, although so far this option is available only at major medical centers. A woman should try to conceive as soon as possible after surgery, before endometrial growths have a chance to reappear.

When tube traps egg: ectopic pregnancy

Sometimes a fertilized egg never makes its way into the womb, a dangerous condition known as an ectopic, or outside-the-uterus, pregnancy. In this situation, the embryo gets stuck in a fallopian tube (or, in rare cases, backs out of the tube and latches elsewhere in the abdomen—say, onto an ovary). Left undetected, a trapped embryo can grow large enough to rupture the tube, setting off life-threatening internal bleeding.

The incidence of ectopic pregnancy has reached near epidemic proportions, with the number of cases almost tripling from 17,800 in 1970 to 52,200 in 1980. One reason for this upward spiral is the dramatic increase in pelvic inflammatory disease and the STDs that cause it, since anything that damages the tubes ups the odds an egg will lodge there.

Other risk factors include: IUDs (they prevent implantation in the uterus, but don't block fertilization in the tubes); a previous ectopic (odds are the tubes are damaged); abdominal surgery, which can introduce a bacterial infection in which the tubes swell; increased age (the older you are, the more likely you've been exposed to other risk factors); use of the morning-after Pill; and, surprisingly, sterilization. Infrequently, tubes that have been sealed off to prevent conception rejoin enough to allow fertilization, but not enough to give the embryo a clear shot at the uterus.

Use of the mini-Pill further increases the risk of ectopic pregnancy since it slows egg transit time, and if it fails to prevent pregnancy an embryo may have a chance to grow too big to squeeze out of the tube. Some experts feel women whose mothers took DES while pregnant are also vulnerable since these women were more likely to be born with slightly malformed tubes.

Because ectopics are so hazardous, sexually active women—particularly those who are at risk and/or are trying to conceive—should be aware of the two classic warning signs: a) dull one- or two-sided abdominal pain and b) a skipped period followed a few days later by light spotting, explains Eberhard Muechler, M.D., associate professor of obstetrics and gynecology, the University of Rochester School of Medicine and Dentistry, New York. Some women also notice milder-than-normal pregnancy symptoms—like breast tenderness and bloating.

If the tube ruptures (usually anywhere from five to 14 weeks into the pregnancy), pain will suddenly switch to being extremely sharp and one-sided, and may radiate to the shoulder. It can be coupled with any or all of the following: dizziness, nausea, a weak pulse, clammy skin. This situation demands an *immediate* trip to to the emergency room and usually requires surgery to have internal bleeding stemmed and, sometimes, part or all of the tube removed. Increasingly, doctors are leaving the ovary in place—a necessity should a woman want to undergo *in vitro* fertilization later on, says Dr. Muechler.

Ectopics in which the tube has not ruptured are more insidious since the symptoms can be easily confused with those for a variety of other problems, such as appendicitis or even the flu.

And, in some instances, early symptoms are too mild to pick up or absent altogether. Nevertheless, recent diagnostic advances have brought down the death rate from ectopics markedly by making it possible to uncover many more before they rupture.

Diagnosis at this stage begins with a pregnancy test. The best option is a recently devised blood test called beta HCG—quite an advance since it can detect pregnancies of just eight days (compared with 14 to 28 days for less sophisticated varieties) with virtually 100 percent accuracy. Positive test results, or negative ones if symptoms persist and a less accurate test was used, are followed by ultrasound, culdocentesis and/or laparoscopy.

Ultrasound can detect pregnancies of six weeks or more. If the picture is too fuzzy (or it's too early) to make a definitive diagnosis, culdocentesis may be in order. In this case, fluid is removed from behind the uterus and checked for blood, which indicates whether or not a tube is beginning to bleed into the abdomen. In still-questionable cases, a look at the tubes through a laparoscope is advisable. The relatively recent advent of laparoscopy has also helped make ectopics more readily detectable since formerly a larger abdominal incision (which doctors were more reluctant to make) was required.

Once diagnosed, an ectopic pregnancy must be removed. Any tubal surgery, however, results in the formation of scar tissue, which can compromise fertility. Some experts feel laser surgery, which involves less bleeding and scarring, or microsurgery (done with tiny tools and a high-powered microscope) offers a better chance of keeping fertility intact. If one is available, choosing a surgeon who specializes in infertility may also be wise.

When the tube is unruptured and the pregnancy is in the outer portion, some doctors prefer to sidestep surgery and squeeze an ectopic pregnancy out. A majority of experts don't recommend this, though, since there's a risk some tissue will be left behind and continue to grow, according to Dr. Muechler.

Despite recent fine-tuning of tubal surgical procedures, only about half the women who want to conceive after an ectopic will be able to do so since whatever caused scarring in one tube has likely affected the other. Of the women who do conceive, 15 to 20 percent will develop another ectopic. Before a woman tries, experts recommend that she wait at least three months (to give the tubes a chance to heal), keeping in close contact with a gynecologist and reporting any unusual symptoms immediately.

Tying and untying the tubes

On the flip side of the fallopian tubes' importance in conception is their role in contraception. "Tying" off the tubes to block an egg's path from the ovary to the uterus is the most common as well as the most effective means of birth control around.

There are actually several different methods of female sterilization—ranging from having the fallopian tubes burned closed with an electric current to having them sealed off with a silicone band. A gynecologist will usually choose the one with which he's most familiar.

The two main ways to gain access to the tubes are with laparoscopy and mini-laparotomy. During laparoscopy a gas (usually carbon dioxide) is pumped into the abdomen to puff it up, giving the physician a clear look at the area. The tubes are then sterilized through the laparoscope or via a second tiny cut. In mini-laparotomy, the tubes are sterilized directly through a horizontal one- to-two-inch incision just above the pubic hair line.

Both operations last between 15 and 30 minutes, may either be performed on an outpatient basis or involve an overnight hospital stay. They can be done under local or, more commonly, general anesthesia (depending upon your and your doctor's choice), with costs ranging from $500 to $1,300. Several insurance companies do cover the costs.

While there may be some abdominal tenderness for about 48 hours after surgery, aspirin should be enough to ease the ache. You may return to work in two or three days and resume love-making as soon as it's comfortable. Expect menstruation to recur as usual. There's a slight chance of developing an infection, so you'll be asked to keep an eye out for the warning signs—fever, redness, inflammation at the incision site and increasing abdominal pain, points out Douglas Huber, M.D., medical director of the Association for Voluntary Surgical Contraception.

While the decision to be sterilized should be the result of careful consideration, occasionally a woman changes her mind. For the small percentage who subsequently want to conceive, there's an operation that may be able to restore fertility, and it's successful more often than might be expected.

After making a three- to four-inch incision, a surgeon (usually a gynecologist trained in microsurgery) focuses in on the fallopian tubes with a microscope. He then rejoins the lining of each tube (which in some places is as narrow as a pinhead) with sutures so tiny they're tough to see with the naked eye. This procedure is done under general anesthesia, requires a short hospital stay and costs considerably more than sterilization, although some insurance companies will foot the bill.

Bypassing troubled tubes

Irreparably damaged tubes have been a stumbling block as far as fertility is concerned, but in the past decade, scientists have made great strides in making childbearing possible for women with this problem. The most well established option, *in vitro* fertilization, bypasses the tubes altogether. Eggs are retrieved from the ovary, fertilized outside the body and inserted into the uterus in the hope that at least one will implant. For unexplained reasons, however, this works only about 20 percent of the time. So in an attempt to give women more options, researchers are exploring other possibilities.

One breakthrough occurred last year when Sherman Silber, M.D., reproductive microsurgeon at the St. Luke's Hospital in St. Louis and author of *How to Get Pregnant,* conducted the first successful ovary/fallopian tube transplant. This was done between identical twins, who have precisely the same genetic makeup, preventing rejection of transplanted organs. While the donee started ovulating recently, so far she has not become pregnant.

Still in the animal testing stages is an option with more widespread possibilities: tube transplants between unrelated parties. In this case, drugs to suppress the immune system are taken so the donor tube is not rejected. While the number of animals being studied is too small to estimate a realistic success rate, so far quite a few pregnancies have occurred, reports study director James R. Scott, M.D., professor and chairman, department of obstetrics and gynecology, the University of Utah School of Medicine, Salt Lake City. He hopes human trials will get under way within the next five years. However, doctors will first have to be certain the drugs to be used are safe for a fetus should conception occur. In a similar vein, researchers at the University of Utah are conducting animal experiments using artificial tubes that contain tiny pumps to propel eggs from ovary to uterus—a far-off mechanical substitution for two anatomical wonders whose health it's worth your while to preserve.

SEX, WITH CARE

■ *"Sometimes, right before I ask a guy up to my apartment for a drink,"* reports Janice, 30, an advertising executive in Boston, *"I look at him and ask myself, 'Is this guy worth two weeks on penicillin?' Most of the time, I have to say no. That's why I'm looking for a guy to settle down with, to finally make that kind of question moot."*

America's affair with casual sex, that two-decade adventure launched by the Pill, is giving way to a time of caution and commitment.

From the singles bars of Boston to the campuses of California, more and more young people are counting fewer partners. For many, the one-night stand is out and courtship is in. Behind their shift toward monogamy: Primarily a greater appreciation of traditional values but also a growing fear of what indiscriminate sex can do to health.

According to a number of sociologists, the sexual free-for-all that started among some young people in the early 1960s began slowing before this decade arrived. San Francisco therapist Alexis Rabourn says many who took part realized that "being sexually uninhibited didn't make them all that happy." Some felt humiliated after sleeping with people who never called back. For others, the sexual revolution eventually meant boredom. Some, heading toward their 40s, simply settled down and sought the rewards of careers and family life.

Now, the move toward conservative ways is accelerated by a new concern. Single people in their 20s and 30s are worried by what public-health professionals call STD's, or sexually transmitted diseases. Not since the early years of this century, when pregnancy and childbirth were still considered major risks, have so many Americans viewed promiscuity as a hazard to health—and for good reason.

According to the federal Centers for Disease Control (CDC), the nation is in the grip of an STD epidemic that infects an average of 33,000 people a day. That figures to 12 million cases a year, up from 4 million in 1980. At this rate, 1 in 4 Americans between ages 15 and 55 eventually will acquire an STD. Millions will suffer from a painful infection that even doctors until recent years had never heard of—chlamydia, with its risk of infertility and botched pregnancies. Others will be pestered for life by herpes lesions. Thousands will be stricken and, unless a cure is found, die from acquired-immune-deficiency syndrome, or AIDS.

It is a "staggering" problem, one health leader says, and what's needed to fight it is more money for research and cures plus a greater awareness by the public of what the diseases do.

No authority in public health is urging adults to shun sex. Such counsel was offered—and ignored—during venereal-disease outbreaks in past decades. What's stressed now is "safe sex," practicing hygiene, limiting partners and knowing more about them.

Fear of AIDS has prompted significant, well documented changes in the lifestyles of homosexual men, who comprise three fourths of its victims. Surveys show gays having fewer sex partners and making greater use of condoms, generally considered the most effective shield against STD's.

More difficult to assess is the impact of STD's on heterosexual conduct. A *Los Angeles Times* poll of adults

> Casual affairs fade
> and courtships blossom as singles
> experience a new appreciation
> of old values and a growing fear
> of an epidemic of sexually
> transmitted diseases

across the U.S.—marrieds, singles, heterosexuals, homosexuals—found 4 percent making major changes in their lives because of AIDS and 13 percent making lesser changes. Eighty-one percent reported no change—no surprise since most Americans, the authorities say, don't need to change. All along, a majority of adults have endorsed monogamy and the idea that sex should be accompanied by commitment.

Still, a growing number of psychologists and public-health authorities report significant behavioral changes, primarily among single baby-boomers in big cities and on campuses. For some singles, care became a watchword when alarms rang out over herpes. For many more, especially in areas with large gay populations, AIDS is the catalyst.

In Houston, Dr. James Haughton, the public-health director, reports that "the fear of AIDS, herpes and other STD's has done more to change habits than has 100 years of preaching."

In Chicago, public-health administrator Jeanette Restagno counts more gays and heterosexuals having blood tests for AIDS. "The pendulum has swung," she says. "The Pill changed attitudes in the '60s and '70s. AIDS is helping to change attitudes in this decade."

In Boston, Dr. Luisa Fertitta, assistant professor of gynecology at Tufts University, finds many young women rethinking their sex lives in the wake of bouts with chlamydia and herpes. "We

are seeing, very definitely, the downside of the sexual revolution," she says.

What to fear and what not to fear are much debated among experts in medicine, psychology and public health.

Doctors wish that more women were aware of chlamydia—pronounced kleh-mih-dee-uh—which has become the No. 1 STD in America, striking from 3 to 10 million people a year. A Pap smear can detect it and antibiotics can cure it. The problem is that the bacterial infection often has no symptoms and victims can go for years not knowing they have it. If not treated, it can cause pelvic-inflammatory disease (PID), which can lead to ectopic, or tubal, pregnancy and bring pneumonia and eye diseases to children born to infected mothers.

There is less concern now about genital herpes, which accounts for 500,000 new cases a year. In fact, many therapists consider the herpes scare of the early '80s overblown. Except for AIDS, it's the only STD without a cure, but the severity of its outbreaks can be controlled. Many with herpes suffer only one outbreak in a lifetime. For a woman, the greatest danger is a severe outbreak just before childbirth. That could cause physical or mental damage to the infant.

No disease rivals AIDS in stirring confusion and alarm. "Even intelligent people," says Atlanta therapist Stephen Sloan, "think herpes or gonorrhea can turn into AIDS." One woman recently phoned Virginia's Alexandria Hospital

in a dither, asking whether she would die if she used her false teeth, which had fallen to the floor in a dentist's office.

"AIDS is quite different from any other disease," notes Allan Brandt of Harvard, assistant professor of medical history. "It strikes down people in their very early years very, very quickly and kills them." As a result, "it is affecting the way people think about sexuality and the way people act sexually."

Physicians and psychologists stress that fears of catching AIDS from heterosexual sex far outweigh the chances of that happening. Since 1981, the CDC has counted 266 cases spread by heterosexual contact—47 men and 219 women. That's roughly 1 percent of all AIDS victims.

Still, much remains a mystery. The CDC notes there is not evidence that saliva can transmit AIDS. But the virus has been found in saliva, and Dr. George Pazin of the Univeristy of Pittsburgh Medical School says it may be years before anyone knows for sure the disease can't be passed on through long kisses with someone carrying the AIDS virus. Before starting a sexual relationship, he says, one should ponder the prospects of it enduring.

Legitimate or not, scares are prompting a sharp rise in cases of what psychologists call ISD—inhibited sexual desire. "Ten years ago," observes Houston psychologist Alice Gates, "women were dealing with men the same way men had dealt with women—they were sexually aggressive.

America's most troublesome sex diseases

Until recent years, public-health experts counted barely five types of sexually transmitted diseases. Now, they know that more than a score exist. Causing the most concern—

■ AIDS ■

Acquired-immune-deficiency syndrome, since first reported in the U.S. in 1981, has each year doubled its number of new victims. AIDS damages the body's immunity against infection, leaving its victims without a defense against a host of serious diseases.

Cause: A virus called HTLV-III/LAV. However, not everyone exposed develops AIDS. Many of the estimated 1 million people infected by the virus so far have no AIDS symptoms.

Symptoms: Tiredness, fever, loss of appetite, diarrhea, night sweats and swollen glands.

When do they occur? From about six months after infection to five years and possibly longer.

How is it diagnosed? Doctors look for certain kinds of infections, do tests to reveal AIDS antibodies and show damage to white blood cells.

Who gets it? Three largest groups are sexually active gay men, 73 percent of cases; intravenous drug users, 17 percent; blood-transfusion recipients, 2 percent.

Treatment or cure: Nothing yet.

■ CHLAMYDIA ■

The "disease of the '80s," chlamydia hits between 3 million and 10 million Americans a year.

Cause: The bacterium *Chlamydia trachomatis*, spread to adults by sexual contact and to babies of infected mothers during birth.

Symptoms: For men, discharge from penis or burning sensation during urination. For women, vaginal itching, chronic abdominal pain, bleeding between menstrual periods.

When do they occur? Sometimes two to four weeks after infection. But many men have no symptoms. Four of 5 women won't notice one until complications set in.

Complications: In both sexes, possible infertility. In women, pregnancy problems that can kill a fetus and, occasionally, the mother. In babies, infections of the eyes, ears and lungs, possible death.

Diagnosis: For men and women, a painless test at a doctor's office. Symptoms need not be evident.

Cure: Usually with the drug tetracycline or doxycycline.

■ GONORRHEA ■

The number of cases of this ancient disease rose last year for the first time since 1978.

ONE YEAR'S TOLL

New cases of sexually transmitted disease expected in 1986

Disease	New cases
AIDS	15,000
Syphilis	90,000
Genital herpes	500,000
Venereal warts	1,000,000
Gonorrhea	1,800,000
Trichomoniasis	3,000,000
Chlamydia	3,000,000
Other STD's	2,450,000

Note: Pelvic-inflammatory-disease cases are included in figures for chlamydia and gonorrhea.
USN&WR—Basic data: Centers for Disease Control

They were into one-night stands. Now, my patients don't want to sleep with anyone. They are worried about AIDS and dying.''

In New York, many who seek counseling are young, single, upwardly mobile heterosexuals—and "real, real scared," says Maryellen Duane, a psychologist at the Postgraduate Center of Mental Health. They used to boast about the joys of sexual liberation. Now, most refuse to date anyone. "To hear someone say, 'I haven't had sex in a year' is not unusual. It's common."

Many therapists consider long-term abstinence drastic and unwarranted. The change that's much more common, one welcomed by physicians and psychologists, is simply a shift toward a more discriminating, less adventuresome lifestyle. "If you ask people how many partners they have, they often say, 'One, and I plan to keep it that way,' " reports John Potterat, an STD-control officer in Colorado Springs, Colo. "Monogamy is in."

Settling down is on the minds of many, if not most, sexually active singles. "They are looking for bonding and for a Mr. or Mrs. Right," says Gale Golden, a psychiatrist at the University of Vermont. She says sex is their way—"not necessarily the right way"—of searching for that mate.

"People want more commitment, whether in a marriage or not," says the Rev. Arthur Van Eck, director of the Commission on Family Ministries and Human Sexuality for the National Council of Churches. "They're looking for someone they can rely on to care about and be cared for."

Many who marry want to stay wed, some because of STD fears. "A lot of my friends say they're glad that they aren't still out there," says Linell Juliet, a psychotherapist in Boulder. "They say things like, 'I think I'll work on this relationship.' They don't want to be single again."

At the University of California at Berkeley, health educator Cathy Kodama finds women looking to marriage and motherhood—goals less evident when she was a student in the '70s. Today's co-eds worry that STD's could make them infertile, she says.

There's a growing awareness, reports Dr. Lawrence Laycob of Denver, "that when you're casual about sex, chances are that the person you're casual with has been casual with someone else. So there's a third, fourth or fifth party out there that you have no knowledge of."

For many people, dealing with what is "out there" is not easy. Ben, a Philadelphia bartender who spent years on the sexual prowl, finally decided to marry, as did most of his former drinking buddies. "It's a matter of settle down or die," he says. Carole, an artist in Pennsylvania, keeps spurning invitations from a man she deems attractive. "I find myself trying to pick up clues about him—the way he turns his head or moves his hands." She suspects that he is bisexual and could give her AIDS. Joan, an assistant buyer in New York, worries that an STD will keep her from someday becoming a mother. But she risks one-night stands, never asking a lover about his sex life. Although STD's hit every economic group, she tells herself that he is safe if he holds a good job.

Counselors are advising singles that they should not be intimate physically unless they can be intimate verbally. Here's what Paul Pearsall, who teaches sex education at Dearborn's Henry Ford Community College, suggests that his students say to partners: "I have never had, nor do I now have, any symptoms of sexually transmissible disease, nor have I knowingly been intimate with anyone who has. Have you?"

Traditional candlelight conversation it's not, but Abigail Van Buren of "Dear Abby" fame says such a quiz is prudent. "You have to be very careful about your companions nowadays," the advice columnist notes.

How do you know that a partner is being truthful? "You don't," says Martha Gross, a psychologist in Washington, D.C. "And that's all the more reason for slowing down the sexual pace. A person is more likely to talk about a bisexual relationship after six months than on the first night."

Even an honest answer to an intimate

Cause: The bacterium *Neisseria gonorrhoeae.*

Symptoms: For males, a puslike discharge. Most infected women show no symptoms.

Complications: Many, from back pains and urination problems to arthritis and sterility. Babies of infected mothers may be born blind.

Diagnosis: Cell-culture tests.

Cure: Penicillin works in most cases. A sharp increase, however, is occurring in a strain of gonorrhea, called PPNG, that resists penicillin.

■ GENITAL HERPES ■

Twenty million Americans have genital herpes. Recurrences are frequent in some, rare in others. Some persons have only one outbreak in a lifetime.

Cause: Herpes-simplex viruses in skin-to-skin contact with infected area.

Symptoms: Blisters in genital area form and become open sores. Initial outbreak sometimes is accompanied by swollen glands, headache and fever, and its lesions may last weeks.

Later outbreaks are shorter and less severe.

Diagnosis: A physician can make a test while sores still exist.

Cure: None is known. Acyclovir reduces severity of flare-ups.

■ TRICHOMONIASIS ■

Some 3 million men and women get this disease each year.

Cause: The parasite *Trichomonas vaginalis.*

Symptoms: For women, a frothy discharge, itching, redness of genitals. Men usually have no symptoms.

Diagnosis: Pap smear or microscopic examination.

Complications: None in men, gland infections in women.

Cure: Drug metronidazoile.

■ VENEREAL WARTS ■

Although often painless, these growths on and around the genitals can be dangerous and need medical attention.

Cause: HPV's, the human papilloma viruses.

How are they found? Some look flat. Some look like tiny cauliflowers. Some only a doctor can see. It takes a Pap smear to detect warts on the cervix.

What harm do they do? Babies exposed during childbirth may get warts in the throat. Some researchers believe that venereal warts caused by some types of HPV's increase risk of cancer of cervix, vulva, penis and anus.

Cure: Doctors can remove with the drug podophyllin. Some require surgery. Over-the-counter drugs for other skin warts should be avoided.

■ SYPHILIS ■

This once rampant disease is now on the decline, but it still can be life threatening.

Cause: The bacterium *Treponema pallidum,* an organism that can be killed with soap and water.

Symptoms: In two stages and usually in three weeks. First, a painless pimple, blister or sore where the germs entered the body. Then, a rash, hair loss, swollen glands.

Diagnosis: Blood test, microscopic examination.

Complications: Brain damage, heart disease, paralysis, insanity, death. Babies born to untreated women may be blind, deaf, crippled by bone disease.

Cure: Penicillin.

■ PID ■

Pelvic-inflammatory disease is described by the Centers for Disease Control as the "most common serious complication" of STD's.

Causes: Infections from any of several diseases, including chlamydia and gonorrhea, that result in inflammation and abscesses of a woman's Fallopian tubes, ovaries and pelvis.

Possible harm: One in 7 women with a PID attack becomes infertile. After three attacks, up to 75 percent cannot conceive.

Diagnosis: Examinations of abdomen and pelvis, laboratory tests.

Cure: Antibiotics for some cases. Severe cases often require surgery that results in infertility.

question is no guarantee that a person is safe. While dormant in one person, an STD can be transmitted to another. Dr. Edward Wiesmeier, director of the UCLA Student Health Center, warns students that one chance encounter can infect a person with as many as five different diseases.

That's why nearly every campaign against STD's stresses the use of condoms. AIDS has prompted a dramatic increase in condom sales to gay men. Many women in New York carry condoms in their purses, says psychotherapist Shirley Zussman. "It's kind of like a security blanket."

Physicians are complaining, though, that condoms too often are shunned. Dr. Steven R. Mostow, director of the University of Colorado's STD clinic, stockpiled 1,000 last summer and has tried ever since to give them away. But "we rarely get a taker," he laments.

As one who sees people who get STD's and not those who avoid them, Mostow is convinced that habits aren't changing enough. One problem is that many people are aware of STD's but refuse to believe that any could hit them.

Example: A married couple, in their 30s, showed up at Mostow's Denver clinic, both with chlamydia. After learning they recently had experienced sex with others, the doctor asked that they return in a week and bring their partners. They did—with nearly 30 men and women, all clad in the jackets of a swingers' club. "They felt that because they knew each other the risks were lower than if they picked someone up in a bar," says Mostow, who gave each swinger a chlamydia treatment.

What's ahead for STD's? Public-health professionals fear that the epidemic will get worse before it gets better. The CDC unit in charge of fighting STD's is getting 9 percent less money than it did in 1980, taking inflation into account. But the unit is dealing with three times as many cases plus AIDS, a disease that absorbs 15 percent of its $53.5 million budget. The AIDS battle also is siphoning government scientists from other STD projects.

The chlamydia epidemic can be curbed, reports Dr. James Mason, director of the CDC, but only with more money. The disease would be harnessed, he told Congress on May 19, if the government would start a control program such as the one that checked gonorrhea in the mid-'70s. But Mason sees little chance of getting the $50 million needed. The CDC is holding chlamydia spending to $4.5 million, he said. "This is one of our efforts to get that deficit under control."

Another problem: Many doctors still know little about fighting STD's. In a survey in the *Journal of the American Medical Association,* Dr. King Holmes

KINGS AND QUEENS AND AL CAPONE

Syphilis treatment in 17th century: Time in a fumigation chamber

3,000 years of sex scourges

It was Moses who started the war on STD's, back when his soldiers came home from defeating the Midianites and brought with them thousands of captive women. He quickly saw a problem—"a plague among the congregation"—and acted. He invoked a one-week quarantine and condemned "every woman that hath known man by lying with him."

Some 3,000 years and many sex plagues later—in fact up till the 1900s—even skilled physicians didn't know what to do about STD's. Many didn't want to know. To treat a sex disease, they felt, was to sanction sin.

STD's maimed kings, queens and Popes plus chunks of armies, navies and cities. Victims in the past 100 years ranged from Adolf Hitler and Al Capone to Oscar Wilde and Wild Bill Hickok.

More than once, history was altered. Sixteenth-century Russia had been put on a progressive path by an enlightened Ivan IV until syphilis turned him into Ivan the Terrible.

STD origins have long been debated. After syphilis swept Europe in the 1490s, many called it the Naples disease. The English termed it French pox. Some French knew it as the Spanish

A World War II message

disease, claiming that Columbus's crew carried it from America to Spain—an issue still in dispute.

Cure after cure was tried. German men in the 15th century hoped to purge syphilis in bathhouses, but nude women did the scrubbing and the disease multiplied. The year 1900 found Americans relying on Unfortunate's Friend and other quack remedies laced with alcohol.

To keep men fit for World War I, the U.S. detained up to 30,000 prostitutes in camps, many with barbed wire, reports Harvard historian Allan Brandt—a move akin to the interning of Japanese Americans in World War II.

Major progress came in 1938 when Congress funded local venereal-disease-control programs. Soon, every state was requiring blood tests for marriage licenses.

Only 5 percent of draftees entered World War II with VD, compared with 13 percent reporting for World War I. "Knock out VD" was a '40s slogan, and penicillin's debut in 1944 nearly did.

But STD's never die. Diseases change and require new cures, notes Brandt. "It's a constant problem keeping up with the microbes that are on this planet."

WHERE TO GET HELP

American Social Health Association—260 Sheridan Avenue, Suite 307, Palo Alto, Calif. 94306. Telephone (415) 321-5134 between 8 a.m. and 4:30 p.m. PDT for free brochures. For information on herpes, chlamydia, PID and other diseases, call (415) 328-7710 from noon to 4:30 p.m. PDT.

Planned Parenthood Federation of America—Affiliates, listed in phone books, provide screening, treatment, counseling.

U.S. Public Health Service's AIDS hot lines—For recorded message on disease symptoms, (800) 342-2437. For counselors and referrals, (800) 447-AIDS. In Atlanta, 329-1295 between 9 a.m. and 7 p.m. EDT

VD national hot line—(800) 227-8922. In California, (800) 982-5883. Referrals for doctors and clinics nationwide.

of the University of Washington at Seattle found that medical students, on average, received less than 3 hours of training in diagnosing and treating sexually transmitted diseases. Until recently, that training included virtually nothing on chlamydia.

Better tests are helping physicians to diagnose more cases of STD, especially chlamydia. Doctors at the University of California at San Francisco have developed a treatment, with the drug erythromycin, to keep pregnant women from passing chlamydia on to their babies. Stanford researchers are encouraged about tests, just under way, in which genital warts are treated with interferon. A half-dozen teams are at work on the development of a vaccine to prevent gonorrhea.

More is being done to find what the nation wants most—a vaccine to prevent AIDS—but few specialists look for anything effective before 1990. Even more elusive is a cure for the disease, which has stricken nearly 20,000 Americans, 10,500 of whom are now dead.

But what goes on in labs is only part of the STD battle. As far as public-health authorities are concerned, more Americans need to put care back into sex. "The major challenge for society in the next five years," says Dr. Willard Cates, director of the CDC's STD division, "is to help individuals realize that the choices of sexual activities they make today are going to affect their lives later on."

by Lewis J. Lord with Jeannye Thornton, Joseph Carey and the domestic bureaus

A Gift from Mother Nature

Menstruation isn't a curse. It isn't something that requires the banishment of women. And it certainly doesn't cause broken violin strings.

Barbara Gastell, M.D.

Barbara Gastell is a medical writer and editor who lives in Washington, D.C. Her article originally appeared in Women's World.

What sours wine, blights crops, kills bees, rusts bronze and drives dogs mad? Menstrual blood, claimed the Roman scholar Pliny the Elder. Sex during one's period was thought to cause the birth of a monster, and even as late as the 1970s, many women were told they suffered cramps because they hadn't accepted their "proper roles."

For centuries, menstruation has been shrouded in myth and mystery. Today, however, we have a better understanding of what this normal process is and how it works. And new research keeps adding useful knowledge.

Fear and Wonder

"In the beginning," write co-authors Janice Delaney, Mary Jane Lupton and Emily Toth in 'The Curse: A Cultural History of Menstruation,' "the menstrual process inspired fear and wonder in human beings." But primitive cultures seemed to consider the bleeding far more awful than awesome. A menstruating woman was viewed as an impure and dangerous being whose mere presence could ruin hunts, spoil food and in general, invite disaster.

Thus, early societies throughout the world banished women to special huts during their periods. Others developed customs to keep them from causing harm, such as forbidding menstruating women to bake bread. In fact, the very word "taboo" is thought to come from a Polynesian term for menstruation.

Yet menstrual blood has also been considered a cure for diseases such as leprosy, warts and gout. And it has even been used as a love charm and an offering to the gods.

"Don't take a bath. And don't touch flowers, or they'll wither and die."

A mother to her child

Menstrual superstitions have persisted even into this century. In the 1920s, the superstition circulated that a permanent wave wouldn't take during menstruation. Some musicians still blame broken violin strings on their own or their wives' periods. And one mother recalls that her own mother warned her : "Don't take a bath. And don't touch flowers, or they'll wither and die."

Myths and taboos about menstruation undoubtedly have many roots. One may be the fear of blood, one mysterious aspect of the process—especially to men.

Slang expressions used to refer to menstruation suggest that even today the topic is still embarrassing and poorly understood. Men often use expressions like "on the rag," which has come to mean cranky as well as menstruating, or phrases that echo the old taboo against sex for the duration of a woman's period.

Even among themselves, many women do not mention menstruation directly. Instead, they often refer to a female or male visitor ("Aunt Tilly is here," or "Herbie's over") redness ("red-letter day"), nature ("Mother Nature's gift") or pain and calamity ("falling off the roof"). "The curse" refers to an old superstition, often stemming from Eve's expulsion from the Garden of Eden, and expressions such as "sick time of the month" and "being unwell" perpetuate the myth that menstruation is an illness rather than a normal bodily function.

Misinformation

In light of these deep-seated attitudes, it's not surprising that young girls have often been misinformed—or not informed at all—about menstruation.

From *St. Raphael's Better Health*, January/February 1986, pp. 9-12. Reprinted with permission of the Hospital of St. Raphael Magazine, New Haven, Connecticut.

Long before their first periods, according to Diane N. Ruble, Ph.D., of the University of Toronto's psychology department, many girls have picked up negative beliefs that may become "self-fulfilling prophecies."

Like Meggie in Colleen McCullough's *The Thorn Birds,* the young woman whose first period comes as a total surprise may fear she has a dread disease such as cancer. One woman recalls, "When I found blood on my panties, I was scared to death. I made sure my daughters were better prepared than I was."

But when parents try to describe the process to their children, they may discover how poorly informed and embarrassed they are themselves. A mother of two teen-age daughters remembers "I was surprised how little I knew about menstruation when I tried to explain it to my kids. I had to first look up the information in reference books."

"When I found blood on my panties, I was scared to death. I made sure my daughters were better prepared than I was."

A mother

What actually happens during the menstrual cycle? Dr. Ervin E. Nichols, now director of practice activities at the American College for Obstetricians and Gynecologists, sometimes explains the menstrual process to his patients by having them imagine that the inside of his office is a uterus. He tells them to pretend that the floor, walls and ceiling are covered with stalks of wheat, which first grow tall and then ripen. Later a threshing machine comes through and cuts down the stalks. "The wheat goes swooshing out the door—and that's menstruation," Dr. Nichols concludes.

Of course, a woman's womb isn't lined with wheat. In reality, the menstrual cycle—which only humans, apes and other primates experience—involves complex interactions among several glands and organs. Each month, the lining of a woman's uterus thickens so that a fertilized egg can implant there and grow. If conception does not occur, the uterine lining, known as the endo-

metrium, is shed through the vagina in the form of menstrual fluid.

The four stages

In a simplified manner, the menstrual cycle can be viewed as having four stages. The first stage is called the proliferative phase. Early in the cycle, the hypothalamus, which is part of the brain, signals the pituitary gland, which is located at the base of the brain, to release FSH (follicle-stimulating hormone). This hormone causes an egg to ripen in one of a woman's ovaries. Concurrently, a group of cells known as a follicle develops around the egg and begins secreting the hormone estrogen. This substance, in turn, makes the uterine lining grow, or proliferate.

The second stage of the cycle is called ovulation, the time when the egg is released from the ovary. Near the middle of the typical cycle, the pituitary—still on the direction of the hypothalamus—releases a surge of another hormone called LH (luteinizing hormone). Shortly thereafter, the egg is released and is swept into the nearby fallopian tube, where conception usually takes place.

It is at this time of the cycle—not during menstruation as was once thought—that women are most likely to conceive. "Ovulation is the peak of fertility," says Mary Jane Gray, M.D., the gynecologist for student health services at the University of North Carolina. "But some people still think that at the time they bleed women get pregnant."

When the egg is released, a woman may feel a little pain, called mittelschmerz, German for "middle pain." Occasionally, the discomfort is so severe that is mimics appendicitis. A little bleeding from the vagina may also occur around the time of the woman's ovulation.

The third stage of the cycle is called the secretory phase. After ovulation, the follicle in the ovary turns into a corpus luteum ("yellow body") which secretes estrotervals of between 25 and 35 days, but some have shorter or longer cycles, and others never establish truly regular patterns. Although the total length of the cycle can vary considerably, the time from ovulation to menstruation is almost about 14 days. But cycles can occur without ovulation and be very irregular, especially during the first and last few years of menstruation.

Missed Periods

Many factors—including, of course, pregnancy—can delay a woman's period. Among them are excessive dieting, recent use of birth control pills, thyroid conditions or other illness, excessive exercise, and psychological factors.

Emotional stress, in particular, can affect the menstrual cycle. Elizabeth Crisp, M.D., a gynecologist in Washington, D.C., notes that a young woman may not menstruate for an entire year after she leaves for college. A singer from New York recalls, "I used to be like clockwork. Then I moved to Europe and didn't get my period for three or four months."

It's also important to keep records, says Dr. Crisp. Like many other doctors, she gives her patients menstrual record charts—simple calendars to note the days of each period. By consulting such a record, a woman and her doctor can easily see whether she's maintaining the pattern that's normal for her.

"I wouldn't say that menstruation should interfere with athletics any more than with other activities."

Bonnie Kestner
Swimming/Diving coach at Sweet Briar College

When menstruating, women need not avoid their usual activities. "They can do anything they're comfortable doing," says Dr. Gray. Many women can recall being excused from gym during their periods, as if they were extra frail or ill. But although a woman may choose to be less active if she's uncomfortable, there's no medical reason to avoid sports.

"I wouldn't say that menstruation should interfere with athletics any more than with other activities," says Bonnie Kestner, swimming and diving coach at Sweet Briar College. "Women in the Olympics have achieved top performances at all phases of the menstrual cycle," she notes. Similarly, the research fails to support the belief that women are less competent in school or at work during their periods.

What about sex when one is menstruating? Most experts agree that it's simply a matter of personal choice. It doesn't pose any special risk to the woman, the man or future children—and some women find that sex relieves cramps. A diaphragm can be used to hold back menstrual blood. It's also possible, though rare, for pregnancy to result from sex during menstruation. Thus, a woman who does not want to conceive should make sure she is adequately protected.

New Research

"There's a terrific blossoming of research on the menstrual cycle," says Alice Dan, Ph.D., a psychologist at the University of Illinois College of Nursing and president of the Society for Menstrual Cycle Research. "I credit it to the women's movement. There was a demand to answer some of the questions asked by women."

Some of the most useful research has been on menstrual cramps. Scientists have recently found that substances known as prostaglandins (PG) cause uterine contractions and pain. Now medications with anti-PG action are being used to control cramps.

Menstruation is thus becoming less and less of a mystery and is now being recognized as a normal and healthy part of a woman's life. The true curse for far too long has been ignorance.

A Consumer's Guide to Over-the-Counter Tests

When to Be Your Own Lab Technician

EMILY GREENSPAN

Emily Greenspan is a free-lance writer specializing in health and sport topics.

FEW OF US ENJOY A VISIT TO the doctor. Routine tests seem to cost more than they should, and waiting rooms are famous for just that—endless waits. Many people have latched on to a new trend, medical testing at home, as a way to save time and money. On the shelves of your local drugstore you can find tests to help you pinpoint ovulation, a kit that suggests how to choose a child's sex by altering the timing and positions of intercourse, and tests that will tell you if you are, in fact, pregnant. If you are diabetic or have high blood pressure, there is now over-the-counter equipment you can use at home to monitor these conditions. Still other tests, like those for urinary tract infections and colorectal cancer, can help you detect symptoms between visits to the doctor. Americans are already spending more than $500 million on home-use tests each year, and additional tests for strep throat and chlamydia are on the way. New products are constantly entering the market while others just as quickly disappear. But is this do-it-yourself medicine truly beneficial? What *are* the advantages, and possible risks, of self-testing?

SELF-TEST, DON'T SELF-DIAGNOSE

The main danger of self-testing arises when consumers use the test to diagnose themselves. Doctors, knowing that no test is 100 percent accurate, evaluate test results along with information from a physical examination, a history,

and possibly other tests. Dr. Michael Policar, medical director of Planned Parenthood for Alameda and San Francisco Counties in California, warns about pregnancy testing: "It's a fallacy to think that you can make the diagnosis of pregnancy on the basis of a pregnancy test alone. The diagnosis depends on a number of factors taken together—including a positive blood or urine test *and* the finding on a pelvic examination that the uterus is soft and enlarged."

Adds Dr. James C. Hunt, chancellor of the University of Tennessee in Memphis and author of a report on self-administered blood pressure measurement: "The diagnosis of hypertension can only be made by a physician who interprets the significance of self-obtained blood pressure readings. And those who do have hypertension and see a drop in their readings should never decide to stop taking their medication without first seeing their doctor."

Another problem with home tests involves their utility in cases where a disturbing and chronic symptom is present. Some people may be reassured by a negative result on a home test, perhaps thinking that the nagging symptom will go away. In the case of ectopic pregnancy—when the embryo becomes implanted in a Fallopian tube instead of the uterus—a negative result on a pregnancy test is common, and ignoring the feeling that something is wrong can be dangerous, even fatal. Similarly, the package insert for the male test for gonorrhea states, "If you are having symptoms, discharge, or pain on urination, see your physician or local health clinic immediately for diagnosis and

treatment." Where disturbing symptoms persist, a home test is an unnecessary step. It makes more sense to see a doctor immediately.

Is self-testing, then, a good thing? The answer is a qualified yes. For example, blood pressure and glucose levels, which can rise and fall at different times of the day and in different situations, can be monitored more closely (and less expensively) at home than with isolated trips to the doctor. As a result, people with high blood pressure and diabetes who monitor their condition at home often become more aware of the effects of certain changes in diet and activity on their bodies. As they become more involved with their own health care, they may experience a psychological lift as well, since it is empowering to be able to perform a test oneself.

Fecal blood tests are usually done on three consecutive bowel movements and thus are not easily performed in a doctor's office. Even though the home tests are sometimes inaccurate, if used annually, it's estimated they could detect nearly 90 percent of bowel cancers, improving the five-year survival rate for people with these cancers from 43 percent to 84 percent. For this reason, many physicians give home kits to their patients who are over 50 years old or who have a family history of colorectal cancer.

The bottom line on home medical tests is that with proper monitoring by the FDA and some wariness on the part of the consumer, they can increase our participation in our own health care and reduce unecessary visits to physicians. But when you know you have a disturbing symptom that doesn't disappear, a visit to a doctor *is* necessary and the home test is probably a waste of time and money. The objective of home tests should not be to shun the medical establishment, but to work with physicians to ensure the best health care both in and out of the doctor's office.

To report a problem with a home test, be sure to contact both the manufacturer and the FDA at the following address: U.S. Pharmacopeial Convention, 12601 Twinbrook Parkway, Rockville, Maryland 20852; call toll free (800) 638-6725; in Maryland (301) 881-0256 (collect). For more information on medical tests, consult *The People's Book of Medical Tests*, by David S. Sobel and Tom Ferguson (Summit Books).

A CLOSER LOOK AT HOME TESTS
Ovulation Monitoring
Product names: First Response, QTest, Rabbit, Cue, Peak.

What they do: First Response and QTest measure the amount of luteinizing hormone (LH) in urine, which increases suddenly midway through the menstrual cycle, triggering ovulation. Rabbit electronically records and stores basal body temperature (BBT), which rises slightly after ovulation. Cue and Peak register changes in vaginal mucus and saliva that occur around ovulation. By monitoring these physiological changes, women can determine when pregnancy is most likely to occur.

Procedure: First Response and QTest—once a day for about a week in the middle of the menstrual cycle, liquid chemicals or a treated strip are exposed to a urine specimen. When an LH surge occurs, the urine or the strip will change color. Rabbit—each morning you take your temperature with an electronic thermometer. The result is flashed on a mini-screen, stored in a microprocessor, and the accumulated monthly data are displayed as a chart on the screen. Cue and Peak—the daily process involves touching a specialized sensor to the tongue for a few seconds and taking note of a digital readout. Subsequent vaginal readings, taken primarily to confirm oral predictions of ovulation, use the same monitor with a tampon-type sensor.

Time for results: First Response and QTest—20 to 40 minutes. Rabbit—45 to 60 seconds. Cue and Peak—10 to 20 seconds.

Cost: First Response and QTest—$25 to $30 for a one-week kit. Rabbit—$159 (not available in drugstores; consult your physician or, to order, write to Rabbit Computer Corp., 1180 South Beverly Drive, Suite 501, Los Angeles, Calif.

90035). Cue—$495, or $59 to rent (Zetek, Inc., 794 Ventura Street, Aurora, Colo. 80011). Peak—$295 (Micron Technology, Inc., 2805 East Columbia Road, Boise, Idaho 83706).

Comments: the electronic basal body thermometers represent a technological improvement over regular basal body thermometers because they take a minute or less for results and eliminate errors in reading the thermometer or in charting the results. The urine tests are slightly more accurate, because they react to the hormone responsible for ovulation, rather than to a secondary temperature change that results from the shift in the hormonal balance. But they take more time than a BBT thermometer, and may not detect LH in diluted urine. So keep liquid intake fairly constant, urinate every three hours or so, and avoid excess liquid intake just before collecting the urine. Optimally, urine samples should be collected first thing in the morning. Cue and Peak, although expensive, are the latest technology on the market. Fast and accurate, they predict ovulation five to six days in advance.

Pregnancy Tests
Product names: Answer and Answer Plus, Advance, e.p.t., First Response, QTest.

What they do: measure the amount of a hormone called human chorionic gonadotropin (HCG) in urine. This hormone is produced by the developing placenta and excreted in the urine.

Procedure: a urine sample is taken and mixed with chemicals in a test tube. With one-step tests, the solution will change color if the result is positive. In some tests, a dipstick is inserted into the mixture, rinsed, and then placed in a special developing solution. If the result is positive, the solution, or an indicator on the strip itself, will turn blue.

Time for results: 10 to 20 minutes for the color-change test; 30 minutes for the dipstick test.

Cost: about $8 to $12 for a single test, or $10 to $17 for a double test kit.

Comments: the first morning sample of urine contains the highest concentration of HCG, and therefore should give the most reliable result. Any traces of soap in the container can produce a false result. Home pregnancy tests are particularly useful for women who must wait several weeks to get a doctor's appointment. Some manufacturers report that their tests will pick up a positive result the same day as a missed period.

Urinary Tract Infections
Product names: Microstix-Nitrite Reagent Strip, Chemstrip LN.

What they do: indicate the presence of bacteria in the urinary tract. One type detects the presence of nitrites. (The nitrate in our diet is converted into nitrite by some types of bacteria.) Another type of test detects leukocytes (bacteria-fighting cells) in the urine.

Procedure: on three consecutive mornings, the pad at the end of a plastic dipstick is immersed in a urine sample. The color of the test pad is compared with a standard color chart.

Time for results: 30 seconds for nitrite dipstick; one minute for leukocyte dipstick.

Cost: from $4 for kit with three test strips to $24 for kit with 100 strips.

Comments: urinary tract infections produce symptoms of pain or burning during urination, a puslike discharge, frequent urination, or the sudden, repeated urge to urinate. If this is the first time you've experienced these symptoms, it's best to see a doctor. If, however, you are frequently bothered by urinary tract infections, or are a diaphragm user who has a burning sensation the day after sexual intercourse and wonder if the problem is simply irritation from the diaphragm or an actual bladder infection, home tests are useful. The nitrite and leukocyte tests each will catch about 90 percent of urinary tract infections. For greater accuracy, some physicians suggest using a kit like Chemstrip LN, which contains both leukocyte and nitrite tests. If results are negative but symptoms persist, see a doctor.

Blood Glucose Monitoring
Product names: Finger-sticking devices—Auto-Lancet, Autolet, Glucolet, Penlet.

Visually read test strips—Chemstrip bG, Visidex II.

Glucose meters—Accu-Chek II, Glucochek SC, Glucometer II, Glucoscan 2,000.

What they do: measure the concentration of glucose (a type of sugar) in a drop of blood.

Procedure: the user pricks a finger and places a drop of blood on a reagent pad at the end of a thin plastic test strip. The glucose in the blood reacts with the chemical on the strip to produce a color. The blood is cleaned off the strip and the color on the strip is matched to a color guide. With some kits, the matching is done visually. If you have difficulty comparing your result with the color guide, you can purchase a portable glucose meter that "reads" the strip and indicates blood glucose numerically on a digital display.

Time for results: 1 to 2 minutes.

Cost: $12 to $24 for the finger-sticking

device; $50 to $60 for a box of 100 visually read test strips; $150 to $200 for glucose meters.

Comments: both the visually read strips and the glucose meters are quite accurate—usually within 10 percent of the blood glucose levels measured in a laboratory. Normal blood glucose levels fall between 60 and 140 milligrams per deciliter, but vary depending on changes in diet and activity. If the results are inconsistent with other symptoms, test again; then consult a physician.

Screening for Bowel Cancer

Product names: Early Detector, CS-T.

What they do: detect hidden blood in stools. In Early Detector, a stool specimen is brought into contact with a reagent. Since colon cancers can bleed intermittently, the test should be done on three consecutive bowel movements to increase the chances of detecting hidden blood.

Procedure: a stool specimen is collected, or, with CS-T, a treated pad is laid in the toilet bowl. If hidden blood is present, a color change will appear.

Time for results: 30 seconds to 10 minutes.

Cost: about $7.

Comments: because there are many false positives with this test, there are diet restrictions that should be followed before testing. Also, don't use this test if you are bleeding from hemorrhoids or menstruation. There are also some false negative results with this test, usually caused by a high intake of vitamin C. Despite negative results, see a doctor if you have any other symptoms—such as unexplained weight loss.

Blood Pressure Monitoring

Product names: Marshall Electronics, Inc., distributes three types of blood pressure measuring instruments—mercury column devices, aneroid devices, and electronic devices.

What they do: measure the pressure of blood on the walls of the arteries. The measurement consists of two numbers: the systolic pressure (when the heart is in contraction) and the diastolic pressure (when the heart is relaxing).

Procedure: most kits contain a cuff, a listening device (stethoscope or microphone), and a monitoring device (sphygmomanometer). The cuff is wrapped around the arm just above the elbow and is inflated until it stops the blood flow. The stethoscope is placed on the pulse point of the artery (or the microphone inside the cuff is centered over the artery) to listen for systolic and diastolic pressures, which are heard when the air in the cuff is slowly let out and the blood starts to be pushed through the closed artery. The electronic devices will automatically read out both pressures on a digital display.

Time for results: 2 to 5 minutes.

Cost: $50 to $75 for mercury column devices, $20 to $75 for aneroid devices, and $50 to $250 for electronic models.

Comments: in people 18 to 45, normal systolic pressure is about 120 millimeters of mercury; normal diastolic pressure is near 80 millimeters. In older people, somewhat higher readings are more common. If you repeatedly get readings in which the systolic pressure is over 140 and diastolic pressure is over 90, consult a physician. Eating, drinking, or smoking before the test can influence results, as can extraneous noises. An average of three readings, five to 10 minutes apart, is more accurate than one reading. Finally, a doctor or nurse should observe your technique to make sure that you are doing the test correctly. The device should be checked for accuracy every six to 12 months against a physician's mercury column monitor. The electronic devices should be sent back to the manufacturer annually for recalibration. Regardless of results, don't stop or change blood pressure medications based on home readings without first consulting with your doctor.

Reproduction

- Pregnancy and Childbirth (Articles 18-21)
- Birth Control (Articles 22-26)

The interface of sexuality and reproduction, like so many of the other aspects of sexuality, is today being radically transformed. Contemporary awareness and practices regarding procreation comprise interesting and sometimes even alarming subject matter for our consideration in this section. While human reproduction is as old as humanity itself, there are many aspects of it that are strikingly new.

The rising cost of childbearing is leading many couples to reconsider whether or not to have a family, especially a large one. The decision of having a family is even more difficult for those couples in dual-career situations, yet two incomes may be necessary to raise and educate a child or children today. The future will undoubtedly bring increasing changes—technological, attitudinal, and socio-cultural—to traditional patterns of childbearing.

This section also addresses the issue of birth control. In light of the attitudinal change toward sex for pleasure, birth control is becoming a matter of prime importance. Even in our age of sexual enlightenment, some individuals, possibly in the height of passion, fail to correlate "having sex" with pregnancy. Before sex can become safe as well as enjoyable, people must receive thorough and accurate information regarding conception and contraception, birth and birth control. In addition to such information, it is even more crucial that individuals make a mental and emotional commitment to the use and application of the available information, facts, and methods. Only this can make every child a planned and wanted child.

Despite the relative simplicity of the above assertion, birth control has been, and remains today, an emotionally charged and fervently contested issue in American society. While opinion surveys indicate that most of the public is supportive, individuals who seek abortions often face and bear the brunt of negative stigmatization. Despite Supreme Court rulings toward greater acceptance, new religio-political groups are challenging the basic definitions of human life and its beginnings.

Many of the questions raised in this section about the new technologies of reproduction and its control are likely to remain among the most hotly debated issues for the remainder of this century. The very foundations of our pluralistic society may be challenged. We will have to await the outcome.

The first article in the *Pregnancy and Childbirth* subsection reviews the new techniques of conception. In vitro fertilization is detailed and additional technologies are explained. The next two articles deal with teen pregnancy. The first suggests reasons why teen pregnancy rates in the United States are the highest in the Western world, a record that does not make most people in the country proud. The second article provides a variety of reasons for teen pregnancy. The last article of this subsection addresses women and couples who choose to remain childless, an issue which still received only nominal socio-cultural support.

The first article in the subsection on *Birth Control* focuses on the crisis in developing contraceptives and the misunderstandings surrounding birth control. The next deals with contraception for teens. The pill is receiving more positive support, according to the article by Judy Ismach. Teenage pregnancy is considered in the next selection. The author also relates how society provides confusing messages regarding teen sexuality. The last article of this subsection is concerned with the latest in contraceptive technology—RU-486. This product, while effective in its task, raises religio-moral questions for some groups in American society.

Looking Ahead: Challenge Questions

What are some of the benefits of the new discoveries of improved reproduction? What are some of the dilemmas and problems resulting from the new reproductive technologies? Who will benefit most from the discoveries? Who will benefit least?

Does society have a reason to be optimistic about how teens are handling the consequences of their sexual activity? Why or why not?

Why is choosing not to have children such an issue? Are attitudes changing? Explain.

What can be expected of birth control in the future? Are males or females more likely to be affected by the discoveries?

What is the crisis in contraception? Why is this occurring?

If teen pregnancy isn't the real problem, as stated in Peter Scales' article, then what is?

Is RU-486 a viable form of birth control? Why or why not? What are some of its problems? Who may be affected by the problems? Why or how?

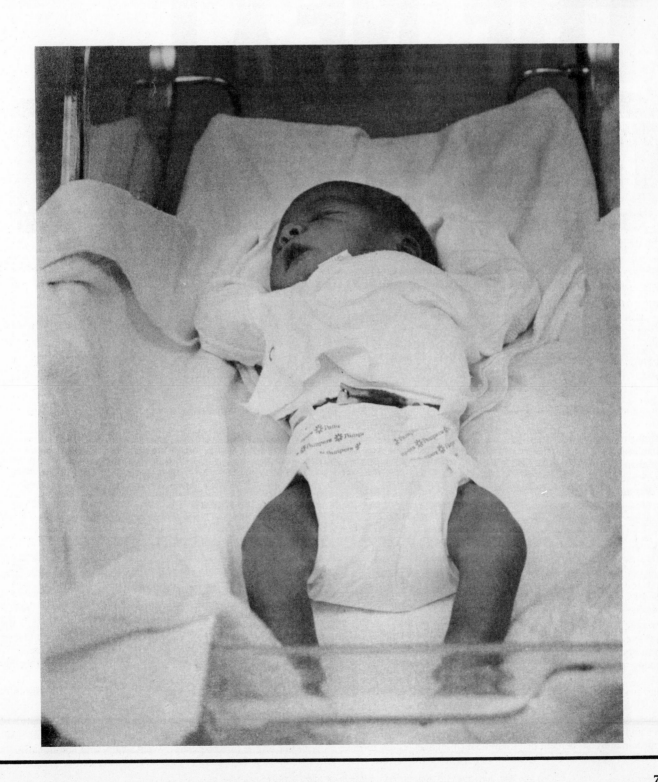

MIRACLE BABIES
THE NEXT GENERATION

MARY GARNER

It's been nine years since the birth of the first "test-tube baby," Louise Brown, rocked the world. At the time, this awesome breakthrough seemed an impossible act to follow. Yet in the intervening years, science has come up with a handful of equally astonishing infertility advances—from deep-freezing embryos to enabling women without ovaries to bear children. "Impossible" pregnancies have become a regular occurrence. The techniques are easier and increasingly successful. And with each new step, more and more fertile couples are able to bring home a baby at last.

Most recent fertility advances involve modifications of the original *in vitro* fertilization, or IVF, procedure. These improvements, coupled with the medical community's growing familiarity with the procedure, have significantly increased IVF's success rate: In the past few years, the odds that a couple will end up taking home a baby have risen from 10 percent to somewhere between 15 and 30 percent (depending on the program), according to John J. Stangel, M.D., program medical director of IVF Australia—a clinic in Port Chester, New York, that's a spin-off of the original pacesetting IVF program at Monash University in Melbourne, Australia. Both places are among the most successful in the world. (A side note on success rates: Some centers base their figures on the number of women who first test positive for pregnancy—not pregnancies that have been ongoing. This can be misleading if you don't expect it since, for unknown reasons, about 25 percent of IVF pregnancies end in spontaneous abortion. Not bad, though, considering approximately 20 percent of "traditional" pregnancies do, too.)

Stunning breakthroughs that are turning infertile couples into families

Couples most likely to benefit from recent IVF advances are those in which 1) the woman's fallopian tubes are damaged or missing (IVF bypasses the need for them altogether); or 2) the man's sperm are too sparse or too sluggish (the technique places sperm next to the egg instead of relying on them to make it through the vagina, cervix, uterus and up into the egg-harboring fallopian tubes on their own).

But real progress is being made with other fertility troubles too—from women who don't ovulate to men with sperm "stranded" inside their body. To top it off, there are a handful of exciting innovations which make existing procedures dramatically easier on the infertile couple—physically *and* emotionally.

New ways "infertile" women are becoming mothers...

One of the most welcome IVF-related advances is known as *ultrasound-guided egg retrieval*. It takes much less of a toll on the infertile woman than the traditional approach because eggs are "harvested" without a surgical incision.

Instead, the doctor uses an ultrasound picture (a video-screen image of the inside of the abdomen painlessly "drawn" by bouncing sound waves off the area) as a road map to maneuver a needle through either the abdomen, the urethra (the tube leading to the bladder) or the vaginal wall and on to the ovary. The eggs are gently drawn from their follicles—tiny bubbles that surface on the ovary as eggs mature—into the needle.

Although this *sounds* uncomfortable, hundreds of women say it's not, according to Dr. Stangel. That's largely because there is no incision, so less tissue is damaged, fewer nerves are disturbed. No incision also means no stitches or scar. Generally, for the vaginal or urethral route, a sedative is all that's needed. If the needle is passed through the more sensitive abdominal wall, a local anesthetic is used as well, according to Mary Martin, M.D., director of the University of California, San Francisco, School of Medicine's IVF program. The fact that egg-gathering is done under a local (at most) also means there isn't the post-op grogginess or nausea associated with general anesthesia.

Most importantly, the technique enables women whose abdomens are clogged with scar tissue (from things like an old infection or previous surgery) to benefit from IVF. In the past, doctors couldn't see to navigate through a scarred pelvis. But scars are virtually invisible on ultrasound (which is designed to picture structures with fluid or spaces between them, like the ovaries). In addition, needles passed through the vagina approach the ovaries from beneath (instead of through the abdomen from above), where there's usually not much scar tissue to begin with. So far, no-surgery egg-gathering is available in about 25 fertility centers, and it's gaining ground fast.

Frozen embryos—having a second chance on hold

Sounds like science fiction, but a couple of places in the U.S. are freezing embryos in conjunction with IVF. The idea behind this technique, known as *cryopreservation,* is to fertilize (with sperm, in a petri dish) *all* of the eggs that are gathered in one harvesting, but to transfer only some of the resulting embryos to the womb. The rest are then frozen in case no pregnancy is achieved the first time around. (If pregnancy is ever going to occur, it usually takes about four tries.)

This is an important advance since experience has shown three to four embryos to be the ideal number to return to the womb. Using more increases the chance of multiple births, but *doesn't* up the odds much that one will implant. Why harvest so many eggs to begin with? Doctors collect all they can (sometimes as many as 12) since only about 70 to 80 percent of them will successfully become fertilized.

Another advantage of freezing: "Saving" embryos spares a woman egg-gathering attempts, says Dr. Stangel. Thus, the emotional and physical difficulty associated with the surgical procedure, and the mostly emotional stress of the ultrasound version, are kept to a minimum.

The freezing itself is surprisingly straightforward. The embryos are immersed in a fluid designed to insulate their cells from damage. They're then cooled to -230°F and kept chilled indefinitely in a vat of liquid nitrogen.

About 60 percent of embryos survive regardless of how long they've been frozen. (For unknown reasons, the rest fragment.) But should we worry that those that make it through a freeze/thaw cycle are at high risk for miscarriage and/or birth defects? "We suspect only the hardiest embryos will survive, meaning they'll be strong and likely to develop normally," says Dr. Stangel. Because the technique is cutting-edge new, so far in the U.S. there's been only one healthy birth associated with it, although a handful of women are pregnant now.

Another way scientists hope to make each egg-gathering go further: splitting fertilized eggs in half to create two separate but genetically identical embryos. Sounds fantastic, but if it's done within a couple days of fertilization, both halves develop perfectly normally. In fact, this is exactly what happens naturally in the case of identical twins. The technique is still being tested in animals, says Eberhard Muechler, M.D., director of the IVF program, the University of Rochester School of Medicine and Dentistry, New York.

Borrowing eggs—for women who can't make their own

Amazingly enough, now women without any ovaries to produce eggs can actually get pregnant via a procedure called *ovum transfer* (OT). This "donor egg" technique can also be useful for women whose ovaries don't trigger ovulation, whose eggs have been damaged by radiation therapy or who are concerned about passing on a genetic disease. It may also be worth a shot if traditional IVF fails: There is a slight chance IVF didn't work because of an undetectable defect in the woman's eggs, a stumbling block ovum transfer neatly sidesteps.

The technique starts off with the infertile woman taking hormones 1) to synchronize her cycle with that of the egg donor and 2) to ready her uterus to receive an embryo when the transfer takes place. At ovulation, the donor is inseminated with the partner's sperm by way of a tube that is wended painlessly through the vagina and cervix. Five days later, the egg donor's uterus is sprayed with fluid and then gently "washed" in hope of recovering an embryo.

The donor is never officially pregnant because fertilized eggs don't embed on the wall of the uterus until the sixth day after conception, explains John E. Buster, M.D., professor of obstetrics and gynecology, University of Tennessee School of Medicine, Memphis, who helped pioneer the procedure. (To be on the safe side, though, the donor woman is given a dose of hormones after her uterus has been washed. This ensures that, in the unlikely event an embryo does implant, it will be absorbed by the uterine wall and shed during menstruation.)

Next, the embryo is transferred to the infertile woman's uterus—by way of a thin tube slipped through the vagina. At this point, it's natural for a woman's hormones to kick in and maintain the pregnancy (although some centers augment this with hormone shots). Women with faulty or no ovaries, though, must be given compensatory hormones throughout the pregnancy.

Because the fertilized egg is both rinsed out of the donor's uterus *and* slipped into the infertile woman's womb without a surgical cut, the procedure is painless for everyone involved. Sparing the scalpel makes it cheaper, too: $2,000 per shot, vs. up to $5,000 for IVF.

So far OT is being done in only a handful of places, and has a success rate of just 10 percent. While the numbers look small, experts are in the process of developing refinements they're confident will up the success odds.

Borrowing a uterus—when there is an egg, but no place to grow it

Even newer on the scene is a technique designed to help a slightly different group of women—those with healthy ovaries but no uterus (either because they were born without one, or because it had to be surgically removed). This "host uterus" technique begins like IVF in that the infertile couple's egg and sperm are paired in a petri dish. Here's the twist: Should fertilization take place, the embryo is transferred to another woman's uterus in hope that she will be able to carry it to term.

While this sounds a lot like currently controversial surrogate motherhood, there's one major, significant difference: The baby is genetically related to both halves of the infertile couple—*not* to the woman who carries the baby, explains James Goldfarb, M.D., who's head of IVF at Mount Sinai Medical Center in Cleveland. (Scientifically, surrogate motherhood isn't even a new procedure. All it involves, from a medical standpoint, is artificial insemination, which has been around for many years.) Because the "host uterus" technique is so new, only one baby has been born this way so far.

The "gift" technique—doctor-aided "natural" fertilization

Another IVF spin-off is known as *gamete intrafallopian tube transfer,* or GIFT. As with IVF, the woman takes fertility drugs to stimulate extra egg production and, just before ovulation, the eggs are retrieved via a laparoscope, a slender tube introduced into the body via a tiny surgical cut. Then, while the scope is *still in place*, the eggs are transferred to a dish and the sperm added in. Within minutes, the egg/sperm mixture is slipped *back* through the laparoscope and into the fallopian tube for fertilization.

When GIFT first came on the scene several years ago, its pioneers hoped it would be more successful than IVF because fertilization occurs in the fallopian tubes, as it does naturally, not in a dish. As it's turned out, only a few experts have had better-than-IVF results. Others claim GIFT is on par with or less successful than IVF.

In any case, GIFT is easier on the woman than laparoscopic IVF since it's a one-step procedure. IVF requires a return trip to have the embryos transferred to the womb. But there are drawbacks: 1) GIFT can only be done in women whose tubes aren't damaged; 2) it requires a laparoscopy when some places can provide nonsurgical egg retrieval; and 3) if pregnancy doesn't occur, there's no way to figure out (and try to correct) what went wrong. Did the egg never get fertilized? Did it get fertilized, but fail to make it to the uterus, or to implant on the uterine wall?

How "infertile" men are becoming fathers

Half of all infertility can be chalked up to faulty sperm—there are too few of them or they're sluggish swimmers, for example. These problems lead to infertility since, as nature's law of averages has it, it takes millions of vigorous, healthy sperm in order for just one to penetrate an egg. Recently, there have been a couple of advances that help diagnose sperm problems more effectively. And pinpointing the problem is the first step toward correcting it.

First off, there's *videomicrography.* Traditionally, scientists sized up sperm samples simply by looking at them under a microscope—a rather inexact approach. With this new technique, a videocamera records a continuous picture of highly magnified sperm while a computer tracks precisely how many sperm there

> A carriage full of hope: This year more fertility-troubled couples became parents than last— and *next* year's bound to beat every record so far

are and how fast they're swimming. That way doctors can better diagnose whether infertility is a result of inadequate sperm.

Another technique used to size up sperm's viability is known as the *hamster penetration test.* Sperm are tossed in with a hamster's egg, since hamster eggs are the only nonhuman animal eggs that can be fertilized by human sperm. If the human sperm are not able to fertilize the animal egg, they will most likely be unable to penetrate a human egg. If they can, the doctor knows to look elsewhere for the source of fertility trouble, explains Neri Laufer, M.D., director of the IVF program at Mount Sinai Medical Center in New York City.

Medical muscle for sluggish sperm

Should sperm be deemed defective, there are several exciting ways scientists have devised to get around the problem. The first three of the following techniques are still in the animal-testing stages; the last two have just gone into human trials.

1. *Easy-access eggs:* With the *zona drilling* technique, a doctor uses a high-powered microscope and a needle finer than a human hair to deposit a drop of acid on an egg. The acid eats away a tiny window of the egg's protective coating, or zona, upping the odds a slow-swimming or sparse sperm sample will result in fertilization. But will this technique cause birth defects by allowing weak sperm to penetrate an egg? "While more studies are needed, so far no defective births have occurred," reports Jon W. Gordon, M.D., associate professor in the department of obstetrics, gynecology and reproductive science at Mount Sinai Medical Center in New York City.

2. *Direct injection:* Again, tiny instruments and strong magnification are used, but this time a sperm is injected right into an egg. This makes fertilization possible with only *one* sperm, instead of the usual *millions*.

3. *Sperm "uppers":* Scientists have also been incubating sperm with stimulants to increase motility. Details are sketchy since researchers haven't completed their studies or officially reported

on their work so far, says Donna Howlett, senior embryologist, IVF Australia, Port Chester, New York.

4. *Help for stranded sperm:* Sometimes sperm, while perfectly healthy, get trapped inside the body—when, for example, scar tissue from sterilization or cancer surgery closes off the tubes through which sperm travel during ejaculation. Recently, researchers at the IVF program in Melbourne have gotten around this problem by surgically extracting sperm from the body. So far, there's been one baby born with sperm retrieved this way.

5. *Electric ejaculation:* Stateside, there's a new procedure that's enabled four men who are paralyzed from the waist down (and therefore can't ejaculate at all) to father children. The technique involves sliding a probe into the rectum and passing a gentle electric current through it. (Sounds awful, but men reported feeling only a mild sensation of pressure.) The current simply "jump-starts" the nerves responsible for ejaculation into action, explains Carol J. Bennett, M.D., instructor of urology, University of Michigan Medical Center, Ann Arbor.

Recent fertility advances have targeted men and women, the majority of infertile couples and the select few. They can be time-consuming, expensive, and physically and emotionally draining. They've also, in the end, brought the unmatchable joy of a child to thousands of couples who would otherwise have none. And even those couples who can't yet be helped by current techniques can have hope—that as science continues to make strides, they might be among those the *next* breakthrough will turn into a family.

New Study of Teenage Pregnancy

36 Other Developed Countries Suggests Reasons why U.S. Teen Pregnancy Rates are the Highest in the Western World

Jane Murray and Barbara Parks

The United States leads nearly all other developed nations of the world in rates of teenage pregnancy, abortion and childbearing. The rates for white U.S. teenagers alone are much higher than those in most industrialized nations with similar rates of teenage sexual activity. Moreover, the maximum difference in birthrates between the U.S. and other countries occurs among the most vulnerable teenagers, girls under 15. The U.S. is the only developed country where teenage pregnancy has been *increasing* in recent years, with the U.S. rate for 15-19-year-olds standing at 96 per 1,000 (83 per 1,000 for whites) compared to 14 per 1,000 in the Netherlands, 35 in Sweden, 43 in France, 44 in Canada and 45 in England and Wales. It is notable that the teenage abortion rate *alone* in the U.S. is as high as or higher than the combined abortion and birthrates of any of these countries. Those developed countries with the most liberal attitudes toward sex, the most easily accessible contraceptive services for teenagers and the most effective formal and informal programs for sex education have the *lowest* rates of teenage pregnancy, abortion and childbearing.

These are among the major findings of a massive comparative study of teenage sexual activity and fertility in the United States and 36 other developed countries, performed during the last year and a half by the Alan Guttmacher Institute (AGI), with the assistance of researchers from Princeton University's Office of Population Research, and funded by the Ford Foundation. The study was undertaken to explore the reasons for disparities between U.S. teenage pregnancy rates and those of other countries, and to see if any lessons could be drawn from the experience of countries with lower rates that might be applied in the U.S. The study report, released today, will be published in the upcoming issue of *Family Planning Perspectives,* the bi-monthly professional journal of the Institute.

The findings emerged from a two-stage study, the first a statistical examination of factors associated with adolescent fertility in 37 developed countries, and the second an in-depth examination of the issue in the United States and five approximately comparable countries: Sweden, France, the Netherlands, England and Wales, and Canada. The statistical study showed that low levels of socio-economic development, pro-natalist fertility policies, generous maternity leaves and benefits, and early marriage are associated with high levels of teenage fertility, a pattern which the United States, despite its high teenage fertility rates, does not fit.

Several other factors related to high teenage fertility, however, more closely align with the profile of the United States, including a lack of openness about sex in the society, a relatively inequitable distribution of income to the poorest 20 percent of the population, a high degree of religiosity, and restrictions on teenagers' access to contraception and teaching about birth control in the schools.

The second stage of the study, which looked at these and other factors in the five selected countries and the United States, yielded a mass of evidence that contradicts or refutes many widely-held beliefs in this country about the determinants of teenage pregnancy:

- Young teenagers in these other countries are *not* too immature to use contraceptives effectively;
- The availability of welfare benefits and services (in all five countries, more generous than those in the U.S.) does *not* act as an inducement to teenagers to have babies;
- Low teenage birthrates in these other countries are *not* achieved by greater recourse to abortion—on the contrary, all have much lower teenage abortion rates than the U.S.;
- Teenage pregnancy rates are *lower* in countries with *greater* availability of birth control and sex education;
- Teenage pregnancy in the U.S. is *not* primarily a black phenomenon, since white rates alone far outstrip those of the other five countries, which themselves have sizable minority populations with disproportionately high fertility;
- High teenage pregnancy in the U.S. cannot be ascribed to teenage unemployment, since unemployment among the young is a very serious problem in all the countries studied.

In all five countries, government actions have demonstrated a determination to minimize the incidence of teenage pregnancy, abortion and childbearing, though each has developed its own unique approach to the problem. In the Netherlands, the country with the lowest rates of any of the five, for example, sex education in the schools is perfunctory, but clear, complete information about contraception is widely promulgated in all the media, and mobile sex education teams operate under the auspices of a government-subsidized family planning association. In Sweden, which liberalized its abortion laws in 1975, a concerted effort was made to assure that teenage abortion rates did not rise as a result, with the primary vehicle being a link between schools and contraceptive clinic services for adolescents (as a result, the teenage abortion rate *declined* dramatically after 1975.) More remarkable,

however, are the similarities in the policies and programs of the five countries. All make confidential, free or virtually free contraceptive services easily accessible to teenagers. In all, the pill is accepted by the medical profession as the most appropriate method for teenagers and is widely prescribed, often without the requirement of a pelvic examination. In all, abortion services for teenagers are free or subsidized. In all but the Netherlands and Canada, there is a national policy encouraging (in the case of Sweden, requiring) sex education in the schools.

The authors note that a number of other characteristics shared by the five study countries may have contributed to their success in developing effective policies and programs for achieving lower rates of teenage pregnancies, abortions and births than those found in the United States. All appear to be more tolerant of teenage sexual activity than the United States and, according to measures used in the study, may be considered more open about sex in general. In each, however, there is a broad consensus that teenage *pregnancy* is undesirable and that teenagers require help in avoiding pregnancy. In all the countries, the governments have perceived their responsibility to be the provision of contraceptive services to sexually-active teenagers, and in France, the Netherlands and Sweden, the decision to develop such services was specifically linked to the desire to minimize abortions among teenagers. In no country has the government attempted to reduce or eliminate teenage sexual activity or placed any restrictions on confidential access to birth control.

The authors conclude that, though the specific approaches used vary from country to country, increasing the legitimacy and availability of contraception and sex education (in its broadest sense) has been effective in reducing teenage pregnancy rates in other developed countries, and that there is no reason to believe that such an approach would not be successful in the United States. They note that "American teenagers at present have inherited the worst of all possible worlds regarding their exposure to messages about sex. [The media] tell them that sex is romantic, exciting, titillating . . . yet at the same time [they] get the message that good girls should say no. Almost nothing they see or hear about sex informs them about contraception or the importance of avoiding pregnancy."

Young, Innocent and Pregnant

*TEENAGERS GET PREGNANT FOR A VARIETY OF REASONS,
FROM AMBIVALENCE AND IGNORANCE ABOUT SEX
TO WANTING TO FILL A VOID IN THEIR LIVES.*

ELIZABETH STARK

*Elizabeth Stark is an assistant editor
at* Psychology Today.

One out of ten teenage girls in the United States becomes pregnant every year and almost half of these pregnancies result in births— 30,000 of them to girls under the age of 15.

Part of the reason for the high rate of teenage pregnancy is obvious: Teenagers are becoming sexually active at younger ages. During the 1970s, the number of sexually active teenagers increased by two-thirds. Today, among 15- to 17-year-olds in this country, almost half of the boys and a third of the girls are sexually active.

Unfortunately, teenagers' sense of responsibility and ability to plan for the future have not kept pace with their sexual sophistication. Only 14 percent of teenage girls use contraceptives the first time they have intercourse. Most wait until they have been sexually active for nine months or more before they visit a birth-control clinic. And a major reason for a visit to a clinic is for a pregnancy test.

Among teenagers who do use contraceptives, many depend on such unreliable methods as withdrawal or rhythm. All in all, nearly two-thirds of unwed sexually active teenage girls either never or inconsistently practice birth control. Why are teenagers so lax about using contraception?

"The first time, it was like totally out of the blue.... I mean, you don't know it's coming, so how are you to be prepared?" a 16-year-old girl told Ellen Kisker, a demographer at the Office of Population Research at Princeton University.

"If I did [use a contraceptive] then I'd have sex more. Then it would be too easy.... I don't feel it's right. I haven't been raised that way," said another teenager, reflecting a major reason for the delay in obtaining contraceptives—ambivalence. As Karen Pittman, a sociologist at the Children's Defense Fund in Washington, D.C., explains it, "Many teenagers can reconcile their sexual activity if it's spontaneous or unplanned."

Studies that support this idea have been conducted by psychologists Donn Byrne, at the State University of New York in Albany, and William Fisher, at the University of Western Ontario in London, Ontario. In many cases, they find, a teenager's desire for completely spontaneous sex is tied to the belief that being "swept off your feet" or "carried away" is forgivable, but having premeditated sex is not. According to Fisher, "many adolescents are comfortable enough to have intercourse, especially with the aid of lust, love or liquor, but they are not comfortable enough to plan for it in advance."

Byrne and Fisher found that college students with negative attitudes toward sex were less likely to use birth control than those with more positive attitudes. The reason those who have negative attitudes are more likely to risk unwanted pregnancy, Byrne and Fisher believe, is that their negative feelings, while not strong enough to inhibit them from having sex, prevent them from going through the steps necessary to use contraception. They deny the possibility that sex may occur, are too embarrassed to get birth control or to discuss it with their partners and are inhibited about using birth-control devices. "The more guilt and anxiety you have about sex, the less likely you are to use contraception," Byrne says.

Young teenagers are simply not capable of internalizing contraceptive information, according to Irma Hilton, a psychologist at the Ferkauf Graduate School of Psychology. She believes that "young people just don't have the psychological strength to recognize the consequences of their actions." Teenagers tend to be impulsive and have trouble deferring gratification and making long-range plans, Hilton says. She points out that the older teenagers are when they initiate sexual activity, the more likely they will be to use contraceptives.

Another reason, according to Hilton, is that "maybe deep down they want to get pregnant." For those who feel isolated, the prospect of a baby offers the possibility of someone to love. Pregnancy also brings attention to a girl who may be feeling neglected. The ploy of entrapping a reluctant suitor may motivate some teenagers. Others may see pregnancy as a way to assert their independence from their parents or to become their mothers' equal. Some may want to keep up with their pregnant girlfriends. Unfortunately, says Hilton, most teenage girls who see someone else's cute, cuddly baby are in for a rude awakening when their own baby cries through the night and interferes with their social life.

Gerard Kitzi, director of the Adolescent Resources Corporation in Kansas City, Missouri, which runs three school-based health clinics, agrees that many teenage pregnancies are on some level deliberate. He says that they have teenagers who come in for a pregnancy test and "are disappointed when the test is negative."

And it is not only teenage girls who may desire a child. In one study Hilton found that teenage fathers were generally happy about their girlfriend's pregnancy, whether or not they had any intention of caring for the child. They felt that the pregnancy affirmed their manhood.

Many of the motivations for a teenage pregnancy are born of hopeless-

MANY ADOLESCENTS ARE COMFORTABLE ENOUGH TO HAVE SEX, BUT ARE NOT COMFORTABLE ENOUGH TO PLAN FOR IT.

ness, the feeling that opportunities in life are few and limited and one might as well have a baby as do anything else, according to Fisher. These feelings, many experts believe, are most common among lower-income teenagers who see success in school or work as impossibilities for themselves. "They're people who've fallen out of the system," Fisher says. Studies have shown that teenagers who are behind academically in school are three times more likely to become unwed parents.

"The bottom line is kids don't feel good about themselves, especially those in lower-socioeconomic groups, who have no feeling of the future," says Kitzi. "So they do something that for them seems 'temporary': go out and start a family."

In addition, Hilton believes that lower-income teenagers are more likely to become pregnant because of attitudes within the family. According to her studies, a tolerant family attitude toward early sexual activity and pregnancy predicts high rates of teenage pregnancy. But if a teenage girl has a good relationship with her mother and

SOME KIDS DON'T FEEL GOOD ABOUT THEMSELVES, SO THEY GO OUT AND DO SOMETHING THAT FOR THEM SEEMS TEMPORARY: START A FAMILY.

if her mother is opposed to teenage pregnancy, it is less likely.

The first step in combatting teenage pregnancy, many experts agree, is teaching children about sex and sexuality from an early age. Although some school administrators claim that parents are opposed to sex education, 85 percent of the people polled by Louis Harris in the summer of 1985 said they wanted sex education taught in the schools. In addition, 78 percent said that television should air messages about birth control, and 67 percent thought that schools should establish links with family-planning clinics so that teenagers can obtain and learn about contraceptives.

Between 60 and 75 percent of students in this country receive some type of sex education before they graduate from high school, but the effectiveness and quality of these classes are questionable, according to Douglas Kirby, director of the Center for Population Options. Many schools that claim to offer sex education just provide one biology or health class on basic reproduction and do not address the real questions teenagers have about sex. (See "What Kids Need to Know," this issue.) Not all programs discuss birth control, and even when they do, they are unlikely to affect teenagers' use of contraception.

The most effective sex-education classes don't just teach basic reproduction and contraception; they discuss dating and relationships, as well as beliefs and life goals, according to Kirby, who did an evaluation of 13 sex-education programs in the United States. The attempt in the past to teach sex education free of values may have been a mistake, Kirby says. He believes it is important to discuss basic values such as "all people should be treated with respect and dignity" and "no one should use subtle pressure or physical force to get someone else to engage in unwanted sexual activity."

Although these sorts of sex-education classes appear to help, they are most effective in reducing teenage pregnancies and births when combined with the resources of a clinic, according to Kirby's report.

There are about 50 school-based clinics in the country, and many of them show promise in reducing pregnancy rates and keeping teenage mothers from dropping out of school or becoming pregnant again. The prototype of such clinics, the St. Paul Maternal and Infant Care Program in St. Paul, Minnesota, began its school-based clinic more than a decade ago. It was originally set up to offer prenatal and postpartum care to pregnant teenagers at an inner-city high school. The focus soon shifted to preventing pregnancies by offering contraceptive counseling, but students were reluctant to attend since "there was no question why someone was going in there," says Ann Ricketts, program administrator. So the clinic quickly expanded to include more health services, such as athletic and college physicals, immunizations and weight-control programs, to broaden its appeal and to encourage more teenagers to visit.

There are now four school-based clinics in St. Paul. Each has a core group made up of a nurse practitioner, social worker and technician. A nutritionist, pediatric nurse, pediatrician and obstetrician visit once a week. The clinics offer sex-education courses in the school, and participation in the clinics is completely voluntary, confidential and free for all students.

The clinics have helped reduce pregnancies among their students by more than 50 percent, have kept pregnant teenagers from dropping out of school (80 percent return to school and graduate after their delivery) and have increased teenagers' use of contraceptives. Most impressive, the percentage of repeat pregnancies among students is less than 2 percent.

Laurie Schwab Zabin, director of the Social Science Fertility Research Unit at the Johns Hopkins School of Medicine, and her colleagues recently completed an evaluation of an adolescent pregnancy prevention program that ran for three years in Baltimore's inner city. The health program was based in two schools—a junior and senior high. A social worker and a nurse practitioner taught sex-education classes in the schools and provided birth-control information and devices at the nearby clinics. In addition, seven "peer resources" students publicized the centers and acted as counselors. The program was extremely successful. Among high school students involved with the program for at least two years, the pregnancy rate decreased by 30 percent, while the rates rose 58 percent at similar schools in the area, according to Zabin.

Another encouraging finding was

SOME SCHOOLS THAT CLAIM TO OFFER SEX EDUCATION JUST PROVIDE ONE BIOLOGY OR HEALTH CLASS ON BASIC REPRODUCTION.

the high attendance at the clinic of boys, especially at the junior high school level. Various researchers have pointed out the importance of getting teenage boys motivated to use contraception since two of the most popular methods among teenagers, condoms and withdrawal, depend on male cooperation. Many have claimed that it's impossible to get young men interested in practicing contraception, but Zabin says that this isn't true "if you get them interested at young ages."

One result of the program, which surprised some, was that those who participated in it became sexually active on average seven months later than did teenagers attending schools with no such programs. According to Zabin this "once and for all refutes the notion that these sorts of programs encourage sex."

She explains that "the staff was willing to tell kids that they thought sex was inappropriate at young ages. It was discussed in the context of future goals. We tried to develop values in these kids. The focus was 'make a life for yourself before you make another life.'"

TEENAGERS AT ONE SCHOOL-BASED CLINIC BECAME SEXUALLY ACTIVE LATER THAN THOSE WITHOUT SUCH PROGRAMS.

Various programs around the country encourage teenagers to "say no" to sex. One called "Will Power/Won't Power" helps 12- to 14-year-olds deal with the pressures of becoming sexually active and increases their assertiveness and skills in saying "no." In other programs teenagers learn responses to come-ons and pressures to have sex by role-playing and following scripts. But a few researchers question the effectiveness of such programs.

"I'm not saying it's a bad idea," says Byrne. "Society might be a better place for it. But in our present society with movies, TV and magazines glamorizing sex, the idea of just telling kids to say no is not realistic."

Pittman believes simply telling teenagers to say no is "naïve as a single strategy, but can be important as one of many strategies, especially among younger teenagers. There are teens who didn't want to do it but were pushed into it. We should support those teens who don't want to be sexually active."

Fisher suggests that teenagers who aren't ready for sexual activity should be encouraged to pursue "virginity with affection," in which they achieve orgasm without intercourse. Various other programs have promoted the same sort of idea, which is sometimes referred to as "outercourse."

Fisher also believes that society needs to develop fantasies that involve birth control. Most of our fantasies don't include contraception, he says, and if they do they're often "bad" fantasies, as in the awkwardness of buying condoms in *Summer of '42* or the horror of having a parent discover a diaphragm, as in *Good-bye Columbus.* "It's possible to replace those bad fantasies with good ones," he says. But he admits that this is not the total solution, especially among lower-income teenagers. "They need the possibility of jobs and a future. No amount of pro-contraception fantasy can change that," he says.

Almost everyone who has looked at the problem agrees that poverty-stricken teenagers need to know that opportunities await them before they can be motivated to avoid pregnancy. As Pittman puts it, "all kids don't have equally compelling reasons to delay parenthood." She believes that programs that help increase teenagers' self-esteem and their abilities to succeed in the working world will lower teen pregnancy rates. If they feel valued as human beings they will be less likely to get pregnant to fill a void in their lives.

According to Pittman, the movement to help these teenagers find positive alternatives to pregnancy must go beyond the schools into churches, youth groups, summer camps, recreation centers, after-school centers and of course the home—any place where a teenager's self-esteem can be bolstered and where he or she can be offered possibilities for the future.

"The more teens, male or female, think they have to lose with a pregnancy," says Pittman, "the more likely they will try to avoid parenthood."

TRAGIC CONSEQUENCES

Women have always had children while still in their teens (although usually their late teens), but until recently it wasn't economically as important for them to finish school or to be able to earn a living. Chances were they would marry the fathers (if they weren't already married), who would then support them, or else they would put the baby up for adoption. But today only one-third of pregnant teenage girls marry the fathers of their children and few consider adoption.

As a result of illegitimate births, teenage mothers usually drop out of high school and are unable to find jobs to support their children; unmarried teenage fathers rarely contribute financially to their children's upbringing. Families headed by young mothers are seven times more likely to be living below the poverty level than other families, according to the Alan Guttmacher Institute.

Even if teenagers do marry, they usually have a hard time supporting themselves. Among married couples younger than 25, those with children are four times as likely to be poor as childless young couples, according to the Children's Defense Fund in Washington, D.C. On top of that, teenage marriages

A BLACK PROBLEM?

In 1983 the birth rate for unmarried black teenagers was 86 per 1,000; for unmarried white teenagers it was 19 per 1,000, according to the National Center for Health Statistics (NCHS). Despite this, Karen Pittman, a sociologist at the Children's Defense Fund in Washington, D.C., is opposed to labeling teenage pregnancy a "black" problem. "It's not a cultural phenomenon," she says, "it's an economic one."

It is the circumstances of poverty that encourage teenage pregnancy, Pittman claims, pointing out that "no one has looked at these data from an economic standpoint."

In addition, birth rates have been declining among unmarried black teenagers, while they have been increasing among unmarried white teens, according to Stephanie Ventura, a statistician at the NCHS. The birth rates for unmarried white teenagers increased by 40 to 65 percent between 1970 and 1981 while the birth rate dropped by 14 percent among unmarried black teen-

agers, according to Ventura.

In fact, the recent rate of increase in sexual activity has been highest among white adolescent girls, whose sexual activity almost doubled during the 1970s, according to the Alan Guttmacher Institute, a private New York corporation that does research on family-planning issues. A recent study from the Guttmacher Institute points out that even if the pregnancy rates of white teenagers are taken alone, they are still higher than the teenage pregnancy rates in other developed nations.

The teenage pregnancy rate in the United States is almost twice that for France, England and Canada, three times that of Sweden and seven times that of the Netherlands. Teenagers in these countries are just as sexually active as teenagers in the United States, the study claims, but they have easier access to birth control and sex education. Unlike us, the Europeans do not focus on "the morality of early sexuality," the researchers say.

are a high risk for divorce. In 1983, 35 percent of all divorces involved women who married in their teens.

In addition to facing economic hardships, teenage mothers are more likely to have birth complications and are less likely to receive adequate prenatal care than are older mothers. Low-birth-weight babies and premature births, which can lead to problems such as childhood illnesses, neurological defects and mental retardation, are common to teenage mothers.

As a group, children born to teenage mothers tend to have lower IQ's than those born to women older than 20. Studies have also shown that children of teenage parents are at an increased risk for child abuse; teenage parents are often completely unprepared or too immature to care for a baby.

In about 45 percent of the cases,

pregnant teenagers have abortions, the major reason that although the teenage pregnancy rate is increasing, the birth rate has declined. In fact, about 30 percent of all abortions in this country are performed on teenagers. Although many people see abortion as preferable to teenage parenthood, it carries a host of emotional consequences, aside from any moral issues. Teenagers often don't seek abortions until late in the pregnancy, increasing the risk of complications and emotional distress.

In addition to the dire individual consequences of teenage pregnancy is the economic burden on society as a whole. According to the Center for Population Options in Washington, D.C., teenage childbearing cost the United States $16.65 billion in 1985.

Saying No to Motherhood

You like babies. You're the last person who can carry on the family genes. You think it's selfish to not have children. Still, something deep down inside you votes against it. Deciding against having children is a relatively recent option for women. With this advice, you can examine your options practically and emotionally and learn how to live with your choice.

VICKI LINDNER

Vicki Lindner is a freelance and fiction writer and the coauthor of Unbalanced Accounts: Why Women Are Still Afraid of Money.

I don't remember when I first realized I didn't have an instinctive drive to give birth to a baby. When I was a child, I played with dolls, but I saw myself not as their mother but as their creative prime mover. If someone had asked me if I expected to marry and have children, I would have said *yes*, because that was what all girls raised in the fifties did when they grew up. I saw no adult women in my New Jersey suburb who were doing otherwise.

When I was 28, I became pregnant while living and working in Japan. In Japan at that time, birth control pills, which I'd run out of while traveling through Asia, were illegal, and the easiest to obtain form of contraception was a cheap abortion. The father and I were in love. Months later, when our transcultural romance came to its confusing close, he looked at me with bewildered eyes and asked, "Why didn't you want to have the baby?" I'd had the nausea, lethargy, and inexplicable terror in my gut extracted like an aching tooth; I'd never thought of *it* as a child.

As I edged into my 30s, and friends began to marry and have children, no biological clock ticked inside me. Either I hadn't grown up yet or I hadn't grown up to be like other women. About the time the proverbial clock should have been sounding a shrill alarm—age 36— my younger brother married a woman who didn't opt for motherhood either. So certain was she that she wouldn't change her mind that my sister-in-law had her tubes tied before she was 30. The responsibility to carry on the Lindner genes fell to me, and I didn't want it. I *wanted* to want it; I wanted to be a normal female, part of a world of close, fertile families, joyfully reproducing themselves. Instead I was a writer, living alone, creating not living beings but characters in books and short stories. On my good days, I thought of myself as a Brave New Woman in a Brave New World, paving the way for others who wished to be different. On my bad days, I felt like a neuter alien from a science-fiction novel.

I'm not sure I ever chose not to have

children. That is, I never sat down, counted up the minutes left on my biological clock, and said, "Do I or don't I?" Instead, I feel that my childlessness evolved from a series of life choices, which resulted in a lifestyle and personal temperament that are incompatible with motherhood. I'm not married. I live in a tiny, rent-controlled apartment in Manhattan, and I support my fiction by working as a freelance writer; my income is modest and often unpredictable. I need silence to work (actually, it would be more honest to say I love silence). I'm one of the rare people who like being alone, and I love travel and freedom, too. I want to learn instead of teach, and I am as hungry for new experience as any child; in that sense, I want to remain one. What would I be doing if I had a child? Who would I be? I might be somebody different, somebody more satisfied, or less satisfied, but I would not be the person I define as myself.

Sometimes I like to get off the hook by believing that childlessness chose me. My mother's pregnancies, one of which I witnessed, were nightmares of nausea and anemia. Her mother, my maternal grandmother, died at 44 of a heart attack in the ninth month of a troubled pregnancy. My mother told me the story—of how she

technology have made it possible for women not to have children, society still persuades and pressures us to believe that motherhood is a duty, a virtue, and a delight—our natural calling. Few women dared to consider childlessness, or sup-

quate, a woman who loves her career, or who needs to earn money, might reject the time-consuming responsibilities of raising children. She may look at an exhausted "supermom" friend, struggling to work and raise a child, and say, "I don't want to take this on myself." In short, women who have decided to say *no* to motherhood do not believe kids are compatible with self-fulfillment or necessary to happiness.

The woman who chooses childlessness chooses alone and may feel defensive, ambivalent, and confused, as friends and relatives pressure her to make a pro-baby decision.

had watched her mother die gasping on the floor and had run barefoot through the snow to phone the drunken rural doctor—when I was very young. Yet, it wasn't until I was 35 and searching for convincing reasons to explain my childlessness that I became aware of how these long-known facts (with buried significance) had made me fear pregnancy. For me, the maternal condition conjured specters of sickness and death.

As I write my reasons for choosing childlessness, I imagine my readers, who have bravely overcome their own reluctance and fears to produce lovable namesakes, saying, "What nonsense!" I imagine their faces, bemused, even angry, as they mutter, "Selfish! Neurotic! Doesn't want to grow up! Doesn't know what she's missing. Will die alone and lonely, buried in the sheaves of dried-up manuscript!" The truth is that I don't know whether it is the voice of my readers I hear or a voice inside myself, not yet reconciled to my unusual decision—the part of me that feels guilty! The part of me that believes I had no right to make such a choice.

Recently, I held a baby at a dinner party. I was in awe. This miraculous infant of my species, so helpless, so pliable, seemed made to fit into my body's curves, to merge with them. Too young to know the difference between her mother and other women, she reached for my breast. I handed her back quickly, saying, "I don't want to get my hormones in an uproar!" The guests all laughed, but it wasn't really a joke. Having made my choice, I am afraid that what the world has told me might be true and that a force springing from my female biology, over which I have no control, might still rise up and punish me with regrets.

Why It's So Difficult to Choose Childlessness

■ Not only does the childless choice flout centuries of tradition and social expectations, but also it is a relatively new option. (Birth control was not legally available until the 1930's, and abortion was legalized nationwide only in 1973.) Even though the law and medical

port this option, until the 1970's, when concern about the world's burgeoning population gave some a legitimate excuse to speak out. Author Betty Rollin was one. She wrote a controversial article for *Look* magazine titled, "Motherhood: Who Needs It?" Readers were outraged. "In 1970," Rollin says, "to support childlessness was equivalent to supporting communism. I wasn't antimotherhood, but I suggested that life could be good without having children. My article got more hate mail than any article *Look* had published, except for one about Hitler. People called me a monster!"

Rollin believes that it is easier to make the childless decision now than it was then. "Though pressures to have children are still very great, and there is a lot of guilt attached to not being a mother, it is not totally freakish to choose childlessness in the eighties," she says. Rollin, whose recent book, *Last Wish,* describes her terminally ill mother's suicide, believes strongly in choice—"in diversity, differences, and tolerance. Motherhood is a perfectly good choice, and nonmotherhood is a good choice too. There's no reason why we can't have both."

Why Women Choose Childlessness

■ According to Jean Veevers, a Canadian sociologist who has studied childless couples, most couples who choose childlessness believe they are opting for a pleasant lifestyle over an unpleasant one. They see child raising versus a freewheeling lifestyle as an either/or choice. *Either* they can have the freedom and money to seek experience, travel, and change or quit jobs, *or* they can commit themselves to supporting a stable family. Some, who enjoy deep intimacy with their mates, fear a child's presence would sabotage it. Others think they would sacrifice important career goals for children. As Susan Brownmiller writes in *Femininity,* "Motherhood and ambition have been seen as opposing forces for thousands of years." Since studies show that most fathers shoulder little of the burden of child care, and day-care facilities are expensive and inade-

According to experts, however, the childless choice is often made unconsciously, before we are old enough to form adult lifestyles and beliefs. Some choose childlessness because early childhood experiences or perceptions have made them see parenthood as unrewarding or threatening. Some view pregnancy and birth as repulsive, frightening, or, as I do, dangerous. "They do not see their bodies as being sturdy and resilient," says Lois Kennedy, a New York City psychotherapist. "They do not believe they will survive physical changes."

Others reject parenting because they feel their parents were less happy or prosperous because they had large families and devoted their lives to their offspring. Modern women may feel that their own mothers would have enjoyed richer lives if their interests and talents hadn't been submerged by domestic duties. According to Kennedy, mothers who do not see their own womanhood in a positive light, or who resent their maternal roles, communicate a negative sense of what it meant to be a woman to their daughters. These daughters often identify with their fathers and reject traditional female activities—including having children.

On the positive side, the childless may have known "Auntie Mames," who lived intriguing lives without children. They grew up more able to see themselves as nonmothers than did women without inspirational role models.

Making the Decision

■ The social push to have children is strong, and there are no support groups to help the childless. (The one that existed, the National Alliance for Optional Parenthood, is now defunct.) As a result, the woman who chooses childlessness chooses alone and may feel defensive, ambivalent, and confused, as friends and relatives pressure her to make a pro-baby decision. Instead of regarding her choice as positive or inevitable, she is tempted to blame it on others or on herself. Some defend their own lifestyles by downgrading mothers. "Isn't it better to be doing what I'm doing," they ask, "than scraping Gerber's off the walls?" Others blame children themselves for their lack of desire to have them: kids are noisy, irritating, and expensive. Who would want one? Some say their mates would be terrible fathers. Most of the childless women I interviewed say their own negative qualities—impatience or bad tempers—would make them unfit mothers. Others ask, who would want to raise a child in such an unpredictable and dangerous world? Sometimes the childless offer *all* of the above reasons.

Given the difficulties, how does a woman manage the traumatic decision-making process? Let's look at some women who made the childless choice.

Practical and Emotional Research

Merry Bruns, a commercial model and graduate student in anthropology, presented me with the reading list and pile of books that helped her choose childlessness. "I think people should talk more openly and honestly about this issue," she says. "Most of my friends are either dying to have children or are ambivalent. I feel like I belong to a secret club."

Merry grew up "not thinking about having children." When she was 20, the "big decision" seemed "twenty-five years away. When I turned thirty, my friends started having babies left and right," she says. "At my wedding, people asked not *if* we were going to have them, but *when* we were. 'I have to think about this,' I said to myself, and I researched my decision like I would a term paper." After reading extensively, Merry wrote down the reasons why she wanted a child in blue and why she didn't in black; the black column was much longer. Tops on the black list was, "I like to have complete freedom and control of my life."

Though Merry sees her decision as practical, she researched it emotionally, too. Because she is wholesome and blond, with bright blue eyes, she is often cast as a mother, holding an infant, on modeling assignments. "I would say to myself, 'On a scale of one to five, how do you feel about this baby?' " When her nephew was born, she enjoyed a special relationship with the little boy: "I'd look at Alec and ask, 'Does loving him make me want to have children?' and I'd honestly have to answer *no*. But I tried to stay in touch with new feelings."

A pregnancy, followed by an abortion, which proved physically and emotionally painful, made Merry face up to her choice. Though her husband, who has two adult children by a first wife, didn't want more and was willing to have a vasectomy, Merry opted for a tubal ligation. "I thought it was my responsibility," she says. "I wanted to know *I* wasn't going to get pregnant."

Her father accepted her decision, saying proudly, "You're really your own woman!" But what about her mother? Merry's vivacious smile fades. "I gave

How to Say No

● Write down all the reasons why you don't want children. Don't prejudge them as selfish or superficial. Then write down the reasons why you do. Make sure the *pros* belong to you, not someone else.

● Discuss your feelings about not wanting children with other women who don't want them either or who have serious doubts. From them you will get the support and validation you need. If you can, find an older woman who opted for childlessness and discuss the issue with her. It will help if you learn she has no regrets.

● Hit the bookstore or library (most of the books on the subject are out of print) for information and support. Recommended reading: *Childless by Choice,* by Jean Veevers (Butterworth & Co., 1980); *Pronatalism: The Myth of Mom and Apple Pie* (a collection of essays), edited by Ellen Peck and Judith Senderowitz (Thomas Y. Crowell, 1974); *The Parent Test: How to Measure and Develop Your Talent for Parenthood,* by Ellen Peck and William Granzig (G. P. Putnam's Sons, 1978); *Making up Your Mind about Motherhood,* by Silvia Feldman, Ed.D. (Bantam, 1985); and *Childless by Choice* by Marian Faux (Doubleday, 1984).

● When casual acquaintances or people you sense are unsympathetic to your choice ask why you haven't had children, don't feel obliged to answer this very personal question. Usually they are asking not because they really want to know, but because they disagree. Say firmly but politely, "I can't," and indicate the subject is closed. It will only make you feel insecure to argue this issue.

● Don't let insecurities about your choice lead you to make unsympathetic remarks about children or parenting to parents—including your own. They will respect your choice more if you indicate that you respect theirs.

● When relatives pressure you to provide grandchildren, ask them if and how they are willing to help. Ask for specifics. This tactic may backfire, as some parents want heirs enough to offer child care and financial aid, but often it will discourage further harassment.

● If you don't want children, make sure your boyfriend understands and accepts that before you make a serious commitment.

● Remember, it's 1987—you have a right to say *no* to motherhood. It's not illegal or immoral to remain childless when the world population is increasing by 78 million a year. Think of your decision as positive and appropriate for you. Don't take it to heart when others suggest you are abnormal or selfish. "Society teaches women that they should put the needs of others first; and when they don't, they're selfish," says feminist psychotherapist Annette Lieberman. —*V.L.*

her my list of reasons and told her to consult them whenever she's inclined to protest. She'll get over it, but right now she thinks I'm selfish."

Fighting Urges

Some women choose childlessness in spite of yearnings to have children. Betty Tompkins, 41, an artist who has let her clock tick with no regrets, ignored "biological urges" because they conflicted with her desire to paint. "When these urges visited, they were very strong," she says, "and I didn't want them. I'd look glowingly at some crying child in the supermarket. I'd have to wait until those feelings went away, because they never had anything to do with what was happening in my life."

Betty, like Merry, viewed her choice as a practical one that had to be weighed against other plans and obligations that, for her, came first. Like most women who choose nonmotherhood, she leads a busy, satisfying, creative life with specific goals. "It would have been naive to think I could be a full-time exhibiting painter, earn money somehow, and be a full-time mother, too," she points out. "I would have needed another day in every day to do what I'm doing and have a baby."

Though this modern woman chose a twentieth-century option, she respected her body's messages. "I've always been careful with birth control," she says, "because if I got pregnant, I'm not convinced I'd have the courage to have an abortion."

"Postponing" the Choice

Sociologist Veevers found that many women who don't want children postpone the decision indefinitely. They evade pressures by pretending to others—and sometimes to themselves—that they may one day become pregnant. One 36-year-old woman played this complex game. "Let's say my decision is *no* until I change my mind," she says. "I think I will never make a decision *not* to have a child, until biology catches up with me."

According to this woman, her "ambivalence" helps her to avoid uncomfortable moments with friends who are thrilled with new babies and to enjoy a "richer fantasy life. Because I've never made an official decision, I can say, 'Oh, what a cute little baby! What a wonderful thing it is to have your own child,' and imagine doing it myself. But all it takes is for a new mother to say, 'You should have one too,' and the fantasy dissolves. I don't want to do what everybody else is doing, what my mother did! I'm too delicate. I would feel crowded by a baby. Actually, I've made a conscious decision to move in other directions." This woman, who is a photographer, fears she would lose "creativity to maternity."

Some women eventually realize that continued ambivalence implies a negative decision. A California woman says her husband helped her make her childless choice. "He thought having a child might be a romantic idea," she says. "I was curious. What would it be like to have a child with this man? How would it turn out? On my thirty-ninth birthday I said to him, 'I still can't decide. I'm still thinking about it.' And he said, 'Then the answer is *no*.' "

Coping with Fears and Pressures

The greatest fear for women who are childless by choice is that they'll regret their decision in later years. One childless woman's therapist reduced her anxiety by asking if regretful feelings had ever made her want to jump off buildings in the past. "At that point I realized regret was not a lethal emotion," she says. "Fear of regret was not a positive reason to have a child."

Most women who don't want children marry men who don't want them either. But some fear that their mates will change their minds. "I'm afraid that ten years from now he'll divorce me and have a child with a younger woman," says one woman. "Whenever we see a baby, I test the waters. I ask, 'Isn't he adorable? Don't you want to have a baby too?' He always reassures me by saying firmly, 'No, I don't.' "

Those who pressure the childless to have children prey on such fears. These pressures prevent many women from making the childless decision or from feeling comfortable about it. Most of the women I interviewed confessed to feelings of guilt or shame. Many said they felt selfish or had been told they were. Though some labeled negative emotions as "society's trips," others found it hard to distinguish between their own feelings and the feelings of those who were disappointed or angry. "Almost everybody else in the world rejects your choice," says Kennedy. "That's pretty hard to come up against and say, 'I know I'm right.' "

Why do others feel they have an obligation to convince the childless to change their minds? According to Kennedy, those who resort to pressure tactics may have an ax to grind. "Parents see the childless decision as a rejection of their lifestyles and major life accomplishment," she says. "People who love you, and who are happy with their own babies, want you to discover this happiness too. They have trouble acknowledging differences and think you can't possibly know what you're missing." Kennedy believes that no one in our culture can raise children without ambivalence and stress. "It's a very hard job," she says. "Parents get little help from society. Those who experience difficulty raising children need to be validated. They feel that you may hold them in contempt, having made a choice that is more rebellious or creative. They will ask you to explain, but no answer you give will satisfy them, because they are really looking for validation."

The Crisis in Contraception

ELIZABETH B. CONNELL

ELIZABETH B. CONNELL, M.D., is professor of gynecology and obstetrics at Emory University School of Medicine in Atlanta. She has served on the FDA's Obstetrics and Gynecology Advisory Committee and the executive board of Planned Parenthood, and as an advisor to the U.S. Agency for International Development.

THE United States has led the world in contraceptive research and development for many years. Americans have provided most of the basic scientific data, expertise, and manufacturing capability for contraceptive technologies now in use around the world. However, the United States is losing its leadership role in this area—with potentially disastrous consequences for women and men in this country and elsewhere.

The increasingly litigious climate in this country is one major reason for our technological slippage in this field. The growing number of lawsuits against companies that manufacture contraceptives has prompted many to withdraw products such as intrauterine devices (IUDs) from the marketplace. As a result, there are fewer contraceptive options available to Americans than there were a decade ago.

Fear of litigation has also discouraged companies from introducing safer and more convenient contraceptives to the domestic market, although they continue to test and sell new products abroad. It is particularly ironic that a number of excellent products developed by Americans, such as Depo-Provera (an injectible contraceptive) and the copper-bearing IUDs, are now available virtually everywhere in the world *except* the United States.

This situation has been aggravated by widespread public misunderstanding about the risks and benefits of certain birth-control methods. This is particularly true of the pill, whose risks have been grossly exaggerated in proportion to its benefits.

A steady decline in federal funding for contraceptive R&D in recent years has further exacerbated the situation. In 1985, for instance, the National Institutes of Health (NIH) allocated only $7.5 million for contraceptive research, down from $38 million spent by the U.S. government in 1974. The Reagan administration has sliced contraceptive funding for both research and services because of political pressure from religious groups and right-wing organizations.

For all of these reasons, the United States is facing a crisis in the development and use of contraceptives. While everyone is affected, two groups are suffering the most. The first is our teenage population. The United States now holds the dubious distinction of having the highest rate of teenage pregnancies anywhere in the developed world. Our rate is seven times higher than that of the Netherlands, and more than twice as high as that of Canada, Denmark, England, Finland, New Zealand, and Sweden, even though our teenagers are not more sexually active. More than 1 million U.S. teenagers become pregnant each year, with almost half of the pregnancies ending in abortion. If current trends continue, 40 percent of today's 14-year-old girls will be pregnant at least once before age 20.

Political pressures and litigation are driving contraceptives off the market and stifling research and development in this area.

The vast majority of teenagers don't give their babies up for adoption, and they face all the medical and socioeconomic problems that occur when children have children. The Center for Population Options in New York estimates that the cost to the public of teenage childbearing was $16.65 billion in 1986. This figure does not include the costs of housing, day care, special education, and numerous other needs, all of which are steadily increasing as more and more teenagers keep their babies.

While inadequate sex education programs and the lack of easily available contraceptive services play a role in this epidemic, many pregnant teenagers say they failed to use birth control because either they didn't know there were safe and effective methods or they didn't know how to obtain them. Educating teenagers about contraceptives becomes even more of an urgent priority with the looming threat of AIDS and other sexually transmitted diseases.

A different problem exists at the other end of the age spectrum. Women who are beyond the age when the pill is deemed appropriate—35 to 40—still face 10 to 15 years of potential fertility. Yet the options available to these women are narrowing. As a result, many of them (or their husbands) will undoubtedly resort to possibly irreversible sterilization procedures for which they are not psychologically ready. Furthermore, while a vasectomy has some risks of minor side effects, a tubal ligation—a surgical procedure often done under general anesthesia—carries a small but real risk of significant complications.

The current crisis is also creating problems for other countries. Since many developing nations do not have a regulatory agency such as the Food and Drug Administration (FDA), they have traditionally looked to the United States for guidance in evaluating new drugs and devices. So when birth-control methods are discontinued here for economic reasons, or are not approved by the FDA for political reasons, other countries often get the impression that they are unsafe or ineffective. Thus, the decline in contraceptive development and use in the United States is resulting in fewer contraceptive options for those countries. To make matters worse, the current administration has refused to fund any international family-planning organizations that offer abortion counseling or referrals along with other forms of birth control. This could have particularly serious repercussions for nations with uncontrolled population growth.

Sneezing to Prevent Pregnancy

Ever since our ancestors concluded that there was a causal relationship between sexual intercourse and the birth of a baby, both men and women have searched for ways to control their fertility. Some of these techniques seem ludicrous in light of today's knowledge, while others were scientifically quite perceptive. Some were extremely dangerous and even lethal.

Every country had its own superstitions. In Rome around the sixth century B.C., women wore the testicles of a cat in a tube around their waist. Women in other regions believed that sneezing and jumping after intercourse would prevent conception, and still others claimed success from burning moxa-balls (small packets of medicinal herbs) on the abdomen. Barrier devices that prevented sperm from entering the cervical canal were made of numerous plant and animal materials such as cabbages, pomegranates, leaves, animals' ear wax, and elephant dung. The ingestion of heavy metals for contraception killed many women during the Middle Ages, and many women died as a result of mutilating sterilization procedures.

Condoms, in one form or another, have been employed ever since prehistoric times, but the use of modern condoms began with the industrialization of rubber. A modern version of the diaphragm was developed in the late nineteenth century, and spermicides, made from chemicals toxic to sperm, were introduced for contraceptive use around the 1930s and 1940s.

Before the development of the pill and IUDs, barrier contraceptives were the only reliable methods of birth control. But they have to be used with every act of intercourse, and many users find them inconvenient and aesthetically unattractive. Furthermore, these devices are not completely effective in preventing pregnancy—condoms occasionally tear and diaphragms fitted or used improperly do not always prevent sperm from getting into the cervical canal. For these reasons, barrier methods were rapidly replaced by oral contraceptives and IUDs when they became available.

The FDA approved the first oral contraceptive in 1960. The pill contains two female hormones: estrogen, which blocks ovulation, and progestin, which promotes cyclic bleeding. The pill seemed safe and effective during initial clinical tests. However, data accumulated during the mid- and late 1960s, when the pill became more widely used, indicated that there were risks for certain individuals. For instance, use of the early oral contraceptives resulted in a seven fold increase—to 3 in 100,000—in women's annual death rate from thromboembolism, a blood-clotting disease. Pill use also caused a fourfold increase in users' risk of stroke, and a threefold increase in their risk of heart attacks.

However, the risks of heart attacks and strokes appeared only in 35-year-old women who smoked and 40-year-old women who did not: there have been no reported deaths from the pill owing to these cardiovascular diseases in women under the age of

25. Long-term risks apply only to women who have additional risk factors such as age and smoking. Thus, for women without these risk factors, it is far safer to take the pill than to carry a pregnancy to term.

Making a Safer Pill

After these initial risks came to light, researchers modified the pill, lowering the dosage first of estrogen and then of progestin. The amount of estrogen, for instance, declined from more than 100 micrograms to 30 micrograms. As a result, the incidence of serious side effects is considerably lower in the pills sold today. And as the newer, low-dosage pills become more widely used, we can look forward to even fewer long-term cardiovascular side effects. Yet the almost 100 percent effectiveness rate of the early oral contraceptives, when taken properly, has been maintained.

Despite this track record, the use of oral contraceptives has declined. This is largely because the pill's early risks received a disproportionate share of public attention. The first major assault against the pill took place during U.S. Senate hearings held by Sen. Gaylord Nelson's Subcommittee on Monopoly of the Select Committee on Small Business in 1970. In the opening days of these hearings, witnesses antagonistic toward oral contraceptives such as Hugh Davis, inventor of the Dalkon Shield, testified about their risks. This early testimony received extensive media coverage. Only later in the hearings did witnesses such as myself and Alan Guttmacher, president of Planned Parenthood, present a more balanced view of the pill's risks and benefits. But by then the damage had been done.

The legacy of these hearings and later reports about adverse side effects was vividly documented in a 1985 Gallup poll commissioned by the American College of Obstetricians and Gynecologists. The poll showed that the public's fears far exceed the real dangers of oral contraceptives. For example, about 75 percent of the men and women interviewed thought that the pill posed a serious threat to health. Of these, one-third believed that women taking these agents are at risk of developing cancer.

This viewpoint is particularly disturbing because, according to recent studies, the opposite is true. The pill not only does not cause malignancies but actually protects against cancer of the endometrium, the tissue lining the uterine cavity, and the ovary, the latter disease being almost always fatal. Howard Ory, of the Centers for Disease Control (CDC), has estimated that 1,700 hospitalizations for ovarian cancer and 2,000 for endometrial cancer are prevented each year by the use of oral contraceptives. In addition, 23,490 admissions for benign breast disease are averted annually, according to CDC estimates. Studies have shown that the pill continues to offer this protection for at least 10 to 15 years after women stop taking it.

Clinical studies have revealed other health benefits from the use of oral contraceptives. It is now well established that these potent hormonal agents protect against a number of medical conditions including ectopic pregnancy, a potentially fatal condition in which the fetus develops outside the womb in one of the woman's two fallopian tubes. The pill also protects against numerous conditions, including ovarian cysts, fibroid tumors of the uterus, pelvic inflammatory disease, excessive menstrual bleeding, and weakening of the bones (osteoporosis). Yet under intense pressure from some consumer groups, the FDA has not allowed information about these significant health benefits to be included in the packaging for oral contraceptives.

Similarly, the vaginal contraceptive sponge was attacked by two activist consumer groups shortly after its approval by the FDA in 1983. The Associated Pharmacologists and Toxicologists in Washington, D.C., and the Empire State Consumer Association in Rochester, N.Y., claimed that the sponge contained three carcinogens, that its use carried a high risk of toxic shock syndrome, and that it had been inadequately evaluated by the FDA.

These charges culminated in hearings before the House Subcommittee on Intergovernmental Relations and Human Resources in July 1983. All the allegations were essentially refuted by the manufacturer of the sponge, VLI Corp., based on its research data. The NIH, which provided funding for the sponge's development, found no reason for concern. The FDA did not withdraw its approval nor recommend any alterations in the product's labeling. The media, however, focused primarily on the alleged risks of the device and the public once again became alarmed.

In my opinion, the concern about contraceptives—

The pill's early risks received a disproportionate share of public attention.

and indeed all new medications—can be traced to a general belief that all drugs and devices should be totally safe and effective. Given the great scientific advances made in recent years, many people believe there should be no risks associated with medical care. This, unfortunately, will never be true, since it is impossible to develop any agent powerful enough to produce a desired biologic effect that will not have an adverse effect on a few susceptible people. Therefore, every treatment has and will always have its own risk-benefit ratio for any given individual.

The Disappearance of the IUD

The first intrauterine device was invented in the early 1920s. Several centuries before, camel drivers somehow learned that placing pebbles in the uteri of their female camels would keep them from getting pregnant while crossing the Sahara. Foreign bodies inserted into the uterine cavities of women were later shown to induce biochemical changes that were either toxic to sperm or did not allow the implantation of a fertilized ovum.

Like the pill, the early IUDs seemed to be highly effective and safe. However, studies with larger numbers of users soon revealed adverse effects, particularly in the case of the Dalkon Shield. This plastic device was found to be very dangerous because its tail, composed of hundreds of small filaments encased in a sheath, acted as a wick, allowing bacteria from the vagina to ascend into the uterus. Hundreds of cases of pelvic infections resulted from the use of the Dalkon Shield, causing sterility and a number of deaths among women using this IUD.

At least 12,000 lawsuits and more than 325,000 claims were filed against A.H. Robins, the manufacturer of the Dalkon Shield, forcing it to withdraw the IUD and later file for bankruptcy. In this particular case, there seems to be clear evidence of corporate irresponsibility. According to internal memos released during litigation, Robins officials had known of the dangerous wicking tendency of its IUD before they marketed the device.

All the other marketed IUDs had monofilament (single filament) tails, which do not have as much potential for infection. There are two major types of IUDs: the earlier, non-medicated devices made of plastic such as Saf-T-Coil and Lippes Loop, and the more recent medicated devices made out of plastic

to which copper (Copper-7 and Tatum-T) or a progesterone (Progestasert) have been added to increase their effectiveness. The medicated devices are smaller and better tolerated, producing fewer cases of cramping and bleeding than their predecessors. Furthermore, two studies published in the *New England Journal of Medicine* in 1985 showed little or no increased risk of tubal infertility from the use of copper IUDs in monogamous couples. The Saf-T-Coil and Lippes Loop have since been removed from the market for economic reasons.

However, fears aroused by the Dalkon Shield fiasco have prompted a number of lawsuits against the widely used Copper-7. The suits claim a variety of injuries, primarily related to pelvic infections. Most of these suits have been decided in favor of the manufacturer, G.D. Searle.

Despite these favorable judgments, Searle decided in January 1986 that it was no longer economically feasible to continue producing the Copper-7 and the Tatum-T. While sales of the Copper-7 amounted to $11 million in 1985, the successful defense of just four of the Copper-7 lawsuits cost the company $1.5 million. With more than 300 lawsuits pending, Searle found product-liability insurance for both products to be virtually unobtainable.

One decision in a 1986 lawsuit against Searle may discourage some future IUD litigation. U.S. District Court Judge Joseph H. Young in Baltimore declared that the evidence submitted on behalf of 17 Copper-7 users who had sued Searle was nothing but a "series of alternative unsubstantiated theories." He concluded that the "plaintiffs had failed to present sufficient evidence of causation" and rendered a verdict in favor of Searle.

Unfortunately, that court decision will probably not change the decision of Searle and other pharmaceutical companies to stay out of the IUD market. As a result, the newest IUD—the Copper T Cu 380A—may never be brought to the U.S. market. Yet this IUD is the best of the copper devices (it has the highest rate of effectiveness) and has already been approved by the FDA.

At present, at least 2.3 million American women use an IUD. When those devices need to be replaced, most of these women will have to find some other form of contraception. Jacqueline Forrest of the Alan Guttmacher Institute, a New York-based research organization, has statistically estimated that

*I*UDs are no longer available in the U.S. because companies cannot obtain liability coverage.

160,000 unintended pregnancies will occur from the discontinuation of IUD production in the United States, resulting in 72,000 live births and 88,000 abortions.

The Controversy over Depo-Provera

Another unfortunate victim of the current medical-legal climate is Depo-Provera (depo-medroxy progesterone acetate), a long-acting injectable progestin that acts by blocking ovulation. The injection is given by a health-care provider once every three months. This route of administration not only allows for long-term effectiveness but is particularly desirable in many areas of the world where medications are perceived to be of value only when given by injection. Depo-Provera has been shown to be extremely safe and virtually 100 percent effective. This agent has been used by more than 11 million women in over 80 countries for more than 20 years with no reported deaths. Yet it has never been approved in the United States because of political reasons.

The FDA's scientific advisory committees, the World Health Organization, and numerous other national and international groups have reviewed the data on Depo-Provera and recommended its use as a contraceptive agent. However, the drug has been the target of various consumer and feminist groups such as the National Women's Health Network, *Mother Jones* magazine, and the Institute for Food and Development Policy.

These opponents have cited animal data on malignancy that are probably irrelevant to women. For instance, beagles given high doses of Depo-Provera developed breast tumors. However, the beagle has a high spontaneous rate of breast lesions, and British scientists have recently stated that it is not an appropriate animal for testing hormonal agents. Two of fifteen rhesus monkeys receiving 50 times the contraceptive dose developed endometrial cancer, but in a tissue not found in the human female. Moreover, this tumor has also been reported to occur in untreated animals. While critics maintain that Depo-Provera can cause birth defects, there is no evidence that this has occurred. Furthermore, this agent is so effective as a birth-control method that the risk of exposing a fetus to the drug is extremely low.

Opponents have also claimed that Depo-Provera causes permanent sterility, but studies have shown normal pregnancy rates approximately one year after stopping the medication. Most women do experience irregular menstrual cycles, and sometimes a complete absence of menses, while using this contraceptive. But this has not been shown to have adverse effects on their health or future fertility.

Despite the agent's long-term record of safety, an FDA Public Board of Inquiry recommended in 1985

that Depo-Provera not be approved without more research to establish its long-term safety. The Upjohn Co. is currently preparing a new application to the FDA based on recent international studies that document Depo-Provera's safety and efficacy.

Other contraceptive agents currently under attack are spermicides, which work by chemically disrupting the membrane covering the head of the sperm. These are manufactured as jellies, creams, and foams and are used either alone or with a diaphragm, condom, or in the vaginal sponge. In 1985, in a nonjury trial in Atlanta, a judge awarded $5.1 million to a woman who claimed that her child's congenital defects resulted from the use of Ortho Gynol, a spermicide made by the Ortho Pharmaceutical Corp. In his decision, the judge cited a study published in 1981 that purportedly showed a link between congenital anomalies and spermicides. However, this study has many methodological flaws and lacks statistical validity. Moreover, the judge made this award even though most of the evidence presented at the trial showed that there is no proven association between the use of spermicides and fetal damage.

Spermicides are low-profit items, and one or two more suits of this magnitude might be enough to convince U.S. companies to discontinue production. Thus, we face the potential loss of these valuable contraceptive agents as well.

In the meantime, there is little chance that new contraceptives will become available in the near future. It is very difficult and sometimes impossible to obtain funds to pursue promising leads for new contraceptive technologies. Two factors are to blame. First, as I mentioned, federal funding of basic research—in both government and university labs—has steadily declined over the last six years. Second, the development of a new product is very expensive (it costs approximately $50 million) and very time consuming (it takes about 15 years to bring an idea to market). Unless companies expect a product to produce a reasonably good financial return, they are unwilling to make a major investment.

Even if U.S. companies decide to develop and test new contraceptives, they may not be able to obtain liability insurance for them. And there is always the fear of litigation, which can occur regardless of the product's safety record in clinical tests.

For these reasons, the number of pharmaceutical companies working in the field of contraception has dropped precipitously over the last decade. The Ortho Pharmaceutical Corp. is the only major U.S. company now committing significant amounts of money to developing contraceptives.

A classic example of this dilemma is a biodegradable contraceptive capsule known as Capronor, developed with NIH funding. This agent is implanted under the skin of the arm and releases a progestin, which also blocks ovulation, for a year. The product has been ready for clinical testing for more than two years, but no company has been able to obtain product-liability insurance in order to supply clinical researchers with the implant.

The same situation will probably apply to IUDs. A new tailless magnetic IUD has been developed by researchers at Emory University and the Georgia Institute of Technology. The magnet is used to detect and remove the IUD, so the tail—which can allow bacteria to pass into the uterine cavity—is no longer necessary. This new device is also almost ready for clinical trials. Yet it is unlikely that this or any other promising new IUD will undergo clinical trials in the United States, at least in the foreseeable future.

The current political climate is also inhibiting the availability of completely new technologies. This is particularly true in the case of RU 486, a steroid compound developed by the Roussel-Uclaf Co. of France and soon to be marketed there. RU 486 acts by suppressing the corpus luteum—a structure that develops in the ovary following ovulation and produces progesterone, a hormone essential to the development of a fertilized ovum.

Taken as an oral tablet, this agent interrupts the normal menstrual cycle and can prevent the implantation of a fertilized ovum. It can also be used to terminate pregnancy. Early data from clinical trials in other countries suggest that terminations induced by this agent carry lower complication rates than those linked with the few abortions performed late in the first trimester and in the second trimester.

However, RU 486 is highly controversial because it places control of pregnancy in the hands of women themselves. It thus circumvents any legislative authority and renders the whole abortion debate moot. Needless to say, antiabortion groups are vehemently opposed to introducing this agent in the United States. Given the current administration's anti-abortion stance, it is highly unlikely that such an agent will be studied and approved in the near future.

Another contraceptive that may not make it to the American marketplace is the Cavity Rim cervical cap, used with a spermicide. Studies conducted with approximately 2,000 American women showed pregnancy rates with this device comparable to other barrier methods. And there are no adverse health effects. Some women prefer the cap to the diaphragm because it is smaller and therefore less apt to affect the vaginal walls. And unlike the diaphragm, it does not put pressure on the urethra and bladder, which can cause urinary tract infections.

However, the FDA classified the cap as experimental in 1981. Therefore, anyone who wished to manufacture this device must accumulate all the data from the various centers where the cap was tested and submit the information to the FDA. This is a time-consuming and expensive exercise. Since the cap—like other barrier methods—would probably not be a major income producer, and insurers would assign manufacturers the same liability as that for the sponge and other vaginal contraceptives, it is unlikely that any U.S. company will pursue FDA approval.

Other contraceptives such as an implant encased in biocompatible plastic, a steroid-containing vaginal ring, and an antipregnancy vaccine have been investigated for more than a decade. But for the same reasons, these products are not likely to reach the American marketplace.

A Male Contraceptive?

Activist women's groups have often charged that there are no male contraceptives available today because most of the researchers are men who only want to work on methods for use by women. In reality, much time and money has been spent trying to develop safe and effective birth control for men.

It is much more difficult to control male fertility. A woman produces only one egg per month and is fertile for only about 12 hours. A man, however, produces as many as 30 million sperm per day and is almost constantly fertile. Preventing the development of a single egg is less difficult than reducing the sperm count to zero for long periods of time.

The World Health Organization has predicted that it will be more than 20 years before a male contraceptive becomes available for general use. Even if one is marketed, it would not eliminate the need for good female methods. Many women may not want to entrust their sexual partners with the sole responsibility for preventing pregnancy.

As the contraceptive crisis worsens, American women are being forced to leave the country to ob-

*The current administration
has cut funding for contraceptive research and services
largely because of pressure from religious
and right-wing groups.*

tain contraceptives. This is already happening with the IUD. The Copper T Cu 380A is now available in Canada, the United Kingdom, and continental Europe, and American women are traveling to these countries to obtain the device. While this solution may not pose an inordinate problem for middle- or high-income women, it does for poorer women. This de facto discrimination cannot fail to have serious social and economic repercussions.

The current crisis is also hurting family-planning activities worldwide. When devices such as the copper IUD are discontinued in the United States for purely economic reasons, other countries believe that they are not safe or effective. Similarly, because of the consistent failure of the FDA to approve Depo-Provera, grave doubts about its safety have begun to affect its use in various parts of the world.

To make matters worse, the U.S. government has drastically reduced funding for international family planning in recent years. In December 1984, the Reagan Administration abruptly terminated 17 years of support for the International Planned Parenthood Federation (IPPF) because it would not renounce its members' rights to carry on abortion-related activities with their own funds. The following year the U.S. Agency for International Development (AID) cut $10 million from support for the United Nations fund for population activities because of its program with China. AID claimed that China coerced women into obtaining abortions, sterilizations, and IUD insertions so the country could attain its population goals. Since the United States has been a primary source of support for such programs for many years, these cuts are hurting many countries' efforts to curb population growth. It is impossible to talk with international colleagues without becoming acutely aware of the immense negative impact we are having on contraceptive programs abroad.

Improving Public Understanding

The track record of the present administration suggests that very little will be done in the next two years to alleviate the contraceptive dilemma. One hopes that the next administration will better understand the need to support the development and use of safe and effective contraceptives. With that in mind, several potential solutions can be explored.

First, efforts must be undertaken by government agencies and the health-care profession to improve the public's understanding of the risks and benefits of available contraceptives. For instance, public ed-

ucation programs, using every type of media to reach the widest audience, should be launched to inform consumers that today's oral contraceptives are extremely safe and effective. Such programs should also spread the news that copper IUDs are safe and effective for monogamous individuals, who have a lower potential for contracting infections, and that no data exist linking spermicides to fetal defects.

People must also be informed that the condom offers our best defense against the spread of AIDS and other sexually transmitted diseases. U.S. Surgeon General C. Everett Koop has taken an admirable stance in advocating extensive public education programs about AIDS and the use of condoms.

The media should also attempt to cover contraceptives in a more balanced and responsible way. Television is perhaps most in need of improvement. Television executives who broadcast programs and ads that sell sex to teenagers should recognize how hypocritical they are in refusing to run public-service announcements about contraception.

Second, ways must be found to curb the increasing number of lawsuits that claim an association between a product and some sort of damage even though there is no scientific evidence for such a link. The public must be made aware that insurance companies do not have unlimited funds in their "deep pockets," and the public ultimately pays the price for unwarranted judgments.

Some so-called experts testify against drugs and devices without any scientific evidence to back up their claims. Many of these "hired guns" would not be allowed to testify if the courts imposed stricter criteria on expert witnesses' training and experience.

One approach to the product-liability quagmire would be to indemnify manufacturers of high-risk medical therapies against certain types of risk. This has already been suggested for manufacturers of vaccines and might also work for developers of contraceptives. Both vaccines and contraceptives carry an unavoidable risk to a very small percentage of users. Some policymakers have suggested a national fund to compensate the few individuals who sustain damage from these otherwise safe and effective drugs.

Finally, federal agencies such as the NIH and the Department of Health and Human Services should increase funding for contraceptive research and services. There is no reason why the United States should lose its leadership status in this area. And there is certainly no reason why women in this country must bear unwanted children because they do not have satisfactory options for birth control.

Kids and Contraceptives

The alarming rate of teenage pregnancy and the inexorable spread of AIDS has raised troubling moral questions and given new urgency to the debate over how best to protect our children

In Boston, where 13 percent of all births in 1983 were to girls 19 and under, the controversy over a plan to distribute birth-control devices in the city's schools is intense. The same kind of furor has accompanied the opening of many clinics that dispense contraceptives or provide family-planning counseling in at least 76 schools around the country. "We have no choice," says School Committee member Abbie Browne, the mother of two teenagers, who favors the plan. But fellow committee member Joe Casper, a father of five, is adamantly opposed to giving condoms to teenagers. "What are we going to do next?" he says. "Put them on for them, too?"

On national television, the 17-year-old hero of "Valerie" lusts after his sultry blond girlfriend. They get into bed together. But there's a little hitch: she doesn't have "protection." The boy decides to postpone their lovemaking until he can buy some condoms. Later, when his mother finds the package of contraceptives, they have a heart-to-heart talk. "Just make sure whatever you do, it's the right time in your life," she advises her son.

Every week more than 130 girls—some of them as young as 12—receive birth-control pills at one of the three clinics for teenagers run by the Chicago Board of Health. Peer pressure to have sex is unrelenting in the South Side ghetto, says director Cheryl Walker. "If a girl gets to be 15 or 16 years old and she hasn't had a baby yet, [her friends think] there must be something wrong with her," Walker says. So Walker takes the angry words of the critics in stride. "We holler when 12-year-olds come in here for contraceptives," she says. "But we holler louder when they come in here pregnant."

Contraceptives in the schools. Teenagers using condoms on television. Twelve-year-olds receiving birth-control pills—at the taxpayers' expense. A decade ago it would have been unthinkable. But the alarmingly high rate of teenage pregnancy and the fear of AIDS and other sexually transmitted diseases have opened up the debate over what to do about the precocious sexual activity of young people; what was once a matter of morality has become a matter of public health. Politicians, educators, doctors and parents have the best interests of their children at heart. And everyone, it seems, wishes that their kids would just say no to sex until they understand the possible consequences. But that's as far as the agreement goes: Abstinence? More sex education? Free access to contraceptives? What is best for the kids—and for all of us?

The statistical portrait of sex and the American teenager will stagger many parents. Each year for the past decade, more than a million teenage girls have become pregnant. Even though the teenage-pregnancy rate has remained fairly steady for the last few years, it is still very high—indeed, it is the highest in the Western world. The number of illegitimate births has soared. In 1984, 56 percent of teen births were out of wedlock, compared with only 15 percent in 1960. About 500,000 teenagers actually become mothers each year; the rest of the pregnancies end in miscarriages or abortions. A shocking one-third of all abortions performed annually in this country are done on teenage girls.

The outlook for the babies, and for the young mothers, is grim. They are most likely to come from low-income households, and chances are that other members of the family—their mothers or their older sisters—have been teenage mothers. If they drop out of school to have their babies, as most girls do, they probably will never finish their education and they will come to depend on public assistance to survive. A third of all teenage mothers have a second child before they turn 20. Because teenage mothers usually do not have access to any prenatal care, they do not know about nutrition; their babies are likely to have low birthweights, which in turn increases the risk of health and developmental problems. The huge number of teenage mothers is one reason why the United States has a high infant-mortality rate: 10.8 infant deaths for every 1,000 live births. According to a report released last week by the Children's Defense Fund, the United States ranked with Belgium, East Germany and West Germany for the highest infant-mortality rate among 20 industrialized countries.

High risk: A potentially more serious threat—AIDS—has forged unlikely alliances in the battle over teenage sex. Public-health experts worry openly that sexually active teenagers will be the next AIDS "high risk" group. In October Surgeon General C. Everett Koop—known for his conservative views on abortion and birth control—came out in favor of early and explicit sex education in schools; he also advocated the use of condoms as protection against AIDS (page 64). In December a distinguished panel of researchers from the National Research Council issued a report that advocated making contraceptives available to teenagers.

It is now much more acceptable to talk publicly about contraception (page 82). In the last few weeks, condom ads have begun appearing on some television stations and in major newspapers and magazines, including NEWSWEEK. The new openness is mandated by serious public-health concerns. "When it comes to pregnancy and decisions about abortion or whether to bear a child at a young age, then the stakes are high," says Leroy Walters of the Kennedy Center for Biomedical Ethics. "The stakes are even higher with an infection that could be lethal within five to 10 years."

In this atmosphere, it has also become acceptable to talk about chastity—long out of fashion. "Abstinence is our first choice," says Patricia Davis-Scott, who runs a teen health clinic that dispenses contraceptives at DuSable High School in Chicago. The National Research Council panel also endorsed programs that stress delaying sexual activity, although the panel noted in its report that "there is little available evidence to document their effectiveness." Other groups, such as the Washington-based Center for Population Options, which helps schools set up clinics, have made extensive efforts to get kids to postpone sex. The center publishes a booklet called "Make a Life for Yourself" that lists 10 reasons to wait. Among them are: "You don't want to"; "You're not ready"; "You want to wait until you're in love or married"; and "You're not using birth control." Says the center's Debra Haffner, coauthor of the booklet: "We believe in abstinence. There's no question that kids should delay having sex because most adolescents are not ready to have sex." That message seems to be getting across to at least a few stu-

dents. "We tell the kids the best kind of safe sex is abstinence," says Amy Weitz of Planned Parenthood in San Francisco, "and we're seeing more of it." Tina, a 16-year-old from Oakland, Calif., says that fear of AIDS and other diseases has made some of her friends chaste. "We call it the 'Straight Age'," she says.

But most health-care professionals aren't counting on teenagers to stay away from sex. "After food and sleep, you are dealing with the third most powerful drive we have," says Dr. Sheldon Landesman, an AIDS researcher in New York. "And sex is the most powerful nonsurvival drive." There are other forces pushing teenagers into each other's arms as well. A recent Harris poll of U.S. teenagers indicated that more than half have had intercourse by the time they are 17—primarily because they felt pressure from their peers. "My friends say, if you haven't done it, you're not in with the 'in' group," says Nekell McGrith, a 16-year-old sophomore at Harry S. Truman High School in the Bronx.

Jeans ad: Still, only a third of the teenagers who were sexually active said they used contraceptives all the time. Nearly as many (27 percent) said that they never use them. The rest said they used birth control "sometimes" or "most of the time." It's not because birth control is unavailable. Any kid who's not too embarrassed can pick up a package of condoms in the local drugstore. Sometimes kids avoid contraceptives because of ill-founded concerns about their safety. There are other prevalent myths about birth control. Last year the Detroit Free Press asked high-school students to write letters about what was wrong with their schools. Pregnancy was a major topic and many of the responses included popular misconceptions about sex. At Clintondale High School in Mt. Clemens, Mich., for example, some girls thought that you couldn't get pregnant if you wore high heels during intercourse. Other misguided ideas about sex: You can't get pregnant the first time. Douching afterwards will prevent pregnancy. You can't get pregnant standing up. You can't get pregnant if you don't kiss. Many health-care professionals say the level of ignorance among teenagers is astounding—and yet most of these children have had some kind of sex-education class in school. The sexual innuendoes in everything from blue-jean ads to MTV are "overwhelming," says June Osborn, dean of the University of Michigan's school of public health. "Pregnant kids know all about sexuality but they do not know what makes them pregnant."

First clinic: What's the best way for them to learn? Most experts say sex education should start at home, although they concede that few parents feel comfortable talking about sex. Classrooms are another important source of information, but a lot

depends on the quality of the instruction. No study has ever borne out a prevalent notion among adults: that sex education has any effect on students' rate of sexual activity. However, classes combined with school-based clinics offering contraceptives or information about birth control have been proven effective in delaying sex and lowering pregnancy rates. After the first school clinic to offer birth control was started at Mechanic Arts High School in St. Paul in 1973, birthrates were cut nearly in half. "In the schools, you have a beautiful system for follow-up because the nurse in a school has access to kids in a hallway to say, 'How's it going?' " says Gail Fearnley, a nurse-practitioner at school clinics in Muskegon, Mich.

It may turn out that the best hope for getting control of the problem is the most controversial approach. The very idea of school birth-control clinics raises troubling moral questions for many people. When the Portland, Ore., school district opened its first on-campus health clinic a year ago at Roosevelt High School, there were angry pickets. Clinic coordinator Mary Hennrich faced taunts of "devil worshiper" and "whoremonger" on her way to work. "They're well-meaning, concerned people with tunnel vision," says Hennrich of the protesters. "They think all kids are from ideal families in the suburbs and that all parents can talk openly with the kids about sex. It's not at all like that out there." The clinic at the all-black DuSable High School in one of Chicago's poorest neighborhoods

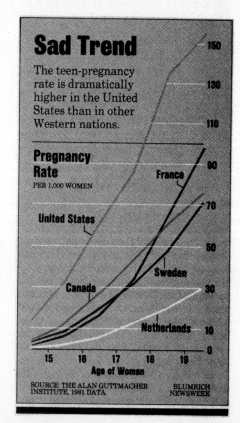

Sad Trend

The teen-pregnancy rate is dramatically higher in the United States than in other Western nations.

Pregnancy Rate
PER 1,000 WOMEN

France

United States

Sweden

Canada

Netherlands

Age of Women
15   16   17   18   19

150
130
110
90
70
50
30
10
0

SOURCE: THE ALAN GUTTMACHER INSTITUTE, 1981 DATA.

BLUMRICH NEWSWEEK

is under attack in the courts; 13 black ministers from churches in the area have filed suit to close down the facility, alleging that it is a "calculated and pernicious effort to destroy the very fabric of family life among black parents and their children"—a charge denied by clinic director Patricia Davis-Scott. She says students can participate in the family-planning program only if a parent or legal guardian gives permission. "We are a school which is intimately involved with children and their families," she says. "We're not trying to circumvent parental authority."

Black leaders: Sometimes the opposition spreads beyond the schools themselves. In Boston a task force convened last fall by Schools Superintendent Laval Wilson recommended that clinics be established in two middle schools and two high schools. A powerful lobby lined up against the clinics. Included were Mayor Ray Flynn, members of the school board, local conservatives, prominent black leaders and religious leaders. The Roman Catholic Church set up its own task force and compiled a thorough report arguing that clinics are not only morally wrong but ultimately ineffective. In a letter he sent last fall to Wilson, Cardinal Bernard Law, archbishop of Boston, argued that the clinics would "place the Boston public schools in the position of implicitly condoning or encouraging sexual activity among students." Wilson is expected to decide whether or not to open the clinics in the next two weeks.

Whatever Wilson's decision, school-based clinics will probably continue to grow in popularity—and not just because they give out contraceptives. Many are located in low-income areas, where a substantial portion of the students have no health insurance. Often, the clinics provide the only medical care the kids will get. At Chicago's DuSable clinic, director Davis-Scott says that family planning is only one of 10 health programs—including regular physical examinations and prenatal care. In fact, she says, 80 percent of the students who use the clinic do not participate in the contraceptive program. The demand for clinics like the one in Chicago appears to be great. Wanda Wesson of the Support Center for School-based Clinics in Houston, which has been advising schools on how to open clinics since 1985, says that the center gets about 100 requests for help a month from schools wanting to begin new projects.

But school-based programs are not the only resource available to teens. There are about 5,000 community family-planning clinics around the country that distribute contraceptives to teenagers—often on a confidential basis. At The Hub in the South Bronx, teenagers participate in an after-school program that includes aerobics, karate and computer lessons as well as group discussions about sex and the need for contraceptives. The neighbor-

hood, one of the poorest urban areas in the nation, has a serious teen-pregnancy problem. In 1980, the last year for which such data is available, 179 out of every 1,000 teenage girls in the South Bronx got pregnant—compared to 112 out of 1,000 for all of New York City. (The national rate in 1983 was 108 per 1,000.)

Peer pressure: "They have a lot of family problems—unemployment, alcoholism, suicide," says The Hub's director, Mary Morales. "Our focus is to give these people options other than early child rearing. We want them to know there is more out there than just having kids. If they have self-esteem, they can learn to say no. And children have to be given credit if they withstand peer pressure." With the high rate of drug use in the area, AIDS is also a very real danger for teenagers. Intravenous drug users are one of the major risk groups for the disease and are also thought to be among the main carriers of AIDS to the heterosexual population. "Maybe the best

way to get the message across about contraceptives is to say use condoms—if you get AIDS, you're dead," says Morales.

At least some of the youths who use the center seem to have gotten the message. One day last week, five teenagers took part in a group discussion about attitudes toward sex and birth control. All agreed on the need for contraception, but most seemed to think the girl should take care of it. Clive McKay, an 18-year-old high-school senior, talked about "spontaneity" and how hard it is to stop and put on a condom. Dorothy Guttierrez, 19, responded angrily: "Now you have to carry a condom for him! You can stop to go to the bathroom if you have to. Why can't you protect yourself at the same time? Why should it be just the responsibility of the girl?"

Getting boys involved has been difficult in recent years. A generation ago, if a teenage girl became pregnant, she married the father. Now, says Stanford law Prof. Robert Mnookin, a member of the National

Teenagers, Birth Control and AIDS

Americans 13 and older are split over whether schools that dispense birth control encourage sex. But they overwhelmingly believe that parents unable to prevent their child from having sex should help the teenager get birth control.

How worried are you that AIDS will spread widely among the nation's teenagers?

48%	Very worried
24%	A little worried
15%	Not very worried
9%	Not worried at all

If a school dispenses birth-control devices, do you think that will make teenagers more likely to engage in sexual activities or not?

45%	More likely
47%	Not more likely

At what age do you think young people should be first able to get birth-control devices?

3%	8-11
31%	12-15
54%	16-18

Has the fear of AIDS affected the social life and dating habits of teenagers greatly, to some extent or not at all?

13%	Greatly
43%	To some extent
29%	Not at all

Which do you think is the best way to limit AIDS and unwanted pregnancies? By emphasizing:

51%	Sex education
43%	Advocating abstinence

What method of birth control do you think is most appropriate for teenagers?

	13- to 17-year-olds	Total
The Pill	69%	42%
Diaphragm	1%	4%
Condom	26%	34%
Foam	1%	1%
The sponge	2%	2%
Abstinence	0%	8%

If parents are unable to prevent their teenage child from having sexual relations, is it better for them to help the teenager get birth control or not?

76%	Help
16%	Not help

Should teenagers be able to get birth-control devices at the following places, only with their parents' permission or not at all?

	Should be available	Should not be	Only with parents' OK
Family doctor	52%	5%	42%
Clinic	50%	9%	39%
School	24%	41%	32%
Local drugstore	34%	34%	31%

For this NEWSWEEK Poll, The Gallup Organization conducted telephone interviews with a representative sample of 606 Americans over the age of 13 on Feb. 5 and 6. The margin of error is plus or minus 5 percentage points. Some "Don't know" and "Other" answers omitted. The NEWSWEEK Poll © 1987 by Newsweek, Inc.

Research Council panel, "it's more common for her to abort or be a single parent, and for the boy to become difficult to find or wash his hands of responsibility." Mnookin says the attitude of most young boys is: "You take the Pill, you take the risk. If you don't want to have a baby, you have an abortion." Mnookin recommends the enforcement of child-support laws to make it clear to young men one "mistake" can mean 18 years of paying bills.

But other experts say that work with boys has to begin on an even more basic level. Louise Flick, an associate professor at the St. Louis University School of Nursing, has reviewed studies conducted over 15 years on teenagers' attitudes toward sexuality. Boys tend to be less well informed about sex and contraception than girls and have more trouble discussing sex—although they may cover up their discomfort with "macho" talk. The boys' role is crucial in contraception. "Girls say they don't want to use contraceptives because their partners don't want them to," says Morales of The Hub. "The boys say condoms don't feel good, destroy the sensation, are artificial. The condoms made today are so thin, you can't feel them."

Some groups are making special efforts to reach boys. It's not easy. Charles Ballard, who runs the Teen Fathers Program in Cleveland, says that one day he asked a group of 15 boys how many were fathers. Only two raised their hands. When he asked how many had babies, 14 hands went up. "They just don't think like fathers," Ballard says. "They don't connect pregnancy with marriage or husbanding or fatherhood." At least 65 percent of his clients never really knew their own fathers. "No man has ever touched their lives except a policeman," he says, "and he was approaching them with a gun or billyclub in his hand."

Although many boys seem to be able to ignore the responsibilities of parenthood, AIDS has made them think about condoms. Fear of dying isn't the only reason; teenagers often have a hard time believing in their own mortality. "They're terrified of getting AIDS and being labeled homosexual," says Medora Brown, who runs the sex-education program at Como High School in St. Paul, Minn. "That's the issue—they are more afraid of having people call them gay than they are of dying."

Comic strip: Family-planning groups and condom manufacturers are taking advantage of this increased receptivity to contraceptives. A series of Planned Parenthood ads featuring comic strips of young people urges readers to "protect your love with condoms." Condoms are coming out of the wallet; not only are manufacturers placing ads in mainstream publications and TV stations like KRON in San Francisco, they are trying to appeal to younger audiences, experimenting with packaging and hipper slogans. Rev. Carl Titchener of suburban Buffalo dispensed condoms during a sermon on AIDS last Sunday.

Condoms have begun to appear on regular television programs as well—a move that health-care experts say is particularly important since teenagers get many of their ideas about sex from television and movies. In the Harris poll, substantial numbers of teenagers said that they thought television presented an accurate portrayal of sexually transmitted diseases, pregnancy and birth control. Younger teenagers were more likely to believe in television than older teens. "TV has become the major form of sex education," says Dr. Victor Strasburger, head of the American Academy of Pediatrics task force on children and television. The problem is, sex on television isn't very realistic.

Koop and Bennett Agree to Disagree

Secretary of Education William Bennett and Surgeon General C. Everett Koop, two of America's most visible and voluble conservatives, have clashed in recent weeks over the issue of sex education for teenagers. Two weeks ago, in an attempt to head off a looming feud, the two issued a joint statement. They managed to agree on this much: "Education has a fundamental role to play in teaching our young people how to avoid that threat [of AIDS]." On the important questions that lie just beyond, however—what kind of role education should play and how far it should go—they seem to have agreed to disagree. Curiously, it is not the education secretary but the surgeon general who has taken a broader view of what students should learn about AIDS in school.

Last week, at the convention of the National Religious Broadcasters, Koop was out once again stumping for the use of condoms to prevent the spread of AIDS. He repeated the joint statement's position that "the safest approach to sexuality for adults is to choose either abstinence or faithful monogamy." But in the absence of such a choice, he went on, "an individual must be warned to use the protection of a condom." The Koop-Bennett statement had made no mention of condoms, which the surgeon general in November had called the best protection short of abstinence. "Strong, honest and family-centered" sex education (which Koop prefers to call "health and human development") should begin in kindergarten, he told the religious broadcasters, and explain the dangers of sexually transmitted diseases—specifically AIDS—in junior high school.

Moral context: Bennett is moving more cautiously. He says schools should stress abstinence and should teach about sex only as a part of marriage. "In matters like this," he says, "I trust the judgment of the local community instead of the sexperts." Even where sex education is taught, he adds, contraception, abortion and condom-protection should not automatically be made part of the curriculum, nor should contraceptives be dispensed in school. (Koop has not taken a position on contraceptive distribution.) To do so "encourages those children who do not have sexual intimacy on their minds to have it on their minds," he said in a speech last year. Sen. Paul Simon, Democrat of Illinois, who plans in this Congress to reintroduce his bill calling for federal funding of school clinics that might offer family-planning services, suggests that "It's been too long since [Bennett] was a teenager." But Bennett argues that sex education should be taught "in a moral context" and that to dispense contraceptives in schools "is to throw up one's hands and say, 'We give up'."

Koop and others argue, in effect, that sex is a fact of life. Last week, speaking to the religious broadcasters, the surgeon general cited a Michigan State University study that found that large numbers of 9th- and 10th-grade girls watch one to two hours of soap operas every day; the programs show or discuss sex between unmarried partners an average of 1.5 times an hour. "You as Christians will continue to be tested by tremendous questions that arise from the turmoil of current events," he said and urged them to face squarely the sensitive intertwining of sexuality and public health. For non-Christians too, these are frightening issues. And short of a cure, education may be the only answer.

BILL BAROL *with* MARY HAGER *and* PAT WINGERT *in Washington*

Lovers usually hop into bed quite spontaneously—with little thought of the consequences. Teenagers raised on these scenes of impulsive romance think they're watching the only course of true love. Last October Planned Parenthood launched an ad campaign with slogans like "When J.R. took Mandy for a roll in the hay, which one had the condom?" and "They did it 20,000 times on television last year. How come nobody got pregnant?" Says Faye Wattleton, president of the Planned Parenthood Federation of America: "Just as sex is integrated into most programming, prevention should be also. It should go hand in hand."

Some television executives are beginning to make changes, partly in response to pressure from groups like Planned Parenthood. "We were avoiding the issues," concedes Al Rabin, executive director of the soap opera "Days of Our Lives." "We had teens losing their virginity. When we wanted her to get pregnant, she'd get pregnant, but we never mentioned contraception." Rabin developed a new story line where a young girl wants to make love with her boyfriend and discusses it with her grandmother, her brother, a doctor and a married girlfriend—all of whom urge her to use birth control. The program even showed her boyfriend buying a condom.

There are changes on prime time as well. The producers of the NBC show "Valerie" say it wasn't easy to convince the network's censors to let them use the word "condom" on a sitcom. "If you can talk about it on the 6 o'clock news," says coexecutive producer Thomas Miller, "why can't you talk about it on 8 o'clock sitcoms?" Miller finally won, but when the show ran Sunday, it was preceded by an advisory from the network that parents watch the show with their children. It won't be the last time condoms appear on television. In April, ABC is going to air a movie called "Daddy" that shows a teenage boy passing a condom to a friend. " 'Daddy' is not a two-hour movie dealing with an unwanted pregnancy that never produces a baby," says Ted Harbert, ABC's vice president for motion pictures. "In our movie, [a teenage girl] has the baby in the first hour and you spend the next hour watching her deal with the consequences." The 22-year-old star, Dermot Mulroney, says he didn't have to do a lot of research on the subject to prepare for his role. "I went to high school in Virginia where, my senior year, there were 52 pregnancies," Mulroney says. "An unplanned pregnancy is as devastating as a death in the family. It changes your life forever."

Low income: As well-intended as all these efforts are, they may be treating only the symptoms, not the disease. Teenagers who begin sex early and don't use contraceptives are likely to come from low-income homes or single-parent families. "They're little kids with grown-up problems," says Kim Cox, a health educator at Balboa High School in San Francisco. They are moved to sex, many of them, not by compassion or love or any of the other urges that make sense to adults, but by a need for intimacy that has gone unfulfilled by their families. "Sex," says Cox, "is an easy way to get it."

Teenagers make important decisions about their lives on their own—without much help from parents. It's not just that adults are uncomfortable discussing sex with their kids, although many probably are. The teenagers don't think they can talk to their parents. In the Harris poll, 64 percent of teenagers said they had never discussed birth control with their parents.

Parents are also reluctant to assert their authority in a positive way. Dr. Catherine Deangelis, a professor of pediatrics and adolescent medicine at Johns Hopkins University in Baltimore who runs an inner-city health clinic for teenagers, says she often sees 13- and 14-year-olds come into her clinic with their mothers—both dressed in jeans. "My first question is how does she know you're her mother? I mean, psychologically, that you are her mother, not her friend?" Deangelis tries to teach parents that they must set limits for their children and teach them right from wrong.

As the problems of teenage pregnancy and the fear of AIDS grow worse, the dilemma will deepen as well: where to draw the line between the rights and responsibilities of parents and society's need to protect itself. Our children—and their children—will be waiting for the answer.

BARBARA KANTROWITZ *with* MARY HAGER *and* PAT WINGERT *in Washington,* GINNY CARROLL *in Detroit,* GEORGE RAINE *in San Francisco,* MONROE ANDERSON *in Chicago,* DEBORAH WITHERSPOON *in New York,* JANET HUCK *in Los Angeles and* SHAWN DOHERTY *in Boston*

A Second Look at the

ROBERT LESSER

With the recent ban on IUDs, millions of women will have to reconsider the pill . . . in its improved low-dose form.

Judy Ismach

Judy Ismach is an associate editor of Physician's Weekly.

First came the scare headlines: "Pill Linked to Cancer," "Pill Users at Risk for Fatal Blood Clots." Millions of couples went racing for other kinds of birth control: IUDs, diaphragms, condoms and sterilization—the most effective method.

But now IUDs, for the most part, are on the way out. The Dalkon Shield has been linked to deaths, and the apparent complications of other IUDs have led to a rash of lawsuits. Though G.D. Searle & Co. calls these suits "unwarranted," it has stopped selling its IUDs in the U.S.; insurance and legal costs ran too high. The only remaining American IUD is Progestasert, manufactured by Alza Pharmaceuticals. But many doctors believe it's no substitute—its progesterone limits the number of users and it must be replaced every year. (See "IUDs: **Chaos in Contraceptive Land," next page.**)

The virtual disappearance of IUDs raises a tough question: Should women reconsider the pill? Many are still scared of it. Three-quarters of 1,000 women surveyed in a Gallup Poll last year believe the pill is risky. Their main concern: cancer. Among women with partners, pill use dropped from about 7 million in 1973 to roughly 4 million in 1982, according to the National Center for Health Statistics.

Much of the pill's early bad publicity was probably deserved. Inadequately tested at first, it was promoted—and received—as the great sexual emancipator. Then the bad news hit: The pill was associated with blood clots and other cardiovascular disorders.

But 26 years of experience have changed both the pill and the way it's used. Today, say the experts, the pill remains unsafe for some women—but quite safe for many. The key is knowing the best version of the pill to use and whether it's risky for *you*.

A New, Improved Pill

The best thing that's happened to the pill since 1960 has been a drop in its estrogen and progesterone. They're the hormones that were linked to cardiovascular disease in earlier studies, says Dr. Philip D. Darney, an associate professor of obstetrics and gynecology at the University of California, San Francisco. The new lower-dose pills work like the earlier ones: They suppress ovulation and bring about other changes, such as making the uterine lining inhospitable to implanting the fertilized egg. But they do this by combining smaller and less potent amounts of a synthetic version of the hormone progesterone—called progestin—with only 20 to 35 mg of estrogen, about one-fifth the amount in the original pill.

Then there are the new biphasic and triphasic combination pills. These also have less estrogen than earlier pills. And they vary hormone levels to reflect normal hormonal variations, which may lower the risk of side effects. No contraceptive is completely risk-free—including the risk of pregnancy—but with the new lower-dose pills, complications are far below researchers' predictions in the '60s and '70s. A National Institutes of Health study estimates the decrease in the

Low-dose pills:
Are they right for you—
or are they risky?

risk of heart attack and stroke may be as great as 80%.

Another alternative: the minipill—no estrogen, just progestin. It works, doctors believe, by changing cervical mucus so sperm can't penetrate, and by inhibiting uterine-lining development so that if an egg *is* fertilized, implantation can't occur. But because it's less effective and causes spotting, even better chemical solutions are being sought (see "Future Pills," next page).

Even if the new pill is safe for the cardiovascular system, what about cancer—most women's main concern? In fact, there's no convincing evidence that the pill causes any kind of

malignant tumor. And there are even studies to show it somehow *protects* against ovarian and endometrial cancer, says Dr. David B. Thomas, an epidemiology professor at the University of Washington in Seattle.

A few researchers have found higher breast cancer rates among women who used the pill in their teens or before their first pregnancy. But others haven't. Overall, more than a dozen studies show the breast cancer rate is the same for both groups.

Researchers have looked for a link between the pill and melanoma, as well as cancers of the pituitary, thyroid and gall bladder—but have found nothing.

Although some have also eyed the pill as a cervical cancer risk, the findings are regarded as inconclusive because women who've used oral contraceptives tend to have more sex partners, a risk factor in cervical cancer.

The pill may also have some real benefits: Benign breast lumps, ovarian cysts and possibly rheumatoid arthritis are less likely to occur with pill use. And the pill may protect some women against pelvic inflammatory disease (PID) caused by gonorrhea.

Who Should Be Cautious?

Short of surgical sterilization, which usually can't be undone, the pill's certainly the most effective contraceptive. In actual use, the failure rate—from both real contraceptive failure and improper use of the method—is 2% for estrogen/progestin pills. For the minipill: 3%. For the closest competitors, the diaphragm and condom: 10%.

The pill is so convenient and effective many women may stick with it even if they experience side effects. And many side effects are avoidable, or at least harmless. For example:

■ *Breakthrough bleeding.* The new, low-dose estrogen version and the minipill have a higher rate of breakthrough bleeding, due to lower—or nonexistent—amounts of estrogen. Bleeding's an inconvenience, but not dangerous. It happens while the body adjusts to the pill's hormones. Ask your doctor about switching to a different brand or to one with slightly higher estrogen. You may also cut down on bleeding by switching to the newer biphasics and triphasics that release different amounts of the hormones at different times of the month.

■ *Nausea, bloating, fatigue, breast*

IUDS: CHAOS IN CONTRACEPTIVE LAND

Saying goodbye is never easy. And it wasn't when Searle, citing high litigation and insurance costs, pulled the plug on some of the last IUDs.

The first mass-produced IUDs—the plastic Lippes Loop and Saf-T-Coil—came out in the mid-1960s when the pill's safety was first questioned. Almost as effective as the pill, they could be forgotten until check-up time. Although no one's really sure how IUDs work, researchers suspect they prevent pregnancy by causing chronic inflammation of the uterine lining.

But complications surfaced: uterine perforation, IUDs embedding in the uterine lining, too many infections. In fact, pelvic inflammatory disease (PID) has been two to seven times more common in IUD users. IUD strings facilitate the movement of harmful organisms from the vagina, spreading eventually to the fallopian tubes. In the process they often cause

scarring, infertility or ectopic pregnancy. A.H. Robins' Dalkon Shield was linked to thousands of cases of PID, as well as spontaneous septic abortions (miscarriages)—some fatal.

But the Dalkon Shield's design was defective. And despite the hazards, IUDs have scored high with older women who've had families but reject sterilization. Because they're monogamous and unlikely candidates for sexually transmitted diseases (STDs), they're at the lowest risk for infectious complications.

With these women in mind, many physicians stocked up on IUDs, so you can probably still locate one if you want to. There's also no reason to remove Searle's CU-7 or TATUM-T (or any other FDA-approved IUD, except the Dalkon Shield) before you would ordinarily get your replacement.

In 1980, the Population Council, a nonprofit group, developed several copper IUDs now marketed in other countries. But unless the group can find a U.S. company to manufacture its IUDs, you may have trouble finding a replacement when it's needed.

tenderness or fullness for up to three months. Here's the downside of estrogen/progestin pills and minipills. You may also gain or lose weight or experience mood swings. Try switching brands if they don't go away.

■ *Chloasma.* The skin darkens across the nose and cheeks, a hyperpigmentation that also occurs in pregnancy. It happens with minipills and the combination varieties, but it's rare and not dangerous. You may want to switch your birth control method if this happens. If you go off the pill, the darkening usually fades. But see your doctor if any pill symptoms last longer than three months.

For some women, though, potential side effects are far more serious:

■ If you smoke and are over 35, most experts agree, all birth control pills are dangerous. The death rate for women in that age group who smoke and take the pill is four times higher than for nonsmoking users; almost all of the pill's cardiovascular complications—blood clots, strokes and heart attacks—occur after 35. Any artificial hormone, including those in the minipill, may increase the risk of these diseases. Studies from the American College of Obstetricians and Gynecologists cite a pill-related death rate (among women using higher dose pills) of 84 in 100,000 smokers ages 35 to 44. In contrast, the pill-related death rate for nonsmokers in the same age group is 23 in 100,000. For nonsmoking pill-users 15 to 24: 0.6 in 100,000.

■ Even if you don't smoke, most doctors agree: Skip the pill if you're over 40. Cardiovascular problems start showing up at that age. Play it safe.

■ Look elsewhere if you have clotting or circulation problems, severe varicose veins or thrombophlebitis (clots that can travel from the legs to the lungs), heart disease, heart defects or a history of stroke. Check out other options, too, if you have breast or reproductive-organ cancer or undiagnosed, abnormal genital bleeding. Oral contraceptives may speed tumor growth, though they don't appear to *cause* cancer.

■ Hepatitis, liver tumors and other liver diseases are more reasons to stay away from the pill. The liver must be healthy to metabolize estrogen and progesterone.

■ Women with pregnancy-related or chronic diabetes and those with a strong family history of the illness should discuss the pill's pros and cons with a doctor. The pill may affect a diabetic woman's insulin needs, and her cardiovascular risk is already high. But pregnancy also carries potential dangers.

More cautions: Consider skipping the low-dose estrogen pill if you have migraine headaches, high blood pressure, asthma, epilepsy, sickle cell anemia or kidney disease. It may aggravate these conditions.

Stop using the pill in any form if there's a chance you're pregnant. If you're nursing, most oral contraceptives can decrease your milk supply and the amount of protein, fat and calcium you feed your baby. The minipill, however, isn't a problem.

Despite new research and many improvements, taking the pill still involves a serious decision. But it's not a decision to make by the headlines. Every woman should take an informed look at the choices that are right for her body—and then decide with her doctor whether today's new pill is right for her.

FUTURE PILLS: THE NEXT 25 YEARS

At a time when contraceptive choices are shrinking, researchers are working on some promising alternatives.

One is Norplant, a small, permeable, removable silicon rod filled with progestin and implanted under the skin of the arm. It presumably works by thickening cervical mucus, blocking sperm and inhibiting ovulation.

Scientists are also testing a synthetic form of gonadotropin-releasing hormone (GnRH), the master reproductive hormone of both sexes. Delivered in a daily nasal-spray pump or implanted, it inhibits ovulation by directly affecting the pituitary gland.

RU 486, a steroid compound, blocks the effects of progesterone, needed for implanting and maintaining a fertilized egg. Studied abroad for inducing abortion, the controversial agent is likely to run into roadblocks in the U.S.

Last year, researchers isolated and reproduced an elusive protein called inhibin. Although its natural role is unclear, in laboratory tests inhibin blocks sperm and egg cell development without interfering with the natural hormonal balance. Someday the substance may provide safe hormonal contraception for women *and* men.

What about vaccines? Edinburgh researcher John Aitken is at work on two. One produces antibodies to the zona pellucida, the translucent shell surrounding the egg. In animal studies, he found that those antibodies keep sperm from penetrating the egg. Aitken's second approach: finding sites on sperm crucial to fertilization and blocking these with antibodies.

HOW WE CAN PREVENT TEEN PREGNANCY (AND WHY IT'S NOT THE REAL PROBLEM)

Peter C. Scales, Ph.D.
Executive Director
Family Connection, Inc.
Anchorage, AK 99508

Abstract

Research on the relationship of sexuality education and contraceptive availability to teen pregnancy prevention is reviewed in light of charges that each has encouraged higher teen pregnancy rates. It appears that neither sexuality education nor contraceptive availability can be blamed for teen pregnancy rates, and that in fact the overwhelming weight of research evidence is that these factors have helped limit or reduce teen pregnancy rates. The current debate focuses more upon teen sexual activity than it does upon teen pregnancy, and if public policy interest is truly in preventing teen pregnancy, models currently exist which can contribute to that goal. Comprehensive programs, including but not limited to school-based clinics, are capable of reducing teen pregnancy rates. Programs which focus exclusively upon helping young people "say no to sex" are criticized. The costs of instituting a widespread national campaign of comprehensive programs are compared to the current costs annually of paying for families begun by teen pregnancy.

The United States has the highest teen pregnancy rate in the developed world. I hope that shocks people. At 96 pregnancies per 1,000 young women aged 15–19, our rate is three times Sweden's and seven times that of the Netherlands. It is double the rate of Canada and England. That is pregnancy rate, not birth rate, so those nations' lower figures are not due to having more teen abortions. In fact, it's just the opposite: those countries have a lower teen pregnancy rate *and* a lower teen abortion rate. The United States has the highest teen abortion rate in the developed world (Jones et al., 1985). Even further, all these countries with lower teen pregnancy and abortion rates also have lower infant mortality rates than the United States (Anchorage Daily News, 1986b).

The reasons for these differences are clear. Sweden has comprehensive, early sexuality education and the Netherlands has easy access to contraception, along

with plenty of advertising. Clearly, if you are pro-life and pro-health, you've got to be pro-sexuality education. The main reason, however, seems to be that these nations are not wasting policy time debating whether adolescents should have sexual relationships. They acknowledge that a sufficiently large proportion will, regardless of adults' wishes; and that adults who fail to assist young people in learning about their sexuality are the ones guilty of irresponsibility, not the youth. Each of those countries views sexuality education as a life-long process, and views sexuality as a positive force capable of enriching and fulfilling human lives in noncoercive, mutually enjoyable ways. When these countries provide sexuality education, their motives are both to help youth avoid problems and also to learn how to enhance pleasure (gasp!). That context is completely different from how we go about it in the United States.

The net effect of a sexuality-positive climate, and not necessarily a *sex act*-positive one, is to make it more acceptable to talk about sexuality, to seek information and advice openly, and to *plan* how sexuality will or will not affect various relationships. All this helps young people take personal responsibility for their actions. In the United States, by way of contrast and particularly for young women, a veneer of magical, other-worldly influence—fate, romance, being "swept away"—seems to be necessary, as revealed in the too-often heard, plaintive explanation: it "just happened" (Cassell, 1985).

Some of our educators have realized this, of course, but they have hardly been rewarded for their insights. Over 40 years ago, sex education pioneer Lester Kirkendall convened a national conference under the auspices of the U.S. Office of Education. The final recommendation of the meeting was that sexuality should be covered in a "positive and affirming" manner "resting on fulfilled living" rather than on avoiding "social evils." It should come as no surprise that to this day, those conference recommendations have never been published (Kirkendall, 1984).

Let it be said very clearly: we have never tried good sexuality education in this country.

In 1979, I was with Mathtech, Inc., a Washington, DC research firm. After conducting the most extensive survey ever of all the data available on sexuality education, we concluded that no more than 10% of the nation's teenagers ever had a "comprehensive" course. Comprehensive meant that no subjects were forbidden or censored, the course lasted the better part of a semester, and teachers were free to respond to any question students raised (Kirby, Alter, & Scales, 1979). A few years ago, the Urban Institute repeated much of the same type of survey, but also collected new data from 179 large school districts around the country. This time, they defined "comprehensive" to be 75% of the students taking the course by the 9th grade; it was at least 10 hours in duration; and it covered most of a long list of subjects. The bottom line? No more than about 15% of the students could be said to have a comprehensive course by those standards (Sonenstein and Pittman, 1984).

Yet, a good many conservative leaders are still guilty of saying that sex education has caused the teen pregnancy problem. Common sense tells us something different. Only 15% have had uncensored, comprehensive sexuality education, but over 55% have had intercourse by the time they graduate from high school, according to the Johns Hopkins University research that is considered the most solid source of such figures (Zelnik & Kantner, 1980). Only one study to date has suggested that sexuality education is somehow associated with starting sexual activity. That finding was only marginally significant, was limited to a subgroup of 15–16 year olds, and is contrary to the findings of every other similar study. In fact, that study found that having a fundamentalist Protestant upbringing bore more relation to first intercourse at age 16 than having a sex education course did (Marsiglio & Mott, 1986).

Study after study shows that sex education does not stimulate sexual behavior. Sexual behavior patterns simply do not change much as a result of a course, suggesting that a single sex education course has a modest influence on such complex behavior (Kirby, 1984). More to the point, our common sense tells us that knowledge leads to responsible actions and that ignorance produces irresponsibility. The research, difficult as it is to summarize because of differences in quality and method, backs up that conclusion.

If anything, the evidence suggests that sex education helps delay sexual activity. Students who take a sex education course do increase their factual knowledge about sexuality. Knowledge alone may not lead to wise choices, but wise choices are impossible without a factual base to stand on.

More importantly, students' values for their own sexual behavior do not seem to change after involvement in a sex education program. In other words, if you don't believe in having premarital sex prior to a course, you probably won't believe in it afterwards. Students do seem to have a better idea of what their values are following a course. Knowing where they stand gives them strength to resist experiences which contradict and violate those values.

Moreover, there is evidence that youth who have had a sex education course are more likely to know about contraception, use it more regularly, and use the most effective methods. Finally, some courses have had the impact of increasing communication between parents and children about sexuality. That would hardly dispose young people toward sexual activity (Dawson, 1986).

A 1986 study of interstate differences in teen pregnancy rates also concluded that when a higher proportion of high school seniors had taken a sex education class, the teen pregnancy rate was lower. In fact, *a 10% greater proportion of students receiving sex education translated to a state teen pregnancy rate 5 points lower than states with lower sex education enrollment* (Singh, 1986).

Although it is obvious from research, as well as from personal anecdote, that there is very little quality, comprehensive sex education in this country, there has been an increase in the number of students receiving something in schools, and probably an increase in the depth at which it is covered. Perhaps, given the positive outcomes of sex education described earlier, this has had a beneficial impact upon our teen pregnancy rates. Clearly, we could be doing more. However, if the teen pregnancy rate is calculated only on the sexually active (who, after all, are the only ones who can get pregnant), then the U.S. rate essentially stayed the same between 1974 and 1982 (latest figures at this writing), going down in one period and up in another (Select Committee, 1985). Without even this less than adequate sex education, perhaps it could be assumed that the rate would have gone up even more.

Conservatives cannot have it both ways. Even in a 1986 Reagan Administration report on the family, which charges liberalism with bringing on ruin, the conservative author used data from the National Center for Health Statistics to show that the proportion of sexually experienced teens went down from 1979 to 1982, and concludes, solemnly, that "adolescent sex [sic] is on the decline" (Anchorage Times, 1986a). Yet the data cited earlier in this paper show that the extent and depth of sex education increased slightly in those years. The inescapable conclusion is that *while sex education increased, teen sexual activity decreased.*

Nonsensically enough, contraception is also blamed for causing teen pregnancy, which is like saying that fire extinguishers cause fires. It is difficult to support that reasoning when ⅔ of teenagers who have had intercourse either *never* use contraception or use it poorly (Zelnik & Kantner, 1980). That pattern even continues into their 20s: 17% of single women in their 20s never use contraception, and ⅓ have been pregnant at least once (Anchorage Daily News, 1986a). The clinics which provide contraception and counseling are also blamed, but only 15% of teenagers ever go to a clinic before starting to have intercourse. How can the clinic cause a behavior that started before they ever got there?

For more than ⅓ of teenagers, their very first visit to a clinic is because they think they are already pregnant. The median average delay between first intercourse and first clinic visit is one full year (Zabin, et al., 1984). That astonishing gap is one reason why the National Academy of Sciences recommended in 1986 far more widespread availability of low cost, confidential contraceptive services for teenagers. They pointedly stated that there is no evidence that contraceptive availability encourages earlier teen sexual activity (N.A.S., 1986).

So neither comprehensive sexuality education nor the availability of contraception can be blamed for this country's teenage pregnancy problem. Partly because some people believe that they are to blame, however, the "saying no to sex" movement has mushroomed over the last few years. Sexuality educators have been pointing out for years that the best programs have always included saying no as an important part of the program, but the new wave is devoted exclusively to saying no. The National Academy of Sciences report found "little evidence" that this approach works. Unlike more comprehensive sexuality education, almost no evaluation studies have been done on the "saying no" programs. The one evaluation now being done of an Atlanta program may not, according to some experts, be designed well enough to provide useful answers.

But what does saying no really mean? The two questions around which these programs dance lightly are: 1) saying no until when? and 2) saying no to intercourse or to all sexual activity? Are we really expecting all young people to say no until marriage, when the average age at marriage, now in the mid-20s, is the oldest since the statistics were first collected back in 1890 (U.S. Bureau of Census, 1985)? Perhaps this might have been plausible 20 years ago, when polls showed that 85% of Americans thought "premarital" sex was wrong. The social context is different today, with the Harris and Yankelovich polls showing that only about 30% of Americans think "premarital" sex is wrong. Significantly, it is parents of school-age children who are the *least* likely to agree that it is wrong!

The real reason we have guaranteed the ineffectiveness of sexuality education so far; the real reason why we have not yet mounted a coordinated, multi-faceted national campaign to reduce unplanned teen pregnancy, is that the debate is not over teen pregnancy. The issue is really teen sexual activity.

The debate has been strong enough to affect young people, leaving many guilty and ashamed of their sexual desires, feelings and activities. Research has shown repeatedly over the past 20 years that guilt does not prevent sexual intercourse, but it does prevent planning ahead contraceptively (Gordon, Scales, & Everly, 1979). I would also argue that guilt actually prevents young people from thinking clearly enough about their sexuality to say no more often.

If the debate were really about teen pregnancy, we have enough data now to know that at least one approach is promising. It does prevent teen pregnancy. That is the model where a school sexuality education program is linked with an adolescent health clinic located either in the school itself or nearby. The extensive Mathtech research (Kirby, 1985) clearly demonstrates this, as do more recent studies from the Center for Population Options, and an important Baltimore study. In the latter study, 28 months into the program, "experimental" group students had a 30% decline in their number of pregnancies, while students in the "control" group showed a whopping 58% increase. What's more, those students in the program who were virgins *delayed* their first intercourse 6 months longer than students who were also virgins but not in the program (Sexuality Today, 1986; Zabin, et al., 1986). These results were noted 2½ years into the program. Researcher Douglas Kirby (1985) has demonstrated that no sexuality education program alone, no matter how good, has yet come close to achieving these impressive results in just one year, and no sex education program alone (without a clinic component) has been studied for its impact over three years.

These data and emerging data from a Ford Foundation-Carnegie Corporation project are showing that we have methods that "work," comprehensive services linking sexuality education with clinics and other occupational and medical resources (Ford Foundation, 1985). These approaches work both by delaying sexual activity and by making contraception more available. They also link young people with dropout prevention, job training, and other medical and social services. They provide opportunities which demonstrate better than any lecture how teen pregnancy and parenthood can wipe out options, hopes and dreams, and lessen one's control over one's life.

Incredibly enough, these programs are already being attacked as causing teen pregnancy (Education Daily, 1986). We are hearing the same foolishness about school-linked clinics as we have heard about sexuality education for years. If we allow our moral politics to prevent us from using this model, we have only ourselves to blame. Our common sense ought to prevail. If we imbed the sexuality education component within a life skills approach, and we begin early enough (by the fourth grade), supplemented by clinic and other links to community resources in the junior and senior high schools, we will help young people get control over their lives. That achievement will help us reduce teen pregnancy, and other social ills in the process.

Some will say, even if we can get past the debate over sexual activity, that a national program of such efforts would cost too much. Based on doubling the average published costs of providing these comprehensive programs, it could take about $30,000 per year per every 100 teens who needed it (Pittmman, 1986). About 30% of young people seem to be handling these choices adequately already, so perhaps less costly options would suffice to reinforce what they have already learned. If we initiated programs for the remaining 70%, or about seven million teens, then we would spend about $2.1 billion. That is just one-eighth the price we're paying now each year trying to help families begun by teen pregnancy.

If we made that kind of financial commitment for five years or so, we would recoup far more than a 8:1 return on our investment, because we might begin to affect patterns generationally, and affect far more than just teen pregnancy. We apparently already recognize that it may take $3 billion or more to deal effectively with drug abuse (Weinraum, 1986), so I do not think the hope for this kind of investment is wildly misplaced.

In the book *Crime and Human Nature*, James Q. Wilson concludes that the best crime prevention strategies are policies and programs that strengthen family life. A 1986 Southern State Legislators Conference shows that key justice officials are also seeing the connection between crime and the family weakening influence of teen pregnancy. They are citing crime prevention down the road as a payoff from preventing teen pregnancy today (Anchorage Times, 1986b). The national consensus is emerging.

People whose lives are in order, whose burdens do not exceed their developmental or financial readiness to shoulder them, and who see hope and opportunity without limit, end up giving more to society than they take from it. It is time to dedicate ourselves to helping our young become these types of people.

References

Anchorage Daily News (1986a). 40% of single women abort 1st pregnancy, study finds. June 2, 1986.

Anchorage Daily News (1986b). Scandanavian countries have lowest infant mortality rates. September 17, 1986.

Anchorage Times (1984). Neighborhood schools get best rating. June 23, 1984.

Anchorage Times (1986a). Family report released. November 13, 1986, p. A3.

Anchorage Times (1986b). States meet to discuss growing teen pregnancy problem. November 18, 1986.

Cassell, C. (1985). *Swept away.* New York: Simon and Schuster.

Dawson, D.A. (1986). The effects of sex education on adolescent behavior. *Family Planning Perspectives, 18,* (4), 162–170.

Education Daily (1986). School birth control clinics a mistake, report asserts. *Education Daily.* August 27, p. 5, Alexandria, VA: Capitol Publications.

Ford Foundation (1985). Preventing teen pregnancy. *Ford Foundation Letter,* December 1, p. 6.

Gordon, S., Scales P., & Everly, K. (1979). *The sexual adolescent: Communicating with teenagers about sex.* North Scituate, MA: Duxbury.

Jones, E.F. et al. (1985). Teenage pregnancy in developed countries: Determinants and policy implications. *Family planning perspectives, 17,* (2), 53–63.

Kirby, D., Alter, J., & Scales, P. (1979). *An analysis of US sex education programs and evaluation methods.* Springfield, VA: National Technical Information Service.

Kirby, D. (1984). *Sexuality education: An evaluation of programs and their effects.* Santa Cruz, CA: Network Publications.

Kirby, D. (1985). The effects of selected sexuality education programs: Toward a more realistic view. *Journal of Sex Education and Therapy, 11,* (1), 28–37.

Kirkendall, L.A. (1984). The journey toward SIECUS: a personal odyssey. *SIECUS Report, 12,* 1-4.

Marsiglio, W. & Mott, F.L. (1986). Sex education for American youth: Its availability, timing and relationship to teenage first intercourse and premarital pregnancies. *Family Planning Perspectives, 18,* (4), 151–162.

N.A.S. (1986). *Risking the future.* Washington, DC: National Academy of Sciences.

Pittman, K. (1986). *Preventing adolescent pregnancy: What schools can do.* Washington: Children's Defense Fund.

Select Committee (1985). *Teen pregnancy—What is being done?* Washington, DC: Report of the Select Committee on Children, Youth and Families, US House of Representatives, December.

Sexuality Today (1986). School-based clinic achieves dramatic decrease in teen pregnancies. *Sexuality Today,* July 14, 1–2.

Singh, S. (1986). Adolescent pregnancy in the United States: An interstate analysis. *Family Planning Perspectives, 18,* (5), 210–220.

Sonenstein, F.L., and Pittman, K.J. (1984). The Availability of Sex Education in Large City School Districts. *Family Planning Perspectives, 16,* (1), 19–25.

U.S. Bureau of the Census (1985). Marital status and living arrangements: March 1984. *Current population reports,* Series P-20, no. 399.

Weinraum, B. (1986). Reagan says nation's schools have improved. *New York Times,* September 7, 1986.

Zabin, L.S., Hardy, J.B., Streett, R., & King, T.M. (1984). School-, hospital-, and university-based adolescent pregnancy prevention program. *Journal of Reproductive Medicine, 29,* (6), 421–426.

Zabin, L.S., Hirsch, M.B., Smith, E.A., Streett, R. & Hardy, J.B. (1986). Adolescent pregnancy prevention program. *Journal of Adolescent Health Care, 7,* 77–87.

Zelnik, M. & Kantner, J.F. (1980). Sexual activity, contraceptive use and pregnancy among metropolitan-area teenagers, 1971–1979. *Family Planning Perspectives, 12,* (5), 230–237.

RU-486: the unpregnancy pill

WILL the latest "contraceptive miracle" survive the pressures of politics, economics, and international rivalry?

SUE M. HALPERN
Sue M. Halpern is associate research scholar at the Center for the Study of Society and Medicine at the Columbia University College of Physicians and Surgeons.

imagine being pregnant, swallowing a pill, and—presto!—not being pregnant any longer. If your imagination is this good, then it will not be difficult to picture why a new drug, mifepristone, has family-planning and reproductive-rights advocates ecstatic, and opponents of abortion distressed. Developed by a team of French researchers under the sponsorship of the Swiss company Hoechst-Roussel Pharmaceuticals, mifepristone, commonly referred to as RU-486, produces a chemical abortion. *The New England Journal of Medicine* calls it a "major advance that will...provide new options" for women. Congressman Robert Dornan (R.-Calif.) calls it "the French death pill." Not since the introduction of the IUD has a breakthrough in reproductive research generated so much excite-

ment; never has it piqued such political controversy.

Of course, we've heard rumblings of the birth-control revolution before. They preceded the Pill, the IUD, and the sponge with claims that the ultimate form of birth control had been discovered; that it was safe, reliable, convenient, and inexpensive; that it had the potential to change our lives. Yet while earlier innovations in contraceptive and reproductive methods enhanced the lives of many women, they proved, more significantly, to be hazardous to the health of women and their offspring. Once use of them was linked to, among other things, cancer, sterilization, and toxic shock syndrome, the revolution they promised was forfeited.

The excitement created by the prospect of RU-486 is, therefore, both

familiar and unusual. In light of the record of contraceptive research, one might realistically expect any new method of birth control to be met with skepticism, if not dismissal. This is hardly the case with RU-486. While a few women's-health advocates, like Judy Norsigian of the Boston Women's Health Book Collective (which produced *Our Bodies, Ourselves*) and Ruth Hubbard, Ph.D., a feminist biology professor at Harvard University, are voicing caution, most are greeting the prospect of RU-486 with uncritical optimism. By far, the major challenge to the testing and marketing of RU-486 comes not from those concerned with women's health, but from the right-to-life movement.

Congressman Dornan, one of the movement's supporters, typifies their position. Despite its obvious extravagance, his "French death pill" epithet contains the kernel of truth on which right-to-life supporters base their objection to the drug: RU-486 is not technically a contraceptive; it is a contragestive. That is, it does not act to prevent the union of sperm and egg but, rather, acts to prevent the implantation of the egg in the womb once it has been fertilized. If the egg is already implanted, it will be expelled. In other words, it induces abortion.

The drug, an antiprogesterone steroid, blocks the cells in the uterus from receiving the hormone progesterone, which is needed to mature the uterine lining in order to support the fertilized egg. In the absence of progesterone, the body is tricked into doing what it would normally do at the end of a menstrual cycle in which no egg has been fertilized—shedding the lining of the uterus. Within 48 hours of the first dose of RU-486, uterine bleeding begins. The difference, of course, is that with RU-486, the fertilized egg is expelled, too.

esearchers envision that RU-486 will be used both as an abortifacient—an agent that induces abortion—to be taken orally or intravenously within the first five to six weeks of pregnancy, and a once-a-month pill, taken a few days before the expected onset of menses. In the latter case, it would enable women to terminate a pregnancy without the knowledge that they were pregnant. In the former, it would allow women to abort privately, without surgical intervention. These properties, claims Dr. Etienne-Emil Baulieu, the French physician who pioneered the development of the steroid, make it likely that "abortion . . . should more or less disappear as a concept, as a fact, as a word in the future."

While Baulieu's claim may be dismissed as the exaggeration of an overzealous parent (since RU-486, which is only effective in the first two months of pregnancy, will not eliminate the need for later-term surgery), it is being treated with unfaltering respect by members of the National Right to Life Committee and other antiabortion groups. In the past, these organizations have won supporters by exploiting the effects of surgical abortion on a fetus in films like "The Silent Scream." As Dr. John Wilke, president of the National Right to Life Committee, conceded on "The MacNeil-Lehrer Report," "It's clearly easier for us to show a picture of what's left after an abortion, let's say right after she misses her second period. You can identify little fingers and hands and ribs." There is no public relations value in a menstruating woman.

Even if abortion as we know it does not disappear as a consequence of RU-486, the drug's widespread use may serve to decimate the ranks of abortion foes. Because RU-486 causes the abortion early in the gestational process, before the fertilized egg has been implanted in the uterus, it is unlikely to seem to most of its users like abortion at all.

This prospect has the pro-life forces understandably edgy. "Since opinion polls show that the public supports contraception but is deeply split over abortion," writes Richard D. Glasow, the education director for National Right to Life, in a pamphlet on the new pill, "proponents of RU-486 are eager to tie it to the former. Moreover, if RU-486 becomes identified in the public's mind with contraception, then right-to-life opposition to the drug could be portrayed as 'reactionary' and 'out-of-touch' with the mainstream of Americans."

At the very least, public acceptance of RU-486 as a legitimate form of birth control is likely to further confuse, if not obscure or possibly moot, the debate over when life begins. This debate is central to the antiabortion argument.

Ironically, it is through right-to-life efforts to discredit RU-486 that we are getting information about the drug's effect on women's health.

To date, clinical trials in 15 countries over five years have revealed RU-486 to be free of major side effects, but such evidence is both relative and inconclusive. According to Dr. Andre Ulmann, one of the principal researchers of the drug for Hoechst-Roussel, "The only way to be sure of the absence of side effects is to test a large number of women in many conditions and to define which is the minimal dose which can be used to induce abortion. So far in these 400 women treated with RU-486, we had no report of any severe side effects—*I mean by severe side effect, any life-threatening side effect.* [Author's italics.] So we are very much confident that the drug is safe."

It is too early in the trial and development process to know if Ulmann's confidence is warranted. What is known, however, is that RU-486 can cause such

---

RU-486's widespread use may decimate the ranks of abortion foes.

"nonsevere" side effects as dizziness, nausea, painful contractions, and hemorrhaging that requires hospitalization and blood transfusion. As Dr. Phillip Stubblefield, chief of ob-gyn at Mt. Auburn Hospital in Cambridge, Massachusetts, and associate professor of ob-gyn at Harvard Medical School, points out, "People don't realize how dangerous natural miscarriage is."

Also problematic is the drug's rate of failure. At best, when paired with a prostaglandin (to induce contractions), RU-486 has fostered complete abortions in 90 percent of subjects during the first six weeks or less of pregnancy. Its rate of success falls precipitously later on in the term. Yet even when it is administered at the most propitious time—within 10 days of a missed period—it has a failure rate of 10 to 15 percent, which researchers cannot account for. In a study of 100 women at the University of Paris (Paris-Sud), reported in *The New England Journal of Medicine*, 15 women did not abort. According to the researchers, "There were no differences between the 85 women who responded to RU-486 and the 15 who did not in regard to age, date of pregnancy, or previous history of pregnancy." Such a finding is alarming, for it indicates critical gaps not only in the researchers' understanding of how the drug operates, but also in their understanding of how the reproductive system functions.

Significantly, the drug's failure to work optimally does not mean that it has failed to have an effect. All 15 subjects in the Paris-Sud study who failed to abort nevertheless reported some uterine bleeding. Similarly, a study of 44 women at the State University Hospital in Utrecht, the Netherlands, found that while 17 percent of them did not abort, all of the latter's pregnancies were affected. Potentially, failure to abort completely is dangerous because it leaves the woman susceptible to infection that may ultimately compromise her ability to bear children in the future.

Since RU-486 has only been tested on human subjects for five years, its safety over time is unknown. In the estimation of Ruth Hubbard, it is also unknowable, for "there is really no way to predict the long-term effects of a drug such as this that interferes in fundamental ways in the molecular biology and cellular biology of a variety of cells in the human organism." She suggests that until we know more about it, RU-486 would best be used as a backup for barrier methods of birth control, rather than as a regular, monthly method itself. However, because the drug is being developed in conjunction with the private, multinational pharmaceutical industry, whose research interests are driven by market forces, Hubbard is afraid that the opposite will occur. The same forces may be responsible for the premature verdict on the safety and efficacy of RU-486.

That private industry is behind the development of RU-486 is more a reflection of the state of publicly funded birth-control research in the United States than an indication of private-sector interest in contraceptive research. The American government, which is the largest supporter of reproductive and contraceptive research in the world, has been prohibited since 1974 from supporting research on abortifacients. (For example, clinical trials to test RU-486 at the University of Southern California are funded by the nonprofit Population Council.) Politicians allied with the antiabortion movement have been vigilant in their efforts to restrict research protocols to ensure that no public funds are expended on RU-486.

Jacqueline Derroch Forrest, director of research at the Alan Guttmacher Institute, believes that people are "overexcited" about the prospect and promise of RU-486. For one thing, it will not eliminate the need for later surgical abortion. For another, it is unlikely that the drug will become available in the United States in the foreseeable future—if ever. She points out that the American market is inhospitable to investing in new methods of birth control. It can cost upward of $45 million and take 10 to 15 years for a contraceptive to be developed and granted approval by the Food and Drug Administration. In that time, drug companies are susceptible to economic and political pressure exerted by the antiabortion movement, including boycotts, picketing, and lobbying. Moreover, even if the political climate were to cool, the prohibitive cost of liability insurance coupled with an increasingly litigious public would serve as serious disincentives to investment. Private pharmaceutical companies like G.D. Searle and Upjohn have all but deserted the American contraceptive market over the past few years. At present, no pharmaceutical company, either domestic or foreign, has expressed plans to seek marketing approval for RU-486 in the United States.

In the meantime, Americans are advised to turn their attention to Europe, where the constraints that exclude RU-486 from the American market are not in effect. Later this year, in Holland and Sweden, RU-486 will be offered under close medical supervision as an alternative to surgical abortion at family-planning clinics—as it is currently in France. Its record in Europe might well indicate if RU-486 is indeed the harbinger of a revolution in fertility control, or another vanquished hope.

Whatever happened to the IUD?

Ginnie T., a certified nurse midwife, has imported 100 Cu-7 ("Copper-Seven") intrauterine birth-control devices (IUDs) from Canada. She gives them to her patients, whom she sees in affiliation with a doctor at her clinic, just as she used to dispense similar Cu-7 IUDs before their manufacturer decided it could no longer afford to sell them in the United States. Ginnie T. is trying to give her patients the best medical care possible; she is also breaking the law.

G.D. Searle and Company says that it stopped selling its IUDs here for business, not medical, reasons. "Our IUDs are safe and effective," claims Searle spokesman Steven Dickinson. "We've discontinued sales here only because liability insurance has become unavailable and our legal expenses have become unaffordable."

Searle estimates that about one million women were using the Cu-7 or its close cousin, the Tatum-T, when both were taken off the market on January 31, 1986. Because these had been the only nonhormonal IUDs remaining on the U.S. market, Searle's decision left these women with no access to replacements.

IUD supporters and detractors alike agree that bad publicity and multimillion-dollar lawsuits against the notoriously dangerous Dalkon Shield have done much to push safer IUDs off the market. But feminist health activists remain divided about the IUDs' withdrawal. Some note that women need more birth-control options, not fewer, and that the IUD has been many women's preferred contraceptive. "Each woman deserved the right to assess the risks and benefits of the IUD and decide if it's right for her," says Ginnie T.

Others believe that no IUDs should be on the market. They note that many IUD users have experienced serious health problems, that manufacturers have been slow to investigate and publicize IUD side effects, and that doctors have often given IUDs to women for whom they are particularly risky.

The most common, and most controversial, serious risk associated with the IUD is pelvic inflammatory disease (PID), an infection that can cause sterility. The poorly designed Dalkon Shield is associated with the highest PID rate of all the IUDs; the Cu-7 has the lowest. Also at increased risk for PID are women who have more than one sexual partner. How these factors interact is unclear. And the heated legal atmosphere surrounding IUDs has made objective information hard to find.

The National Women's Health Network recommends that women approach IUDs with extreme caution. "Women should consider using an IUD only if they have no previous history of PID, do not plan to have children in the future, are over thirty, and have only one, long-term sexual partner," says the network's executive director, Victoria Leonard.

—*Tricia Andryszewski*

Interpersonal Relationships

- **Establishing Sexual Relationships (Articles 27-30)**
- **Responsible Quality Relationships (Articles 31-33)**

Most people are familiar with the term "sexual relationship." It denotes an important dimension of sexuality on which this section focuses attention: interpersonal sexuality, that is sexual interactions occurring between two (and sometimes more) individuals.

No woman is an island. No man is an island. Interpersonal contact forms the basis for self-esteem and meaningful living; conversely, isolation generally spells loneliness and depression for most human beings. People seek and cultivate friendships for the warmth, affection, supportiveness, and sense of trust and loyalty that such relations may provide.

Long-term friendships may develop into intimate relationships. The qualifying word in the previous sentence is "may." Today many people, single as well as married, yearn for close or intimate interpersonal relationships but fail to find them. Fear of rejection causes some to present a "false front" or illusory self that they think is more acceptable or socially desirable. This sets the stage for a "game of intimacy" that is counterfeit to genuine intimacy. For others a major enigma may exist: the problem of balancing closeness with preservation of individual identity in a manner that at once satisfies the need for personal as well as interpersonal growth and integrity. In either case, relationship partners may be well-advised that the development of interpersonal awareness (the mutual recognition and knowledge of others as they really are) rests upon self-disclosure: letting the other person know who you really are and how you truly feel. In American society this has never been easy and is especially difficult in the sexuality area.

The above considerations regarding interpersonal relationships apply equally to achieving meaningful and satisfying sexual relationships. Three basic ingredients lay the foundation for quality sexual interaction. These are self-awareness, sharing that awareness with one's partner, and accepting the partner's state of awareness. Without these, misunderstandings may follow, bringing into the relationship anxiety, frustration, dissatisfaction, and/or resentment. Indeed, those three basic ingredients, taken together, may constitute sexual responsibility. Clearly, no one person is completely responsible for quality sexual relations.

As might already be apparent, there is much more to quality sexual relations than our popular culture recognizes. Such relationships are not established on penis size, beautiful figures, or correct sexual techniques. Rather, it is the quality of the interaction that makes sex a celebration of our sexuality. A person-oriented (as opposed to genitally-oriented) sexual awareness, coupled with a leisurely, whole body/mind sensuality and an open attitude toward exploration make for quality sexuality.

The subsection on *Establishing Sexual Relationships* begins with an article about the inadequacy of the way many people learn about sex in the first place. Next, the differences in male-female thinking about love and sex are highlighted. This is followed by a *Psychology Today* article which looks at commitment, intimacy, and passion as three components of love. The last article in this subsection considers the dynamics of friendships. It suggests a need for openness and flexibility to ease hurt feelings.

The first article in the *Reasonable Quality Relationships* subsection gives advice for maintaining and improving relationships. Here, Masters and Johnson provide sixteen steps to better sex. Sex in the workplace is discussed in the next article. The dangers of such activity are noted. Finally, Barbara DeAngelis offers some help for couples who may be bored with their relationship in its present form.

Looking Ahead: Challenge Questions

How do you feel about your childhood sexual information and/or experiences? Do you agree or disagree with the points made in the article by Carol Mithers?

What do you think are the reasons for the differences in male/female thinking about love and sex? Are attitudes improving?

What are the different aspects of love? How can the relative presence or absence of each of these aspects change the type of love that is in a relationship?

Are there some good ways to heal bruised friendships?

What Masters and Johnson tips did you find most valuable? Do you disagree with others?

What are the particular aspects that make an office romance different from any other?

What can you do to improve your sex life in an intimate relationship? How do couples get into "traps" to begin with?

Unit 4

Considering the Way Most of Us Learned About Sex, It's a Wonder We Can Do It, Do It Well or Have Any Interest in Doing It at All

Carol Lynn Mithers

Carol Lynn Mithers is a free-lance writer who lives and works out of Los Angeles and New York.

The Film was an elementary school legend. One day in fifth grade you were marched to the auditorium to see it. You needed a permission slip from home to go. No boys were allowed. The Film was something so secret, so shameful, so tantalizing, no girl who'd seen The Film would discuss it.

The night before I saw it, my mother decided it was time for a talk. As long as I was going to learn about blood, eggs and fallopian tubes, I might as well know the rest. My father, embarrassed, fled the house. I couldn't understand why. The act my mother described—which explained why my parents behaved so oddly when my sister and I, desperate for a brother, begged my father to "give Mommy a baby sometime when she's not looking"—wasn't particularly embarrassing. It was peculiar, but if that's what it took to make a baby, I guessed I could live with it. My father came home and pretended nothing had happened. When I saw The Film the next day, its information was old hat. Life went on as ever.

Well, not quite. Despite the fact that my friends and I couldn't figure out why, something about The Film, the glossy pamphlets the teachers passed out to us and the peculiar act my mother described, was endlessly fascinating. During gym class, separate huddles of boys and girls made jokes about blood and organs, and people getting stuck together. Suddenly it became vital that girls wear bras and that boys snap them, and it was rumored that the popular crowd met at someone's house for after-school make-out parties.

One day I went to my mother with a question that was starting to bother me: I'd more or less grasped what she's told me about this going into that, but how did it *get* there? What exactly happened after it did? How would I know what to do unless I got some real instructions?

"When the time comes, you'll know," was all she said.

I wasn't the only one who found the answer unsatisfactory. Compared to what our parents had been told when they asked about sex—it's dirty, don't do it, let's change the subject—my friends and I, children of The Film and immoral times, were eleven-year-old sexual sophisticates. But we didn't feel that way; we were filled with a growing curiosity about sex. And what we'd been told didn't come close to satisfying. With official information sources exhausted, like generations before us, we turned to those less than official: anyone or thing we could find. With a single-minded thirst for knowledge that would have thrilled our teachers, we began the search for answers.

Even before we knew what to call it, there had been hints of something strange out there, something that had vaguely to do with private parts and babies, something dirty. There were the senseless cocktail-party jokes that made our parents roar, and the innocent questions—for instance, why do those machines in public bathrooms sell sanitary napkins (why can't everyone just use paper towels after going to the toilet?)—that made them blush and clam up. Most of all, there were inexplicable differences in the way

Schools have not been able to effectively fulfill the role of sex education teacher, and a large number of parents do not adequately inform their children about sexuality. As a consequence, much information about this very basic and important human topic comes from peer groups.

Film—or The Book or The Heart-To-Heart Talk—was supposed to do. Sometimes it did: "In sixth grade, the kids at school said sex was someone putting their penis in your butt," recalls Patty. "When I asked my mom about it, what she said didn't shock me at all—it was a lot better than what I'd heard."

But more often the explanations just caused new confusion. "My mother," says Janet, "gave me a copy of *Ann Launders Talks to Teenagers About Sex*, and told me to ask if I had any questions. The book said that people even have sex in cars. The way it explained sex being done—you're lying on your back and you start feeling 'real loving' didn't make sense; people don't lie down and feel loving in their cars. Plus, I'd never seen a man naked, so I had no idea what the book was talking about. I figured there must be part of a man that came off of him, that he could *use* on you somehow."

We had been taught all about reproductive biology. But what we wanted to know about was *sex*. How did it start? What did it feel like? Descriptions of eggs dropping and "loving feelings" never explained how and why male organs could grow to apparently monstrous proportions, how they then fit into the part of a woman's body that had to be coaxed to receive a junior Tampax, and most of all, aside from making a baby, why anyone would *want* this union to happen.

And as our hormones started perking in earnest, when the idea of people "doing it" in cars didn't seem so far-fetched, the need to know became more urgent. But if parents and sex classes had been little help before, when it came to action, etiquette and technique, they were completely useless.

Older brothers and sisters gave sometimes dubious help. "Before I went out on my first date, I asked my sister how to kiss," Denise recalls. "She told me, 'Don't just glue your lips together; you have to keep your mouth moving.' So when the boy and I kissed, I twisted my lips around in this ridiculous manner. I don't know what the guy thought, but we never went out again."

Sometimes, the scholarly approach provided useful information. For boys desperate for a roadmap of a

boys and girls were built. "I never saw a woman without a bra on, either at home or on TV," remembers my friend Jim. "So in early childhood I decided that women wore bras because they didn't have nipples. Bras were what kept their breasts from falling apart and slushing out."

Here and there, rumors of the forbidden act would make the rounds. But since most of us were working with a limited understanding of physiology, the early reports often involved a basic confusion of anatomy and orifices. Gentle correction of such information was, of course, what The

woman's body, *Playboy* showed where everything went. But when it came to describing what things felt like— particularly for women—books often made everything more confused. "There were lots of orgasms in *Valley of the Dolls* and *Lolita*," remembers Rose. "No one could figure out what they were talking about. Your eyes would flutter and fall back into your head and you'd breathe real hard and lose consciousness. When did you wake up?"

In adolescence, boys, whose bodies sometimes took them by surprise, began to understand some of the mystery of the orgasm. Girls first had to learn that there *was* such a thing as female orgasm, and that a fairly inconspicuous body part triggered it (minor details The Film had neglected to mention). While male orgasm is a verifiable thing, female climax— "two- to four-second muscle-spasm contractions . . . followed by rhythmic contractions at intervals of 0.8 of a second," as described in *The Naked Ape*—seemed far more vague.

Of course, questions about sex could always be referred to your peers. Among girls, there was a kind of weird split—we shared the most intimate menstrual information, coyly confessed what base our young lovers had managed to get to the night before and offered tips on how to keep them from going farther ("When the fingers start moving from back to front, move your arm *down*"). But when it came to details, it was different. Those who had done it might worry loudly about overdue periods, but never deigned to share hows and whys with virginal sisters, who veered be tween anticipation and terror of what lay in store for them.

Boys, on the other hand, could always be counted on to give the gory details—whether or not they knew what they were talking about. "None of us knew how you could come unless someone was stroking your penis," says Jim. "So we theorized that in order to have sex you jerked off until you were about to come, then got inside the woman."

Ultimately, all of us ignorant and misguided explorers fell back on what sociologists call "field research," otherwise known as trial and error. Along the way there were surprises, like French kissing. The first time it happened to a girlfriend of mine at a party, Lisa remembers, "she walked around the whole night spitting into a napkin."

When the time came for me to do it, in a way, my mother was right: Without a carefully diagrammed instruction book, I managed to accomplish the sexual act. But my questions had been valid, successfully getting this into that was not the same as knowing what to do. Just about nothing I had heard about sex—including the slang "screw," which led me to expect certain movements that never materialized—described its reality.

In my surprise, as in my earlier curiosity, I wasn't alone. "In books, the man always knows what to do," Anne says. "The man I lost my virginity with didn't know a whole lot more than I did. The first few times we made love I couldn't help thinking 'it doesn't actually fit that well. You have to work to get it in.' In fact, no one ever told me that you had to work at the whole thing, that it takes a while before you get good at it."

In the end, in settings far different from darkened auditoriums and raucous locker rooms, old misconceptions about sex got corrected. All the questions were answered, and the real surprise—even miracle—was that all of us "overeducated" and misinformed children finally did learn to "do it," even, perhaps, do it well.

Or maybe that wasn't such a miracle after all. Because the one thing few of us had been told, none of us had believed—and all of us quickly learned—was that sex is like a lot of the best things in life: Until you've done it, there's no way you can know what it's like. And even the best descriptions, says a friend of mine, "are nothing compared to the real thing."

When Men and Women Think About Sex: WAYS THEY DIFFER

You'd think that after all those years of lusty lib, followed by today's more cautious trend, male-female views on Le Sport *would have converged. But in fact, men remain amazingly unlike us when it comes to love . . .*

Katharine Merlin

The French have a joyous way of putting it: *Vive la différence!* And most of the time, the differences between the sexes *are* a celebration—life's most magic magnet.

On the other hand, there are times when those very differences can make you feel as distant from a man as earth from Mars. Language fails, you're totally out of sync—baffled by the strange, infuriating behavior that's considered "typically male."

Take the night you and he fell into bed after playing out all the ritual moves. You were aroused and inspired, felt as if you were perfectly matched. But just when you were poised on the brink, he murmured, *"Don't have any expectations."*

It's puzzling that even in the eighties, we're as polarized by the gender gap as ever. We've accumulated a wealth of sexual knowledge and are free, within reason, to follow any inclination. But men *still* play out the role of the promiscuous sex, while women remain strung out on dreams of true love. Is it because both sexes *think* about sex in conflicting ways, and if so, are these differences skin-deep or much more fundamental?

M E N
•
The Locker-Room Mentality

Men apparently think about sex *a lot*—about six times an hour, says one survey. "This tendency to eroticize is set in motion by the particular quality of male sexual awakening," says Ron Murphy, a psychologist with the Human Sexuality Center of the Long Island Jewish–Hillside Medical Center.

When the differences that distinguish the men from the boys announce themselves, they aren't exactly subtle. "In my teens, I started having erotic dreams, sometimes climaxing in my sleep," says twenty-nine-year-old Chris. "And sometimes I'd get an erection just *looking* at some girl in class. It was very disturbing and thrilling."

At nature's invitation, male attention is invariably drawn *downward* to the source of such new power and excitement. "Not surprisingly, boys develop a lively interest in their own and their friends' genitals," says psychologist John Nicholson, author of *Men & Women: How Different Are They?* "They're a favorite topic of conversation, and masturbation contests and mutual masturbation are commonplace among young boys."

Ninety-three percent of all men masturbate, and many start as soon as they're able. Youthful camaraderie—joking about it, looking at pinups—is a fillip that's traditional and may also set the stage for the typically masculine mindset.

"I don't remember exactly when I began masturbating," says thirty-two-year-old Shawn, "but there were all these girlie magazines circulating. It was kind of a shared experience—learning to masturbate, drooling over pictures of naked women, lots of crude jokes."

Testosterone levels are highest—and male sexual powers peak—in the late teens and early twenties. "The drive is very urgent and demanding," says Ron Murphy, "and the way a young man typically goes about sex stems from this physical fact. The tendency is to look at sex in impersonal terms . . . which doesn't exactly encourage romance and tenderness."

For the male of the species, loss of virginity is both a tribute to manhood and fulfillment of a new and overwhelming need. The focus is much more on *having* the experience than on whom to have it *with*. What's more, men seem to take to sex swimmingly—and usually look back on their first encounter with a mixture of both pleasure and glee.

"I didn't last more than a minute, but I'll never forget how fantastic it felt," says twenty-three-year-old Jeff, who first made love at seventeen. "I was high—really flying. I couldn't wait to do it again."

Adds thirty-year-old Rob, "In my teens, the urge to 'make it' was both a physical and social pressure. I guess because of that, I really strong-armed a lot of girls. And when one finally gave in, I was so thrilled, it really didn't bother me that she wasn't someone I especially cared about."

Any Warm Body

Since men virtually support the eight-billion-dollar pornography industry, they apparently derive considerable pleasure from erotic pictures and scenes. One reason for this is that "male arousal mechanisms tend to be set off by visual stimuli, like body images," comments Barbara DeBetz, M.D., assistant professor of psychiatry at Columbia University.

When it comes to sexual attraction, the purely visual also seems to play a major role. A survey in *Psychology Today* reports that the three things men notice first about a woman are her figure, her face, and how she's dressed. According to another survey, this one in *Ms.*, good looks was listed first by males as the trait they most desired in a partner.

Says thirty-three-year-old Craig, "Looks are definitely important to me in my choice of women, although I'm not as hung up about them as I was when I was younger. But when you start out fantasizing about those gorgeous airbrushed nudes in *Playboy*, I guess it programs you to look for that image."

"If a woman is really attractive, it's enough to arouse my interest—at least sexually," adds twenty-nine-year-old Vern. "The reaction is involuntary, like a knee jerk."

Male emphasis on the visual aspect of attraction goes hand-in-hand with the mentality of the brief encounter. Sex can be based purely on physical attraction *without* the complexities of relationship and feeling. "Some men tend to use sex as an outlet for tension," says Ron Murphy. "Often, its purpose is simply to experience release."

The starkest example of this, of course, is men who visit prostitutes. And according to a 1983 *Playboy* sex survey, 21 percent (roughly one-fifth) of the respondents had been with a prostitute in the past five years.

Most men *don't* buy sex, but the idea that, in a pinch, any warm body will do—at least, if it's attractive enough—is one that seems typically male.

"I wouldn't ever admit this to my girlfriend," confesses twenty-seven-year-old Seth, "but I could easily have sex with any good-looking girl and then just forget about it when it was over. Maybe that's insensitive, but that's the way it is."

Adds thirty-five-year-old Mick, "There have been times when I didn't want involvement or even to know the woman, just to experience the excitement and pleasure of being with someone different and new."

Variety—a constant diet of new women—is also a male aphrodisiac, which, according to the *Playboy* survey, was the main reason offered by men for cheating on their wives. And while many philanderers apparently have no intention of endangering their marital bonds, another survey reports that they attribute their infidelities to boredom.

Traditionally, sex for sport and fun has always been—and remains—a popular masculine pastime. The quick release of tension, the ego boost of conquest . . . both encourage the love-'em-and-leave-'em philosophy. But, according to the experts, there's a hidden agenda: Reducing sex to a mere game keeps threatening feelings—like dependency and vulnerability—at bay.

"In general, men have problems with intimacy because they fear that their inner lives—being needy or 'soft'—will be the basis for rejection," says Murphy.

According to Gabrielle Brown, author of *The New Celibacy*, for many men sex takes the place of other outlets by working as a sort of release valve for anxiety and tension *while* covering hidden fears. "Quite simply," she says, "sex becomes a way for men to *avoid* intimacy."

Since social conditioning tacitly encourages men to use sex as a form of recreation and to close off tender and vulnerable emotions, men often have to break down inner barriers and overcome habits before they can truly unite sex with feeling. Some men may never achieve this, but for many it's a product of experience and maturity. Midlife is the stage at which most men discover the value of intimacy, relationships, and caring.

Aftermath: The Sexual Revolution

In the fifties—before women changed the rules and began to enjoy sex instead of just putting up with it—Kinsey's findings showed that the average duration of intercourse was a scant two minutes. By the seventies—according to sex researcher Morton Hunt's survey, *Sexual Behavior in the 1970s*—it had gone up to about ten minutes. Aware that women expected more—and with their reputations on the line—men began making more of an effort to *please*.

Generally, men have been more-than-willing participants in the sexual revolution, but there's been a hitch. They've also begun showing up at sex clinics in unprecedented numbers, concerned about sexual performance, premature ejaculation, and especially, impotence.

Some sex researchers, including Hunt, blame men's new anxieties on women's growing assertiveness. And it's true that in the past men didn't feel nearly as pressured to prove their lovemaking skills.

Though the sexual revolution has had the salutary effect of making men intent on being not just lovers but *good* lovers, "sadly," says Gabrielle Brown, "some men . . . mistake that for being *good performers*."

"I think the pressure to be good in bed is pretty intense for most men now," says twenty-nine-year-old Rick. "I always try to bring a woman to climax, even if it means holding back my own release for a long time."

Adds thirty-three-year-old Jack, "It's extremely humiliating to go to bed with a woman and then not be able to perform. This happened to me a few years ago, and for weeks afterward, I was afraid to *have* sex."

The male response to the sexual revolution has been mainly to bone up on sexual mechanics: to perform better and make more efforts to please women *in bed*. Period. But there are other trends as well. Because sex is readily available—not a rare commodity—the masculine role of predator isn't necessarily the rule anymore. Having a chance to live out their fantasies, and discovering they're not always up for it, is changing the way men have traditionally thought of sex: a constant, urgent *goal*.

WOMEN

●

Gender Gaps

In contrast to men, many women don't have glowing memories of their first sexual encounter but instead remember the experience as embarrassing, uncomfortable—and often disappointing.

"When I lost my virginity, the main thing I felt was that sex was about the most awkward, overvalued experience in the world," admits twenty-six-year-old Sara.

"When I first started having sex, I liked the feeling of closeness, but I had no idea how pleasurable making love could be," adds thirty-year-old Claire. "In fact, I thought it was kind of a washout, until I started having orgasms—that was a few years later."

A time gap between the loss of virginity and the discovery of sexual pleasure seems to be a common feminine theme. Unlike men, for whom orgasm is usually a given, for women it seems more like a prize to be won.

One reason for this, says psychologist Ron Murphy, is that in contrast to men, many women aren't especially orgasmic in intercourse. "Orgasms stems from the clitoris," he points out, "and for women, oral sex, masturbation, and the use of vibrators may be much more direct—and successful—forms of stimulation."

Traditionally, women have looked to men to awaken their slumbering erotic senses. But since it takes a truly skilled lover to push all the right buttons, the awkward boy to whom they lose their virginity isn't likely to succeed. Instead, many women wait until someone more knowledgeable and experienced comes along—unless they learn how to satisfy themselves on their own.

But, though the majority of men start masturbating in their teens, women—if they do masturbate—tend to begin when they're older. According to statistics, by the age of forty-five, only 62 percent of all women have ever masturbated, the practice being much more common among older women.

Some experts believe that this gender gap results from a combination of biology and conditioning. "When a girl begins to menstruate, the physical changes she undergoes are not likely to bring her obvious pleasure," says psychologist and author John Nicholson. While boys are experiencing titillating erections and sharing their sexual discoveries in an atmosphere of camaraderie and male bonding, "there is not the same tradition among girls of discussing the development of their genitals," he comments.

In fact, though boys often boast about their newfound powers and sometimes masturbate together, if a girl does happen to stumble on the pleasure of bringing herself to orgasm, she's hardly likely to tell.

"No one I ever knew in high school or college talked about masturbating," says twenty-five-year-old Jenny. "It would have been considered gross. I have no idea how many actually did masturbate, but I doubt that it was very many."

"I started masturbating when I was pretty young," says thirty-year-old Maura, "but I would never have told anyone. I don't even talk about it now."

Though there is a current trend toward women beginning to masturbate at a much earlier age, it's still not the matter-of-fact rite of passage that it has always been for males. And since today "many sex researchers believe that the pattern of an adult's sex life is set by his or her early pattern of masturbation," says Nicholson, "the reason men in general are more sexually active than women in general is that boys tend to masturbate more than girls."

Other patterns may also be set in place by early experiences. While adolescent boys' fantasy fare tends to be *Playboy* or *Penthouse*, girls don't encourage each other to turn themselves on by collectively gawking at pictures of naked men.

Is this something women would even *choose* to do if it were an accepted rite of passage? Kinsey's research indicated that four times as many men as women were aroused by erotic pictures—the conclusion being that this form of fun was one for the boys. But more recent research—and more accurate tests—cancel out Kinsey's findings. "When sexual arousal is measured physiologically," says Nicholson, "women are found to react no less strongly than men to a film of a couple copulating." What's more, whether the film portrays the couple as being in love or as complete and total strangers, in both cases women are equally aroused, although they are reluctant to admit it.

Poppies to Orchids

Unlike men, women don't come into full erotic bloom until their thirties, but when they do—somewhere between ages thirty and thirty-four—"they daydream about sex even more frequently than men," says Joyce Brothers in her book *What Every Woman Should Know About Men*.

Although in general women often take a while to learn to enjoy sex—to climax, communicate in bed, take pleasure instead of passively awaiting it—once they do, their interest equals, and sometimes surpasses, men's. Equipped by nature to experience nearly limitless enjoyment (the clitoris, after all, is the only organ in the animal kingdom that has the sole function of giving its owner sexual pleasure), many women are startled by the discovery of their own erotic depths.

"I used to think men were somehow more sexual than women, but I'm beginning to change my mind," says thirty-three-year-old Miranda. "Since I've loosened up and learned more about myself, I not only enjoy sex more—I *want* it more. My drive has become really intense."

Adds twenty-nine-year-old Liz, "Sometimes I find myself wondering if I actually get more pleasure out of sex than my husband does. I mean, he obviously enjoys it, but he always tries to hold off his orgasm until I climax, and then I often have several orgasms while he just has one. And his seems so quick; mine last longer."

While Masters and Johnson have found many similarities between male and female orgasms, the main difference is that while men have a refractory period after ejaculation before they can achieve another erection, women can orgasm in rapid succession. Women's orgasms also seem to be more *varied* than men's. As Masters put it, the male orgasm is a rose-is-arose-is-a-rose sort of thing, but the female's goes all the way from poppies to orchids.

In the field of brain research, recent findings are leading to speculation that there are neurological differences between men and women that may actually trigger a more complex and exciting orgasm in females. Though a mere three decades ago popular opinion pivoted on the premise that men were basically more sexual than women, scientific research has begun to overturn this myth.

Historians point out that the idea of women's being less erotic than men is, in fact, a fairly recent invention—namely, a Victorian one. Earlier literature is full of complaints, not about women's lack of interest but about their excessive sexuality and recklessness. Von Krafft-Ebing, in his famous *Psychopathia Sexualis*, warns that if women were free to pursue sexual pleasure, "all the world would be a bordello and marriage . . . unthinkable." And in his *Moral Essays*, Alexander Pope writes that "every woman is at heart a rake."

Although women enjoy sex as much as (or possibly even more than) men, sex for sport and fun remains a typically masculine pursuit. For some reason, the majority of women still haven't come round to the view that sex is just an exciting form of entertainment—and are much more inclined to romanticize.

Connecting

"If I meet a really attractive man and he turns out to be wimpy or dumb, I immediately get turned off," says twenty-eight-year-old Anne. "I appreciate a well-built man, but I'd never sleep with someone *just* because he had a great body."

Adds thirty-year-old Nicki, "Of course, I'm turned on by gorgeous men. But I only sleep with men I can relate to—who turn me on emotionally as well as physically."

Unlike men, women don't tend to get sexually aroused simply by looks but respond to other qualities ranging from wealth or power to warmth. From the first, women's motivations in choosing to have sex tend to differ from men's. Attractions generally aren't only physically based but involve thoughts—not just of sex itself but of what might happen before and *after*.

"In my fantasies, I sometimes have sex with perfect strangers," says twenty-eight-year-old Lisa. "But in real life, I either get emotionally hooked or I feel uncomfortable about the whole thing."

"I enjoy sex a lot," adds thirty-one-year-old Molly. "But I just can't be as matter-of-fact about it as most men seem to be. I always feel there should be *meaning*—not just the meeting of two bodies."

Though many women might feel they'd truly enjoy trying out a range of partners or experiencing sex for its own sake, in practice most find casual sex both a disappointing and upsetting experience.

The female conflict about acting on sheer lust may stem partly from a healthy need to find closeness and intimacy. But sex researcher and author Nancy Friday also points out that—for women—this behavior is still quite new.

One reason for women's uneasiness with sex for its own sake is that "they acted on new attitudes *before* these ideas had become integrated into our deepest value system," says Friday. "The feeling of what is right, what is wrong, comes to us from parents. They got it from *their* parents. That changes very slowly and is beyond superficial intellectual decision."

"General thinking is that most sexual behavior is a highly learned response pattern," adds Murphy. And though it's true that the sexual revolution has practically institutionalized the casual encounter, many women feel that the double standard remains today.

"I was fairly promiscuous a few years ago," says twenty-seven-year-old Celeste. "And during that time I had an intense affair with a musician who I knew sometimes slept with other women. We had a wonderful rapport and magic sex, but when he realized I was also sleeping with other men, he started acting cold and then dropped me. It was a big shock, but I learned that men still expect a woman to be purer than they are—and if you're not, they label you as no good."

Adds twenty-nine-year-old Becky, "I've noticed that if I sleep with a man on the very first date, he's much more likely to treat me uncaringly than if I hold off. I used to be impulsive and have sex on the spur of the moment, but I've stopped doing that, since I don't like the way men act toward me in those situations."

When it comes to a choice between finding love and commitment or being sexually free, most women *will* opt for love. And a woman is more likely to repress any desire to stray once she's settled down—not only because men are more likely to leave an unfaithful wife than are women to leave a philandering husband, but because, for the most part, women's self-esteem and identity *still* remain more invested in being successfully married.

●

The gender gap is constantly reenforced by how differently men and women think about sex. Many sex researchers, like Nancy Friday, believe that even today cultural facts—not biology—are the *cause*. Women may experience sexual desire just as intensely as men. But it remains true that men still have problems dealing with intimacy, and women remain conflicted about the consequences of acting out their sexual urges.

Many experts are hopeful, though, that in time social change will come full circle. The gradual redefinition of sex roles will narrow the gender gap and free both sexes to embrace *all* the possibilities. Meanwhile, scientists continue to probe nature's designs, trying to puzzle out the reasons men and women act as they do. "The truth is, no one really knows," says Ron Murphy. But no matter how we explain the mystery—or how changing trends affect us—men and women still seem to remain endlessly fascinated by each other.

The Three Faces of Love

*COMMITMENT, INTIMACY AND PASSION
ARE THE ACTIVE INGREDIENTS
IN STERNBERG'S THREE-SIDED THEORY
OF LOVE.*

ROBERT J. TROTTER

Robert J. Trotter is a senior editor at Psychology Today.

Brains and sex are the only things in life that matter. Robert J. Sternberg picked up that bit of wisdom from a cynical high school classmate and appears to have taken it to heart. "I spent the first part of my career studying brains, and now along comes sex," he says, claiming to be only partly facetious.

Sternberg, IBM Professor of Psychology and Education at Yale University, has, in fact, made a name for himself as one of the foremost theoreticians and researchers in the field of human intelligence (see "Three Heads are Better than One," *Psychology Today,* August 1986), but in recent years he has turned a good deal of his attention to the study of love. Why? Because it's an understudied topic that is extremely important to people's lives. "It's important to my own life," he says. "I want to understand what's happening."

Sternberg began his attempt to understand love with a study for which he and graduate student Susan Grajek recruited 35 men and 50 women between 18 and 70 years old who had been in at least one love relationship. Participants rated their most recent significant love affair using the well-tested scales of loving and liking developed by psychologist Zick Rubin and the interpersonal involvement scale developed by psychologist George Levinger. The participants also rated their love for their mothers, fathers, siblings closest in age and best friends of the same sex.

Sternberg and Grajek found that men generally love and like their lover the most and their sibling the least. Women tend to love their lover and best friend about the same, but they like the best friend more than they like the lover. Sternberg thinks he knows why. "Women are better at achieving intimacy and value it more than do men, so if women don't get the intimacy they crave in a relationship with a man, they try to find it with other women. They establish close friendships. They can say things to another woman they can't say to a man."

Sternberg and Grajek concluded that, while the exact emotions, motivations and cognitions involved in various kinds of loving relationships differ, "the various loves one experiences are not, strictly speaking, different." In other words, they thought they had proved that love, as different as it feels from situation to situation, is actually a common entity. They thought they had discovered the basis of love in interpersonal communication, sharing and support.

This research generated a lot of publicity in 1984, especially around St. Valentine's Day, and earned Sternberg the appellation "love professor." It also generated a lot of phone calls from reporters saying things like, "You mean to tell me the way you love your lover is the same as the way you love your 5-year-old kid? What about sex?" Sternberg had to rethink his position.

He analyzed various relationships to figure out what differentiates romantic love from companionate love, from liking, from infatuation and from various other types of love. He finally concluded that his original theory accounted for the emotional component of love but left out two other important aspects. According to Sternberg's new triangular theory, love has motivational and cognitive components as well. And different aspects of love can be explained in terms of these components (see "How Do I Love Thee?").

Sternberg calls the emotional aspect of his love triangle intimacy. It includes such things as closeness, sharing, communication and support. Intimacy increases rather steadily at first, then at a slower rate until it eventually levels off and goes beneath the surface. Sternberg explains this course of development in terms of psychologist Ellen Berscheid's theory of emotions in close relationships.

According to Berscheid, people in close relationships feel increased emotion when there is some kind of disruption. This is common early in a relationship primarily because of uncertainty. Since you don't know what the other person is going to do, you are constantly learning and experiencing new things. This uncertainty keeps you guessing but also generates new levels of emotion and intimacy. As the other person becomes more predictable, there are fewer disruptions and less expressed, or manifest, intimacy.

An apparent lack of intimacy could mean that the relationship and the intimacy are dying out. Or, says Sternberg, the intimacy may still be there in latent form. The relationship may even be thriving, with the couple growing

*T*HE LOVE OF A PARENT FOR A CHILD IS DISTINGUISHED BY A HIGH, UNCONDITIONAL LEVEL OF COMMITMENT.

together so smoothly that they are hardly aware of their interdependence. It may take some kind of disruption—time apart, a death in the family, even a divorce—for them to find out just how they feel about each other. "Is it any wonder," Sternberg asks, "that some couples realize only after a divorce that they were very close to and dependent on each other?"

The motivational side of the triangle is passion, which leads to physiological arousal and an intense desire to be united with the loved one. Unlike intimacy, passion develops quickly. "Initially you have this rapidly growing, hot, heavy passion," Sternberg says, "but after a while it no longer does for you what you want it to—you get used to it, you habituate."

Passion is like an addiction, Sternberg says. He explains it according to psychologist Richard Solomon's opponent process theory of motivation, which says that desire for a person or substance involves two opposing forces. The first is a positive motivational force that attracts you to the person. It is quick to develop and quick to level off. The negative motivational force, the one that works against the attraction, is slow to develop and slow to fade. The result is an initial rapid growth in passion, followed by habituation when the more slowly developing negative force kicks in. "It's like with coffee, cigarettes or alcohol," Sternberg says. "Addiction can be rapid, but once habituation sets in, even an increased amount of exposure to the person or substance no longer stimulates the motivational arousal that was once possible.

"And then when the person dumps you, it's even worse. You don't go back to the way you were before you

met the person," Sternberg explains. "You end up much worse off. You get depressed, irritable, you lose your appetite. You get these withdrawal symptoms, just as if you had quit drinking coffee or smoking, and it takes a while to get over it." The slow-starting, slow-fading negative force is still there after the person or the substance is gone.

The cognitive side of Sternberg's love triangle is commitment, both a short-term decision to love another person and a long-term commitment to maintain that love. Its developmental course is more straightforward and easier to explain than that of intimacy or passion. Essentially, commitment starts at zero when you first meet the other person and grows as you get to know each other. If the relationship is destined to be long-term, Sternberg says, the level of commitment will usually increase gradually at first and then speed up. As the relationship continues, the amount of commitment will generally level off. If the relationship begins to flag, the level of commitment will decline, and if the relationship fails, the level of commitment falls back to zero. According to Sternberg, the love of a parent for a child is often distinguished by a high and unconditional level of commitment.

Levels of intimacy, passion and commitment change over time, and so do relationships. You can visualize this, says Sternberg, by considering how the love triangle changes in size and shape as the three components of love increase and decrease. The triangle's area represents the amount of love and its shape the style. Large amounts of intimacy, passion and commitment, for example, yield a large triangle. And in general, Sternberg says, the larger the triangle, the more love.

Changing the length of the individual sides yields four differently shaped triangles, or styles of love. A triangle with three equal sides represents what Sternberg calls a "balanced" love in which all three components are equally matched. A scalene triangle (three unequal sides) in which the longest leg is passion represents a relationship in which physical attraction plays a larger role than either emotional intimacy or cognitive commitment. A scalene triangle with commitment as its longest leg depicts a relationship in which the intimacy and passion have waned or were never

HOW DO I LOVE THEE?

Intimacy, passion and commitment are the warm, hot and cold vertices of Sternberg's love triangle. Alone and in combination they give rise to eight possible kinds of love relationships. The first is nonlove—the absence of all three components. This describes the large majority of our personal relationships, which are simply casual interactions.

The second kind of love is liking. "If you just have intimacy," Sternberg explains, "that's liking. You can talk to the person, tell about your life. And if that's all there is to it, that's what we mean by liking." It is more than nonlove. It refers to the feelings experienced in true friendships. Liking includes such things as closeness and warmth but not the intense feelings of passion or commitment.

If you just have passion, it's called infatuated love—the "love at first sight" that can arise almost instantaneously and dissipate just as quickly. It involves a high degree of physiological arousal but no intimacy or commitment. It's the 10th-grader who falls madly in love with the beautiful girl in his biology class but never gets up the courage to talk to her or get to know her, Sternberg says, describing his past.

Empty love is commitment without intimacy or passion, the kind of love sometimes seen in a 30-year-old marriage that has become stagnant. The couple used to be intimate, but they don't talk to each other any more. They used to be passionate, but that's died out. All that remains is the commitment to stay with the other person. In societies in which marriages are arranged, Sternberg points out, empty love may precede the other kinds of love.

Romantic love, the Romeo and Juliet type of love, is a combination of intimacy and passion. More than infatuation, it's liking with the added excitement of physical attraction and arousal but without commitment. A summer affair can be very romantic, Sternberg explains, but

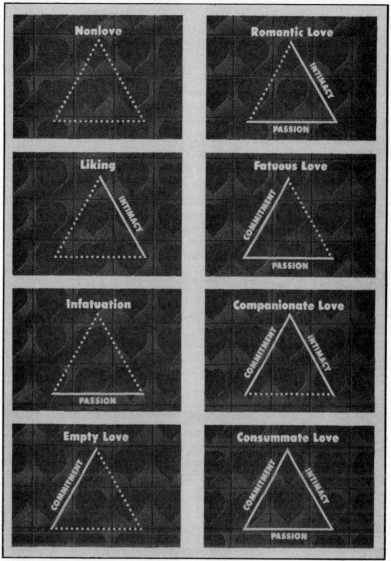

you know it will end when she goes back to Hawaii and you go back to Florida, or wherever.

Passion plus commitment is what Sternberg calls fatuous love. It's Hollywood love: Boy meets girl, a week later they're engaged, a month later they're married. They are committed on the basis of their passion, but because intimacy takes time to develop, they don't have the emotional core necessary to sustain the commitment. This kind of love, Sternberg warns, usually doesn't work out.

Companionate love is intimacy with commitment but no passion. It's a long-term friendship, the kind of committed love and intimacy frequently seen in marriages in which the physical attraction has died down.

When all three elements of Sternberg's love triangle come together in a relationship, you get what he calls consummate love, or complete love. It's the kind of love toward which many people strive, especially in romantic relationships. Achieving consummate love, says Sternberg, is like trying to lose weight, difficult but not impossible. The really hard thing is keeping the weight off after you have lost it, or keeping the consummate love alive after you have achieved it. Consummate love is possible only in very special relationships.

LOVE'S PROGRESS

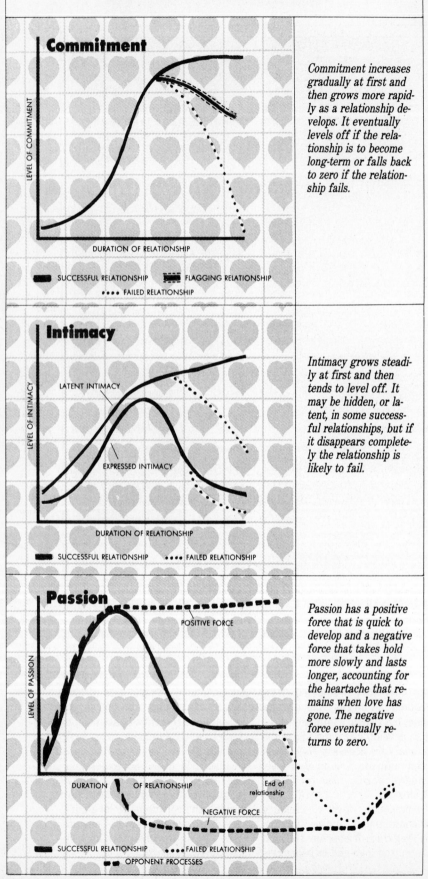

Commitment

Commitment increases gradually at first and then grows more rapidly as a relationship develops. It eventually levels off if the relationship is to become long-term or falls back to zero if the relationship fails.

LEVEL OF COMMITMENT

DURATION OF RELATIONSHIP

▬▬ SUCCESSFUL RELATIONSHIP   ▬▬ FLAGGING RELATIONSHIP
•••• FAILED RELATIONSHIP

Intimacy

Intimacy grows steadily at first and then tends to level off. It may be hidden, or latent, in some successful relationships, but if it disappears completely the relationship is likely to fail.

LEVEL OF INTIMACY

LATENT INTIMACY

EXPRESSED INTIMACY

DURATION OF RELATIONSHIP

▬▬ SUCCESSFUL RELATIONSHIP   •••• FAILED RELATIONSHIP

Passion

Passion has a positive force that is quick to develop and a negative force that takes hold more slowly and lasts longer, accounting for the heartache that remains when love has gone. The negative force eventually returns to zero.

LEVEL OF PASSION

POSITIVE FORCE

DURATION OF RELATIONSHIP

End of relationship

NEGATIVE FORCE

▬▬ SUCCESSFUL RELATIONSHIP   •••• FAILED RELATIONSHIP
▬ ▬ OPPONENT PROCESSES

---

*T*HERE CAN BE A VARIETY OF EMOTIONS, MOTIVATIONS AND TYPES OF COMMITMENT IN A LOVING RELATIONSHIP.

there in the first place. An isosceles triangle (two equal sides) with intimacy as its longest leg shows a relationship in which emotional involvement is more important than either passion or commitment. It's more like a high-grade friendship than a romance.

Sternberg admits that this triangle is a simplification of a complex and subtle phenomenon. There can be a variety of emotions, motivations and types of commitment in a loving relationship, and each would have to be examined to completely diagnose a relationship. Beyond that, he says, every relationship involves several triangles: In addition to their own triangles, both people have an ideal triangle (the way you would like to feel about the person you love) and a perceived triangle (the way you think the other person feels about you).

Sternberg and graduate student Michael Barnes studied the effects these triangles have on a relationship by administering the liking and loving scales to 24 couples. Participants were asked to rate their relationship in terms of how they feel about the other person, how they think the other person feels about them, how they would feel about an ideal person and how they would want an ideal person to feel about them. They found that satisfaction is closely related to the similarity between these real, ideal and perceived triangles. In general, the closer they are in shape and size, the more satisfying the relationship.

The best single predictor of happiness in a relationship is not how you feel about the other person but the difference between how you would ideally like the other person to feel about you and how you think he or she actually feels about you. "In other words,"

Sternberg says, "relationships tend to go bad when there is a mismatch between what you want from the other person and what you think you are getting.

"Were you ever the overinvolved person in a relationship? That can be very dissatisfying. What usually happens is that the more involved person tries to think up schemes to get the other person up to his or her level of involvement. But the other person usually sees what's going on and backs off. That just makes the overinvolved person try harder and the other person back off more until it tears the relationship apart. The good advice in such a situation is for the overinvolved person to scale down, but that advice is hard to follow."

An underlying question in Sternberg's love research is: Why do so many relationships fail? Almost half the marriages in the United States end in divorce, and many couples who don't get divorced aren't all that happy. "Are people really so dumb that they pick wrong most of the time? Probably not," he suggests. "What they're doing is picking on the basis of what matters to them in the short run. But what matters in the long run may be different. The factors that count change, people change, relationships change."

Sternberg can't predict how people or situations will change, but he and his assistant Sandra Wright recently completed a study that suggests what will and won't be important in the long run. They put this question, what's important in a relationship, to 80 men and women from 17 to 69 years old, and divided them into three groups according to the length of their most recent relationship. The short-term group had been involved for up to two years, the mid-term group between two and five years, the others for more than five years.

Among the things that increase in importance as a relationship grows are willingness to change in response to each other and willingness to tolerate each other's imperfections. "These are things you can't judge at the beginning of a relationship," Sternberg says. "In the beginning," he explains, "some of the other person's flaws might not seem important. They may even seem kind of cute, but over the long term they may begin to grate on you. You both have to be willing to make some changes to make the relationship work and you both have to be willing to tolerate some flaws."

Another thing that becomes increasingly important is the sharing of values, especially religious values. "When you first meet," says Sternberg, "you have this love-overcomes-all-obstacles attitude, but when the kids come along you have to make some hard decisions about the religion issue. All of a sudden something that wasn't so important is important."

---

*I*T IS NECESSARY TO EXPRESS LOVE; WITHOUT EXPRESSION EVEN THE GREATEST OF LOVES CAN DIE.

Among the things that tend to decrease in importance is how interesting you find your partner. "In the beginning," Sternberg says, "it's almost as if the other person has to keep you interested or the relationship will go nowhere. Later on, it's not quite as critical because there are other things in your life that matter."

In addition to asking what is important at different times, Sternberg and Wright asked how much of these various things people had at different times in their relationships. The answers were not encouraging. The ability to make love, for example, often goes just at the time when it is becoming more important. In fact, Sternberg says, almost everything except matching religious beliefs decreased over time. The ability to communicate, physical attractiveness, having good times, sharing interests, the ability to listen, respect for each other, romantic love—they all went down. "That may be depressing," says Sternberg, "but it's important to know at the beginning of a relationship what to expect over time, to have realistic expectations for what you can get and what is going to be important in a relationship."

And Sternberg feels that his triangular theory of love can help people in other ways. "Just analyzing your relationship in terms of the three components can be useful," he says. "Are you more romantic and your partner more companionate? It's helpful to know where you and your partner are well-matched and where you are not and then start thinking about what you can do to make yourselves more alike in what you want out of the relationship."

If you decide to take steps to improve a relationship, Sternberg offers a final triangle, the action triangle. "Often there's quite a gap between thought or feeling and action," he explains. "Your actions don't always reflect the way you feel, so it could help to know just what actions are associated with each component of love."

Intimacy, he suggests, might be expressed by communicating inner feelings; sharing one's possessions, time and self; and offering emotional support. Passion, obviously, is expressed by kissing, hugging, touching and making love. Commitment can be expressed by fidelity, by staying with the relationship through the hard times that occur in any relationship or by getting engaged or married. Which actions are most important and helpful will vary from person to person and from relationship to relationship. But Sternberg feels it is important to consider the triangle of love as it is expressed through action because action has so many effects on a relationship.

Citing psychologist Daryl Bem's theory of self-perception, Sternberg describes how actions can affect emotions, motivations and cognitions. "The way we act shapes the way we feel and think, possibly as much as the way we think and feel shapes the way we act." Also, he says, certain actions can lead to other actions; expressions of love, for example, encourage further expressions of love. Furthermore, your actions affect the way the other person thinks and feels about you and behaves toward you, leading to a mutually reinforcing series of actions.

"The point," Sternberg concludes, "is that it is necessary to take into account the ways in which people express their love. Without expression, even the greatest of loves can die."

Bruised Friendships

How to ease hurt feelings

While friendship has never been more in demand than it is today, it demands a real freedom and flexibility in order to thrive. If you approach with rules and rigid expectations—what a friend must be and do—you could end up with more former *friends than* old *friends. Keep an open heart and mind and you stand a good chance of reaping the rewards of growth, self-esteem and greater intimacy. "Friendship is about openness," says Edward M. Shelley, M.D., assistant clinical professor of psychiatry at the Columbia University College of Physicians and Surgeons in New York City. "Being open draws people to you because they feel they can trust you." Here, how to put that quality to use in negotiating some common friendship restrictors.*

Judith Jobin is a regular contributor to Self.

When a New Love Puts Old Friends on Hold

A serious new romance always puts a strain on an old friendship, but doesn't have to snap it. "Good friends can withstand the stress as long as they share their feelings," says psychologist Marilyn Ruman, Ph.D., director of Clinical and Consulting Associates in Encino, California.

Those feelings can get pretty intense for both people. If one is without a partner she is bound to feel the loss of her formerly single friend. *Not fair*—her world shrinks while her friend's expands; her self-esteem may falter while her friend's rises. "It's natural to feel abandoned, hurt, envious and angry for awhile," says Hanna E. Kapit, Ph.D., a psychotherapist at the Post-graduate Center for Mental Health in New York City.

But it's also natural for the person in love to want to put her friendships on hold temporarily. "A normal part of 'new love' is the need to merge and be isolated with the person," explains Dr. Ruman.

Generosity and sensitivity on both sides can help you ride out the awkward period. If you're the smitten one, you need to keep some perspectives on the importance of your other relationships and not exclude your friend completely or treat her like a second-class citizen. Including her in some outings with your new man is one solution, but you need to save her some just-the-two-of-us time as well.

If you're the left-behind pal, you've got a responsibility, too. Don't do a vanishing act out of anger or insecurity; continuing to call occasionally and initiating dates shows self-respect and caring for your friend, too. Using your extra time to reach out to new people and try new activities can not only take the pressure off your friend, but expand your own resources.

The best way to maintain closeness, though, is simply to keep a dialogue going, according to Dr. Ruman. No disappearing without a word for 3 months, no stiff-upper-lip forbearance: "It's the ability to share something that's the hallmark of a good friendship. Getting through conflicts doesn't mean that one of you gives up something for the other, but that you register your feelings. That's what intimacy is."

Ground Rules for Surprise Visits

Casual drop-in visits can enhance an already-close friendship with feelings of privilege, intimacy and coziness. But whether and when you can handle drop-ins depends on your temperament and other obligations and priorities. Some people will *always* flinch when the doorbell rings unexpectedly: "They may simply find it difficult to switch gears when they get surprise company," says Eva Margolies, a therapist and author of *The Samson and Delilah Complex*.

Instead of feeling bound by etiquette-book ideas of hospitality, you and your friends need to negotiate your own ground rules. If you dislike spur-of-the-moment visits, you have to be direct, according to Dr. Shelley: "Your friend probably doesn't give it a lot of thought. She assumes you'll be delighted to see her under any circumstances. You simply have to say, 'Paula, I love having you over, but I'd rather you call first, since there are times when I'd like to be alone or am right in the middle of something.' " No one is likely to feel wounded by that. "Drawing the line isn't rejection and most people don't take it that way," says Dr. Shelley. But if you want to gentle your request even more, make it mutual—"Let's agree to call in advance."

Even if you *like* finding people on your doorstep, you undoubtedly have limits. One way to enjoy the surprise without the inconvenience is to let friends know there are certain times when company is welcome, say, 5 or 6 o'clock, after dinner, Sunday evenings. Otherwise, try suspending ordinary manners to make a spontaneous relationship comfortable for both of you; agree ahead of time that if one of you is too tired, busy or preoccupied for a visit, you'll say so without having to apologize or explain. If you're cleaning closets or fixing dinner when the doorbell rings, feel free to keep at it while she grabs a soda, chats, or pitches in. "There's nothing impolite about that," points out Dr. Shelley. In fact, it suggests a special, inner-circle intimacy.

Unfortunately, these strategies don't always prevent problems—a friend who comes by too often or stays too long, or one who keeps showing up without notice when you've asked her not to. What to do? If her clinging is something new, perhaps you can ride it out. "When a friend sits and sits and sits, she might have a problem she hasn't raised and you might be able to help by drawing her out," Dr. Shelley suggests. If not, you've got to be firmer. "The key thing is to be clear about your limits and not assume that your friend can read your mind," says Margolies. If you are ambivalent, it could be because your ego is fueled by your friend's dependency. "Maybe you're afraid that you won't be wanted or needed if you don't open your house at all hours," she says. In that case, do a reality check. Surely you'd like your friend if she wasn't available to you 24 hours a day. Chances are, she feels the same.

When a Friendship Ends

The loss of a close friend, for whatever reason, cuts deep, and while society may not acknowledge your grief, *you* must: "If you don't mourn, the emotions and conflicts you feel remain below the surface and may come back to haunt you," says Dr. Shelley. Since every friend has a little piece of you, every loss is sad, even if you broke in anger or over an important point of ethics: "You can take some comfort in having done the right thing," Dr. Kagle says, "but being right doesn't prevent you from being sad."

By trying to understand where you're hurting and what's missing, you can also start looking for ways to compensate for the loss. If your best friend is moving cross-country, you may be stuck with a big empty space in your life, but you don't have to write off your special connection. "When friends share more than proximity," points out Margolies, "a move will end the day-to-day intimacy but not the good feeling." It takes commitment to maintain long-distance ties, but a surprising number of people do it, according to researcher Elizabeth Aries, Ph.D., associate professor of psychology at Amherst College in Massachusetts: "They might see each other only once a year, but they keep in touch by letter and phone. They still feel like best friends, that they are still there for each other."

If a friendship is really *over*, you can't erase the loss but you can try to figure out what special quality your friend had—humor, motivation, optimism—and try to find that in a new friend. "Sit down and think about what you're missing," Dr. Kagle says. "With luck, you can find it somewhere else. Or better yet, cultivate it in yourself."

Change, challenge and conflict bring a risk of loss and sad goodbyes, but if you don't face them down you take a worse risk. Tough times reveal us to ourselves and others—and revelation fuels intimacy, says Dr. Ruman. "The only way a friendship can grow is by going through the various stages and changes of life."

Caring for a Relationship That's Soured

When a once-intense friendship seems empty or troubled, or a friend hurts or betrays you, you may want to close the door on the friendship. And sometimes that's necessary—but as a last step. First steps: patience, soul-searching, a recognition that conflict can be productive as well as painful.

Carelessly discarding friends who don't measure up may reflect fear and insecurity, according to Linda Tschirhart Sanford, a psychotherapist in Boston: "If there is some sudden disagreement, some people may fantasize, 'She doesn't like me anymore and is planning to dump me, so I'll protect myself by getting out first.' Conflict makes them push the panic button." Others feel repeatedly disappointed by friends because their expectations are unrealistic: "They expect their friends to be all things to them, to give unconditioned love, to parent them," says Sanford.

Slow down, pull back when you suddenly sour on a friend. There are times in any relationship when all you see are flaws; perspective soon returns. "See how it goes for awhile," advises Marian Starrett Matunas, Ph.D., a clinical psychologist in private practice in New York City. "Let it play out. Your friend—or you—could be going through a phase." It's also possible that a change in your life or hers is triggering feelings that will soon subside—one of you has a new job, for instance, and the other feels edgy, competitive. Very common. Friendships wax and wane naturally, as friends change, grow, enter new phases. Periods of closeness and distance alternate. "Given time," Dr. Kapit notes, "friendships usually change to accommodate new situations."

But if there's too much distance and no more basic glue in your friendship, gradually reducing contact is the sensible approach. "There's nothing to confront," points out Dr. Matunas. "The friendship will die like an unwatered plant." One caution: Don't let guilt about leaving prompt an unnecessary blowup. "Sometimes people feel they can leave a relationship only if it's terrible, so they contrive a way to make it terrible," observes Sanford. "They exaggerate something small like a forgotten birthday or an unreturned phone call and act wounded to prove that the other person doesn't deserve their friendship."

On the other hand, some people hold onto and still get some small pleasures from old but now-limp friendships; in such cases, no need to scuttle them. "We all have people in our lives who have meaning because they're part of our history," Dr. Ruman points out. "If you don't feel very intimate anymore, limit the frequency of your meeetings and plan activities you'll both get pleasure from." Catch a play, meet for a sport, explore your city.

When there is conflict, not merely distance, between friends who still care, you need to confront it. Walk away without sorting things out, warns Arlene Kagle, Ph.D., a psychologist in private practice in New York City, and "you'll carry around excess baggage—feelings that will contaminate future relationships." You'll also miss the chance to move a faltering friendship through a crisis. "If you can talk about your differences, the friendship probably can survive," Dr. Kapit says, "provided you keep in mind that friends don't have to agree on everything—their ability to understand and explain their differences can be bond enough."

You're the only authority on when a friendship of yours *must* end. We vary enormously in our ability to overlook betrayals or differing moralities—a friend who gossips about you, finagles an apartment or job you were in line for, has an affair with your husband. Sometimes we ease up with age: "As we mature," says Dr. Ruman, "we realize that people often do things not out of malice, but out of stupidity." But attempts to continue a friendship probably don't make much sense when fundamental values are at stake: "They're the things you feel 'absolute' about—whether lying is ever justifiable, how much loyalty friends owe each other," she says. "There's no compromising. When a value at that level is violated it is usually impossible to forgive and forget. You can't give up your own identity."

Although there's no point in dwelling on unhappy endings, they do merit a private review before moving on. Figuring out what role each of you played in the conflict can improve the way you choose and deal with friends. This is especially true when you feel you were betrayed. "If you pick up the pieces of the puzzle that you ignored at the time, you'll gain a level of awareness that will keep you safer next time, and make you more confident," explains Dr. Ruman.

Friends for the Wrong Reasons

Since we bring largely the same needs and vulnerabilities to friendship as to romance, it's as easy to take up with a Ms. as a Mr. Wrong. "It's amazing how similar the patterns are," says Dr. Matunas, "including the self-deception." Ms. Wrongs can take a heavy toll on personal growth and self-esteem, so it's important to spot them. But this requires a real *hard* look, because there's always something about the friendship that feels good, at least for awhile. Here are some common patterns to watch for:

• You're in the grip of a manipulator. "The controlling person sets the pace and the terms of the friendship," explains Dr. Matunas. "She chooses all the activities, does the arranging, and fits you in around her needs. You often end up keeping your life on hold." The insidious appeal of this kind of person is often apparent only to you. She may have something—looks, talent, lifestyle—that you long for, and you can bask in the reflected glow when you're with her, according to Dr. Shelley: "You admire and value her. She lends you something you feel you lack, so her promise outweighs the pain." Some manipulators play a come-on game. "At first she seems like everything you ever wanted in a friend—sensitive, affectionate, understanding," says Dr. Matunas. "But all that is withdrawn after a few days or weeks. You hang on because you want to get that wonderful time back or because you think you'll change her. You won't."

• Your main link is shared misery or inadequacy. Say, you are both unhappy in your jobs and feel unfulfilled. A good pairing if you and your friend can motivate each other to improve matters, but not so great if the friendship makes your unhealthy rut feel too comfortable, or if an improvement by one will be regarded as a betrayal by the other. The price of this friendship is too high. Sticking with it means staying stuck.

• One of you plays the helper, nurturer; the other is the problem-ridden, helpless one. There are lots of versions, from mild to extreme, of this unequal relationship, but the basic mechanism, according to Margolies, "is a confusion of dependency with intimacy." It's another easy but costly mistake. One gets all her needs for a perfect parent met, but sacrifices independence, growth, competence. The other comes away with a feeling of power, superiority and being needed, but gives up the chance to be liked for who she is apart from what she gives. Both women can enjoy their closeness—this kind of association can be a fair enough fit for a short while; we all have periods of neediness and we all can take pleasure in nurturing others.

When pain beings to outweigh pleasure, however, or a jump in self-esteem quiets old needs and prompts new insights; the destructiveness of such relationships becomes apparent. However, if there's some real caring on both sides, the friendship might be able to be saved. Share your insights and your determination to change the nature of the bond, and help your friend understand that she'll be better off, too, if you can relate to each other more equally. But if she can't or won't change, don't hang on out of loyalty. "Sometimes you have to break up with a woman friend," says Dr. Kagle, "just as with a man." Fortunately, once you spot this pattern, you're not likely to repeat it.

MASTERS & JOHNSON'S
new guide to better loving

America's foremost sex researchers, who have counseled thousands of couples, share with you 16 surefire steps to better sex

WILLIAM H. MASTERS, M.D.,
VIRGINIA E. JOHNSON AND
ROBERT C. KOLODNY, M.D.

William H. Masters, M.D., and Virginia E. Johnson are codirectors of the Masters & Johnson Institute in St. Louis, where, since 1958, they have pioneered in the treatment of sexual dysfunction. Their books include *Human Sexual Response* (a Bantam paperback) and *Masters & Johnson on Sex and Human Loving* (Little, Brown), from which this article is excerpted.

Half of all American couples are troubled by some form of sexual distress, ranging from disinterest to outright sexual dysfunction. While some people need sex therapy to overcome their difficulties, we feel confident that many couples can learn to increase their personal satisfaction on their own—if they go about it in a sensible way. Here are 16 specific steps to take, based on our experience advising thousands of couples.

1. Always remember that good sex begins while your clothes are still on. This doesn't mean that sensuous stripteases are necessary for satisfying lovemaking. It's simply a reminder that the buildup of sexual desire and the atmosphere that will be carried into the bedroom largely depend on what happens not just in the moments before deciding whether to make love but over the hours or days preceding a sexual interlude. In this sense, "getting in the mood" is not a deliberate act of playing romantic music or dining by candlelight (although there's nothing wrong with such activities) but is part and parcel of an ongoing closeness between partners that is both psychological and physical. Being able to express tenderness and affection, both verbally and nonverbally, without its being a direct invitation to sex is a particularly important ingredient.

2. Take time to think about yourself as a sexual being. One of the problems people often have with sex is that they compartmentalize it as something that happens to them in isolation from the rest of their lives. If you can spend time thinking about your sexuality in its many different dimensions, you can better appreciate that as long as sex is only a discrete activity, like a game of tennis, it will be a somewhat fragmented, disjointed experience rather than part of the fabric of your life and your relationship. In addition, if you think of yourself as sexual, you are, in effect, learning to accept your sexuality as a fact about your being instead of simply seeing it as an impulse or urge that arises in you from time to time.

3. Take responsibility for your own sensual and sexual pleasure. As much as you might like to think that it is someone else's duty to turn you on and give you joyful paroxysms of sexual pleasure, in actuality we are each responsible for our own eroticism. While men seem to have an easier time accepting this aspect of sex, women often slip into a culturally dictated role of passivity in which they expect their partner to sweep them off their feet and to be the expert in sex, relieving them of any responsibility except to respond on command. This notion of sex as something one person does *to* the other—or the somewhat kinder notion that sex is something one person does *for* the other—can lead to problems. By taking responsibility for your own sensual and sexual needs, you actually are paying your partner a terrific compliment: In effect, you're saying to him, "I care enough about you to want to keep you from having to guess at what I want, what I like and what can make me happy."

4. Talk with your partner about sex. One of the most amazing things to us about sexual behavior is how reticent most people are to talk with their lovers about sex. It's as though talking about sex would somehow spoil it or take away its spontaneity. Instead we see many, many instances where one partner doesn't have the foggiest notion of what the other wants or likes sexually. We also see plenty of couples whose well-intended caresses fall short of the mark because they're too much, too soon, too little, too light-handed, too far off the mark—all matters that could be easily corrected by a few words, discreetly murmured, at the right time.

One note of caution: When we say that talking with your partner about sex is apt to be beneficial, we don't mean that this should be done immediately after you've had sex together, as a sort of postmortem or critique. In fact, it's best to avoid sounding critical entirely. That almost invariably gives your partner the message "Look what you're doing wrong," which is likely to put him on the defensive. Instead, we're suggesting that talking about sex can help establish a number of useful understandings ranging from how you can handle intense sexual feelings when your partner isn't much interested, to developing a repertoire of code words or signals that convey sexual messages if this seems to be useful.

5. Make time to be together regularly. Many couples find their sexual desire on the decline because they forget to create unencumbered pockets of private time together. It's all too easy to relegate our primary relationship to a backseat as we look after the kids, try to get ahead at work, spend time socializing with friends and pursue our hobbies—but the cost of this sort of benign neglect can be high. If sex is always last on your agenda, it's safe to say that you'll be tired out and frazzled by the time you think about it, if you even think about it at all. This certainly doesn't set the stage for a satisfying, relaxed lovemaking session. Likewise, if you don't spend much quality time with your partner outside the bedroom, it's hard to create a sense of closeness and affection the instant you're ready for sex. This doesn't mean that every time you're together with a bit of privacy you have to seize the opportunity for sexual action—in fact, it's much more sensible to let your feelings and needs dictate just what you do with this time together—but it doesn't hurt to have the option available more often than once or twice a week.

6. Don't let sex become routine. For too many couples, sexual dissatisfaction is a direct reflection of boredom, the result of an absence of variation or creativity in their sexual interaction. To avoid too much "sameness" in sex, don't always try to get amorous at the same time of day; change the scenery on occasion (for instance, try sex someplace other than your bedroom, even if you check into a hotel for a night or send the kids to sleep at friends' homes so you can make love in front of the living room fireplace), and vary the action:
• One partner should not always be the aggressor while the other is passive; try switching these roles at times, or even try having *both* partners be aggressors.
• Initiate sexual opportunities with unexpected kinds of invitations. This might be a phone call home from the office saying, "I'm feeling kind of romantic, so tonight before dinner I'd really like to make love," a love note pinned to a pillow, or a verbal invitation at an unusual time.
• Introduce new options into your sexual interactions in ways that are comfortable to

you and your partner. This might mean experimenting with sensual massage, watching erotic videotapes together, trying new sexual toys such as vibrators, or creating mutual sex fantasies that you proceed to perform. It can also include types of sexual activity you've rarely or never tried before, if they are appealing to you both.
• Try different positions. This strategy may provide an additional turn-on not just during intercourse but also during other kinds of sexual play.
• Don't be trapped into thinking that sex has always got to include intercourse to be meaningful or gratifying. By occasionally omitting intercourse from a lovemaking session, you may even discover other pleasures that are equally arousing.
• Use different tempos at different times. There's no rule that says that good sex must always be a long, leisurely, teasing process. At times, a throw-off-your-clothes, rush-into-bed quickie can be the height of passionate abandon, while at other times a slower-paced session suits your mood better. Just remember, too much sameness can reduce pleasure in sex as in other matters—dining on *pâté de foie gras* and butter-dipped lobster every day would soon become incredibly boring for most of us. Use your best creative thinking to avoid letting sex become just another dull, routine affair.

7. Use fantasy—you'll find it's one of the best aphrodisiacs. Fantasy can be used in a wide variety of ways to enhance excitement and bring variety to your life. Whether it's used as a prelude to a sexual encounter—as a means of whetting your sexual appetite—or incorporated into your lovemaking sessions directly, your imagination can help you transform ordinary sex into something far more stimulating. In some instances, fantasy can be quite useful in getting you or your partner beyond minor sexual inhibitions, too.

8. Understand that working at sex doesn't work. Herein lies the tale of many people's sexual woes. Most of us tend to try to deal with sexual anxieties or frustrations by working harder to overcome them. This approach usually backfires—although it may be eminently successful in dealing with other problems in our lives—because working at sex usually makes it so goal-oriented that it loses its fun and spontaneity.

You shouldn't, however, ignore any sexual problems you're having, hoping they will magically disappear. It may take some effort on your part (and some understanding from your partner) to make the sort of changes in your sex life that we're discussing here. The distinction between making the effort to do something different and *working* at sex may seem slim, but there is more than just a semantic difference. Working at sex almost invariably means carrying a mental checklist into every sexual encounter and then watching yourself to see if you're performing

properly. In effect, it involves pushing yourself into the spectator role. Implementing changes in your sex life, in contrast, may involve making an effort to plan different types of opportunities, but leaving the performance checklist out of the process. If there's no goal that *must* be attained right now, there's far less pressure to perform and far less of a need to be a spectator to check up on how you're doing.

9. Don't carry anger into your bedroom. Sometimes, as we all know, the sweetest, most delirious erotic moments come as we rush into our partner's arms to make up after a fight. But those who withhold sex or demand sex to try to settle a score that has provoked considerable anger are asking for trouble in the long run, no matter how satisfying it may be to gain a temporary sense of revenge. The best thing to do, of course, is to try to minimize the amount and duration of anger that you and your partner feel by recognizing its source and trying to handle it while it is still at the level of hurt or frustration. If your anger is not so easily prevented or dissipated, however, it is usually best to acknowledge it and temporarily avoid sex unless both partners are willing to engage in a relatively impersonal version. There's nothing wrong with impersonal sex once in a while, but if it becomes the rule rather than the exception in a relationship, chances are that it will result in less sexual satisfaction for both parties.

10. Realize that good sex isn't just a matter of pushing the right buttons. It's tempting to think that there's some magical formula for foolproof sex, but this just isn't true. In fact, we tend to overemphasize the mechanical aspects of sex and underplay the emotional components that are probably far more important in terms of how we actually experience sex. People who get preoccupied with matters of sexual technique frequently find that sexual satisfaction becomes more and more elusive to them, which is not surprising, because sex for them becomes more and more depersonalized. While careful attention to mechanical detail may help straighten your golf swing or improve your bowling score, it's often more of a hindrance than a help when it comes to sex.

11. Nurture the romance in your life. While working at sex usually produces dismal results, as we've already said, working at being romantic is another matter entirely. Creative ingenuity and plain old-fashioned thoughtfulness can go a long way in this direction. Preserving romance is an ongoing process that involves everything from those little nonsexual exchanges of affection that are so easy to forget about to the out-of-the-ordinary special gestures like a love poem written for an anniversary, flowers sent for no reason at all, or a surprise gift. These gestures are not just ceremonial; they make the

William H. Masters, M.D., and Virginia E. Johnson are America's foremost sex researchers. They have counseled thousands of couples and have done pioneering work in the area of sexual dysfunction.

recipient feel special and loved. In fact, the lavish attention we bestow on our loved one during courtship has a great deal to do with the passionate feelings that are present at that time; thus, it's no surprise that as we fall into nonromantic complacency in our relationships, our sexual interests and passions are apt to dwindle, too.

12. Don't make sex too serious. The seriousness with which we regard sex is a definite drag on our sexual satisfaction, and a by-product of our goal orientation and performance anxieties, our work ethic and the guilt we seem to attach automatically to having a good time. If people could only take themselves a bit less seriously in the bedroom and allow themselves to experience sex as a pleasurable pastime or adventure rather than

a task with predetermined objectives (excite your partner, reach orgasm), they might be surprised to find that sex is more enjoyable. And they also might be able to accept their sexual shortcomings and foibles without a fear that the world is coming to an end. Consider, for a moment, the difference between going on a leisurely, relaxed walk in the woods with no expectations versus deciding that you want to spot a yellow-bellied warbler. If you never see the elusive warbler, you're apt to be disappointed and rate your experience a failure, whereas if you set no goals, you could simply enjoy the scenery.

13. Don't always wait to be "in the mood" before agreeing to have sex. As revolutionary as this may sound, it's a little silly to think that you always must feel sexy before

getting into a sexual situation. For one thing, it's perfectly reasonable to accommodate your partner's needs when you're not feeling particularly in the mood. For another, while you may not feel very sexy at the moment your partner has invited you to fool around, if you give yourself a chance to get into the situation, you may be surprised to find that your feelings can change quite rapidly. If you keep the opportunity from ever developing except when you feel in the mood, you prevent yourself from being able to enjoy your sexual appetite rising when you least expect it.

14. Realize that you and your partner don't have to see eye to eye sexually. For a variety of reasons, not everyone shares the same sexual tastes and preferences. If your partner won't participate in some form of sex that you find quite appealing, the important thing to remember is that he is *not* rejecting you, only the activity. Try to talk out the problem without using an accusatory tone, because it may be possible to find some compromise solution. For example, a woman may be willing to try fellatio if she has her partner's assurance that he won't ejaculate in her mouth. If talking with your spouse about the problem doesn't result in any progress, a visit to a qualified sex counselor or therapist may be helpful.

15. Don't be afraid to ask for help. There's little question that the vast majority of people have times when they're temporarily out of commission sexually. The reasons may be physical—fatigue, infection, acute illness— or related to factors such as high levels of stress, grief, depression, preoccupation with school or job, family problems, and so forth. Most of the time, these episodes of sexual distress appear to be relatively transient and disappear within a matter of weeks. There's no reason to get all worked up if you or your partner feel a temporary loss of appetite, but if difficulties persist for more than a few months without showing definite signs of improvement, it's time to seek out professional advice. The longer a problem lingers, the less likely it is to disappear by itself; furthermore, a professional will usually be able to make a rapid diagnosis of what's going on. In fact, sometimes a sexual problem can be the first sign of a medical condition that requires treatment. In any event, the sooner the cause of the problem is identified and appropriate treatment is started, the easier it generally is to cure it.

16. Try to keep your sexual expectations realistic. If you're looking for every sexual encounter to be sheer ecstasy for you and your partner, you're setting yourself up for failure. If, instead, you can accept the fact that sex isn't always the great passionate joining of souls that Hollywood would have us believe—that it's sometimes rather feeble, awkward and even unsatisfying—then you won't be a prisoner of unrealistic standards. In real life every orgasm isn't a stupendous, earth-shattering event—some are more like small, ordinary twitches. If we keep in mind that we are human beings rather than machines, we can accept the ups and downs, the ebb and flow, of our sexuality.

Sexual dilemmas of the modern office

■ The late Margaret Mead, America's most renowned anthropologist, anticipated the management problems related to the growth of women in the workplace nearly a decade ago. She called for a taboo on sex at the office. "You don't make passes or sleep with the people you work with," she wrote. Without such taboos, it would be impossible for "women . . . to work on an equal basis with men." Ironically, Mead didn't follow her own advice—her second and third husbands worked closely with her—and neither have lots of others.

Office romance is just one of the vexing sexual dilemmas facing managers and workers alike. What do you do when two married subordinates are the targets of office gossip? Or when you want to fire a manager, but his wife is one of your most valued employes? Or when your top salesperson is dating a customer or the vice president of a competing firm? Or when your colleague, the one you suspect is sleeping with the boss, gets the promotion you covet?

As managers well know, bungling any of these situations can result in massive morale problems, the loss of key employes, even million-dollar lawsuits against the company. Nevertheless, the subject is rarely discussed openly by business. "Companies would rather ignore it more than any other issue," says career consultant Betty Harragan, author of the career guide *Games Mother Never Taught You.*

Mixing matters of the heart and careers is already a persistent problem. In a 1985 survey of 100 white-collar employes by Prof. Phillip Hunsaker of the University of San Diego, 90 percent *thought* they knew of a romance in their organization. Whether a couple is having an affair isn't the issue; mere speculation is enough to wreck careers, divide office loyalties and disrupt normal workplace routines.

> Mixing work and romance is dangerous. So why do so many do it, and how should companies handle the conundrums?

A perceived romance between Bendix Corporation chief executive William Agee and his Harvard M.B.A. protégé Mary Cunningham six years ago contributed to the pair's eventual ouster. They're now married.

Only 1 out of 4 respondents in Hunsaker's survey thought office affairs were positive, and those involved single people of equal rank who worked in different departments. Viewed most negatively were liaisons between married workers. Co-workers reacted by sabotaging projects, complaining to supervisors and gossiping. And with more women working, and at higher levels, the dilemmas arising from sex in the workplace won't go away.

Women now account for 45 percent of the civilian work force, compared with 38 percent in 1970. They earned 31 percent of all master-of-business-administration degrees awarded last year, and a third of the lawyers in the top 250 law firms are now women. Despite this progress, women often still find themselves the victims of sexual double standards in the office.

Office romance, career risks

Common sense would indicate that office romances carry big risks, but many get involved anyway. Why? For many people, there are few better places than the office to size up a potential mate's grace under pressure, future career prospects, the amount in his or her paycheck and the likelihood of transmitting a social disease. Working long hours on a shared project can be a lot more stimulating than exchanging small talk with someone who doesn't understand what you do all day, even if that someone is your spouse. "Work is sexy, engrossing. Office romances are intensified by the thrill of the forbidden and meeting in secret places," notes Baila Zeitz, a New York psychologist. But a romantic haze can blind a couple to their colleagues' ire.

A romance that supersedes the organizational power structure is the most dangerous. "It raises the perception that it's a rigged game," says Eliza Collins, an editor of the *Harvard Business Review* and author of a recent study on office romance. "Jealous co-workers feel aced out. They don't feel they have a fair shot at the boss." Resentments fuel gossip. The subordinate, no matter how talented, is often viewed as using sexual favors to get special treatment; both parties are criticized for using poor judgment.

Take the case of one managing partner and an associate at a prestigious Washington, D.C., law firm. He was in his 40s and married; she was in her 30s and separated. Their work relationship blossomed, and he left his wife. A year later, the associate was passed over for partnership and told that unless she transferred to another city, it would happen again.

"Our relationship cast suspicions on his earlier, glowing evaluations of me," she says. They're married now, and she's a part-time lawyer at a federal agency with regrets about her career. Her husband is still managing partner, but some of his partners no longer throw him the business they did before his affair.

Those are the problems that arise when a romance goes well. A breakup really gets messy. Harry Newton, publisher of *Teleconnect,* a trade magazine in the telecommunications industry, recounts a disastrous breakup between two members of his staff. "It was office

SEXUAL HARASSMENT

Crossing the line into verboten territory

Until recently, many corporate managers didn't take charges of sexual harassment seriously. Those days are over as a result of a Supreme Court decision last June and big-dollar legal settlements.

In the Supreme Court case, *Meritor Savings Bank v. Vinson,* Mechelle Vinson was a bank-teller trainee who rose to assistant branch manager in Washington, D.C. She says she was forced to yield to her supervisor's sexual advances. Eventually, she left the bank and sued. Disputes over facts will be settled in an upcoming court trial, but the decision gave Vinson the right to sue and endorsed the concept that sexual harassment is a form of sex discrimination.

The case put businesses on notice that they are liable for harassment even if the company claims ignorance. Merely having a grievance procedure and a general policy against sex discrimination isn't enough to guard against lawsuits. The case also underscores that sexual harassment doesn't have to be linked to promises or threats about job advancement. A "hostile or abusive work environment" is sufficient ground for an employe's harassment claim, the Supreme Court ruled.

Wolf whistles and worse

Studies indicate that the atmosphere at many workplaces may be hostile. The National Organization for Women asserts that at least 50 percent of all working women experience sexual harassment, which it defines as anything from having to look at pornographic pictures on the wall to sexual advances. A 1980 survey of federal workers concluded that 42 percent of 294,000 female federal employes had been sexually harassed at work. The number of

complaints filed with the Equal Employment Opportunity Commission rose from 4,272 in 1981 to 7,273 last year, which doesn't tell the whole story.

"Like rape, it's grossly underreported," asserts lawyer Gloria Allred, who specializes in cases involving women's rights. Experts estimate that harassment is about 90 percent male to female—the rest involves female superiors' making advances to male subordinates and gay men harassing other men.

Sexual harassment hits companies in their wallets. The average size of jury decisions or settlements is in the $60,000-to-$75,000 range, but some have gone as high as $500,000. That was the amount the ABC television network reportedly agreed to pay to resolve a case with Cecily Coleman, a special-projects director who made $60,000 a year and said that she was fired after complaining about her boss's sexual advances.

In another case involving a large cash settlement, Elizabeth Reese, 33, won a $250,000 judgment last October in a U.S. district court against her former company, the Washington branch of architectural firm Swanke, Hayden & Connell. Reese quit her job as marketing director after incidents that she says included her supervisor's encouraging her to sleep with leasing agents to land business. Her firm is appealing the case.

When is a pass wrong?

Still, the arena of sexual harassment is not always clear-cut. Sometimes, it's difficult to tell harassment from normal romantic overtures, says psychologist Judith Waters of Fairleigh Dickinson University. One essential difference is that harassment is persistence in the face of clear rebuffs. "Normal people take 'No' for an answer," Waters adds.

It's a bit easier to draw the line when a supervisor makes overtures to an underling, which is "fraught with overtones of sexual harassment," says Marsha Levick of NOW. Says Waters: "What one person defines as offensiveness, another sees as flattery and still another as humorous."

It gets even trickier to define harassment when former mutually consenting lovers turn on each other or in cases of "reverse sexual harassment." That's when co-workers sue because they feel they have been discriminated against while the career of the boss's lover advances unfairly. In four cases this year, federal judges have upheld the right of co-workers to sue for this reason.

Company confusion and concern have spurred a growth industry in training videos, seminars and consultants. Chase Manhattan Bank discourages employes from touching each other and runs a 2-hour harassment-awareness program for managers. Atlantic Richfield distributes a film and training materials to corporate divisions, but the level of activity in each division varies.

While the ambiguity surrounding sexual harassment perplexes many managers, it's a boon to the companies that market videotapes and training programs. How helpful educational tools will be in sensitizing companies to the management problems related to sex in the workplace is an open question. But, at the very least, they indicate corporate America's dawning awareness that the old rules about sex in the workplace are getting tougher.

by Art Levine and Beth Brophy

warfare. Half the staff sided with her, the other half sided with him. It screwed up morale and prevented work from getting done until the woman left after three months."

Hell hath no fury like a scorned lover. Consider the West Coast marketing manager who had a tempestuous romance with the married president of her company. "As the personal relationship deteriorated, our business relationship fell apart. When I tried to pull back, he wanted all or nothing. He cut me out of meetings, belittled my sales ability, put barriers in my path."

Finally, she allowed him to buy out her 12 percent stake in the business. She was out of work for six months. "I went from being part owner to being a manufacturer's representative. It was quite a culture shock." In another case, a female manager took revenge on her former lover, a group vice president, by writing a letter to the chairman of the board, saying that he used company funds to buy her dinner. Both had to resign.

How a manager should handle such turmoil is not clear-cut. "We intervene when the bank's reputation is at stake

or when we think the company might be open to a sexual-harassment lawsuit," says William Caldwell, senior vice president of human resources of Commerce Union Corporation in Nashville. "If one or both are married, we explain we're not making moral judgments, but people talk." The bank is more concerned about appearances when the couple have jobs with community contact, such as lending officers.

Does office gossip or complaints from other employes constitute an office disruption? "I wouldn't stick my nose in before at least three workers complained," says Janice Beyer, a management professor at the New York University School of Business. "Then, the best outlet is for the manager to suggest counseling through an employe-assistance program, if the company has one."

The double standard lives

Just because the boss hasn't mentioned it doesn't mean the affair has gone unnoticed—or will go unpunished. "Careers get screwed up because bosses won't say openly that the situation makes them uncomfortable," says consultant Marilyn Moats Kennedy of Career Strategies, Inc., in Wilmette, Ill. "There may be quiet, internal sanctions. Nothing is said, but they won't get promoted," adds Collins of *Harvard Business Review.*

Female professionals are more likely than men to suffer career fallout. Says Andrea Warfield, associate professor of management at Ferris State College in Michigan: "Women have had to subdue their sexuality to advance in a corporation. Being perceived as a sensual figure would mean a loss of respect within the organization."

Another reason a double standard operates is that no matter how high up the woman is, her lover is usually higher. "There was no question I would be the one to leave the firm," says the woman lawyer. Her husband, after all, had "16 years invested in the firm and was earning multiples of my income. It was easier for me to take a small pay cut than for him to take an enormous cut."

Not everyone agrees that sexual attraction is harmful to productivity, particularly if it's not acted upon or acknowledged. "Over all, sexual tension is positive. It can bring energy into the workplace and fuel creative work," says Kathy Kram, a management professor at the Boston University School of Management, who has studied 75 mentor pairs in large corporations.

She found that sexual attraction was often an element in the relationships, but it was usually not acted on. The most benign office romances, in terms of office reactions, are between two single people of equal rank. But even those affairs aren't all smooth sailing. For example, a Washington, D.C., research analyst dated a co-worker who sat a few offices away. But when they broke up a year later, she turned her back every time he passed by.

Red flags for co-workers

Soon, he left for a better job and, for several years anyway, kept his vow to avoid office romance. Then, he had another brief romance with a colleague. "Never again," he declares. "It's awkward for your co-workers because they can't discuss the other person's work with you objectively, which gets in the way. And it raises red flags to your colleagues about your emotional stability. Who needs that?"

Another problem with dating colleagues is that co-workers and bosses may view a liaison between two workers as a business team. "Two peers together have more influence than each does separately," says Leslie Aldridge Westoff, author of the book *Corporate Romance.* Adds Warfield: "If one is bruised, then the other is unhappy. Whatever decisions the boss makes are a political double whammy."

Some companies circumvent the problems caused by a husband and a wife reacting as a team by forbidding it. At Greyhound Corporation, spouses can't work in the same department under the same boss, and couples working at the same level in different departments need special dispensation from the chief executive.

Michigan Bell has no formal policy and allows married couples to work together, but it frowns on couples in a supervisor-employe relationship. However, each supervisor decides how to handle a particular situation. Pharmaceutical firm Merck & Company restricts relatives from supervising each other but employs several husband-wife research teams. Du Pont Company does not object to spouses working together.

Companies that forbid spouses to work together sometimes base their policy on concerns about financial malfeasance. Banks are particularly sensitive to the situation. At Amcore Bank in Rockford, Ill., Richard Catlin, senior vice president for human resources, says that "when handling funds, one spouse can influence the other's judgment." Thus, if two co-workers marry, one will be moved to another department.

A few companies take a radically different view of family ties. Says Ronald Assaf, president and founder of Sensormatic Electronics Corporation, a 1,000-employe company in Boca Raton, Fla.: "We found that having family members work in the same organization is a definite plus. It creates a good atmosphere." In fact, Assaf married his manager of international operations and shifted her responsibilities so she reported directly to him.

"I thought that having my wife report to a vice president who reported to me would put undue pressure on the vice president," he explains. In February, former marketing manager Leon Rawitz, 29, and accounting supervisor Marlene Mazza, 31, also plan to marry.

They report no problems but say that they kept the romance secret at first because of rivalries between the two departments.

Caught in the middle

Sometimes, bedfellows make for strange office politics. Ellen Gumbiner, 32, a San Francisco real-estate agent, married her boss, a co-owner of the agency, three years ago. Her husband no longer works at the agency, but when he did, she was "put in the middle of agent-owner problems, such as disputes over commissions. Agents would tell me their side of the story so I would tell Richard. I didn't want any part of it."

Another time, a furor arose when she won a sales contest. To avoid the appearance of favoritism, the prize was scaled back, even though she had won it fair and square.

The trickiest problem facing a company that employs couples is how to dump one without alienating the other. When one spouse must be fired, employers can minimize the traumas by bringing in outplacement counselors to help the employe find a new job. "If the fired person lands another good job, the other spouse will be less upset with the company," says consultant Kennedy.

For the couple, though, problems don't end with one's departure, even when it's a voluntary exit. Biting the hand that signs the spouse's paycheck can lead to marital discord. "The ex-employer is like an in-law you must tolerate but feel no affection for," says a Chicago free-lance writer who used to work at the same newspaper that employs her husband. Soon after she left, the wife criticized the paper to friends, angering her husband. "He doesn't want to hear me bad-mouthing his employer," she says.

At least married couples know where they stand regarding company rules. When it comes to dating clients, or peers at competing companies, the guidelines are murky.

By the time an employe realizes he or she has transgressed an invisible boundary, it can be too late. A case in point: Virginia Rulon-Miller was a rising star at IBM until she began dating a former co-worker who had gone to work for a competitor. Rulon-Miller's boss informed her that the relationship was a conflict of interest. She had to choose her job or her boyfriend. Rulon-Miller was fired and sued IBM. The jury awarded her $300,000 for "wrongful discharge and intentional infliction of emotional distress."

Romance by the rules

The precedent set by the IBM case—a

clear ruling in the employe's favor—has made companies understandably nervous about firing employes who date competitors. Still, there are ways to make employes' lives miserable, short of firing them.

"A manager can start nailing a person until he voluntarily quits, which only increases the company's liability should an employe sue," says San Francisco lawyer Cliff Palefsky, who represented Rulon-Miller in the IBM case.

A senior executive with a California medical-equipment company hopes she won't suffer career setbacks as a result of dating a man who is a potential financer of the equipment. She keeps the relationship secret. "I don't want anyone to think I'm throwing large commissions his way as a result of our personal relationship," she says.

The culture of a company plays a large role in determining what's acceptable behavior—and only an insider can gauge the career risks. Advice from experts on how to handle a potential conflict of interest runs the gamut from full disclosure to stonewalling.

In the absence of a written policy or clear company precedents, employes would be wise to talk to a supervisor privately before the rumors start flying, says Professor Beyer. Many people, no doubt, would view discussions with the boss as an invasion of their personal lives. Consultant Kennedy recommends the opposite tack. "Neither deny nor confirm. If someone brings the relationship up directly, ask where they heard it. That will put them, not you, on the defensive."

As more and more managers are discovering, negotiating the tricky boundaries between employes' private and public lives is no easy task. Yet pretending that issues related to sex in the workplace don't exist won't make these problems disappear. As former Bendix executive Mary Cunningham notes: "Sexual accusations are serious ones. They can ruin personal lives, and they can ruin careers."

---

by Beth Brophy with Nancy Linnon
and Marilyn A. Moore in Miami

MAKING LOVE: 5 TRAPS TO AVOID

If sex often seems like just another routine, it's time to give your love life a makeover. Hundreds of couples have managed to bring back the old magic—you can too!

Barbara De Angelis

Barbara De Angelis is director of the Los Angeles Personal Growth Center, which offers seminars, courses and workshops on relationships for couples and singles. She also hosts a program on KABC-Radio in Los Angeles.

Most "sexual problems" are not sexual at all. They begin with problems we bring into the bedroom from our adolescence, from that awful date in college, from what our parents told us about how men and women should behave. In other words, they often originate as misconceptions about the way sex *should* be.

In my years of counseling hundreds of people, I've seen how easily perfectly good sex lives can be ruined. I also know that the damage can be repaired. Making love can be a deeply satisfying experience if we can let go of five common assumptions. I call them "sexual traps" because they trap us into behavior patterns that contribute to sexual problems.

1. MAKING LOVE MEANS HAVING SEX

Try this exercise: After you read this sentence, close your eyes and picture a couple making love. If you're like most people, you probably imagine a couple having intercourse. But this is the first "sexual trap"—the belief that making love means only that one thing. Some couples won't be tender or affectionate—which is all part of making love—unless they think it's a preamble to sex. Yet making love is something you can experience in or out of bed. If you think, "Why bother with it if we don't go all the way?" you deny yourself and your partner the innumerable ways in which to enjoy each other.

Don't wait until you're in bed to express your love and attraction for each other. Celebrate your relationship. Think back and remember something you both used to do together and really enjoyed, like dancing, bowling or eating at a special restaurant. Plan for this activity again. Surprise your partner with a gift when he or she least expects one. Send a love letter. Use every moment in your relationship as an opportunity to make love.

2. IF MY PARTNER REALLY LOVES ME, HE'LL KNOW JUST WHAT TO DO TO MAKE SEX WONDERFUL

Did Dr. Zhivago need to be told how to satisfy his lover, Lara, when they made love? No, he just *knew*. Unfortunately lovers like Dr. Zhivago don't exist in real life. In real life we don't always intuitively know what our partners want. "But," you may protest, "talking takes all the romance out of it!" This idea implies that your partner may not be a true soulmate if he or she doesn't know how to make perfect love to you. This puts unnecessary pressure on both of you, which can lead to resentment and frustration.

A woman named Linda* whom I counseled fell into that category of people I call "sexual martyrs." They rarely have satisfying sexual experiences, blaming their partners for not being sensitive to their needs. Yet they never express these needs out loud. I asked Linda what she wanted from her husband, and at first all she could tell me was, "I want him to love me." No wonder she didn't ask for what she wanted—she didn't even know! I then asked her to make a list of the things she liked and disliked sexually. This was difficult for her because she had been brought up to think that girls who wanted sex were "bad." Expressing what she really wanted in bed meant acknowledging that her desires were O.K.

---

*All names in this article have been changed.

From *Family Circle*, March 3, 1987, pp. 20, 114-115. From the book HOW TO MAKE LOVE ALL THE TIME, by Barbara De Angelis. Copyright © 1987, Barbara De Angelis. Published by Rawson Associates. Reprinted by permission of the author's agent, Harvey Klinger, Inc.

Linda's list turned out to be one and a half pages long! Once she got free of the sexual martyr role, she knew exactly what she wanted—she'd just been too afraid to ask for it. Two months later Linda called me and sounded like a different person. She had discovered that when she asked for what she wanted, she was able to have much more enjoyable sex.

Follow Linda's example and try to explain to your partner, at a time when you're both feeling especially close and loving, exactly what you like to feel and when.

3. THERE'S ONLY ONE REASON TO MAKE LOVE

John and Sue go out for a romantic dinner. They go to a nice restaurant, complete with candles and strolling guitarist. At the table they hold hands and every once in a while give each other a tender kiss. After dinner they take a long walk with their arms around each other. They stop at a nightclub to dance for a while. Then they return home. Sue puts soft music on the stereo; John spends a long time seducing her. Finally they make love. Afterward, while they lie silently entwined, John asks, "Honey, was it good for you?"

Does he mean, "Did you enjoy the evening we spent together?" Of course not! What he really means is, "Did you have an orgasm?" I choose to tell you this story because I think it perfectly illustrates this sexual trap. Orgasm is the natural release of built-up sexual energy, but it is just one part of the total experience of making love. Most people remember their most cherished lovemaking experiences because of how loved and appreciated they felt, not because of the final orgasm. Sue and John had just finished *four hours* of lovemaking, yet they were falling into the trap of judging the entire evening by whether or not they achieved orgasm.

There are many elements involved in sexual satisfaction: feeling safe, appreciated and not pressured to perform. Breaking out of this sexual trap means realizing that making love encompasses much more than orgasm.

4. NOVELTY IS THE KEY TO AN EXCITING SEX LIFE

Judith cried as she sat in my office, trying to understand what had gone wrong in her marriage to Ted. It seemed that early in the relationship, Ted felt that he and Judith had to keep a constant sense of novelty in their sex life so it wouldn't get boring. As soon as the couple became comfortable making love in a particular style or setting, Ted would insist that they change. "We've had sex in the kitchen, den, even the laundry room," said Judith. "I can't stand it anymore. Why can't he just love me and our sex life for what they are? Rather than bringing us closer, I feel that this is driving us apart!"

Ted was unable to really enjoy sex because he felt it always had to involve something new or unusual. But the truth is, sex becomes boring when partners forget how to be attentive to each other. We all change, year to year, month to month, day to day. It's not the place that makes sex really exciting, it's knowing and loving your partner and feeling loved in return.

5. SEX SHOULDN'T BE PLANNED, IT SHOULD JUST HAPPEN

This is one of the most common sexual traps. Most of us have hectic lives: We work, we take care of kids, we handle all the financial and personal affairs necessary to keep a household going. Yet we still believe it is unromantic to plan for sex. While we're just sitting around after dinner, we imagine that we should suddenly be seized with so much passion that we rush to the bedroom.

But who actually has time to sit around after dinner? One or both of you probably has to clean up, entertain the kids, do extra work brought home from the office or go out to a meeting or to a class. The only thing that may seize you after dinner is a strong urge to get into bed—and sleep!

The solution is to create the opportunity for sex to happen—but not to force it. Plan for time to be alone together. Turn on the answering machine, put a DO NOT DISTURB sign on the bedroom door. Ask a neighbor to take the kids for the evening. Just doing this will probably make you feel very special and loved, and may be all you need to put the spark back into your love life.

Sexuality Through the Life Cycle

- Youth and Their Sexuality (Articles 34-38)
- Sex in and out of Marriage (Articles 39-43)

Individual sexual development is a lifelong process that begins at conception and terminates at death. Contrary to popular notions of this process, there are no latent periods during which the individual is nonsexual or noncognizant of sexuality. The growing process of a sexual being does, however, reveal qualitative differences through various life stages. It is with respect to these stages of the life cycle and their relation to sexuality that this section devotes its attention.

As children gain self-awareness, they naturally explore their own bodies, masturbate, display curiosity for the bodies of the opposite sex, and show interest in the bodies of mature individuals such as their parents. Such exploration and curiosity is an important and healthy part of human development. Yet, it is often difficult for adults (who live in a society that is not comfortable with sexuality in general) to avoid making their children ashamed of being sexual or showing interest in sexuality. Adults often impose their conceptualization and ambivalence upon the children's innocuous explorations into sexuality. Thus, distortion of an indispensable and formative stage of development occurs, which often makes difficult a full acceptance of sexuality later in life.

Adolescence, the social status accompanying puberty, proves to be a considerably stressful period in life for many individuals as they attempt to develop an adult identity and forge relationships with others. Because of the physiological capacity for reproduction, adolescent sexuality tends to be heavily censured by parents and society at this stage of life. This is especially true for the female. Standard injunctions that all sex is evil or that all adolescents are sexually irresponsible fail to contribute toward healthy and/or responsible sexuality. To the contrary, they are much more likely to contribute to the feelings of guilt that may stay with the individual for the remainder of his or her life. The benefit of experience and knowledge of the adult generation needs to be honestly and constructively mobilized. For this knowledge and experience to be useful, though, trust across the generations must be established.

Finally, sexuality in adulthood, at least within marriage, becomes socially acceptable. Yet, for some, routine and boredom exact a heavy toll on the quality of sexual interaction. Extramarital sexual encounters are often sought and established despite the fact that such activity is conventionally stigmatized as infidelity. The problem of infidelity is not an easy one to solve. Current scholarly opinion maintains that infidelity and extramarital relations are two separate phenomena.

Sexuality in the later years of life is again socially and culturally stigmatized by the prevailing misconception that sex is for young married adults. Such an attitude is primarily responsible for the apparent decline in sexual interest and activity as one grows older. Physiological changes in the aging process are not, in and of themselves, detrimental to sexual expression, as noted by the saying, "Just because there is snow on the rooftop, doesn't mean that there is not fire in the chimney." A life history of experience, health, and growth can make sexual expression in the later years a most rewarding and fulfilling experience.

Youth and Their Sexuality begins with an article about sexual abuse. The author argues in favor of early sex education designed to teach values. The next article provides helpful advice on providing adequate sex education for youth, from the very young to the teens. It deals with problems that parents and schools need to overcome in providing this valuable, much needed information. The next two articles focus on teen pregnancy: the first discusses the problem from a sociological point of view; the second looks at the issue of "teen lust" and its consequences. The last article in the subsection emphasizes the importance of informal sources of sexual learning for promoting sexual responsibility.

Sex in and out of Marriage explores some sex myths and the reality behind them. The next article considers why many females in their mid-life question their sex life and their sexuality. More myths are discussed by Susan Squires who focuses on sexual misinformation about men and sex and aging. The last two articles explore relationships, sexual activity, and aging. The point is made that while there are changes in these areas as we grow older, sexual relationships among the older generation are very similar to those of younger generations.

Looking Ahead: Challenge Questions

How would you describe some of the problems that youth have in dealing with their sexuality? What do some parents need to change in order to help their adolescents? How would you support or disagree with the statement that sexual knowledge is the best weapon against irresponsible sexuality?

How would you summarize what appears to disturb women in mid-life about their sexuality?

Should we change our thinking about extramarital sex? Infidelity? Why or why not?

How does advancing age affect romantic relationships? Sexuality? Can sex for older people bring new freedoms, experiences, and joys? How or why not?

SEX IN CHILDHOOD: AVERSION, ABUSE, OR RIGHT?

Dean D. Knudsen, Ph.D.
Department of Sociology and Anthropology
Purdue University
West Lafayette, IN 47907

Abstract

Childhood sexuality has become a new focus of attention with the public awareness of child sexual abuse, but there are many unresolved issues. First, the incest taboo is no longer an adequate control on adult-child sexual activities. Second, definitions of sexual abuse are imprecise and inconsistent across county and state lines, resulting in varied levels of enforcement or legal action. Third, an emphasis focused only on the right to say no denies the choice that is inherent in the concept of "rights." A major conclusion is that sex education designed to teach values about sexuality is essential and must begin very early.

Sexual behavior by children has been a problem for parents, schools, and law enforcement for generations. In recent years, the concern about sexual abuse by adults has refocused the issue of child sexual activities. One approach has been to define all activities involving adult-child sexual contact as sexual abuse, giving law enforcement and child protective services an easy way to deal with such behavior. Many questions remain concerning other issues of sexuality in childhood, however. Some consensus exists about the extreme behaviors that should be defined as abusive, but even such terms as *incest, molestation,* and *rape* have several meanings. In addition, there are some persistent issues, including consent versus victimization and the rights of children to engage in sexual activities, that are largely unresolved.

This paper is directed toward the general issue of sex in childhood. Three perspectives will be examined: 1) that the incest taboo and the natural aversion among humans to sex with intimates—especially with adults and family members—provides an adequate and appropriate level of control over sexual abuse; 2) that sexual activities for children—especially with adults—is harmful to children, and thus protection and control of children are essential; and 3) that sexual activities are a right of the child if the child desires them—even with adults. Each of these views will be examined, and research that supports or contradicts the various positions will be noted.

Background

Public concern about childhood sexuality is of relatively recent origin. Prior to the eighteenth century, little attention was paid to such sexual activity, but after religious moralists and medical personnel condemned it, child sexual behavior gradually became defined as sinful or harmful (Fishman, 1982). Masturbation, for example, was seen not only as evil but also as the cause of many illnesses, including epilepsy, hysteria, sterility, and insanity (Neuman, 1975). Parents were encouraged to discipline their children to eliminate such self-abuse and thus prevent sickness and disease. Through the years, various techniques, including fear, brutality, and superstition were employed to eradicate masturbation, though with limited success at best (Schultz, 1980a; Gagnon & Simon, 1973).

Heterosexual behaviors and relationships similarly were controlled on the ground that children lacked the physical maturity and cognitive abilities to deal with such experiences, and the concept of "age of consent" was applied, especially to girls, to preserve their moral innocence. Originally "age of consent" apparently referred to the male's ability to enter into commercial agreements or to bear the armor required

*The author wishes to express appreciation to Barbara Carson and members of the Sorento Seminar for their helpful comments on an earlier draft of this paper.

From *Journal of Sex Education and Therapy*, Vol. 13, No. 1, Spring/Summer 1987, pp. 16-24. Copyright © 1987, JSET. Reprinted by permission.

for battle. Only later, during the thirteenth century, was it applied to females under the age of 12, and by the sixteenth century the age of 10 was established as the legal age of consent for males and females in England and America. However, the economic conditions that spawned childhood prostitution were so severe and prostitution was so widespread that as late as 1880 no charge of sexual assault could be made against a man if a child, regardless of age, gave voluntary consent to sexual intercourse (Schultz, 1980b).

Criminal laws were enacted in the late nineteenth century to eliminate childhood prostitution and other forms of sexual abuse by adults. By increasing the age of consent, the laws were designed to protect children from sexual exploitation and effectively denied children the right to engage in any sexual activities (Schultz, 1980a). Changing conceptions of childhood and the concern for protection and control that characterized the child-saving movement (Platt, 1969) also were incorporated into the juvenile justice system by the beginning of the twentieth century, resulting both in a paternalism and in an ambiguous legal status for children and youth.

Since 1900, laws in most states have offered protection of girls and young women through "statutory rape" codes and relatively high ages of consent, and more recently, by child protective services. Despite changing laws, however, and the new legal definitions of childhood that extend it to ages 16–18 in most states, few efforts are made to protect females over the age of 14 (Russell, 1984). The use of higher ages would technically classify those young women who voluntarily or willingly engaged in sexual intercourse below the age of 16—about one third to one half of all females (Zelnick, Kim and Kanter, 1979; Furstenberg, 1976)—either as victims of criminal behavior with possible prosecution of their partners, or as incorrigible individuals subject to possible incarceration (e.g, Wooden, 1976). As a result, few efforts are made to prosecute consensual sexual activity among teenagers.

Most of the current concern about excluding children from sexual experiences is directed toward younger ages, especially those under 12, whose physical and emotional immaturity is viewed as sufficient reason for their protection. This approach is buttressed by beliefs about the natural asexuality of infants and children, by moral codes, and by a genuine concern about the negative effects of early sexual stimulation. Some recent research offers challenges to these beliefs, however, concerning both the physiological functions of small children and the inevitability of negative consequences from early sexual experiences.

Physiological Capabilities of Children

Many adults believe that most sexual functions are possible only with the onset of puberty, though research now suggests that a wide range of sexual behaviors can occur at very early ages. Martinson (1976) has noted that male infants are capable of penile erections and that vaginal lubrication has been recorded for female babies, functions that indicate a physical capac-

ity for sexual activities and intercourse almost from birth. Other observations among small children have indicated that autoerotic behavior such as masturbation or exhibiting may occur by age 2, and is common among boys and girls by 6–7 years of age. In addition, heterosexual play among preschool children involving exploration, genital manipulation, and coital training, that is, positions and movements associated with coitus, has been reported (Langfeldt, 1981a). Though Freud termed these years "the Latent Period," it is clear that many preadolescent children have sexual capacities—including orgasms and even pregnancy (Borneman, 1983; Janus and Bess, 1976; Kinsey, Pomeroy, & Martin, 1948).

To say that children are physically capable of sexual activities does not imply that they interpret such behavior in the way that most adults view sexuality, however, because children lack both knowledge of and experience with the cognitive and emotional dimensions of sexuality. Researchers have described this ability in various ways—as imagery (Byrne, 1977) and as sexual maturity (Borneman, 1983) or as concept formation (Langfeldt, 1981b)—all of which refer to erotic fantasies that appear at very young ages and develop over time, through social experiences, into adult sexuality. At the physiological level, the entire range of sexual activity including sexual intercourse appears to be possible for most humans at very young ages; it is the social and cognitive aspects of sexuality that distinguish adult and child sexual understandings of sexual behavior.

Sociohistorical Factors in Defining Appropriate Child Sexuality

Numerous historians and researchers have noted that children and childhood have different meanings today than in the past (e.g., Aries, 1962; deMause, 1974; Demos, 1971; Pollock, 1983; Postman, 1982; Suransky, 1982; Synott, 1983). While several historical eras might be constructed on the basis of varied criteria, the changing perspective of childhood sexuality is represented by the development from "property," to "protection," to "personal" paradigms (Lee, 1982). In preindustrial society, children were viewed as property whose sexuality was recognized and accepted as a part of life. With the development of schools and changes in families as a part of the industrial revolution, the protection of childhood innocence was sought through the removal of children from the sexuality of adult life. Protection became an adult responsibility that included both the observing and making of decisions in the "best interests" of children. With the emergence of individual rights—especially the right of a child to veto the parental choice of marriage partners—the shift toward a personal paradigm was begun, in which personal rights for children would replace adult protection. One consequence of this movement is the view that young children should be able, if they wish, to choose to engage in the entire range of sexual activities available to adults (e.g, Holt, 1974).

The current ambiguity in legal definitions of sexual abuse and consent and in parental understanding of child sexuality, in part reflects a failure to address the changed understandings and increased knowledge about sexual abuse, incest, molestation, and sexual activities. In the United States, for example, the term *incest* may be used to describe diverse sexual activities that range from an unwanted touch to sexual intercourse; that occur once or over long periods; that occur between nuclear family members as well as consanguineous, affinal, or step-relatives; and that may be consensual or involve force or threats (Bixler, 1983). The genetic factors that often have been cited as a basis for the incest taboo are more scientifically and clearly understood now than when most legal definitions were written. Similarly, the social factors noted to be associated with incest—such as family role conflict, sibling or spousal jealousy, or extrafamilial alliances—that once were cited as reasons for the incest taboo (e.g, Davis, 1949), no longer appear to affect family patterns in an era of mobility and high divorce. While the concept of sexual abuse has obscured some difficult issues, much ambiguity remains about appropriate sexuality for children. In addition, little consensus exists among legal jurisdictions, intervention agencies, and protective service units about the appropriate means of dealing with either children or adults involved in sexual activities or the effects of those sexual experiences on children (e.g. Finkelhor, Gomes-Schwartz, and Horowitz, 1982).

Definitions of Sexuality

Various positions have been taken regarding childhood sexuality and the protection of children from sexual exploitation. Historically, the incest taboo and the assumed natural aversion to sex among intimates have been the means by which children were protected from sexual abuse by family members. The emergence of child abuse as a social problem redefined child protection less as a family responsibility, and social services were developed to supplement or replace the incest taboo as a form of control over sexuality of and against children. A third view defines sexual activities as a right for children, and the decision to become involved is left to the child. Each of these perspectives will be developed more fully and evaluated by examining the existing research literature.

Childhood Sexuality as Aversion

Aversion to sexual activities with family members, usually associated with the incest taboo, is frequently expressed by incest victims who felt that those experiences were "bad" or "wrong"—even as they occurred. Some researchers see these feelings as a natural consequence of intimate social experiences in all small groups, and especially in private family life (e.g., Bettelheim, 1969). Other researchers, however, view the incest taboo as a defense and a social control mechanism against a natural sexual attraction among primary family members. They see the taboo as necessary to prevent sexual activities that would have important social, biological, and psychological consequences

(DeMott, 1980; Renshaw & Renshaw, 1977). Both views would suggest that a genuine aversion to intrafamily sex exists and is buttressed—if not created—by the incest taboo and its strong moral and legal supports.

It has become evident that incest is not rare, suggesting that aversive feelings about intrafamilial sexual behaviors clearly are no longer powerful enough to prevent adults from engaging children in consensual and forced sexual behaviors. The failure of incest taboo in recent decades has been tied to the social changes that have occurred in Western societies in the past 50 years. The sexual revolution and the increased divorce rate with the complementary increase in step-parents have had important consequences for higher levels of sexual contact (e.g., Finkelhor, 1979b, Russell, 1984). Similarly, the contemporary pattern of small, mobile, vertical family units and the loss of extended family ties may foster incestuous relationships because each individual's need for affection and physical intimacy must be satisfied largely from within the nuclear unit (Henderson, 1972; Parker & Parker, 1986). Other researchers suggest depersonalization and compartmentalized life-styles (Taubman, 1984) as factors in the declining power of the incest taboo.

In general, the aversion argument proposes such social changes as sexual permissiveness, changing sex and gender roles, disrupted and reconstructed families, the emphasis on economic success, and the dependence on the family for non-ego-threatening abuse. Not all males in chaotic social settings persistently seek sexual experiences with children, however, suggesting that other individual factors are involved as well. Efforts to deal with this question focus on the breakdown of inhibitions or prohibitions against sexual behaviors directed toward children by adults. Araji and Finkelhor (1986) have suggested that disinhibition theories offer explanations at both the individual and sociocultural levels. At the individual level, impulse disorder, senility, alcohol problems, psychosis, situational stress, and the failure of incest avoidance mechanisms have been identified. Cultural tolerance, pornography, and patriarchal prerogatives are seen as sociocultural conditions that contribute to disinhibition. It may also be that the incest taboo is not learned by all members of society, leading to different levels of strength or salience of the prohibitions against sex with family members, just as other norms have uneven adherence.

Responses of excitement, participation, or disgust to adult overtures reflect earlier experiences with sex and the degree to which these behaviors were rewarded, ignored, or punished (Howells, 1981). Because of the adult's ability to manipulate the child, there is little evidence of physical force being used—at least initially—in most sexual abuse (Plummer, 1981), though it is common for threats, coercion, or bribes to be used to maintain a relationship. Adults may interpret the initial acceptance of contact by children as interest or desire, whether or not such views are supported by the child's behavior following the contact. Such submission is important, for as Frude notes, "the most powerful factor in reducing inhibitions may be a daughter's apparent acceptance of the behavior"

(1982). Others (e.g., Meiselman, 1978; Finkelhor, 1979b) also have reported on the passivity or willing participation of young women in sexual activity with fathers. Because reactions to sexual activity on the part of the offender as well as the child are learned, the lack of immediate negative responses may be viewed as an apparent willingness of young children to participate, thereby further encouraging the perpetrator. Such processes are probably more descriptive of opportunistic abusers rather than of pedophiles who engage in continued or repeated sexual acts with children and probably are not affected by incest taboos in their behavior (e.g., DSM–III, 1980). The fact that boys learn different responses than girls to touch and body contact at early ages also may be a factor in gender victimization in sexual abuse. By the early years of elementary school, the male response to touch is aggressive physical action, whereas females respond with deference and acceptance (Gunderson, Melas, and Skor, 1981).

It is clear that the incest taboo has not prevented adults from seeking sexual activities with children within their kinship group, and intrafamily intimacy has not resulted in a universal aversion to sexual behavior with kin. Thus, several proposals that would emphasize the legitimacy of child sexual activity have been made. Johnson (1977), for example, has suggested that the traditional approach to the sexuality of the young—trying to eliminate it—has failed and that responsibility and enhancement of sexual expression are preferable. Separating abuse from normal or acceptable sexual activity has obvious merit; however, the ambiguity of intentions has presented an important problem for those responsible for protecting children.

Childhood Sexuality as Abuse

The concern with child protection rests on the perspective that children are primarily victims of adult actions and that exposure of a child to any type of sexual activities before the child reaches an appropriate level of maturation has serious negative consequences and thus should be defined as abuse. This view has been based on one or more of several judgments: 1) that adult-child sex is wrong because physical or maturational differences result in damage or harm to the child, 2) that premature sexualization draws the children into adult life and deprives them of the freedom of childhood, 3) that sex at an early age leaves emotional and psychological damage that often appears in later life, and 4) that children cannot give informed consent to sexual activities with adults because by their nature children lack the power and knowledge to give consent (Finkelhor, 1979a). In essence, children are seen as incapable of, disinterested in, or too immature for appreciating the significance of sexual activities and the consequences of their sexual behavior; thus they must be protected from too early exposure and its effects.

Despite the obvious appeal of such an approach to childhood sexuality, some serious questions remain. The first argument, that adult-child sex is unnatural due to size difference and that it produces physical harm and damage to the child, primarily applies only to that small proportion of the cases that involve attempted or achieved sexual intercourse. Schultz has noted that "no more than 5 to 10 percent of sexual abuse involves physical injury" (1980). Other types of physical effects such as AIDS, gonorrhea, or syphilis, are serious and cannot be ignored. Unfortunately, these problems are not unique to child abuse or child victimization where their control would appear to be more feasible than among adults; in fact, on the basis of current public health concerns, it is apparent that adulthood does not necessarily bring a greater ability to deal with them.

The second issue, premature sexualization, ignores the fact that children have extensive interest in sexual activities, however immature and exploratory they may be. The exposure of children to television and the varieties of sexuality expressed through that medium probably have reduced the adult-child differences in sexual understanding that once existed (e.g., Postman, 1982). Though premature sexualization may be an irrelevant issue to many children who have been exposed to a wide range of sexual activities from infancy, other children may be incapable of understanding the full meaning of sexual behaviors, with some serious consequences for their behavior. Unfortunately, data are inadequate to assess the extent or importance of this problem.

Third, the evidence also is far from convincing in the documentation of psychological damage (Conte, 1985). Early reports about sexual abuse came from clinical observations that emphasized the severe negative impact of child sexual abuse, especially coerced sexual activities. These studies suggested that there is a wide range of short- and long-term reactions of victims: anxiety and fear, guilt and shame, depression, grief, sense of stigma, somatic complaints, and learning and behavioral problems (Browne and Finkelhor, 1986). The significance of such reports must be qualified by the fact that the population under observation is selective, that is, the very persons most likely to experience emotional reactions and thus seek assistance in dealing with them are the subjects for these research reports. The lack of representative samples of control groups in most of these studies precludes generalizations about the extent and severity of trauma of sexual experiences with adults, because no comparable evidence is available from those people not traumatized by such activities. Nevertheless, some careful, recent clinical research supports the conclusion that sexual abuse produces trauma for children (e.g., Friedrich, Urquize, & Beilke, 1986; Husain & Chapel, 1982; Rogers & Terry, 1984; Rosenfeld, 1979; Ruch & Chandler, 1982; Scott & Stone, 1986; Sgroi, 1982).

Other clinical studies, as well as much research based on larger, representative samples, are less consistent in documenting the pervasive, negative consequences of sexual abuse, however. Indeed, the evidence about the extent and inevitability of trauma is contradictory at best. Several recent studies indicated that perhaps one third of the children who have engaged in some form of sexual activities with adults do not define the experience as negative (e.g, Bernard, 1981; Brunold, 1964; Constantine, 1981; Curtois, 1979; Emslie & Rosenfeld, 1983; Gagnon, 1965; LaBarbera, Martin & Dozier, 1980; Mayer, 1983:15–16; Ramey, 1979; Trepper & Traicoff, 1983:15; Tsai, Summers, & Edgar, 1979; Yorukoglu & Kemph, 1966). Such findings strongly suggest some modifications of the general conclusions drawn from clinical samples that *all* sexual contacts between children and adults have negative consequences for children. Evidence indicates that factors that appear to contribute to trauma for both sexes are: 1) the use of force, and 2) fathers or stepfathers as perpetrators (Browne & Finkelhor, 1986).

A few studies of boys also suggest early experiences may be related to homosexuality (Sandfort, 1982; Ingram, 1979), though such interpretations lack sufficient data to be convincing (DeJong, Emmett, & Hervada, 1982; Farber, Showers, Johnson, Joseph, & Oshins, 1984). It is too early to draw conclusions about long-term consequences for young children who have been victimized without obvious trauma. Though clinical studies often have documented the negative effects for adults of sexual contacts during childhood, such data also are inevitably selective and it remains to be determined if serious problems will develop for all children who experience early sexualization with adults.

No adequate explanation has been offered for these diverse findings, but the nature and intensity of reactions by parents and professionals to the situation is often mentioned as an important factor in generating trauma among victims (Colonna & Solnit, 1981; Conte & Berliner, 1981; Constantine, 1981; Elwell, 1979; Walters, 1975). Additional support for the idea that adult reactions are important comes from a study of communes (Berger, 1981) that suggested that sexuality expressed freely among and between children and adults had few negative consequences—unless the contact had been forced.

Clearly, the attitudes and actions of parents and children toward all sexual activities are important, not only those responses to events that are classified as sexually abusive. Because the term *sexual abuse* is often applied to a range of activities—sexual intercourse, fondling, oral-genital contact, indecent exposure to a child, involvement of a child in obscene performances, and even suggestive, provocative speech—the age and maturation of the child is an important factor in the reactions by both adult and the child to the incident or activity. Some studies attempt to incorporate maturation as a part of the definition of victimization and limit abuse to behavior between adults and children whose ages are at least 5 years apart (e.g., Finkelhor, 1979b; Mrazek and Kempe, 1981), though the psychiatric definition of pedophilia refers to age differences of 10 years or more between participants (DSM–III, 1980). Other researchers have focused on all unsought sexual experiences and include actions by age peers or perpetrators who are even younger than the victims (e.g., Russell, 1984). Current research,

however, offers no consistent evidence that there is greater trauma either for those of younger ages at the onset of abuse or for those whose sexual experiences were of longer duration (Browne & Finkelhor, 1986).

Finally, there is an unfortunate lack of data that would help clarify the issue of age at which the average child can give informed consent. Classifying all sexual activities involving young children—whether with peers or adults—as abuse rests upon a system of age stratification and age segregation that assumes privacy and isolation of children from the adult world. The idea that 12-year-old children are unable to give consent because they lack the knowledge and capacity to make responsible decisions or to accept the consequences of sexual behavior assumes an ignorance and immaturity about sex and life that probably no longer exists for many, if not most children.

If, as some supporters of early sex education claim, the issue of sex is treated as a natural and normal part of life, children of very young ages exposed to sexuality—either as observers or participants—may see a wide range of sexual behaviors as acceptable. Thus, many activities currently defined as abusive, such as parental nudity, exposure to sexual activities of parents, or even fondling or caressing, all of which are often considered abusive and may account for 90% of all sexual experiences of small children (Plummer, 1981), would not be considered inappropriate by parents or the child who had been exposed to these from infancy. To be sure, this perspective does not address the issue of acceptance or responsibility for the consequences of sexual behavior that is implied by the concept of consent; nevertheless, the reality that most sexual practices between children and adults are neither exploitive nor misunderstood by children is an important qualifier to the perspective that *all* adult-child contact is child sexual abuse.

Ironically, the emergence of child protective services in response to parental abuse of children and the development of programs to treat and prevent sexual abuse coincide with changes in modern societies that threaten to eliminate childhood as a distinctive period of life. A large number of recent publications have noted a blurring of childhood and adult life due to communication media, especially television (Postman, 1982); to early education experiences (Suransky, 1982); and to changing patterns of family life (Schultz, 1977); all of which have eroded the dependency, segregation, and innocence of children. Causal linkages between the observation of sexual behaviors by a child and his or her initiation of personal sexual activity remain inadequately specified. For a child who has been exposed to television and movies during the past 20 years, however, sexual behaviors, pregnancy, childbirth, drug use and abuse, rape, physical and sexual violence, abortion, alcoholism, suicide, and the possibility of a nuclear holocaust—all problems that once were reserved for consideration by those recognized by adults (Meyrowitz, 1984; Rooke & Schnell, 1983), are no longer secrets. As a result, childhood for most children in modern societies probably is not as innocent and carefree as parents assume. Instead, it involves many experiences that accelerate learning—preschools, enriched curricula, and television programs, all of which result not only in social skills, but also in a basic knowledge of sexuality (Allgeier, 1982; Goldman & Goldman, 1982) and a curiosity and interest in it. Unfortunately, the new knowledge gained through mass media ultimately may provide a more violent and exploitative and a less humane and sensitive view of sexuality than that taught by peer groups.

Childhood Sexuality as a Right

The children's rights movement probably reached its zenith in the late 1960s and early 1970s. Despite its relative dormancy for over a decade, however, the idea of sexual rights for children has been and continues to be attacked from various sources, so that any discussion of childhood sexuality is viewed as a campaign by pedophiles to justify their behavior (e.g., Constantine & Martinson, 1981; DeMott, 1980). *Time* magazine, for example, noted: ". . . a disturbing idea is gaining currency within the sex establishment: Very young children should be allowed, and perhaps encouraged, to conduct a full sex life without interference from parents or the law" (1981).

Unfortunately such attacks obscure some important issues. First, this view tends to group and define all sexual activities of children as abuse, even those based on curiosity. In addition, there is an unstated assumption that sexual abusers are "dirty old men" who prey on strangers, a perspective that is contrary to the evidence of most research. Indeed, most studies report that at least three fourths of sexual abuse victims are abused by family members or friends who are loved and trusted. Those children who are victimized by strangers or acquaintances tend to be emotionally deprived, socially isolated, desirous of tenderness and affection, or largely ignored by parents (Finkelhor, 1981). In short, they are very vulnerable to attention and expressions of affection—"easy targets."

There appears to be little middle ground between those who advocate sexual rights for children and those who define all sexual experiences of children before an age of consent as abusive. As noted earlier, much research has documented that child sexual contact with an adult does not always result in negative emotional or social consequences. Some studies have reported that trauma, guilt, shame, and deception occur when force or coercion is used by the offender, or in situations in which the child has little sexual knowledge or defines sex as dirty or shameful, especially in families that are characterized by marital disputes or poor communication (e.g., Constantine, 1981; Colonna & Solnit, 1981; Emslie & Rosenfeld, 1983; Trepper & Traicoff, 1983). Some cases may produce a form of the "self-fulfilling prophecy"; that is, those who believe that a child is too immature for sex or who believes such experiences inevitably produce psychological trauma often create the circumstances and conditions that result in those problems for the child.

Fundamental human rights of children, for those who espouse this view, include sexual rights, or the right to choose to be sexual, that is, to engage in a range of sexual actions if they choose to do so. In the words of Mary Calderone (1977), these rights include the right to know about sexuality, the right to be sexual, the right of access to educational and literary materials, and the right of the unwilling or inappropriate audience to have its privacy or peace of mind protected.

Defenders of the sexual rights of children include those whose ideological position is that childhood sexual contact is beneficial to the child (Summit & Kryso, 1978). Noting that the physiological capacity for sexual activities exists in very young children, they argue that understanding the social significance of sex involves learning and experience that can occur at nearly any age if parents and other adults are able to approach sexuality in a rational and consistent manner. Thus nearly all sexual activities should be seen not as abusive, but in fact, as important experiences in the maturation process that enable children so exposed to recognize and avoid exploitative sexual relationships. Such a view has important implications for child protection services.

Recent materials for sexual abuse prevention have emphasized the rights of children over their bodies but have ignored some implications of such an approach. Illusion Theater in Minneapolis, for example, uses the TOUCH Continuum as a tool to identify "good," "confusing," and "bad" touches, and gives the message to children that ". . . NO ONE, whether stranger, acquaintance or relative, has the right to force or trick them into sexual contact or touch" (Anderson, 1981:2). The King County Rape Relief program in Seattle also emphasized the child's right to say NO to unwanted touch (Fay et al., 1979). Empowering children in this way may well prevent some unwanted sexual contact and exploitation. Nevertheless, the concept of right includes the issue of choice, and thus the emphasis on the *right* to say no implies that a child also has the right to say yes to wanted touches and the pleasures that go with them. For a sizable proportion of children, yes may be their choice if the concept of rights is emphasized. Further, if rights to say yes are recognized, is the right for children to initiate sexual behavior included as well? Such total control over one's body is a power that many parents are unwilling to grant to their teenagers, to say nothing of prepubertal children, in part because of the ambiguity about the final result of sexual activity, for example, sexual intercourse, the fear of premature sexualization of the child, pregnancy and unwanted parenthood, and the stigma of having an unmarried child become a parent.

Issues about children's rights, and the age at which they should be recognized, derive from a lack of consensus about competency, consent, and maturity, and how to define and measure them, as well as from different values about sex. The general confusion about values and appropriate sexual behavior—for children, youth, and adults—also presents ambiguous expectations to children, especially given the fact that most mass media expose people of all ages to the same images of sexuality. Emphasis on sexual rights for young children demands early education to provide knowledge and awareness of the meaning and responsibilities associated with sex. Only then can ignorance be eliminated, thus enabling children to prevent adult exploitation of them. Such a program could be effectively begun by parents before school age and continued throughout childhood.

Summary and Conclusion

Three perspectives regarding childhood sexuality have been presented here. Each reflects a different view of childhood and sexual behavior. In addition, definitions of sexual abuse that include all sexual contact between a child and an adult are not correct because they assume that all children who have sexual experiences are innocent victims of adult manipulation and exploitation that the children would have avoided had they been given the opportunity or been empowered to do so. Such interpretations *may* include a majority of cases, but clearly do not include all types of adult-child sexual activity. Further, conditions of modern life have weakened familial controls over children and have altered family patterns that have protected children from exposure to sexual activities in the past. In short, parents and child protection personnel cannot predict when abusive situations will occur or how to identify a sexual offender (Howells, 1981) and lack the ability to control the circumstances in which sex abuse may occur. Thus children are exposed to sexual activities and to sexual experiences that are assumed to have serious negative consequences but which cannot be totally eliminated, leaving children vulnerable to exploitation if they are not able to protect themselves.

Finally, despite the opposition to granting children rights to express their sexuality because of moral grounds or immaturity, the "best interests" of the child may be served by emphasizing children's rights. Parents and professionals should recognize that knowledge and information are the best ways to prevent exploitation of children. Extending rights to include decisions about sexual behavior demands that children have a more complete knowledge of sexuality and that adults examine their assumptions about the appropriate role of sexuality in childhood. Ultimately the best prevention is the child's ability to sense potential exploitation and to confront it. A society that cannot offer the social control over adults and children that existed a half-century ago provides choice de facto; appropriate choices can only be made with adequate information, suggesting that a program of education is mandatory.

A further implication is that the definition of sexual abuse can and should be revised to focus on *Unwanted* sexual contact between children and between children and adults. In one sense, this is a slight extension of current practice, because sexual contact is rarely reported if it is enjoyed by the child, and often is defined as abusive only after the child grows older or is sexposed to information that causes him or her to revise earlier views.

Unfortunately, there is no simple answer to this complex issue. However, the importance of providing information about sex, of teaching values, and of sensitizing children to their possible exploitation cannot be overemphasized. Only then can the genuine problem of sexual abuse be addressed adequately.

References

Allgeier, E.R. (1982). Children's interpretations of sexuality. *Siecus Report, 10* (5/6),8–10.

Anderson, D. (1981). *Touch and sexual abuse: How to talk to your childrem.* Minneapolis, MN: Illusion Theatre, Sexual Abuse Prevention Program.

Araji, S., & Finkelhor, D. (1986). Abusers: A review of the research. In D. Finkelhor (Ed.), *A sourcebook on child sexual abuse.* Beverly Hills, CA: Sage.

Aries, P. (1962). *Centuries of childhood: A social history of family life.* New York: Alfred A. Knopf.

Berger, B.M. (1981). Liberating child sexuality: Communal experiences. In L. Constantine & F. Martinson (Eds.), *Children and sex.* Boston: Little, Brown and Company.

Bernard, F. (1981). Pedophilia: Psychological consequences for the child. In L. Constantine & F. Martinson (Eds.), *Children and sex.* Boston: Little, Brown and Company..

Bettelheim, B. (1969). *Children of the dream.* New York: Macmillan.

Bixler, R.H. (1983). Multiple meanings of incest. *The Journal of Sex Research 19*(2), 197–201.

Borneman, E. (1983). Progress in empirical research on children's sexuality. *Siecus Report, 12*(2), 1–5.

Browne, A., and Finkelhor, D. (1986). Initial and long-term effects: A review of the literature. In D. Finkelhor (Ed.), *A sourcebook on child sexual abuse.* Beverly Hills, CA: Sage.

Brunold, H. (1964). Observation after sexual traumata suffered in childhood. *Excerpta Criminologica, 4,* 5–8.

Byrne, D. (1977). The imagery of sex. In J. Money & H. Musaph (Eds.), *Handbook of sexology.* New York: Elsevier/North-Holland Biomedical Press.

Calderone, M.S. (1977). Sexual rights. *Siecus Report, 5*(1), 23.

Colonna, A.B., & Solnit, A.J. (1981). Infant sexuality. *Siecus Report, 9*(4), 1–2, 6.

Constantine, L.L. (1981). The effects of early sexual experiences: A review and synthesis of research. In L. Constantine & F. Martinson (Eds.), *Children and sex.* Boston: Little, Brown and Company.

Constantine, L., & Martinson, F. (1981). Childhood sexuality: Here there be dragons. In L. Constantine & F. Martinson (Eds.), *Children and sex.* Boston: Little, Brown, 1981.

Conte, J.R. (1985). The effects of sexual abuse on children: A critique and suggestions for future research. *Victimology, 10*(1–4), 110–120.

Conte, J.R. & Berliner, L. (1981). Sexual abuse of children: Implications for practice. *Social Casework, 63,* 601–606.

Curtois, C.A. (1979). The incest experience and its aftermath. *Victimology, 4*(4), 337–347.

Davis, K. (1949). *Human Society.* New York: Macmillan.

DeJong, A.R., Emmett, G.A., & Hervada, A.A. (1982). Epidemiological factors in sexual abuse of boys. *American Journal of Disease of Children, 136*(11), 990–993.

deMause, L. (Ed.). (1974). *The history of childhood.* New York: Psychohistory Press.

Demos, J. (1971). Developmental perspectives on the history of childhood. *The Journal of Interdisciplinary History, 2*(2), 315–327.

DeMott, B. (1980). The pro-incest lobby. *Psychology Today, 13*(10), 11–12, 15–16.

DSM–III (1980). *Diagnostic and Statistical Manual of Mental Disorders* (3rd ed.). Washington, DC: American Psychiatric Association.

Elwell, M.E. (1979). Sexually assaulted children and their families. *Social Casework, 60*(2), 227–235.

Emslie, J., and Rosenfeld, A. (1983). Incest reported by children and adolescents hospitalized for severe psychiatric problems. *American Journal of Psychiatry, 140*(6), 708–711.

Farber, E.D., Showers, J., Johnson, C.F., Joseph, J.A., & Oshins, L. (1984). The sexual abuse of children: A comparison of male and female victims. *Journal of Clinical Child Psychology, 13*(3), 294–297.

Fay, J., Adams, C., Flerchinger, B.J., Loontjens, L., Rittenhouse, P., & Stone, M.E. (1979). *He told me not to tell.* Renton, WA: King Co. Rape Relief.

Finkelhor, D. (1979a). What's wrong with sex between adults and children? Ethics and the problem of sexual abuse. *American Journal of Orthopsychiatry, 49*(4), 691–697.

Finkelhor, D. (1979b). *Sexually victimized children.* New York: Free Press.

Finkelhor, D. (1981) *Four preconditions of sexual abuse: A model.* Paper presented at the National Conference of Family Violence Research, Durham, NH.

Finkelhor, D., Gomes-Schwartz, B., & Horowitz, J. (1982). *Agency management of sexual abuse: Responses and attitudes from a survey of Boston professionals.* Paper presented at the annual meeting of the Massachusetts Psychological Association, Boston.

Fishman, S. (1982). The history of childhood sexuality. *Journal of Contemporary History, 17*(2), 269–283.

Friedrich W.N., Urquize, A.J., & Beilke, R.L. (1986). Behavior problems in sexually abused young children. *Journal of Pediatric Psychology, 11*(1), 47–57.

Frude, H. (1982). The sexual nature of sexual abuse: A review of the literature. *Child Abuse and Neglect, 6,* 211–223.

Furstenberg, F.F., Jr. (1976). *Unplanned parenthood: The social consequences of teenage childbearing.* New York: Free Press.

Gagnon, J. (1965). Female child victims of sex offenses. *Social Problems, 13*(2), 176–192.

Gagnon, J., & Simon, W. (1973). *Sexual Conduct: The Social Sources of Human Sexuality.* Chicago:: Aldine.

Goldman, R., & Goldman, J. (1982). *Children's sexual thinking.* Boston, MA: Routledge and Kegan Paul.

Gunderson, B.H., Melas, P.S., & Skor, J.E. (1981). Sexual behavior of preschool children: Teacher's observations. In L. Constantine & F. Martinson (Eds.), *Children and sex* (pp. 45–61). Boston: Little, Brown and Company.

Henderson, D. (1972). Incest: A synthesis of data. *Canadian Psychiatric Association Journal, 17,* 299–313.

Holt, J. (1974). *Escape from childhood.* New York: Dutton.

Howells, K. (1981). Adult sexual interest in children: Considerations relevant to theories of aetiology. In M. Cook & K. Howells (Eds.), *Adult sexual interest in children.* New York: Academic Press.

Husain, A., & Chapel, J.L. (1982). History of incest in girls admitted to a psychiatric hospital. *American Journal of Psychiatry, 140*(5), 591–593.

Ingram, M. (1979). Participating victims: A study of sexual offenses with boys. *British Journal of Sexual Medicine, 6,* 22–26.

Janus, M. (1983). On early victimization and adolescent male prostitution. *Siecus Report, 13*(1), 8–9.

Janus, S.S., & Bess, B.E. (1976). Latency: Fact or fiction. *The American Journal of Psychoanalysis, 36*(3), 339–346.

Johnson, W.R. (1977). Childhood sexuality: The last of the great taboos? *Siecus Report, 5*(4), 1–2, 15.

Kinsey, A.C., Pomeroy, W.B., & Martin, C.E. (1948). *Sexual behavior in the human male.* Philadelphia: Sanders.

LaBarbera, J.D., Martin, J.D., & Dozier, J.E. (1980). Child psychiatrists' view of father-daughter incest. *Child Abuse and Neglect, 4* 147–151.

Langfeldt, T. (1981a). Processes in sexual development. In L. Constantine & F. Martinson (Eds.), *Children and sex.* Boston: Little, Brown and Company.

Langfeldt, T. (1981b). Sexual development in children. In M. Cook & K. Howells (Eds.), *Adult sexual interest in children.* New York: Academic Press.

Lee, J. (1982). Three paradigms of childhood. *Canadian Review of Sociology and Anthropology,19*(4), 592–608.

Martinson, F.M. (1976). Eroticism in infancy and childhood. *The Journal of Sex Research, 12,* 251–261.

Mayer, A. (1983). *Incest: A treatment manual for therapy with victims, spouses and offenders.* Holmes Beach, FL: Learning Publications.

Meiselman, K. (1978). *Incest: A psychological study of causes and effects with treatment recommendation.* San Francisco: Jossey-Bass.

Meyrowitz, J. (1984). The adultlike child and the childlike adult: Socialization in an electronic age. *Daedalus, 113*(3), 19–48.

Mrazek, B., & Kempe, C.H. (Eds.). (1981). *Sexually abused children and their families.* Oxford: Pergamon Press.

Neuman, R.P. (1975). Masturbation, madness, and the modern concepts of childhood and adolescence. —*Journal of Social History, 8*(1), 1–27.

Parker, H., & Parker, S. (1986). Father-daughter sexual abuse: An emerging perspective. *American Journal of Orthopsychiatry, 56*(4), 531–549.

Platt, A. (1969). *The child savers: The invention of delinquency.* Chicago: University of Chicago Press.

Plummer, K. (1981). Pedophilia: Constructing a sociological baseline. In M. Cook & K. Howells (Eds.), *Adult sexual interest in children.* New York: Academic Press.

Pollock, L.A. (1983). *Forgotten children: Parent-child relations from 1500 to 1900.* Cambridge: Cambridge University Press.

Postman, N. (1982). *The disappearance of childhood.* New York: Delacorte Press.

Ramey, J.W. (1979). Dealing with the last taboo. *Siecus Report, 7*(5), 1–2, 6–7.

Renshaw, D.C. & Renshaw, R.Y. (1977). Incest. *Journal of Sex Education and Therapy, 3*(2), 307.

Rogers, C.M., & Terry, T. (1984). Clinical intervention with boy victims of sexual abuse. In I. Stuart & J. Greer (Eds.), *Victims of sexual aggression: Treatment of children, women and men.* New York: Van Nostrand Reinhold.

Rooke, P.T., & Schnell, R.L. (1983). *Discarding the asylum: From child rescue to the welfare state in English-Canada, (1800–1950).* Lanham, MD: University Press of America.

Rosenfeld, A.H. (1979). Incidence of a history of incest among 18 female psychiatric patients. *American Journal of Psychiatry, 136*(6), 791–795.

Ruch, O., & Chandler, S.M. (1982). The crisis impact of sexual assault on three victim groups: Adult rape victims, child rape victims, and incest victims. *Journal of Social Service Research, 5*(1/2), 83–100.

Russell, D. (1984). *Sexual exploitation: Rape, child sexual abuse, and workplace harassment.* Beverly Hills, CA: Sage.

Sandfort, T. (1982). Pedophile relationships in the Netherlands: Alternative lifestyle for children? *Alternative Lifestyles, 5,* 164–183.

Schmidt, G. (1977). Introduction, Sociohistorical perspectives. In J. Money & H. Museph (Eds.), *Handbook of sex-*

ology (pp. 269–281). New York: Elsevier/North-Holland Biomedical Press.

Schultz, L.G. (1980a). The sexual abuse of children and minors: A short history of legal control efforts. In L. Schultz (Ed.), *The sexual victimology of youth.* Springfield, IL: Charles C. Thomas.

Schultz, L.G. (1980b). The age of sexual consent: Fault, friction, freesom In L. Schultz (Ed.), *The sexual victimology of youth.* Springfield IL: Charles C. Thomas.

Schultz, L.G. (1980c). Diagnosis and treatment—Introduction. In L. Schultz (Ed.), *The sexual victimology of youth,* Springfield, IL: Charles C. Thomas. (1986).

Scott, R.L., & Stone, D.A. (1986). MMPI measures of psychological disturbance in adolescent and adult victims of father-daughter incest. *Journal of Clinical Psychology, 42*(2), 251–259.

Sgroi, M., (Ed.). (1982). *Handbook of clinical intervention in child sexual abuse.* Lexington, MA: D.C. Heath.

Summit, R., & Kryso, J. (1978). Sexual abuse of children: A clinical spectrum. *American Journal of Orthopsychiatry, 48*(2), 237–251.

Suransky, V. (1982). *The erosion of childhood.* Chicago: University of Chicago Press.

Synott, A. (1983). Little angels, little devils: A sociology of children. *Canadian Review of Sociology and Anthropology, 20*(1), 79–95.

Taubman, S. (1984). Incest in context. *Social Work, 29*(1), 35–40.

Time (1981). Cradle-to-grave intimacy. September 7, p. 69.

Trepper, S., & Traicoff, M.E. Treatment of intrafamily sexuality: Issues in therapy and research. *Journal of Sex Education and Therapy, 9*(1), 14–18.

Tsai, M., Summers, S., & Edgar,M.(1979). Childhood molestation: Variables related to differential impacts on pychosexual functioning in adult women. *Journal of Abnormal Psychology, 88*(4), 407–417.

Walters, D.R. (1975). *Physical and sexual abuse of children: Causes and treatment.* Bloomington, IN: Indiana University Press.

Wooden, K. (1976). *Weeping in the playtime of others: America's incarcerated children.* New York: McGraw-Hill.

Yorukoglu, A., & Kemph, J.P. (1966). Children not severely damaged by incest with a parent. *Journal of the American Academy of Child Psychiatry, 5*(1), 111–124.

Zelnick, M., Kim, Y.J., & Kantner, J.F. (1979). Probabilities of intercourse and conception among U.S. teenage women, 1971–1976. *Family Planning Perspectives, 11*(3), 177–183.

What Kids Need to Know

*MOST PARENTS AND SCHOOL SYSTEMS
FAIL TO PROVIDE TEENAGERS WITH
RELEVANT SEX EDUCATION.*

SOL GORDON

Psychologist Sol Gordon, Ph.D., is professor emeritus at Syracuse University. He has written many books for teenagers, including The Teenage Survival Book *(Times Books) and* When Living Hurts *(Union of American Hebrew Congregations).*

If you tell kids about sex, they'll do it. If you tell them about VD, they'll go out and get it. Incredible as it may seem, most opposition to sex education in this country is based on the assumption that knowledge is harmful. But research in this area reveals that ignorance and unresolved curiosity, not knowledge, are harmful.

Our failure to tell children what they want and need to know is one reason we have the highest rates of out-of-wedlock teen pregnancy and abortion of any highly developed country in the world. And we pay a big price monetarily and otherwise in dealing with the more than one million teenage pregnancies every year, as well as several million new cases of sexually transmitted diseases.

Poor education, of course, is only one cause of teenage pregnancy. Such factors as poverty, racism and sexism are even more crucial. But there is ample evidence to show that relevant sex education is part of the solution to teenage pregnancy.

At the Institute for Family Research and Education at Syracuse University, we have been studying questions related to sex education for more than 15 years. Some people still seem to think they can and should be the only sex educators of their children. My response is, "How can that be? You'll have to wrap your children in cotton and not allow them to leave their bedrooms, watch TV or read newspapers or current magazines. You certainly can't allow them to have any friends or go to any public school bathroom."

The idea that kids get information about sex from their parents is completely erroneous. Even the college-educated parents of my Syracuse University students offer very little. In survey after survey in a period of 12 years involving more than 8,000 students, fewer than 15 percent reported that they received a meaningful sex education from their parents. Usually girls were told about menstruation.

The rest of the teaching could be summed up in one word: DON'T. The boys were on their own except for an occasional single prepuberty talk with Dad, who made vague analogies involving the birds and bees and ended the talk with "if worst comes to worst, be sure to use a rubber."

One reason parents have for not educating their children is discomfort with their own sexual feelings and behavior. Part of this discomfort derives from the fact that they themselves received little or no sex education as children. Without one's parents to draw upon as a model, the cycle of noncommunication is repeated from generation to generation.

If parents don't do the job, do kids get their sex education through the media? Of course not. TV is full of antisexual messages of rape, violence and infidelity. This is especially true of the soaps, watched by an increasingly large number of teenagers via delayed video recordings. When was the last time you saw a really good sex-education program on TV or an article in your local newspaper? There are a few exceptions to this sex-education wasteland. Teenagers who read, particularly girls, do get some good information from Judy Blume and her novels, such as *Forever* and *Are You There God? It's Me, Margaret,* and magazines such as *Teen* and *Seventeen.*

What about schools? Probably fewer than 10 percent of American schoolchildren are exposed to anything approaching a meaningful sex education. There are some good programs and some dedicated and well-trained teachers, but I doubt there are a dozen school districts that have a kindergarten through 12th-grade sex-education program that even approaches those available in Sweden. American teenagers typically score abysmally low on sex-knowledge questionnaires.

Sex education in the United States today, where it exists at all, is usually a course in plumbing—a relentless pursuit of the fallopian tubes. The lack of real education is obscured by the answers to surveys that ask students if they've had sex education in their schools. More than half respond, "Yes." What most surveys don't ask—

University, we have reviewed more than 50,000 questions teenagers from all over the country have submitted, anonymously, to us and to their teachers. Not one teenager has ever asked a question about fallopian tubes. Young people want to know about homosexuality, penis size, masturbation, female orgasm, and the answers to such questions as how can I tell if I'm really in love, what constitutes sexual desire, what is the best contraceptive, when are you most likely to get pregnant and various questions about oral and anal sex. Recently, the most frequent one seems to be why boys are only interested in girls for sex.

Before I talk to teenagers about questions like these, I try to place the issue of sexuality in a proper framework. I tell kids that of the 10 most important aspects of a mature relationship, number one is love and commitment. Number two is a sense of humor. (I advise parents not to have teenagers unless they have a sense of

sex before they finish high school, I say to them, if you are not going to listen to me (or your parents) about postponing sex, use contraception.

The simple message—No, Don't, Stop—doesn't work. The double message—No, but....—is more effective. Look at how alcohol education is now being handled by many parents and school organizations. They say, "I don't think you should drink, but if you get carried away and you drink anyway, don't drive. Call me and we'll arrange alternate transportation." When it comes to premarital sex, a parent might start with "No" and try to convince the teenager to hold back but also provide the "But"—reliable contraceptive information. As the Talmud says, expect miracles but don't count on them.

Masturbation is one of the biggest concerns of young people. They should learn that masturbation is, most of the time, a normal expression of sexuality at any age. (When I was growing up we were told that masturbation gave you acne, tired blood, mental illness and blindness. Maybe that's why I wear glasses.) Nobody believes these stories anymore, but most parents still don't like the idea of their children masturbating. Some parents even suggest that it's all right if it's private, and ... pause ... if you don't do it too much. But how much is too much? Once a year, twice a week, after every meal?

There are folks who suggest that masturbating too much will make you shy, retiring, narcissistic and that you won't have any friends. But how long does it take to masturbate? Why should it interfere with friends? Most of my friends are masturbators; some others I know never masturbate and they have no friends. Virtually all teenagers have strong sexual urges. Why give them dumb solutions, such as: "Go take a cold shower." Why not tell them to masturbate? It's a much more effective solution to the problem.

Any form of behavior can become compulsive. Some people eat too much, not because they are hungry but because they have high levels of anxiety. Some people drink too much, not because they are thirsty but because of anxiety, and many become alcoholics. And there are those who masturbate too much, not because they are aroused but because of tension. My point is that if you absolutely must

WITHOUT ONE'S PARENTS AS A MODEL, THE CYCLE OF NONCOMMUNICATION IS REPEATED FROM GENERATION TO GENERATION.

or if they do, what doesn't get reported—are the really important questions such as:

(Q) How much sex education did you have?

(A) Two classes in menstruation for girls only in the sixth grade.

(Q) How effective was the education?

(A) I slept through it.

(Q) By whom was it taught?

(A) One gym teacher proclaimed to the boys, "Hey fellows, the thing between your legs is not a muscle—don't exercise it."

Useful sex education should tell children what they want and need to know. And we know what they want to know. At the Institute for Family Research and Education at Syracuse

humor.) Number three is meaningful communication. Sex is somewhere down on the list, just ahead of sharing household tasks together.

I also tell them that I, like most parents, don't think teenagers should engage in sexual intercourse. They are too young and too vulnerable. They aren't prepared to handle the fact that the first experiences of sex are usually grim. Almost no one will have an orgasm. The boy gets his three days later when he tells the guys about it.

Fewer than one in seven use a reliable form of contraception the first time they have sex. In contrast, the large majority of Swedish teenagers use contraception the very first time and consistently afterwards. But knowing that most teenagers will have

have a compulsion, please choose masturbation rather than overeating or overdrinking. Nobody has ever died from overmasturbating.

I joke to make a point, but the issue is more important than it appears. In my 30 years of clinical work, research and therapy, I have yet to hear about a rapist, a child molester or a chronically sexually dysfunctional person who grew up feeling comfortable about masturbation.

It's also important for young people to learn that while behavior can be abnormal, thoughts in and of themselves are not. All people experience weird thoughts and fantasies, often emanating from the unconscious and often involuntary. If we realize that these phenomena are normal and cannot harm us, they pass, and nothing happens. If

taught that masturbation is evil, it only increases the tension. Finally, it becomes intolerable, and he sexually abuses a child to relieve the tension.

Some researchers have suggested that masturbation in itself provides a powerful stimulus for sexual abuse. In my clinical work, I have found this to be true only if the molester despises masturbation and/or feels guilty about it.

What else do we need to tell young people? Tell the boys not to worry about penis size. You can't tell the size of the penis by observing its detumescent state. (Freud got it wrong—men are the ones with penis envy.) Reassure girls about their vaginas—one size fits all.

One or a few homosexual experiences or thoughts don't make a person

Love is blind. I think love is blind for only 24 hours. Then you have to open your eyes and notice with whom you're in love.

Love at first sight. I advise people to take another look.

You can fall in love only once. This silly idea can have tragic results. How many young Romeos and Juliets have committed suicide after the breakup of a torrid love affair, thinking that life is over for them? No, I tell them, you can fall in love at least 18 times.

Will I know when I'm really in love? Certainly. If you feel you are in love, you are. (Parents should never trivialize a teenager's love affair. However brief, it's always serious.) But I tell teenagers there are two kinds of love—mature love and immature. Mature lovers are energized. They want to please each other. They are nice to parents who are nice to them. Immature love is exhausting. Immature lovers are too tired to do their schoolwork. They are not nice to those they should care about—parents, siblings, even their dogs and cats.

Sex-education courses that cover even a few of these real concerns are being taught almost nowhere in this country. It's up to parents to make a start, whether they are comfortable with the subject or not. You don't have to be comfortable to educate your children. I daresay most of us are uncomfortable about a lot of things these days, but we keep doing our jobs anyway. We should at least teach teachers, psychologists, clergy, social workers and others who work with youngsters how to respond to young people's questions.

We owe it to our children and their children to provide them with the information they need in a manner they will accept. I sometimes use humor. It helps reduce anxiety and puts teenagers in a receptive mood. An old Zen expression says, "When the mind is ready a teacher appears."

I F YOU FEEL YOU ARE IN LOVE, YOU ARE. PARENTS SHOULD NEVER TRIVIALIZE A TEENAGER'S LOVE AFFAIR. HOWEVER BRIEF, IT'S ALWAYS SERIOUS.

we feel guilty about them, they often reoccur and become embodied in obsessions that lead to inappropriate behavior or sexual dysfunctions.

Let me illustrate. A male teenager feels guilty because he gets sexually aroused when he plays with young children. He knows he is supposed to have sex with girls his age, not little kids. The more he "knows" his arousal is wrong, the more his preoccupation takes hold. He tries to relieve himself by masturbating, but since he's been

homosexual. Homosexuals are people who in their adult lives are attracted to and have sexual relations with others of the same sex. The preference is not subject to conscious control. Sexual orientation is not a matter of choice. It's not OK to be antigay.

For teenagers, few questions are as urgent as: How can I tell if I'm really in love? I've probably listened to more nonsense in this area than any other. I've heard the same rubbish so many times that I've come up with some standard responses to the following:

Children Having Children

Teen pregnancies are corroding America's social fabric

The rhythm of her typing is like a fox trot, steady and deliberate. It is a hot summer day in San Francisco, and Michelle, a chubby black 14-year-old, is practicing her office skills with great fervor, beads of sweat trickling down her brow. She is worried about the future. "I have to get my money together," she frets. "I have to think ahead." Indeed she must. In three weeks this tenth-grader with her hair in braids is going to have a baby. "I have to stop doing all the childish things I've done before," she gravely resolves. "I used to think, ten years lobbying her mother for permission to attend a rock concert, asking if she can have a pet dog and complaining she is not allowed to do anything. The weight of her new responsibilities is just beginning to sink in. "Last night I couldn't get my homework done," she laments with a toss of her blond curls. "I kept feeding him and feeding him. Whenever you lay him

down, he wants to get picked up." In retrospect she admits: "Babies are a big step. I should have thought more about it."

Before the baby came, her bedroom was a dimly lighted chapel dedicated to the idols of rock 'n' roll. Now the posters of Duran Duran and Ozzy Osbourne have been swept away and the walls painted white. Angela Helton's room has become a nursery for six-week-old Corey Allen. Angie, who just turned 15, finds it hard to think of herself as a mother. "I'm still just as young as I was," she insists. "I haven't grown up any faster." Indeed, sitting in her parents' Louisville living room, she is the prototypical adolescent, from now I'll be 24. Now I think, I'll be 24, and my child will be ten."

It is early afternoon, and the smells of dirty diapers and grease mingle in the

bleak Minneapolis apartment. The TV is tuned to All My Children, and Stephanie Charette, 17, has collapsed on the sofa. Her rest is brief. Above the babble of the actors' voices comes a piercing wail. Larissa, her three-week-old daughter, is hungry. In an adjacent bedroom, Joey, 1½ years old and recovering from the flu, starts to stir. Stephanie, who is an American Indian and one of ten children herself, first became pregnant at 15. It was an "accident," she explains. So too was her second baby. "I'm always tired," she laments, "and I can't eat." Before Joey's birth, before she dropped out of school, Stephanie dreamed of being a stewardess. Now her aspirations are more down-to-earth. "I want to pay my bills, buy groceries and have a house and furniture. I want to feel good about myself so my kids can be proud of me." It has been a long, long while, she confides, "since I had a good time."

They are of different races, from different places, but their tales and laments have a haunting sameness. Each year more than a million American teenagers will become pregnant, four out of five of them unmarried. Together they represent a distressing flaw in the social fabric of America. Like Angela, Michelle and Stephanie, many become pregnant in their early or mid-teens, some 30,000 of them under age 15. If present trends continue, researchers estimate, fully 40% of today's 14-year-old girls will be pregnant at least once before the age of 20. Says Sally, 17, who is struggling to raise a two-year-old son in Los Angeles: "We are children ourselves having children."

Teenage pregnancy has been around as long as there have been teenagers, but its pervasiveness in this country, the dimensions of its social costs and the urgent need to attack the problem are just beginning to be widely appreciated. According to a Harris poll released in November, 84% of American adults regard teenage pregnancy as a serious national problem. The news in recent weeks illustrates the growing concern:

▶ In Wisconsin last month, Governor Anthony Earl signed landmark legislation designed to combat unwanted teen pregnancies and, as he put it, to "limit thousands of personal tragedies that are played out in our state every day." The law, which won unanimous approval in the state legislature, provides funding for sex education in public schools, repeals restrictions on the sale of nonprescription contraceptives and provides $1 million for counseling pregnant adolescents. It also takes the unusual step of making grandparents of babies born to teenagers legally responsible for the babies' financial support. "All of us," said Earl, "young people and parents of young people, have a responsibility for our actions."

▶ At Chicago's DuSable High School, controversy erupted when school officials decided to establish an on-campus health clinic, authorized to dispense contraceptives to students who have parental permission. The school, which serves one of the nation's poorest neighborhoods, is battling a veritable epidemic: each year about one-third of its 1,000 female students are pregnant. The clinic has elicited picketing and protest, mostly by religious and antiabortion groups, but the school has refused to back down. Says Principal Judith Steinhagen: "All I can say is, we're trying to keep some young ladies in school and off welfare."

▶ The school board in Los Angeles announced that it too plans to open a health clinic offering contraceptives to high school students. So far, nine schools around the U.S. have taken this step, and others are expected to follow suit. Says School Board Member Jackie Goldberg: "There's an appalling number of teen pregnancies. I hope to upgrade the quality of teen medical care, and I hope that young men and women will consider the ramifications of being sexually active."

Such strong and controversial measures reflect the magnitude of the problem and its consequences. Teen pregnancy imposes lasting hardships on two generations: parent and child. Teen mothers are, for instance, many times as likely as other women with young children to live below the poverty level. According to one study, only half of those who give birth before age 18 complete high school (as compared with 96% of those who postpone childbearing). On average, they earn half as much money and are far more likely to be dependent on welfare: 71% of females under 30 who receive Aid to Families with Dependent Children had their first child as a teenager.

As infants, the offspring of teen mothers have high rates of illness and mortality. Later in life, they often experience educational and emotional problems. Many are victims of child abuse at the hands of parents too immature to understand why their baby is crying or how

"**I** was going to have an abortion, but I spent the money on clothes."

**SONYA LYDE, 18
CHICAGO**

their doll-like plaything has suddenly developed a will of its own. Finally, these children of children are prone to dropping out and becoming teenage parents themselves. According to one study, 82% of girls who give birth at age 15 or younger were daughters of teenage mothers.

With disadvantage creating disadvantage, it is no wonder that teen pregnancy is widely viewed as the very hub of the U.S. poverty cycle. "A lot of the so-called feminization of poverty starts off with teenagers' having babies," says Lucile Dismukes of the Council on Maternal and Infant Health in Atlanta, a state advisory group. "So many can't rise above it to go back to school or get job skills."

Among the underclass in America's urban ghettos, the trends are especially disturbing. Nearly half of black females in the U.S. are pregnant by age 20. The pregnancy rate among those ages 15 to 19 is almost twice what it is among whites.

Worse still, nearly 90% of the babies born to blacks in this age group are born out of wedlock; most are raised in fatherless homes with little economic opportunity. "When you look at the numbers, teenage pregnancies are of cosmic danger to the black community," declares Eleanor Holmes Norton, law professor at Georgetown University and a leading black scholar. "Teenage pregnancy ranks near the very top of issues facing black people."

The shocking prevalence of teenage pregnancy among white as well as black Americans was brought to light earlier this year, when the Alan Guttmacher Institute, a nonprofit research center in New York City, released the results of a 37-country study. Its findings: the U.S. leads nearly all other developed nations in its incidence of pregnancy among girls ages 15 through 19. As a point of comparison, AGI investigators looked at five other Western countries in detail: Sweden, Holland, France, Canada and Britain (see chart). Though American adolescents were no more sexually active than their counterparts in these countries, they were found to be many times as likely to become pregnant. And while black teenagers in the U.S. have a higher pregnancy rate than whites, whites alone had nearly double the rate of their British and French peers and six times the rate of the Dutch. Observes AGI President Jeannie Rosoff: "It's not a black problem. It's not just an East Coast problem. It's a problem for all of us."

It is also a complex problem, one that strikes many sensitive nerves. The subject of teenage pregnancy seems to raise almost every politically explosive social issue facing the American public: the battle over abortion rights; contraceptives and the ticklish question of whether adolescents should have easy access to them; the perennially touchy subject of sex education in public schools; controversies about welfare programs; and the precarious state of the black family in America. Indeed, even the basic issue of adolescent sexuality is a subject that makes many Americans squirm.

To understand the nature of the problem, one must look beyond statistics and examine the dramatic changes in attitudes and social mores that have swept through American culture over the past 30 years. The teenage birth rate was actually higher in 1957 than it is today, but that was an era of early marriage, when nearly a quarter of 18- and 19-year-old females were wedded. The overwhelming majority of teen births in the '50s thus occurred in a connubial context, and mainly to girls 17 and over. Twenty and 30 years ago, if an *unwed* teenager should, heaven forbid, become pregnant, chances are her parents would see that she was swiftly married off in a shotgun wedding. Or, if marriage was impractical, the girl would discreetly disappear during her confinement, the child would be given up for

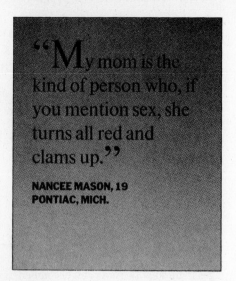

"My mom is the kind of person who, if you mention sex, she turns all red and clams up."

**NANCEE MASON, 19
PONTIAC, MICH.**

adoption, and the matter would never be discussed again in polite company. Abortion, of course, was not a real option for most until 1973, when the Supreme Court ruled it could not be outlawed.

All this has changed. Today if a girl does not choose to abort her pregnancy (and some 45% of teenagers do), chances are she will keep the baby and raise it without the traditional blessings of marriage. "The shotgun marriage is a relic of the past," observes Mark Testa, of Chicago's National Opinion Research Center. With teen marriages two to three times as likely to end in divorce, he explains, "parents figure, why compound their mistake?" In 1950 fewer than 15% of teen births were illegitimate. By 1983 more than half were, and in some regions of the country, the figure exceeds 75%. Unwed motherhood has become so pervasive that "we don't use the term illegitimate anymore," notes Sister Bertille Prus, executive director of Holy Family Services, a Los Angeles adoption agency for pregnant teens.

With the stigma of illegitimacy largely removed, girls are less inclined to surrender their babies for adoption. In fact, fewer than 5% do (compared with roughly 35% in the early 1960s). "In earlier times if a girl kept her child, society would treat her like an outcast," reflects Sister Bertille. "The fear and guilt are not the same as before."

Unwed motherhood may even seem glamorous to impressionable teens. "They see Jerry Hall on TV, flinging back her hair, talking about having Mick Jagger's second [out-of-wedlock] child, and saying what a wonderful life she has," bristles Daphne Busby of Brooklyn, founder of the Sisterhood of Black Single Mothers. A succession of attractive stars, including Farrah Fawcett and Jessica Lange, have joined Hall in making a trend of extramarital pregnancy, something that 35 years ago helped get Actress Ingrid Bergman blackballed in Hollywood.

But if unwed motherhood has lost much of its notoriety, premarital sex has

over the same period become positively conventional. Like it or not, American adolescents are far more sexually active than they used to be. Guttmacher statistics show that the incidence of sexual intercourse among unmarried teenage women increased by two-thirds during the 1970s. Moreover, the sexual revolution seems to have moved from the college campus to the high school and now into the junior high and grade school.* A 1982 survey conducted by Johns Hopkins Researchers John Kantner and Melvin Zelnick found that nearly one out of five 15-year-old girls admitted that she had already had intercourse, as did nearly a third of 16-year-olds and 43% of 17-year-olds. "In the eyes of their peers, it is important for kids to be sexually active. No one wants to be a virgin," observes Amy Williams, director of San Francisco's Teenage Pregnancy and Parenting Project (TAPP). The social pressure even on the youngest adolescents can be daunting. Says Stephanie, 14, of suburban Chicago, now the mother of a four-month-old, "Everyone is, like, 'Did you lose your virginity yet?' "

Social workers are almost unanimous in citing the influence of the popular media—television, rock music, videos, movies—in propelling the trend toward precocious sexuality. One survey has shown that in the course of a year the average

"Everyone is, like, 'Did you lose your virginity yet?' "

**STEPHANIE, 14
SUBURBAN CHICAGO**

viewer sees more than 9,000 scenes of suggested sexual intercourse or innuendo on prime-time TV. "Our young people are barraged by the message that to be sophisticated they must be sexually hip," says Williams. "They don't even buy toothpaste to clean their teeth. They buy it to be sexually attractive."

And yet, for all their early experimentation with sex, their immersion in heavy-breathing rock music and the erotic fantasies on MTV, one thing about American teenagers has not changed: they are in

many ways just as ignorant about the scientific facts of reproduction as they were in the days when Doris Day, not Madonna, was their idol. In a study funded by the Rockefeller Foundation, Demographer Ellen Kisker of Princeton University found that teenage girls are awash in misinformation. Among the commonest myths: that they could not become pregnant the first time they had sex, if they had it only occasionally or if they had it standing up. Adolescents are especially foggy on the subject of contraception. A National Opinion Research Center survey of teenage mothers found that few were familiar with the IUD, and most, says Researcher Pat Mosena, "didn't even know what the diaphragm was." Mistaken notions about the health risks of the birth control pill are rampant. All this may help explain why, according to Johns Hopkins researchers, only about one in three sexually active American girls between ages 15 and 19 uses contraceptives at all. And many who do use them have a rather weak grasp of the methodology: one-quarter of the girls in the NORC survey said they were using birth control at the time they became pregnant.

It is this naiveté and ineptitude coupled with less openness in American society generally about birth control that, according to Guttmacher researchers, constitute one of the most striking differences between American adolescents and their European peers. In Sweden teenagers are sexually active even earlier than they are in the U.S., and they are exposed to even more explicit television. However, the Swedish National Board of Education has provided curriculum guidelines that ensure that, starting at age seven, every child in the country receives a thorough grounding in reproductive biology and by age ten or twelve has been introduced to the various types of contraceptives. "Teachers are expected to deal with the subject whenever it becomes relevant, irrespective of the subject they are teaching," says Annika Strandell, the board's specialist in sex education. "The idea is to dedramatize and demystify sex so that familiarity will make the child less likely to fall prey to unwanted pregnancy and venereal disease."

In Holland, sex is similarly demystified. While the country has no mandated sex-education program, teens can obtain contraceptive counseling at government-sponsored clinics for a minimal fee. In addition, the Dutch media have played an important role in educating the public, says Dr. Evert Ketting of the Dutch Mental Health Center, citing frequent broadcasts on birth control, abortion and related issues. "We've been told that no Dutch teenager would consider having sex without birth control," says Guttmacher Spokeswoman Jane Murray. "It would be like running a red light."

The signals are quite different for American teenagers. Last summer, when the American College of Obstetricians

---

*One factor in the trend toward earlier sex: the average American girl now reaches puberty at age twelve or 13, in contrast to 14 or 15 at the turn of the century, thanks in part to a better diet.

and Gynecologists unveiled a new public service announcement designed to combat teenage pregnancy, all three major TV networks balked. The reason: the announcement included the word contraceptives. These are the same networks that, as one ABC official put it, routinely depict intercourse to "the point of physical motion under the covers of a bed." Network officials have since relented, but the offending word has been dropped.

How to explain this skittishness? "We are still very much governed by our puritanical heritage," answers Faye Wattleton, president of the New York–based Planned Parenthood Federation. "While European societies have chosen to recognize sexual development as a normal part of human development, we have chosen to repress it. At the same time, we behave as if we're not repressing it." In studying various cultures, the Guttmacher researchers found that the highest teen-pregnancy rates were in countries with the least open attitudes toward sex. "The ambivalence our society is projecting about sex is costing us a lot," concludes Institute President Rosoff.

People who work directly with teenagers agree. "We maintain this incredible double standard with teenagers about sex," says Alice Radosh, coordinator of pregnancy and parenting services in the New York City mayor's office. "If you're swept away by passion, then you didn't do anything wrong. But if you went on a date after taking the Pill or with a diaphragm, then you're bad. You were looking for sex, and that's not permitted."

The message that contraception is bad is often reinforced by parents, who

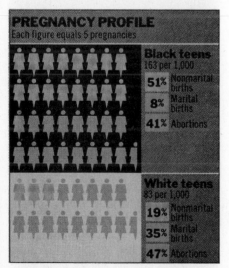

PREGNANCY PROFILE
Each figure equals 5 pregnancies

Black teens
163 per 1,000
51% Nonmarital births
8% Marital births
41% Abortions

White teens
83 per 1,000
19% Nonmarital births
35% Marital births
47% Abortions

are loath to admit that their children are sexually experienced. "I went to my mom five different times to see if she could at least get me to a doctor to get me on birth control," recounts Nancee Mason, 19, from Pontiac, Mich., who has a nine-month-old son. "By my mom is the kind of person who, if you mention sex, she turns all red and clams up."

The Reagan Administration has taken

steps to make it difficult for teenagers to obtain contraceptives. Since taking office, the President has repeatedly tried to restrict the availability of family-planning services. One-third of the women who seek such services at federally funded clinics are teenagers. In 1983 the Administration further attempted to control teenage access to contraceptives by issuing what quickly became known as the "squeal rule." The regulation required federally funded clinics to notify parents within ten days of prescribing contraceptives to minors. However, the squeal rule was squelched in the courts on the ground that it would have increased unwanted pregnancies and abortions.

Even without the risk of being squealed on, many young girls are embarrassed about going to a public clinic. "I chickened out," confesses Debra Stinnett, 18. "I just never went back to Planned Parenthood for the pills." She now has a one-year-old daughter. Studies show that, on the average, teens wait twelve months after first becoming sexually active before they seek contraception. By then it is often too late. "When you're young," says Kim Adalid, 19, of Lawndale, Calif., a wise old mother of two, "all you think about is the weekend."

When they do become pregnant, many girls simply hide the fact, denying it even to themselves. For Angela Spencer, 16, of Lawndale, reality did not hit home until five months into her pregnancy, when she entered a special school for young mothers. "A lot of the girls had already had their babies," she relates. "When I walked in that classroom, it was like the first time I realized what was happening to me." Unable to grasp their situation, adolescents frequently wait too long even to consider having an abortion. The gravity of such a decision often eludes them. "I was going to have an abortion, but I spent the money on clothes," confesses Sonya Lyde, 18, of Chicago, now the mother of a seven-month-old boy.

According to the most recent statistics, almost 30% of U.S. abortions are performed on teenagers. Abortions seem to be commonest among the affluent. "Upper-middle-class girls look at abortion as a means of birth control," says Myra Wood Bennett, a county health official in southern Illinois. The poorer girls, she notes, simply cannot afford it. Federal funding of most abortions for low-income women was barred by Congress in 1976; only nine states have stepped into the breach, providing for abortions without restrictions.

There is for many young girls another, less tangible factor in the sequence of events leading to parenthood: a sense of fatalism, passivity and, in some cases, even a certain pleasure at the prospect of motherhood. Such attitudes are especially prevalent among the poor. Take Zuleyma, 16,

of Los Angeles, who gave birth last May: "I thought I might want to have a baby," she says. "I was thinking more in the future, but things happen." Or Derdra Jones of Chicago, who gave birth at 15: "Part of me wanted to get pregnant," she confesses. "I liked the boy a lot, and he used to say he wanted a baby." Or Marquel, 17, of Hawthorne, Calif.: "I had birth control pills in my drawer. I just didn't take them," she says. "My life was getting boring. I wanted a baby."

For young girls trapped in poverty, life offers few opportunities apart from getting pregnant. High school may seem pointless. Even graduation is little guarantee of a job. Their lives are circumscribed in every sense. Says Social Worker Lisa Rost, who counsels such youngsters at Project Hope in Chicago: "Some of these kids have never seen Lake Michigan." Pregnancy becomes one of the few accessible means of fulfillment. "Nobody gets more attention than a little girl who's pregnant," observes Bishop Earl Paulk of Chapel Hill Harvester Church, a Protestant church in Atlanta that sponsors a program for pregnant teens. "It feels good to be the center of things."

Youngsters who get pregnant often have a history of feeling deprived and neglected. Many have been abused or raped. "Their getting pregnant has nothing to do with sex," observes Pat Berg, director of a Chicago program for homeless youth. "It's attempting in a perverse sense to get some security and nurturing needs met ... It's like when kids get puppies." Finally, there is little social pressure to persuade them to postpone childbearing, notes Joy Dryfoos, who has conducted research for the Rockefeller Foundation. Middle-class girls tend not to have babies, she says, "because Mother would kill them if they did." For the lower socioeconomic groups, she says, "it's the big shoulder shrug. They don't get abortions. They don't use contraception. It's just not that important; they don't have a sense of the future."

No wonder teenage pregnancies have reached epidemic proportions in some ghetto areas. According to Guttmacher statistics, black American teenagers have the highest fertility rate of any teenage population group in the entire world. (Israeli Arabs come in a distant second.) One in four black babies in the U.S. is born to a teen mother, most of them unwed. "In the black community, the phenomenon of teen marriage is almost gone," observes Mark Testa of NORC. "Eventually these girls get married, but it might be years later and not to the father of the child." Young black women under age 24 are facing "a shrinking pool of marriageable— that is, economically stable—young men," explains Sociologist William Julius Wilson of the University of Chicago, who coauthored a 1985 study titled *Poverty and Family Structure.* The reasons he cites for the dearth of eligible candidates: unemployment, incarceration and an appalling rate of murder, the leading cause of death of black males age 15 to 44.

Wilson is part of a new breed of black

AN AMERICAN DILEMMA
Pregnancy rates per 1,000 teenage females
Each figure equals 10 pregnancies

U.S.	
Britain	
Canada	
France	
Sweden	
Netherlands	

Pregnancies ending in abortion

TIME Charts   Source: Alan Guttmacher Institute

academicians and leaders who have begun to acknowledge teenage pregnancy as a major issue for the black community. The National Urban League has declared it its No. 1 concern and last spring, on Father's Day, launched a program aimed at teenage boys, the often forgotten partners in the problem of teen pregnancy. Says League President John Jacob: "We cannot talk about strengthening the black community and family without facing up to the fact that teenage pregnancy is a major factor in high unemployment, the numbers of high school dropouts and the numbers of blacks below the poverty line."

This public recognition from black leaders is a significant departure from the past. Back in 1965 when New York Senator Daniel Patrick Moynihan, then Assistant Secretary of Labor, released a study depicting instability in the black family and stressing the problem of the absentee father, he was roundly accused of racism for ignoring the economic basis of the situation. In the heyday of the civil rights movement, admits Jacob, "teenage pregnancy was not the kind of subject we were willing to deal with publicly. We felt the black community would be blamed." That lack of attention was unfortunate, as black leaders now acknowledge. In the years since the Moynihan report, observes Eleanor Holmes Norton, the status of the black family has deteriorated. In 1965, she points out, only about one-third of black children were born to single mothers. Now more than half are. She insists that the black family remains strong, but admits "there have been important structural changes that will be hard to reverse."

Some blame the welfare system for contributing to the disintegration of the black family by providing an incentive for young women to have babies. While rules vary from state to state, indigent girls generally become eligible for public assistance in their third trimester of pregnancy. Most social-service workers argue,

however, that the welfare system is at most a minor factor in teenage pregnancy. "It's possible that with no assistance, we would see fewer kids going to term," says Radosh of New York City's mayor's office. "But I don't think you'd see fewer getting pregnant."

Guttmacher researchers concur, pointing out that countries like Holland, Sweden and France provide far more generously for indigent young mothers, yet have low pregnancy rates. Research by Sociologist Frank Furstenberg of the University of Pennsylvania further refutes the notion that teenagers who become pregnant are simply looking for a handout. In following 400 young black mothers in Baltimore, Furstenberg discovered that most were "surprisingly motivated to get off welfare." In fact, 17 years after bearing a first child, only one-quarter were receiving public assistance.

Despite the discrepancy in statistics, teen pregnancy, as black leaders are quick to point out, should not be seen as a specifically black problem. Rather, says Jacob, it is a poverty-related problem. "It has a greater impact on the black community because it is a poor community." Indeed, poor whites as well as blacks tend to have high rates of teenage pregnancy. In the largely white community of North Adams, Mass., an old mill town where unemployment has been high, teen pregnancy is reaching epidemic levels. One out of five births at North Adams Regional Hospital is to an adolescent, and 90% of the young mothers wind up on welfare. "I'm seeing a world where kids feel being pregnant is a viable option," sighs Maggie Bitman, who runs a parenting program in North Adams. "They feel their lives are in disarray." The situation is similar in the mostly white, down-at-the-heels southern counties of Illinois, and in white, working-class areas where the work has disappeared. The underlying reasons for the pregnancies are no different from those in urban ghettos: lack of opportunity, absence of interesting alternatives to childbearing. The girls feel "locked into their stations in life," says Health Official Wood Bennett of southern Illinois. "They're not motivated to break out."

Needy girls who imagine that having a baby will fill the void in their lives are usually in for a rude shock. Hopes of escaping a dreary existence, of finding direction and purpose, generally sink in a sea of responsibility. With no one to watch the child, school becomes impossible, if not irrelevant. And despite the harsh lessons of experience, many remain careless or indifferent about birth control. About 15% of pregnant teens become pregnant again within one year; 30% do so within two years. "You ask, 'Why didn't you come in for the Pill?' and they say, 'I didn't have time,' " says an exasperated Kay Bard of Planned Parenthood in Atlanta. "Their lives begin to spiral out of control."

The problems faced by children of such parents begin before they are even born. Only one in five girls under age 15 receives any prenatal care at all during the vital first three months of pregnancy. The combination of inadequate medical care and poor diet contributes to a number of problems during pregnancy, says Dr. John Niles of Columbia Hospital for Women in Washington: "Teenagers are 92% more likely to have anemia, and 23% more likely to have complications related to prematurity, than mothers aged 20 to 24." All of this adds up to twice the normal risk of delivering a low-birth-weight baby (one that weighs under 5.5 lbs.), a category that puts an infant in danger of serious mental, physical and developmental problems that may require costly and possibly even lifelong medical care.

Infants that escape the medical hazards of having a teenage mother do not always manage to negotiate the psychological and social perils. Desirée Bell, 19, of New York City, had her first son at age 15 and her second the following year. Her elder son Eddie has a learning disability and was almost autistic as an infant. Bell, who has managed heroically to complete high school and secure a good job with the city, blames herself for his problems. "I hated the fact that I was pregnant," she recalls. "I was resentful of my unborn child. I used to punch myself in the stom-

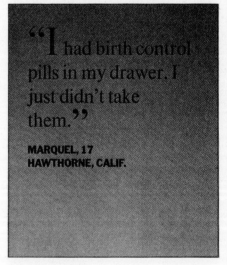

"**I** had birth control pills in my drawer. I just didn't take them."

**MARQUEL, 17
HAWTHORNE, CALIF.**

ach. Poor Eddie," she muses, "the first year I wouldn't play with him. He didn't talk until he was nearly two; he would just grunt. I would say, I traumatized my own son."

Desirée Bell has recognized her error and tried to give her son the extra attention he needs. Not all teenagers do. According to the Children's Aid Society in New York City, one of the oldest family agencies in the country, a large number of babies delivered to teenage mothers wind up in foster care. "Teenagers get excited about this little, adorable person that's all theirs," explains Barbara Emmerth of the New York City-based Citizens' Committee for Children, "but when the kid is in the terrible twos and the mother wants to go out on dates instead of taking care of the little monster, they change their minds.''

Often the state must intervene in cases where abuse or neglect is suspected. Two-year-old Ana Marie seemed to be perpetually falling and hurting herself. ''I didn't pay her enough attention,'' admits her mother Kim Adalid, 19, who also has a three-year-old son and expects a third child in January. After one of Ana Marie's mishaps, Kim took her daughter to a doctor, who quickly discovered that the child's arm was broken. Believing that the girl had been neglected (a charge that Kim vigorously denies), the doctor filed a report with the California courts. Ana Marie was taken away and placed with a temporary guardian.

Such interventions come at a considerable cost. In Illinois, state officials calculated that teenage pregnancy cost $853 million in medical care, day care, welfare and other social programs last year. It has been estimated that overall, the U.S. spends $8.6 billion on income support for teenagers who are pregnant or have given birth.

Most programs addressing the problem of teen pregnancy are directed at the group easiest to identify and help: adolescents who are already pregnant or have given birth. The goals: to ensure that the girls obtain adequate prenatal care, continue their education and learn how to be good parents. Providing prenatal care has become a bigger problem since 1982, when the Reagan Administration reduced the appropriation for the Feeding Program for Women, Infants and Children, which offers nutritional supplements and medical care to low-income expectant mothers. The cuts, say critics, will prove expensive in the long run, because caring for undersize, ailing infants through Medicaid is many times as costly as preventive prenatal measures. In recent years, private organizations and local governments have attempted to fill the gap left by WIC cutbacks. San Francisco's TAPP, a model program that the state plans to extend to other cities, has helped reduce the incidence of low-birth-weight infants to about 4% among the teenagers it counsels, against a national average of 17%.

Keeping young mothers in school has proved to be a stickier problem. Among TAPP counselees, for example, nearly half who were not enrolled in school were persuaded to resume their education. Unfortunately, an additional 31% who had been attending decided to drop out. In New York City, special public high schools have been established for pregnant teenagers to encourage them to stick with it. New York has also established day-care facilities at 18 of its 117 high schools, so that mothers can continue to attend after they have given birth.

Increasingly, conservative religious organizations have got into the business of aiding pregnant teenagers as a way of discouraging abortion. Jerry Falwell's Moral Majority has, for example, developed a nationwide $4 million program called Save-a-Baby, run in conjunction with an adoption agency. ''We agree to assist girls who are fixing to have an abortion, if they will let the baby live,'' says Jim Savley, the program's executive director.

Other programs for teen mothers emphasize careful instruction in family planning to prevent more unwanted pregnancies. Some go so far as to send a social worker to the hospital shortly after the girl has given birth in order to present gifts of condoms and contraceptive foam, along with something for the baby. Increasingly, programs like the Door in New York and Crittenton Center in Los Angeles have extended their contraceptive-counseling programs to teens who have not yet become pregnant. Crittenton purposely holds discussion groups that mix young mothers with other adolescents to reinforce the lessons on birth control. ''When they see how hard it is to be a mother,'' says Executive Director Sharon Watson, ''they don't get pregnant.''

Many believe that such lessons should be a regular part of the curriculum in public schools. According to a TIME poll taken by the research firm of Yankelovich, Skelly & White, Inc., 78% of Americans respond yes to the question ''Do you favor sex education in the schools, including information about birth control?'' And yet, despite the majority opinion, the subject of sex education remains a divisive one. On one side are those like Wattleton of Planned Parenthood who argue that Americans should learn to accept adolescent sexuality and make guidance and birth control more easily available, as it is in parts of Europe. On the other side are those who contend that sex education is up to the parents, not the state, and that teaching children about birth control is tantamount to condoning promiscuity. Sex-education classes are simply ''sales meetings'' for abortion clinics, says Phyllis Schlafly, a leading right-to-lifer. In addition, she claims, there is simply no way to tell youngsters about contraception

''**I** want to feel good about myself, so my kids can be proud of me.''

STEPHANIE CHARETTE, 17 MINNEAPOLIS

''without implicitly telling them that sex is O.K. You've put your Good Housekeeping seal on it.''

The conflict has contributed to riotous clashes at school-board meetings whenever the sex-education curriculums come up for review. Last year, for example, when New York City developed a program designed to help combat a runaway rate of teenage pregnancy, religious groups presented a list of 56 objections. In middle-class San Juan Capistrano, Calif., the fray over sex-education reform grew so heated last spring that conservative opponents showed up at a school-board meeting dressed in Revolutionary War garb and bearing a cannon.

In 1981 the Reagan Administration instituted a program to, in its words, ''encourage teenagers not to engage in sexual activities'' and foster ''good communication between parents and child about sexual matters.'' The plan has won favor with conservative church groups but has been derided by family-planning advocates as an unrealistic ''chastity act.'' Terrance Olson, professor of family sciences at Brigham Young University in Provo, Utah, is using funds from the new program to develop a conservative sex-education curriculum. Olson's offering stresses abstinence, and, he says, ''we try to involve teenagers with their parents in understanding the issues of marriage, family and reproduction.'' The program has been tested in selected schools in Utah, California and New Mexico since 1982, but, he admits, ''we don't have a lot of evidence yet that we've changed behavior.''

Changing human behavior is, of course, always an elusive objective. When Researcher Douglas Kirby, head of the Washington-based Center for Population Options, studied the behavioral effects of sex education, he found them to be few and far between. Sex-education graduates certainly knew more about reproduction, but that did not significantly affect their habits. There was, however, one important exception. Kirby found that when sex-education programs are coupled with efforts to help teenagers obtain contraceptives, the pregnancy rate drops sharply.

The model for this type of program was the Mechanic Arts High School in St. Paul, which in 1973 became the first public high school in the U.S. to have its own full-service health clinic in the building. Set up by St. Paul–Ramsey Medical Center, it offered everything from immunizations to sport physicals to treatment for venereal disease. Significantly, it also advised teenagers on contraception and dispensed prescriptions for birth control devices (provided that parents had agreed beforehand to allow their children to visit the clinic).

Such clinics now exist at four other St. Paul high schools (Mechanic Arts High has been closed). The results have been dramatic. Between 1977 and 1984, births to female students fell from 59 per thousand to 26 per thousand. Even girls who did become pregnant seemed to benefit from the counseling. At Mechanic Arts High, their dropout rate fell from 45% to 10%, and only 1% had another unwanted pregnancy within two years of the first. The controversial clinic at Chicago's DuSable High School and ones at other schools around the country were modeled after St. Paul's pioneering program.

For all their apparent success, in-school clinics do not necessarily get at the emotional wellsprings of teenage pregnancy: the sense of hopelessness and resignation felt by many underprivileged girls. In Milwaukee, Janice Anderson, a successful black businesswoman, is trying to do something about it. Anderson, 36, was inspired to act last March when she read that her hometown led the country in birthrates among black teenagers. "I sat up in bed at 2 a.m. and wrote down the name of every black professional woman I knew," she recalls. "I came up with a list of 42 names and wrote to each one, asking them to come help their sisters." Anderson's early-hour inspiration evolved into Reach for the Stars, a volunteer program that pairs inner-city adolescents with black role models who are successful achievers.

Similar groups have begun to appear around the country. In New York, the Family Life program, co-sponsored by the state and the Children's Aid Society, is attempting to give dead-end kids a sense of self-esteem, says Michael Carrera, its energetic director. Since the program's initiation last February, not one of the 55 participating youngsters has become pregnant or fathered a child.

These efforts are aimed at what may be the true root of the teenage pregnancy problem: not simply lack of sex education or access to birth control but a sense of worthlessness and despair. Recounts Watson of Crittenton Center: "The girls tell me, 'Before I was pregnant, I was nothing. Now I am somebody. I'm a mother.' " As long as adolescents look in the mirror and see nobody there, they are likely to seek identity by becoming—ready or not— somebody's mother.   —*By Claudia Wallis.*
Reported by Cathy Booth/New York, Melissa Ludtke/Los Angeles and Elizabeth Taylor/ Chicago

TEEN LUST

ELLEN WILLIS

Ellen Willis is a senior editor of "The Village Voice." Her first article for "Ms." appeared in June, 1973.

In the age of just-say-no, as the focus of moral hysteria shifts from group to group—AIDS sufferers, women who have abortions, pornographers, drug users— one target remains constant: sexually active teenagers. In the public mind, kids who have sex are by definition "promiscuous"; they never have love relationships, let alone monogamous ones. They are responsible for a rampant social disease, "the epidemic of teenage pregnancy." And sometimes, we are warned, the wages of sin are, literally, death: WILD SEX KILLED JENNY blared a New York *Post* headline after 18-year-old Jennifer Levin was strangled during what may or may not have been a sexual encounter in Central Park. Last fall, a couple of months after the Levin murder, teenage sex panic once again surfaced in New York City. The occasion was the revelation that an on-site health clinic at a city high school had been giving out contraceptives. The Catholic hierarchy and outraged parents and school board members protested. The liberals responsible for the clinic's policy, caught with their secular humanism showing, responded by assuring everyone in sight that they, too, were all for abstinence. They argued that making birth control available does not encourage teenagers to have sex. Did anyone—educator, doctor, birth control provider, social service agency—suggest that teenagers' sexual desires (you

know, sexual desires, those sort of primal impulses responsible for humanity's continued existence) are as legitimate as adults'? That making it possible for teenage girls to enjoy sex without fear of pregnancy might actually be a positive thing? Hey, don't all talk at once!

In the end, the city's Board of Education came up with an ingenious compromise: school clinics could, with parental consent, give out prescriptions for contraceptives, but not the contraceptives themselves. Apparently, allowing teenagers access to birth control is okay in principle, but only if it's made as inconvenient, not to mention as expensive, as possible.

All this pusillanimity drove me to satire, in the form of an article for *The Village Voice* called "Teenage Sex: A Modesty Proposal." In it I denounced society's gutlessness in the face of our Teenage Sex (TS) plague. It was time, I wrote, "to move beyond toothless moralizing . . . time, in short, to make war on TS." I proposed a 12-point program of "benign terrorism," which included indoctrination beginning at birth (". . . the best way to prevent Teenage Sex is to scare the shit out of children. But in recent years . . . parents have been told not to slap an infant's hand when it wanders down there, not to tell little kids to stop

touching it or you'll cut it off . . . the Victorians had the right idea"); prosecuting TS as child abuse, with jail or compulsory marriage for those convicted; random vaginal testing; the death penalty for contraceptive dealers who sell to minors; castration for a second TS offense.

It wasn't exactly subtle; I was a little worried that maybe I was being too heavy-handed. Then, the day after it appeared, I got a phone call.

A male voice: "I was *outraged* by your article."

"Oh. What outraged you?"

"I thought some of what you had to say made sense, but your *proposals* . . . !"

I didn't know what was more unnerving—that he had taken the whole thing seriously or that he thought it wasn't all bad.

Usually, when I write a piece of satire, I get one or two straight-arrow responses; this time I got at least a dozen. Several accused me, in essence, of being over 30 (the sixties live!)—a dried-up, frustrated old bag who was jealous of teenagers and their beautiful young bodies. But some of the letters were not so much polemics as pleas for understanding. "Sex with someone you love, who loves you, with the proper contraception can be the most wonderful

"Sex can be a wonderful feeling – better than drugs."

feeling in the world—better than drugs," wrote a 19-year-old woman. "Sex isn't dirty; ignorance is."

Clearly, something else was going on besides careless reading, humorlessness, or not having heard of Swift. And when I thought about it, I realized what the problem was: I had assumed that my curmudgeonly persona's antisexual rantings were manifestly absurd, and in making that assumption had seriously underestimated the impact of the hysteria I was trying to ridicule.

Rereading the batch of angry letters, most from kids in their teens or just out of them, I saw that not all the writers had taken my article literally. Several knew I was making some kind of joke, only they assumed that it was at their expense—that I was merely emphasizing my hatred of teen sex (or perhaps sex in general) by indulging in a bit of hyperbole. As one woman (whom I'd guess to be in her twenties) put it, getting into what she thought was the spirit of the discussion, "Of course it was humor, wasn't it? I'm sure most mothers out there would go along with prison terms and castration for their licentious teens." Today's teens and postteens are growing up in a relentlessly mean-spirited time; it's no wonder that some of the kids who read my piece could only see it as one more nasty put-down.

The source of teen sex panic is not really teenage pregnancy. On the contrary, a central aspect of the current panic is fear that if those liberal do-gooders have their way, pregnancy will no longer serve as a self-enforcing deterrent—or failing that, punishment—for "illicit" sex. In recent years the teen pregnancy rate has actually stabilized; the reason it's suddenly an "epidemic" and a social crisis is the rise in pregnancies among *unmarried* teenagers. Under present social conditions, teen-

age childbearing is at best a serious obstacle to the mother's prospects (assuming she had some to begin with) for an education, economic mobility, and psychic independence, but no one worried much about that so long as the mothers in question were married—they were just embracing (or submitting to, what difference did it make?) women's destiny a little early.

Part of the concern now is economic, since unwed teenage mothers are likely to end up on welfare. But ultimately even proposals to cut off welfare benefits for teen mothers are aimed less at reducing costs than at ending this public subsidy (with its implied tolerance) of "immorality." For sexual conservatives, what matters is maintaining a social and moral norm, however honored in the breach, that condemns sexual activity outside marriage. And whatever else the 1960s sexual revolution may or may not have accomplished, it destroyed that norm for (heterosexual) adults. In the cultural mainstream, sex before marriage is now a taken-for-granted part of growing up, nor does anyone expect the legions of divorced people to be celibate; when bishops and right-wing columnists oppose TV ads for condoms on the grounds that such ads would "encourage premarital sex," they sound laughably out of touch. Clearly, traditionalists' frustration and resentment at having lost this battle are being displaced with special vehemence onto teenagers. Though most teens do in fact have sex, the social and moral norm still dictates that they're not supposed to, at least not till they're 18 or so—and beleaguered conservatives are determined to hold the line.

I say "adults" and "teenagers," but of course I mean "especially women and girls." Neither premarital sex for men nor the age at which they start having it

has ever been a serious issue: the basic impulse underlying the anti-teen-sex crusade is maintaining social control over female sexuality. This is most obvious in the debate about teen pregnancy and birth control, but it's also implicit in the rhetoric about teenage "promiscuity"—a label promiscuously applied to women and gay men, rarely to straight men, for whom it's considered natural to sleep with as many women as possible.

Public discussion of the contraceptives-in-the-schools question, especially in the mass media, has been notably lacking in any sort of feminist perspective. While conservatives make speeches about chastity, and liberals call for pragmatism, one crucial point is lost: as a matter of simple justice, women of any age have a right to the means of controlling their fertility. Without that right, teenage girls cannot hope to have equal freedom and power in their relations with boys or their relation to the world. Beyond this most basic of principles, a feminist approach to the issue of teenage sex would assume that girls ought to have the power to define their needs for sexual pleasure, emotional satisfaction, and (in the age of AIDS) safety—and to resist male pressure for sex on any terms that violate those needs. In short, we need not only contraceptives and sex education in our schools, but feminist consciousness-raising—and a feminist movement.

From this point of view, I take some comfort in the response to my article. The letter writers may have been confused about where I stood, but their anger at the authorities they thought I represented is heartening. These are young people who, despite the ongoing barrage of guilt-and-fear-provoking propaganda, are defending their right to sexual love. And half of them are female.

FORMAL VERSUS INFORMAL SOURCES OF SEX EDUCATION: COMPETING FORCES IN THE SEXUAL SOCIALIZATION OF ADOLESCENTS

Jeremiah Strouse, Ph.D. and
Richard A. Fabes, Ph.D.

Jeremiah Strouse, Associate Professor, Department of Home Economics, Family Life, and Consumer Education, Central Michigan University, Mt. Pleasant, MI 48859.

Richard A. Fabes, Assistant Professor, Department of Home Economics, Arizona State University, Tempe, AZ 85287

Most of the research evaluating formal sex education has shown that these programs have failed to achieve their intended purpose of promoting responsible behavior, especially in young teenagers. This paper examines some of the plausible reasons for this lack of success and reviews literature which suggests that the informal sources of sexual socialization, especially television, may dilute the impact of school programs. The influence of parents is also discussed. The authors conclude that educators and parents need to recognize and consider the importance of the informal sources of sexual learning in order to promote sexual responsibility in adolescents.

According to Penland (1981), the sex education movement in the United States began around 1900. The educational philosophy of this early era was characterized by antisexual lectures which focused primarily upon the dangers of sex and loss of control. These lectures were given to groups of boys only. By the 1940s, sex education began to focus on family life, reproduction, hygiene, and venereal disease. While the emphasis was still very moralistic, the purpose was to promote healthy sexual adjustment within the family.

The "youth revolution" of the 1960s served as a catalyst to once again alter the scope and purpose of sex education. The "new sex education" of the '70s and '80s has

been characterized by the impartial teaching of factual information, nonjudgmental discussion, and values clarification (Otto, 1971). The purpose has been, and continues to be, to promote healthy sexual relationships, encourage responsible decision-making, and reduce the incidence of unintended teenage pregnancies and sexually transmitted diseases (STDs). It seems that the underlying assumption of sex education in America has been that if young people have factual information about the nature and possible consequences of various sexual actions and have discussed and formulated individualistic values of sexual conduct, they will either avoid experimentation or protect themselves against unintended pregnancies by utilizing contraceptives.

The bulk of the research to date does not support this assumption. While some studies have found that exposure to sex education can increase knowledge and tolerant attitudes, such programs do not have much impact upon sexual behavior (Bidgood, 1973; Kirby, 1983). Moreover, in their comprehensive review of the literature on sex education, Kirby, Alter, and Scales (1979) concluded that there are several serious methodological limitations to most studies. First, they usually do not have adequate control groups; second, they tend to evaluate single programs; third, any negative findings are not likely to be reported; and fourth, they do not measure the long-term effects of the programs. In one of the few studies which did utilize a nationally representative sample of teens, and was con-

Portions of this paper were presented at the annual meeting of the National Council on Family Relations, October, 1983, in St. Paul, Minnesota. The authors would like to thank Mary Hicks for her reactions to the issues presented in this paper.

From *Adolescence*, Volume XX, No. 78 (Summer 1985) pp. 251-263. Reprinted by permission.

161

ducted at various periods of time after the programs were finished, Zelnick and Kantner (1977) concluded that the "transfer of knowledge in formal settings may be likened to carrying water in a basket" (p. 59), thus emphasizing the limitations of sex education.

At the same time that the new discussion-oriented programs were being implemented, the U.S. was experiencing what some sources have termed an "epidemic" increase in teenage pregnancies (Alan Guttmacher Institute, 1981). Studies revealed that throughout the 1970s, more teenagers were engaging in sexual intercourse, at earlier ages, and having more pregnancies, more abortions, and more births than ever before. In her recent review of adolescent fertility, Baldwin (1983) concluded that, "More teenagers appear to have sex before marriage . . . and the chances that an unmarried teen will have a baby have increased" (p. 2). While the association between current sex education programs and teenage sexual behavior discussed above does not in itself provide evidence of a cause-effect relationship, it, along with a plethora of related data, does suggest that we should seriously question the validity of the underlying assumptions of the formal sex education model.

The purpose of this paper is to review data from a variety of sources which examine these basic assumptions. In addition, the authors suggest that one possible reason for the apparent ineffectiveness of formal sex education is that the informal sources (i.e., parents and TV) exert a more powerful and frequently contrary influence. Research examining these informal sources of sexual socialization will also be reviewed.

Why Has Formal Sex Education Apparently Failed to Achieve Its Intended Purpose/Goals?

Perhaps the first question to be asked is whether sex educators should even promise behavioral results with teenagers. Most other educational programs that attempt to achieve behavioral outcomes have a high rate of failure. Researchers examining health education, for example, have long reported a discrepancy between health knowledge and personal health behavior (Hamrick, Anspaugh, & Smith, 1980). These studies have shown that although many adults "know" that they should exercise, that they should not smoke cigarettes, overeat, drive without using seat belts, or speed, they do not necessarily act upon this information. This evidence suggests that knowledge alone does not motivate intended behavioral action. One possible reason is that the educational programs are not adequately designed. While recent studies show that most schools in the United States offer some type of sex education, most of the programs are not very comprehensive or adequate. Gordon (1983) estimates that only 10% of the programs are minimally adequate. He therefore asserts that we are unable to accurately assess the effects of sex education on a national scale.

Kirby (1983), however, reports rather discouraging results for the Mathtech Project, which included a careful study of exemplary programs. To achieve the basic goal of this research project, the authors set out "to find, improve, evaluate, and describe effective approaches to sexuality education" (p. 11). They had 200 chosen professionals rate what they considered to be important features of good programs. They then selected 9 quality programs, attempted to improve each one as much as possible, and then carefully studied and evaluated their effectiveness. Although they qualify the tentativeness of their findings, they report that the programs had very little impact on knowledge and attitudes, and that "most (nonclinical) programs did not have any impact upon whether or not teenagers had sex, how often they had sex, or how often they used birth control" (p. 22). This is important in light of the fact that the researchers had identified the reduction of unintended pregnancies as one of two important goals of the programs.

Another plausible explanation of the apparent failure of sex education is that very young teens (who have experienced the greatest increase in unplanned pregnancies) may be too cognitively immature to engage in the logical, premeditated thought processes necessary to assume the desired level of responsibility for their sexual behaviors. As Cvetlovich, Grote, Bjorseth, and Sarkissian (1975) pointed out, many adolescents entertain a "personal fable" of sterility and do not comprehend the probabilistic relationship between sexual intercourse and pregnancy. Because of this egocentrism, adolescents may not be able to conceive of themselves as mature sexual beings who are capable of impregnating or becoming pregnant. Moreover, many teens, especially males, may fixate on the most immediate and salient consequences of their sexual actions (release of sexual tension and the accompanying pleasure) and ignore the more distal and much less probable consequences (partner pregnancy or STDs).

Very closely related to the level of cognitive development is the level of moral development. As Gilligan (1974) has stated, sexual choices are influenced by an individual's level of moral reasoning. Kohlberg (1974) has been critical of the use of values clarification in that it is relativistic and does not promote the development of the underlying moral principles themselves. He suggests that in addition to careful analysis of the possible consequences of various sexual choices, adolescents should be exposed to models who portray characteristics of thinking found at the stage of moral development above their own so as to stimulate moral growth. To the extent that Kohlberg is correct, our laissez-faire approach to values clarification may be a limiting factor for sex education. Group discussion by youthful cohorts may simply lead to a sharing and reinforcing of a common pool of values which are based upon immature levels of reasoning and limited perceptions of reality.

Regardless of the reasons, based upon the measured rates of adolescent pregnancies, abortions, and STDs, one is left with the inescapable conclusion that sex education in the United States has fallen far short of achieving its intended goals. The authors believe that one of the main reasons is that there are simply too many invalidated assumptions built into the formal education model. Further, we believe that there has been too much disregard for the informal sources of sex education, which may overshadow the formal.

Informal Sources of Sex Education

The sexual socialization process is very complex and is influenced by many factors other than classroom instruction. Nearly all studies examining sources of sex information show that peers are rated as the most important source (Thornburg, 1981). Further, in reviewing a variety of selected studies since 1915, Darling and Hicks (1982) suggest that the peer group has diminished in importance while the media and literature have increased in importance as sources of sexual information. Other studies (e.g., Roberts, Kline, & Gagnon, 1978) have indeed found that television is regarded as at least second in importance to parents as a source of sexual influence.

The remainder of this paper will focus primarily upon parents and television as the major sources of informal sex education, for the following reasons. First, parents are the primary agents of socialization and exert the most control over their children's early exposure to other sources of influence, such as television, peers, and school. Second, although peers exercise a strong influence over teens, they should be regarded as secondary sources of processors of values and information.

The pervasive influence of television cannot be ignored. A report of the National Institute of Mental Health (NIMH, 1982) indicates that more American homes have television sets than they have indoor plumbing or refrigerators. Various surveys show that television has altered our eating, sleeping, elimination, socializing, recreational, and educational activities; and that young people spend more time watching television than participating in any other activity except sleeping (NIMH, 1982). By the time of graduation from high school, the average person has spent one and one-half times as many hours watching TV as the total hours spent in school (Liebert, Sprafkin, & Davidson, 1982). More importantly, heavy TV viewers tend to believe that what they see on television represents reality (Buerkel-Rothfuss & Mayes, 1981). With the steady increase in the volume of sexual messages on television (Sprafkin & Silverman, 1981), it is suggested that television may play a very influential role in sexual socialization.

For the most part, television presents sexuality as a distorted, recreation-oriented, exploitive, casual activity, without dealing with the consequences. Various studies which analyzed the content of television programs have found that male characters outnumber female characters by a ratio of 3 to 1 (Liebert, et al., 1982). Women tend to be typecast either as mothers, housewives, or lovers. Aside from the blatant gender stereotypes, some studies (Silverman, Sprafkin, & Rubinstein, 1979) have shown that prime-time televisionn presents sex mainly via innuendos and contextual references to intercourse. Further, children have been found to spend more time watching prime-time television than any other programming and are thus widely exposed to these sexual messages. In addition, it is important to note that the programmers of soap operas are increasingly successful at attracting a larger and more youthful audience where the main sexual content is heavy, explicit, erotic petting (Lowry, Love, & Kirby, 1981). Of all the alleged incidences of sexual intercourse on television soap operas, 49% involved lovers, 29% strangers, and only 6% involved marital partners (Greenberg, Abelman, & Neuendorf, 1981), and marital infidelity is presented as the major family problem (Katzman, 1972). The National Federation for Decency (1977) reports that on prime-time television, 89% of all sex is presented outside of marriage. Further, it is frequently not presented within the context of a caring, loving, considerate relationship. Sex is most often presented as an overwhelming, uncontrollable, physical attraction and desire. The only recent TV characters who were cast in a "hard-to-get role" were Laverne and Shirley, and they were presented as "goofy and unattractive" role models for young people. In contrast, nearly all of the other popular sexual characters on TV are "beautiful people" whom the youth of America frequently attempt to emulate. Fabes and Strouse (1983) found that these "beautiful" people represented an important source of what adolescents considered appropriate sexual role models.

What Are the Effects of Television Sex on Youth?

In recent years, entertainment television has become a source of concern as to its sexual socializing influence on youth. One study (Roberts, Kline, & Gagnon, 1978) found that the majority of parents believe that, next to themselves, television is the second most important source of sexual learning. A majority of these same parents also believe that TV sex is inaccurate and unreliable. To date, however, there have not been any studies of the direct effects on children's behavior. However, there is an abundance of related studies which indicate that entertainment television may be exerting a powerful influence on the sex education of youth.

The early studies of the effects of TV were spawned by the upsurge of violence and social disorder during the late 1960s. Early research and the Surgeon General's report indicated that there was a positive correlation between TV viewing and aggressive behavior. During the 1970s, about 2,500 articles on the influence of TV were published (NIMH, 1982). A recently published summary of this research (NIMH, 1982) concluded that after 10 years, the consensus of researchers is that watching violence on television does lead to aggressive behavior in youths. The many laboratory experiments and field studies indicate that, although the effects are not long-lasting, "a causal link between televised violence and aggressive behavior now seems obvious" (p. 6).

On the other hand, parallel research has examined the effects of television programming on prosocial behavior in children. Nearly all studies have found that prosocial TV (such as "Mister Roger's Neighborhood") can achieve desirable results in children (Liebert et al., 1982). The evidence is persuasive that children can learn to be friendly, altruistic and self-controlled by watching TV programs depicting such behavior (NIMH, 1982). Therefore, it seems that by selective TV viewing, young people can learn to be either more aggressive or less aggressive.

One may be tempted to infer that if TV can affect both antisocial and prosocial behavior, it can also affect sexual behavior. Before considering such an inferential conclusion, however, it is important to note that in 1969 and 1970 two presidential commissions reported seemingly contradictory conclusions. The first report by the National Commission on the Causes and Prevention of Violence concluded that those who viewed violent TV programs were more likely to behave violently. The second report by the National Commission on Obscenity and Pornography, which did not deal with television per se, concluded that exposure to sexually explicit materials did not influence sexual behavior. The latter report used a catharsis model to guide its research; this theory, in contrast to social learning theory, states that exposure to certain behavioral acts purges the viewer of the tendency to commit such acts. While the former report has stood the test of time, the latter has attracted many critics of the research design, subjects, and methodology, as well as the bias of the authors in the direction of protecting freedom of speech (Liebert et al., 1982). Moreover, a growing body of experimental research suggests that exposure to sexually explicit materials, especially when associated with violence, can influence people's judgments of sexual scenarios, as well as their sexual behavior (Allgeier, 1983).

While regular network TV programming does not offer explicit depictions of sexual behavior, it does present a nearly constant stream of more or less implicit sexual messages. Since most programming includes plots revolving around relationships, sexuality is interwoven into the fabric of the meanings and feelings of such relationships (Roberts & Holt, 1977). These aspects of sexuality have been found to be of extreme concern to adolescents and are thus highly relevant to them (Fabes, 1982).

While sometimes subtle, television presents a well-financed and well-orchestrated light and sound show that establishes a mood which captures the attention of the target audience. Various studies have shown that young persons, especially, attend to TV scenes that have a high degree of salience (Liebert et al., 1982). Toddlers, for example, will usually ignore an ongoing TV program until there is a scene of high salience, such as a commercial. Hence, it is little wonder that many young toddlers learn the jingles of a commercial before they can pronounce their own name.

A second illustration of the effects of what might be regarded as salient sex-role stereotyping is found in the results of a study by Miller and Reeves (1976). They asked young children which TV characters they prefer and which characters they "would want to be like when you grow up." None of the boys chose opposite-sex models, while 27% of the girls chose male models. When queried about the reason for their choices, girls most often said it was the physical attractiveness, and boys said it was physical aggressiveness.

A third example of the powerful impact of combining high salience video and sound is the skyrocketing commercial success of Music Television, or MTV. According to the Nielsen Home Video Index (The Wall Street Journal, August 24, 1983, p. 10) within the two years of its existence, MTV has become the number one cable channel for those 12-20 years of age. It is widely credited with rekindling sales for the record industry and is now regarded as a crucial promotional tool for new releases. In a recent weekly survey, 47 of the top 50 rock albums were promoted by videos. While the videos were initially purely promotional for the audios, they have been so successful that the video-tapes themselves have become a promising retail item (Kneale, 1983).

Although the authors are unaware of any noncommercial studies of MTV, there has been an early expression of concern in a smattering of letters to the editor of The Wall Street Journal (10/5/83, p. 29). The films are variously described as weird, bizarre, extreme, low-budget, talented, art, and junk. A casual watching of the programming leaves one with the impression that the characters, who are largely walk-ons, engage in extreme gestures and provocative sexual gyrations. Whatever effect MTV may be having on the sexual attitudes and behavior of the rock-and-roll youth, it certainly has captured their attention as well as their purchasing power.

In summary, it can be said that television watching is the major activity of young people. Its multimodal appeal has affected nearly every facet of behavior that has been studied. The authors suggest that when evidence from studies of social learning and observational learning is related to sex on TV, the results will show that young people are influenced by the sexual behaviors of their favorite characters. Further, this effect can be expected to increase as television increasingly serves as a surrogate parent.

Parental Influence on Sexual Socialization

Parents are generally regarded as the chief transmitters of cultural values. However, recent changes in the family structure may have affected this function. First, mothers of over half the families now work outside the home (Superintendent of Documents, 1980). Second, about one-half of the parents are getting divorced, and about half are involved in extramarital sexual affairs. Finally, with a quarter of all families having single parents, one has to question whether parents are as significant as role models as they were in the past (Hicks & Williams, 1981).

Youth of America have little opportunity to observe adult sexual behavior, and hence, may be forced to depend upon the mass media as a source of sexual learning (Bandura & Walters, 1963). It is not surprising then, that one recent study (Pocs & Godow, 1977) found that a majority of college students either believe that their parents are not sexually active or are involved in a very low level of sexual activity. It follows then, that if young people do not view their parents as sexual beings, they cannot serve as models of sexual conduct. Fabes and Strouse (1983) recently found additional evidence supporting this conclusion in that the adolescents in their study perceived parents as models of sexuality half as often as they perceived them to be models of behavior in general.

Although parents may not be perceived as significant sexual models or sources of sexual information, they nevertheless convey influential sexual messages, even by their silence, to young people. Darling and Hicks (1982) report that by both verbal and nonverbal means, parents communicate positive and negative sexual messages to their children, and these messages affect their adolescent and adult levels of sexual satisfaction. Both the positive and negative messages were found to influence the males' level of sexual involvement and satisfaction in a positive fashion. For the females, however, positive and negative messages did not influence sexual involvement, but positive sexual messages were inversely related to their perceived level of sexual satisfaction. Coincidentally, the Youth Values Project (1978) found that, if teenagers' sexual activity was discovered by their parents, the females expected their parents to be very upset, while the males expected that they would give tacit approval. However, research suggests that when parents do intervene directly in their childrens' sexual development, they can exert a very powerful influence. Various studies (see Darling & Hicks, 1982) have shown, for example, that the most important variable in determining whether or not a female delays first intercourse or uses contraception, is for the parents, especially the mother, to talk to the daughter about such matters. These studies have demonstrated that parental involvement can either directly or indirectly serve as a source of sexual socialization. The authors suggest that by default, many parents are yielding to the more accessible influence of the mass media, especially entertainment television.

Recommendations for Improvement

Sex educators and parents need to work in tandem to counteract the distortions of the media and to compensate for the reduced contact with real-life parental models. In order to do so, the following suggestions are offered. First, educators must recognize the reality of television and treat this powerful source of influence with respect. They can no longer ignore the fact that a neutrally presented, 50-minute session cannot compete with 28 hours of million-dollar television programs each week. Sex educators can incorporate TV programming into their classroom discussions and highlight their unreal and exploitive features. Further, they must recognize that the home is the most important source of sexual learning, and the classroom can never be any more than a supplementary or remedial source. Finally, as Green (1983) has suggested, sex educators can attempt to positively influence television productions of sexual themes, and can offer workshops for parents to practice "active viewing" and to develop discussion skills.

On the home front, parents can and should monitor the television viewing of their children. Further, television can serve as a catalyst for parent-child communication. Research has demonstrated that positive parental intervention can enhance or limit what children learn about social roles by viewing family television shows (Buerkel-Rothfuss, Greenberg, Atkin, & Neuendorf, 1982).

Third, educators should become more assertive in directly teaching about immoral and irresponsible sexual conduct, rather than just conducting discussions of relativistic issues. This may be especially true in the case of very young teens whose cognitive skills limit their ability to draw their own conclusions regarding sexual responsibility. As Gordon (1983) has repeatedly pointed out, there is a distinction between being moral and being moralistic. Educators can promote universal values without proselytizing individual values. As Gordon (1983) has stated, "a sex education without values is valueless" (p. 2).

Fourth, divorced and single parents need to be more discreet about their adult sexual liaisons. Visher and Visher (1979) have pointed out that teenagers may feel aroused and confused about their parent's passionate display of affection in their presence. Perhaps such activity conveys a signal to young persons that sex outside of marriage is condoned. Data show that teenagers in such families are more active sexually than those from intact families (Alan Guttmacher Institute, 1981).

Finally, we need to encourage and promote positive models of responsibility. We can no longer ignore the fact that much of what young people learn is from observation and imitation of favorite adults. As Fabes and Strouse (1983) reported, young persons tend to view media characters as their main sexual models.

Summary and Conclusions

This paper has sought to point out some of the limitations of formal sex education, especially when contrasted with the influence of informal sources. The authors are not opposed to sex education; we fully support the SIECUS statement that young people have a right to know and a right to be sexual. Nor are the authors opposed to television. The issue is not whether television is good or bad. Television is an integral part of family life and is an influential force that needs to be recognized as such. The tremendous potential of television has yet to be harnessed and used beneficially by many parents and educators. Furthermore, sexuality educators must recognize that their brief and frequently remedial programs cannot, in isolation, counteract the barrage of negative sexual messages from negative sexual models. In order to more adequately enhance responsible sexual behavior in adolescents, parents and educators need to consider these informal sources and deal with them constructively.

References

Alan Guttmacher Institute. *Teenage pregnancy: The problem that hasn't gone away.* New York: Planned Parenthood Federation of America, Inc., 1981.

Allgeier, E.R. Violent erotica and the victimization of women. *SIECUS Report,* May-July 1983, 7-10.

Baldwin, W. Adolescent fertility—facts, fads and fallacies. *Impact '83-84* (Syracuse, NY: Syracuse University) 1983, *6,* 2.

Bandura, A., & Walters, R.H. *Social learning and personality development.* New York: Holt, 1963.

Bidgood, F.E. The effects of sex education: A summary of the literature. *SIECUS Report,* March 1973 *1*(4).

Buerkel-Rothfuss, N., Greenberg, B., Atkin, C., & Neundorf, K. Learning about the family from television. *Journal of Communications,* Summer 1982, 191-201.

Buerkel-Rothfuss, N.L., & Mayes, S. Soap opera viewing: The cultivation effect. *Journal of Communications,* Summer 1981, 108-115.

Burleson, D. Evaluation in sex education—a wasteland? *SIECUS Reports,* 1973, *4*(10).

Cvetkovich, G., Grote, B., Bjorseth, A., & Sarkissian, J. On the psychology of adolescents' use of contraceptives. *The Journal of Sex Research,* August 1975, *11*(8), 256-270.

Darling, C.J., & Hicks, M. Parental influence on adolescent sexuality: Implications for parents as educators. *Journal of Youth and Adolescence,* 1982, *11,* 231-245.

Darling, C.J., & Hicks, M. Recycling parental sexual messages. *Journal of Sex and Marital Therapy,* 1983, *9,* 233-243.

Fabes, R.A. Adolescents' questions about sexuality. *Journal of Sex Education and Therapy,* 1982, *8,* 39-41.

Fabes, R., & Strouse, J. *Adolescent sexuality, sexuality education, and modeling.* Manuscript submitted for publication, 1983.

Fernandez-Collado, C.F., Greenberg, B.S., Atkin, C.K., & Korzenny, F. Sexual intimacy and drug use in TV series. *Journal of Communications,* Summer 1978, 30-37.

Fleishman, N. Population and sexuality: The Hollywood connection. *SIECUS Report,* May-July 1983, 3-4.

Gebhard, P. The acquisition of basic sex information. *The Journal of Sex Research,* 1977, *13,* 148-169.

Gilligan, C. Sexual dilemmas at the high-school level. In M.S. Calderone (Ed.), *Sexuality and human values.* New York: Association Press, 1974.

Gordon, S. The case for a moral sex education [Letter to the editor]. *Impact '83-84,* 1983-84, *2.*

Green, D. Sex on television: A case for involvement. *SIECUS Report,* May-July 1983, *1,* 5-6.

Greenberg, B., Abelman, R., & Neuendorf, K. Sex on the soap operas: Afternoon delight. *Journal of Communication,* Summer 1981, 83-89.

5. SEXUALITY THROUGH THE LIFE CYCLE: Youth and Their Sexuality

Greenberg, B., Graef, D., Fernandez-Collado, C., Karzenny, F., & Atkin, C. Sexual intimacy on commercial television during prime time. *Life on Television*, Norwood, N.J.: Ablex Publishing Company, 1982.

Hamrick, M., Anspaugh, D., & Smith, D. Decision-making and the behavioral gap. *Journal of School Health*, October 1980, 455-458.

Health Care of Southeastern Massachusetts. *Sex on TV: A guide for parents*. Santa Cruz, CA: Network Publications, 1982.

Hicks, M.W., & Williams, J.W. Current challenges in educating for parenthood. *Family Relations*, October 1981, *30*(4), 579-584.

Katzman, N. Television soap operas: What's been going on anyway? *Public Opinion Quarterly*, 1979, 200-212.

Kirby, D. The Mathtech research on adolescent sexuality education programs. *SIECUS Report*, 1983, *12*, (1), 11-12, 21-22.

Kirby, D., Alter, J., & Scales, P. *An analysis of U.S. sex education programs and evaluation methods*. Springfield, VA: National Technical Information Service, 1979.

Kneale, D. Weirder is better in the red-hot land of rock videos. *The Wall Street Journal*, October 1983, *1*, 17.

Kohlberg, L. Moral stages and sex education. In M.S. Calderone (Ed.), *Sexuality and human values*. New York: Association Press, 1974.

Liebert, R., Sprafkin, J., & Davidson, E. *The early window effects of television on children and youth* (2nd ed.). New York: Pergamon Press, 1982.

Lowry, D., Love, G., & Kirby, M. Sex on the soap operas: Patterns of intimacy. *Journal of Communication*, Summer 1981, 90-96.

Mace, D. The long, long trail from information-giving to behavioral change. *Family Relations*, 1981, *30*, 599-606.

Miller, M., & Reeves, B. Dramatic TV content and children's sex-role stereotype. *Journal of Broadcasting*, Winter 1976, *20*(1), 35-50.

National Federation for Decency. *Sex on television*. Tupelo, MS: 1977.

National Institute of Mental Health. *Television and behavior: Ten years of scientific progress and implications for the eighties* (DHHS Publication No. ADM 82-1195). Washington, DC: U.S. Government Printing Office, 1982.

Otto, H.A. (Ed.), *The new sexuality*. Palo Alto, CA: Science & Behavior Books, 1971.

Penland, L. Sex education in 1900, 1940, and 1980: An historical sketch. *Journal of School Health*, April 1981, 305-309.

Pocs, O., & Godow, A.G. Can students view parents as sexual beings? *The Family Coordinator*, 1977, *26*(1), 31-36.

Roberts, E.J., & Holt, S.A. TV's sexual lessons. In J. Fireman (Ed.), *The television book*. New York: Workman Publishing Co., 1977.

Roberts, E.J., Kline, D., & Gagnon, J. *Family life and sexual learning*. Cambridge, MA: Cambridge University, 1978.

Scales, P. How we guarantee the ineffectiveness of sex education. *SIECUS Report*, March 1978, *6*, 1-3.

Scales, P. Sex education in the '70s and '80s: Accomplishments, obstacles and emerging issues. *Family Relations*, 1981, *30*, 557-566.

Scales, P. Sense and nonsense about sexuality education: A rejoinder to the Shornacks' critical view. *Family Relations*, April 1982, *32*, 287-295.

Silverman, L., Sprafkin, J., & Rubinstein, E. Physical contact and sexual behavior on prime-time TV. *Journal of Communication*, Winter 1979, 33-43.

Sprafkin, J.N., & Silverman, L.T. Update: Physically intimate and sexual behavior on prime-time television: 1978-79. *Journal of Communications*, 1981, *31*(1), 34-40.

Superintendent of Documents. *Social and economic characteristics of American children and youth*. Series P-23, 114. Washington: U.S. Government Printing Office, 1980.

Thornburg, H. Adolescent sources of information on sex. *Journal of School Health*, April 1981, 274-277.

Visher, E., & Visher, J. *Step-families: A guide to working with step-parents and step-children*. New York: Brunner/Mazel, 1979.

Waters, H.F. Life according to TV. *Newsweek*, December 1982, *6*, 136-140.

Youth values project. Susan Ross (Project Director), New York: States Communities Aid Association, 1978.

Zelnick, M., & Kantner, J. Sexual and contraceptive experience of young, unmarried women in the United States, 1976 and 1971. *Family Planning Perspectives*, 1977, *9*(2), 55-71.

DON'T LET SEX MYTHS HURT YOUR MARRIAGE

We may have had a "sexual revolution," but there's still lots of misinformation around—and, say Masters and Johnson, it can harm even a good marriage. Now this renowned husband-and-wife team separates the facts from the fiction.

An Interview With Masters and Johnson

JANE GASSNER PATRICK

Jane Gassner Patrick is a freelance writer who specializes in psychosexual subjects.

Twenty years ago a landmark book was published that dramatically altered the way we think, feel and behave sexually. *Human Sexual Response* (Little, Brown), by William I. Masters, M.D., and Virginia E. Johnson, exploded commonly held beliefs and made known new facts that enabled men and women to understand and feel more comfortable about their sexuality. At the time, it was believed that their research was going to usher in a new age in which openness and understanding about sex would replace secrecy and ignorance.

Yet, despite all that has been written and said about sex in the last 20 years, Masters and Johnson continue to find that a major cause of sexual problems between husbands and wives is a blind acceptance of misinformation. Here they explain how the most widely believed myths can damage a happy sex life.

MYTH: Women are less interested in sex than men.
TRUTH: "A woman has an infinitely greater physiological capacity to respond to sexual stimulation than a man does," say Masters and Johnson. Moreover, given good health and enough time and energy, women either equal or exceed men in their physical desire for sex. However, women have not been encouraged to make sex a priority. Women generally have so many more daily responsibilities than men—taking care of the children, preparing the meals and, often, going out to work—that sheer exhaustion might mean women want sex less often because they simply do not have the energy or time for it.

Why is this myth so pervasive? It has almost everything to do with our social conditioning. Women have not been taught to fulfill their sexual potential the way men have. Girls are encouraged to ignore or repress their sexual feelings, while boys are encouraged to express them. Even as enlightened adults, many women find it difficult to overcome the initial conditioning that sex should not be important to them.

MYTH: The harder you work at your sex life, the better it will be.
TRUTH: There is nothing further from the truth. If you try to work at sex, you'll be unable to truly participate in it. If you're busy thinking about how you should be moving, where you should be touching, what your partner is feeling, you will feel little yourself. "The best sex," say Masters and Johnson, "occurs when you are totally immersed in the moment, with no distractions, be they physical or mental."

MYTH: Sex gets boring with the same partner year after year.
TRUTH: Sexual boredom is the unavoidable result of *not* knowing your partner well enough, of investing too little of yourself and too little in the relationship. Most couples develop a kind of sexual script that they follow every time they make love. This tightly structured routine generally evolves out of knowing the easiest ways to give each other pleasure. But when sex becomes routine, instead of inventive, it gets boring. Who can look forward to sex when both partners know exactly when and how it's going to happen?

Masters and Johnson believe that the creativity and freshness that make for good sex with a lifelong partner come from both partners allowing their feelings to be expressed at the moment. If you're feeling sad or depressed, you may make love more slowly, with much more holding and touching. When you're joyful or celebrating, you may be very playful, full of laughter and teasing. And when you just want sexual release, you may be much more direct in your passion. Whatever your mood, if you and your partner are open and allow your feelings to affect how you make love, sex can be different each time.

MYTH: Good sex happens when each person takes responsibility for his or her partner's pleasure.
TRUTH: "Sex," they point out, "is something two people do *with* each other." You can't be totally responsible for another person's satisfaction. However, they add, you can add to your partner's pleasure by responding to the needs and desires he or she communicates to you.

5. SEXUALITY THROUGH THE LIFE CYCLE: Sex in and out of Marriage

MYTH: Men hit their sexual peak at 18 and go downhill from then on.
TRUTH: Most men are in top physiological form when they're about 18. Testosterone, the male hormone that influences sexual excitement, is usually at peak production then. However, a man's sexuality doesn't depend on physiology alone. Psychological and social stimulation are major factors as well.

How a man feels about himself, his partner and about sex in general has a greater influence on his sexual interest and capability than how efficiently his body responds to stimulation.

Thus, say Masters and Johnson, the older man who is in good health, who understands his sexuality and who has an interested and interesting partner may be at a higher peak of his sexual powers than the 18-year-old who experiences sex merely as a physical act.

MYTH: Independent women make their men impotent.
TRUTH: From the male point of view, the most stimulating partner is one who is sexually active. The woman who is more likely to make her man impotent is the dependent one who does nothing sexually for herself or for him other than to be available.

MYTH: Sex should always be a passionate, physical and emotional communion between two people.
TRUTH: There are two myths here—that the best sex is some cosmic kind of union and that this cosmic union must be the goal every time we make love. The truth is that only in fiction is sex always a total, passionate, physical and emotional communion between two people. In real life, it's wild, mild, a peak experience, a hand-holding comfort; it's good, bad, indifferent and all points in between.

To feel inadequate because our own lovemaking doesn't match up to the drama on the screen or in the book actually denies us the pleasure of what we *did* experience. Equally important, it dooms us to constant feelings of inadequacy and failure. "Making the goal of sex a total emotional communion is, in itself, a distraction," say Masters and Johnson. "It can almost guarantee that that kind of experience will not happen."

MYTH: Sex should always be spontaneous.
TRUTH: It is a fantasy to assume that to be truly romantic sex must "just happen," that we must be swept away by our desires and that to plan for sex is cold-blooded. But as all too many couples are now discovering, today's busy schedules allow almost no time for lovemaking. "If you insist on sex being spontaneous," Masters and Johnson point out, "chances are you're going to find your sex life dwindling away to nothing."

Masters and Johnson don't say you should plan sex: That's too contrived. But they do advocate planning time for sex. They compare it to planning for a picnic. If you want to go on a picnic, you must plan a time for it to take place and you must prepare the food you'll take with you. But once you're on the picnic, you just let the good times happen. Once you've made time for making love, you can allow the pleasure to emerge out of the moment.

Sexual Passages

The most important factor in sustaining sexual desire is regular sexual activity. The more sex a woman has, the more she'll maintain her sexual fitness.

Jane Fonda

with Mignon McCarthy

From a purely physical perspective, a woman's sexual desire should *increase* as she ages. And, indeed, there is mounting evidence to support the fact that for most women there *is* more sexual interest, pleasure, and capacity for orgasm. In fact, for many the desire for and enjoyment of sex appear to rise continuously into our middle years and remain stable from that time on. This, of course, overthrows the old concept that sexuality somehow disappears as we get older.

A whole constellation of factors contributes to a heightened sexual response. Sexual conflicts may be resolved, releasing the hold that old inhibitions may have had on our sensuality. Energies previously tied to child rearing are more available for opening, renewing, or deepening intimacies with a partner, and a mature woman is likely to give more priority to lovemaking in all its dimensions.

Desire Killers

But desire isn't static. It varies from day to day. It can come and go in different periods in your life. More often, though, we become sexually inactive because problems have intervened and need to be addressed—including:

● Boredom from sexual "routine."
● Too much food or drink (either can be a desire killer).
● *Stress*—money worries or excessive work demands.

● Fear of not measuring up to the new "sexual Olympics" or problems with self-esteem in regard to aging.
● Medication, such as tranquilizers, antihypertensives for high blood pressure, and antihistamines for allergies.

However, the most important factor in sustaining sexual desire is regular sexual activity. The more sex a woman has, the more she'll maintain her sexual fitness as well.

Physical Changes

Following menopause, a number of physical changes begin to occur as a result of our bodies' new hormonal environment, as well as the aging process in general. None of these changes, however, need alter our status as sexual beings. Our lowered production of estrogen means subtle alterations in the reproductive tissues—how subtle depends largely on genetics, good health, and the general state of our physical and sexual fitness. The changes come about gradually and differently for each woman.

Overall, there is a small decrease in the size of both the internal and external sexual organs—the vagina, uterus, and the ovaries, as well as the inner and outer vaginal lips and the clitoral hood—though there is no loss of sensation in the clitoris. Lubrication during sexual activity may take longer. And the walls of the vagina may generally become smoother, thinner, less moist, and less elastic. During lovemaking, if you need to add to your body's own ability to lubricate, there are a variety of good products to use. *Vegetable and fruit oils* are among the best. Try coconut, apricot kernel, safflower, and even baby oil. *Vitamin E* oil, which you can take from a vitamin E capsule, is a good healer in between times of sexual activity for fragile vaginal tissues that may have torn, and it also relieves dryness.

Some women also have a tendency toward more urinary or vaginal infections, but there are several natural solutions. For a urinary infection, drink lots of *water* to flush bacteria out of the urinary tract. Drinking lots of *cranberry juice* can also help to prevent bothersome bacteria and other microorganisms from flourishing. It's also a good idea to empty your bladder immediately after sex to keep bacteria from entering the urethra. For vaginal infections many women report success treating the vagina with *yogurt*. The plain lactobacillus acidophilus kind is best. (Ask about it at your health food store.) You can use one to two tablespoons in warm douche water, or several teaspoons of yogurt inserted with a vaginal-medication applicator, foam applicator, or tampon container, allowing it to remain in the vagina for a few minutes.

Last, the pelvic muscles that contain and support the vagina and its surrounding organs may slacken. These muscles are hormone-sensitive, as well as inactivi-

From *New Woman*, March 1986, pp. 92, 94, 95. Copyright © 1984 by Jane Fonda. Reprinted by permission of Simon & Schuster, Inc.

ty-sensitive. This muscular relaxation may also be the result of having given birth. One of the most common results of a loss of pelvic muscle tone is the occasional, uncontrolled loss of a little urine. Referred to as urinary or stress incontinence, this is caused by a relaxation of the muscles around the neck of the bladder. Some women may have already encountered this during or after pregnancy. As many as half of all mid-life and older women now experience urinary incontinence, most frequently while coughing, sneezing, lifting, or laughing, and it's twice as common in women as in men. But such urinary leakage is not inevitable, even though the urinary tract thins with age as does the vagina. Proper exercise, discussed later in this section, is a strong preventive.

All of these changes are possibilities. Women may have a reluctance to talk about these physical changes and may be unaware of their connection to menopause—partly accounting for our relative lack of information. We do know that these pelvic changes can begin anytime in the ten years following the last menstruation and as early as the first year.

The strong belief among authorities now is that sexual activity, defined in its broadest sense, can make a difference in significantly slowing or even postponing the normal, but modifiable, sexual aging process.

Arousal and Orgasm

In sexual activity, as we get older, men take longer to reach orgasm and orgasms are spaced more widely apart, unlike the process for women, whose ability to experience multiple orgasms seems to increase with age (!). If men don't understand or expect these changes of pace, they can develop a tremendous anxiety over "performance" and a fear of impotence. But actually this slowing down contains the wonderful possibility of a more neatly matched sexual relationship with women. More time is usually needed by both men and women for sex in each of its phases, which means more time for tender and imaginative lovemaking. The *process* of lovemaking itself can become more important than the *out-*

come, and there is more room for emotional closeness to grow as well. When orgasm does occur, there is a faster loss of erection, a smaller volume and less force to the ejaculation, and over time there are fewer sperm and still fewer that are capable of fertilizing an egg—though most men remain fertile throughout their lifetimes. None of the changes need mean a lessening of sensual pleasure or sexual satisfaction.

Sexual Fitness

Most of us are unaware of the muscle deep in our pelvic area, much less the need to exercise it.

The pubococcygeus (pew-bo-cox-uh-*gee*-us), or PC muscle, is a broad band of tissue that stretches like a taut hammock from the pubic bone in front to the tailbone or coccyx in back. Sometimes called "the love muscle," it supports all of the internal pelvic organs and includes the muscles of the vagina. And like any muscle group, this one needs to be kept strong.

If this muscle is not exercised, in both women and men, it will, like any muscle, weaken and eventually atrophy. A lack of PC muscle tone may cause urinary incontinence. It can also mean the lessening of sensitivity in the vagina and hence the lessening of sexual pleasure. Decreased sensation can also be caused if the PC muscle is held in a chronically tense state. *Weak* muscles and *tense* muscles both can inhibit strong active pelvic movement and block the flow of physical and even emotional feelings that are part of healthy sexual release and activity.

Regular exercise of the PC muscle is a way to reverse all of this. With conditioning, the entire pelvic area will become stronger, more limber, and less tense. It will allow a greater flow of blood to the genitals, which is so important for orgasm. The muscles themselves become healthy and toned so you will have a healthy vagina, more pleasure in sex, firm placement of the pelvic organs, and an end to urinary troubles. It also means better posture and a stronger lower back.

Sexual intercourse exercises the PC muscle naturally. There are also specific exercises that similarly work this muscle.

The PC Exercise

To *improve* your PC muscle tone, squeeze and release the PC muscle 200 times a day in slow movements and in rapid movements.

1. The Slow Squeeze. Squeeze for ten seconds, relax for ten seconds. Do ten times. (Begin, if you can, with three seconds and gradually build to ten seconds. Always be sure the duration of your release equals the duration of your contraction.)

2. The Quick Squeeze. Squeeze and relax the PC muscle as rapidly as you can. Do for two minutes. (Begin with as many seconds as you can and gradually build up to two minutes.)

3. Make Your Personal Plan. Design whatever plan will work best for you that insures you will have done a total of 200 contractions by the end of the day.

4. Breathe Normally during the exercises.

The PC exercise can be done spontaneously anytime—driving the car, watching TV, sitting at your desk, or relaxing in bed.

It's important to begin gradually but to do the exercises regularly. In a short time, you'll notice how much better you've become at identifying and controlling the muscle during the exercises.

In the 1940's, the physician Arnold Kegel developed a series of exercises as a nonsurgical alternative for urinary incontinence. These have proven a success in slowing the unwanted flow of urine—and, in addition, some women have reported experiencing orgasm for the first time after doing the exercises!

The Kegel exercises, as they are called today, involve the concentrated contraction and release of the PC muscle, which you can activate when you squeeze your vagina as though trying to interrupt a flow of urine. With good muscle tone and good muscle control, you will be able to start and stop your flow of urine at will. If you place your finger inside your vagina to test yourself, you will be able to feel the muscle tighten.

Some Hard (and Soft) Facts About Sex and Aging

Susan Squires

There are two tragedies in a man's life. The first time he can't do it twice . . . and the second time he can't do it once. As a man ages, the joke may not seem so funny. But new evidence suggests that the best predictor of how active your sex life will be later is how active it is now. Just remember that sex at 50 will be somewhat different from sex at 20.

For one thing, it will take slightly longer to achieve an erection, you may need more direct manual stimulation to do so, and you won't get as hard, probably due to a reduction in blood supply to the penis. (Erection is simply a reflex phenomenon that results from blood surging through millions of tiny blood vessels into the corpora cavernosa, the two shafts that provide support for the penis.)

Of course, there are a few other downers that come with aging. You can expect the intensity of orgasm and the amount of semen to decrease. In the mid-thirties, there's a gradual decline in sperm count. (For most men, however, this has no effect on fathering children.) You'll feel less of a physical need to ejaculate, and may not do so every time you have sex. The refractory period—the time between ejaculations—will lengthen.

You can even study the charts that compare, decade to decade, the "average" number of orgasms (104 per year at age 20, 121 at 30 and 52 at 50) or the "average" angle of tumescence (the angle of erection is 20 percent above horizontal at 50).

But "averages" have little to do with individuals. All you really need to know when it comes to sex and aging is that, very gradually, you'll begin to slow down. By age 20, a man is having sex on an average of three times a week, even though, biologically, he's passed his sexual peak. By 30, the average is two and a half times a week; by 40, less than twice weekly; and by age 50, one and a half times. Rest assured, this has little effect on your sexual performance. Although it will take longer to reach orgasm, you will probably sustain an erection longer, resulting in more pleasure for both you and your partner.

This physiological slowdown usually begins after age 40, sometimes even well into the fifties. Under 40, it's possible that certain medical problems—such as diabetes, infections, anemia, nutritional deficiencies, overindulgence in alcohol or adverse drug reactions—can affect your sexual performance. But as a general rule, the younger you are, the more likely that sexual problems stem from a psychological cause.

What does begin to change in your twenties and thirties is not the state of your love muscle but the state of your mind. "You begin to move from the sexual self-involvement of adolescence and early adulthood to a greater interest in the communicative part of sex," says Myrna Lewis, coauthor of *Love and Sex After Forty* and an expert on the psychological effects of aging on sexuality.

One 37-year-old single man says he has yet to notice any physiological differences, but his feelings about sex have altered over the past ten to fifteen years. "I don't crave conquest the way I used to," he says. "That's the good news—I'm less insecure, so I don't need to convince myself that women want to make love to me, and I don't have to kill myself trying to satisfy someone just to get her to tell me how great I am. The bad news is I get bored more easily with the physical act unless I'm really in love."

Your fantasies also begin to change. Leonard Giambra, Ph.D., a psychologist at the National Institute on Aging's Gerontology Research Center in Baltimore, is the author of a series of recent studies on daydreams. The majority of his subjects were middle- and upper-middle-class, college-educated men and women. Though Giambra wasn't concerned with the specific content of daydreams, he did examine what categories dominated in different age groups.

For men aged 17 to 23, sexual daydreaming was number one. From 24 to 29, "problem-solving" daydreaming tied with sex for first place. In the thirties, problem-solving stayed at number one, while sex dropped off to second place. That's where it stayed until the sixties, when it slid into third; in the seventies, it declined to fourth. (For women, problem-solving was the top category across all age groups.)

Such mental shifts in sexual focus, which begin in the twenties, can help ready a man for the physiological slowing that occurs in the forties and fifties. As you begin to perceive that sex has something more to offer than a necessary physical release, your body prepares you for a fuller, more leisurely experience.

"You're more relaxed, and you're not as single-minded about orgasm as when you were younger," says a 44-year-old working on his second marriage. "You discover that the thrill lies in the ride as much or more than in the destination. But there's a scary transition period. I was just turning 40 when I started noticing that it was taking me longer to get an erection and I wasn't as hard. I worried that I was losing my virility entirely. But I got through that period and came to like the trade-off: less excitement, but more pleasure."

If you're not aware of the changes to come, turning 40 can be a particularly vulnerable time. "Since rumor has it that after age 40 a man is 'over the hill' sexually, many men begin to check their sexual performance for signs of wear and tear," claims Masters and Johnson's *Sex and Human Loving*. "Once a man begins to question his sexual capabilities, the odds are that he will experience difficulty getting or keeping an erection. This, of course, 'proves' the correctness of the underlying concern, and a vicious cycle is set in motion." But if you're prepared for the slight sexual slowing that usually begins in middle adulthood, you'll be less likely to misinterpret a normal change as abnormal and wind up with needless performance anxiety and other psychological problems.

An occasional component of the turning-40 period that might affect performance, according to Masters and Johnson, is sexual burnout, which affects up to 20 percent of men and women, married and single. Burnout is not simply boredom; it's a satiation with sexual routine that's characterized by physical and emotional depletion, a negative sexual self-image and a sense of hopelessness that nothing can be done to spark your libido. According to Bill Young of the Masters and Johnson institute, sexual burnout occurs when sex has been the sole form of communication for the individual or couple. Burnout usually triggers a reevaluation of

self and partner, of what you need sexually, which leads to a reawakening of the sex drive within three months to a year for the vast majority. The few who don't recover their libido remain sexually inactive on a permanent basis and are in fact probably happier being celibate, say the scientists.

But chances are you'll turn 40 and you'll realize that you're just fine. In fact, being older can even give you a distinct advantage. Your pace may be a bit more leisurely than it was when you were 17, but your capacity for sustained sexual pleasure will have deepened. So, one hopes, will your sense of humor.

Never Too Late

*SINGLE PEOPLE OVER 65 WHO ARE DATING
AND SEXUALLY ACTIVE BELIE THE NOTION THAT
PASSION AND ROMANCE ARE ONLY FOR THE YOUNG.*

KRIS BULCROFT AND MARGARET O'CONNER-RODEN

Kris Bulcroft is a sociologist at St. Olaf College in Northfield, Minnesota. Margaret O'Conner-Roden is a sociology doctoral candidate at the University of Minnesota in Minneapolis.

What is the age of love? The star-crossed lovers Romeo and Juliet were teenagers; Anthony and Cleopatra's torrid affair occurred at the prime of their health and beauty; Lady Diana Spencer was barely 20 when she married her Prince Charming. How old is too old for the sparkle in the eye and the blush in the cheek?

The message our culture often gives us is that love is only for the young and the beautiful—people over 65 are no longer interested in or suited for things such as romance and passion. Few of us imagine older couples taking an interest in the opposite sex other than for companionship—maybe a game of bridge or conversation out on the porch. But, in fact, there are quite a few older single people who not only date but are involved sexually with someone.

Statistically there are good reasons for older people to be dating. At the turn of the century only about 4 percent of the total American population was 65 years of age or older. Today that number has soared to approximately 11 percent, with the total expected to increase to about 20 percent by the year 2050. In addition, older people are living longer and staying healthier, and they are less likely than before to have children living at home. And an increasing number of divorces among the elderly is casting many of these older people back into the singles' pool. All of these factors create an expanded life stage, made up of healthy and active people looking for meaningful ways to spend their leisure.

The question of whether older people date, fall in love and behave romantically, just as the young do, occurred to us while we were observing singles' dances for older people at a senior center. We noticed a sense of anticipation, festive dress and flirtatious behavior that were strikingly familiar to us as women recently involved in the dating scene. Although our observations indicated that older people dated, when we looked for empirical research on the topic we found there was none. We concluded this was due partly to the difficulty in finding representative samples of older daters and partly to the underlying stereotype of asexual elders. So we decided to go out and talk to older daters ourselves. Once we began looking, we were surprised at the numbers of dating elders who came forward to talk to us. We compared their responses to those from earlier studies on romance and dating, in which the people were much younger.

Dating, as defined by our sample of older people, meant a committed, long-term, monogamous relationship, similar to going steady at younger ages. The vast majority of elderly daters did not approach dating with the more casual attitude of many younger single people who are "playing the field." All respondents clearly saw dating as quite distinct from friendship, although companionship was an important characteristic of over-60 dating.

One of our major findings was the similarity between how older and younger daters feel when they fall in love—what we've come to call the "sweaty palm syndrome." This includes all the physiological and psychological somersaults, such as a heightened sense of reality, perspiring hands, a feeling of awkwardness, inability to concentrate, anxiety when away from the loved one and heart palpitations. A 65-year-old man told

When they fall in love, older daters experience the same emotional somersaults, sweaty palms and beating hearts as do younger couples.

us, "Love is when you look across the room at someone and your heart goes pitty-pat." A widow, aged 72, said, "You know you're in love when the one you love is away and you feel empty." Or as a 68-year-old divorcée said, "When you fall in love at my age there's initially a kind of 'oh, gee!' feeling . . . and it's just a little scary."

We also found a similarity in how both older and younger daters defined romance. Older people were just as likely to want to participate in romantic displays such as candlelight dinners, long walks in the park and giving flowers and candy. Older men, just like younger ones, tended to equate romance with sexuality. As a 71-year-old widower told us, "You can talk about candlelight dinners and sitting in front of the fireplace, but I still think the most romantic thing I've ever done is to go to bed with her."

A major question for us was "What do older people do on dates?" The popular image may suggest a prim, card-playing couple perhaps holding hands at some senior center. We found that not only do older couples' dates include the same activities as those of younger people, but they are often far more varied and creative. In addition to traditional dates such as going to

the movies, out for pizza and to dances, older couples said they went camping, enjoyed the opera and flew to Hawaii for the weekend.

Not only was the dating behavior more varied, but the pace of the relationship was greatly accelerated in later life. People told us that there simply was "not much time for playing the field." They favored the direct, no-game-playing approach in building a relationship with a member of the opposite sex. As one elderly dater commented, "Touching people is important, and I know from watching my father and mother that you might just as well say when lunch is ready . . . and I don't mean that literally."

Sexuality was an important part of the dating relationship for most of those we spoke to, and sexual involvement tended to develop rapidly. While sexuality for these couples included intercourse, the stronger emphasis was on the nuances of sexual behavior such as hugging, kissing and touching. This physical closeness helped fulfill the intimacy needs of older people, needs that were especially important to those living alone whose sole source of human touch was often the dating partner. The intimacy provided through sex also contributed to self-

esteem by making people feel desired and needed. As one 77-year-old woman said, "Sex isn't as important when you're older, but in a way you need it more."

A major distinction we found between older and younger daters was in their attitudes toward passionate love, or what the Greeks called "the madness from the gods." Psychologists Elaine Hatfield, of the University of Hawaii in Manoa, and G. William Walster, of Los Gatos, California, have similarly defined passionate love as explosive, filled with fervor and short-lived. According to their theory of love, young people tend to equate passionate love with being in love. Once the first, intense love experience has faded, young lovers often seek a new partner.

For older daters, it is different. They have learned from experience that passionate love cannot be sustained with the same early level of intensity. But since most of them have been in marriages that lasted for decades, they also know the value of companionate love, that "steady burning fire" that not only endures but tends to grow deeper over time. As one older man put it, "Yeah, passion is nice . . . it's the frosting on the cake.

But it's her personality that's really important. The first time I was in love it was only the excitement that mattered, but now it's the friendship ... the ways we spend our time together that count."

Nonetheless, the pursuit of intimacy caused special problems for older people. Unlike younger daters, older people are faced with a lack of social cues indicating whether sexual behavior is appropriate in the dating relationship. Choosing to have a sexual relationship outside of marriage often goes against the system of values that they have

WHEN MY GIRLFRIEND SPENDS THE NIGHT SHE BRINGS HER CORDLESS PHONE, JUST IN CASE HER DAUGHTER CALLS.

followed during their entire lives.

Older couples also felt the need to hide the intimate aspects of their dating relationship because of a fear of social disapproval, creating a variety of covert behaviors. As one 63-year-old retiree said, "Yeah, my girlfriend (age 64) lives just down the hall from me ... when she spends the night she usually brings her cordless phone ... just in case her daughter calls." One 61-year-old woman told us that even though her 68-year-old boyfriend has been spending three or four nights a week at her house for the past year, she has not been able to tell her family. "I have a tendency to hide his shoes when my grandchildren are coming over."

Despite the fact that marriage

WHO'S WHO IN THE SAMPLE

For our study we interviewed 45 older people in a Midwestern metropolitan area who were widowed or divorced and had been actively dating during the past year. Fifty-four percent were men and 46 percent were women; all were white. The age of the subjects ranged from 60 to 92; the average age was 68. Although most of the group was middle-class, some were affluent and others lived solely on Social Security. Names were obtained through a variety of methods, including a membership list of a singles' club for older persons, senior citizens' centers, newspaper ads and word of mouth. The face-to-face interviews were, for the most part, conducted in the home of the older person. We asked people questions about how they met, what they did on a date, how important sexuality was in their relationship and what family and friends' reactions were to their dating.

would solve the problem of how to deal with the sexual aspects of the relationship, very few of these couples were interested in marriage. Some had assumed when they began dating that they would eventually marry but discovered as time went on that they weren't willing to give up their independence. For women especially, their divorce or widowhood marked the first time in their lives that they had been on their own. Although it was often difficult in the beginning, many discovered that they enjoyed their independence. Older people also said they didn't have the same reasons for marriage that younger people do: beginning a life together and starting a family. Another reason some elders were reluctant to marry was the possibility of deteriorating health. Many said they would not want to become a caretaker for an ill spouse.

Contrary to the popular belief that family would be protective and jealous of the dating relative, family members tended to be supportive of older couples' dating and often included the dating partner in family gatherings. The attitude that individuals have the right to personal happiness may be partially responsible for families' positive attitudes. But more importantly, many families realize that a significant other for an older person places fewer social demands on family members.

Peers also tended to be supportive, although many women reported sensing jealousy among their female friends, who were possibly unhappy because of their inability to find dating partners themselves and hurt because the dating woman didn't have as much time to spend with them.

Our interviews with older daters revealed that the dating relationship is a critical, central part of elders' lives that provides something that cannot be supplied by family or friends. As one 65-year-old man told us, "I'm very happy with life right now. I'd be lost without my dating partner. I really would."

Our initial question, "What is the age of love?" is best answered in the words of one 64-year-old woman: "I suppose that hope does spring eternal in the human breast as far as love is concerned. People are always looking for the ultimate, perfect relationship. No matter how old they are, they are looking for this thing called love."

love, sex and aging

A surprising and reassuring report.

EDWARD M. BRECHER

Science writer, social historian and investigative reporter, Edward M. Brecher, the author of Love, Sex and Aging, *also wrote the award-winning* Licit and Illicit Drugs, *a Consumer Union report published in 1972.*

The popular concept for years, nurtured by earlier Victorian attitudes and later television diets—that young is beautiful and old is, well, just respectable—has contributed to the terror of growing older, the fear of losing the capacity to love and to make love.

Surveys conducted by Dr. Alfred Kinsey a quarter of a century ago did little to alleviate these fears, for they did not reach beyond middle age. Questions such as, "At what age do men and women begin to lose interest in sex?" and, "At what age do they begin to lose their capacity for sexual enjoyment? went unanswered. Six years ago, Edward Brecher of West Cornwall was commissioned by Consumer Union to secure answers to sex-and-aging questions. Sixty-six years old at the time, Brecher had a personal as well as professional interest in the research, and in cooperation with the editors of Consumer Reports Books, he drafted and mailed 10,000 questionnaires to men and women between ages 50 and 93 all across the country. A staggering 42 percent of the surveys was returned—and the answers were as unique and individual as they were revealing. Taken together, they confirmed the heretofore unsaid: Men and women are as sexually active when they can be for as long as they want to be.

Following are highlights of the surprisingly reassuring findings, from *Love, Sex and Aging: A Consumers Union Report* (Little, Brown and Company and Consumer Reports Books, 1984).

COMING OUT OF THE CLOSET

The late humorist Sam Levinson once recalled: "When I first found out how babies were born, I couldn't believe it! To think that my mother and father would do such a thing!... My father, maybe; but my mother—never!"

It is hardly surprising that today's young people, taught to think of their parents as nonsexual even when those parents were in their 20s and 30s, continue to think of their parents (and other older people) in their 50s and beyond as *still* nonsexual.

A 58-year-old husband and father wrote to us: "It has been my experience that children in the 15-to-25-year range are horrified if not disgusted at the thought of their 45-to-60-year-old parents having intercourse." He recalled that he, too, was disgusted, decades ago, when he first realized that *his* parents were having sex—and that his wife had reacted similarly when she first realized this about *her* parents. "Something should be done—and I can't suggest what," he continued, "to convince (young people) that a married couple having intercourse in their 50s, 60s, and later is normal, natural, even beautiful, but definitely not dirty or weird or odd."

Many older people have devoted themselves to keeping the secret of their sexuality not only from their children and other young people, but from one another as well. The result is that they themselves are seriously misled about the nature and extent of sexuality in their own generation. Some of them even wonder whether their continuing sexuality is "abnormal" or "perverted." "I must be an animal to (still) desire sex," wrote a troubled 71-year-old widower.

How can such misconceptions about love and sex after 50 be corrected? Clearly, older people themselves must supply the data, demonstrating that their sexuality is no longer something to hide or be ashamed of.

"Let us silver-haired sirens out of the closet!" implored a 54-year-old divorcée. "We have a lot to 'show and tell' the world."

SEXUAL CHANGES WITH AGE

What proportion of men and women experience a decline in sexual function after the age of 50? For men, the answer is: *all men*. What's more, for most men past 50, this is not a recent phenomenon. Most of them have experienced a progressive decline ever since sexual function peaked in their early 20s, or before. This decline is visible in many ways:

- It takes most older men longer to get an erection.
- When fully erect, the penis is not as stiff as formerly.
- The erection more frequently disappears prior to orgasm.
- It takes more stimulation of the penis to reach orgasm.
- Sex more frequently terminates without orgasm.
- The refractory period (the time it takes to have another erection after orgasm) is longer.

In addition, interest in sex and desire for sex tend to decrease.

Among women, vaginal lubrication during sexual arousal is the precise physiological equivalent of male erection—and, as might be expected, the quantity of lubrication goes down as women age. The details, however, have not been worked out for vaginal lubrication. No one knows, for example, whether it takes older women longer to lubricate, or whether they more fre-

From *Connecticut Magazine*, November 1984, pp. 66-69. Based on the book, LOVE, SEX AND AGING, by Robert M. Brecher and the Editor of Consumer Reports Books. (Little, Brown and Consumer Union, 1984.)

> ## 'Let us silver-haired sirens out of the closet!
> ## We have a lot to "show and tell" the world.'

quently lose lubrication during sexual arous-al, or whether it takes more physical stimu-lation to achieve lubrication in the later years. Nor has the female "refractory pe-riod" following orgasm been studied dec-ade by decade. There is evidence of a mod-est decline in sexual interest and desire among women as among men in their 60 s and 70 s.

What is astonishing, however, is not the *decline* in sexual function. Rather, it is the high proportion of women and men who *re-tain* an interest in and an enjoyment of sex even in their 70's and 80's. The tables pro-vide the details.

TABLE A shows the proportion of men and women in the Consumers Union study who remain sexually active (either with a partner or through masturbation or both) during the decades from age 50 on. Even among those past 70, 65 percent of the wom-en and 79 percent of the men report contin-uing sexual activity.

TABLE B shows the *frequency* of sexual activity. Even among those past 70, more than half of those sexually active report sex once a week or more often.

TABLE C presents similar data for sex-ual *enjoyment*. Sixty-one percent of the sexually active women past 70 and 75 per-cent of the men continue to rate their own enjoyment of sex as "high."

Many of those who filled out the Con-sumers Union questionnaire, moreover, have refused to sit idly by as age has pro-gressively dampened their physiological responses. Instead, they have sought and found techniques for maintaining and in some cases even enhancing their sexual en-joyment despite functional losses.

SEXUAL FANTASIES

More than half of the sexually active men and women who filled out the Consumers Union questionnaire said that they sometimes, usually, or al-ways engage in fantasy during sex with a partner. Among those who masturbate, moreover, more than 75 percent of both men and women reported that they en-gage in sexual fantasy during masturba-tion.

An example is supplied by a 52-year-old husband who wrote: "I need an attrac-tive female to stimulate (arouse) me. Phys-ically, I am as fit as I was thirty years ago, while my wife has deteriorated into a pot-bellied slob. Seeing her in clothes turns me off—let alone seeing her in the nude."

He accordingly conjures up for himself a fantasy woman who is "young...long hair, pleasant voice, obvious and firm breasts (not necessarily large), firm belly and 'Oriental' navel, shapely legs...small feet. This dream creature indicates friend-liness so there is no risk of rejection. We engage in tentative touching, leading to caresses, and slowly proceed to the ulti-mate union....

"A less frequent dream: I am 'captured' by a bikini-clad maiden who proceeds to manipulate my body until I reach an agonizing ecstacy."

A 64-year-old wife wrote similarly: "The sexual side of my marriage was never very good." So she engages in fantasies like this one:

"I see myself (younger than I am) with a man who is strong and sure and tender. I see us dancing, driving, park-ing on the cliff to watch and hear the sea crashing on the rocks—always aware of each other, always reaching toward the ultimate, wondrous culmi-nation, yet prolonging the anticipation. I feel his hands gently removing my dress, my underclothes, lingering on my body, caressing me as I caress him. I feel his body against mine and desire rises, rises, filling me, filling me, and I want that moment to last forever and ever. And I dream that this time, *this* time, there will be that perfect, earth-shaking realization of sexual love. An overwhelming joy in each other, then quiet and peace and sleep in each other's arms."

An 82-year-old widow described her wish-fulfillment fantasy more briefly: "While masturbating, it's fun to pretend that the relationship is with a loved one who lives far away. Murmuring sweet

THE FOUNTAIN OF ETERNAL YOUTH

The slim young man I married
Has slowly gone to pot;
With wrinkled face and graying pate,
Slender he is not!
And when I meet a mirror,
I find a haggard crone;
I can't believe the face I see
Can really be my own!

But when we seek our bed each night,
The wrinkles melt away:
Our flesh is firm, our kisses warm,
Our ardent hearts are gay!
The Fountain of Eternal Youth
Is not so far to find:
Two things you need—a double bed,
A spouse who's true and kind!
　　　　　　　—74-year-old wife

nothings, encouraging him to hold out a bit longer—and imagining I'm holding him close at the climax."

Many of the fantasies reported by these older men and women are "reruns" of ac-tual experiences years earlier. Thus a 69-year-old husband still likes to rerun in fan-tasy "an experience with a girl when I was 37. She was fantastic in bed—a passion-ate, manipulating, hot-blooded sylph."

An 85-year-old widow recalled simi-larly that 15 years ago, when she was 70, "I had a sudden, violent love affair that lasted about three months. It remained my fantasy for over ten years!"

Many of the reruns reported, however, were not of extramarital affairs but of prior sexual encounters with one's own spouse. Thus a 67-year-old husband wrote: "It may sound unusual, but when I have [a fantasy during] sex with my wife, it in-cludes her." A special feature of these re-runs, of course, is that in the fantasy, both partners are young and fresh again. A 55-year-old wife explained: "I need to think 'sex' thoughts to get into a mood where I can get aroused and complete the sex act, including orgasm. I think back to when we were first married, were young and more attractive physically."

Men, too, have such "rejuvenation fan-tasies." One 72-year-old husband, after describing his gradual loss of sexual po-tency, added that in his fantasies "I'm young again—a straining, eager bull."

In marked contrast to such experienced fantasizers is the 66-year-old wife who wrote: "I can honestly say that I have *never* had sexual fantasies." Another wife, aged 59, asked in bewilderment, "What is a sexual fantasy?"

Many women and men who use por-nographic materials appear to fall between these extremes; they can fantasize on their own—but find pornography helpful for fantasy enrichment.

WHY SOME WIVES AND HUSBANDS STAY FAITHFUL

The religious, legal, social, and eco-nomic penalties against adultery no doubt help keep some spouses from engaging in extramarital sex. Dearth of acceptable or available partners may be another factor. But the reasons given by our respondents were for the most part much more personal; they seemed to arise directly out of the circumstances of each particular marriage.

"I cannot approve of sex outside mar-riage," wrote a wife of 54. "That is 'defil-

> 'I'm young again—a straining, eager bull,'
> says a 72-year-old husband of his fantasies.

ing' my marriage bed whether it be done by my husband or me."

A second 54-year-old wife echoed these views: "Sex is such an intimate part of our marriage, I could not help but feel the marriage diminished if either of us had sex with someone else."

A 65-year-old wife wrote: "I find my love for my husband has more depth, a stronger feeling and mellowed like rare wine. If either partner of the marriage has to seek outside for sex, then that marriage should be ended."

Other wives reported that they have remained faithful—but expressed some small regrets. A 70-year-old wife wrote: "At times I regret having known only one man sexually; but if I had my life to live over, I would probably do the same."

"I sometimes wish I had had more heterosexual experience," a 56-year-old wife wrote. "I have not done so out of loyalty to my husband but would have liked to."

A 67-year-old wife recalled: "I tried to get my husband's permission for outside sex after he could no longer function. He was shocked—and refused! I have too much respect for him, and we together have other 'fun activities'—so it isn't important. Our being together is important."

Our faithful husbands expressed a similar range of views. One wrote, at age 59, that "trust and fidelity outweigh the satisfaction of conquest and change of partners that seem so attracting." Another, 55, said: "I have a very healthy and active sex life with my wife. After being married for thirty-five years, I feel that my sex life now is better than ever before. In view of this situation, I have never found it necessary to seek activity outside my marriage."

A husband of the same age wrote: "If the husband wishes sex outside of marriage...the wife should have the same prerogative, which I doubt many men would accept. Marriage is more fruitful and fulfilling if there is no outside sex by either spouse."

A faithful 50-year-old husband said he would engage in extramarital sex if the opportunity came along: "[My] wife never was enthusiastic about sex. About five or six years ago, she began to say it was "undignified" or "like animals" or "not suitable at our age" and gradually stopped completely....Because of the above, I would feel justified in having sex with someone else, but never have—mainly because I don't know how to find a partner without fear of discovery, embarrassment, etc."

A 54-year-old husband sadly reported that his wife is not sexually aroused by his efforts. He continued:

"It has occurred to me many times to have an affair but I have never done so. My reasons for contemplating this action are (1) to prove that I am still viable sexually; (2) [to prove] that I could be attractive to another female; (3) [to prove] that my technique was adequate...; (4) to test my theory that some other woman would be more easily aroused by my sexual advances. I also fear this sort of encounter to the extent that I cannot tolerate rejection in any form. On a higher level, I firmly believe in the institution of marriage, family and all that this entails. Furthermore, my wife would not be understanding or compassionate to this sort of frailty."

WHY SOME WIVES AND HUSBANDS SEEK (AND FIND) EXTRAMARITAL SEX

We had expected to compile an anthology of reasons given by our adulterous respondents for engaging in outside sex paralleling the reasons given above for refraining. Such reasons might include a spouse who is no longer physically able to have sex, marital incompatibility, boredom with marriage, a desire for variety, a feeling that life is slipping past, and so on. Some respondents did give such reasons, but for quite a few others, adultery "just happens"

—and for still others, it arises out of a complex set of circumstances that cannot be summarized simply.

Adultery takes two markedly different forms. Many of our adulterous wives and husbands have engaged since 50 in the activity commonly known as *cheating*—sex outside marriage without the knowledge or consent of the spouse. Others have engaged in sex outside their marriage with the knowledge and sometimes with the consent of their spouse. In a few marriages, indeed, adultery is a mutual and cooperative enterprise.

A much higher proportion of husbands than of wives in our study (23 *vs.* 8 percent) reported one or more extramarital affairs since age 50. For many husbands, however, these are likely to be mere brief and casual encounters. One husband of 60, for example, said he is in love with his wife and enjoys sex with her once a week —but in addition, he has had "five or six" encounters with other women since age 50. He explains: "Sex outside marriage is exciting and fun. Makes one feel younger for a while."

A 67-year-old husband wrote: "I have been faithful to my present wife since 50 except for one occasion which more or less fell into my lap. I was anxious to see whether I was still functioning—and very pleased with the results." His partner was also married. "We both decided not to continue [due to] constant fear of being

---

QUALITY OF COMMUNICATIONS

That open, constructive communications become increasingly important during the later years of a marriage was noted by several respondents—including a 55-year-old husband, married for 35 years, who wrote: "When you are young, love is predominantly influenced by sexual activities. In later life, you still relate love to sex—but other things become more important. These things are companionship, doing things together, communicating [with] and relating to your wife."

A 70-year-old wife, married for 43 years, wrote: "[Nowadays] we travel together more, spend more evenings together at home reading, and we feel less need to entertain friends or relatives....When we were young we bought fewer books, read less and discussed what we did read with more heat and less mature judgment, it seems to me....We are more honest with each other [now] on likes and dislikes...and yet we are more considerate of each other's feelings. We really know each other better."

Communications need not always be verbal, of course—as one husband points out: "Problems of all kinds are seen through together. You have this background, and you communicate with each other by a look, a touch, a feeling."

But for some wives and husbands, nonverbal communication, however tender, is not enough. They need the communication of verbal sharing, and love withers in its absence. Wrote an unhappy wife: "I find myself at a total loss for want of anything to talk about [with my husband]. We can spend the entire evening together —he staring at the boob-tube....I reading or needlepointing—and I can't think of one word to say to him even if you paid me a dollar a word."

'I tried to get my husband's permission for outside sex after he could no longer function. He was shocked—and refused.'

found out—and it really wasn't that much fun for a long-time relationship."

When adultery is found out, of course, it sometimes leads to divorce—but not always. Nearly 250 of our wives and husbands remain married despite the fact that one spouse knows of the other's adultery. A smaller number reported that *both* wife and husband have had outside sex with each other's knowledge and consent. Half a dozen of these older couples reported engaging in "swinging": outside sex as a sort of cooperative adventure, in each other's presence or even in the same bed.

This broad spectrum of responses—ranging from wives and husbands for whom lifelong monogamy is the only acceptable lifestyle to those who accept outside sex for both partners—is a dramatic example of a theme that runs throughout our study:

All older people are not alike. No stereotype of "the aging" or "the aged" can do justice to the richly variegated patterns of life as it is actually being lived by many in their later years.

"BETTER TO WEAR OUT THAN RUST OUT"

I have been in love with the same woman for 53 years, and we have never cheated or been untrue to each other. We have complete trust in each other. The only trouble with a relationship like this is, when one of us passes on, it is going to be catastrophic for the one left behind."

So writes an 80-year-old husband of his 75-year-old wife. Asked what he regretted in his life, he reached back 60 years to recall his one and only encounter with a prostitute. "It was the most disgusting sexual experience I ever had." He added, however, that if he hadn't had that experience, "I wouldn't know how disgusting it could be."

Both he and his wife reported that they have no intimate friends and no desire to make new friends; they are too busy and hardly ever lonely. Both said that they are currently in love—with one another, of course.

"Participating in sex interests me only with my wife," the husband stated. They have sex about once a week; the husband says he reaches orgasm "almost always." His wife confirmed this, adding that she reaches orgasm "every time." She continued:

"Love in the later years is an enduring love—not the great passionate love of the teens but a greater love. You enjoy the knowledge that you are loved and wanted, that you are still beautiful to your husband. You have shared happiness, sorrows, death—watching your sons leave for the wars, seeing your friends grow old and feeble, then dying. You hold out your hand and your husband clasps it, then draws you near. Sleeping close together.

Having sex whenever you want...."

The husband summed up:

"My wife and I both believe that keeping active sexually delays the aging process. Neither of us is troubled with false modesty....We keep our interest alive by a great deal of caressing and fondling.... We feel it is much better to wear out than to rust out."

TABLE A
PROPORTION OF MEN AND WOMEN WHO REMAIN SEXUALLY ACTIVE (WITH A PARTNER OR ALONE) AFTER AGE 50

	In their 50s	In their 60s	Age 70 and older
WOMEN	93%	81%	65%
MEN	98%	91%	79%

TABLE B
FREQUENCY OF SEX (WITH A PARTNER OR ALONE) AMONG SEXUALLY ACTIVE MEN AND WOMEN AFTER AGE 50

	In their 50s	In their 60s	Age 70 and older
WOMEN Sex at least once a week	73%	63%	50%
MEN Sex at least once a week	90%	73%	58%

TABLE C
ENJOYMENT OF SEX BY SEXUALLY ACTIVE MEN AND WOMEN AFTER AGE 50

	In their 50s	In their 60s	Age 70 and older
WOMEN High enjoyment of sex	71%	65%	61%
MEN High enjoyment of sex	90%	86%	75%

Old/New Sexual Concerns

- Sexual Orientation (Articles 44-45)
- Sexual Abuse and Violence (Articles 46-51)
- Focus: More AIDS (Articles 52-55)

The final section deals with several topics that are of interest or concern for different reasons. In one respect, however, these topics have a common denominator: They have all recently emerged in the public's awareness as "social issues." Unfortunately, public awareness of issues is often a fertile ground for misinformation and misperceptions. Recognizing this, it is the overall goal of this section to provide for the reader some objective insights into pressing sexual concerns.

The first article on *Sexual Orientation* deals with lesbian affairs. The author points out that most people are not entirely heterosexual or homosexual, but are somewhere in between, and suggests that women having lesbian affairs is not an uncommon occurrence. The next article shows the widespread existence of homophobia, even on college campuses across the nation.

Sexual abuse and violence is another topic of ongoing concern. Most commonly—but not exclusively—it is directed toward women and children. These acts can be especially pernicious when an acquaintance, a relative, or a parent is involved. The trust that may have existed is destroyed and the relationship may be destroyed beyond repair. The psychological scars may last for years and may not heal without professional help.

Some of the most devastating and flagrant violations of individual sexual and personal integrity arise from the misuse of sex as a means of humiliation and violence. Such is the case of rape. Public awareness of the threat and incidence of rape, for the present, may best be directed toward preventive measures and avoidance of potentially vulnerable situations. It must be emphasized that rape is not a sex act; it is a crime of violence.

Incest and the sexual abuse of children have been receiving widespread public attention only recently, even though the problems have existed for centuries. These instances of abuse are not easy to define or determine since they too are subject to individual interpretation. Revelations by several nationally known females of their experiences as children have kept this topic in the news. Now, researchers are taking a closer look at this problem and finding that it is much more widespread than most people suspected. The majority of the victims of child sexual abuse state that no other event had more impact on their life. Child sexual abuse has been identified as the "hurt that keeps hurting," at least psychologically, even in adulthood.

Sexual Abuse and Violence begins with an article on date rape among college students—a phenomenon that may be more dangerous to women than walking through dark alleys. The next article takes a look at rape's aftereffects on women's sexual functioning.

The last half of this subsection deals with child abuse in its many forms. Meredith Maran's article deals specifically with incest and provides some characteristics of the offenders, many of which are quite surprising and unexpected. The remaining three articles focus on sexual abuse, prostitution, and pornography. It is pointed out that the latter two practices are growing and have become very lucrative fields, always involving child abuse in one form or another.

The focus topic of this edition again deals with Acquired Immune Deficiency Syndrome (AIDS). AIDS has been a very prominent topic in the media during the past two years, and it is currently the focus of a great deal of emotional debate. Its causes and origins are examined in this section. Also discussed are how one gets AIDS, what the chances are of getting it, and how AIDS victims are being treated—medically and socially. The first article gives the facts about AIDS. The next focuses on particular dangers to the college student. The last two articles present a symposium of national experts and information about drugs which may hold answers to the cure or prevention of AIDS.

The articles in this section have been selected for the purpose of providing objective insights into some of the ongoing concerns related to sex and sexuality. Clearly, social awareness regarding these issues is changing. Hopefully, in the future, our society will find more humane ways of perceiving and more effective ways of dealing with these continuing sexual and social concerns.

Looking Ahead: Challenge Questions

Why do so many individuals in American society experience homophobia? Does the negative attitude toward homosexuals permeate most of our social institutions?

Is date or acquaintance rape a problem for many college women? What are some of its causes and what

YOU CAN'T LIVE ON HOPE.

relationship changes may prevent it? What are some long-lasting effects of rape?

What are some of the main problems for parents, for society, and for the victims of child sexual abuse? What are some solutions to combat this problem? What can make incest even worse than other types of sexual abuse?

In general, how has society reacted to the discovery and spread of AIDS? Will the existence of AIDS change the way people think about sex and express themselves sexually? How?

How are AIDS and STDs changing the sexual practices among people, especially college students?

Are there some medical findings that suggest an improvement in the AIDS crisis? What suggestions do you have for future sexuality until AIDS has been conquered?

Women Who Have Lesbian Affairs

You and a pretty girlfriend are gabbing, laughing . . . then suddenly somebody is *kissing* somebody. Not possible, you say? Listen to these stories from women who stumbled innocently into surprisingly *delicious* same-sex liaisons!

Kiki Olson

When Anne Marie's divorce became final, she used the settlement money to realize a long-cherished dream—her own glittery gourmet shop. She hired Judy, a bright business-school grad to help her manage it, and they worked side by side for weeks, accumulating inventory and arranging the wall hangings and ficus trees. Opening day was exhausting but exhilarating, and afterward, Anne Marie popped open a bottle of celebratory champagne.

"We were in the back of the shop joking about the poor little candy salesman who had a terrible crush on me," Anne Marie recalls, "when Judy took me quietly in her arms and kissed me—a gorgeous, easy, velvety kiss. I was confused, to say the least, but giddy from the Moët and strangely thrilled by her touch. When we finally closed the shop, Judy squeezed my hand and, smiling like a schoolgirl, suggested we finish the party at my house. Soon we were sitting in front of my fireplace, sipping champagne. And what followed was wonderful . . . and very, very strange.

"To begin with, I was at least a dozen years older than Judy. I was supposed to be experienced, worldly—at least that's the image I've always tried to project. Judy was just out of college, a baby, yet she was the one who took the lead, urging me to relax, brushing her lips against my skin. I can't say *we* made love. She made love to *me*, kissing and caressing every inch of my body. She knew, without my having to tell her, that I'd never had an experience like this before. After-

ward, we fell asleep holding hands like children.

"The next morning, I tried to put the incident out of my mind. I was angry with myself for going to bed with an employee, but mostly I was shocked and worried that I'd taken a woman as a lover—and enjoyed it so much. My God, I thought, driving to work—am I a lesbian? Have I always been one and just never known?"

Twenty years ago, the Kinsey Institute of Sex Research estimated that some 12 percent of women had had a lesbian affair. Today, that number is undoubtedly higher. But while many women may share Anne Marie's guilty worries, psychologists hold that one—or even several—gay affairs don't establish a homosexual identity.

"It's much easier for a woman to slip in and out of same-sex relationships than it is for a man," says Matti K. Gershenfeld, president of the Couples Learning Center in Philadelphia and adjunct professor at Temple University. "Easier because it's always been acceptable for women to hug and kiss each other, stroll arm and arm down the street, or share dressing rooms. Men can't be physically close in these ways—with women it's considered 'sisterly.' "

Should that closeness drift into a sexual attraction, it doesn't necessarily mean a woman is lesbian. "If a woman has a continual attraction to other women, she may certainly be considered bisexual," Gershenfeld states. "But if she's had thirty affairs with men in her lifetime and

three with women, she's by and large a heterosexual."

Maddi-Jane Sobel, a clinical social worker in private practice in Philadelphia, agrees, adding that women who find themselves in lesbian relationships are usually looking for a different kind of love and not just a sexual adventure. "Often, they're basically heterosexual women who haven't been able to get men to give them the love and attention they need. Unfortunately, most men still can't be fully nurturing partners."

Anne Marie's affair continued, and so did the special gratification it brought. "Judy and I had drifted into having sex once a week, and it was the warmest, most comfortable of relationships. I never felt I had to look my best or be incessantly 'on' or constantly cheerful—attitudes that had tended to mark my relationships with men. I began to wonder—had I *always* been lesbian and simply been lying to myself? Finally Judy and I sat up one night and talked it all out.

"Judy *was* gay, had been since her teens—her sexual commitment to women was total—and mine, I realized, was not. My affair with Judy had been a sort of lucky 'accident.' I'd been hungry for love and caring, and she'd been *there*, willing to provide it.

"Judy and I didn't make love that night, or ever again. Shortly afterward, she left to take a job in another state. And I began going out with men—nobody special, but I'm having fun. The odd thing is how much I learned from Judy. She taught me I can be myself—not always charming or well turned out—and still be deserving of love."

Often, women involved in a lesbian relationship see it as a "rest stop" between heterosexual entanglements. For them, the relationship is less sexually compelling than it is warmly reassuring. Their "sisterly" arrangement affords an opportunity to sort out complicated—and perhaps negative—feelings toward men. Elaine, a trim, attractive magazine editor, explains her affair with an old girlfriend this way.

"I was mired in a destructive relationship and a dead-end job, and I just felt trapped," she says. "I needed to jettison everything—so I left the man, quit my job, and flew off to visit my old college roommate, Nancy. She had a terrific public-relations job in London and a darling little flat, and wasn't particularly involved with anyone either. We were thrilled to see each other and settled into a relaxed, easygoing routine—rather like a long pajama party. We'd stay up late watching old movies and making popcorn and giggling.

"Well, one night there wasn't anything on the telly, and the weather was too rainy and discouraging for us to want to go out. We were talking about sex, and Nancy asked me if I'd ever tried a vibrator. When I confessed I hadn't, she smiled and got hers out—it was very sophisticated, with loads of attachments—and asked me to lie back on the couch, loosen my robe, and relax. It was fantastic! Then it was my turn to satisfy her. After that, we just fell into each other's arms and made love all night."

Although her affair continued for several weeks, Elaine never worried that she might "secretly" be gay. "Nancy and I both knew it had been just for fun, just a lark. Really, it didn't feel that different from the camaraderie of high-school days—you know, when young girls get together to discuss bra sizes or what they did on dates. True, we were both a little teary at the airport when I finally decided to come home—but we also knew we'd go right back to dating men.

"I'm in a good relationship with a man now, but if the opportunity comes along to have a woman lover—and it all feels as right as it did in London—I wouldn't turn away from it."

When Matti Gershenfeld of the Couples Learning Center was told about Elaine's experience, she found nothing surprising in it. "The right person at the right time can trigger homosexual desires," Gershenfeld explained. "Most people aren't totally homosexual or heterosexual. They're somewhere in between." Adds Judith Sills, a Philadelphia clinical psychologist and author of *How to Stop Looking for Someone Perfect*

and Find Someone to Love, "Freud believed that we are all born *pansexual*—capable of finding stimulation from a wide variety of experiences. It's just a matter of whether or not we act on diverse sexual impulses."

Not all women are left unscathed by a venture into lesbian sex. It must be remembered that this is a sort of activity society does not condone and that being discovered can lead to unpleasant consequences. Or so Laura, a part-time art teacher married to a wealthy investment banker, found out.

"My husband, Walter, has been blatantly unfaithful to me for years," Laura explains. "Everyone—friends, neighbors, even employees—has heard him boast about his conquests. The children are the only reason, really, that I've stayed with him.

"Over the years, I'd gotten into the habit of confiding in Barbara, the wife of Walter's partner (another disgraceful philanderer). One day we were crying on each other's shoulders, just as we always did, but somehow the hugs of consolation turned into passionate embraces. And even though we were both hesitant and shy, we finally became lovers. For a few months, we were very happy. Then Walter came back early from a business trip and found us in bed together.

"There was no explaining away what had been going on, since Barbara and I were both naked. Shocked and embarrassed, we hid ourselves under the sheets. But Walter was delighted and began to undress. He wanted a threesome! Whatever good, loving feelings Barbara and I had shared suddenly seemed dirty. I screamed at Walter to get out, Barbara began to cry, and the next few minutes were full of shouting and slamming doors and tearful torrents.

"I called Barbara the next day, but our conversation was halting and strained. We both knew that whatever we had had together was lost. I'm heartsick over what happened and angry at myself—I've only given Walter more ammunition to humiliate me with. Now I'm afraid to *ever* leave, because he'll bring Barbara's name up in court and try to get custody of the children. I feel trapped and guilty and *so* unhappy."

For other women, woman-love brings a guiltless pleasure. It's an opportunity to discover—and revel in—long-buried desires. Harriet, an energetic thirty-seven-year-old advertising executive, is one woman who claims that her peccadilloes with women are unfettered by guilt.

Now on her second marriage, she admits, "I've always needed a lot of sex—both flirting and the occasional full-fledged affairs—but in the last few

years, I've found myself wondering, 'Where have all the men gone?' Then I realized they were all chasing younger women! I missed the thrill of the chase and the glamour of seduction. Certainly I didn't feel ready to retire—thrills and glamour were still definitely my thing.

"Then one night I was at a party my husband's boss was giving when I began chatting with Alice, a beautifully stylish woman about my own age. We'd gone into the powder room together, and I was just putting on fresh lipstick when she took my hand and said, 'Before you do that . . . ,' and kissed me, full on the mouth. It felt wonderful—I think the naughtiness of that kiss only made it that much more exciting. She invited me to her house the next day for tea, and we ended up making love on her silk chaise longue. I've *always* enjoyed sex—but no one was ever as sensitive to every nuance, every texture as Alice was. It was like discovering a whole new world."

Harriet says she soon found herself involved in a fascinating subculture of married and divorced women who were having gay affairs. What motivated these dalliances? Harriet explains: "There's the excitement of doing something a bit risqué and daring, along with the ego gratification that comes when someone finds you irresistible. Also, these affairs are curiously relaxing, partly because you're with another woman but mainly because you're *safe*. My husband isn't going to get jealous if he happens to see me hold Alice's hand, and if we spend hours on the phone, he'll dismiss it as a gossip fest."

Though Harriet is without guilt, she does consider herself something of a sexual pioneer. "Women," she concludes, "are beginning to finally take advantage of all the sexual options available to them, whether that means dating a younger man or going to bed with another woman. I've *loved* knowing I can be romantically involved with women. Probably I've been bisexual all my life but never had the time or opportunity to explore this side of my nature. If Alice hadn't kissed me that night, I might never have known. And I wonder how many other women are just now discovering this facet of their erotic natures.

"Alice and I were joking about this the other day. We were taking a tennis lesson with a group of girls down at the club, and the pro was a handsome, beautifully built young man—every woman there wanted to grab him up and drive off to the nearest motel. 'Too bad there's not enough of him to go around,' I whispered to Alice. 'Well,' she said, pressing my hand, 'at least we have each other.' We grinned at each other, slyly. And I'll bet we weren't the only women at the club exchanging that same secret smile."

HOSTILE EYES

What is behind the anger and fear triggered by homosexuality?
A report on homophobia on American campuses.

Peggy Bendet

Peggy Bendet is a reporter for The Knoxville Journal *in Tennessee.*

A chilly breeze cut through the autumn twilight as Dennis and Steve, shouldering their way out of the crowded deli, headed back across campus to their dorm. Dennis was busy buttoning his padded jacket, a thrift-shop find, so he didn't notice the young man who hurried past them into the lengthening shadows. Steve would remember later that the guy had stood behind them in line at the deli.

Dennis and Steve (not their real names) were both sophomores at a large Southeastern state university. They had been friends for a year and roommates, at that point, for just two weeks. Outgoing, tall, and lean, Dennis was a psychology major with a deep appreciation of people's differences, including his own. He loved to dress in flashy clothes that stood out as badges of nonconformity in this conservative town. Other students thought he was a little strange, but that was more than okay with Dennis: better to celebrate being different than to pretend he wasn't.

Steve, an advertising major, admired the ease with which his friend embraced life, but he couldn't quite pull off the nonchalance himself. Fair-haired and muscular, Steve emulated Dennis, but with restraint. His clothes were colorful but coordinated, and although he was friendly at parties, he couldn't just go up to a stranger and strike up a breezy conversation the way Dennis could.

As the two friends walked through the courtyard of their dorm on this night in 1984, they noticed someone leaning beside the glass doors that led to the lobby. When they reached the door, the guy

straightened up, surveyed them from head to foot, and spat out one word: "Faggots."

Steve and Dennis froze. The man merely strode through the lobby to the elevator without looking back.

"I don't even know him," Steve said, bewildered. But in his heart he knew that didn't matter. He and Dennis weren't lovers, but they were, in fact, gay. Verbal assaults weren't new to either of them.

"People always react when they find out you're gay," Dennis said later. "Even people who know you well."

But the incident would soon become more than an unprovoked insult. Over the following months, at least 20 young men in the dorm participated in a deliberate and escalating campaign of harassment. Scores of other students witnessed the abuse and did nothing either to curb it or to offer support to the victims. And no one seemed to notice that anything was wrong—no one, that is, but Steve and Dennis. This is their story.

Hostility toward lesbians and gay men has long been taken for granted by most heterosexuals as a natural response to "sick and dangerous" behavior. A decade ago, the American Psychiatric Association removed homosexuality from its list of mental disorders, but even as recently as this past June, the U.S. Supreme Court upheld state laws that deny the right of lesbians and gay adults to express themselves sexually.

However, such homophobia is beginning to be closely scrutinized by researchers who wonder why homosexuality threatens so many people so deeply.

Homophobia is defined as an irration-

al fear of homosexuals. But that description is inadequate, according to Dr. Gregory M. Herek, a psychology professor at the City University of New York (CUNY) who has written numerous articles on the subject. Fear is involved, he says, but it's not the most telling component.

"Something like agoraphobia—the fear of leaving your house or even of getting up out of your chair—that's a phobia," says Herek. "But with homophobia, you're also talking about hostility and prejudice, housing and job discrimination, and threats—even acts—of violence."

As a lecturer at Yale University, Herek last spring conducted a survey of 200 gay and lesbian students there. Ninety of the students—nearly 50 percent— reported that they'd experienced some kind of antigay harassment. A majority of the 200 said they feared for their safety on campus because of the threat of violence.

One Yale student, a lesbian, reported being followed on campus by five men in a car who told her they wanted to teach her about sex. They then graphically outlined what they wanted to do to her and what they wanted her to do to them. Another student said a group of men accosted her and a lesbian friend at a campus party and demanded that they kiss each other. A third student said that he regularly received obscene phone calls and that one time his jacket was taken from the common room and trampled in the dirt. It was a jacket he'd marked with an inverted pink triangle—the symbol homosexuals were required to wear in the Nazi death camps.

The survey's results were presented to Yale's governing body in support of a request that the school include sexual orientation in its official antidiscrimination policy, for which gay students and faculty members had been lobbying for 15 years. Last spring, the measure finally passed.

"Rule changes aren't the most effective way to deal with prejudice," comments Herek, "but they *are* an important step."

An even bigger step is education. Homophobia, for those who think homosexuality is unnatural, is often rooted in sheer ignorance. Sexuality, like skin and eye color, is not a choice. Researchers say that sexual orientation is set in place by a series of genetic and environmental cues so complex that no one understands why one person is homosexual, another heterosexual, and still another bisexual.

According to studies conducted by the Kinsey Research Institute, at any one time between 4 and 12 percent of the American population is primarily homosexual; about 50 percent is primarily heterosexual; and the rest of us fall somewhere in between.

The statistical probability of reversing any of these orientations, say experts, is zero. It's been tried. Through the centuries, homosexuals have been subjected to everything from electroshock treatment to exorcisms in attempts to "cure" them of their so-called deviant behavior. If you are heterosexual, try imagining what could possibly move you to become permanently and genuinely attracted to others of your own gender, and perhaps you'll understand why records fail to show one instance of such "cures" achieving their goal. Homosexuality is not the norm, experts say, but it *is* normal.

Even people who know this, however, experience homophobic feelings ranging from outright disgust to smug tolerance of gays as long as they keep their homosexuality out of public view. Why does homophobia seem so deep-seated? Researchers are only now beginning to piece together some answers.

Immediately after the incident in the courtyard, Steve and Dennis began finding explicit photographs of female body parts tacked up on their dorm-room door. Other times they'd come home to find condoms filled with hand cream, or globs of shampoo smeared on the doorknob. One night someone pounded on their door. When Steve answered it, he found an article about AIDS lying on the floor outside.

As fall passed into winter, each day brought some new offering from their nameless, faceless antagonists. Dennis's

natural buoyancy protected him, but Steve found his frustration building, as if he was barely holding his own in an all-too-serious game of psychological warfare. He wanted to confront someone, to stand up for himself, but Dennis talked him out of it: why ask for more trouble? For all his forthrightness, Dennis tended to extend himself only when he felt safe. And this wasn't one of those times. Reluctantly, Steve agreed to lie low.

Then, one evening in January, the situation worsened.

They were walking through the dorm lobby where students habitually hung out. Just as they reached a table full of students playing Trivial Pursuit, one of the players called out, "Faggot!"

At this point Dennis and Steve made what they later realized was a tactical error—they pretended they hadn't heard the slur. To the other guys, this just meant it was open season.

At least once a day, a group of men (but not always the same men) would eye Steve and Dennis as they walked through the lobby on their way to the elevator. Just as they passed, the men would simultaneously cough. Or they would abruptly stop talking until someone broke the heavy silence with the one-word epithet: "Faggot!" Or for variety, "Queer!"

Other times the men would turn their heads in unison to watch Steve and Dennis walk past, the two friends swallowing hard as they ran the gauntlet of hostile eyes. That little torture was the hardest to bear because it seemed to encompass everyone in the lobby. There were 500 men and women living in the dorm that year. Steve and Dennis felt that all the students knew what was happening and that their very silence was an expression of approval.

The two men started taking the stairs instead of the elevator, walking four flights up and four flights down several times a day just to avoid the lobby. When the harassment moved to the cafeteria, Steve and Dennis began eating in another dining hall clear across campus. Surely, they thought, it would all end soon.

Noting that lesbians and gay men will always be a minority group, CUNY's Herek says that "there is a high correlation between homophobia and a reluctance to accept other minority groups. People who are homophobic are more likely to be prejudiced against blacks, against Jews, against anything other than the norm in gender roles." That is, against anything that's perceived as different.

Herek's view is backed up by the work of the man who coined the word "homophobia": Dr. George Weinberg, psychologist and author of *Society and the Healthy Homosexual*. According to

Weinberg, homophobia is partially the result of a condition he calls "acute conventionality."

"Those who condemn homosexuals are really giving you a Rorschach test of their own shakiness, their own lurking fear that there is another way to live [than what they consider normal]," Weinberg says. "The rigidity is a reaction to a fear that they are losing their grip. The insistence that they have *the* way to do it is really a response to a terror that their way may *not* be the only way."

This societal pressure to conform is felt even by those who champion the right of lesbians and gays to live as they choose but who find themselves uncomfortable when a gay person gets too close. As one heterosexual man says of a former friend who told him he was gay, "The other guys started giving me grief about it. Everyone knew he was gay, and I didn't want anyone to think *I* was gay. I don't feel right about it, but I stopped being his friend."

But fear of the unconventional is only one basis for homophobia. As Herek says, "Homophobia is not a monolithic phenomenon. People react negatively to lesbians and gay men for many different reasons."

One reason Herek and other researchers cite is the common discomfort felt by many heterosexual people regarding their own fleeting, natural homosexual impulses. Most people don't want to acknowledge these feelings, much less explore them, so anything reminiscent of them is unconsciously threatening. This is *not* to say that all homophobes are latent homosexuals. Only in extreme cases might a severely homophobic person be a homosexual who cannot bear the existence of those feelings and who will act with hatred against anyone who represents them.

Sex itself is a threatening subject in American culture. Homophobic people, ignoring the emotional and intellectual ties lesbians and gay men sustain with their partners, tend to react to homosexuality as a purely sexual issue.

Another tributary to homophobia is the difficulty people have in giving up cherished ideas that seem vital to their sense of selves. For example, Christians who believe that the Bible condemns homosexuality as a sin often cannot reconcile their love for a gay relative or friend with their love of God. Unless such people are willing to reexamine their beliefs in light of new information concerning homosexuality, they will hold onto their homophobic feelings on moral grounds.

Homophobia comes from many sources; it is also expressed in many different ways. Gay-bashing has always been a favorite pastime of more violent homophobes, and as Herek's Yale study showed, it's a problem on college campuses as well. But on a day-to-day basis, homophobia assumes other forms.

Only 47 universities bar discrimination on the basis of sexual orientation (as does only one state, Wisconsin). Admittedly, lesbian and gay studies are offered at about 30 schools, and there are nearly 300 lesbian and gay student organizations. But many of these groups function under a cloud of controversy, and most exist without the official recognition necessary for office space and funds.

At Georgetown University in Washington, D.C., for example, a lawsuit brought against the school by the student group Gay People of Georgetown University (GPGU) is holding up the sale of city bonds needed for the construction of a long-awaited $43 million student center. The administrators refused to officially sanction GPGU, despite a vote in its favor by the student government and despite a city civil rights law banning such discrimination. Administrators contend that recognition would put the Jesuit school in the untenable position of condoning a "homosexual life-style."

Georgetown students, originally tolerant of GPGU, have been struggling with a rising tide of homophobia now that some students blame the gays for the construction delay. Last spring, angry letters filled with antigay rhetoric showed up weekly in various student publications. But the homophobic atmosphere at Georgetown has been mild compared with that at some other schools.

Students at the University of Kansas still talk about the vicious campaign launched two years ago against Gay and Lesbian Services of Kansas (GLSOK). In September of 1984, a KU student distributed T-shirts emblazoned with the slogan FAGBUSTERS. A campus political party, Young Americans for Freedom, ran a slate of student government candidates on a platform that included the promise to stop GLSOK's funding, which the organization had only started receiving after five years of petitions to the administration.

At the height of the conflict, a disc jockey in a popular student hangout played the *Ghostbusters* theme over and over again one night, turning the volume down on the chorus while he screamed "FAAAG-busters" into the microphone. One of the bartenders there, who was gay, left in disgust only to be pelted with rocks outside a gay bar in another part of town.

Another gay KU student barely avoided major injury that autumn when he suddenly lost a wheel while driving his car. Upon inspection, the student found

that the lug nuts had been loosened. After that, he started receiving phone calls from people threatening his life. When he complained to the campus police, they told him it would "take some time" before they could get to the case.

He dropped out of school. As he told a friend, "I'm a student here. I'm trying to get an education. Somebody's trying to kill me, and nobody cares."

The Saturday before finals week late in the winter semester, Steve and Dennis decided to turn in early. They wanted to get a good night's rest so they could study all day Sunday. About 11 p.m., Steve, a light sleeper, heard a noise at the door.

"Who's there?" he called out. Instead of an answer, he heard the scuffling of running feet. He opened the door. No one was there, so he went back to bed.

A little later, Steve heard another sound. This time he tiptoed to the door and tried to open it without making any noise. But the lock clicked as he tripped it, alerting whoever was outside.

This went on until 3 a.m. Dennis, as usual, wanted to ignore the whole thing, but Steve decided he'd had enough. He picked up a can of hair mousse and leaned toward the crack under the door, intending to give whoever was outside a good dousing. Just then, a flame shot up through the crack, brushing a poster tacked to the door and, more alarmingly, coming within inches of the aerosol can in Steve's hand. Outside the door, a group of men ran away; it had taken them a while, but their handmade acetylene torch had gone off as planned.

Badly shaken, Steve called downstairs to report the torching of the door. But the student on desk duty that night neither recorded the call nor notified anyone else. Three days later, Steve and Dennis came home to find that the lock on their charred door had been filled with glue. It was only while they were arranging with the floor's resident assistant to have the lock changed that a report on the fire itself was finally filed. Eventually at least one student was expelled in connection with the arson attack. The exact number isn't known because few people within the administration today will confirm any details.

The administrator who was responsible for prosecuting the case in the student judiciary system refuses comment. "Any students who are charged with a violation like this have a right to the university's protection," he says.

The dorm's chief resident assistant, the student responsible for discipline and morale in the building, likewise refuses to discuss the case.

One housing official at first claims not to remember the incident, then says, "It

was a very stupid prank." He smiles wryly at a reminder that the handmade torch had been fashioned from a prophylactic, but seems surprised when told that Steve and Dennis were never contacted about the incident by an representative of the university.

"Naturally it's our policy to follow up on something like this," he says. "I don't know why we didn't in this case.

"Of course, it wasn't because they were homosexuals."

In the fall of 1984 a group of students at the University of Massachusetts at Amherst launched a "Heterosexuals Fight Back" rally. They also tried to get finals week designated as "Hang a Homo" week and put up posters that read THE GAYBUSTERS ARE COMING. Instead of interpreting these actions as pranks, members of the administration took some unusual steps to confront and deactivate the tension.

Felice Yeskel of the student affairs office spent the next several months looking at causes of homophobia at UMass. She published a report the following June in which she called for a series of 15 actions, including the creation of a visiting faculty position to teach gay and lesbian studies; the acquisition of relevant library materials; and the welcoming of lesbians and gays to an alternative dorm floor devoted to those wishing to live with others of diverse backgrounds.

The thrust of the report was that the school had the responsibility for establishing healthy communication between gay and lesbian students and the rest of the student body.

"That's really vital in this issue," says Kevin Berrill, the manager of an ongoing project on violence for the National Gay and Lesbian Task Force (NGLTF). "The notion that gay and lesbian students ought to be carrying the ball, educating the people who are prejudiced against them, handling the acts of violence that come up, is simply wrong. Homophobia is not a gay problem. It is a societal problem."

By spring, Dennis was coping with his dormmates' relentless animosity by planning a move to off-campus housing at the end of the semester. But Steve was feeling the heat. His grades began dropping. His concentration was diffused by vague depression. No matter what he tried, he just couldn't seem to keep the climate of hostility from seeping into and corroding even the little pleasures of his daily life. Maybe, he thought, he should just drop out of school.

In a final effort to reclaim his peace of mind and salvage his education, Steve spent two hours talking with the director of the school's student-counseling service, a crusty old man who convinced Steve that he had everything to gain by meeting his tormentors head on.

And so he did. For Steve, the pivotal confrontation began like so many others. A young man heading down in the elevator called out contemptuously just as the door was closing on Steve's floor, "You faggot!"

This time Steve raced down the stairs and stopped the guy as he left the elevator for the lobby.

"What did you call me?" he said loudly, looking his adversary in the eye. Students milling nearby couldn't help noticing the exchange.

"Never mind," the man said. He started to walk away.

"I'm talking to you!" Steve yelled. "What did you call me?"

The other guy kept walking.

"You coward!" Steve yelled.

That got him. "Don't you call me that," the man said, turning around with an unexpectedly fragile look on his face.

Steve was a little taken aback; the man looked as if he was about to cry.

"Well, what did you call me?" Steve said in a calmer voice. "How do you think I felt about that?"

The man didn't exactly apologize, but he never hassled Steve again and even took to saying a friendly "hello" on occasion. After two more confrontations—and after the school's investigation into the arson attack—Steve discovered that an unspoken truce had been established. The harassment ended as suddenly as it had begun.

Today, in their senior year, Dennis lives on the outskirts of campus and Steve rooms without trouble in an upperclassmen's dorm. But though their particular time of trial may be over, the campus atmosphere remains unchanged.

Just last spring, in the same dorm courtyard where Steve and Dennis were first harassed, a pre-election rally was held for several student-government hopefuls. One vice-presidential candidate stood up and made a campaign pledge to tear down a gay bar near campus in order to create more parking.

"I'm sorry," he told the crowd. "But I'm not a homosexual. These guys can take their AIDS and get out. Burn them. Execute them. I want no part of them."

He didn't win the election, but he did get 7 percent of the votes—more than his presidential running mate.

Even highly educated people can be homophobic, as proven by the U.S. Supreme Court's 5-to-4 decision last June to uphold a Georgia law prohibiting sodomy. Although sodomy is defined legally as oral and anal sex, not uncommon among heterosexuals, laws against sodomy are almost exclusively applied to gay men. In fact, Justice Byron R. White, who wrote the decision, specifically stated that the court was addressing the issue of "homosexual sodomy."

"This decision is a legal and moral disgrace," says Kevin Berrill of NGLTF. "I think it's an attack on the entire basis of our civil rights laws, not just for gay Americans, but for all Americans. It is a blatant act of prejudice by the five justices who voted for it."

The U.S. Justice Department has also dealt a blow to enlightened public treatment of gays and lesbians. The department ruled last spring that an employer can fire someone who has AIDS if the employer fears that the person will spread the disease to other workers.

Given that AIDS is transmitted only by semen or large amounts of blood, Berrill points out that the fear of its being spread under normal working conditions is starkly irrational—a hallmark of homophobia. "The ruling will be used as a tool to discriminate not only against AIDS victims but also against anyone who is gay or lesbian," he says.

When it comes to America's campuses, Berrill says that the climate for homosexuals has never been better—and it's never been worse.

"It's good," he says, "in that more gay and lesbian student organizations are forming, more schools are adopting non-discrimination clauses, more schools are offering gay and lesbian courses. But the violence is getting worse."

In a 1984 NGLTF survey of 2,074 gay men and lesbians in eight cities, 82 percent they'd been threatened with physical violence. In 1985, another survey found that 20 percent of gay men and 10 percent of lesbians polled had been the victims of antigay physical abuse. Berrill, who oversees a national hotline for college students concerned about such violence, has noticed a change since the 1985 survey was conducted.

"There were almost no calls before that time, and now it's a deluge," he says. Whether there is actually more violence or merely better reporting of it is unclear, but Berrill's hunch is that increased media attention to gays in the wake of the AIDS crisis has given more homophobes the excuse to attack homosexuals.

"But the increased visibility doesn't cause the violence," he emphasizes. "That's the same flak women get when they're told that they bring rape on themselves. It's antigay prejudice that causes the violence."

If the fear of violence doesn't drive lesbians and gay men further into obscurity, perhaps their increased visibility will eventually work in their favor. Herek cites a simple lack of exposure to gay friends, family members, or co-workers as another important factor in homophobia.

Visibility is a funny thing, however, when you're talking about some 20 million Americans. Notes Ron Najman, the media director for NGLTF, "It's not that people don't know someone who is gay. Everybody knows someone who is gay.

"It's just that they don't *know* they know someone who is gay."

DATE RAPE AND OTHER FORCED SEXUAL ENCOUNTERS AMONG COLLEGE STUDENTS

Bonnie L. Yegidis, M.S.W., Ph.D.
Associate Professor, Department of Social Work
University of South Florida
Tampa, FL 33620

Abstract

This survey explores the incidence of date rape and other forms of forced sexual behavior among college students at a large urban university. It is estimated that approximately 10% of college females surveyed had experienced some form of forced sexual encounter within the previous year. Penetration occurred in half of these cases. In addition, nearly 6% of the males surveyed admitted forcing a date to engage in some form of sexual activity within the last year. The nature of force used by the perpetrators and experienced by victims is also described. Finally, the perceptions of date rape victims and perpetrators are described with respect to this phenomenon.

Within the last several years, date rape has emerged in the professional literature as a major type of non-stranger rape. Minimal data are available on the specific incidence of date rape, although there is a preponderance of information on other forms of acquaintance rape. There are difficulties encountered in the use of public crime rates in establishing incidence estimates. Variations in definitions, crime enforcement activity levels, police and public attitudes, local legal codes, and recordkeeping and reporting all contribute to varying estimates of the true incidence of date rape. In addition, it has been suggested that 50% of all rape victims may know their offenders and that underreporting bias is directly related to victim-offender relationships (Rabkin, 1979).

The incidence of rape is "ecologically bound" (Amir, 1971), occurring between people who live in the same neighborhoods and who are members of the same race. The underreporting of rape is believed to be due to variations in the characteristics of the offender, the act, and the victim, but mostly is due to the nature of the victim-offender relationship. There is an assumption that females who experience forced sexual intimacy are less likely to label the incident as a rape when the perpetrator is previously known to them. This association between victim and offender has led in the past to a victim-blame model discussed by Amir (1971) in his concept of "victim-precipitated" rape. Feminist theory holds that acceptance of rape myths, sex-role stereotyping, sexual conservatism and acceptance of sexual violence against women all create an atmosphere which fosters the acceptance of rape and other forms of sexual assault (Burt, 1980; Check & Malamuth, 1983; Clark & Lewis, 1977; Shotland & Goodstein, 1983). These social and psychological factors probably all contribute to the underreporting of date rape.

Between ¼ and ⅕ of college women surveyed over a 20-year period by various investigators have reported forceful attempts at sexual intercourse by their dates (Kanin, 1957; Kanin & Parcell, 1977; Shotland & Goodstein, 1983). Similar findings have been reported by others. For example, Wilson and Durrenberger (1982) found that of 447 college females studied, 15% had been raped and 18% had experienced an attempted rape by a date. Russell (1984) reported that 44% of a randomly selected sample of 930 women had been subjected to at least one rape or attempted rape at some time in the course of their lives. By far the most likely offender was an acquaintance (14%) or a date (12%).

The purpose of my study was to investigate the incidence of date rape and other forms of sexual battery among college students and to provide a description of the nature of force used in date rapes.

*This study was supported by the Research Enhancement Program, University of South Florida, Tampa, Florida.

Subjects

In order to select a representative sample of college students, data were gathered from students enrolled at a large southern state university. A list of spring semester classes with a student enrollment of at least 100 was secured from the university registrar's office. Data were gathered from each of the classes where instructors gave permission for this activity. Only two instructors refused. Ten classes with a total of 648 students (348 females and 300 males) comprised the final sample. The sampling plan may best be characterized as a nonprobability one. The plan led to a sample of students reasonably similar to the university population as a whole with respect to age, race, and sex. Tables 1 and 2 display these variables for the sample studied and the university population.

Methodology

The data gathering instrument was a brief, anonymous, self-administered questionnaire. Students were asked to respond to a series of questions about their experiences with forced sexual activities while dating. Force was operationalized on a continuum ranging from verbal persuasion" to "use of a weapon." Sexual activities were defined as fondling, oral sex, intercourse and "other." There were separate items constructed for male and female respondents. The instrument had been field-tested and revised earlier in the project year.

Data were gathered at the beginning of the regular class meeting times to insure a high completion rate. The questionnaire was distributed by the investigator, completed by the students, and returned to the investigator in a student-sealed envelope.

Results

Data analyses were directed toward describing how frequently each form of sexual battery occurred within the previous year and over the course of one's lifetime. In addition, methods of force used were also identified. The major findings follow.

Incidence of Sexual Battery in the Last Year. Of the 348 women who completed the questionnaire, 34 (9.8%) students reported experiencing a forced sexual encounter within the previous year. A frequency distribution of these forced sexual encounters is displayed in Table 3. Seventeen of these 34 women (4.9%

of the female sample) reported having been forced into either oral sex or intercourse within the previous year. Both of these acts meet the State of Florida's legal definition of felonious sexual battery punishable by life imprisonment or a term of imprisonment up to 40 years (Florida Statutes, 1984). If this estimate of the incidence of forced sexual battery is accurate, then perhaps as many as 494 women (4.9% of 10,087 students) are victims of sexual battery in a given year on the campus used for this study.

Incidence of Sexual Battery Over the Course of One's Lifetime. Students were also asked if any of the four specific sexual acts had ever been forced on them by a date. A total of 77 women (22%) reported having been forced to engage in the forms of sexual activity presented in Table 4. In addition, 40 of the 77 women reported having been forced to have either intercourse or oral sex at some time in their lives with a date.

The Nature of Force. As previously indicated, the kind of force was measured on a continuum, from less to more serious in terms of the potential for physical harm to the victim. The frequency distribution for the types of force experienced by the victims in a given sexual encounter is presented in Table 5. The three most frequently used methods of force were verbal persuasion, physical intimidation or roughness, and the use of drugs or alcohol by the victim or the perpetrator. Twenty-two of the female victims described in writing how they perceived the forced sexual experiences they were presented with, and what if anything they were able to do to prevent the attack. A content analysis of their responses showed that the incident was most likely to have occurred in the male's apartment or room, with the next likely location being the female's apartment or room. Only a very few attacks (less than five) occurred in a car or outside. Drugs and/

Table 2
Selected Characteristics of the USF Population
(n = 19,881)

		N	%
Sex	Male	9,794	49.0
	Female	10,087	51.0
Race	White	17,067	85.8
	Black	817	4.1
	Hispanic	1,139	5.7
	Other	858	4.3

Median undergraduate age = 22

Table 1
Selected Characteristics of the Sample
(n = 648)

		N	%
Sex	Male	300	46.0
	Female	348	54.0
Race	White	567	87.5
	Black	37	5.7
	Hispanic	8	1.2
	Other	16	2.5

Median undergraduate age = 20

Table 3
Number of Females Forced into Sexual Encounters by Specific Act
(n = 34)

Act	Frequency
Fondling	27
Oral Sex	10
Intercourse	11
Other activity	7

Table represents 34 women forced into 55 sexual acts

or alcohol were used by either the victim or perpetrator or both in nearly all incidents. A total of 11 women reported being able successfully to prevent a rape through saying "no," crying or screaming, talking the attacker out of the assault, or physically resisting.

The Male's Perspective. A total of 17 men reported forcing a female (date) to engage in sexual activity within the previous year. This represented 5.7% of the male sample. If this estimate is accurate, then in any one year perhaps as many as 588 college men on the campus used for this study force a date into sexual activity. Thirty-three (11%) of the male respondents reported having forced a date into sexual activity at some time in their lives. As was true for the females' responses, most of the forced sexual encounters were classified as fondling. However, 22 of the 33 males reported having forced a woman to engage in either oral sex or intercourse, both felonious assaults.

Data relevant to the nature of force used by the perpetrators are presented in Table 6. Again it can be seen that the most commonly used methods of force was verbal persuasion, followed by the use of alcohol or drugs. Only a very few males indicated displaying any form of physical roughness with their dates.

Twelve males provided brief written descriptions of the forced sexual encounters they initiated. Seven of these men stated that they did not actually use force. Rather, they viewed the situation as an opportunity for more intense sexual activity. Furthermore, they suggested that their dates had placed themselves in the situation by turning them on, engaging in fondling, or getting drunk or high with them. Only three of these respondents admitted actively using force or manipulation to gain sexual access. Two men indicated that their dates "owed" them sex in return for the money spent on the date.

Discussion and Conclusions

The data gathered in this study reveal that about 10% of the college women studied are at risk of sexual victimization by their dates in a given year. A total of 22% of the women studied reported being subjected to a forced sexual encounter by a date at some point in their lives. These estimates are somewhat lower than the estimate reported by Kanin & Parcell (1977), but similar to those reported by Wilson & Durrenberger (1982). As previously indicated, researchers generally assume that most rapes go unreported (Ageton, 1983; Rabkin, 1979; Schultz, 1975). If this is the case,

Table 4
Number of Females Ever Forced into Sexual Activity by Specific Act
(*n* = 77)

Act	Frequency
Fondling	51
Oral Sex	23
Intercourse	27
Other Activity	14

Table represents 77 women forced into 115 sexual acts

Table 5
Nature of Force Experienced by Victims
(*n* = 77)

Type of Force Experienced	Frequency
Verbal persuasion	46
Verbal threats	11
Physical intimidation	12
More than one perpetrator	2
Use of alcohol or drugs	29
Some physical roughness (pushing, slapping)	14
Extreme physical roughness (beating, choking)	5
Displayed a weapon	1
Injured with a weapon	1

Forty of the 77 women reported two or more forms of force used against them

then perhaps the 10% estimate found in this study is an underestimate of the true incidence of sexual battery on campus.

The role of force in date rape was investigated because the legal definition for sexual battery typically includes reference to it. In short, if there is no evidence of force, threat of force, or rendering the victim helpless, then victim consent cannot be legally ruled out. In date rape the variable of force may not be clearly present. This study showed that most of the sexual encounters were forced through verbal persuasion-protestations by the male to "go further" because of sexual need, arousal, or love. A small percentage of women reported successfully preventing the assault through saying no or offering physical resistance. Others did not resist because they "felt intimidated."

The data presented in this study support that date rape is a contemporary problem among college students. Practically speaking, there are implications for educators and counseling practitioners on college campuses. The literature on rape shows that rape victims experience guilt, depression and some level of personal dysfunctioning as a result of the incident (MacDonald, 1971; McCahill, Meyer & Fischman, 1979). Of course the possibility of physical harm or retaliation from the perpetrator is paramount in the minds of the

Table 6
Type of Force Used To Control Victims
(*n* = 33)

Type of Force Used	Frequency
Verbal persuasion	27
Verbal threats	1
Physical intimidation	5
More than one perpetrator	2
Use of alcohol or drugs	15
Some physical roughness (pushing, slapping)	3
Extreme physical roughness (beating, choking)	2
Displayed a weapon	1
Used a weapon	1
Other (not specified)	6

Ten respondents reported using at least two types of force

victims (Peters, 1973). Moreover, some rape victims report a delayed stress reaction to the incident presenting a serious obstacle to their functioning (Burgess & Holmstrom, 1974).

In the date rape situation, the primary reaction of the victim is likely to be guilt (Kirkpatrick & Kanin, 1957). Because she accepted a date with the perpetrator, the victim believes she is responsible for creating the context that permits the assault to occur. Therefore, she feels partially or wholly to blame and consequently guilty. Also, since women have been socialized to "hold the line" in the area of sexual intimacy in dating, then victims feel they have failed at a crucial courtship task. Professionals working with college students should be sensitive to the possibility of date rape and to the reactions that victims have to it.

It may be that date rape occurs because of men's expectation for sexual intimacy which may be reinforced by environmental stimuli, such as the availability of an isolated locale. If the victim does not offer verbal or physical resistance, or in other ways is perceived as a willing participant, then the situational context may be set for sexual intimacy to occur. If this is, in fact, how forced sexual encounters occur in dating, then there are educational strategies that may be planned on campus to deal with the problem. For example, educational seminars or workshops on sexual intimacy in dating might be conducted. These activities would likely have wide appeal among students, and could provide a forum for discussing the expectations that students have for dating.

References

Ageton, S. (1983). *Sexual Assault Among Adolescents.* Lexington, MA: D.C. Heath and Co.

Amir, M. (1971). *Patterns in Forcible Rape.* Chicago: The University of Chicago Press.

Burgess, A. & Holmstrom, L. (1974). Rape trauma syndrome. *American Journal of Psychiatry 131,* 981–986.

Burt, M. (1980). Cultural myths and supports for rape. *Journal of Personality and Social Psychology 38* (2), 217–230.

Check, J. & Malamuth, N. (1983). Sex role sterotyping and reactions to depictions of stranger versus acquaintance rape. *Journal of Personality and Social Psychology 45* (2), 344–356.

Clark, L. & Lewis, D. (1977). *Rape: The Price of Coercive Sexuality.* Toronto: The Women's Press.

Florida Statutes (1984). *Sexual Battery,* Chapter 794 (FS 794.011).

Kanin, E. (1957). Male aggression in dating-courtship relations. *American Journal of Sociology 63:* 197–204.

Kanin, E. & Parcell, S. (1977). Sexual aggression: A second look at the offended female. *Archives of Sexual Behavior 6,* 1.

Kirkpatrick, C. & Kanin, E. (1957). Male sex aggression on a university campus. *American Sociological Review 22,* 52–58.

MacDonald, J. (1971). *Rape Offenders and Their Victims.* Springfield, IL: Charles C. Thomas.

McCahill, T., Meyer, L. & Fischman, A. (1979). *The Aftermath of Rape.* Lexington, MA: D.C. Heath and Co.

Peters, J. (1973). *The Philadelphia Rape Victim Study.* A report presented at the First International Symposium on Victimology, Israel. Mimeographed copy from The Center for Rape Concern, Philadelphia General Hospital.

Rabkin, J. (1979). The epidemiology of forcible rape. *American Journal of Orthopsychiatry 49*(4), 634–646.

Russell, D. (1984). *Sexual Exploitation: Rape, Child Sexual Abuse, and Sexual Harassment.* Beverly Hills, CA: Sage Publications.

Schultz, L. (ed.) (1975). *Rape Victimology.* Springfield, IL: Charles C. Thomas.

Shotland, R. & Goodstein, L. (1983). Just because she doesn't want to doesn't mean it's rape: An experimentally-based causal model of the perception of rape in a dating situation. *Social Psychology Quarterly 46* (3), 220–232.

Wilson, W. & Durrenberger, R. (1982). Comparison of rape and attempted rape victims. *Psychological Reports 50,* 198.

Women's Postrape Sexual Functioning: Review and Implications for Counseling

Barbara Gilbert and Jean Cunningham

Barbara Gilbert is a graduate student in the Counseling Psychology PhD Program, Southern Illinois University at Carbondale. Jean Cunningham is an assistant professor in the Clinical Psychology Program, Southern Illinois University at Carbondale.

The authors present a literature review concerning the effects of rape on sexual functioning and suggestions for facilitating sexual recovery of rape surivors in counseling.

Since the publication of Susan Brownmiller's *Against Our Will: Men, Women and Rape* in 1975, the number of studies of sexual assault on women has skyrocketed, and more attention than ever before has been focused on the effects of rape on the functioning of survivors. Additionally, many suggestions have been offered for those who counsel survivors (this term is preferred to *victim* because of the implication of helplessness in the latter). Although the aftereffects of rape can extend into many areas of survivors' lives, it seems apparent that sexual attitudes and behaviors are especially vulnerable to disruption after such an assault. As Whiston (1981) has pointed out, the brutal and terrifying experience of rape may change the attitude of the woman who previously viewed sex as a "desirable, pleasurable and intimate method of expressing love" and may also confirm the negative view of the woman who previously perceived sex as "a necessary evil for a man's pleasure and ego" (p. 364).

In this article several aspects of the recent literature concerning sexual problems resulting from sexual assault of women are reviewed. First, prevalence, types, and duration of post-assault sexual problems are discussed, followed by consideration of data concerning survivors' sexual satisfaction. Finally, suggestions for counseling rape survivors on the sexual aspect of their recovery are made. The articles cited here were identified through a search of *Psychological Abstracts* from 1975 to 1985;

virtually all the articles that specifically addressed postrape sexual functioning are reviewed. This article does not provide specific descriptions of methods of sex therapy; rather, integration of sexual recovery into more general recovery from rape is discussed.

PREVALENCE AND TYPES OF DYSFUNCTIONS

Three studies have focused primarily on rates and types of sexual dysfunctions among rape survivors. Becker, Skinner, Abel, and Treacy (1982) compared survivors of rape or incest to women who had never been sexually assaulted on number and types of sexual dysfunctions. Whereas only 11.1% of the non-assaulted group reported one or more dysfunctions, 56% of the rape-incest survivors reported one or more sexual dysfunctions. Furthermore, 71% of the sexually dysfunctional rape survivors reported that the assault had definitely precipitated the sexual dysfunction. For these women, fear of sex and lack of desire or arousal were the most common problems. Burgess and Holmstrom (1979) studied a group of women who had been sexually active before the rape and found that 71% had decreased levels of sexual activity after the rape, with 38% completely abstaining from sex for at least 6 months after the rape. Specific sexual acts that had occurred during the rape were now distressing to 35% of these women, and 41% reported problems with sexual arousal and orgasm. Miller, Williams, and Bernstein (1982) considered the impact of rape on the sexual functioning of couples. In their study 14 of 18 couples

(78%) reported that sex had become a major problem in their relationship after the female partner had been raped, with 53.3% of the women and 20.9% of the men reporting individual sexual problems. Avoidance of sexual relations was also a common postrape pattern among the couples in this study: 58.1% reported this problem.

It is apparent from these findings that some form of disruption in sexual functioning is a very common sequel to rape and that although a variety of dysfunctions may result, many survivors' problems involve fear, avoidance, or lack of desire for sex.

SEXUAL SATISFACTION

Several studies have provided data concerning sexual behaviors and have also included the important dimension of sexual satisfaction, which may not always be apparent from reports on behavior alone. For example, Feldman-Summers, Gordon, and Meagher (1979) found no differences between groups of raped and nonraped women in rates of engaging in sexual activities and experiencing orgasm, but women who had been raped reported significantly decreased levels of satisfaction with almost all activities after the rape. Women who had survived rape, however, continued to find autoerotic and primarily affectional behaviors (e.g., holding hands) as satisfying as they were before the rape. Similarly, Orlando and Koss (1983) found that sexually victimized (not necessarily raped) women were less satisfied with sexual behaviors than were nonvictimized women.

Norris and Feldman-Summers (1981) studied change both in frequency of sexual behaviors and in sexual satisfaction after rape. In their sample oral sex was engaged in less frequently than before the rape by 25.5% of the participants, intercourse frequency dropped for 29.4%, and frequency of orgasms dropped for 21.7%. Overall, 32.7% of the participants reported a decrease in sexual satisfaction after rape.

DURATION OF POSTRAPE SEXUAL PROBLEMS

Although it is clear that both sexual behavior and sexual satisfaction decrease significantly for many women after they are raped, the previously cited literature does not make clear the duration of such problems. Are these problems relatively time limited, occurring mostly in the few months directly after the rape, or does rape have a long-term impact on sexual functioning? Nadelson, Notman, Zackson, and Gornick (1982) interviewed 41 women who had been raped 1 to 2½ years earlier. Only 24% of these women reported that they had not experienced postrape sexual problems, whereas 51% had developed problems that were still present at the time of the interview. Another 17% had developed sexual problems after the rape that had been resolved by the time of the interview. Similarly, Becker, Skinner, Abel, Howell, and Bruce (1982) compared the impact of attempted versus completed rape on survivors who had been assaulted more than 1 year earlier and found that sexual problems were reported by 25% of survivors of attempted rape and 50% of survivors of completed rape. The Burgess and Holmstrom study cited above provided more evidence

pertaining to this question: The more sexual symptoms the survivor developed, the longer the time before recovery. Even 4 to 6 years after the assault, 26% of their participants had sexual problems. Becker, Skinner, Abel, and Treacy (1982) noted that one participant had assault-related sexual problems 35 years after the rape.

Thus, although some women may return to prerape levels of sexual functioning very quickly, others report long-term problems with sexuality that do not subside even years after the rape. The question of what factors are responsible for these individual differences in vulnerability to sexual dysfunction has been addressed in a few articles, which are reviewed below. The identification of such factors has important implications for counselors, because these data indicate that some women will not recover quickly (or perhaps ever) if untreated.

PREDICTION OF INDIVIDUAL RESPONSE

Becker and Skinner (1983) stated that attempts to identify specific characteristics of survivors of sexual assaults that may be related to the development of sexual problems have been largely unsuccessful. In various studies, no predictive value has been found for such factors as (a) whether the rape was reported, (b) the survivor's vulnerability to claims that she was responsible, (c) the survivor's belief that she lives or works with supportive others (Norris & Feldman-Summers, 1984), (d) the survivor's level of sexual activity before the rape (Burgess & Holmstrom, 1979), (e) level of victimization, and (f) perception of self as a rape victim (Orlando & Koss, 1983). Some of Burgess and Holmstrom's participants did believe that sympathetic understanding and a gentle, nonpressuring approach to sex by their partners contributed to their recovery. One participant who reported no sexual problems after the rape said she believed it was because she had never equated the rape with sex. Although it is certainly clear that more research is needed in this area, the major implication for counselors from the findings reported above is that no woman can be assumed to be invulnerable to sexual problems after rape.

IMPLICATIONS FOR COUNSELORS

Counseling rape survivors concerning their sexual functioning cannot be separated from counseling rape survivors in general. The survivor's emotional tolerance for dealing with the incident in depth, her interpretation of what has happened to her (including any tendency she has to blame herself for the attack), and the involvement of significant others in her recovery are all important issues in postrape counseling. Some issues of particular importance to the sexual aspect of postrape recovery, however, deserve special attention.

The research reviewed above indicates that problems with sexual functioning are very common among rape survivors. What is not as apparent, however, is that unless the counselor asks specifically about these problems, he or she may never know they exist. For example, Nadelson et al. (1982) found that when asked specifically, more than half of their group of women, who were interviewed 1 to 2½ years after the rape, reported current sexual problems. These problems were not mentioned spontaneously, however, by most of the participants. The authors remarked:

> The fact that many victims did not spontaneously volunteer this information but that it was easily elicited by direct questioning is not surprising because sexual functioning is clearly not an everyday topic of conversation for many people, and for those who have been sexually traumatized, it has special meaning and negative implications, (p. 1269)

Thus, counselors need to convey that they are comfortable and ready to discuss sexual functioning and problems, and they should not assume that the survivor will raise these issues herself. Counselors may find it helpful to let survivors know that many other women in their situation have experienced problems with sex but should avoid the implication that such problems are inevitable or indicative of a serious, long-term dysfunction.

The case of the woman for whom sexual assault has been her first experience of intercourse requires special attention (Burgess & Holmstrom, 1979). Particularly in college settings, it is important for counselors to recognize the possibility that the client had not been sexually active before the rape and thus may be unusually distressed and embarrassed by the experience itself and by discussion of it. If the client has placed high value on sexual abstinence before marriage, the meaning of the rape may be complicated by her feelings about the loss of her virginity. Such clients may find discussion of the sexual aspects of the assault particularly difficult, and although the counselor must respect the client's decision concerning what she discusses and discloses, such material may serve an important function in preventing future problems. For example, the client who has been maintaining her virginity despite a loved partner's desire for intercourse may feel a need to reevaluate her desire and her right to refuse sex and may be concerned over her partner's acceptance of her decision. If the client does not plan to become sexually active in the foreseeable future, discussion of how the rape may affect her sexual functioning when she does become active may forestall problems that could otherwise occur.

Another important issue is the involvement of the rape survivor's partner in counseling. As Masters and Johnson (1970) have pointed out, sexual problems inevitably affect and involve both partners in a relationship. Studies of sexual functioning in rape survivors support that viewpoint: Worry over their partner's response was reported as a rape-related problem by approximately half of Burgess and Holmstrom's (1979) sample, and Miller et al. (1982) found that sexual functioning became a major relationship problem for couples after the woman was raped.

Silverman (1978) specified four ways in which counselors may help couples after rape: (a) encourage the partner to express his affective response; (b) facilitate the partner's understanding of what the rape means to the survivor; (c) educate the partner concerning the crisis and likely sequelae; and (d) provide individual counseling for profoundly affected partners. (Although Silverman refers to male marital partners of rape survivors, these points would seem equally applicable to unmarried partners of either sex—homosexual women are not immune to rape.)

When counseling addresses sexual adjustment after

rape, the partner's emotional reaction to the rape cannot be overlooked. Burgess and Holmstrom (1979) listed a variety of frequently observed partner reactions, from such a strong identification with the survivor that the partner also feels raped to defining the rape as an act of sexual infidelity and seeing the survivor as "degraded and soiled." Whereas the counselor must understand the partner's response to facilitate the couple's sexual recovery, he or she must also work to avoid what Silverman termed *revictimization* of the survivor via the partner's response.

Once communication about the rape is established, a basic issue for the couple is their return to sexual activity. Miller et al. (1982) described a dysfunctional but common Way of dealing with this issue, whereby

> The male partner is concerned about openly requesting sex, fearing that his wife or girlfriend is not ready. All too often, the victim herself is starting to feel desire to resume her sexual relationship but is reluctant to initiate sex, because her partner has not expressed interest. Once again, the failure to communicate prevents each partner from understanding the current needs and desires of the other. (p. 57)

Because long-term avoidance of sex is a frequent result of rape, the counselor's help in raising this issue seems of great value in preventing such problems. Regardless of the length of time involved before a return to sexual activity, couples may also need help in anticipating problems that might arise and in planning how they might handle them. In dealing with these issues, the counselor needs to balance a realistic concern over potential sexual problems with an overly pessimistic view, which might suggest that serious problems are inevitable.

A final issue of concern in counseling survivors of sexual assault is that working on any aspect of the experience may bring about a temporary, but uncomfortable, emotional reaction in the client. Such reactions might be unanticipated by clients who were assaulted in the distant past but are only now dealing with the effects of the assault on sexual functioning. By anticipating depressed or anxious reaction from clients, counselors can reassure them that such reactions are temporary by-products of the counseling and can prevent premature termination because of such discomfort.

For some women, sexual problems may persist despite an otherwise successful experience in postrape counseling. In these cases a more specialized approach may be needed. Becker and Skinner (1983) described a treatment program aimed specifically at sexual dysfunctions in rape survivors. Their program employs a variety of treatment techniques, many of which were developed for sex therapy with the general population. For the counselor who has not had specialized training in sex therapy, a timely referral of such clients to a qualified sex specialist is advisable.

Because postrape sexual functioning is a relatively new area of focus for research, there are few studies in which counseling interventions for these problems have been evaluated. In the two studies cited here in which outcome is mentioned, the authors do so very briefly. Miller et al. (1982) found gains in marital and sexual adjustment immediately after treatment consisting of conjoint marital counseling with rape survivors and their spouses, but these gains were not maintained at 6-month follow-ups. Becker and Skinner (1983) reported that of the first 43 women to complete their time-limited (10-week), behaviorally oriented treatment program for sexual dysfunction, 92% made progress toward their self-defined sexual goals. Certainly, more research is needed in this area, and treatment methods and outcome measures must be more precisely defined if counselors are to base their interventions with sexually dysfunctional rape survivors on empirically evaluated methods.

CONCLUSION

In this article we have reviewed research related to problems with sexual functioning after rape. It is clear that such problems are common among women who have been sexually assaulted and that these problems are not necessarily brief or easily resolved. Although many authors point out that a methodological problem in such research is that participants who volunteer to participate may represent a subgroup of survivors who are more concerned and more troubled by problems resulting from assault than are women who have been raped but do not volunteer, this issue is of little importance to counselors. Postrape counseling is most likely to take place when the survivor sees herself in need of help in dealing with the aftereffects of assault. Although such immediate psychological problems as intense fear may need to be the initial focus of counseling, full recovery cannot be said to have been achieved until the survivor is once again comfortable with her own sexual functioning. To this end,

counselors must be aware of and prepared to deal with sexual issues in postrape counseling.

REFERENCES

Becker, J.V., & Skinner, L.J. (1983). Assessment and treatment of rape-related sexual dysfunctions. *Clinical Psychologist, 36,* 102–105.

Becker, J.V., Skinner, L.J., Abel, G.G., Howell, J., & Bruce, K. (1982). The effects of sexual assault on rape and attempted rape victims. *Victimology, 7,* 106–113.

Becker, J.V., Skinner, L.J., Abel, G.G., & Treacy, E.C. (1982). Incidence and types of sexual dysfunctions in rape and incest victims. *Journal of Sex and Marital Therapy, 8,* 65–74.

Brownmiller, S. (1975). *Against our will: Men, women and rape.* New York: Simon & Schuster.

Burgess, A.W., & Holmstrom, L.C. (1979). Rape: Sexual disruption and recovery. *American Journal of Orthopsychiatry, 49,* 648–657.

Feldman-Summers, S., Gordon, P.E., & Meagher, J.R. (1979). The impact of rape on sexual satisfaction. *Journal of Abnormal Psychology, 88,* 101–105.

Masters, W.H., & Johnson, J.E. (1970). *Human sexual inadequacy.* Boston: Little, Brown.

Miller, W.R., Williams, A.M., & Bernstein, M.H. (1982). The effects of rape on marital and sexual adjustment. *American Journal of Family Therapy, 10,* 51–58.

Nadelson, C.C., Notman, M.T., Zackson, H., & Gornick, J. (1982). A follow-up study of rape victims. *American Journal of Psychiatry, 139,* 1267–1270.

Norris, J., & Feldman-Summers, S. (1981). Factors related to the psychological impact of rape on the victim. *Journal of Abnormal Psychology, 90,* 562–567.

Orlando, J.A., & Koss, M.P. (1983). The effects of sexual victimization on sexual satisfaction: A study of the negative-association hypothesis. *Journal of Abnormal Psychology, 92,* 104–106.

Silverman, D. (1978). Sharing the crisis of rape: Counseling the mates and families of victims. *American Journal of Orthopsychiatry, 48,* 166–174.

Whiston, S.K. (1981). Counseling sexual assault victims: A loss model. *Personnel and Guidance Journal, 59,* 363–366.

THE INCEST CONTROVERSY

Can Daddy Come Home Again?

Meredith Maran

Meredith Maran is a free-lance journalist who often writes about child sexual abuse.

*T*HREE YEARS AFTER the secret came out, Roberto and I are still speaking," says Elena Martinez (not her real name), a nurse's aide at a San Jose, California, hospital. "We even go to counseling together when something comes up with the girls. But there are days when I picture him doing what he did to my daughters—those are the days when I'd like to kill him."

In May 1982 Elena's five teenage daughters told her that their father had been sexually molesting them for the past fifteen years. "They'd never talked to each other—or me—about it because he'd promised each of them that if she didn't tell he'd leave the others alone. They kept the secret to protect each other. But then when Sarah—the youngest—was thirteen, Roberto started trying to penetrate her. Sarah told her oldest sister, and right away Robin got the five of them together. That's when they found out that Roberto had been abusing all of them since they were babies."

Elena was devastated by the disclosure that the man she'd loved since high school had betrayed her and their children in this hideous way. Despite Roberto's drinking problem and frequent infidelity, she'd struggled to keep the family together so her daughters could have the devoted father that Roberto appeared to be. "He was their hero, the one they called their best friend," Elena says. "I was the one who made them do their homework and clean their rooms. Sometimes I resented the closeness between him and the girls, but I put my own feelings aside for their sake."

When Elena confronted Roberto, he cried and swore it would never happen again. She thought about calling the police, but her daughters threatened to deny everything. "They said they didn't want to lose their dad—they

Reprinted from *New Age Journal*, May 1986, pp. 39-43, by permission.

just wanted him to stop molesting them," Elena says. "I knew I should report it, but I couldn't stand the thought of telling the world that my husband was a child molester! Besides, he was our breadwinner. My income barely covered the groceries."

Elena installed dead bolts on the girls' bedroom doors and ordered them to lock themselves in at night. For the next six months she questioned her daughters daily to make sure that Roberto was no longer bothering them.

Then on Christmas Eve Sarah came to Elena crying that Roberto had once again begun begging her for "special back rubs." Two days later, on the basis of his victims' six-hour testimony, Roberto was booked on three counts of felonious child molestation.

Experts estimate that incest occurs in 100,000–250,000 U.S. families each year. Defined broadly as "any sexually arousing intimate physical contact between family members who are not married to each other," incest is most

often committed by males whose age, physical size, and position of authority provide them with access to their younger, female victims. In her book *Father-Daughter Incest*, Judith Herman likens incest to rape: "Because a child is powerless in relation to an adult, she is not free to refuse....Therefore, any sexual relationship between the two must take on some of the coercive characteristics of rape."

Sociologist Diana E. H. Russell reported in a 1978 study that 16 percent

One Family's Therapy

WHEN ELENA MARTINEZ made the desperate decision to report her husband's molestation of their daughters, the first phone call she made was to Parents United, which she'd seen a television special about several years earlier. The counselor who answered that call advised Elena that a jury trial and further trauma could be avoided if Roberto confessed and left home willingly; an hour later a trained team of offenders-in-treatment from Parents United arrived and convinced Roberto to do so. Roberto turned himself in to the San Jose Police Department, where he was booked and released on the condition that he observe the no-contact order prohibiting him from seeing his daughters.

While awaiting Roberto's sentencing, the entire family was court ordered into therapy at Parents United, where they were assigned to therapist Theresa Bell. "The classic symptoms," Bell says, "were there: a dysfunctional marriage, father-daughter closeness at the expense of the mother-daughter bond, secrecy and deception—all hiding behind a facade of the happy family."

Each member of the Martinez family was assigned to an appropriate Parents United support group to combat the isolation typical of incestuous families and thereby lessen the likelihood of future unreported molestation. Simultaneously, individual counseling began. "We spent the first six months working through the initial chaos following disclosure," Bell recalls. "As is often the case when the molester is removed from his home, when Roberto left, his victims turned their rage on their mother. The girls accused Elena of not protecting them, of not keeping Roberto sexually satisfied, of not loving and understanding them as their father had done. No two members of the family could sit in the same room together. It's the secret that keeps an incestuous family balanced. Disclosure destroys that balance."

In January 1983 the judge in charge of Roberto's case asked the five Martinez daughters to recommend a sentence for their father. The maximum was nine years in state prison. The girls told the judge that they didn't want Roberto sent to a state prison, but they did want him to serve the maximum sentence of one year in the county jail. Roberto was sentenced to the one year, though his confession, clean police record, and regular attendance in therapy qualified him for work furlough,

with his weekend labor donated to Parents United.

After Roberto's sentencing the Martinez family settled into group and individual therapy. "In his weekly individual sessions Roberto remembered that he'd been molested by an uncle at the age of five, and he relived the feelings of powerlessness he'd had at the time," Bell says. "Elena realized that the barriers she'd built around herself when she was beaten by her father made it difficult for her to bond intimately with Roberto or her children. The girls stopped trying to make the problem just go away and started accepting that they'd never have the ideal parents they wished they had."

Bell also sought to restore the relationship among the family members. "Incest had just about destroyed the connection between Elena and the girls," she says. "Creating relationships between them took a long time because of the number of victims, the severity of the molestation, and the extreme isolation of Elena within the family and of the girls from each other."

Perpetrator-victim counseling begins only when the perpetrator has taken full responsibility for the molestation and the victims have moved past self-blame. Once the family is ready, confrontation gives the victims a chance to express their rage and to hear the offender say clearly that what happened was his fault, not theirs. In the case of the Martinez family, it took a year and a half of therapy to bring the entire family together for the first time and another six months to give each victim the time she needed to confront her father.

From there Bell began family therapy with the Martinezes and marriage counseling with Elena and Roberto. "The goal at this stage, Bell says, "is to get everyone to talk openly and to move on to forgiveness—of self and of others. For families who want to get back together, this letting-go process is the last step before reconciliation.

"Elena says she wants a divorce," Bell continues, "but she still hasn't filed. Maybe she and Roberto will reconcile after the girls leave home. But the important thing is that they've worked through the trauma together; they have real relationships with each other. Thanks to the hard work this family's done," she concludes, "I believe that those young women will avoid the self-destructive pattern that so many untreated incest victims fall into."

—M.M.

of the randomly selected women she interviewed had been incestuously abused in childhood. Twenty-three percent of the incidents were "very serious" (vaginal, oral, and anal intercourse; cunnilingus); 41 percent were categorized "serious" (genital fondling; simulated intercourse; manual penetration); 36 percent were categorized "least serious" (intentional sexual touching of body parts, including genitals; kissing). The most prevalent

---

Elena installed dead bolts on the girl's bedroom doors and ordered them to lock themselves in at night.

---

perpetrators of incest were uncles, followed by fathers, stepfathers, first cousins, brothers, and grandfathers—women made up fewer than 5 percent of offenders in Russell's and most other studies.

Incest is a key link in the chain of multigenerational emotional, physical, and sexual assault that plagues our culture. For instance, Parents United, a nationwide incest-treatment agency, reports that 80 percent of the perpetrators and 80 percent of the mothers of victims it treats were themselves sexually assaulted in childhood. It is estimated that more than 50 percent of child prostitutes and teenage runaways leave home to escape incestuous abuse.

In the past ten years therapy designed to heal the wounds of incest has emerged as a distinct specialty. Experts in the field are scattered throughout the country in social-service agencies, sexual-abuse crisis centers, university hospitals, and private practices. The goal of therapy is to prevent or heal the repercussive trauma of untreated incestuous abuse.

"There are two dominant views about what makes incest happen," says Sandra Butler, author of *Conspiracy of Silence: The Trauma of Incest*. "One is the 'family dysfunction–cycle of incest' theory. This theory sees power-imbalanced families as being the primary cause of incest, along with the childhood abuse experiences of the perpetrator and/or his wife. The treatment model based on this view encourages families to reconcile after

they've changed their family dynamics through therapy.

"The second view," Butler continues, "has its origins in the women's movement against rape. It's based on a sociocultural feminist analysis. It looks at the predominant dynamic of male as perpetrator and female as victim and concludes that *families* don't molest children and that most *women* who were abused as children don't molest children—men do. This perspective is supported by current research indicating that incest perpetrators are not just wounded souls in dysfunctional families; they are men who because of a complex array of psychological and social factors are addicted to having sex with children. This treatment model puts the emphasis on controlling offenders' behavior, strengthening mothers, and healing child victims —not putting child molesters back into families."

Treatment of offenders—as a supplement to or substitute for incarceration—requires them to disclose, analyze, and develop techniques to control their abusive behavior. Nonoffending parents, usually mothers, are urged to work on building the weak relationships that typically exist between them and their abused children. Treatment of child victims is aimed at counteracting self-blaming, a leading cause of the self-destructive behavior that devastates many untreated adult survivors of child sexual abuse.

Parents United bases its therapy on the belief that incest perpetrators can be reconciled with their families. It has organized support groups in 155 cities, each of which seeks the sponsorship of local family-service or juvenile-probation departments to form an integrated treatment system.

Parents United begins by treating each family member individually, then progresses to counseling the family as a unit. Because incestuous fathers are themselves viewed as victims of dysfunctional families, offender treatment focuses on uncovering and healing the childhood traumas—especially physical or sexual abuse— which may have caused them to become molesters.

Henry Giarretto, who founded and directs Parents United with his wife, Anna, says that the whys of incest are elusive. "Sexual tension exists in every family," he explains. "Tender feelings and sexual responses can't be separated by the body. Every offender would prefer to be a good father, but if he came from an abused or emotionally deprived child-

hood, he feels that no one can possibly love him. He senses a separation widening between him and his wife, maybe his job is going poorly. . . . finally he turns to his daughter, feeling she is the only one he can trust.

"Sexual abuse of children is self-abuse," Giarretto continues. "Parents who molest their children are like neglected children who destroy a favorite toy. You're never going to change [a molesting father] until you accept him as a human being who can be taught to stop that behavior."

Many experts believe that Giarretto's view downplays the risks of returning a convicted molester to his family and to society. The first thing to address in an offender's treatment is the need to change his sexual attraction to children, says Lucy Berliner, a social worker for the Sexual Assault Center at Harborview Medical Center in Seattle. Although, she adds, many health professionals are so uncomfortable with this that they don't want to acknowledge it. Many therapists, Berliner says, treat offenders too sympathetically. "These people put up a good front; they seem so normal. But they've gotten so good at denial that they can easily lie to anyone. Offenders are far more dangerous as a group than we have been willing to acknowledge."

Rich Snowdon, now training director of the Child Assault Prevention Training Center in Oakland, California, led a weekly counseling group for incest perpetrators in San Francisco throughout 1981. He agrees with Berliner's view, describing the men in his group "as facile as professional por-

---

"We believe that these men are incurably addicted to their sexual behavior. We treat them with the goal of controlling, not curing them."

---

nographers, the way they justified their own abuses." "They blamed their demon nymphet victims, their frigid, unloving wives," he says. "But the truth is that incest offenders are men much like other men: they use their power to take what they want."

The addiction model is the basis for offender treatment at Northwest Treatment Associates in Seattle, a partner program to Berliner's agency. "Unlike Parents United, we see no difference between incestuous fathers and other child molesters," says therapist and codirector Steven Wolf. "Clinical and empirical evidence show that incest perpetrators are sexual deviants; whether they ever admit it, most of

them have committed multiple sex crimes by the time they get caught for incest."

Wolf cites a recent study done by Gene Abel while he was director of the Sexual Behavior Clinic at Columbia University, which shows that 44 percent of heterosexual incest perpetrators had molested children outside their families and that 18 percent of them had committed rape. "We believe that these men are incurably addicted to their sexual behavior," Wolf says. "We treat them with

the goal of controlling, not curing them."

Reflecting the view that the primary cause of incest is not family dysfunction but sexual deviance, Northwest uses behavior modification and treats offenders only. These men are mostly first-time convicted sex offenders who are court ordered into therapy as a condition of work furlough, parole, or probation. Therapy is directed at what the agency defines as the two elements of sexual addiction: character issues, which are addressed in peer-led weekly group-therapy sessions;

Adult Survivors of Incest

THE TREATMENT OF ADULTS who were incestuously abused as children is a growing subspecialty within incest therapy. The urgency of providing such treatment is evident in the historically high incidence and low report rates of incest—and in its documented impact on adult lives. Judith Herman, author of *Father-Daughter Incest,* reported that in her sample 65 percent of adults molested as children showed major depressive symptoms, 55 percent suffered sexual dysfunction, and 45 percent became alcoholics or drug addicts.

Incest survivors present a particular challenge to therapists because most of them are unidentified, even to themselves. Years of threats to "keep the secret, or else," combined with the tendency of the childhood psyche to repress trauma, destroys many memories. Often the only visible sign of abuse is chronic self-destructive behavior. "Many male survivors find themselves in the criminal-justice system," comments Terri Muessig of Parents United. "Many females find themselves in the mental-health system." Therapist Sandra Butler says, "Many survivors don't have a memory—only a certainty. And that's all they need to begin work on healing."

When Barbara first went to see San Francisco therapist Padma Moyer in 1984, she had no memory of having been molested by her father. She sought therapy because of an increasing terror of men she'd experienced since her husband's death ten years ago. "I knew I wasn't normal, and I knew my weirdness came from something in my childhood, but I didn't know what it was," she says. "When Padma and I were working on my mother's physical abuse of me, I kept telling her how my father always tried to protect me, how he was the only one who ever loved me. And then I started having nightmares about being held down by a man, about a crack of light coming through a door. Padma asked me a lot of questions about my father, and I remembered some things: his coming into my bedroom at night in his underwear, me as a teenager in the bathroom with him while he took a bath. When Padma first asked if my father had molested me, my response was 'Oh god, no—it can't be true!' But then I read a story in *Conspiracy of Silence* by Sandra Butler about a woman whose father had told her he was teaching her about sex, and I could *hear* my father saying those words. I shook and cried for two days."

Now, as her memories return, Barbara is experiencing both anguish and relief. "It's all finally starting to make

sense: why I kept trying to kill myself when I was eight and nine, why my father refused to come to my wedding, why it took three years of marriage and a lot of alcohol before I could undress in front of my husband or touch him, why I'm still terrified of men and of sex. I haven't had a moment of peace since I started therapy with Padma. There have been times I've asked her if I could stop this and go back to not remembering. But then there's the hope that I could be a woman, a sexual being, not a scared kid who gets terrified when a man comes in the room."

"What's ahead for Barbara now," Moyer says, "is anger, which is difficult to feel because the source of the sexual abuse was also the source of the most human contact in her family. We're trying to find a group for her to join that will accelerate her progress."

Incest specialists recommend a combination of individual and group therapy for adults who know or suspect that they were molested as children. "As Judith Herman says, incest is a social as well as an individual wound," says Ellen Bass, author of *I Never Told Anyone,* a book about incest. "Survivors need to break down their sense of isolation, to get rid of the stigma and shame, to feel compassion first for the other women in the group and then to extend that compassion to themselves."

The first therapeutic step is what Bass calls the "getting-clear" stage: recognizing that the abuse, regardless of whether its details are remembered, really happened. Then comes a period of learning to believe that the abuse was not the victim's fault. Sandra Butler describes the next phase as learning to understand that coping responses can be creative, not pathological. This concept, therapists agree, is a difficult one for many survivors to integrate. "It's easy to forgive yourself as a child," Bass says, "but the adult manifestations of incest—difficulty trusting in relationships, alcohol and drug abuse, chronic depression, sexual dysfunction, eating disorders, suicide attempts—are harder to forgive."

In the final stages of healing, clients are urged to experience grief and rage with the support of the therapist and other group members. Some clients choose to confront their abusers in role-playing, in writing, or in person. Moyer describes the results of successful therapy as exhilarating. "Clients who have felt shattered all their lives, often without knowing why," she says, "become whole, integrated women."

—M.M.

and sexual-arousal patterns, which are treated in behavioral individual therapy. "First the client must define for himself what his deviance is," Wolf explains. "From there he starts confronting the rationalizations for his behavior and learning the specifics of his pattern—the warning signs that precede a return to deviant behavior. Finally, the client is taught to curb this behavior through various conditioning techniques."

Of the four thousand offenders treated at Northwest who had families, 50 percent returned to them, but half of those marriages dissolved a few years after treatment. "We don't encourage women to take offenders back," Wolf says. "But if families choose to stay together we try to 'perv-proof' them."

"Perv-proofing," Wolf says, involves teaching family members to recognize both the warning signs that precede deviant behavior and the ways the perpetrator covers up such behavior. But an even more important element, according to Wolf, is to strengthen wives and children. This is accomplished through therapy and practical assistance and by proving to them that reported offenders do get punished and reporting victims don't.

"Usually the process takes about two or three years, and any time a kid says stop, it stops," says Wolf. "Nothing matters more to us than protecting children."

This goal—protecting chidren—is primary to all who work with incestuous families. But how best to accomplish this is the subject of some debate. Some experts say breaking up the family only deepens the trauma of child victims by depriving them of restructured, healthy relationships with their fathers. To substantiate this stance, Parents United claims that repeat offenses occur in fewer than 1 percent of families who complete its program. Steven Wolf counters flatly, however, that every client continues to abuse while in treatment. Monitoring the repeat-offense rate of molesters released from treatment is impossible, he says, but the rearrest rate of Northwest "graduates" is 5–10 percent.

At Seattle's Sexual Assault Center, Lucy Berliner sees victims as young as three years old. "What we do with kids is preventive," she says. "We're trying to keep them from developing severe mental-health problems as a consequence of having been victimized." The impact of chronic sexual abuse on a child, Berliner believes, is similar to a soldier's wartime experience—"Like soldiers, molested kids develop defenses to help them survive ongoing trauma. But unlike a nineteen-year-old GI, these kids are still becoming who they are. So their coping responses may actually become integrated into their personalities: the way they think, the way they look at the world." Role-playing and play therapy with anatomically correct dolls are used to convince children that what happened was not their fault and that they have a right to expect not to be abused. "Victims can't recover," Berliner says, "until they've had a chance to respond as normal, healthy kids would—with rage, grief, loss."

Berliner's work with mothers emphasizes that a family doesn't need an offender in it to be a family. "We do urge biological parents to work on their communication in counseling," she says, "because those two people have a lifelong relationship to that child, but we also point out to mothers that agreeing to live with a sex offender means agreeing to be a supervisor for the rest of your life in order to protect the children in your home. We recommend that every mother get a job, so if she stays with an offender it's because the relationship is worth it, not for economic reasons. Generally, the stronger and smarter a woman gets, the less willing she becomes to carry that load."

Shattered Innocence

*CHILDHOOD SEXUAL ABUSE
IS YIELDING ITS DARK SECRETS
TO THE COLD LIGHT OF RESEARCH.*

Alfie Kohn

Alfie Kohn's book, No Contest: The Case Against Competition, *has just been published by Houghton Mifflin.*

No one would claim today that child sexual abuse happens in only one family in a million. Yet that preposterous estimate, based on statistics from 1930, was published in a psychiatric textbook as recently as 1975. Sensational newspaper headlines about day-care center scandals seem to appear almost daily and, together with feminist protests against sexist exploitation, these reports have greatly increased public awareness of what we now know is a widespread problem.

Even so, the most recent scientific findings about child sexual abuse—how often it happens and how it affects victims in the short and long term—have received comparatively little attention. These findings suggest that as many as 40 million people, about one in six Americans, may have been sexually victimized as children. As many as a quarter of these people may be suffering from a variety of psychological problems, ranging from guilt and poor self-esteem to sexual difficulties and a tendency to raise children who are themselves abused.

The startling figure of 40 million is derived from several studies indicating that 25 to 35 percent of all women and 10 to 16 percent of all men in this country experienced some form of abuse as children, ranging from sexual fondling to intercourse. In August 1985, *The Los Angeles Times* published the results of a national telephone poll of 2,627 randomly selected adults. Overall, 22 percent of respondents (27 percent of the women and 16 percent of the men) confided that they had experienced as children what they now identify as sexual abuse.

Some victims of abuse may be reluctant to tell a stranger on the telephone about something as traumatic and embarrassing as sexual abuse, which suggests that even the *Times* poll may have understated the problem. When sociologist Diana Russell of Mills College sent trained interviewers around San Francisco to interview 930 randomly selected women face-to-face, she found that 357, or 38 percent, reported at least one instance of having been sexually abused in childhood. When the definition of abuse was widened to include sexual advances that never reached the stage of physical contact, more than half of those interviewed said they had had such an experience before the age of 18.

Confirming the *Times* and Russell studies is a carefully designed Gallup Poll of more than 2,000 men and women from 210 Canadian communities. The results, published in 1984, show that 22 percent of the respondents were sexually abused as children. As

with Russell's study, that number increases dramatically, to 39 percent, when noncontact abuse is included.

John Briere, a postdoctoral fellow at Harbor-University of California, Los Angeles Medical Center, has reviewed dozens of studies of child abuse in addition to conducting several of his own. "It is probable," he says, "that at least a quarter to a third of adult women and perhaps half as many men have been sexually victimized as children."

One reason these numbers are so surprising, and the reason estimates of one family in a million could be taken seriously for so long, is that many children who are sexually abused understandably keep this painful experience to themselves. In the *Times* poll, one-third of those who said they had been victimized also reported that they had never before told anyone. Many therapists still do not bother to ask their clients whether abuse has taken place, even when there is good reason to suspect that it has.

Studies demonstrate that most child sexual abuse happens to those between the ages of 9 and 12 (although abuse of 2- and 3-year-olds is by no means unusual), that the abuser is almost always a man and that he is typically known to the child—often a relative. In many cases, the abuse is not limited to a single episode, nor does the abuser usually use force. No race, ethnic group or economic class is immune.

All children do not react identically to sexual abuse. But most therapists would agree that certain kinds of behavior and feelings occur regularly among victims. The immediate effects of sexual abuse include sleeping and eating disturbances, anger, withdrawal and guilt. The children typically appear to be either afraid or anxious.

Two additional signs show up so frequently that experts rely upon them as indicators of possible abuse when they occur together. The first is sexual

abuse, it is far more difficult to draw a definitive connection between such abuse and later psychological problems. "We can't say every child who is abused has this or that consequence, and we are nowhere near producing a validated profile of a child-abuse victim," says Maria Sauzier, a psychiatrist who used to direct the Family Crisis Program for Sexually Abused Children at the New England Medical Center in Boston. In fact, some experts emphasize that many sexual abuse victims emerge relatively unscathed as adults. Indeed, David

der," people whose relationships, emotions and sense of self are all unstable and who often become inappropriately angry or injure themselves. "Not all borderlines have been sexually abused, but many have been," Briere says.

Briere, working with graduate student Marsha Runtz, has also noticed that some female abuse victims "space out" or feel as if they are outside of their own bodies at times. And he has observed that these women sometimes have physical complaints without any apparent medical cause. Briere points out that these two tendencies, known as "dissociation" and "somatization," add up to something very much like hysteria, as Freud used the term.

Other therapists believe the label Post-Traumatic Stress Disorder (PTSD), which has most often been applied to veterans of combat, may also be an appropriate diagnosis for some of those who have been abused. Symptoms of the disorder include flashbacks to the traumatic events, recurrent dreams about them, a feeling of estrangement from others and a general sense of numbness. "It feels to me like the fit is very direct to what we see with [victims of] child sexual abuse," says Christine Courtois, a psychologist from Washington, D.C. "Many victims ... experience the symptoms of acute PTSD." She describes an 18-year-old client, abused by her father for nine years, who carved the words "help me" in her arm. In the course of dealing with what had happened, she would sometimes pass out, an occasional response to extreme trauma.

AT LEAST 25 PERCENT OF ALL WOMEN AND 10 PERCENT OF ALL MEN IN THIS COUNTRY EXPERIENCED SOME ABUSE AS CHILDREN, RANGING FROM SEXUAL FONDLING TO INTERCOURSE.

preoccupation: excessive or public masturbation and an unusual interest in sexual organs, sex play and nudity. According to William Friedrich, associate professor of psychology at the Mayo Medical School in Rochester, Minnesota, "What seems to happen is the socialization process toward propriety goes awry in these kids."

The second sign consists of a host of physical complaints or problems, such as rashes, vomiting and headaches, all without medical explanation. Once it is discovered that children have been abused, a check of their medical records often reveals years of such mysterious ailments, says psychologist Pamela Langelier, director of the Vermont Family Forensic Institute in South Burlington, Vermont. Langelier emphasizes that children who have been sexually abused should be reassessed every few years because they may develop new problems each time they reach a different developmental stage. "Sometimes it looks like the kids have recovered," she says, "and then at puberty the issues come back again."

While there are clear patterns in the immediate effects of child sexual

Finkelhor, associate director of the Family Violence Research Program at the University of New Hampshire, has warned his colleagues against "exaggerating the degree and inevitability of the long-term negative effects of sexual abuse." For example, Finkelhor and others point out that studies of disturbed, atypical groups, such as prostitutes, runaways and drug addicts, often find that they show higher rates of childhood sexual abuse than in the general population. Yet according to the estimate of Chris Bagley, a professor of social welfare at the University of Calgary, "At least 50 percent of women who were abused do not suffer long-term ill effects."

If 50 percent survive abuse without problems, of course it follows that 50 percent do not. And Bagley, in fact, has conducted a study indicating that a quarter of all women who are sexually abused develop serious psychological problems as a result. Given the epidemic proportions of sexual abuse, that means that millions are suffering.

Briere, for example, has found a significant degree of overlap between abuse victims and those who suffer from "borderline personality disor-

Even when no such serious psychological problems develop, those who were sexually abused often display a pattern of personal and social problems. Abused individuals in psychotherapy have more difficulties with sexuality and relationships than do others in psychotherapy, for instance. And women who have been victimized often have difficulty becoming sexually aroused. Ironically, others engage in sex compulsively.

Abused women often feel isolated, remain distrustful of men and see themselves as unattractive. "Some [victims] become phobic about intimacy. They can't be touched," says Gail Ericson, a social worker at the Branford Counseling Center in Connecticut. "These women feel rotten about themselves—especially their bodies." As a group, adults who were sexually abused as children consistently have lower self-esteem than others. Other studies have found abuse victims to be more anxious, depressed and guilt-ridden.

Might there be a connection between the high incidence of child sexual abuse among girls and the fact that women tend, in general, to score lower on measures of self-esteem than men? Bagley believes that this disparity may simply reflect the fact that in our society, more women are abused: Seven of ten victims are girls, so any random sampling of men and women will pick up more abused women than men,

those in Russell's survey who had been abused as children reported that they were later victims of rape or attempted rape. Abuse victims "don't know how to take care of themselves," Courtois says. "They're easy targets for somebody, waiting for victimization to happen." This may be due to poor self-image, lack of assertiveness or the feeling that they deserve to be punished.

Women, of course, are not to blame for being victims. "In a society that raises males to behave in a predatory fashion toward females, undermining a young girl's defenses is likely to be exceedingly perilous for her," Russell says, since childhood abuse "could

that the prognosis is particularly bad for those who have been abused by more than one person. Counselor Claire Walsh, director of the Sexual Assault Recovery Service at the University of Florida, has paid special attention to this subgroup. She studied 30 women who were in psychotherapy and who had been abused by their fathers, 18 of whom had also been abused by at least one other person. Walsh found a different psychological profile for those who had been molested by more than one person, which included more anxiety, fear and flashbacks. She also believes that PTSD may show up more often when there is more than one abuser.

Another important variable is the age of the abuser. Russell found that victims are most traumatized if their abuser was between the ages of 26 and 50.

Victims seem to experience more serious problems if force is used during the abuse and if the abuser is a close relative, but evidence for these claims is not conclusive.

Obviously, large gaps remain in the research on the long-term effects of child sexual abuse. This is not very surprising given how new the field is. Most of the studies reported here have been conducted since 1980, and the five scholarly journals devoted to the subject have all been launched within the last two years. Only in 1986 was the groundwork finally laid for an American professional society dealing with sexual child abuse.

There is no question that the field already has produced striking findings. "We now clearly know that sexual abuse is a major risk factor for a lot of later mental-health problems," Finkelhor says. "What we don't yet know is who is most susceptible to these problems, how other experiences interact with abuse or what can be done."

Finkelhor adds that research on child sexual abuse "should teach all social scientists and mental-health practitioners some humility. Despite several generations of clinical expertise and knowledge of childhood development, it was only very recently that we came to see how incredibly widespread this childhood trauma is.

"It may make us realize that there are other things about childhood that we don't have a clear perspective on as well," he says.

*S*INCE GIRLS IN OUR SOCIETY ARE ABUSED MORE COMMONLY THAN BOYS, PERHAPS IT'S UNDERSTANDABLE THAT WOMEN, AS A GROUP, HAVE LOWER SELF-ESTEEM THAN MEN.

perhaps enough of a difference to account for the gender gap in self-esteem.

In one study, Bagley discovered that half of all women with psychological problems had been abused. "The reason for the higher rate [of psychopathology] for women is the higher rate of sexual abuse in women," he says. Other researchers might not support so sweeping a conclusion, but Bagley points to a study of his that showed that nonabused men and women have comparable self-esteem.

One of the most disturbing findings about child abuse is its strong intergenerational pattern: Boys who are abused are far more likely to turn into offenders, molesting the next generation of children; girls are more likely to produce children who are abused. Two of five abused children in a study conducted by Sauzier, psychologist Beverly Gomes-Schwartz and psychiatrist Jonathan Horowitz had mothers who were themselves abused.

In addition, victimization can lead to revictimization. Nearly two-thirds of

have stripped away some of [her] potential ability to protect" herself.

Men who were abused, meanwhile, are likely to be confused about their sexual identity, deeply ashamed, unwilling to report the experience and apt to respond aggressively. Says Jack Rusinoff, a counselor in Minneapolis who works with male victims, "I have one 5-year-old boy who's already on the road to being an abuser." This boy, like many others, has displayed sexual aggression, even at this age. Langelier, who has seen more than 200 victims over the last three years, notes that her young male clients are sometimes caught reaching for others' genitals or "making demands for sexual stimulation."

Is there any indication, given this variation in psychological outcome, why one case of childhood sexual abuse leads to serious adult problems while another does not? So far, only two characteristics of abuse have consistently been linked with major difficulties later on. For one, studies by Bagley, Briere and others have shown

Kids for Sale

A shocking report on child prostitution across America

Michael Satchell

Across America, there are tens of thousands of children—boys and girls—working as prostitutes. You can find them in New York City, loitering on the street corners of Times Square and the lower West Side. Or in suburban middle-class areas like the San Fernando Valley of Los Angeles, where—until a recent raid by the Van Nuys police—you could order up a 12-year-old girl from an out-call massage service. Or in placid little towns like Waterville, Maine (population 18,000), where 15-year-old girls occasionally hustle outside the bars on Temple and Water streets.

Kids are for sale everywhere, part of the continuing national tragedy of America's runaway and throwaway child population.

In 1982, my colleague Dotson Rader circled America to chronicle for PARADE the plight of runaway and throwaway children. Four years later, I traced roughly the same path down the East Coast and up the West Coast, focusing on youngsters who had been forced into prostitution—their most common option for survival.

My findings:

• The population of runaways—between a million and 1.3 million Americans under 18 leave home each year—has remained about the same, but social workers are seeing more children in the 12-14 age bracket. The kids are staying away from home longer, resulting in a growing hard-core street population.

• About one youngster in three is a so-called "throwaway," either a child fleeing intolerable home conditions who is not reported missing by his parents or one literally forced out of the house to fend for himself.

• Well over half of the youngsters who have been on the streets for longer than a month become involved in prostitution, which may range from turning an occasional "trick" to regular daily hustling, depending on their needs. Most of the young males say they are not gay, and they are poorly informed about the dangers of catching and spreading AIDS.

• Fear of AIDS and other sexually transmitted diseases is encouraging men to seek younger boys and girls as partners. Unlike neighborhood child-molesters who are vigorously prosecuted, those who sexually prey on street kids have little to fear from the police because prosecuting "johns" is a low priority.

• While there has been progress in recent years, shelter and support programs remain inadequate considering the size of the problem. There are some first class programs run by extremely dedicated social workers, but money is always short, and volunteers are needed.

Just how many juvenile prostitutes work the streets isn't known, but Drs. Daniel Campagna and Donald Poffenberger, using data provided by 595 police departments in 50 states, estimate there are between 100,000 and 200,000 adolescent prostitutes with a median age of 15. Other experts and observers accept the two doctors' figures, published in their book *Sexual Exploitation of Children—Resource Manual.*

But statistics don't convey the realities of life for these young street hustlers. They don't tell of the agony of a bewildered 9-year-old boy, forced into prostitution by his mother. The story of this young victim was related by Judy Turner, a police officer who works in an unusual Miami-Dade County Task Force program that uses a novel approach in helping teenage prostitutes. Turner, a six-year veteran, patrols in plainclothes in an unmarked car with a social worker as her partner. When they spot a youthful prostitute, they interview the youngster and arrange to get the child home. They visit and counsel the parents, plug the family into social-service programs and follow up at regular intervals.

The exploitation of runaway and throwaway children continues to be a searing national tragedy

---

"The 9-year-old boy was the youngest we've worked with," Turner related as we cruised Biscayne Boulevard. "His mother was a drug user, sending him out to get money to support her habit. The neighbors told us that the boy would be forced to sleep on the front steps all night if he didn't come home with enough money. When we investigated, we also found three neighbors, brothers aged 10 through 13, all prostitutes."

Reprinted from *Parade Magazine*, July 20, 1986, pp. 4-6, by permission.

Three young victims from one family is an extreme but not unusual example of child prostitution. During visits to shelter and outreach programs around the country and in interviews with two-dozen teenage hustlers, I heard not only a litany of horror stories but also some encouraging examples of youngsters who are being helped to get out of the gutter and start putting their lives back together. Some programs help.

The largest, and one of the most effective programs, is Covenant House, started in New York 14 years ago by Father Bruce Ritter. It evolved from an offer of refuge in his modest apartment on a freezing winter night to six homeless teenagers with nowhere to sleep. The next evening, there were 10 youngsters stretched out on Ritter's living room floor. This year, more than 18,000 runaway and throwaway kids—well over half of them with experience in prostitution—will find sanctuary in Covenant House shelters in New York, Houston, Toronto and Fort Lauderdale, Fla.

Covenant House is a remarkable example of what can be achieved with determined leadership, committed volunteers and private philanthropy. Last year, it raised $28.8 million from private sources to finance its programs. By comparison, the entire federal government contribution to runaway shelter programs nationwide was $23.2 million, and Gramm-Rudman cutbacks in 1987 will trim that figure to about $17 million.

Besides hot meals, clean beds, clothing and medical assistance, the four shelters offer youngsters comprehensive program services designed to get them into stable living situations; back into school or into jobs. In New York City and Fort Lauderdale, I met two kids—former prostitutes—who are trying to piece their lives together with the help of Covenant House workers.

'The average person can't imagine what goes on in certain parts of the underground'

Peter, 17, has supported himself since he ran away from home at the age of 12 to escape a brutal father. For five years, he worked as a street hustler on Santa Monica Boulevard in Los Angeles and as a stripper, go-go dancer and prostitute in homosexual bars and clubs in Washington, D.C., New York, Atlanta, Florida and California.

"The average person can't imagine what goes on in parts of the gay underground," he told me. "Kids 11, 12, 13, 14 being fed all kinds of drugs and being sexually abused and hurt in the meat-rack bars and at private parties."

Peter (a fictitious name, as are all those used for youngsters in the article) reached bottom in San Francisco as a hustler on Polk Street. Most of his earnings went to support a drug habit, and he was sleeping on the streets. "I woke up one day and said enough is enough," he recalled. "I flew back to New York, went to my mom's,

and my stepfather beat me up and threw me out after a couple of days. I had nowhere else to go, so I came to Covenant House."

Today, Peter is working to earn a high school equivalency certificate and has a modest but steady job as a cashier in a food store.

In Fort Lauderdale, I met Alice, a chubby 15-year-old estranged from her police officer father and beautician mother since the age of 13. A veteran of scores of liaisons in parked cars and motel rooms in this vacation city, she said angrily: "I got to hate the johns—especially the older ones. They'd ask you how old you were, and I'd say 13. They'd say, 'Good, honey, because in a couple of years you ain't gonna be any good.'"

Today, Alice is enrolled in a long-term therapeutic program designed to help her overcome a history of drug abuse and regain her emotional health. She's receiving vocational training and has expressed an interest in becoming a nurse's aide.

Unlike the well-equipped and financed Covenant Houses, most of the nation's 500 or so runaway shelters—about half supported partially by federal funds—tend to be smaller and limited by shoestring budgets. Kids can usually stay from two nights up to a maximum of two weeks. Dedicated staff and volunteers compensate for shabby furniture and threadbare carpets.

While 500 shelters may sound like a lot, it isn't. Los Angeles County, for example, with a population of 7.5 million persons, has just 24 beds in its walk-in shelters. The Chicago area, by comparison, has 68 beds but Seattle only 8. Other random examples: San Francisco, 31 beds; Bismarck, N.D., 3; Nashville, 8; Paterson, N.J., 12; Sacramento, 8; New Orleans, 16; Miami, 24; Galveston, Tex., 16; Philadelphia, 25.

Many cities also have programs designed to find street kids involved in prostitution and steer them back home or into some kind of stable living situation. One of the most successful is Children of the Night, begun in Hollywood in 1979 by Lois Lee in much the same manner as Father Ritter launched Covenant House.

Lee was studying prostitution for a doctoral thesis in sociology and opened her home to teenage girl runaways who had come to Hollywood seeking glamour and wound up working for Sunset Strip pimps. Last year, more than 1600 runaways and throwaways sought help from Lee and her staff of counselors.

"We're seeing more and more throwaways," reports Hida Avent, who runs the Stepping Stone shelter house in Santa Monica. "We see kids whose parents put them out of the house, change the locks and don't allow them to return. "We see kids who are literally dumped—their parents drive into California, pull into some gas station, give the kid a few dollars to buy doughnuts or something, then take off and abandon them."

June Bucy, executive director of the National Network of Runaway and Youth Services in Washington, D.C., describes a recent incident in Galveston where a 13-year-old boy came home from school and found that his parents had hitched up their trailer home and disappeared. "It took three weeks to track the parents," Bucy recalls. "The mother said she was kind of tired of him, and the stepfather didn't want him home at all."

6. OLD/NEW SEXUAL CONCERNS: Sexual Abuse and Violence

In an era of shrinking federal and local tax dollars for social problems as broad and complex as the plight of street kids, Bucy and others working in the field will increasingly rely on volunteer help, public generosity and innovative ideas. One new program that combines all three is Project Safe Place, an idea that has been successful in Louisville and one that professionals are now trying to establish nationwide.

The program employs a distinctive yellow and black logo to inform runaways, throwaways and children in crisis where they can get immediate help. Volunteers throughout Louisville—in fire stations, libraries, gas stations, convenience stores, public and private facilities—are screened and trained to assist youngsters who spot the logo and request help. They make the children welcome, offer a safe, temporary refuge, determine their immediate needs and either transport them to the nearest shelter or arrange for professional help.

"Project Safe Place is an ideal way of involving volunteers, and it also brings in the business community, which becomes interested in the problem and hopefully responds with financial support for the shelter and outreach programs," says Larry Wooldridge, who runs the program. "It uplifts the entire image of the runaway problem and the shelter program. We've had a lot of success involving local businesses, and now we're talking to national corporations, hoping to spread it nationwide."

The Question of Pornography

IT IS NOT SEX, BUT VIOLENCE,
THAT IS AN OBSCENITY IN OUR SOCIETY.

EDWARD I. DONNERSTEIN
AND DANIEL G. LINZ

Edward I. Donnerstein, Ph.D., is a professor of communication studies at the University of California, Santa Barbara. Daniel G. Linz, Ph.D., is coordinator of health services research at the William S. Middleton Memorial Veterans Hospital in Madison, Wisconsin.

In July 1986, the United States Attorney General's Commission on Pornography issued its final report on a subject that is as complex as the human condition. While many people have commented upon the report, few have actually read it and fewer still understand its implications.

As social scientists and two of the researchers whose work was cited throughout the two-volume work, we feel it necessary to point out that the report fell short of our expectations in several important respects. First, there are factual problems with the report, representing serious errors of commission. Several of the contentions made in its pages cannot be supported by empirical evidence. Some commission members apparently did not understand or chose not to heed some of the fundamental assumptions in the social science research on pornography. Second, and perhaps more importantly, the commission members have committed a serious error of omission. The single most important problem in the media today, as clearly indicated by social science research, is not pornography but violence.

The report begins with some history about previous attempts to examine the question of pornography. One of the most important of these was the President's Commission on Obscenity and Pornography, which issued its final report in 1970. "More than in 1957, when the law of obscenity became inextricably a part of constitutional law, more than in 1970, when the President's Commission on Obscenity and Pornography issued its report . . . we live in a society unquestionably pervaded by sexual explicitness," the current report states. It goes on to point out, quite rightly, that the most dangerous form of pornography is that which includes specifically violent themes. But then the report adds: "Increasingly, the most prevalent forms of pornography . . . fit this description . . . . It is with respect to material of this variety that the scientific findings and ultimate conclusions of the 1970 Commission are least reliable for today, precisely because material of this variety was largely absent from that Commission's inquiries."

It is popularly assumed—and the members of the commission appear to share this assumption—that images of violence have become more prevalent in pornography in recent years. Interestingly, there has never been a systematic content analysis of X-rated books, films and magazines that would be needed to support such a conclusion. But there are a handful of studies, concentrating on specific media, that at least call this notion into question.

One of the most recent of these was undertaken by sociologist Joseph E. Scott of Ohio State University. He

From *Psychology Today*, December 1986, pp. 56-59. Adapted from THE QUESTION OF PORNOGRAPHY, by Edward I. Donnerstein, Daniel G. Linz, and Steven Penrod. © 1987 The Free Press, Inc.

*I*T IS POPULARLY ASSUMED THAT IMAGES OF VIOLENCE
HAVE BECOME MORE PREVALENT IN PORNOGRAPHY IN
RECENT YEARS. BUT THERE ARE A HANDFUL
OF STUDIES THAT AT LEAST CALL THIS NOTION INTO QUESTION.

examined the content of cartoons in *Playboy* magazine from 1954 to 1983 and found that there was indeed a period—around 1977—when the violent content peaked. But just as there had been an increase in violence in the years before 1977, there has been a like decrease since. Further, he notes that sexually violent material seems to occur on an average of about 1 page in every 3,000 and in fewer than 4 pictures out of 1,000—a level that would have to be considered barely noticeable.

In addition, there is evidence indicating a different sort of trend in sexually oriented videocassettes. Psychologist Ted Palys of Simon Fraser University analyzed the content of 150 randomly selected home videos, most of which were produced between 1979 and 1983. He divided these films into "Triple X," in which sexual activity is explicit and graphic, and "Adult," in which no explicit sex is shown but nudity and "implied" sexual behavior is allowed.

Palys found that the Adult films actually portrayed a higher percentage of aggressive scenes and more severe and graphic forms of aggression than did the Triple X videos. More important, there was no increase in aggressive images between 1979 and 1983 for either type of video. In fact, as Palys notes, the difference between these two types of videos may be widening over time, primarily because of decreases in sexual violence in the Triple X category.

At least for now we cannot legitimately conclude that pornography has become more violent since the time of the 1970 Pornography Commission. The results of the few studies that have been done are inconclusive and inconsistent, but at least a few of them point in the opposite direction. Perhaps it is because all forms of pornography are more prevalent now than they once were that we are more aware of the sexually violent forms of pornography.

What is so particularly evil about violent pornography? Here, the commission does not mince words: "In both clinical and experimental settings, exposure to sexually violent materials has indicated an increase in the likelihood of aggression." The commission goes on to state that "finding a link between aggressive behavior toward women and sexual violence . . . requires assumptions not found exclusively in the experimental evidence. We see no reason, however, not to make these assumptions." The assumptions include the idea (in the commission's words) that "increased aggressive behavior towards women is causally related, for an aggregate population, to increased sexual violence."

One persuasive reason to be careful about an intuitive leap like this, however, is a closer examination of the empirical evidence—what it says and what it does not say. We have no argument with the commission on its first point. Experiments by psychologist Neil Malamuth at the University of California, Los Angeles, suggest that, especially when the experimenter appears to condone aggression against women, men act more aggressively toward women in a laboratory after having been exposed to sexually violent stories. But a question that the prudent reader might raise is: "How long do these effects last?" In the vast majority of studies, aggressive behavior is measured almost immediately after exposure to the violent pornographic films. But is the effect cumulative or does it disappear over time?

In one study by Malamuth and psychologist Joseph Ceniti, college-aged men were exposed to violent and nonviolent sexual material over a four-week period. They watched two feature-length films each week and read similar materials. About seven days later, they were (according to the researchers' plan) angered by a woman working with the researchers and then given an opportunity to act aggressively against her. Contrary to expectations, the men who had been exposed to pornography were no more aggressive against her than were those not exposed to pornography. For the moment, then, we do not know if repeated exposure has a cumulative effect or if such effects are only temporary. But the evidence, such as it is, points toward the latter conclusion. This fact seems not to have been given sufficient consideration by the commission.

In addition, there is evidence that particular themes in pornography might be especially harmful. Recent research indicates that it is specifically the message that women find force or aggression pleasurable that seems to be important in influencing men's perceptions and attitudes about rape. For example, in a study Donnerstein conducted with psychologist Leonard Berkowitz, men were shown one of two films, both aggressively violent and sexually explicit. In both, a young woman arrives at the home of two young men to study. She is shoved around, tied up, stripped, slapped and ultimately raped by both men. In one version of the film ("positive ending"), the woman is shown smiling at the end and in no way resisting. A narrative added to the film indicates that she eventually becomes a willing participant. In the version with a "negative ending," the reaction of the woman is not clear, but the voice-over indicates that she found the experience humiliating and disgusting.

*I*T IS SPECIFICALLY THE MESSAGE
THAT WOMEN FIND FORCE OR AGGRESSION
PLEASURABLE THAT SEEMS TO BE IMPORTANT
IN INFLUENCING MEN'S PERCEPTIONS AND
ATTITUDES ABOUT RAPE.

Men who saw the positive-ending film interpreted the film itself as less aggressive and said that the woman suffered less, enjoyed herself more and was more responsible for what happened than did the men who saw the negative ending. This seems fairly clear evidence that the different messages in the two films affected the men's attitudes in different ways.

But this literature can be tricky to interpret. In one study by Malamuth, researcher Scott Haber and psychologist Seymour Feshbach, for example, men read several stories, some of which were about a woman being raped. When the men were asked how likely they would be to behave as the rapist did if they knew they would not be caught, more than half indicated some likelihood of behaving that way. Many assume that this surprisingly high percentage was due to the effects of men being exposed to violent pornography. As the commission report concludes, "substantial exposure to sexually violent materials . . . bears a causal relationship to antisocial acts of sexual violence and, for some subgroups, possibly to unlawful acts of sexual violence."

Yet nothing could be further from the truth. In none of the studies by Malamuth has a measure of motivation such as "likelihood to rape" ever changed as a result of exposure to pornography. If the men reported feeling this way, it might be because they were generally callous about rape to begin with. As Malamuth has noted, men who indicate some likelihood that they might commit rape (if not caught) are more sexually aroused by and more attracted to violent materials, but there is no reason to think that exposure to violent pornography is the cause of these predispositions.

Malamuth and psychologist James Check again asked men to read two stories. Some first read a story with a "positive ending," in which the woman becomes sexually aroused; others read a story with a negative ending; then all of the men read a realistic depiction of a rape. But first, the researchers classified the men as "more likely to rape" or "less likely to rape" based upon their answer to the question, "Would you rape if you knew you would not be caught?"

While both groups were more likely to view the woman in the second story as enjoying rape if they had read the positive-ending story first, the "more likely to rape" men seemed much more affected by exposure to this sort of pornography. They agreed much more frequently with statements suggesting that women enjoy rape and enjoy being forced into having sex than did those

who were "less likely to rape" to begin with. This indicates to us that exposure to violent pornography is not necessarily causing callous attitudes about rape but rather may reinforce and strengthen already existing beliefs and values. If aggressive pornography is not the cause of the negative attitudes, then it ought not be blamed for them.

What we have is a picture of violent pornography that is somewhat different from that drawn by the commission. We do not, as yet, know if the detrimental effects of watching pornography are long-lived or only fleeting. We do know that it is specifically the pornographic materials that depict women "enjoying" rape that are especially damaging, but it remains unclear whether all men are affected equally even by these bizarre scripts. Finally, it remains to be seen whether changes in attitudes about women and rape revealed in relatively small-scale tests have any applicability to rape and aggression in the real world.

There is some evidence from the work of Malamuth that these attitudes do have some relationship to real-world aggression, but again, these are attitudes that people already have. The commission members were obviously aware of these issues. In fact, these conclusions, well-grounded in scientific research, are briefly summarized deep within their report, which makes it even more perplexing that they ignore the data in making their 92 recommendations.

Our major criticism of the report and its authors, however, has to do with a subject that has been glossed over in the commission's 1,960-page report. The commission has ignored the inescapable conclusion that it is violence, whether or not accompanied by sex, that has the most damaging effect upon those who view it, hear it or read about it. This is an extremely important distinction, with direct relevance to the work of the commission, because it has implications far beyond violent pornography and pornography in general.

Sexual violence and depictions of women "desiring" rape are not limited to X-rated films, books and magazines. In the popular film *The Getaway,* for example, one of the robbers kidnaps a woman (portrayed by Sally Struthers) and her husband. He rapes the woman, but she is portrayed as a willing participant. Struthers's character becomes the kidnapper's girlfriend and the two of them taunt her husband until he finally commits suicide. The woman then willingly continues with the assailant. Far from being consigned to dingy X-rated the-

VIOLENCE AGAINST WOMEN NEED NOT OCCUR IN A SEXUALLY EXPLICIT CONTEXT TO HAVE A NEGATIVE EFFECT ON ATTITUDES AND BEHAVIOR. VIOLENT RATHER THAN SEXUAL IMAGES ARE MOST RESPONSIBLE FOR PEOPLE'S ATTITUDES ABOUT WOMEN AND RAPE.

aters, this film, originally produced in 1972 and shown in cinemas all over the country, is still shown occasionally on commercial television.

Malamuth and Check tried to determine whether the mildly explicit sexual violence in *The Getaway* and in *Swept Away*, another film with similar content, influenced viewers' attitudes toward women and rape. When the researchers questioned college students who saw both films and students who saw nonviolent films or no films at all, they found that the men who saw violent movies more readily accepted interpersonal violence and more frequently believed that women enjoy rape.

In another study we did with Berkowitz, men saw different versions of a film. The first version contained a scene of sexual aggression in which a woman is tied up, threatened with a gun and raped. The second version contained only the violent parts of the scene, with the sexually explicit rape omitted. The third version contained only the sexually explicit rape scene with the violence deleted.

The most callous attitudes about rape and the largest percentage of subjects indicating some likelihood of raping or using force were found among those men who had seen only the violent coercion. Subjects who saw the X-rated version without violence scored the lowest on both measures, and those who saw both the explicit sex and the violence scored somewhere in between.

Taken together, these studies strongly suggest that violence against women need not occur in a pornograph-
ic or sexually explicit context to have a negative effect upon viewer attitudes and behavior. But even more importantly, it must be concluded that violent images, rather than sexual ones, are most responsible for people's attitudes about women and rape.

As should be obvious to anyone with a television set, the mass media contain an abundance of such nonsexually explicit images and messages. These ideas about rape are so pervasive in our culture that it is myopic to call them the exclusive domain of violent pornography. In fact, one would not have to search much farther than the local 7-Eleven to find numerous bloody murder mysteries in detective magazines that reinforce this point.

And this is where we have our strongest disagreement with the Commission on Pornography. Granted that the charter of the group was to examine the pernicious effects of pornography on society. Granted also that the time, money and other resources of the commission were limited. But it seems appropriate to note that if the commissioners were looking for the most nefarious media threat to public welfare, they missed the boat. The most clear and present danger, well documented by the social science literature, is all violent material in our society, whether sexually explicit or not, that promotes violence against women. Let us hope that the next commission will provide a better example by disentangling sexuality from violence, therefore yielding more useful conclusions.

The Facts About AIDS

THE SPREAD OF AIDS

Proper information and education can prevent thousands of deaths from Acquired Immune Deficiency Syndrome (AIDS).

AIDS was first reported in the United States in mid-1981. Since that time, the Public Health Service has received reports of more than 40,000 adults and 500 children who have contracted AIDS. More than half of these have died. No cure as yet exists. And AIDS is expected to claim increasing numbers of lives.

An estimated 1.5 million people have been infected by the virus that causes AIDS, but many have no symptoms. Current research indicates that at least a third of those infected may develop AIDS within a six-year period. By 1992, authorities project that 270,000 persons will have developed AIDS, and 180,000 will have died. In 1991 alone, a predicted 54,000 persons with AIDS will die.

Fighting AIDS has been designated the number one priority of the U.S. Public Health Service. Researchers in the Service and in many major medical institutions have been working since 1981 to understand AIDS, identify its cause, and develop treatments and preventive measures. These efforts have generated a substantial body of knowledge about the nature of the AIDS virus and how it is transmitted.

Curative treatment or preventive vaccine is likely to take years to develop. Our most effective weapon against both AIDS and the fear of AIDS will be—for years to come—our understanding of how the virus is spread. For this reason it is vitally important for all of us to understand what is known about this deadly disease. It is especially important that educators have complete and accurate information about AIDS.

WHAT IS AIDS?

AIDS is a serious condition characterized by a defect in an individual's natural immunity against disease. AIDS is caused by a virus that attacks the white blood cells that help protect the body from infections. The AIDS virus is now called the Human Immunodeficiency Virus (HIV).

People with AIDS are vulnerable to serious illnesses that are not a threat to those whose immune system is functioning normally. Among the illnesses that become life-threatening to AIDS-infected persons are infections caused by certain bacteria, funguses, viruses, protozoa (one-celled parasites), and some forms of cancer. These illnesses are called "opportunistic": they take the opportunity to attack when natural immunity is weakened. The unexpected presence of such illnesses in groups of young men in 1981 first led to the recognition of AIDS by public health workers.

People infected with the AIDS virus who have no symptoms may nonetheless spread the virus to others through unprotected sexual contact, sharing of intravenous (IV) needles, and transmission during pregnancy or childbirth. Other infected persons may have chronic symptoms such as fever, weight loss, diarrhea, or swollen lymph glands. Such symptoms are sometimes called the AIDS Related Complex (ARC). In one study of persons infected with the AIDS virus, over a period of six years 30 percent developed AIDS, 22 percent developed swollen lymph nodes, 27 percent developed other chronic symptoms, and 21 percent remained free of symptoms.

HOW IS THE AIDS VIRUS TRANSMITTED?

The AIDS virus is transmitted by certain behaviors. In an infected person, virus present in semen and vaginal fluid can be passed to others by intimate sexual contact. Virus in the blood can be passed to others by sharing IV needles contaminated with blood, or can be transmitted from the mother to a fetus during pregnancy. The AIDS virus is not transmitted by any form of casual, nonsexual contact.

SEXUAL TRANSMISSION

The AIDS virus can be passed from infected men to women and from infected women to men through vaginal intercourse (penis in vagina). The virus can also be passed from infected men to other men, principally through anal intercourse (where the penis is inserted in the rectum).

Sexual practices that cause small, often invisible tears in the vagina, penis, or rectum may increase the likelihood of transmission. This fact may explain why anal intercourse, whether involving men or women, greatly increases the risk of transmitting the AIDS virus.

Scientists do not yet fully understand how the virus gets into the bloodstream during sexual intercourse. But they believe the presence of other infections of the penis, rectum, vagina, or cervix (the canal which leads into the uterus, or womb) may be a factor.

Some studies suggest that the AIDS virus may be transmitted more readily from men to women than from women to men. Some sexual partners of persons infected with the AIDS virus have not been infected despite repeated exposure. There is no definitive evidence that the virus is transmitted through oral sex (contact between the penis, vagina, or anus and the mouth), although this possibility cannot be ruled out.

The risk of being infected with the AIDS virus through sexual contact is greatly increased if a person has unprotected sexual contact with persons who share IV needles, with men who have sex with other men, or with prostitutes (many of whom use intravenous drugs). Persons who abstain from sexual relations, as well as couples who are not infected with the AIDS virus and who have sex only with each other, have no risk of infection through sexual transmission.

With virtually all sexually transmitted diseases, the more sexual partners a person has, the greater the risk of infection. The same holds true for AIDS. But for men who have sex with other men and for those who have sex with persons who share needles, even one new sexual partner greatly increases the probability of infection—unless protection is used. The reason: these populations already include a high number of individuals infected with the AIDS virus.

The regular use of latex condoms ("rubbers") can help prevent sexual transmission of the AIDS virus. The effectiveness of condoms may be enhanced if they are used together with nonoxynol-9, a spermicide that has been shown to kill the AIDS virus.

To provide protection, condoms must be used from *start to finish* and must be used *every time*. Condoms made of latex are preferred because the virus is less likely to pass through them. Using two condoms at the same time may also improve effectiveness.

Regular use of condoms can also prevent other sexually transmitted infections that appear to increase susceptability to the AIDS virus. But condoms may fail to protect against infection if they break or leak during contact.

TRANSMISSION FROM INJECTED BLOOD

Persons infected with the AIDS virus usually have large numbers of viral organisms present in their blood. Persons who share needles to inject substances into the blood-stream therefore greatly increase their chances of contracting AIDS.

Some studies of IV drug users show that as many as 60 percent have been infected with the AIDS virus. The sharing of needles in "shooting galleries" is especially dangerous, because many others may have used the same needle. Research also suggests that the use of unsterilized needles for medical injections may be responsible for the spread of the AIDS virus in certain African countries.

Before the discovery that the AIDS virus is found in the blood, a small number of people receiving blood transfusions or blood products (such as persons with hemophilia) were infected with the virus. Some have developed AIDS, accounting for 3 percent of all AIDS cases. Doctors and researchers are now able to detect antibodies to the AIDS virus in infected blood. And high-risk persons are no longer donating blood. The result is that blood and blood products are virtually free of the virus.

But individuals who received blood transfusions from 1978 to 1985 may wish to consult their physicians about having a blood test for antibodies to the AIDS virus, especially if they received multiple transfusions and were living in an area where AIDS is relatively common.

TRANSMISSION DURING PREGNANCY

A pregnant woman infected with the AIDS virus is highly likely to pass the virus to her unborn child, because of the close contact between the mother's bloodsteam and the infant's.

Children born with the AIDS virus are very likely to become seriously ill. For this reason, women at greater risk for having the AIDS virus are strongly urged to have a test for antibodies to the virus *before* considering pregnancy. Women at greater risk include those who share needles and those who have sex with IV drug users or with men who have sex with other men.

HOW THE AIDS VIRUS IS *NOT* TRANSMITTED

Compared to many other viruses, the AIDS virus is weak, fragile, and easily destroyed outside the body. Thus, it is transmitted *only* by sexual contact, introduction into the blood stream, or pregnancy.

AIDS is *not* transmitted by casual contact of any kind, including shaking hands, hugging, social kissing, crying, coughing, or sneezing. Nor is it transmitted from water in pools or baths, from food or beverages, or from sharing bed linens, towels, cups, dishes, straws, or other eating utensils.

You *cannot* get AIDS from toilets, door-knobs, telephones, office equipment, furniture, massages, or any other form of nonsexual contact. The virus is *not* transmitted through vomit, stool, or nasal secretions. Although the virus is also found in small amounts in tears and saliva, no documented cases of transmission from these fluids exist.

In addition, there is no evidence that the virus is transmitted by mosquito or other insect bites. (Unlike diseases that are transmitted by mosquitos, such as malaria and yellow fever, the AIDS virus does not infect the mosquitos' salivary glands.)

WHO IS AT GREATEST RISK FOR INFECTION WITH THE AIDS VIRUS?

The only ways of being infected by the AIDS virus are through sexual contact with infected persons, through the injection of infected blood, or through transmission from mother to child during pregnancy or birth. So the risk of infection is a function of *behavior*. It is *not* a function of genetics *or of sexual preference in itself*.

Men who have sex with men, for example, are more likely to be infected because of the greater frequency of two behaviors in some individuals in this group: having multiple sexual partners (which increases the chance of getting infected and passing the disease to others) and practicing anal intercourse. Men who have sex with men presently make up 65 percent of all persons with AIDS. (An additional 8 percent of cases occur in men who both have sex with men and use IV drugs.)

Anal intercourse is believed to be more likely to transmit the AIDS virus because of the vulnerability of the rectal lining. Heterosexual couples who engage in anal intercourse are also at greater risk. The presence of inflammation due to other sexually transmitted diseases may also increase the risk of infection with the AIDS virus.

For IV drug users, it is the sharing of needles that increases risk of transmitting the AIDS virus. IV drug users make up 17 percent of persons with AIDS. A higher propor-

tion of these cases occur in Blacks and Hispanics because sharing of needles among IV drug users is more common among Blacks and Hispanics than among Whites. Among heterosexual Blacks and Hispanics who do not use IV drugs or have sexual contact with IV drug users, the risk of AIDS is no higher than for the rest of the population. *That is because AIDS is transmitted by risky behavior, not risk groups.*

Most women who transmit AIDS to their children during pregnancy either use IV drugs or have sexual contact with IV users or with men who have sex with men.

The principle that must be kept in mind is that the incidence of AIDS is always a function of *specifically defined behavioral choices, not of genetic or physiological predispositions.* No group is inherently at risk, or inherently susceptible. But *any* group can *become* at risk if the members of the group choose behavioral patterns that are known to increase the susceptibility to AIDS. These facts must be kept firmly in mind if the following statistics are to be properly understood.

Race and Ethnicity of Persons with AIDS (U.S.)
(percentages are by row; some rows don't total 100% due to incomplete statistics on ethnicity)

	White	Black	Hispanic
Men who have sex with men	75%	15%	10%
IV drug users	19	51	30
Both of the above	65	22	13
Heterosexual cases*	14	72	13
Blood clotting disorders	86	5	7
Transfusion recipients	77	14	7
Undetermined	37	42	19
Children with AIDS	20	55	24

Gender of Persons with AIDS (U.S.)

	Male	Female
Men who have sex with men	100%	0%
IV drug users	79	21
Both of the above	100	0
Heterosexual cases*	48	52
Blood clotting disorders	98	2
Transfusion recipients	64	36
Undetermined	78	22
Children with AIDS	55	45

* Heterosexuals represent 4 percent of all AIDS cases in the U.S. Half of these cases are in persons from Africa or the West Indies. The other half are in persons who have had sexual contact with IV drug users, bisexual men, or recipients of infected blood products.

WHAT IS THE GEOGRAPHIC DISTRIBUTION OF REPORTED AIDS CASES?

AIDS cases have been reported from 50 states, the District of Columbia, Puerto Rico, and more than 100 other countries. The disease has been recognized by the World Health Organization as a worldwide epidemic.

Currently, about half of the cases in the U.S. are reported from New York State and California, followed by Florida, Texas, New Jersey, Illinois, Pennsylvania, Massachusetts, Georgia, and the District of Columbia. Over the next four years, it is projected that an increasing proportion of AIDS cases will be in states other than New York and California.

The cities where AIDS is most common are New York (28 percent of cases), San Francisco (10 percent), and Los Angeles (8 percent), followed by Houston, Washington, Miami, Newark, Chicago, Dallas, Philadelphia, and Boston.

IS AIDS SPREAD THROUGH CASUAL CONTACT?

AIDS is *not* spread by casual (nonsexual) contact. Casual contact with AIDS patients or persons who might be at risk for the illness does *not* place others at risk.

No cases have been found where AIDS or the AIDS virus has been transmitted by casual household contact with AIDS patients or infected persons. No cases of AIDS have occurred in persons whose only risk factor was casual contact with someone with AIDS. No family members or others living in close contact with adults or children with AIDS have been infected with the AIDS virus, despite kissing, hugging, sharing dishes, glasses, razors, or toothbrushes, or any other form of close but nonsexual contact.

Additional evidence that the AIDS virus is not spread by casual contact emerges from examining the 5-to-15-year-old population. In this age group, the very few cases of AIDS that have occurred have been due to known risk factors. If the AIDS virus were transmitted by casual contact, many more cases would be expected. The same argument applies to those over age 50.

Although the AIDS virus may be found in small quantities in saliva and tears, no cases of AIDS have resulted from exposure to these substances. Ambulance drivers, police, and firefighters who have assisted AIDS patients, even by mouth-to-mouth resuscitation, have not been infected.

Nurses, doctors, and health care personnel have not developed AIDS from caring for AIDS patients. In a group of 3,000 health care workers in the U.S. who have been studied, including 1,000 with puncture of the skin by needles contaminated with blood from AIDS patients, only one has developed antibodies to the AIDS virus (indicating infection). Three other health care workers with breaks in the skin and persistent exposure to the blood of AIDS patients have also developed antibodies.

Out of 1,800 dentists studied who did not use recommended precautions against exposure to blood, one (in New York City) has developed antibodies. Health workers have much more contact with patients than would be expected from common everyday contact. The fact that these workers have remained uninfected offers further evidence that the AIDS virus is not transmitted by casual contact.

HOW CAN AIDS BE PREVENTED?

AIDS can be prevented by stopping the passage of the virus from one person to another. Since the AIDS virus is transmitted by sexual contact or injection of contaminated blood, transmission can be prevented by eliminating direct sexual contact with infected persons and eliminating the use of contaminated needles.

The Public Health Service recommends the following steps for all persons to reduce their chances of becoming infected with the virus that causes AIDS:

- Recognize that abstinence or mutual monogamy is the best protection against sexual transmission of the AIDS virus.

- Do not have unprotected sex with multiple partners or with persons who have had multiple partners (including prostitutes). The more partners you have, the greater your risk of infection.

- Do not have unprotected sex with persons with AIDS, persons who have engaged in high-risk behavior, or persons who have a positive antibody test for the AIDS virus. If you do have sex with a person you think may be infected, protect yourself by using a latex condom from start to finish.

- Avoid sexual activities that could cause cuts or tears in the lining of the rectum, vagina, or penis, such as anal intercourse.

- Do not have sex with male or female prostitutes; drug abuse is common among prostitutes.
- Use condoms and spermicides to reduce the possibility of transmitting the virus.
- Do not use intravenous (IV) drugs. Do not share needles or syringes.

Infection with the AIDS virus through the medical use of blood or blood products is now being prevented by use of antibody screening tests at blood donor sites. In addition, members of high risk groups are not donating blood. And heat treatment of blood products now prevents infection in patients with hemophilia and other blood-clotting disorders.

There is as yet no vaccine for AIDS itself, and medical experts estimate that it will be at least several years before an effective vaccine is available. But there is good reason to believe that individuals can reduce their risk of infection with the AIDS virus by following the recommendations above.

Communities can help prevent AIDS by vigorous educational efforts, with special emphasis on educational activities for individuals most likely to engage in risky behaviors.

WHAT IS THE RISK FOR HETEROSEXUALS?

It is now very clear that the AIDS virus can be transmitted through vaginal intercourse from a man to a woman and a woman to a man. In one recent study of spouses of persons with AIDS, most spouses who did not abstain

from intercourse or use condoms became infected with the AIDS virus even when only vaginal intercourse was practiced. For spouses not already infected, however, the use of condoms greatly reduced transmission.

Other evidence concerning heterosexual risk comes from studies in certain African countries where equal numbers of men and women have contracted AIDS. In these countries, heterosexual intercourse is believed to be a major factor in the spread of AIDS. Multiple sexual partners and contact with prostitutes appear to increase the risk of contracting the AIDS virus. Other factors that may account for the increased incidence of infection among heterosexuals in these countries include the transfusion of blood infected with the AIDS virus and the use of unsterilized needles for IV injections aimed to remedy common illnesses.

Sexual contact with prostitutes can significantly increase the risk of being infected with the AIDS virus. In a recent study of seven geographic areas in the United States, 11 percent of the prostitutes tested had evidence of infection with the AIDS virus,

and in one area (northern New Jersey) 57 percent were infected. Of those with evidence of infection, 76 percent gave a history of IV drug use.

Current evidence strongly suggests that the presence of other sexually transmitted infections can increase the likelihood of contracting the AIDS virus. And these infections are common among prostitutes.

Four percent of all persons with AIDS are believed to have been infected through heterosexual contact with an infected person. About half of these cases involve persons from other countries (mainly in Africa) where the equal incidence of AIDS among men and women suggests heterosexual transmission. The other half consist almost exclusively of individuals who have been the sexual partners of bisexual men or IV drug users.

One fact indicates the increased difficulty of stemming the spread of AIDS: the number of new AIDS cases arising from heterosexual contact is increasing about one and a half times faster than the new cases in all other categories.

At present, nearly all persons who contracted AIDS through heterosexual contact are the sexual partners of IV drug users or of men who have sex with other men. But this pattern is likely to change unless sexual behavior changes.

Persons infected with the AIDS virus through heterosexual contact with someone in a risk group can set in motion a cycle of heterosexual transmission. In this way the virus can spread, like other sexually transmitted diseases, through all parts of society. Abstinence, monogamy, and the use of condoms are the only ways to prevent this from happening.

HOW DO CHILDREN GET AIDS?

There are currently more than 500 documented cases of AIDS in children under age 13. An estimated 3,000 more children have other serious illnesses resulting from the AIDS virus. And it's estimated that 3,000 additional infected children will be born in 1987.

Eighty percent of all children with AIDS were infected during pregnancy or at the time of delivery; 12 percent received transfusions of infected blood before the blood supply was protected; and 5 percent are hemophiliacs who were treated with blood products before the need to destroy the virus was known.

IS THERE DANGER OF A CHILD'S CONTRACTING AIDS FROM FRIENDS OR SCHOOLMATES?

No. The AIDS virus is difficult to catch, even among people at highest risk for the disease. No cases of AIDS are known or suspected to have been transmitted from one child to another in school, day care, or foster care settings.

Transmission would require direct exposure of a child's bloodstream to blood from an infected child.

The Public Health Service recommends that except in very unusual circumstances, children with AIDS "should be allowed to attend school and after-school day care and to be placed in a foster home in an unrestricted setting."

Each case should be evaluated separately, with individualized attention to the child and the setting. Decisions affecting the schooling of an AIDS-infected child should be made in the same way as decisions for any child having a special problem (such as cerebral palsy). Such decisions should be made by a team that includes the child's parents, teacher, physician, school board members, and local public health officials.

ADDITIONAL RECOMMENDATIONS FOR PERSONS AT INCREASED RISK OF AIDS VIRUS INFECTION

In addition to the recommendations for all persons, the Public Health Service recommends the following precautions for persons at increased risk for infection by the AIDS virus. The population that is especially at risk includes

intravenous drug users and men who have sex with other men, as well as the sexual partners of persons in either of these groups.

The following recommendations are based on the fact that it is possible to carry the AIDS virus without knowing it and, as a result, to transmit it unwittingly to others.

• Consult your physician or public health department and/or local AIDS service organization for counseling. Consider taking the AIDS virus antibody test, which would enable you to know your status and take appropriate actions. This precaution is particularly important if knowing the result would change your behavior. Tests are available in most parts of the country on an anonymous or confidential basis at counseling and testing sites that can be identified by your local health department.

- During sexual activity, protect your partner from contact with the rectum, blood, and semen or vaginal fluids. Use a latex condom from start to finish.

- Do not donate blood, plasma, organs, sperm, or other body tissue.

- If you are a woman at increased risk, consider the risk to your baby before becoming pregnant. Remember that the AIDS virus is easily transmitted from an infected mother to her infant. Before becoming pregnant, you should take the AIDS antibody test. If you do become pregnant, you should consider testing during pregnancy.

ADDITIONAL RECOMMENDATIONS FOR PERSONS WITH A POSITIVE ANTIBODY TEST

In addition to the recommendations for persons at increased risk, the Public Health Service recommends the following additional steps for persons with positive results on the blood test for antibodies to the AIDS virus.

- Seek regular medical evaluation and follow-up.

- Either avoid sexual activity or inform your prospective partner of your antibody test results and protect him or her from contact during sex. Use a condom, and avoid sexual practices that may injure body tissues, such as anal intercourse.

- Inform your present and previous sex partners and any persons with whom you may have shared needles of their potential exposure to the AIDS virus. Encourage them to seek counseling and antibody testing from their physicians or from appropriate health clinics.

- Do not share items that could become contaminated with blood.

- If you use drugs, enroll in a drug treatment program. Needles and other drug equipment must never be shared.

- Clean blood off household or other surfaces with freshly diluted bleach—one part bleach to 10 parts water. (Do not use bleach on the body or on wounds.) Hot water and soap or other disinfectants may also be used.

- Inform your doctor, dentist, and eye doctor of your positive antibody status so they can take proper precautions to protect you and others.

- If you're a woman with a positive antibody test, avoid pregnancy because of the high risk of transmission to your baby.

HOW DOES AIDS COMPARE WITH OTHER SEXUALLY TRANSMITTED DISEASES?

The AIDS virus is only one of many infections transmitted by sexual contact. AIDS is much more serious than other sexually transmitted diseases, but it is actually less contagious.

Like AIDS, the frequency of many other sexual transmitted diseases has been increasing over the last few decades. Reported cases of gonorrhea more than tripled between 1965 and 1976. Between 1966 and 1984 the number of visits to physicians' offices for genital herpes increased sixteenfold; for vaginal infections, fivefold; and for genital warts, sixfold. Between 1956 and 1982 the number of cases of syphilis in men increased sixfold; congenital syphilis cases almost tripled between 1983 and 1986. Hospitalization rates for tubal infections in teenage girls more than doubled between 1970 and 1975. All social classes have been affected by these increases.

Like other sexually transmitted organisms, the AIDS virus is relatively fragile and can invade the body only through sexual transmission or injection into the blood stream. Outside the body, the AIDS virus is easily destroyed by mild soaps or disinfectants, such as a diluted solution of household bleach.

Because sexual contact makes it easier for an organism to enter the body, many other organisms are transmitted only by sexual contact: gonorrhea, syphilis, venereal warts, genital herpes, chlamydia, trichomonas, chancroid, and granuloma inguinale. Other infections transmitted sexually include shiegella, salmonella, guiardiasis, amoebic dysentery, hepatitis-B, scabies, lice, and cyto-megalovirus. Evidence suggests that the presence of sexually transmitted diseases increases the likelihood of infection with the AIDS virus and the development of AIDS.

HOW CAN EDUCATION HELP US STOP AIDS?

Our major weapon against the spread of AIDS has been and will likely continue to be our understanding of the disease and how it is transmitted.

One example of how an understanding of AIDS has generated behavioral change is the virtual elimination of the AIDS virus from the nation's blood supply. The response of persons at risk to requests that they not donate blood has helped ensure a safe supply of blood. Testing of donated blood for the presence of the AIDS virus has shown that members of high risk groups have ceased donating blood.

Two other examples of the effectiveness of education are the sharp decline in other sexually transmitted diseases among homosexual men in certain cities and the decrease among these men of sexual practices that increase the risk of AIDS. The declining rate at which AIDS is spreading in certain cities may also be partly due to the education of high-risk persons.

IV drug users, however, have proved to be a difficult group to reach and influence through educational programs. And many sexually active heterosexuals continue to behave in ways that suggest a denial of the AIDS risk, such as having contact with prostitutes.

DIAGNOSIS AND TREATMENT

WHAT ARE THE SYMPTOMS OF INFECTION WITH THE AIDS VIRUS?

Many individuals infected with the AIDS virus have no symptoms and experience no discomfort. Their defenses against infection are still functioning. Some have remained symptom-free for up to seven years.

If the AIDS virus causes moderate damage to the immune system, symptoms of chronic infection may occur and may include tiredness, fever, loss of appetite and weight, diarrhea, night sweats, skin rashes, yeast infection (candida) of the mouth, and swollen glands (lymph nodes)—usually in the neck, armpits, or groin. Most of these symptoms are quite common and do not usually indicate immune deficiency. Only if they persist *for more than two weeks* should a person see a doctor so that the cause can be identified with certainty.

When damage to the immune system is

substantial, the serious opportunistic infections of AIDS are likely to occur. Most adults with AIDS have had one or both of two rare diseases: a parasitic infection of the lungs known as *Pneumocystis carinii* pneumonia (PCP), or a type of cancer known as Kaposi's sarcoma (KS).

Pneumocystis has symptoms similar to other forms of severe pneumonia, such as persistent cough, fever, and difficulty in breathing or shortness of breath.

Kaposi's sarcoma is a tumor of blood vessels and can occur on the surface of the skin or mouth or inside the body. The tumors may show up as purple, blue-violet, or brownish spots or bumps.

Other opportunistic infections seen in AIDS patients include unusually severe infections with yeast (candida), cytomegalovirus, herpes virus, and various parasites. But milder infections with these organisms, such as vaginal yeast infections, do not suggest immune deficiency.

When the AIDS virus attacks the brain and nervous system, symptoms may include memory loss, indifference, loss of coordination, partial paralysis, or mental disorders. Such symptoms may develop slowly over a long period of time.

Children infected with the AIDS virus tend to have different opportunistic infections than adults. The most common findings in children are poor growth, enlargement of the liver and spleen, and a form of pneumonia in which white blood cells (lymphocytes) are found in large numbers in the lungs. *Pneumocystis* is less common and Kaposi's sarcoma is very rare among children.

HOW LONG AFTER INFECTION WITH THE AIDS VIRUS CAN AIDS OCCUR?

The time between infection with the AIDS virus and the onset of AIDS symptoms (the incubation period) can range from six months to six years or more. The longer a person has been infected with the virus, the more likely he or she is to develop AIDS.

In one study, for those infected for six years, the risk of developing AIDS was 30 percent. Antibodies to the AIDS virus, which are detected by the blood test, may take two weeks to three months to appear after exposure to the virus.

HOW IS AIDS DIAGNOSED?

Infection with the AIDS virus is indicated by the presence of antibodies to the virus in the blood. The diagnosis of AIDS depends on the presence of opportunistic diseases that indicate the loss of immunity. Tests demonstrating damage to various parts of the immune system, such as a decrease in the number of certain white blood cells (T4-lymphocytes), support the diagnosis.

IS THERE A LABORATORY TEST FOR AIDS?

There is no single test for diagnosing AIDS. There is, however, a test that detects antibodies to the virus that causes AIDS.

The current and preferred name for the AIDS virus is Human Immunodeficiency Virus (HIV). Other names that have been used for the AIDS virus are HTLV-III (Human T-Lymphotropic Virus, type III) and Lymphadenopathy Associated Virus (LAV).

Antibodies are substances produced by

white blood cells to fight disease organisms. Unfortunately, the antibodies produced to combat the AIDS virus are not effective in destroying the virus.

The presence of antibodies to the AIDS virus means that a person has been infected with that virus. When a person is infected, it may take from two weeks to three months for antibodies to appear in the blood. *Even if someone has a negative test for antibodies, it is still very important to avoid high-risk behaviors.*

Although the test for antibodies to the AIDS virus is very accurate, it is possible to get a false positive result—indicating antibodies to the AIDS virus even though none exist. This inaccurate result is more likely to occur when the test is performed on persons whose risk of infection is low and may also be more common in pregnant women.

The antibody test is used to screen donated blood to prevent the AIDS virus from being transmitted by blood transfusions or use of blood products (such as Factor VIII) needed by patients with hemophilia.

The antibody test is available through private physicians and most state and local health departments, as well as from local AIDS services organizations. This test is strongly recommended for individuals at high risk who would change their behavior if they knew they were infected.

Confidentiality for those who choose to be tested is, of course, a very important concern. In many testing centers, the test is done anonymously (using a number instead of a name), so that only the person tested knows the result.

IS THERE ANY DANGER OF GETTING AIDS FROM DONATING BLOOD?

No. Blood banks and other blood collection centers use new sterile equipment and disposable needles for each donor.

Today, all blood donors are interviewed, and blood is not accepted from individuals with high-risk behaviors. All donated blood is tested for the presence of the antibody to the AIDS virus. Any blood that tests positive is discarded, and the donor is notified.

This routine testing of blood products has made the blood supply safer than it has ever been with regard to AIDS.

The need for blood is always acute, and people whose behavior does not put them at increased risk for getting AIDS are urged to continue to donate blood as they have in the past. Persons having elective surgery may also wish to consider donating their own blood in advance of the surgery so that it will be available if needed.

HOW IS AIDS TREATED?

Currently there are no antiviral drugs available anywhere that cure AIDS. But the search for such drugs is being pursued vigorously.

Zidovudine (AZT) has been shown to prolong life in some AIDS patients and has been approved for use in certain patients. It does not, however, cure AIDS.

Work is continuing on other drugs that attack the AIDS virus and on drugs that might help restore a damaged immune system. Eventually, a combination of drugs may be the most effective therapy. Though no treatment has yet been successful in restoring AIDS patients' immune systems, doctors have had some success in using drugs, radiation, and surgery to treat the various illnesses AIDS patients suffer.

THE AIDS VIRUS

WHY IS AIDS SUCH A DEVASTATING DISEASE?

Individuals with AIDS are vulnerable to opportunistic infections because the AIDS virus selectively attacks the "helper" T-lymphocyte or T4 cell. This white blood cell is perhaps the single most important element in the body's defense against infection.

Nothing has a more devastating effect on the human immune system than the destruction of the "helper" T-lymphocyte. T-cells are critical to defending against invasion by protozoa (single-celled animals), funguses, viruses, and many bacteria—the organisms responsible for the opportunistic infections seen in AIDS patients.

When a foreign organism is present in the bloodstream, it is picked up by a white blood cell called a macrophage. It is then the job of the T-cell to recognize the infection by means of a special area on its surface called a "receptor site." The T-cell then multiplies to form a "clone" of a thousand or more identical T-cells—all of which have the job of fighting that particular organism.

T-cells produce a number of different substances that help activate the immune system to overcome infection. These substances stimulate other white blood cells to destroy infected cells and invading organisms, instruct B-lymphocytes to multiply and produce antibodies against the invading organism, and stimulate the bone marrow to make more lymphocytes. T-cells also produce substances that help to destroy cancer cells.

Since the cause of AIDS is a virus, it is the job of the T-cell to recognize it as such and to coordinate the different parts of the immune system in order to destroy it. Unfortunately, the AIDS virus has evolved the ability to hook on to the T-cell "receptor site," the very part of the T-cell that normally recognizes a virus infection. By blocking the receptor site, the virus prevents the T-cell from multiplying to form a special group (clone) of T-cells dedicated to attacking the AIDS virus.

This blocking capacity of the AIDS virus may explain why persons infected with the virus are unable to eliminate infection. Some antibodies to the AIDS virus are made by B-lymphocytes (resulting in a positive antibody test), but these antibodies are not effective in destroying the virus.

The AIDS virus may, over a period of months or even years, multiply and destroy T-cells. If a moderate number are destroyed, the infected person may have chronic symptoms such as diarrhea or weight loss. If a large number of T-cells are destroyed by the AIDS virus, then the body loses its ability to effectively fight infections due to protozoa, fungi, viruses, and bacteria that would normally be easily overcome. The presence of these infections helps establish the diagnosis of AIDS.

Powerful antibiotics and drugs may help the AIDS patient overcome one infection. But given the destruction of T-cells these patients have suffered, they are likely to contract another infection within a short time.

Loss of T-cells also makes certain cancers more likely to occur, such as Kaposi's sarcoma (a tumor of blood vessels) and cancers of the lymphatic system.

Even one encounter with the virus may lead to AIDS. But repeated exposure to the virus through sexual relations with infected persons or through injections of infected blood products may increase the risk of infection. The presence of other sexually transmitted diseases may also increase the risk.

WHAT IS THE AIDS VIRUS LIKE?

AIDS is the most serious form of infection caused by the Human Immunodeficiency Virus (HIV).

Viruses are very small particles made of the same material (nucleic acids) as the chromosomes found in the nucleus of each cell in our body. These chromosomes carry our genetic inheritance.

Chromosomes are made of DNA (deoxy-ribo-nucleic acid) and contain coded instructions (genes) for making the proteins that govern the activities of our cells. When a virus enters a cell, it inserts itself into our DNA and instructs the cell to make virus. As the virus multiplies inside the cell, the cell breaks open and releases the new virus particles. Viruses may also interfere with the genes that tell cells when to stop reproducing, so that the cells multiply uncontrollably to form cancers.

The virus that causes AIDS is made of RNA (ribo-nucleic acid) enclosed in a protein envelope. This envelope has the ability to attach to and block the receptor sites on the outer wall of the T-cell. The virus then enters the T-cell and uses an enzyme that it carries (called "reverse transcriptase") to copy itself into the DNA of the cell. (The drug AZT interferes with reverse transcriptase.) At this point, the virus may become inactive and remain hidden in the cell and may not be copied until the rest of the cell's DNA divides. For this reason, a person recently infected with the AIDS virus may be less likely to transfer the virus to others.

Perhaps in response to some new infection or other stress, the virus hiding in the T-cell DNA may suddenly begin replicating, using the chemical machinery of the cell to produce more of the AIDS virus. The increased number of AIDS virus particles then push through the cell wall, destroying the cell. These particles can then travel through the blood stream to infect other T-cells. Rapid multiplication of the virus can begin even several years after the initial infection.

Depending on how many T-cells are destroyed, the infected person may have no symptoms, chronic symptoms (ARC), or full-blown AIDS. Normally, about 950 helper T-cells occupy each cubic millimeter of blood. When this number falls below 400, the likelihood of chronic infection or AIDS is greatly increased.

Even in infected individuals who are free of symptoms, the AIDS virus is usually present in blood and in semen or vaginal fluid. Smaller amounts of the virus may be found in sweat, saliva, and tears, but there is no evidence that these fluids transmit the virus.

AIDS patients, in addition to susceptibility to opportunistic infection and certain cancers, may also develop infections of the brain and nervous system. These infections are due to the ability of the AIDS virus to attach to and infect nerve cells, which have receptor sites similar to T-cells. But the cells of the brain are separated from many of the substances in the blood by the "blood-brain barrier." As a result, infections of brain cells are more difficult for drugs to reach.

WHERE DID THE AIDS VIRUS COME FROM?

As the French biologist Rene Dubos explains in *The Mirage of Health*, new infectious diseases are constantly evolving. The day will never arrive when we have "conquered" infectious disease once and for all.

The organisms that cause infections multiply, mutate, and evolve very rapidly. This rapid rate of multiplication and change explains why bacteria can quickly become resistant to new antibiotics. In addition to AIDS, other new infection-related diseases—Reye's syndrome, toxic shock syndrome, and Legionnaire's disease—have emerged during recent years.

It is reasonable to expect appearances of new infections. And because transmission through sexual intercourse gives infectious organisms an advantage, it is likely that many of these new infections will be sexually transmitted. Syphilis, for example, was virtually unknown prior to the 16th century, and genital herpes and chlamydia (the most common cause of tubal infections) have only very recently become significant problems.

Researchers do not know for certain where the AIDS virus came from. It is a member of a group of viruses called lentiviruses—the "slow" viruses that can leave victims free from symptoms years after infection. The lentivirus that causes visna, a wasting disease in sheep, is similar to the AIDS virus.

Another recently discovered lenti-virus, STLV-III, causes a disease similar to AIDS in the African green monkey and could be a remote ancestor of the AIDS virus. Other viruses similar to the AIDS virus have recently been discovered in West Africa.

These viruses infect humans, and some also cause immune deficiency.

Blood samples drawn in the 1950s from individuals in different countries have been tested for evidence of the AIDS virus. Only those samples collected from a small region of central Africa have tested positive. This finding has led to speculation that the virus may have spread from central Africa to other parts of Africa and then to Haiti, the Americas, and Europe.

AIDS and the College Student: The Need for Sex Education

Sandra L. Caron, PhD, Rosemarie M. Bertran, MSW and Tom McMullen, Syracuse University

Kay comes home from college for the weekend, and on Saturday night runs into her old high school sweetheart, Bill. They spend the night together in his apartment. The next day, while Bill is at the library studying, Kay rummages guiltily through his things to see if he's found a new girlfriend. She finds a card from a local health agency which says he's tested positive for AIDS antibodies. Scared and confused, she panics. What should she do? Confront him and admit she's been going through his stuff? She thinks, "Why didn't he tell me? We could have used a condom." She decides not to tell him because he wouldn't forgive her for sneaking around. Instead, she returns to college to her boyfriend, Jim, without mentioning her "fling." She continues to have unprotected sex with Jim because she fears that if she now insists he wear a condom, he'll know she's been unfaithful.

College students don't need much sex education, right? These modern kids, exposed by the media to all areas of life, already know all about sex. Their own experience has prepared them to be comfortable, open, and mature in their relationships with others. Unlike prior generations, they are knowledgeable and sophisticated.

Wrong. As one can see from the true scenario above, college students struggle with ignorance, misconceptions, doubts, and fears about themselves and others, just as much and just as painfully as did their predecessors. The difference, fortunately, is that today's young people are growing up in a society that permits more open discussion of sexual topics than in previous generations.

As a society, we are now more knowledgeable about our bodies, psychological processes, the interplay of emotion and body, and social processes than ever before. In addition, we live in an "information age" that provides easy access to accurate information. Indeed, we are more likely to be faced with the problem of choosing which facts, among an overabundance, are significant. Among college-educated adults, few sexual topics are in "taboo closets" anymore; many feel more distressed by exposure to and inept handling of sensitive subjects than by prohibitions.

Clearly, in an age touted to be one of great sexual openness,

we still have many problems to solve. It would be naive to suggest that adequate or even ideal (whatever "ideal" may be) sex education at any, and all, levels will solve the social ills of our complex society. Knowledge, however, can be used to alleviate and avoid much human suffering. And putting knowledge in the hands of young people increases their options *and* their capacity to choose among them. We know of no instance in which people, young or old, are better served by ignorance. Choice permits and enhances the individual's ability to develop as a human being; ignorance prohibits choice and adversely affects the quality of life.

Knowledge About AIDS

Just what do college students know about AIDS? Do they believe they are at risk? Has their awareness of AIDS resulted in changes in sexual and dating behaviors? To find out, we conducted a survey of Syracuse University students during the spring term, 1987. The survey consisted of one-to-one interviews with students in bars on "Marshall Street," near the university. Subjects were male and female, mostly undergraduate students. Interviews were generally conducted during the most popular hours of 9 p.m. and 2 a.m.

The instrument was a one-page interview that consisted of structured, open-ended questions regarding the student's opinion and knowledge about AIDS. Interviewers were members of the Peer Sexuality Program at Syracuse University. More than 350 interviews were completed. Returns have not yet been tabulated completely, but our initial impressions are the following.

1. *Most students exhibit a great lack of knowledge and factual data about AIDS.*

2. *Most students fail to see any relevance between ongoing media stories about the growing incidence of AIDS and their personal behavior.* Students frequently indicated that they believed they were not in "high risk" groups and equated this with little or no risk at all. Often unconcerned about risk, they failed to see that high risk *behaviors* placed them in jeopardy. Frequent comments included: "Well, I'm not a slut, I don't sleep around that much, and I'm not gay."

3. *The level of denial among students is high.* For example, students often commented, "Everyone should be concerned about AIDS." But when the interviewer countered with, "Are you?" the answer was almost invariably, "No." Students often reported their conviction that they had the ability to "know" or intuit which sexual partners were "safe." Commonly, they conveyed the conviction that they were personally immune. Only a small minority indicated anxiety about having been exposed. Students often commented that they believed this to be a greater issue for homosexuals than for heterosexuals.

4. *There is a general unreadiness among students to deal pragmatically with the threat of AIDS in their relationships.* Students talked freely about sex and STDs with interviewers, but expressed unwillingness to discuss these topics with their sexual partners. Many reported that generally they had unprotected sex and indicated that they would not talk with a new sexual partner about AIDS, STDs, or the use of condoms. In general, students equated "safer sex" with "not-fun-sex." Some wondered how to bring up the question of AIDS with a new partner without insulting him/her. The unwillingness of students to deal pragmatically with the threat of AIDS is closely related to, and dependent upon, the level of denial discussed above.

5. *Some students reported that AIDS was changing social attitudes regarding sexual and dating behavior.* There is less approval for the "one night stand." "People think twice before picking someone up." Some women indicated increased interest in men who are virgins, wanting to avoid "the guy who's been around" or "the womanizer." It is interesting to see the shift in women's attitudes away from the traditional interest in experienced men, and towards virgins. Some men also indicated their preference for an inexperienced or less-experienced sexual partner, but this is, of course, a more traditional view.

Recommendations for Education

The recommendations, below, are based on our preliminary findings in this study. Those who are planning, and/or developing, educational programs about AIDS for college students are also advised to consider the two recent articles listed at the end of this article.

Our recommendations are directed toward influencing the behaviors of people who do not believe themselves to be at risk of exposure. Ideally, these program recommendations should be carried out in a warm, supportive environment that invites open discussions. Our experience with education suggests that the best approach is a group of peers—students of the same approximate age and educational level—working together. Such programs should be conducted by educators who are knowledgeable about sexual issues and comfortable with open discussion. The following guidelines have been developed from our study.

1. *Provide factual information about the incidence and transmission of the AIDS virus.*
   Most students in our study demonstrated significant factual deficits. Many believed, for example, that AIDS was transmitted through casual contacts, such as sneez-

ing or sharing beer bottles. Presenting solid, clearly stated information will significantly alleviate many fears.

2. *Debunk myths.*
   As stated previously, students widely believe that they are not at risk and/or that they can intuitively recognize which people carry the AIDS virus. Such beliefs permit students to rationalize high-risk behaviors. Education about AIDS should therefore describe high-risk behaviors, explain why engaging in such behaviors jeopardizes the health of the individual, as well as others, and give information on available tests to identify the presence of AIDS antibodies in a person.

3. *Discuss options.*
   Students should be made aware of the potential choices they have to provide varying levels of protection against the AIDS virus. Certainly abstinence should be recognized and discussed as a possible choice. Another option is "safer sex" (which should be clearly distinguished from "safe sex"), which can be achieved through the proper use of condoms with spermicides. Students clearly should understand that this is not 100 percent protection against the transmission of the AIDS virus. Sexually active students, especially, should be made aware of the availability and limits of testing.

4. *Discuss ethical issues.*
   Each individual has a responsibility to himself or herself, as well as to others. Responsible behaviors include taking adequate steps to protect oneself, discussing openly the risk between sexual partners, and not concealing significant information from sexual partners.

5. *Present dramatization of effective coping behaviors.*
   Brief plays, skits, and role-playing all provide opportunities to model responsible sexual behaviors. Actors may be recruited from the drama department, from among peer educators, from the student body at large, or even from the audience. Dramatic presentations should include open discussion of the use of condoms and other protection, frank inquiries about personal risk, and how to deal with casual sexual encounters.

Conclusion

In closing, it is useful to review some basic knowledge: that AIDS is already present in the heterosexual population, as well as among homosexuals; that college students, as a group, tend to be more sexually active than other segments of the adult population; and that college students are a significant proportion of our population, not only in numbers, but also in terms of their future influence. These are our upcoming professionals—the privileged, who will be our future leaders. For their own sake, and for the sake of our society, this group should have the information, knowledge, and wisdom to make sound decisions for themselves and others.

Additional Resources
Hirschorn, M. W. (1987, April 29). AIDS is not seen as a major threat by many heterosexuals on campuses. *The Chronicle of Higher Education.*

The years of living dangerously. (1987, April). *Newsweek—On Campus.*

SPEAKING OUT ON AIDS
A HUMANIST SYMPOSIUM

Unanimity within diversity on the need to face the challenges of AIDS now

In soliciting comments for the symposium that follows, *The Humanist* set out to publicize the wide diversity of opinion that exists over how to deal with the mounting moral, political, economic, ethical, and medical dilemmas that AIDS poses. Invitations for brief comments were sent to a diverse group of medical professionals, psychologists, sexologists, ethicists, and educators. *The Humanist* encouraged each respondent to address any aspect of the AIDS epidemic which he or she felt was relevant. The following was offered as a starting point.

While most people agree that education is the best line of defense against the spread of AIDS, there is less unanimity among humanists over precisely which form such education should take. Which form of education—for example, encouraging "safe" sexual practices, explaining the clinical aspects of the disease, or encouraging sexually active people to alter their life-styles—do *you* advocate? Why? Inasmuch as the AIDS pandemic dramatizes how private behavior and lifestyles can affect us all, how are we to balance individual privacy and rights against the general welfare?

The following responses published by *The Humanist* present an attempt to display the breadth of sentiments humanists have about AIDS. While there is

a wide diversity of opinion about specific responses to the AIDS crisis, there is, it seems, one factor upon which all the respondents are unanimous: AIDS must be dealt with; doing nothing is the worst option with which we are faced. Throughout the responses which follow, reason and compassion fuel a commitment toward making informed, intelligent decisions—admittedly, often choices between two or more equally unpleasant options—in order to best meet the challenges AIDS poses to our future on this planet.

Gina Allen

The AIDS crisis caught us smack in the middle of our fear of sex and our homophobia. Our panicked responses have cost lives. Few seemed overly concerned when the lives lost were those of gays and drug addicts. Some of the inadequate AIDS research money was even earmarked to find a cure not for the disease but for homosexuality.

When the AIDS retrovirus moved into the heterosexual world, panic increased but not good sense. While the number of high school students in the nation testing positive for the AIDS antibodies increases, we try to keep them out of classrooms instead of protecting all students with knowledge and condoms. It's fine to preach celibacy, but

not even Phyllis Schlafly's strident voice speaks louder than hormones at puberty.

Frightened adults are boycotting restaurants that employ gays, calling for a quarantine of all who test positive for AIDS virus antibodies, and taking blood tests every three months which entitle them to carry around "safe sex partner" cards. They need education, too.

The blood test they take doesn't prove that they have not been infected with the AIDS virus. There is no test for the virus. The blood test only proves that there are no antibodies to the virus present at that time. The person tested could be infected for some time before developing antibodies and, during that time, would not be a "safe sex partner."

In the meantime, the experts tell us that AIDS is moving into the straight world from the drug scene via dirty needles and the prostitution (especially male) that supports drug habits. Great Britain has made both the dirty needles and the prostitution unnecessary, as well as preventing many deaths from impure street drugs. Providing drugs to drug addicts has not turned Great Britain into a nation of junkies.

Why do we value our Puritan ethic more than human life? Why have we been arguing about whether or not condom advertisements should appear on television more than seven years after we knew that condoms freely available

This article first appeared in THE HUMANIST issue of July/August 1987, pp. 21-24, 38, and is reprinted by permission.

everywhere could save the lives of our youngsters? Why do we spend millions on nuclear devices that kill and stint on funds for research on AIDS that could prevent death?

The emergency that we now face demands that we accept both heterosexual and homosexual sex as facts of life and deal with the AIDS crisis with all the logic and reason we can muster. This is a war that demands no less—a war we can't afford to lose.

Vern Bullough

The obvious humanist answer to AIDS would be to deal with AIDS as a problem but to put the disease in perspective. We could recommend that everyone observe sexual restraint, but, as a sexologist, I would argue that for a significant portion of the population such advice is unrealistic. It is like telling an alcoholic not to drink or a smoker not to smoke. Sex is part of the process of being human, although sexual urges and needs are highly individualistic. What we should emphasize is that those individuals who do engage in sexual activity with other than a regular partner be educated to take the necessary precautions. At present this would include the use of a condom. We should also advise the drug addict to use sterilized drug paraphernalia or, if we wanted to be effective, we could even give free sterilized needles to drug addicts providing they trade in their used needles for new sterilized ones.

Since we do not know the full meaning of what testing positive for AIDS means, it would be unwise for us to do a mass scale testing of the population. Homosexual bashing is simply stupid and to try to eliminate gays from working as kitchen employees is to label an individual as a carrier without any knowledge of the potential carriers of the disease. Instead, we have to make certain that precautions against the spread of infection normally taken by food handlers are enforced.

"Safe sex" cards, to put it mildly, are a stupid idea and promise a guarantee that no one can give. Medical inspection of prostitutes has never been a guarantee of not receiving a sexually

> *[AIDS] is not "God's curse." It is not from outerspace. It is not a communist plot. It is a communicable disease that is not highly infectious. We need to act accordingly.*

transmittable disease in the past, and there is no indication that the AIDS panic will change this.

What we need to do is to use our common sense and to take precautions. There is still a lot we do not know about AIDS and until we find out more we should avoid contributing to the panic. It is *not* "God's curse." It is *not* from outerspace. It is *not* a communist plot. It *is* a communicable disease that is not highly infectious. We need to act accordingly.

Helen Colton

A truly humanist belief system ideally derives from time, place, and situation. The AIDS pandemic demands, for the greatest good to the greatest number, measures to prevent a decimated human race. Yes, situation ethics requires free distribution of condoms and legally required testing when appropriate, as with prostitutes of both genders.

Theresa L. Crenshaw, M.D.

The AIDS epidemic is the greatest threat to society, as we know it, ever faced by civilization—more serious than the plagues of past centuries, more predictable than nuclear conflict.

The ease and speed of world travel made possible by our modern technology makes this disease more dangerous to humanity than any other disease in history. That same technology in the form of computer-assisted satellite com-

munications systems available to us now, in 1987, gives us rapid response capability never before possible. We have the technology, but time is the enemy. Our weapons are education, research, discipline, courage, integrity, spirituality, and compassion.

However, the AIDS virus isn't as dangerous as our behavior. The disease is not airborne. It will not infect you without your cooperation, and it is therefore preventable. We must reestablish our traditional values and recognize that monogamous relationships with a trustworthy partner will stop the spread of AIDS if everyone becomes educated and cooperates. Then we can concentrate our resources on healing the sick and finding a cure for the millions of people who are already infected.

Here are ten specific steps we must take to deal with AIDS effectively:

1. Make all forms of infection reportable to the public health department.
2. Encourage voluntary testing for the general public, including children.
3. Tell the public the whole truth. The present message of "Calm down, don't panic, but change your sexual behavior" will not work psychodynamically. To motivate sexual behavior change, one must alarm and concern people enough to motivate change and then calm them down with an action plan that demonstrates how they can keep themselves healthy.
4. Modify civil rights issues if necessary for health and survival. Don't let the exercise of the rights of someone who is infected cause someone else to become infected.
5. Stop underestimating this disease. Stop trying to see how much sex or what sexual behaviors one can get away with without becoming infected. Stop playing Russian Roulette. This is no time to be careless.
6. Recognize that sexual behavior can change if the motivation is sufficient and if public leaders expect and recommend it. Death is a powerful motivator.
7. Don't be deluded by condoms, but do use them. Recommend exclusivity in relationships *and* condoms and spermicides unless one can be 100

percent certain one's partner is monogamous and uninfected (which is difficult).

8. Encourage sexual trustworthiness. Don't help a friend arrange a sexual liaison behind his or her spouse's back. The buddy system has to mean something different today.
9. Network among those you care about to discourage casual sex or multiple sex partners.
10. Encourage your government representatives to support research and public education to fight the AIDS epidemic.

In conclusion, our society is in grave danger—not from AIDS but from the experts who have consistently misread this epidemic, disregarded the evidence of Africa, been unwilling to apply traditional epidemiological methods (such as routine testing and contact tracing); from gay leaders who have resisted measures that might limit or inhibit sexual freedoms; from the conservative right which has fought AIDS education in schools and on television; and from ourselves, who have been unwilling to face reality and change our sexual practices radically enough or rapidly enough.

We have a common goal: stop AIDS. We must work together as a nation toward this end and stop drawing battle lines between philosophies.

Albert Ellis

Sex, like many other aspects of life, is both pleasurable and dangerous. So, also, for that matter, is work. There are many obvious advantages to working for a living, but, while working, you can easily get bored, become overly tired, be treated unfairly, and suffer various kinds of physical injury. I need hardly catalog the unique pleasures of sex, but it also can result in unwanted pregnancy, sexually transmitted diseases, marriage to the wrong person, and other ills.

Although sex is supposedly voluntary and you can choose to engage in it or not, the latter choice is hardly a pure option. Certainly, to avoid the dangers of youthful sex, you can decide to be abstinent. But if you are indeed a

> *The AIDS virus isn't as dangerous as our behavior. The disease is not airborne. It will not infect you without your cooperation, and it is therefore preventable.*

healthy and normal adolescent, will you *really* totally refrain? Will you *never* masturbate, fantasize, pet to orgasm, or slip into occasional intercourse? I doubt it. Countless centuries of history have shown otherwise, have proven that young people will think about and have many kinds of sex, no matter how prescriptive their upbringing or how strongly they decide not to engage in copulation.

Is sex among young people, then, inevitable? Of course not—since a few practically never have it. But what a measly few!

Making condoms available to public and high school students, like the sexual and nonsexual behaviors cited above, has distinct disadvantages and it would be foolish to deny them. For example, it gives youngsters a false sense of security, helps them to think that rubbers are absolutely safe, and encourages them to resort to intercourse rather than to noncoital methods of sex. These are real dangers. But as long as boys will (in all probability) be boys and girls will (most likely) be girls, what are our other realistic choices? Millions of unwanted pregnancies? A myriad of venereal diseases—including AIDS? Countless premature (not to mention shotgun-instigated) weddings?

Certainly, doling out free condoms has its evils. But I would guess that the greater evil by far is the alternative of loudly beating the drums for young people's achieving a utopian degree of chastity that they so far have virtually never in human history approached.

Sol Gordon

My message to teenagers on AIDS is simple: no sex. But, if you're going to have sex anyway, don't do it without protection. It's not "romantic" to let it just happen; it's stupid.

If a boy says to a girl, "If you really love me, you'll have sex with me," the girl's response could be, "I really love you, but do you have a condom?" If he says, "I get no feeling out of a condom," the girl's reply should be, "All the other guys I know get plenty of feelings out of a condom—what's the matter with you?"

Lucia K. B. Hall

Even with powerful drugs ranged against them, syphilis and gonorrhea are endemic in the United States, and both are developing resistant strains. Both can cause sterility, both can be passed on to children during birth, and untreated syphilis causes death. Herpes simplex II, although not fatal, is painful and incurable and was until recently the nation's most feared "boogie bug" of sexually transmitted diseases.

Now, it is AIDS. This new virus combines the worst of syphilis, gonorrhea, and herpes. Alarmed at last, people are actually using condoms and talking about sex education as a need rather than as an option—measures which could have prevented the spread of these other venereal diseases.

But this will not be enough. In time, panic about AIDS, too, will fade—when a vaccine is found or when something worse takes its place, such as a natural mutation of the AIDS virus itself. Then, the cycle will continue.

Why? Because the issue is not AIDS at all. It is not sex education, not promiscuity, not homosexuality, not adultery, not the etiology of sexually transmitted diseases. The issue is whether or not the American culture will ever learn a sense of personal responsibility—the same sense of personal responsibility that could have wiped out syphilis and gonorrhea fifty years ago and that could prevent and eradicate herpes now. We must learn the sense of personal responsibility that is virtually absent from the smugness of those who display "Not perfect, just forgiven" bumperstickers, who cannot accept life without a fairytale heaven, who, in short, cannot face up to the reality of reality.

Our culture is steeped in irresponsibility. But those who are irresponsible must learn to *make* themselves responsible—or they will *become* responsible.

Lester A. Kirkendall

Why are the alternatives of encouraging sexual restraint or dispensing condoms categorized? Sex education should emphasize that there are times when sexual activities are acceptable and times when they are not. If they are acceptable, what restraints are in order, why, and who provides them? When they are acceptable, who should be involved in deciding? The educational process should have begun long before an individual becomes a part of a couple facing genital coupling. Educators should recognize that their pupils will become independent decision-makers but that they need factual evidence based upon current knowledge and a humanistic value system so that they will have the necessary background for making informed decisions.

The educator's task is not simply to encourage or discourage genital coupling, but, rather, to help all learners to be at ease with their sexuality and to make decisions which will be advantageous to the couple and hopefully understood and accepted by those around them.

As an educator—whether parent, teacher, or some other—your task is to

> *My message to teenagers on AIDS is simple: no sex. But, if you're going to have sex anyway, don't do it without protection. It's not "romantic" to let it just happen; it's stupid.*

produce learners who think objectively in terms of what is good for themselves and others, not to support or object to a particular pattern of sexual behavior.

In regard to the conflict between mandatory testing for AIDS and individual freedom, I am strongly in favor of abolishing discriminatory practices and in preventing any interference with individual rights. But there does come a time when the maintenance of life itself must take precedence over these other rights. I recall that several years ago, when Mount St. Helens at Longview, Washington, erupted, a lava flow began which later covered the public highways. A bit before the lava flow reached the roads, the police "interfered with the rights of auto drivers" to take the chance that their rapid driving would enable them to use the highway before the burning hot lava covered it. This was interference and, in a sense, discriminatory, but the major concern was to preserve life itself.

I think we must be aware of this conflict with AIDS. From what I have

read about the transmission of AIDS to many, many people of both genders and of all ages, I am not so sure but that we are close to the point of requiring universal testing.

Joan Nelson

As a psychologist and sexologist, I believe thinking men and women can use the fear of AIDS as a bridge rather than as a barrier to intimate communication. The fear is twofold: first is the fear of disease, which can be beneficial in stopping high-risk behaviors; second is the fear of sex, which damages more than it benefits. Moral judgments and guilt about sex exacerbate destructive reactions to AIDS—either denial ("it won't happen to me") or panic (withdrawal from intimate relationships).

In terms of social policy, fear of talking about sex seriously damages safe-sex teaching efforts. To avoid a new Victorian era of socially imposed sexual inhibitions and restrictions, it is necessary to foster realistic internal decision-making. This necessitates talking openly about the pervasive variety of normal sexual behaviors.

The Centers for Disease Control publish guidelines for "low-risk" and "no-risk" sexual behaviors. Low-risk sex includes wet kissing, vaginal and anal intercourse with a condom, urination, fellatio, and cunnilingus. No-risk sex includes massage, hugging, mutual masturbation, dry kissing, body-to-body rubbing, consensual voyeurism, exhibitionism, and fantasy.

The guidelines do not preclude high levels of erotic satisfaction. In fact, even talking about the practices increases human trust and intimate communication. Risking intimate communication is better than risking disease any day.

Fighting the Plague
27 NEW DRUGS TO STOP A KILLER

*AZT and ribavirin are making headlines.
Here's a roundup of other promising drugs.*

Thomas H. Maugh II

Thomas H. Maugh, II *is a science writer for* The Los Angeles Times.

"I've just found out I've been exposed to the AIDS virus," the frantic caller says. "What can I do? How can I get into a clinical trial? If I can't get in, can I get drugs to treat myself?"

Staffers of approximately 40 AIDS hotlines across the nation have had few words of comfort to offer. Treatment options have been limited; chances of getting the experimental drugs, slim. But that's changing now. A broad range of new drugs is beginning to emerge from expanded clinical trials—early tests of a drug's safety and efficacy—at home and abroad.

And under newly proposed government regulations, physicians could administer the more promising of the experimental drugs for any AIDS patient who could benefit. No longer would patients be denied therapy because they were closed out of clinical trials. However, according to the proposed rules, patients would have to pay at least some of the high cost of the drugs.

To AIDS patients who may have only six to 18 months left to live, the promise of fast-paced access answers anguished pleas. But some scientists worry that use of experimental drugs outside controlled studies can skew data needed to prove a drug's worth over the long term. Without proper studies, the effects of a promising drug can go unnoticed or a bad drug could be accepted as effective, says Dr. Samuel Broder, who directs clinical trials of AIDS (and cancer) drugs at the National Cancer Institute.

Though many AIDS researchers investigating new drug treatments are tight-lipped about preliminary studies, about 30 drugs are in clinical trials. And a few more look promising in preclinical (test tube or animal) studies. Conceivably, when the government's new regulations are implemented, a host of new drugs will become more available to AIDS patients.

A generation raised on miracle anti-biotics expects no less. For many, it seems unbelievable that scientists have not already developed effective drugs to combat the AIDS-causing human immunodeficiency virus (HIV, a.k.a. HTLV-III). Though AIDS researchers are pessimistic that a cure will be found soon, many believe drugs that can prolong the lives of AIDS patients are within reach. Today, the antiviral drug azidothymidine or AZT (Burroughs Wellcome's Retrovir) is the first to show good, durable effects in some patients with a pre-disease condition called AIDS-related complex (ARC). (Researchers report patients with full-blown AIDS may also benefit though they're more vulnerable to the drug's severe side effects.) Now interest is growing over two other potential weapons against AIDS: ribavirin (ICN Pharmaceuticals of Costa Mesa, CA) and AZT's less familiar cousin dideoxycytidine or ddC (Hoffmann-La Roche). And many more drugs are succeeding initially in clinical and preclinical studies.

From *American Health*, June 1987, pp. 73-76, 78-80, 83-84. *American Health Magazine* © 1987, Thomas H. Maugh, II.

South of the Border

Last June the government announced it would provide $100 million over the next five years in new funds to increase the number of clinical studies of AIDS drugs at 14 centers. In January, the government added $37.3 million more and designated five additional testing centers.

The program, though, has been exceptionally slow starting. By the end of January, more than 1,000 patients were supposed to have been enrolled in trials—instead there were only 133. Even when enrollment is filled, the total number of AIDS and pre-AIDS patients in the trials will reach only about 2,000. And some of them will receive placebos (sugar pills).

As many as 7,500 of the estimated 13,000 living AIDS victims in the U.S. have received no drugs for their illness—at least not officially. But thousands of AIDS patients, HIV-carriers, friends and sometimes even their doctors, stream across the border to Tijuana to bring back small supplies—or smuggle back bigger loads—of the AIDS drugs they can't get here.

Both ribavirin and isoprinosine—which manufacturer Newport Pharmaceuticals International calls an immune stimulator, but which the FDA says has only minimal effects on immune function—are sold legally in Mexico. (In the U.S. and Canada, an aerosol form of ribavirin, called Virazole, is approved only for use against a serious lung disease in infants.) In January, U.S. Customs ruled that each traveler may bring back a three-month supply of the drugs on each visit. But even before the ruling, the FDA and border agents did not oppose the traffic.

Other AIDS patients have traveled to France, like the late Rock Hudson, for high-priced AIDS treatment with HPA-23 (Rhone-Poulenc) and other experimental drugs. Initial French reports showed HPA-23 inhibited the HIV virus in ARC and AIDS patients, though follow-up studies showed little, if any, therapeutic benefit.

Still other AIDS patients were enticed by claims of West German and

Out of Africa: Tracking A Vaccine

In Central Africa, AIDS is spreading so quickly, the term "high-risk group" no longer holds any meaning. Today, hundreds of thousands of men and women, equally, are infected with the HIV AIDS virus, according to the World Health Organization.

But astonishingly, in Western Africa's republic of Senegal, only five inhabitants came down with AIDS last year. (All had returned home from Central Africa.) Even more surprising: Blood tests of more than 2,000 Senegalese by an international team showed no evidence of HIV infection in most urban areas or rural villages. Instead, the team found hundreds of people with antibodies against a second virus—a close cousin of HIV. It's a never-before-seen virus strain, dubbed HTLV-IV, that researchers hope may act as a natural vaccine against the deadly AIDS virus.

"In some places in Senegal, 40% or more of the prostitutes have antibodies to HTLV-IV," says Harvard epidemiologist Phyllis Kanki, who is spearheading blood-testing studies in Senegal. "But so far as we can tell, the antibody-positive women aren't coming down with any unusual medical conditions—and they aren't developing AIDS."

Further studies by Harvard's School of Public Health, along with the Universities of Tours and Limoges in France, and the University of Dakar in Senegal, show that in areas of Africa where the HTLV-IV virus is prevalent, there is no AIDS epidemic. And where there's AIDS, there's no HTLV-IV.

Even though the newfound AIDS cousin appears harmless, not enough is known about its long-term effects, investigators caution. "HTLV-IV is a retrovirus, a type of virus that remains permanently in the body," explains Dr. Myron Essex, chief of AIDS research at Harvard. "No one would like to intentionally expose people without knowing what might result years later." There's no guarantee it wouldn't cause malignancy 10 or 15 years down the road, he says.

But investigators are working to turn the epidemiologic discovery into a biomedical breakthrough. Dr. Essex believes HTLV-IV may be of enormous help in the worldwide effort to develop a vaccine against AIDS. Reason: The AIDS-causing HIV and the *apparently* benign HTLV-IV have one important feature in common: a genetically similar portion of glycoprotein coating, called gp-120, that stimulates production of HIV-neutralizing antibodies. Such a striking similarity in the two viruses is like siblings who have vastly different temperaments, but share the family nose.

What's more, a key portion of the AIDS virus's gp-120 apparently remains the same though other aspects are genetically wobbly and mutate. "We think we may be able to create a vaccine against HIV using the harmless gp-120 from the HTLV-IV retrovirus," says Dr. Essex. "In theory, the vaccinated person would make antibodies to the gp-120 in the vaccine. And if exposed to HIV later, those antibodies should protect against the disease."

Researchers are wary of killing the AIDS virus and retrieving its gp-120 for fear the virus particles could themselves cause the disease. But Harvard's Kanki is in the midst of testing the apparent protective effect of the African strain's gp-120 in animals.

There may be hundreds of other researchers worldwide developing AIDS vaccines. Though several could be ready for initial safety tests in humans this year or early 1988, most experts agree that it will take years to resolve legal liability issues surrounding widespread use.

—Kristin White

Mexican clinics for unverified "pre-AIDS treatments" costing $1,900.

It was "a national tragedy that people felt they had to go to Mexico or to France to get treatment," says AIDS researcher Martin Hirsch of Harvard Medical School. But now that more drugs are becoming accessible, he believes, "there's no need for AIDS patients to travel for treatments."

Guerilla Clinics give callers recipes for making homemade AIDS drugs.

Aboveboard but Underground

Tom Jefferson, administrative manager of the San Francisco AIDS hotline, Project Inform, goes for his AIDS drug supplies to the Regis Pharmacy, the Olympia Pharmacy or Maxine's Pharmacy, each just a little over a mile from the U.S. border at Tijuana. On each trip, he gets at least 25 boxes of ribavirin (at $26 per box) and 15 boxes of isoprinosine ($7 per box)—a 2 ½ months' supply.

In 1984, Jefferson was diagnosed as having ARC and was told AIDS would be next. Because he was unable to enter a clinical study, he decided to begin treating himself. A year later, Jefferson still had not progressed to AIDS. Wishing to spread the word about self-treatment options, he helped organize Project Inform. Its main mission is to disseminate information about the few drugs that can be readily obtained by AIDS victims.

Today Jefferson says his disease is still in check. He, two paid staffers and a varying number of volunteers answer more than 75 phone calls every day on their hotline (800-822-7422; in California, 800-334-7422). Operating out of a small office on the sixth floor of the Golden Gate Theatre Building in the heart of downtown San Francisco, they mail out 150 packets of information a week explaining how to get the drugs and how to use them.

To date, Project Inform is the only group that provides such information. Most other groups that have state or local funding are prohibited from providing leads to alternative sources, Jefferson says, "so they refer people to us."

Project Inform doesn't tout any particular treatment, he says. "We just

provide callers with information—and recommend that they discuss the information with their own physician and be monitored for side effects."

Currently, Project Inform's formulary includes: ribavirin, isoprinosine, naltrexone (an opiate blocker that, as of the end of March, had no published reports to support claims as an AIDS drug), D-Penicillamine (an arthritis drug) and the photo chemical DNCB, the main ingredient in a homemade anti-AIDS lotion now awaiting funding for clinical studies at the University of California, San Francisco.

Though DNCB's action is unproved, a study described in the *Journal of the American Academy of Dermatology* suggests diluted topical applications might boost the immune-system response in some AIDS patients. The small study suggests a DNCB-based solution helped clear skin lesions among some patients with Kaposi's sarcoma—a skin cancer common among AIDS patients.

Because DNCB is sold in photo supply stores, many desperate AIDS patients began mixing and applying their own DNCB concoctions. There's even an underground network of homes, called Guerilla Clinics, where the lotions are mixed and provided free to AIDS patients. At last count, there were 38 so-called Guerilla Clinics in 15 states, says the network co-founder Blaine Elswood of San Francisco. "Our purpose was to get the medical community to investigate DNCB. And now we've got 17 physicians in New York and California on our Guerilla Clinic directory," he says. "These are doctors who are either using it on their patients, or who are monitoring the results of AIDS patients who use DNCB themselves." (The Guerilla

Clinic phone directory is available from Project Inform.)

Some Guerilla Clinics also will refer patients to underground suppliers of ribavirin from Mexico. And some make available home recipes of other experimental substances, including a lipid-based mixture called AL-721. Praxis Pharmaceuticals of Beverly Hills holds the patent on the actual formula, which it says interferes with HIV infectivity. Homemade frozen mixtures of soy lecithin, fat, and butter "couldn't possibly" work like the actual pharmaceutical, Praxis says. Independent tests on Praxis' AL-721 by doctors at St. Luke's-Roosevelt Hospital, Memorial Sloane-Kettering Cancer Center and Beth Israel Hospital in New York may begin this summer, Praxis says, pending final approval.

"That there is a guerilla movement at all is a telling commentary on the medical establishment's inability to cope with the AIDS epidemic," says Elswood. But clearly, it also indicates the desperation caused by the disease.

A Drug for Life?

Though patients anguish over the slow progress against the AIDS virus, scientists have nevertheless learned a vast amount about the disease in a relatively short time. Now, research teams are engaged in a huge effort to find drugs that can attack, if not conquer, the seemingly invulnerable virus. And some are searching for drugs that will boost depleted immune systems. Most scientists now believe that effective AIDS treatments will require combinations of therapy.

However, few scientists expect to find a drug that will completely rid the patient's body of the virus. Instead,

Some day drugs may control AIDS much as insulin keeps diabetes in check.

most search for drugs that can keep the virus in check by attacking it at some point in its life cycle and that can be taken for years—perhaps decades—without toxic side effects. The hope is that eventually AIDS therapy will control the virus in much the same way daily insulin doses keep a diabetic's blood sugar in check.

Scientists still puzzle over the virus's complexity and ability to attack its victim's immune defenses while resisting counterattack. Like the alien pods in *Invasion of the Body Snatchers*, HIV is insidious. It turns invaded cells into AIDS virus factories and then kills them as infection spreads. Its genetic material not only takes over helper T cells (key immune system sentinels) but may also infect and hide out in other cells, including monocytes and macrophages—those white blood cells that are supposed to devour, not harbour, invading viruses.

The AIDS virus uses a special enzyme—reverse transcriptase—to insert its own genetic material into an infected cell's nucleus. There, it takes over and directs the cell to make new AIDS viruses which, in turn, infect other cells. It literally multiplies itself. Yet, the virus can also remain latent inside a cell's DNA for years before erupting in a burst of infection. Such cunning provides scientists with a target to aim at: Blocking the enzyme's action would keep the virus from replicating and spreading the disease.

Two Media Stars

Enter: AZT. It's a reverse transcriptase-blocking drug. And it's the first anti-retroviral AIDS drug to receive FDA approval as a prescription treatment for some AIDS and ARC patients.

By year's end, say AZT makers, many more patients should receive the drug. And, they say, there will be enough for more than 30,000 patients—at least, for those who can pay. As an experimental drug, AZT was administered free of charge; it will cost $7,000 to $10,000 for a year's supply.

It's still considered the AIDS drug of choice, especially for patients who've had Pneumocystis carinii pneumonia. Burroughs Wellcome explains AZT can cause toxic side effects ranging from muscle pain to reduced red and white cell counts depending upon the bone marrow's condition at the onset of AZT treatment.

But that has not yet interfered with clinical trials—especially tests of AZT's efficacy in combination with other drugs. "It is important to recognize that full-blown AIDS is invariably fatal," says NCI's Dr. Broder. "We can't let a drug be dismissed because it might have some toxicity."

And Broder is testing the combined effects of AZT and another antiviral agent, acyclovir (Burroughs Wellcome), among patients with AIDS and ARC. Acyclovir (Zovirax) is now marketed in the U.S. as an anti-herpes drug. (Chronic herpes simplex infections are common among AIDS patients.) Tests in cultured cells, Broder says, show that acyclovir and AZT are synergistic. AZT could then be used at lower concentrations, possibly reducing side effects. (Still, one patient given the two drugs at Maine Medical Center had such incapacitating drowsiness and lethargy that the acyclovir treatment was discontinued.) Burroughs Wellcome expects to have 2,000 people enrolled in all clinical trial programs by year's end.

And could AZT work in combination with ribavirin? A discouraging pre-clinical test reported in *Science* suggests the two drugs may be antagonistic—at least in the test tube. Ribavirin partially blocked AZT's action in lab studies with infected human cells. The combination treatment, say scientists, might work better in patients if conditions are very carefully controlled.

Researchers believe ribavirin may inhibit HIV replication, though the exact mechanism is unclear. At a Washington press conference, ICN officials announced that the drug could postpone the onset of the disease in some pre-AIDS patients (see Medical News Updates, *AH*, p. 13, May '87).

At press time, ICN had submitted data to the FDA on the clinical trials and requested that ribavirin be given experimental drug status. That would mean wider distribution outside clinically controlled trials.

Meanwhile, Harvard's Dr. Clyde Crumpacker is also studying ribavirin's effect on ARC *and* AIDS patients. Preliminary results show that the drug produced a general improvement in symptoms for both groups and that none of the patients developed other infections while on it. But two of five ARC patients progressed to AIDS within three months of stopping the drug, Crumpacker reports. He's also found that ribavirin crosses the blood-brain barrier. This suggests that future studies might focus on ribavirin's ability to fight the virus in infected brain tissue.

But Broder cautions that although many drugs in early trials appear to help, many may actually have only minimal effects. "Patients must be realistic about what these drugs might be able to do," he says.

Summing up the other side, Richard Dunne, executive director of the Gay Men's Health Crisis in New York City, says: "Researchers don't seem to understand at a feeling level the predicament of a dying person who hears of something promising. Patients ought to be offered virtually anything that holds any promise of being effective. Human beings have a right to make their own decisions."

Patient advocates want AIDS drugs to become available faster.

Other Drugs on Trial

Scientists searching for effective AIDS treatments have made progress on two fronts: drugs that interfere with the AIDS virus's life cycle, like AZT; and agents that boost the patient's immune system so they can fight off deadly secondary infections. The current view is that combination treatment might offer a viable strategy for counterattack. Here are a few drugs under study. (Admission to clinical trials is limited; for information, call the hotlines listed on p. 84.)

Promising Antivirals:

■ **Dideoxycytidine** (Hoffmann-La Roche) and **dideoxyadenosine (ddC** and **ddA)** are nucleoside analogs (like AZT)—they're structurally similar, but not identical, to the biochemical nucleosides that form DNA. As such they appear to fool HIV into incorporating them into the virus's growing DNA chain during replication. Because analogs lack an important biochemical appendage, the virus cannot finish reproducing its nuclear material and is rendered harmless. It appears that ddC is "the most potent nucleoside drug we've found so far," says the NCI's Dr. Broder. "But you can't predict how it will work in people."

In preliminary test-tube studies with AIDS-infected human cells, ddC stopped viral replication at "significantly lower concentrations" than AZT, he says. Now NCI clinical investigators are doing safety studies of ddC among patients with AIDS or AIDS-related complex. Though ddA is still being tested on animals, "it has very little toxicity against cells in vitro," Broder says. "The drug will probably be administered to patients sometime this summer."

■ **CS-85, CS-87** and **CS-91** were developed at Emory University and the University of Georgia. They're closely related to AZT but may be less toxic, according to preliminary studies. In differing degrees, all have proved effective in hindering the virus's spread in AIDS-infected human cells. Now scientists await results of CS-85 and CS-87 animal tests.

■ **Foscarnet** (Sweden's Astra Pharmaceutical Co.) is in clinical trials in Europe for treatment of cytomegalovirus (a herpes virus) and other herpes infections. It's been shown to inhibit AIDS virus replication in cultured cells. Preliminary data from clinical trials indicate Foscarnet also inhibits replication in AIDS patients.

In January, Astra began tests of Foscarnet among San Francisco AIDS patients with cytomegalovirus retinitis, the leading cause of blindness among AIDS victims. Dr. Michael Fanucchi of Memorial Sloan-Kettering Cancer Center in New York City and other researchers say clinical trials with ARC patients are beginning this spring.

■ **Ganciclovir** (Palo Alto's Syntex Corp.), an analog of acyclovir, is being studied in nationwide clinical trials against cytomegalovirus retinitis.

■ **D-Penicillamine** (Degussa Corp. of Teeterboro, NJ) blocked HIV spread in preliminary clinical trials at George Washington University in Washington, DC. Drawback: It also suppressed immune-cell function in some patients. GWU's Dr. David M. Parenti is still giving it to AIDS patients but is alternating monthly between D-Penicillamine and no medication. He hopes the respite will permit immune systems to recover. The drug is available in the U.S. by prescription—for hepatitis and rheumatoid arthritis.

■ **Alpha-interferon** (Hoffmann-La Roche, Nutley, NJ) and **beta-interferon** (Triton Biosciences Inc., Alameda, CA) are naturally occurring substances now mass-produced by genetic engineering. Hoffmann-La Roche is set to begin a trial combining alpha-interferon with AZT.

In a separate study, New York's Memorial Sloan-Kettering Cancer Center tested alpha-interferon in 16 AIDS patients and found it reduced the lesions of Kaposi's sarcoma in about 30% of patients. Also, very preliminary evidence suggests it may suppress the growth of the AIDS virus in patients, reports Dr. Susan Krown.

Small clinical trials with beta-interferon have shown mixed therapeutic results, says Dr. William Lang, who's heading studies at Children's Hospital in San Francisco. Clincial trials are about to be expanded, says Triton's Dr. Stephen G. Marcus.

Immune System Boosters:

■ **Diethyldithiocarbamate, DTC,** is supplied by the Merieux Institute in Paris and Miami. It has "shown a trend toward halting the progression of ARC to AIDS in preliminary studies" at M.D. Anderson Hospital in Houston, Merieux says. Similar results were reported in France. Controlled studies now are in progress at six centers in the U.S.

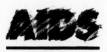

D-Penicillamine, an arthritis drug, may help block the AIDS virus.

Peptide T, studies show, prevents the AIDS virus from entering cells.

■ **Imreg-1** (Imreg Inc., New Orleans) raised immune responses in 15 of 29 patients in a preliminary clinical study, says Dr. A. Arthur Gottlieb, president of Imreg. Full-scale clinical trials have started for 150 patients with AIDS or ARC. Results are due by the end of the year. Imreg's Dr. Clifford Kern reports no observed toxicity in over 100 patients treated.

■ **Thymostimulin** (Serono Laboratories of Randolph, MA) is being tested on ARC patients in clinical trials at four unspecified U.S. hospitals.

■ **Granulocyte Monocyte-Colony Stimulating Factor** (Cambridge's Genetics Institute) is an immune system booster that increases white cells. GM-CSF is now in safety and dosage testing trials with AIDS patients at New England Deaconess Hospital and UCLA. Sandoz Pharmaceuticals of East Hannover, NJ, is sponsoring the trials.

■ **Azimexon** (Boehringer Mannheim) is reported to boost immune system function in some ARC patients. Safety trials have been conducted at the Institute for Immunological Disorders in Houston.

■ **Ampligen** (HEM Research of Bethesda, MD) has been shown to stimulate the body's production of interferon. Hahnemann University in Philadelphia and George Washington University Medical Center in Washington, DC, are conducting clinical trials among AIDS patients.

Too Soon To Tell:

■ **Peptide T**, synthesized by scientists at the National Institute of Mental Health, is the only AIDS drug believed to prevent the virus from entering cells, *Science* reports. Dr. Peter Bridge of the NIMH has filed for FDA approval to begin human safety studies. And in Stockholm, scientists at the Karolinska Institute are set to begin clinical trials.

■ **Thymopentin (TP$_5$)** (Ortho Pharmaceutical Corp. of Raritan, NJ) is now in a 16-week study of combination treatment with ribavirin, headed by Dr. Michael J. Scolaro and colleagues at St. Vincent Medical Center in Los Angeles. The results are not available yet on their study of 30 AIDS patients with Kaposi's sarcoma or secondary infections.

AIDS Information Services

If friend or kin fear AIDS infection, here are numbers to call for information on the disease, available treatments and how to participate in clinical trials. All will lead callers to local counseling, testing and support centers.
■ **Public Health Service:** 800-342-AIDS.
■ **National Gay and Lesbian Crisisline:** 800-221-7044; in NY, Hawaii and Alaska, call 212-529-1604.
■ **San Francisco AIDS Foundation:** 415-863-2437; in Northern California, call 800-FOR-AIDS.
—T.H.M.

This glossary of 330 human sexuality terms is included to provide you with a convenient and ready reference as you encounter general terms in your study of human sexuality which are unfamiliar or require a review. It is not intended to be comprehensive but taken together with the many definitions included in the articles themselves it should prove to be quite useful.

ABBREVIATIONS USED
IN DEFINITIONS

Abbr.	abbreviation
C.	Centigrade, Celsius
e.g.	for example
i.e.	that is
pl.	plural
q.v.	which see
sing.	singular

Abort To terminate a pregnancy prematurely.

Abortifacient A drug or agent that brings about an abortion.

Abortion The removal or expulsion of the products of conception (embryo or fetus and its extraembryonic membranes) before the age of viability, usually 22 weeks. See miscarriage; premature birth.

a., criminal An illegal abortion; one performed contrary to the laws of the state.

a., incomplete One in which there is only partial expulsion of the products of conception.

a., induced One brought about by medicinal or mechanical means; an artificial abortion.

a., interim One occurring between the thirteenth and sixteenth weeks.

a., missed One in which the fetus dies but the products of conception remain within the uterus for two weeks or longer before being extruded.

a., spontaneous One that occurs naturally; one not induced.

a., suction One in which the conceptus is removed by aspiration.

a., therapeutic An abortion that is performed (a) when pregnancy or birth threatens the life or health of the patient or (b) when the likelihood is great that the fetus conceived will be grossly abonormal.

Abortus An aborted fetus; the products of an abortion.

AC-DC Bisexual; ambisexual.

Adultery Voluntary sexual intercourse between a married person and a person other than his or her lawful spouse. It may be *conventional*, which is characterized by deception and is unknown to spouse or *consensual*, which is known to and consented to by spouse.

Afterbirth The material expelled following the birth of a baby consisting of the placenta and embryonic membranes. Also called *secundines.*

Afterplay Activities such as kissing and caressing following coitus that provide psychological and emotional satisfaction greatly enhancing coital pleasure especially in the female.

Agape Nonsexual love; Christian love.

Amatory Of, pertaining to, or associated with love, especially sexual love; expressive of love.

Ambisexual Common to or involving both sexes with respect to structure, feelings, or behavior.

Amenorrhea Absence of menstruation.

Amour A love affair, especially an illicit one.

Anaphrodisiac A substance that allegedly reduces or allays sexual desire, such as cyprosterone, which is effective in males.

Androgyne A person who possesses both male and female characteristics: a hermaphrodite or pseudohermaphrodite.

Androgynous Bisexual; possessing both male and female characteristics; hermaphroditic.

Androgyny 1. A condition in which an individual possesses both male and female characteristics, especially the possession of female characters by a male. *Compare* gynandry. 2. A society that shows little differentiation between the sex roles.

Androphobia Excessive fear of or dislike of males. *Compare* gynophobia.

Anilingus The application of the tongue to the anus.

Annulment The legal invalidation of a marriage; a declaration that a marriage was never valid.

Anorgasmy Inability or failure to reach a climax during coitus.

Apandria An aversion to, or an extreme dislike for males.

Aphrodisiac A substance which stimulates sexual desire and induces an erection in a male. See cantharides.

Artificial Insemination *Abbr.* AI. The injection of semen into the vagina or uterus. The sperm may be provided by the husband (AIH) or by another person called a donor (AID).

Aunt, Auntie *Slang.* 1. An aging homosexual. 2. An old prostitute. 3. A madam.

Autoerotism, Autoeroticism Obtaining sexual satisfaction through solitary sexual activities, as masturbation, nocturnal emissions, and sexual fantasies; autosexuality.

Balanitis Inflammation of the glans penis or glans clitoris.

Bastard 1. An illegitimate child. 2. A child born of unwed parents.

Bawd 1. A prostitute. 2. A woman who manages a brothel; a madam.

B & D Bondage and discipline.

Bigamy The act of marrying another person while still legally married.

Biopsy The examination microscopically of tissue excised from a living body usually performed for diagnostic purposes.

Bisexual 1. Of or pertaining to both sexes. 2. Possessing both male and female sex organs; hermaphroditic. 3. Having sexual relations with individuals of both sexes; heterosexual and homosexual.

Bordello A brothel or house of prostitution.

Buggery Anal intercourse; sodomy.

Butch *Slang.* 1. A bull dyke. 2. An active lesbian who assumes the role of a male.

Cantharides Spanish fly, the dried pulverized bodies of beetles, *Cantharis (Lytta) vesicatoria,* reputed to have aphrodisiac effects. It is a gastrointestinal and urinary tract irritant and highly toxic when taken internally.

Capacitation The process by which spermatozoa, in their passage through the female genital tract, acquire the ability to penetrate the zona pellucida of a recently ovulated ovum.

Castration 1. Removal of the testes or ovaries; orchiectomy, ovariectomy. See Spay. 2. Destruction or inactivation of the testes or ovaries, such as that resulting from irradiation, the effects of drugs, or pathologic conditions.

Celibacy The state of remaining unmarried especially for religious reasons; abstention from sexual intercourse.

Cervical Cap The thimble-shaped, rubber cap shaped to fit snugly over the cervix of the uterus. It is used for contraception.

Change of Life In women, the menopause; in men, the male climacteric.

Chaste Virtuous; abstaining from unlawful sexual intercourse.

Chromosome A self-duplicating body present in the cells of higher animals and plants, especially noticeable during stages of cell division. It is the repository of the genes and of importance in sex determination. See X Chromosome; Y Chromosome.

Circumcision Removal of the prepuce or foreskin from the penis or clitoris.

Clap *Slang.* Gonorrhea.

Climacteric, Female The menopause, q.v.

Climacteric, Male A change in life seen occasionally in men characterized by reduced libido and sometimes marked emotional disturbances. It usually occurs between the ages of 50 and 60 and corresponds to the menopause in women.

Climax The period of greatest intensity of sexual pleasure during intercourse; the orgasm.

Clitoris A small, erectile structure embedded in the tissues of the vulva at the junction of the minor labia. It is homologous to the penis of the male.

Coitus Sexual intercourse between two persons in which the penis is inserted into the vagina.

c. a la veche Rear entry coital position with the woman in a knee-chest position; coitus from behind.

c. interruptus Withdrawl of the penis from the vagina prior to ejaculation.

c. obstructus Delaying an ejaculation by firm pressure on a spot between the scrotum and the anus.

c. reservatus Coition without ejaculation, especially, prolonged copulation and intentional suppression of ejaculation. Also called *karezza.*

Comarital Sex The sharing of mates or the incorporation of extramarital sex in marriage; swinging.

Commune A group of individuals living together and sharing common interests, sometimes involving indiscrimiante sexual relationships.

Concubine A woman who cohabits with a man without being legally married to him. See mistress.

Concubinage Cohabitation without legal sanction.

Concupiscent Sensual, lustful, desirous of sex.

Condom A sheath worn over the erect penis during sexual intercourse. It is usually made of thin rubber and functions as a contraceptive device and as a prophylactic preventing venereal disease infection. Also called *rubber, safety, skin, pro.*

Conjugal Of marriage or the marriage state; connubial.

Contraceptive 1. Of or pertaining to contraception. 2. Any agent or device that prevents conception. *See* Cervical Cap, Condom, Diaphragm, Foam, Jelly, Pessary, Pill, Intrauterine Device.

Contrasexism The compulsion to have the body transformed surgically and hormonally to that of the opposite sex.

Contrectation Sexual foreplay.

Coprology Pornography; scatology.

Copulation Sexual intercourse; coitus.

Courtesan A high-class prostitute whose clientele includes men of the upper classes.

Crabs Pubic lice. See Louse.

Cuckold The husband of an adultress.

Cunnilingus Oral stimulation of the female genitalia, especially the clitoris. Also *cunnilinctus*.

Cunnus The vulva.

Dartos A thin layer of smooth muscle located beneath the subcutaneous tissue of the scrotum.

Detumescence The restoration of a swollen organ to natural size especially the subsidence of the erect penis after ejaculation.

Diaphragm A cup-shaped contraceptive device that fits over the cervix of the uterus.

Dildo, Dildoe An artificial penis.

Dilatation and **Curettage** *Abbr.* D. and C. A method of inducing an abortion involving the dilatation and the cervical canal of the uterus and insertion of a curet by which the embryo is dislodged. The technique is also utilized in securing samples of the uterine endometrium for diagnostic purposes.

Distillatia A clear, viscid, alkaline fluid that appears at the tip of the penis when the male is sexually aroused. It is produced by the bulbourethral glands and functions in alkalinization of the urethra and lubrication of the penis.

Douche A jet or stream of water directed against the body or into one of its cavities, especially one directed into the vagina for cleanliness, contraception, or medicinal purposes.

Drag *Slang.* 1. Female clothing worn by a male especially a homosexual or transvestite. 2. A homosexual party where the participants wear clothes of the opposite sex. 3. A woman accompanying her escort.

D&S Dominance and submission.

Dysfunction Any impairment or disorder in the functioning of a body tissue, organ, or system.

Ecbolic Inducing an abortion or accelerating childbirth.

Ecouteurism Sexual excitement resulting from hearing sounds associated with sexual activities.

Effeminate In a male, possessing the characteristics of a woman.

Ejaculate 1. The fluid discharged during ejaculation; the seminal fluid or semen. 2. To discharge semen.

Ejaculation praecox Premature ejaculation; an ejaculation that occurs before or shortly after penetration.

Electra complex The pathological emotional attachment of a girl or woman to her father. *Compare* Oedipus complex.

Emasculate To castrate; to deprive of masculine vigor; to make effeminate.

Endocrine Gland A gland of internal secretion; a ductless gland whose secretions called *hor-*

mones are discharged into the blood or lymph and distributed throughout the body. The principal endocrine glands are the pituitary, thyroid, parathyroid, adrenal, islets of the pancreas, ovary, and testes.

Endogamy Marriage within a particular tribe, group, or clan; inbreeding. *Compare* exogamy.

Endoscope An instrument for visual examination of a hollow organ or cavity.

Eonism The assumption of feminine traits and mannerisms and the wearing of female clothes by a male; effemination.

Erection The process by which an erectile structure, such as the penis or clitoris, becomes hard and erect, as usually occurs following sexual stimulation.

Erogenous Arousing sexual desire; stimulating sexual activity or response.

Erogenous Zones Regions of the body which, when stimulated, give rise to sexual desire. in the female these include the external genitalia, inner surfaces of the thighs, the breasts, armpits, neck, ear lobes, lips, and mouth. In the male, the external genitalia (penis, especially the glans, scrotum), inner surfaces of the thighs, anal region, breasts, lips, and mouth.

Erotic Of or pertaining to libido or sexual love and desire.

Erotogenic Causing or giving rise to erotic feelings.

Erotomania Nymphomania or satyriasis.

Estrogen, Oestrogen A substance, natural or synthetic, which is capable of inducing estrus in lower animals or changes in the uterine endometrium and the development of female sexual characteristics in humans. The principal estrogens or female hormones are *estradiol, estrone,* and *estriol* produced principally by ovarian follicles and corpora lutea. They are also produced by the placenta, adrenal cortex, and the testes.

Estrus Heat, or the period in female mammals, except primates, during which they are sexually active and receptive to the male. It occurs at the time of ovulation. *Compare* rut.

Eugenics The science that deals with the improvement of the human race through selective breeding. *Compare* euthenics.

Euthanasia The termination of the life of a person suffering from an incurable disease or intractable pain.

Euthenics The science that deals with the improvement of the human race through improvement of the environment. *Compare* eugenics.

Eunuch A castrated person or a person in which there is complete testicular failure.

Eviration 1. Castration; emasculation; demasculinization. 2. The assumption of the feminine role by a male, especially in sexual relations.

Fag, Faggot *Slang.* A male homosexual, especially an extremely effeminate one.

Fairy *Slang.* A male homosexual, especially one who assumes the female role.

Fallopian Tube The uterine tube or oviduct.

Fecund Capable of conceiving and producing offspring.

Fecundate To impregnate.

Fellatio, Fellation Oral stimulation of the penis; irrumation. *Compare* cunnilingus.

Fem, Femme *Slang.* 1. A passive lesbian. 2. A feminine-appearing lesbian prostitute. 3. An effeminate homosexual, male or female.

Femoral Intercourse Intercourse in which the penis is placed between the thighs and not inserted into the vagina.

Fertile Period The period in the menstrual cycle during which conception is most likely to occur, especially the days immediately preceding and following ovulation, which occurs usually between the twelfth and sixteenth days of the cycle. *Compare* safe period.

Fetish An object or a part of the body other than the sex organs that is used to arouse sexual feelings. Objects may include articles of clothing (panties, bras, girdles) or something belonging to the desired person; parts of the body include the neck, breasts, buttocks, and hair.

Flanquette A half-frontal posture in coitus.

Flit *Slang.* A male homosexual, especially one who exhibits female mannerisms.

Foam, Contraceptive A chemical substance usually containing a spermicidal agent that forms as effervescent mass within the vagina. It acts as a physical barrier preventing sperm from entering the cervix.

Foreplay Forepleasure obtained through activities that precede sexual intercourse and tend to lead to an orgasm; contrectation.

Fornication Sexual intercourse between unmarried persons or between two married persons not married to each other. See Adultery.

Frig *Slang.* 1. To have sexual intercourse with a woman. 2. To cheat or trick a person.

Frigidity In women, lack of sexual feelings or desire; coldness; the absence of passion or sexual responsiveness; inability to experience an orgasm. Also called *orgasmic impairment, hyposexuality, sexual anesthesia*.

Frottage The practice of obtaining sexual pleasure by rubbing a part of the body, especially the genitals, against another person or by rubbing an object that serves as a fetish.

Gamete A reproductive cell; a spermatozoon or ovum.

Gay *Slang.* 1. Homosexual. 2. Pertaining to or involving homosexual activity. 3. Licentious; immoral.

Gender Identity The development in a child of a sense of maleness or femaleness depending principally on how a child is reared.

Genitalia The male or female reproductive organs, especially the external sex organs. See vulva, penis.

Genophobia Abnormal fear of sexual intercourse.

Glans A conical structure forming the distal end of the penis or clitoris.

Gonad An organ that products gametes; a testis or ovary.

Gynandry The development of male characteristics in a female; feminine pseudohermaphroditism. *See* Virilism.

Gynecoid Resembling a female.

Gynecologist A physician who specializes in the diagnosis and treatment of diseases of women, especially those involving the sex organs. *Compare* obstetrician. *See* Andrologist.

Gynoid Like or resembling a female; gynecoid.

Gynophobia An abnormal fear of females. *Compare* androphobia.

Harlot A prostitute.

Hedonic Of, pertaining to, or characterized by pleasure.

Hermaphrodite 1. An indivdiual who possesses both male and female sex organs or a combined ovotestis; a monoecious individual. 2. According to Money, a person in whom at least one of five variables of sex is contradictory to the remainder. These are (a) nuclear sex, (b) gonadal sex, (c) hormonal sex and pubertal virilization or feminization, (d) internal accessory reproductive structures, and (e) external genital morphology.

Herpes Simplex An acute, infectious viral disorder of two types: the *labial type* (HSV-1), commonly causing cold sores or fever blisters about the mouth, and the *genital type* (HSV-2), which affects the genital organs. The latter is a venereal disease.

Heterogamy The marriage of unlike individuals; crossbreeding. *Compare* homogamy.

Heterosexual 1. Of or pertaining to the opposite sex, especially with reference to sexual feelings and activities; attracted to the opposite sex. 2. A heterosexual person; a straight. *Compare* homosexual.

Hirsute Hairy; covered with excess hair.

Homoeroticism Homosexuality; lesbianism.

Homogamy 1. The mating of like to like, as in reproduction within an isolated group; inbreeding. 2. The marriage of like individuals, as those of the same race, religion, or social status. *Compare* heterogamy.

Homophile 1. Homosexual, with reference to homosexual associations (homophile societies) that promote gay power and gay liberation movements. 2. A homosexual person.

Homosexual 1. Of, pertaining to, or involving a person of one's own sex. 2. A homosexual person; a lesbian; a gay person; a uranist.

Hymen A membrane that partially closes the external opening of the vagina in virgins; the maidenhead.

Hypersexuality Excessive sexual desire. *See* Nymphomania, Satyriasis.

Hypogamy Marriage to a person of lower social status.

Hysterectomy Partial or total removal of the uterus.

Hysterotomy Surgical incision into the uterus; a Cesarean section.

Impotence, Impotency Inability of the male to perform the sexual act; inability to achieve and maintain an erection to the state of orgasm. It may be due to structural disorders, disease of the genital organs, endocrine dysfunction, systemic disease, or psychic factors.

Incest Sexual relations between closely related persons, as parent and child, or between children of the same parents.

Inseminate To introduce semen into a female. *See* Artificial Insemination.

Insertee A male, passive homosexual.

Insertor A male, active homosexual.

Intersexuality Possessing characteristics of both sexes.

Intrauterine Contraceptive Device *Abbr.* IUCD. A device which, when placed within the uterus, prevents the implantation of the blastocyst.

Invert A homosexual or lesbian.

Irrumation Fellatio.

Ithyphalic 1. With an erect phallus, with reference to graphic representations. 2. Obscene; lascivious.

IUD Intrauterine device.

Jag House *Slang.* A brothel for male prostitutes who cater to male homosexuals.

Jelly, Contraceptive A jelly containing a spermicidal substance, which is placed in the vagina for contraceptive purposes.

John *Slang.* 1. A male customer of a prostitute; a trick. 2. A public toilet, especially one for males. 3. A man who keeps a woman in return for sexual favors. 4. A wealthy, elderly homosexual who keeps a young homosexual as a companion and associate.

Karezza Coitus reservatus or prolonged sexual union. Also *carezza*.

Katasexual Designating sexual relations with a nonhuman.

Labium, *pl.* **Labia** One of two folds of tissue, the outer *labia majora* and the inner *labia minora,* which border the vaginal orifice.

Lactation 1. The secretion of milk by the mammary gland. 2. The period during which a baby feeds from the breast.

Lascivious Lewd, lecherous, tending to excite sexual desire, salacious.

Lechery Excessive indulgence in sexual activity.

Lesbian A homosexual female; a tribade.

Lesbianism Affection of two women for each other; homosexuality between two females, tribadism.

Leukorrhea A disorder common in women characterized by an abnormal, whitish, mucopurulent discharge from the vagina. Commonly called the "whites."

Libertine A dissolute person; one who has no regard for moral or religious restraints.

Libido Sexual desire or sex drive; passion; the force by which the sexual instinct expresses itself.

Licentious Sexually unrestrained; immoral; lewd.

Lochia The discharge from the uterus and vagina during the first few weeks following childbirth.

Lordosis 1. Excessive forward curvature of the spine in the lumbar region. 2. A position assumed by most female mammals preceding and during mating in which the back is arched and haunches elevated thus facilitating reception of the male.

Louse, *pl.* **Lice** A small, wingless insect of the order Hemiptera, which lives as an ectoparasite on man and other mammals. Human lice include the body and head louse, *Pediculus humanus,* and the pubic louse or crab, *Phthirus pubis.*

Machismo A Spanish word implying strength and masculinity especially that demonstrated by the fathering of many children, whether legitimate or illegitimate.

Macrophallus An exceptionally large penis; a macropenis.

Maidenhead The hymen.

Masochism Sexual pleasure derived from submitting to brutality, pain, and humiliating treatment. *Compare* sadism.

Mastectomy Surgical removal of the breast.

Masturbation The obtaining of sexual pleasure, especially the induction of an orgasm by means other than sexual intercourse: autoeroticism. Formerly called *self-abuse*.

Maternal Of or pertaining to the mother; inherited from the mother.

Matrilineal Tracing descent through the female line. *Compare* patrilineal.

Menage The persons living together and comprising a household.

Menage a Trois A triadic relationship involving a married couple and a lover of one of them occupying the same household.

Menarche The onset of menses at puberty.

Menopause The physiological cessation of menstrual cycles and ovarian function in women occurring usually between the ages of 45 and 50. Also called *change of life* or *climacteric.*

Menstrual Cycle The periodic, recurring series of changes that occur in the endometrium of the uterus culminating in menstruation. It averages 28 days in length and includes the phases of repair, proliferation, secretion, and menstruation. It occurs in women from puberty to menopause except during periods of pregnancy and lactation. *See* Menarche, Menopause.

Merkin 1. False hair for the female genitalia. 2. An artificial or substitute vagina.

Microphallus An exceptionally small penis; a micropenis.

Miscegenation Interbreeding or intermarriage between members of difference races; the mixing of races.

Misogamy A dislike for or an aversion to marriage.

Misogynist A woman hater.

Mixoscopia Sexual pleasure obtained from viewing others in coitus.

Monoecious Possessing both testes and ovaries; hermaphroditic. *Compare* dioecious.

Monogyny Having only one wife at a time. *Compare* polygyny.

Mons Pubis An elevated cushion of fat covered with skin, which lies over the pubic symphysis. After puberty, it is covered with pubic hair. Also called the *mons veneris* in women.

Morning-after Pill A pill containing diethylstilbestrol (DES), a synthetic estrogen, sometimes given for contraceptive purposes. It is effective three to five days after coitus but side effects are severe. Also called *abortion pill.*

Muliebrity 1. Possessing a womanly nature or qualities; the condition of being a woman. 2. The assumption of female characteristics by a male; effemination.

Narcissism, Narcism Self-love; excessive love and admiration for one's own body.

Narratophilia A condition in which a person requires or depends on reading or listening to erotic material for the arousal of sexual activity or achievement of an orgasm. *See* Paraphilia.

Necrophilia An attraction to, and often an erotic interest in dead bodies.

Neuter 1. An animal with imperfectly developed sex organs. 2. Neither male nor female. 3. A castrated animal.

Nubile Ready and suitable for marriage, especially with respect to sexuality, with reference to females.

Nuptial Or or pertaining to (a) a marriage or wedding ceremony; (b) mating.

Nymphet A young girl considered sexually desirable; a sexually precocious girl.

Nymphomania Excessive and sometimes uncontrollable sexual desire in a woman. *Compare* satyriasis.

Obstetrician A physician who specializes in the care of women during pregnancy, labor, and the period following childbirth. *Compare* gynecologist.

Oedipus Complex The abnormally strong and persistent attachment of a son to his mother usually involving incestous desire or behavior. *Compare* Electra complex.

Oophorectomy Surgical removal of an ovary.

Orgasm The intense excitement, both physical and emotional, which is experienced at the climax of the sexual act (coitus) or following stimulation of the sex organs. During an orgasm, breathing becomes more rapid, heart rate is increased, blood pressure rises, and blood flow especially to pelvic regions is increased. In the male, ejaculation of semen takes place; in the female involuntary vaginal contractions occur. *See* Sexual Response.

Orgy Wild, unrestrained activity usually involving sexual excesses.

Ovariectomy Surgical removal of an ovary.

Ovary The female organ that produces ova or eggs. It is also the source of hormones (estrogens, progesterone, androgens, and relaxin).

Oviduct A tube in females that conveys eggs from the ovary; in women, the uterine or fallopian tube.

Ovulation The discharge of an ovum from the ovary following rupture of the graafian follicle. It occurs about 14 days prior to the onset of menstruation. *See* Thermal Shift.

Ovum, *pl.* **Ova** A female gamete or reproductive cell; an egg; a cell that, when fertilized, is capable of developing into an individual of the same species.

Panhysterectomy Total removal of the uterus.

Pansexualism The view that all conduct, experiences, and desires are derived from or related to the sex instinct.

Pap Smear A preparation made by taking tissue from the cervix of the uterus and spreading it on a slide that is then examined microscopically, a procedure used in the detection of malignant growths. Also called *Pap test.*

Paramour A lover, especially a lover of a married person.

Parthenophobia An abnormal fear of virgin females.

Partialism A form of sexual behavior in which a person shows an excessive interest in or is obsessed by only one part of the female body, as the breasts, buttocks, or nape of the neck, that part being of especial importance in the arousal of sexual desire.

Paternity The state or condition of being a father; fatherhood.

Patrilineal Tracing descent through the male line. *Compare* matrilineal.

Pederasty Anal intercourse between two males, especially an older man and a boy.

Pedophile A person who directs his sexual desire toward children; a child molester.

Pedophilia Sexual feelings or passion for children; fondness for children.

Penilingus Fellatio.

Penis The male organ of copulation. It also functions in urination. *See* Phallus.

Pessary 1. A device placed within the vagina for various purposes, as support of the uterus. 2. A suppository or cervical cap used for contraception.

Phallus 1. The penis. 2. The embryonic structure that gives rise to the penis or clitoris. 3. An image or representation of the male copulatory organ.

Pheromone A secretion of an organism that is discharged externally and acts on other individuals of the same group initiating certain behavioral, physiological, or developmental responses; an ectohormone.

Pictophilia A condition in which a person requires or depends on seeing erotic pictures for arousal of sexual feelings or achievment of an orgasm. See paraphilia.

Placenta A structure composed of embryonic and maternal tissue attached to the inner surface of the uterus and connected to the fetus by the umbilical cord. Through it the embryo or fetus receives nutritive materials and oxygen from the mother's blood and discharges wastes. It comprises the principal portion of the afterbirth. It also functions as an endocrine gland. See HCG.

Polyandry Marriage of a woman to more than one husband at one time. *Compare* monandry.

Polygamy Marriage of a man or woman to more than one mate at the same time. *See* Polyandry, Polygyny.

Polygyny Marriage of a man to more than one wife at one time. *Compare* monogyny.

Priapism Persistent, prolonged, and frequently painful erection of the penis usually not accompanied by sexual desire.

Progesterone The pregnancy hormone, a steroid hormone produced by the corpus luteum of the ovary that, with estrogens from the follicle, induces progestational changes in the uterine endometrium. During early pregnancy it is also produced by the placenta. It acts to maintain pregnancy and stimulates the development of the mammary glands. It is also produced by the adrenal cortex and the testes.

Progestin Progesterone, or any of a number of synthetic substances that possess the properties of progesterone, especially one that is active when taken orally.

Promiscuous Engaging in frequent and casual sexual intercourse with numerous partners.

Prophylactic 1. Protecting from disease. 2. An agent or device used for prevention of disease, especially a venereal disease; a condom.

Prostate Gland An accessory sex gland in the male located about the urethra at the base of the bladder. Its secretions, which pass into the urethra, comprise the second portion of the ejaculate.

Pseudocoitus Sexual intercourse in which the penis is in contact with the body of a female but not inserted into the vagina.

Puberty The period, also called *pubescence,* during which an individual becomes capable of reproducing, characterized by marked physical and psychological changes. It occurs between the ages of 12 and 16 in males and between 10 and 14 in females. In males, spermatozoa begin to be formed and the first ejaculations occur; in females the first menstruation (menarche) occurs and fertile ova begin to be produced. Secondary sex characteristics in both sexes make their appearance.

Pubes The hairy region that lies over the pubic symphysis; the pubic region.

Pudendum, *pl.* **Pudenda** The external genitalia of a female; the vulva.

Queen *Slang.* An effeminate, male homosexual, especially one who assumes the female role.

Retrocopulation Pederasty.

Retrograde Ejaculation The backward flow of semen into the bladder that may result from weakness of or injury to the sphincter muscle of the bladder or constriction of the urethra.

Sadism Obtaining sexual satisfaction through the infliction of pain on others. *Compare* masochism.

Sadomasochism *Abbr.* S-M. Simultaneous sadism and masochism.

Saline Injection Method A procedure for inducing an abortion in which fluid is withdrawn from the amniotic sac (amniocentesis) and an equal amount of hypertonic saline solution injected, a method employed after the fifteenth week of pregnancy.

Saphism Lesbianism.

Scopophilia, Scoptophilia Obtaining sexual satisfaction through the viewing of sexual acts, genital organs, or erotic pictures. *Compare* voyeurism.

Scrotum The pouch that contains the testes.

Secondary Sex Characteristics Physical structures other than the external genitalia that distinguish a male from a female. These include shape of body, nature and distribution of hair, presence or absence of mammary glands, size of larynx and consequent pitch of voice. Development of these structures depends on hormones produced by the ovaries and testes.

Semen The seminal fluid containing spermatozoa discharged by the male during ejaculation. It is produced principally by the testes, seminal vesicles, and prostate gland. Sometimes referred to as *seed* or *vital fluid.*

Seminal Vesicle A sacular outpocketing of the ductus (vas) deferens close to its junction with the ejaculatory duct just before entry into the urethra. Its secretion which contains fructose and prostaglandins forms an important part of semen.

Serology The science that deals with blood serum, especially antigen-antibody reactions.

Sexologist One versed in the science of sexology.

Sexology The science that deals with sex, comprising the anatomy and physiology of the sex organs and all aspects of behavior, normal or abnormal, associated with their functioning.

Sexual Dysfunction A condition in which ability to perform the sex act is impaired or unsatisfactory responses result during or following the act in one or both partners.

Sexual Inversion 1. The selection of a person of one's own sex as the object of sexual interest; homosexuality. 2. The possession of feelings, thoughts, and behavioral characteristics of the opposite sex.

Sixty-nine Simultaneous *fellatio and/*or *cunnilingus* between individuals of the same or opposite sex; soixante-neuf (69).

Slave In S-M, the masochistic partner.

S-M Simultaneous sadism and masochism.

Smegma A foul-smelling, cheeselike substance, the product of Tyson's glands, which accumulates between the prepuce and glans penis in uncircumcised males, or a similar substance that may accumulate beneath the prepuce of the clitoris in a female.

Sodomy 1. Anal intercourse, especially between two males. *Compare* pederasty. 2. Bestiality. *See* Crime Against Nature.

Spermatocide An agent that kills or destroys spermatozoa.

Spermatozoon, *pl.* **Spermatozoa** A flagellated, mature, male reproductive cell produced by the testis; a male gamete.

Sphincter A muscle surrounding an opening which, upon contracting, closes the opening.

Statutory Rape Sexual intercourse between a man and a girl below the age of consent, usually 18.

Sterile Incapable of producing offspring; not fertile.

Steroid Any of a group of fat-soluble organic compounds, including the sterols, bile acids, D vitamins, and the gonadal and adrenocortical hormones.

Sublimation The process by which unacceptable, instinctual demands are channeled into socially acceptable activities (e.g., intellectual and physical activities) serving as a substitute outlet for sexual activities.

Surrogate A substitute.

Swinger One of a group composed of couples (married or unmarried) who engages in indiscriminate sexual relations with others of the group. *See* Group Sex.

Syphilis A chronic, infectious, venereal disease caused by a spirochete, *Treponema pallidum.* Occurs in three stages, primary, secondary, and tertiary. May be of congenital origin. Also called *lues. See* Chancre.

Tactile Pertaining to or involving the sense of touch.

Testis, *pl.* **Testes** A male reproduction organ or gonad which, after puberty, produces spermatozoa. It is also the principal source of androgens (male hormones).

Testosterone The principal androgen or male sex hormone produced by the interstitial cells of the testes. It is also produced by the adrenal cortex and the ovaries. It is responsible for the development of male secondary sexual characteristics and for the sex drive or libido in both males and females.

Test Tube Baby A baby that develops from an egg that is fertilized externally. The ovum is removed from the ovary and sperm secured from the husband or a donor are added to it in a test tube or glass container.

Titilate To excite by stroking lightly.

Transsexual A person who has been changed externally by surgery from one sex to another; one afflicted with transsexualism.

Transvestism The desire to dress in clothing of the opposite sex and to identify partially or wholly with that sex.

Tribade A lesbian, especially one who assumes the role of the male.

Tribadism Lesbianism.

Troilism Sexual behavior involving three persons (two females and a male or two males and a female), usually combining coitus with oral-genital stimulation. Also *troilism.*

Tubal Ligation The tying off of both uterine tubes, a method of sterilization.

Tubal Pregnancy An ectopic pregnancy in which the embryo develops within the uterine tube.

Umbilical Cord A long cylindrical structure that connects a fetus with the placenta. It contains two arteries, a single vein and a mucous tissue called Wharton's jelly. The arteries carry blood from the fetus to the placenta; veins from the placenta to the fetus.

Unisexual Possessing the sex organs of one sex only; dioecious.

Urethra The tube that leads from the bladder to the outside. In the female it conveys urine; in the male, it traverses the penis and conveys both urine and semen.

Urogenital Of or pertaining to the urinary and reproductive systems.

Urologist A physician skilled in the diagnosis and treatement of diseases of the urogenital organs.

Urophilia A condition in which the sight or smell of urine, or the sight or sound of a person urinating, is essential for the arousal of erotic feelings and the induction of an orgasm; undinism.

Uterus A pear-shaped, female organ located in the pelvic cavity consisting of a lower *cervix,* and an upper *body,* the two separated by a constriction, the *isthmus.* It receives through the uterine tube or oviduct the product of conception (morula or blastocyst) and within it the embryo or fetus develops. It is the source of menstrual fluid discharged monthly through the vagina. Also called *womb. See* endometrium.

Vacuum Curettage Uterine aspiration, a method used for inducing an abortion in which suction is used for the removal of the products of conception.

Vas Deferens, *pl.* **Va Sa Deferentia** The *ductus deferens,* a duct that conveys sperm from the testis (more specifically the epididymis) to the ejaculatory duct and thence to the urethra.

Vasectomy Ligation of or cutting the vas deferens, a method of sterilization in the male.

Venereal Disease *Abbr.* VD. Any disease that is usually acquired through sexual intercourse or sexual contacts, such as gonorrhea and syphilis.

Virilism The development of male traits in a female; masculinity. It is commonly the result of a tumor of the adrenal cortex that results in excessive production of androgens. It occurs to a mild degree following menopause due to reduced production of female hormones. Also called *gynandry.*

Voyeurism Deviant behavior in which a person obtains sexual pleasure and satisfaction from viewing the sexual acts of others or seeing people or pictures of people in the nude. *See* Mixoscopia.

Vulva The structures surrounding the vaginal orifice in a female; the external genitalia or pudendum. These include the labia majora, labia minora, clitoris, vestibule, and mons pubis.

Wasserman Test A specific blood test for the diagnosis of syphilis.

Wean To deprive of a mother's milk; to cause the young to cease to nurse at the breast.

Wet Dream A nocturnal emission; a dream accompanied by the ejaculation of semen.

Wet Nurse A woman who provides milk from the breast to an infant not her own.

X Chromosome One of a pair of sex-determining chromosomes present in all eggs and in half of the sperm. In the zygote, when paired with another X chromosome, it brings about the development of female characteristics. In the male it is paired with the Y chromosome.

Y Chromosome One of a pair of sex-determining chromosomes present in one half of the spermatozoa produced. It is absent from ova and is practically devoid of genes. When present in the zygote, it is paired with an X chromosome and it brings about the development of male characteristics.

Zoophilia Extreme fondness for animals. *See* Beastiality.

Zygote A fertilized egg or ovum.

Source for the Glossary:

The terms in this glossary are reprinted with permission from *Human Sex and Sexuality: With a Dictionary of Sexual Terms,* Steen and Price, pages 263-322. Copyright © 1977 John Wiley & Sons, Inc. Publishers.

Index

Credits/ Acknowledgments

Cover design by Charles Vitelli

1. Sexuality and Society
Facing overview—United Nations/Jane Schreibman.

2. Sexual Biology and Health
Facing overview—New York City Department of Health.
53—Illustration by Bonnie Hofkin.

3. Reproduction
Facing overview—Middlesex Memorial Hospital.

4. Interpersonal Relationships
Facing overview—United Nations/John Isaac. 113—United
Nations. 130—Courtesy of Masters & Johnson.

5. Sexuality Through the Life Cycle
Facing overview—United Nations/Jeffrey J. Foxx. 174—Susan
Gilmore.

6. Old/New Sexual Concerns
Facing overview—New York City Department of Health.

ANNUAL EDITIONS:
HUMAN SEXUALITY 88/89
Article Rating Form

Here is an opportunity for you to have direct input into the next revision of this volume. We would like you to rate each of the 55 articles listed below, using the following scale:

1. **Excellent: should definitely be retained**
2. **Above average: should probably be retained**
3. **Below average: should probably be deleted**
4. **Poor: should definitely be deleted**

Your ratings will play a vital part in the next revision. So please mail this prepaid form to us just as soon as you complete it.
Thanks for your help!

Rating	Article	Rating	Article
	1. 20 Greatest Moments in Sex History		30. Bruised Friendships
	2. New Directions for the Kinsey Institute		31. Masters and Johnson's New Guide to Better Loving
	3. 200 Years of Childbirth		32. Sexual Dilemmas of the Modern Office
	4. Erotic Wisdom of the Orient		33. Making Love: 5 Traps to Avoid
	5. Sex Busters		34. Sex in Childhood: Aversion, Abuse, or Right?
	6. How Important Is Sex?		35. What Kids Need to Know
	7. Re-Making Love: The Real Sexual Revolution		36. Children Having Children
	8. Sex and Schools		37. Teen Lust
	9. What's Your Love-Making IQ?		38. Formal vs. Informal Sources of Sex Education
	10. Hits and Myths in the Bedroom		39. Don't Let Sex Myths Hurt Your Marriage
	11. The Power of Touch		40. Sexual Passages
	12. Prostate: The Misunderstood Gland		41. Some Hard (and Soft) Facts About Sex and Aging
	13. The Secret "Gynecological" Disorders of Men		42. Never Too Late
	14. Fragile Fallopian Tubes		43. Love, Sex, and Aging
	15. Sex, With Care		44. Women Who Have Lesbian Affairs
	16. A Gift From Mother Nature		45. Hostile Eyes
	17. A Consumer's Guide to Over-the-Counter Tests		46. Date Rape and Other Forced Sexual Encounters Among College Students
	18. Miracle Babies: The Next Generation		47. Women's Postrape Sexual Functioning: Review and Implications for Counseling
	19. New Study of Teenage Pregnancy		48. The Incest Controversy
	20. Young, Innocent, and Pregnant		49. Shattered Innocence
	21. Saying No to Motherhood		50. Kids for Sale
	22. The Crisis in Contraception		51. The Question of Pornography
	23. Kids and Contraceptives		52. The Facts About AIDS
	24. A Second Look at the Pill		53. AIDS and the College Student: The Need for Sex Education
	25. How We Can Prevent Teen Pregnancy (And Why It's Not the Real Problem)		54. Speaking Out on AIDS: A Humanist Symposium
	26. RU-486: The Unpregnancy Pill		55. Fighting the Plague: Twenty-Seven New Drugs to Stop a Killer
	27. Considering the Way Most of Us Learned About Sex, It's a Wonder We Can Do It, Do It Well or Have Any Interest in Doing It at All		Glossary
	28. When Men and Women Think About Sex: Ways They Differ		
	29. The Three Faces of Love		

(cont. on next page)

ABOUT YOU

Name_____ Date_____

Are you a teacher? ☐ Or student? ☐

Your School Name _____

Department _____

Address _____

City_____ State _____ Zip _____

School Telephone #_____

YOUR COMMENTS ARE IMPORTANT TO US!

Please fill in the following information:

For which course did you use this book? _____

Did you use a text with this Annual Edition? ☐ yes ☐ no

The title of the text? _____

What are your general reactions to the Annual Editions concept?

Have you read any particular articles recently that you think should be included in the next edition?

Are there any articles you feel should be replaced in the next edition? Why?

Are there other areas that you feel would utilize an Annual Edition?

May we contact you for editorial input?

May we quote you from above?

HUMAN SEXUALITY 88/89

The Dushkin Publishing Group, Inc.
Sluice Dock
Guilford, Connecticut 06437